*Changing
Cities*

Changing Cities

Urban Sociology

Janet L. Abu-Lughod

New School for Social Research

HarperCollins*Publishers*

Sponsoring Editor: Alan McClare
Project Editor: Thomas R. Farrell
Design Supervisor: Heather A. Ziegler
Cover Design: Edward Smith Design
Cover Photo: Courtesy Murphy/Jann, Architects
Production: Linda Murray
Compositor: ComCom Division of Haddon Craftsmen, Inc.
Printer and Binder: R. R. Donnelley & Sons Company
Cover Printer: New England Book Components

CHANGING CITIES: *Urban Sociology*

Copyright © 1991 by HarperCollins Publishers Inc.

Library of Congress Cataloging-in-Publication Data

Abu-Lughod, Janet L.
    Changing cities : urban sociology / Janet L. Abu-Lughod.
      p.   cm.
    Includes index.
    ISBN 0-06-040138-9
    1. Sociology, Urban.   I. Title.
  HT151.A27 1991   90-19835
  307.76—dc20   CIP

91 92 93 94   9 8 7 6 5 4 3 2

Contents

PART THREE   THE CITY AS PLACE   183

PART FOUR   STUDYING COMMUNITY—NOT NECESSARILY A PLACE   267

Preface

Changing Cities examines how cities have changed and why. Using urban ecological methods and social area analysis, augmented by new information about the importance of class, gender, and race/ethnicity in cities, the book demonstrates how these factors affect the behavior of urbanites. New contributions made by network and cluster analysis offer expanded insights into social and physical space and the ways individuals and groups interact with their environments.

Changing Cities is designed to be used in both undergraduate and graduate courses. It is suitable as the primary reading for an undergraduate course and as the introductory section of more advanced graduate courses in a variety of urban studies programs. Technical information and references have been placed in footnotes, and an extensive bibliography has been included at the end to allow faculty members and graduate students to select supplementary readings and to guide deeper research in particular areas of their interests.

The organization has been "pretested" on a generation of undergraduates at Northwestern University, and its usefulness, particularly supplemented by primary sources and field work, has been similarly tested on graduate students at Northwestern and the New School for Social Research.

The book is divided into five sections around which courses in urban sociology are often organized:

Part One sets the stage, examining the definition of the field and tracing its intellectual heritage. It provides historical background concerning the rise and spread of urban civilizations around the world.

Part Two focuses on the development of cities in the United States from the founding of the country to the early 1990s. It contains an analytic historical narrative, together with supporting statistical information, including data drawn from the preliminary returns of the census of 1990. Both are essential to an understanding not only of how cities have changed, but why.

Part Three focuses on the methods and findings of urbanists who have taken an ecological perspective, trying to uncover the spatial order of cities and to trace the effects of that order on the behavior of urbanites. It contains an exposition of conventional census tract analysis methods as well as the later-developed techniques of social area analysis and factorial ecology, demonstrating how those new methods can supplement older and more standard approaches. It theorizes that class, family role, and race/ethnicity must be taken into account in describing the spatial order of any city. The section includes a chapter specifically addressed to questions of race and gender in the contemporary American city.

Part Four focuses on the question of community in the city. It describes some of the methods that have been used to conduct neighborhood participant observation studies and also surveys a wide variety of community studies that have previously been made by urban anthropologists, sociologists, and political scientists. Presenting a new theory of the relationship between social and physical space, it examines the contributions network analysis can make to an understanding of how life is organized in various quarters of the metropolis.

Part Five introduces cluster analysis findings to identify the variations in urban "ways of life" in contemporary America. It presents a deeper theory of social and physical space and a more sophisticated analysis of the ways in which individuals and groups interact than was provided by ecological determinism. It concludes with a chapter on urban planning and some suggestions for how cities might be made more livable and more satisfying.

A number of academics have read the manuscript for *Changing Cities* and shared their suggestions with me. I especially want to thank the following for their helpful comments:

William Schwab, University of Arkansas

Marvin E. Olson, Michigan State University

Donald Deskins, University of Michigan

Rebecca L. Clark, Averett College

Rodger A. Bates, Lamberth College

ACKNOWLEDGMENTS

A decade ago, Noel Gist and Sylvia Fava invited me to join them in preparing the seventh edition of their well-known urban sociology textbook, *Urban Society.* Justifiably flattered, I agreed, thus beginning a fruitful intellectual association with Sylvia Fava that has persisted to this day; Noel Gist died in 1983. Even though the volume originally planned never materialized, the proposed collaboration did start me on the long path that led to this book. What began as a revision of *Urban Society* became *Changing Cities* when Sylvia Fava reluctantly withdrew from the project because of an extended period of eye problems.

Because of this history, there are certain unavoidable parallels between parts of *Urban Society* and portions of *Changing Cities.* In particular, Chapters 2, 7, and 10 of the present book incorporate some materials drawn initially from the sixth edition of *Urban Society.* While these have been modified and rephrased and a substantially new theoretical approach has been introduced, I gratefully acknowledge Sylvia Fava's permission to allow her original work to serve as a partial template.

In the course of our collaboration, Sylvia commented in detail on the first few chapters and provided me with the analysis of data from the Harris Poll. She also read the draft manuscript in its entirety, making suggestions about additional sources, correcting some of the references, and indicating those portions that warranted a more precise footnote to the sixth edition of *Urban Society.* I am grateful for her help and friendship, and regret only that she could not have remained co-author.

It is impossible to acknowledge fully the deeper ways in which earlier editions of *Urban Society* influenced my thinking. That book served as the standard text in the field for decades. Many of today's urbanists began their studies by reading it, and it has shaped our understanding of cities and the way we conceptualize the field. My hope is that the present volume will have a similar impact on the discipline.

JANET LIPPMAN ABU-LUGHOD

Changing
Cities

Chapter
1

Introducing the Field

*T*his book focuses on the contemporary American city, within whose metropolitan web three-fourths of us now live. Americans have always had a love-hate relationship with "the city," which is paradoxically seen as a place in which to make one's mark but also as a place to escape from, whether physically, to the safer suburbs, or, in nostalgia, to an idealized dream of small towns and rural areas.[1]

The city's excitement draws us like a flame at the same time that its noise and crowds repel us. The city's wealth magnetizes us, our noses pressed against its display windows, whereas the city's poverty and crime—perhaps the inevitable underside of its bounty—make us apprehensive and uncomfortable. We celebrate the democracy of disappearing town halls but are all too aware that, today, many of the decisions determining our lives are made in corporate boardrooms and in government chambers of metropolitan centers. We are fascinated by the urban scene, which parades all varieties of life-styles before our eyes, but we are also disoriented, for such variety challenges certitudes and

---

[1]Morton and Lucia White's *The Intellectual Versus the City* (New York: Mentor, 1962) chronicles the long-standing negative evaluation of "the city" that runs deep in western thought. The authors demonstrate that its genealogy goes far back in time, and trace it even to early Hebrew documents.

tells us that there is no one "right" way to be, no one kind of acceptable person. The city may give us freedom—but it also brings confusion and questioning.

Yet love it or not, seek it or flee it, the city has become our home in a way that it never was in the past. Two hundred years ago it was a rare American (only one out of 20) who lived in a city, and cities then were few and small. Now, in contrast, vast stretches of the American landscape are given over to urban forms that mingle so closely (as we view them speeding along the highways that link them) that it is often impossible to tell where one ends and the next begins. Ours is truly an age of cities.

Indeed, the process of urbanization, whether embraced with enthusiasm or, more commonly, viewed with concern, seems irreversible. Where, indeed, would we put the 250 million people who now live in the United States (almost fifteen times more than lived here only 150 years ago), were it not for the density of settlement that cities make possible, and how would we survive without the economic activities of production and commerce that cities support?

If we do not have a choice about whether or not to have cities, we may, however, still have a choice about what kinds of cities we want to create—ones that can minimize the traits we dislike and fear and maximize those we desire. In any case, learning to live in and improve the urbanized society we now have become requires that we understand the city and the forces that create it.

This is not as simple as it may first seem. To begin with, it is often difficult to decide upon a single definition of "the city," even though we may not have trouble recognizing one when we see it. This is because "the city" takes on many different forms and characteristics, depending upon where and when it is found. New York is not Shanghai, nor is the New York of 1790 the New York of 1990. In order to know what a city can be, we need to understand it in its variations as well as its essence, to know what it has been and what it is today.

This brings us to the primary purposes of this book. It seeks to help students understand how cities came to be as pervasive and influential as they now are in American life and to show how cities relate to the societies that produce them. It makes the basic assumption that cities not only reflect the changing socioeconomic basis of our society but influence in fundamental ways how life is currently lived in America.

No deep understanding of the present can be achieved without understanding the past. Therefore, in Chapter 2 we examine cities in earlier times and other places. The city is a special and relatively recent form of human settlement, one that could not appear until human beings achieved a fairly high level of technological and social sophistication. Knowing how cities began helps us to identify three universal prerequisites for their appearance. These same variables continue to determine the persistence and growth of cities. They are:

1. A marked increase in total population density;
2. A transformation in the way wealth is produced; and
3. A radical change in the sociopolitical system designed to harness the new wealth—often at the cost of greater inequality.

Variations in cities also relate to the particular physical environments in which they develop. Urbanists frequently refer to these factors, using a memory aid called POET (where P stands for Population, O for Social Organization, E for Environment, and T for Technology).[2] In this book we have chosen to redefine these factors in a more powerful, analytically useful way.

These urbanizing processes operated over and over again as cities spread throughout the Mediterranean and Asian worlds. The historical survey in Chapter 2 reveals that the trend toward urbanization has been neither smooth nor uninterrupted. From time to time, the "center of gravity" of cities and of their accompanying civilizations shifted dramatically. In some regions, city culture even died out until the prerequisites for its rebirth appeared in different form. This was certainly true in northern Europe in the Middle Ages, where cities were renewed first by commerce, then conquest, but eventually exploded, due to an utterly new and self-perpetuating source of wealth, industrial capitalism.

It was during the nineteenth century that the European industrial city came into its own. For the first time in history, cities became the *typical* abode of people in certain countries, not merely the privileged home of rulers and those who served them. But outside the few urbanizing countries of Europe, most people of the world continued to live in rural places. Such places still house most of the population of Asia and Africa and, until recently, Latin America as well.

In earlier times, the city offered a marked contrast to its unurbanized hinterland; today, the urbanized core countries contrast with the relatively unurbanized and peripheral Third World. However, even this is now changing. Just as European cities earlier expanded to encompass and transform their rural surroundings, so the urbanized world, through colonization, trade, and other contact, has been transforming the rest of the world. By now there are as many cities in Asia, Africa, and Latin America as there are in the industrial West. Increasingly, the world's largest cities are to be found not in Europe and North America but in Asia and Latin America. By the time the next century begins, the city will have become the typical living environment for most of the world's population. This theme is developed in Chapter 3.

The present volume cannot hope to cover all the various patterns that world urbanization is taking.[3] Rather, it focuses on cities in the United States, although it tries to place them in a wider comparative context. The contemporary American city is clearly an object of study in its own right. While American cities share some characteristics of cities in other times and places, in the final analysis they are:

---

[2]Otis Dudley Duncan and Leo Schnore, "Cultural, Behavioral and Ecological Perspectives in the Study of Social Organization," *American Journal of Sociology* 65 (1959), pp. 132–45.

[3]For coverage of urbanization in the Third World, see, for example, Janet Abu-Lughod and Richard Hay, Jr., eds., *Third World Urbanization* (New York: Methuen, 1979), as well as later works such as Josef Gugler, ed., *Urbanization in the Third World* (New York: Oxford University Press, 1988), and Warwick Armstrong and T. G. McGee, *Theatres of Accumulation: Studies in Asian and Latin American Urbanization* (London and New York: Methuen, 1985).

1. The unique outcome of particular historical processes;
2. The product of particular phases in technological and economic development; and
3. The reflection of a particular evolving economic and political system.

Therefore, in Part II we pay special attention to the changing nature of American cities. Chapter 4 traces their development from colonial outposts for European expansion to early export or commercial ports, and then their subsequent absorption of foreign immigrants into a burgeoning industrial structure. Chapter 5 describes the early twentieth-century phase during which an elaborate system of sprawling metropolitan regions, linked together and interlacing the nation, came into being. And finally, Chapter 6 examines the newest phase of this process of urban restructuring, as all parts of the society become "saturated" with urbanism—culturally if not physically. Each of these stages of urban development has left its mark on different regions of the United States, yielding not just one kind of city but many.

Throughout these periods of urban development, the basic economic and political institutions of the United States had to cope with the changing economic base of the country (from agricultural to industrial to informational) and with the changing scale of enterprises (from small to enormous and, finally, to multinational). As these changes occurred, the system of free enterprise capitalism that had built the original cities was bent and stretched to provide an infrastructure to meet public (i.e., collective) needs. Similarly, the original system of agrarian representation and states' rights was hammered into one that could serve a more urbanized society.

URBAN PROBLEMS AND URBAN SOCIOLOGY

Each of these changes in the nature of the city, in the sources of its growth, and in the economic and political mechanisms available for its governance left a residue of unsolved problems. Indeed, when one thinks of the contemporary American city, the closest mental association one has is with the phrase "urban problems." Issues such as crime, drugs, poverty, homelessness, racial tensions, fiscal insolvency, pollution, traffic jams, and suburban sprawl are increasingly associated in our minds with "the city."

These issues cannot be avoided. Indeed, this book is intended to help the student understand the underlying causes of such problems. But its chapters are not organized around these symptoms of distress. Rather, we assume that just as these problems have arisen in the context of the growth and transformation of American cities and within the context of the larger economic and political system that governs them, so a proper understanding of the causes of urban problems must be sought in these wider arenas. Only by grasping the dynamics of urban formation, growth, and change can one come to understand and then proceed to solve the problems that are "urban" largely because we have become an urban nation.

This book, then, is about cities, not urban problems. Furthermore, it examines cities chiefly from a sociological perspective. No single discipline, however, can comprehend an object as complex as a city. A city is many things and needs many ways to study it because, in the last analysis, the city is a real place where people live.

That place has a physical structure, which makes it an object studied by geographers. It contains a population that breeds, is encultured, migrates, and dies, which makes it an object studied by demographers. It is a center in which goods (material and immaterial) are produced, distributed, and consumed, which makes it an object studied by economists, and in which ideas and cultural artifacts are similarly produced, distributed, and consumed, which attracts the attention of humanists. It has governmental structures (formal and informal) for identifying and meeting collectively defined needs, which makes it an object studied by political scientists.

But to a sociologist, a city is primarily a place where social groups live, work, raise families, and interact with or ignore one another. It is these social groups that are distributed—geographically, demographically, economically, politically, and culturally—and are ordered to form a social system. This social system is the chief object of study for urban sociologists.

It should thus be clear that it is impossible (or foolish) to study the city only from the sociological perspective. Since the interactions of individuals and groups are frequently shaped by the physical environment in which they live, some attention to urban geography is required. Since the demographic characteristics of a population (whether young or old; growing, stable, or declining; composed of newcomers or natives) often influence how they live their lives, some attention must be paid to demography. The system of production (the ways people make their living) affects their very existence, and the system according to which wealth is distributed and consumed determines the class and other differences that underlie the social groupings themselves. Hence we cannot ignore economics. Nor can we ignore politics, for in that arena the competing claims of different groups are put forth—some to be rewarded and satisfied, others to be ignored or denied. Such outcomes directly affect the social relations among groups and the social conditions of each group.

In short, a sociological perspective requires an understanding of many other aspects of reality. Sociology, however, always asks how these work together to create a particular social reality, such as a city.

Just as it is impossible to understand the city only from the sociological perspective, so it is also impossible to understand the city only from an urban perspective. Castells made this point when he suggested that the city was not a proper object of study.[4] What he meant was that, just as the geography of a

---

[4]See especially Manuel Castells, "Is There an Urban Sociology?" *Urban Sociology*, ed. C. G. Pickvance (New York: St. Martin's Press, 1976), pp. 33–59, as well as the related discussion in Peter Saunders, *Social Theory and the Urban Question* (New York: Holmes and Meier, 1981). This is so even if one views the city merely as a *node* within a complex network of settlements whose transactions with one another are more important than the geographic place itself, as Manuel

city does not stop at its legal boundaries, so its economic, political, and social life connects with larger systems and other places in a seamless web of interactions and mutual effects.

That fact, however, does not mean that one cannot take the city as a prime object of study. All other fields face the same problem of finding an appropriate "object." A microbiologist studies the cell, even though each cell is connected in an endless chain to the universe. The astronomer studies exploding stars while also acknowledging that each particle in each star might be worth studying. Our point is simple. A scientist can choose to study any arbitrarily selected object, as long as he or she can define it, develop appropriate tools to study it, and relate that object to its wider environment. To study urbanism is no more outlandish than to study individuals or the universe; it is, alas, no easier either.

Our task in this volume, then, is to focus on "the city" while keeping in mind the context in which it exists, and to focus "sociologically" on the city without forgetting the knowledge that other perspectives give us.

THE SOCIOLOGY OF THE CITY—EUROPEAN ANTECEDENTS

The sociological study of the city is guided by a long tradition of scholarship. Over the past one hundred years, a body of ideas and literature (what Foucault has called a "discourse")[5] has grown up around the concept of the city. How sociologists think about the city has been shaped by a distinguished line of thinkers whose views about the city were colored by the particular cities and societies they knew and by the issues and "problems" they identified as pressing. Their ideas may have been appropriate to those times and places, but we may need to correct them when we examine the contemporary city. We have earlier stressed that cities cannot be discussed in the abstract. There is no such thing as "the city" which, everywhere and at all times, exhibits a single set of characteristics. Indeed, the most striking fact about cities is that they have varied so much over time and from place to place, culture to culture. Furthermore, there is no such thing as "urbanism as a way of life" which, independent of the cultural context or the particular inhabitants, leads to predictable forms of social interaction. And finally, particularly at the present time, there is no necessary congruence between the city as a *physical place* and the *social life* that takes place within it.

Many of these points were not recognized when the field was just beginning. The discourse, while claiming to describe universals, was very much constrained by the particular empirical cases examined (at first, British cities, and then Chicago) and by the particular social transformations that were taking place in European society, chiefly in the latter part of the nineteenth century.

Castells contends in his important book *The Urban Question: A Marxist Approach*, revised and translated into English by Alan Sheridan (Cambridge, MA: MIT Press, 1977). Published originally as *La question urbaine* (Paris: Maspero, 1972).

[5]See Michel Foucault, *The Archaeology of Knowledge* (London: Tavistock, 1972).

Empirical Studies

The nineteenth-century transformation of Europe into the first urbanized and industrialized society shook the social foundations of its existence. While there had always been undercurrents of negative attitudes toward the city, the optimistic European reformist philosophers of the eighteenth century had faith that man's rational control over the natural environment would soon be expanded via science to a rational control over his social environment. They were therefore not worried about the city; science and industrial urbanism were expected to usher in a new and unproblematic era of prosperity and happiness for humanity.

In the nineteenth century this outcome seemed less likely. By mid-century, the former peasants of Europe were crowding into the new industrial centers and were becoming impoverished workers in the midst of plenty. Courts of inquiry were established to study the social consequences of their overcrowded housing and their long working hours. Economic crashes and depressions periodically worsened their plight.

It was during this period that Frederick Engels conducted his sociological investigation of the living conditions of the working class in Manchester, England's foremost industrial city,[6] and that Karl Marx began his lifework of unraveling the mechanisms of the capitalist system to explain the recurring economic crises.[7] During the second half of the nineteenth century, English social reformers and muckraking journalists began to document more fully the life of the urban poor. London, in particular, captured their interest. By the end of the century two works of gigantic proportions had been completed by Charles Booth[8] and Henry Mayhew.[9] Novelists such as Dickens provided equally astute (and heart-rending) descriptions of the early industrial city.[10] By then, one of the permanent preoccupations of urban sociologists—to chronicle the "social disorganization" of the urban underclass—was already well established, and scholars had begun to amass information about the appalling conditions under which that class lived and to develop methods for gathering more. (See the relevant section of Chapter 3 for a fuller discussion.)

Theoretical Concepts

In France and Germany, social theorists were more preoccupied with tracing the sociological implications of the transition from rural to urban living. Two

---

[6]Frederick Engels, *The Condition of the Working Class in England* (New York: The Macmillan Company, 1958).

[7]Karl Marx, *Das Kapital*, in three volumes, variously translated and published.

[8]Charles Booth, *Life and Labour of the People in London,* in 17 volumes (London: Macmillan, 1902–1903).

[9]Henry Mayhew, *London Labour and the London Poor* (London: Griffin Bohn and Company, 1861).

[10]Among the more relevant novels of Charles Dickens are *Bleak House* and *Oliver Twist.*

thinkers in particular contributed basic ideas and terms to the evolving discourse, creating the theoretical framework within which the field of urban sociology would develop.

From the German scholar Ferdinand Toennies came a pair of polar terms he applied to two "ideal types" of social solidarity. One, called *Gemeinschaft* (or community), bound human groups together in a warm, caring, familial way. The other, called *Gesellschaft* (or society), bound human beings together through more formal, state-like institutions.[11] While Toennies was careful not simply to equate "community" with rural life and "society" with urban life, he did try to use his contrasting terms to explain why life in Europe was changing from the personalized and family-oriented existence it had previously known (associated with living in agricultural villages and small towns) to the colder, more impersonal, rationally organized and individualistic social life of industrial urbanism.

It was this same change that the French sociologist Emile Durkheim tried to analyze in his *The Division of Labor in Society.*[12] He noted, as others had before him, that the original bonds that formed human groups were those of common kinship, gradually extended to common residence or territory. Durkheim observed that these bonds were beginning to be supplemented by new forms of solidarity based upon differentiated occupations and economic functions. Durkheim distinguished between two types of social solidarity: one growing out of similarity, which he called "mechanical solidarity"; and a second, newer kind, growing out of differences or specialization, which he called "organic solidarity," because in a complex organism, no separate organ can function without the rest.

By this theory, Durkheim was trying to capture the essential transformation that was occurring in European society as national and international markets drew isolated centers of production into a gigantic system of interdependent economies, and as occupational specialization replaced self-sufficient subsistence units. While his study was not about cities as such, Durkheim made a major contribution to urban sociological theory through his relentlessly logical (if flawed) effort to answer the question of how organic solidarity became the dominant social bond in contemporary society. He reasoned that this occurred when population increased, when physical settlements grew more dense, and when improved means of transportation and communication put larger and larger numbers of people in contact with one another. It was from this basic argument that urban sociology later drew one of its crucial theorems: namely, that cities, because they bring together large numbers of inhabitants in dense settlements, *cause* basic changes in the kinds of relationships individuals and groups have with one another.

---

[11]Ferdinand Toennies, *Community and Society,* trans. Charles Loomis (East Lansing: Michigan State University Press, 1957). Written originally in 1887.

[12]Emile Durkheim, *The Division of Labor in Society,* trans. George Simpson (New York: Macmillan, Free Press, 1964). This work was originally written in 1893 as a doctoral dissertation. The basic flaw in his reasoning was to confuse (or rather equate, in operational measurement) physical density with his true variable, moral or interactional density.

Combined with the ideas of Toennies, this theorem was later transformed into one of the most persistent (yet incomplete) theoretical propositions of early American urban sociology: namely, that rural areas are warm, friendly, and socially cohesive while cities, because of their size and density, are cold, formal, and barely held together through law, the police, and the mass media.

Two additional writers contributed to this growing theory. One was Georg Simmel, a brilliant intellectual maverick from Berlin, whose sensitive essay on "The Metropolis and Mental Life" was early translated into English.[13] The other was Louis Wirth, a German immigrant who came to study urban sociology at the University of Chicago and remained to write its most definitive and influential treatise on the city, an essay entitled "Urbanism as a Way of Life."[14]

Simmel's essay explored the psychological consequences of urban living—with its crowds, multiple stimuli, constant pressures and possibilities. Himself an ardent lover of the city, he defended the freedom it offered to individuals to shape their own unique personalities. But he was not blind to its costs. He noted that city residents could be cold and impersonal with one another, that they reacted "with the head" rather than "with the heart," that they were blasé from overstimulation, and that, because of their loneliness in the crowd, they had to devise eccentricities to set themselves apart. These consequences were combined with Toennies's and Durkheim's causal factors of size, concentration, and industrial organization, to make up what Louis Wirth called "urbanism as a way of life." (A fuller exposition of Wirth's theory is given in Chapter 10.)

THE CHICAGO SCHOOL OF URBAN SOCIOLOGY

In analyzing the developing discourse in the field of urban sociology, we cannot ignore the special contributions of the Chicago School of urban sociology, which made its major mark in the period between about 1913 and 1940, when it literally defined the field.[15] This school and the exemplars it established, both for theoretical problem formulation and for empirical research on the city, did not merely derive from European schools, however. While linked to Europe through literature, travel, and even study, the Chicago School was a new

---

[13]Georg Simmel, "The Metropolis and Mental Life," written originally in 1902–1903; first English translation by Edward Shils in 1936. This essay is not understandable, however, except in the context of Simmel's larger theoretical study of the transformation of Western society through capitalism, presented in his *The Philosophy of Money*, which was not available in English translation until 1978.

[14]Louis Wirth, "Urbanism as a Way of Life," *American Journal of Sociology* 44 (July 1938), pp. 1–24.

[15]For a survey of and background on the Chicago School, see Robert E. Faris, *Chicago Sociology: 1920–1932* (Chicago: University of Chicago Press, 1970). An evaluation of the Chicago School can be found in "The Chicago School: The Tradition and the Legacy," a special issue of *Urban Life* 11 (January 1983), edited by Jim Thomas. See also Martin Bulmer, *The Chicago School of Sociology: Institutionalization, Diversity, and the Rise of Sociological Research* (Chicago: University of Chicago Press, 1984).

venture, shaped as much by the characteristics of the evolving American city as it was by the ideas of earlier thinkers.

What kind of city was the Chicago they used as their model of urbanism? First, it was an industrial city—"hog butcher of the world" and home of the blazing open hearth of steel manufacture. Second, it was a city of slums whose physical conditions were every bit as miserable as those that Booth and Mayhew had described in London half a century earlier. Following in the tradition of these earlier social investigators were women social worker–reformers (among them, Edith Abbott, Sophonisba P. Breckinridge, Florence Kelley, and Jane Addams) who contributed landmark studies on housing and urban poverty in Chicago at the same time that they worked to ameliorate the suffering.[16] And third, it was a city populated by migrants. Almost every Chicagoan had been born in the countryside, whether stateside or in Europe, and that included most of the sociologists who were to formulate the theory of the city and to conduct the empirical studies of life in cities.

The fact that most of Chicago's population in 1920 had been born abroad or were children of immigrants influenced beyond measure both the theoretical definition of the city that would guide sociological work and the empirical investigations that would preoccupy its first students. Notably, Louis Wirth's definition of the city stressed social and cultural heterogeneity (while virtually ignoring class and family-cycle differences). The fact that most urbanites at that time had been born and raised in rural areas, either at home or abroad, heightened the preoccupation of these scholars with contrasting urban and rural ways of life and with questions of rural-to-urban adjustment. Often, members of the Chicago School blamed the social problems experienced by immigrants on urban life itself, rather than on the cultural disabilities or the low status of the migrants in the expanding and callous industrial system.

In any event, the Chicago School urbanists remained fascinated with the symptoms of social disorganization—family breakdown, crime, juvenile delinquency, prostitution, psychoses, and alcoholism—which they found in abundance among newcomers to urban life. Like the reformers and muckrakers of their times, they often oversimplified the causes of distress, blaming such "urban" facts as inadequate and overcrowded housing, lack of parks, unwholesome neighborhoods, and the like for problems actually issuing from poverty and the unprotected status of labor in early capitalism.[17]

---

[16]The most remarkable of these studies, however, was the collective volume edited by Jane Addams, entitled *Hull-House Notes and Papers* (1895), which in the late nineteenth century did for the immigrant area on the near west side of Chicago what Booth's study had done for comparable quarters in London. These early social workers were heavily influenced by the British settlement house tradition; some had spent time in England, where they were surely exposed to the work of Booth as well as others. In turn, they exerted a seldom-acknowledged influence on the founders of the Chicago School of urban sociology. See Mary Jo Deegan, *Jane Addams and the Men of the Chicago School, 1892–1918* (New Brunswick, NJ: Transaction Books, 1988).

[17]It is to the credit of W. I. Thomas, a highly influential colleague of both Park and Burgess at the time they were generating their theories of the city, that he never fell into this trap. Because he

Two scholars at the University of Chicago played particularly important roles in setting the agenda and devising methods for urban sociology: Ernest Burgess and Robert Park. Their collaboration, begun in 1916, produced not only the "definitive" textbook in sociology but some very influential essays on the city which, when gathered together in 1925, became the first American text in urban sociology.[18] Park and Burgess trained the first generation of American urban sociologists who, in turn, taught the next.

Between the two of them, they set out the two somewhat different research agendas urban sociologists would follow in the decades to come and the two somewhat different methods that would be used to pursue these agendas. Part III of this book focuses on the first of these agendas, which we have termed the City as Place. Part IV stresses the second agenda, which we have termed the City as People. While, as we shall see, these cannot be neatly separated, they have generally been approached by different scholars using different methods of research.

The City as Place: The Focus of Urban Ecology

Urban sociologists (as well as geographers) studying the City as Place focus their attention on discovering the physical pattern of the city and the distribution of population in it. They ask such questions as:

How does the city grow?

Are there predictable or at least generalizable patterns to the distribution of people in the city?

Do the poor always live near the center and the rich on the outskirts? Why?

How does the area in which one lives affect one's behavior, one's interactions with others, one's physical and, even more, one's mental health?

Why do some areas with good housing become slums while other areas are rehabilitated and even upgraded?

What is the relationship between a city and its surroundings (hinterlands)?

---

devoted so much of his scholarly attention to the pains and burdens of immigrant adjustment, as in his magnum opus, *The Polish Peasant in Europe and America* (with Florian Znaniecki; 5 vols., Boston: Richard G. Badger, 1918–1920), he never falsely attributed their problems to urbanism per se, although he, too, tended to overlook the effects of the industrial system into which his immigrants were fed.

[18]Park and Burgess, *An Introduction to the Science of Sociology* (Chicago: University of Chicago Press, 1921). This is a collection of excerpts, primarily from European social scientists, organized around topics that have become some of the standard fields of sociology. The first urban sociology text was *The City* (Chicago: University of Chicago Press, 1925), edited by Park, Burgess, and Roderick McKenzie, which included such pieces as Park's original 1915 essay, somewhat rewritten, and Burgess's 1923 paper, "The Growth of the City."

And in all these questions, they ask: How can generalizations be made, how can these phenomena be measured, and how can uniformities be explained? This focus of urban sociology came to be called *urban ecology.*

Chapter 7 describes the methods that urban ecologists, using demographic and other statistical sources, have devised to study the spatial organization of cities. We show how these methods grew out of certain theoretical assumptions, were addressed to certain practical goals, and were limited by the types of data available. As theoretical issues and practical goals changed and as new types of data became available, these methods were refined, drawing inspiration and models not only from the fields of urban sociology and urban geography but from economics and political economy as well. Chapter 7 not only traces the development of these methods and data sources but also indicates how students can use them in their own studies of the city.

Chapter 8 looks more closely at the processes that have brought about the particular spatial configurations observed in contemporary American cities. Several competing theories are presented, each of which claims to "explain" why cities come to exhibit the spatial configurations they do under conditions of advanced capitalism. In this chapter we take a closer look at the market for land and housing in contemporary American cities, since all analysts, regardless of theoretical position, assume that this underlies the distribution of classes in metropolitan America.

The distribution of family types and racial groups is less well explained by political and economic variables. Thus, in Chapter 9 we look at the important issues of gender and race in U.S. cities, as they work through or distort "normal" economic mechanisms of capitalism. Just as in Chapter 7 we saw development of method, so in Chapters 8 and 9 we see increased sophistication in theoretical understanding of the factors that create urban spatial structures.

The City as People: The Community Study

The second focus of early urban sociology was on the various ways of life in the city. Robert Park framed the agenda for this subfield in a 1915 essay entitled "The City: Suggestions for the Investigation of Human Behavior in the City Environment."[19] Possibly because he had been a newspaperman before he became a sociologist, Park was attracted by exotic urban types—those who could serve as subjects for a human interest story (the denizen of skid row, the hobo, the taxi-hall dancer). Furthermore, he was a great walker in the city, fascinated by exotic urban neighborhoods—slums, ethnic enclaves, and the like. Out of this focus came the great urban sociology tradition of the "community case study," which uses anthropological fieldwork methods, such as participant observation, to analyze how life is lived in various subareas of cities.

What united these two strains in early urban sociology was a common set

---

[19]Robert Park, "The City: Suggestions for the Investigation of Human Behavior in the City Environment," *American Journal of Sociology* 20 (March 1915), pp. 577–612.

of theories or, more properly speaking, assumptions that have come to be known under a somewhat misleading shorthand term, "human ecology." Park borrowed the idea of ecology from geographers, who had in turn borrowed it from botanists. Just as botanists marveled at the order and balance in nature, an order no human had created but rather one that had grown out of the competitive and symbiotic relationships among various organisms, so Park and Burgess marveled at the same kinds of order they believed they were finding in the city. They believed that complex cities were made up of physically distinctive "natural areas" and that each of these small areas constituted a "social world" that could be explored by sociologists. The sum total of these physical and social worlds made up an urban mosaic of different neighborhoods and ways of life. Early urban sociologists assumed that the spatial organization of the city and its neighborhoods had direct social consequences for how different lifeways developed within the city. At times they even appeared to be saying that urban spatial organization "determined" social life. One of the premature theories in urban sociology was that there was a one-to-one correspondence between the spatial (physical) organization of cities and the social life that could go on in them.

Many later scholars have criticized these views of the organization of the city as being too naive and uncritical, for forgetting that people with different social characteristics can respond differently to the same physical setting, and for ignoring the importance of economic and political power in creating a human ecology quite different from what was found in "nature."

Chapter 10 addresses this controversy. It explores the extent to which social interactions are determined by or independent of the particular spatial settings in which people live. It surveys the findings of various empirical studies that have related physical factors, such as territoriality and the size and density of groups, to specific social behavior. While some of these findings are striking, they fail to prove conclusively that space alone is the determining factor in social interactions. Only when the demographic and social characteristics of people and their cultural patterns are very similar does spatial organization "determine" their social interaction.

These findings have cast doubt on "ecological determinacy," that is, the belief that increases in population, density, and heterogeneity—physical changes associated with the growth of cities—inevitably lead to a reduction in intimate social relations and in feelings of "community." The findings of many of the community studies that have been conducted in urban subareas have also served to undermine this belief. Indeed, many studies of the forms of communal life that have continued to exist in city neighborhoods have reached conclusions that are at odds with this assumption.

Chapter 11 surveys these community studies, showing what has been learned from them but also suggesting that in recent times they have had reduced scope and validity. It has become increasingly difficult for urban sociologists to find the small encapsulated urban neighborhoods most suited to older methods developed in community studies. Today, many urbanites have social relations that extend far beyond their residential neighborhoods and that enmesh them in far-flung networks oriented around scattered kin, workplaces which may be far from their homes, and leisure-time interests and other volunteer and social activities. New methods for uncovering nonspatial communities in the city are needed to capture these forms of community.

In Chapter 12, then, we explore some of these new techniques, especially those in the growing field of urban network analysis. This approach offers a way to make sense out of the diverse patterns that have been found over the past few decades in studies of social life in subareas of American cities.

NEW THEORIES AND A RESEARCH AGENDA FOR URBAN SOCIOLOGY

In the many years since the Chicago School set the two agendas for urban sociology, American cities have changed in dramatic fashion, and so has urban sociology. The accepted verities of the Chicago School have proven inadequate to explain the multi-centered metropolitan regions in the United States, let alone the explosive urban growth in the Third World. All these changes have created environments for which older theories and research agendas have proven increasingly inadequate and even deceptive because they point us in wrong directions. New sources of data must be tapped and new theoretical frameworks must be devised to address the two basic problematics of urban sociology, which remain:

1. *The City as a Consumed Environment.* How is it consumed and with what consequences? This is the problematic of how the built environment, in all its complexity, affects people having different psychological, social, and cultural characteristics.
2. *The City as a Produced Environment.* What produces it? This is the problematic of the political economy of space and the built environment.

Not only has the changing city presented new aspects to be investigated, but there have been numerous methodological innovations that have revealed what was previously unknown. While researchers continue to use the tools developed by the earliest urban sociologists (duly refined and improved), their studies are now being supplemented by others that focus on institutional, legal, economic, and political policies that affect the provision of urban facilities and services.

The critiques of the Chicago School have shaken the very foundations of the field. Some scholars have announced the death of urban sociology as a field—far too prematurely, we believe. Others have called for abandoning the older and increasingly discredited paradigms, arguing that a veritable scientific revolution is required. When a field is changing as dramatically as urban sociology has been, there is always the problem of how a text will handle competing paradigms. Shall they be handled separately and dispassionately? Or shall they be synthesized to ask new questions and point the way to new answers? We have tried to follow the second procedure.

In Part V we attempt to update and modify the field by incorporating the new perspectives that have recently been introduced into urban sociology. It is the most innovative portion of the book, attempting nothing less than a new theoretical approach to the field of urban sociology, one which can not only integrate new empirical findings about urban differentiation but also offer new ways to think about the causes and consequences of contemporary urban life.

Chapter 13 reviews new techniques for identifying life-style differences in America today and offers an estimate of how they are distributed numerically and geographically in contemporary American society. Far more complex than the usual ways of differentiating types of urban areas, the method of cluster analysis offers a new way to select cases for community studies that can capture the variations in ways of life that arise from the *combined* effects of the physical setting (inner city, outer city, suburban, small town, exurban or rural) *and* the socioeconomic, ethnic, and demographic characteristics of residents who have selected such residential settings.

Chapter 14 attempts to build upon the knowledge already presented to develop some theoretical concepts that could, if duly researched, move the field of urban sociology to a new level of synthesis and understanding with respect to the first problematic. It focuses on ways to study how space in the city is *consumed,* and how urban residents actively *participate* in the psycho-sociological *creation* of the physical and social environments that influence their behavior. Rather than assuming that the ecological setting has a direct effect on social life, the discussion posits two types of environment, a physical one and a social one, and suggests that human beings have behavioral responses to both types of environment that are mediated by their beliefs, their perceptions, and their actual activities in city space.

Chapter 15 focuses on the second problematic, examining in greater detail how the built environment is actually *produced,* and exploring the roles played by various interacting agents—builders; investors; political actors; businesspeople and industrialists of different types; urban planners; legal structures; local, state, and federal programs; and so on—in creating our urban environments. In this portion of the text we pose, although clearly cannot answer, the crucial question of how we can get the kinds of cities we want, assuming that only if we understand the processes that have created problems in our cities can we act effectively to solve them.

THE PLACE OF VALUES IN THIS BOOK

The study of cities, like the study of any other cultural phenomenon, is embedded not only in the object itself (which is changing) but in the values of those who study it. There is no way, then, that we can avoid making value statements about the city and about the forces that have created it. "Value-free" social science is probably not possible, nor perhaps even desirable.

Our values have shaped this book in inevitable ways. Values, however, are not the same as biases. Values shape and select. Biases distort and falsify. We hope that we have been able to maintain that distinction and to avoid bias in presenting the material.

In one area we wish to make our values explicit. The title of this book was chosen because it has a double meaning. If one reads "changing" as an adjective, it conveys the fact that cities are continually undergoing transformations. That we believe. But if one reads "changing" as a verb, it conveys the idea that, since cities are human creations, they can be changed by us. It is *our* actions, through economic and political policies and through our own ways of relating to the urban environment, that have made our cities what they are. If we find them unpleasant, unjust, and inhuman, we must learn to change them. But to do that, we must know them better. The agenda for changing cities is the logical end point for urban sociologists and probably the main reason you decided to take this course. It is also the reason this book was written.

PART
ONE

Historical Development of the City

Chapter
2

The Origin and Development of Cities

WHERE AND WHEN CITIES FIRST APPEARED

The first "true" cities date back only to 4000–3000 B.C., that is, some five or six thousand years ago.[1] Although this includes the entire period of written history, it is very short when compared either with the 300,000 to 400,000 years of human evolution or with the 40,000 years that homo sapiens sapiens (the mod-

---

[1] Parts of this chapter have been adapted from Noel Gist and Sylvia Fava, *Urban Society,* 6th ed. (New York: Thomas Y. Crowell, 1974), although certain facts have been corrected in light of later research. It must be recognized that later revisions will also be needed as new evidence is uncovered. There is great uncertainty over the dating of all events before written history. For example, many authorities would assign a date of 700,000 to 1,000,000 years for the appearance of the human species on earth. Authorities also differ on the dates for the beginning of the Neolithic Era in various parts of the world, the first emergence of cities, of metal-working, and so on. Dating through radioactive carbon is beginning to substitute real for speculative dates, but still gives only a broad range of possibility. Gist and Fava have generally followed the dating suggested in Robert Braidwood and Gordon Willey, eds., *Courses Toward Urban Life* (Chicago: Aldine Publishing Company, 1962), Graham Clarke and Stuart Piggot, *Prehistoric Societies* (New York: Knopf, 1965), and David Harris, "New Light on Plant Domestication and the Origins of Agriculture: A Review," *Geographical Review* 57 (January 1967), pp. 90–107.

ern human) has existed. Thus, the 6,000 years of urban existence represent only 1–2 percent of total human existence on earth and 12–15 percent of our existence as physically modern.

Despite their late appearance, cities were hardly a unique "invention" monopolized by one region and passed on to others. Although the earliest cities appeared in approximately 3500 B.C. in southern Iraq (called Mesopotamia, "between the rivers," because the land lay between the Tigris and Euphrates rivers), other urban civilizations later developed in such widely separated places as the Nile Valley (now Egypt), the Indus Valley (now Pakistan), and the Yellow River Valley (in China). In all four cases, cities developed on rich river-irrigated land. This alerts us to one ecological prerequisite for the appearance of cities, namely, extensive cereal agriculture.

There seem, however, to have been several possible routes to urbanization. While the earliest cities were found in river valleys, later urban centers arose along major trade routes and at ceremonial sites. And in the case of Central America, whose cities developed even later, location on lakes as well as rivers occurred (Figures 2.1 and 2.2).

While the "invention" of cities did not require diffusion, the appearance of cities was associated with the development of more sophisticated means of transportation and with the expansion of control over a wide area surrounding the city. Both of these trends drew previously isolated societies closer together, permitting them to learn from one another. Although the archaeological record is still far from complete, every year additional evidence is discovered that places urbanization earlier in time, that suggests cities were denser and more numerous in certain regions than was previously thought possible, and that uncovers connections between centers of urban culture formerly believed to have been quite independent.

Thus, precursors to the Egyptian political institution of kingship, an institution that helped create urban developments at Memphis by about 2700 B.C., have now been found much farther upstream in Nubia (the Sudan) and much

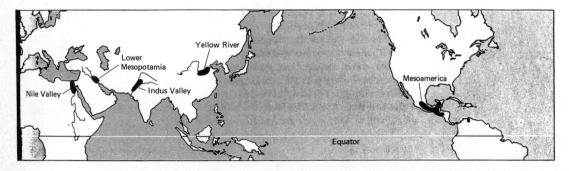

Figure 2.1 Locations of the world's earliest urban developments: in the Nile Valley (Egypt), lower Mesopotamia (now Iraq), the Indus River Valley (now Pakistan), the Yellow River (China), and Mesoamerica (now Mexico). (*Source:* Gideon Sjoberg, "The Origin and Evolution of Cities." Copyright © 1965 by Scientific American, Inc. All rights reserved. Reproduced from N. Gist and S. Fava, *Urban Society,* 6th ed. 1974.)

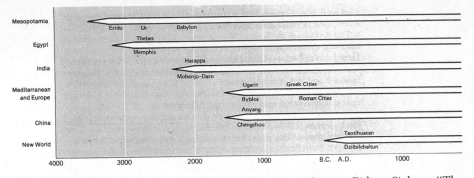

Figure 2.2 The sequence of urban evolution by region. (*Source:* Gideon Sjoberg, "The Origin and Evolution of Cities." Copyright © 1965 by Scientific American, Inc. All rights reserved. Reproduced from N. Gist and S. Fava, *Urban Society,* 6th ed., 1974.)

farther back in time, circa 3300 B.C. This suggests that the idea of the city did not diffuse to Egypt from Mesopotamia, but rather, that changes indigenous to the Nile Valley itself were sufficient to account for the rise of cities there. Eventually, however, contacts between the two river valley civilizations did occur, which greatly enhanced the culture of each.

On the other hand, Mesopotamian society apparently helped to diffuse urbanism elsewhere. On the land bridge of Iran archaeologists have excavated centers for long-distance trade that date back to the fourth millennium. The existence of these transit towns makes it easier to understand how Mesopotamia could have influenced the third millennium development of such Indus Valley urban centers as Mohenjo-Daro and Harappa, even though evidence of direct contact between the two centers of civilization is still modest.[2] Connections between Mesopotamia and urbanizing regions to the north and west (in Syria and Anatolia, now Turkey) have also been coming to light. Italian archaeologists digging near Aleppo in northern Syria uncovered evidence of Ebla, a previously unknown urban commercial civilization that apparently rivaled Egypt by the second millennium.[3] More and more smaller urban centers are being uncovered on the lands intervening.

---

[2]C. C. Lamberg-Karlovsky and Martha Lamberg-Karlovsky, "An Early City in Iran," in Kingsley Davis, ed., *Cities: Their Origin, Growth, and Human Impact* (a special collection of articles from *Scientific American* published in San Francisco by W. H. Freeman in 1973), pp. 28–37. Proof of the connection between Mesopotamia and the Indus Valley has recently been strengthened by the excavations at Dilmun on the island of Bahrain in the Arab Gulf; this town was apparently a crucial link in the trade between the two areas. See Geoffrey Bibby, *Looking for Dilmun* (New York: Knopf, 1970). The most exciting archaeological findings, however, come from recent excavations in Afghanistan that suggest proto-urban precursors to the Indus Valley that may date back to the seventh millennium B.C.

[3]See Paolo Matthiae, *Ebla: An Empire Rediscovered,* trans. Christopher Holme (Garden City, NY: Doubleday, 1981); Howard La Fay, "Ebla: Splendor of an Unknown Empire," *National Geographic* 154 (December 1978), pp. 730–759; Tor Eigeland, "Ebla: City of the White Stones," *Armaco World Magazine* (April–March 1978), pp. 10–18; and for the first announcements of the find, *The New York Times*, October 25, 1976, p. 8 and December 30, 1976, pp. 1 and 14.

Urbanization first developed, then, in a densely settled region that stretched from Anatolia and Egypt on the west to the Indus Valley on the east. Interlaced by long-distance trade routes, small local empires flourished, each supporting a few urban centers and many more small towns and villages. By 2500 B.C. to 1700 B.C., remarkably advanced cities coexisted in different cultural regions and were in indirect, if not direct, contact with one another.

Toward the end of this period (circa 1850 B.C.), a parallel development began in the Yellow River Valley of northeast China. Between 1750 and 1100 B.C. the Shang dynasty controlled much of northern China. At least one of the major capitals of their empire, the city of Cheng-Chou, has been excavated and is being intensively studied.[4] We return to this important case later.

The New World, in contrast to Asia, lagged far behind. Evidence of that region's first towns dates back only to 300 B.C., when major urban centers appeared along the lakes of the Mexican central plateau. (Proto-cities existed even earlier in the Oaxaca Valley along the river.) It has been traditional to treat these developments as completely independent from other urban centers, but at least one writer has argued that migrations from China may have influenced New World urbanization.[5]

Even though cities appeared in a number of places, they were so rare and unusual in human history that their emergence must be explained. The facts are that (1) the city emerged relatively recently; (2) some 2000 years elapsed between its first appearance in Mesopotamia and the point in time when one could say that this prototype had spread or made multiple appearances along the route between Egypt and China; and (3) except for this admittedly large swath of terrain across Asia between the 20th and 35th parallels, the world had no cities . We are then forced to ask: How did cities come into being, and why did they appear where they did, rather than elsewhere? In answering these questions we may come closer to understanding the essential nature of cities and the prerequisites for their development.

WHY CITIES APPEARED WHEN AND WHERE THEY DID

Throughout most of history, human beings were nomadic, the men hunting wild animals, the women gathering edible plants. Technology was simple

---

[4]Chang, Kwang-chih, *The Archaeology of Ancient China* (New Haven: Yale University Press, 1977), pp. 218ff. There is now a 1988 edition of this fine source.

[5]It is no longer disputed that the Indian populations of central America originated in the Orient, but whether they brought "urbanism" with them or reinvented it in the New World is not known, although the former seems unlikely. However, Betty Meggers has argued that there are such strong parallels between Shang culture in China and Olmec culture (the precursor of Aztec culture) in Mexico about 1200 B.C. that she believes that Mesoamerican civilization originated in the Yellow River Valley and was carried to the New World via a trans-Pacific route. See her "The Transpacific Origin of Mesoamerican Civilizations: A Preliminary Review of the Evidence and Its Theoretical Implication," *American Anthropologist* 77 (March 1975), pp. 1–23.

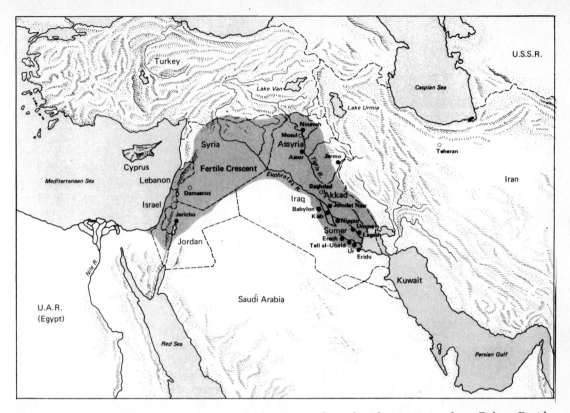

Figure 2.3 The Fertile Crescent and its cities. (*Source:* Adapted with permission from Robert Braid-wood, "Agricultural Revolution." Copyright © 1960 by Scientific American, Inc. All rights reserved. Reproduced from N. Gist and S. Fava, *Urban Society*, 6th edition, 1974.)

and the natural environment was still undergoing drastic transformations. The last of these transformations occurred about 9000 B.C. when the glaciers retreated, which caused great changes in climate, wildlife, and rainfall distribution. The effects of these changes were not felt uniformly. In northern Europe, for example, forests grew on what had been tundra, and mammoths, rhinoceri, and giant bears became extinct. Other parts of the world were inundated by water. In still other places, the climate became more benign. This was particularly true for the Middle East, a zone encompassing (present-day) Egypt and the Sudan on the southwest, Turkey on the northwest, but having as its heartland the region that has been called the "Fertile Crescent," the land arching between the Sinai desert at the Mediterranean and the marshy outlet of the Tigris-Euphrates at the Arabian Gulf that leads to the Indian Ocean. (Figure 2.3)

It was in the Middle East that humans apparently made the first difficult shift from food gathering to food production, and it was here that, several thousands of years later, the first cities appeared. By 7000 B.C. inhabitants of the region had already domesticated the wild ancestors of barley, wheat, sheep, goats, and cattle, although the first methods of agriculture and animal husbandry were so primitive that people still depended heavily on hunting and gathering. Tools were largely made of stone, although better grinding techniques gave them a sharper edge. Clay was fired to produce hardened pottery and weaving was invented to supplement items made from animal skins. During this period in human history, called the Neolithic (New Stone) Age, occurred what has been called an "agricultural revolution."

While this "revolution" was neither rapid nor tumultuous, it was indeed revolutionary, in the sense that the increased food production permitted much larger numbers of persons to settle in permanent and more dense communities. It is estimated that the technology of the earlier Paleolithic Age (stone-using, hunting and gathering) had permitted the support of human populations at average densities of only one person for every two square miles of territory. In contrast, neolithic technology allowed thirty or more persons to be supported per square mile of resources.[6] Thus, the new means of production permitted the emergence of comparatively large and permanent settlements in the Middle East—for the very first time in history.

Evidence of numerous neolithic settlements that were older, larger, and more closely spaced than previously anticipated is still being uncovered throughout the Middle East. One of the most important finds was made by James Mellaart in 1958 when he was excavating in southern Anatolia (Turkey). The town he found, called Catal (pronounced Chatal) Huyuk, is currently believed to have been the largest neolithic settlement in the region, covering some thirty-two acres. It is certainly one of the very oldest neolithic communities, since radiocarbon dating has established its existence as early as 6800 B.C.

What can we learn from this proto-city of Catal Huyuk? Quite a bit, thanks not only to archaeological evidence but also to the fact that its inhabitants left us a wall painting believed to represent the town (see Figure 2.4). It shows that their rectangular mudbrick houses were "built one against the other, presenting to the outside world a blank wall which gave the settlement the appearance of a fortress."[7] Rooms were about ten by thirteen feet in size, and each dwelling had its own storehouse. The town included at least forty structures identified by Mellaart as cult centers or domestic shrines (dedicated to female deities), indicating that religion was as central to the belief system of the town's inhabitants as were agriculture and the domestication of animals to their economic subsistence. And finally, since Catal Huyuk was close to rich deposits of ob-

---

[6]V. Gordon Childe, "The Urban Revolution," *Town Planning Review* 21 (April 1950), pp. 4–5.

[7]Quotation from U. Bahadir Alkim, *Anatolia from the Beginnings to the End of the 2nd Millennium*, trans. James Hogarth (Cleveland, OH: World Publishing Co., 1968), p. 52. For additional information on Catal Huyuk, see James Mellaart, *The Archaeology of Ancient Turkey* (London: Bodley Head, 1978), and his *Catal Huyuk: A Neolithic Town in Anatolia* (New York: McGraw-Hill, 1967).

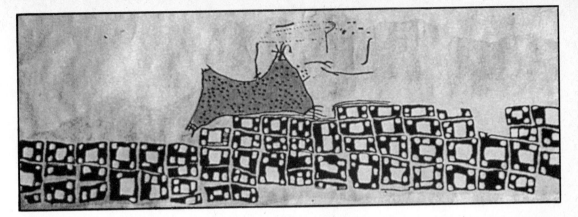

Figure 2.4 Rendering of wall painting showing the town plan of Catal Huyuk and a volcanic eruption, found at Level VII (c. 6200 B.C.). (*Source:* James Mellaart, *Earliest Civilizations of the Near East* [London: Thames and Hudson, 1965] and also in James Mellaart, *Catal Huyuk: A Neolithic Town in Anatolia* [New York: McGraw-Hill, 1967]. Copyright by James Mellaart. Reproduced here with permission of the author.)

sidian, a volcanic glass with a cutting edge much harder and sharper than stone, it is likely that the town was also involved in long-distance trade.

The appearance in the early neolithic period of so complex a settled community as Catal Huyuk, with its almost urban character, belies the older image of neolithic settlements as mere farming villages. But one must recognize that it was exceptional. Far more typical for the time was the small village of Jarmo on the Iranian plateau, where some 150 people lived about 6500 B.C. But even in this tiny settlement of some twenty-five mud houses were found tools and stone objects of fine workmanship based on new stone-working techniques, as well as products of weaving and clay-working. Clay figurines used as religious cult objects were abundant, as were tools of obsidian, even though the nearest source of this material was some 200 miles away. Clearly, items originating in such places as Catal Huyuk were reaching tiny settlements such as Jarmo.[8]

By 5000 B.C. the Fertile Crescent and nearby areas of the Middle East were studded with agricultural villages like Jarmo, and there were proto-cities like Catal Huyuk that had begun to foreshadow the emergence of "true" cities. These settlements were like cities in that they were permanent, well populated, and densely occupied. Like the cities that followed them, they were organized primarily around agriculture, even though the surplus they were able to produce was still very modest. Female-focused religions were a central feature of life, as indicated by the presence of multiple shrines and ceremonial altars, but

[8]The description of Jarmo is based on Robert Braidwood and Bruce Howe, "Southwestern Asia Beyond the Land of the Mediterranean Littoral," in Braidwood and Willey, eds., *Courses Toward Urban Life* (1962), pp. 132–146; and Robert Braidwood, "The Agricultural Revolution," *Scientific American* 203 (September 1960), pp. 130–152.

centralized temple complexes dedicated to male gods had not yet appeared. Trade, even long-distance trade, was not entirely lacking, but it dealt with necessary items such as tools, rather than with luxury goods. In short, these proto-cities were small, existed at near-subsistence levels, and were egalitarian in social organization.

THE TRANSITION TO "TRUE" CITIES

In contrast to the proto-cities described above, the "true" cities that followed were bigger and more complexly organized. Their larger populations enjoyed a higher standard of living, which even included luxuries for some. They developed systems of written notation and expressed themselves through decorative art and architecture well beyond functional necessity. In general, the first true urbanites began to create what we call "civilization," a term that derives from the Latin *civitas*, meaning city. How did mankind make the transition from proto-cities to true cities? What was required, beyond a benign environment and some technological competence?

It is sobering to recognize that what was needed to create cities out of the neolithic farming villages that had by then proliferated in areas well endowed with a water supply was the *concentration of power*, which some (Mumford and Eisler, among others) hypothesize came from nomadic invaders with a very different type of social organization. However instituted, the new system was characterized by the existence of a small class of individuals who had assembled power and used it to extract "surplus" wealth from others. This privileged group devoted itself to such nonagricultural activities as making war, supervising religious observances, trading, and keeping records of transactions. From these activities came greater wealth, elaborate art and engineering, and the development of a written literature—all associated with urban civilization.

Usually, when scholars discuss the origin of cities, they attribute the appearance of a surplus (that is, more food and other necessities than were absolutely required for simple subsistence) to improvements in the environment and to changes in technology, such as the invention of the plow. Social inventions, such as the more complex social division of labor and the emergence of priest-kings at the top of a developing social hierarchy, are viewed as the beneficial results of the surplus.

This does not seem to be a very satisfactory explanation. Consider your own lives. How much "surplus wealth" does your family have that it would voluntarily give away to support others? If with all the wealth of the twentieth century we do not feel ourselves endowed with "surplus," how could neolithic people, living under primitive and brute conditions, suddenly have felt rich enough to give their "surplus" away? The fact is that surplus is almost never given; it is much more likely to be taken, in the form of tribute or taxes.

"Real" surplus was created out of "potential" surplus when powerful individuals, utilizing fear of the gods or of invaders, were able to force or cajole

Table 2.1 TIME SPENT BY MARRIED MEN AND WOMEN
PER DAY IN ACTIVITY

Activity	Hours spent daily by			
	Married men		Married women	
Total work	6.0		7.4	
food preparation		0.2		2.4
food production		4.4		1.8
manufacture		1.4		2.1
child care		0		1.1
Leisure	3.6		3.9	
hygiene		0.3		0.6
visiting		1.0		0.8
idle		2.3		2.5
Total day	9.6		11.3	

Source: Allen Johnson, "The Allocation of Time in a Michiguenga Community," mimeographed 1974 paper as cited in M. Harris, *Culture, People, Nature* (New York: Thomas Y. Crowell, 1975), p. 254.

essential food away from people, thus requiring them to work longer hours to grow the additional food needed for their own use. If neolithic people had to work full-time to meet their own daily needs, no amount of force could have produced this "surplus." But it appears that their working hours were relatively short.

While the workdays of neolithic men and women in 7000 B.C. clearly cannot be reconstructed at this late date, those of groups now living under similar technological conditions have been studied. One anthropologist has provided the accompanying table (Table 2.1), showing the time devoted to various activities per day per married adult in a present-day neolithic village in upland Peru.[9] As can be seen, each adult has almost four hours during which he or she could have worked but instead remained idle or went visiting. Robert Adams has argued much the same thing. He notes that in Mesoamerica, traditional swidden agriculture requires only about 150 man-days of annual work for subsistence; in Iraq (Mesopotamia), families actually spend only 249 man-days per year and would require only about half of that to meet their "immediate subsistence requirements."[10] More recently, a study of the contemporary hunting and gathering society of the ! Kung bushmen of Africa reveals that women gather

---

[9]Allen Johnson, "The Allocation of Time in a Michiguenga Community," mimeographed (1974), as reproduced on p. 254 of Marvin Harris, *Culture, People, Nature*, 2d ed. (New York: Thomas Y. Crowell, 1975). See also Marshall Sahlins, *Stone Age Economics* (Chicago: Aldine, 1972).

[10]Robert McC. Adams, *The Evolution of Urban Society: Early Mesopotamia and Prehispanic Mexico* (Chicago: Aldine Publishing Company, 1966), p. 42.

edible roots only three days each week and that men hunt game only one week out of four in order to subsist.[11]

This considerable gap between the labor-time needed by neolithic people to subsist and the amount of time at their disposal, if only someone could "convince" them to work during their leisure hours, provided the potential for the development of cities. It was political power via supernatural or physical force that evidently mobilized this surplus.

The development of the city was thus the result not only of technological innovations and environmental potential but also of social inventions and the emergence of a class structure. Cities came into being when dominant individuals and groups, such as warriors and priests, succeeded in getting others to work longer hours. A surplus was thus extracted or "created" from within the society itself.

Such surplus, however, could be supplemented by three other means. The labor of others might be coerced through conquest and direct slavery. Surplus might also be extracted after conquest through the collection of "protection money," indemnities, or tribute.[12] And finally, surplus might be captured by trading locally produced goods that required little labor power for goods produced by others in more distant places.[13] In any case, no matter how and from whom the surplus was obtained, the appearance of cities was inextricably linked to the emergence of an institutionalized system of power whereby rulers and priests were able to transform the potential surplus made possible by the agricultural revolution into a real surplus placed at their disposal.

The Prerequisites for True Cities

Perhaps the best way to understand how true cities differed from their precursors is to look more closely at some early examples, namely, at cities that appeared in the subarea of the Fertile Crescent variously called Mesopotamia, Sumer, Babylonia, and now, Iraq. Three characteristics stand out in the detailed accounts of the birth of cities in Mesopotamia after 3500 B.C.

---

[11]See Marjory Shostak, *Nisa* (Cambridge: Harvard University Press, 1980).

[12]Conquest and the ability to use the labor of captives are obvious ways, but one must also recognize that penalties and tribute payments were hidden methods to obtain the fruits of others' labor. Such payments were often excessive. For example, there is evidence that in the third millennium B.C. a Mesopotamian city-state called Umma paid a fine of 10,800 metric tons of grain to the neighboring city-state against which it had tried to revolt. And in a later period, from Mesoamerica there is evidence that the Aztec capital received 52,600 tons of foodstuffs annually, as well as clothing and luxuries of all kinds, all paid as tribute from subordinate neighboring states. See Bruce Trigger, "Determinants of Urban Growth in Preindustrial Societies," as reprinted in Ruth Tringham, ed., *Urban Settlements: The Process of Urbanization in Archaeological Settlements* (Andover, MA: Warner Modular Publications, 1973), pp. 580–81.

[13]Jane Jacobs, in her *The Economy of Cities* (New York: Random House, 1969), makes trade the primary source of early surplus, ignoring the crucial role played by confiscation, enslavement, and tribute—what Marxists term "primitive accumulation."

Population Growth and Density   First, there was a marked increase in total population and settlement density. Technological improvements, including flood control, irrigation,[14] and the invention of the plow, led to a dramatic increase in total population throughout the region between 6000 and 4500 B.C.[15] As this population spread out, neighboring groups began to come into contact and then to compete with one another for space. To protect themselves from the conflicts that arose, and also to guard their produce from the depredations of other groups who were still nomadic, the population congregated into centralized zones of dense settlement, some of which were ringed with fortifications and all of which came under the protection of priest-kings who oversaw defense and who guarded the surplus in storerooms associated with sacredly protected space in the temples.[16]

Sociopolitical Hierarchy and Spatial Differentiation   Second, a sharply defined hierarchy of sociopolitical positions associated with differential wealth replaced the earlier more egalitarian social system of neolithic times. Those in charge of protection and spiritual direction accumulated the surplus, and this inequality was translated into spatial arrangements. Whereas in Catal Huyuk houses were fairly uniform in size and there were many scattered religious sites, in the true cities of Mesopotamia that followed there were monumental palace complexes and elaborate centralized temples. (See Figure 2.5 showing the temple at Ur.) Their existence offers irrefutable evidence of the heightened social differentiation associated with urbanization.

The importance of the temple in Mesopotamia cannot be overestimated. While Childe's contention—that "most of the land of each community belonged to the temple of a deity and was tilled on behalf of the god by tenants, share-croppers or day-laborers under the superintendence of his servants, or priests"[17]—is no longer accepted as unquestionable, there is little doubt that "the oldest decipherable documents from Mesopotamia are . . . the accounts of temple revenues kept by priests . . . [that] reveal the temple as not only the

---

[14]Adams has claimed that too much has been made of irrigation and the need to coordinate it as an explanation for early urban growth. He notes, from detailed studies of the drainage system of Mesopotamia, that the valley between the Tigris and Euphrates did not require such large-scale coordination. See Robert McC. Adams, *Land Behind Baghdad* (Chicago: University of Chicago Press, 1965).

[15]T. Cuyler Young, Jr., in his "Population Densities and Early Mesopotamian Urbanism," claims that "a simple site count suggests population increased some thirteen-fold between c.6000 and 4500 B.C." See Peter Ucko, Ruth Tringham, and G. W. Dimbleby, eds., *Man, Settlement and Urbanization* (London: Gerald Duckworth and Company, Ltd., 1972; Cambridge, MA: Schenkman Publishing Co., 1972), p. 830.

[16]Scholars as diverse as archaeologist Bruce Trigger, in "Determinants of Urban Growth in Preindustrial Societies," in Tringham, ed., *Urban Settlements* (1973), and Max Weber, in *The City*, ed. and trans. Don Martindale and Gertrud Neuwirth (New York: Colliers Books, 1962), which deals with European medieval cities, point to defensive walls as a key characteristic of early cities.

[17]V. Gordon Childe, *New Light on the Most Ancient Middle East* (4th ed., London: Routledge & Kegan Paul, 1964; first pub. 1928), p. 118.

Figure 2.5 Ziggurat of the Temple at Ur, Mesopotamia, originally built c. 1500 B.C. (*Source: Iraq: A Tourist's Guide* [Baghdad: Tourism and Resorts Administration, n.d.].)

center of the city's religious life, but also the nucleus of capital accumulation."[18] Apparently, the temples employed large numbers of agricultural workers, gave loans to small farmers, financed long-distance sea trade, and also ran numerous workshops for production. It would be a mistake, however, to think of the temple as only a religious institution. Postgate reminds us that "the political ruler, by virtue of his office, was also the head of the temple."[19]

Imperial Control   The third characteristic of a true city, as contrasted with a proto-city such as Catal Huyuk, was that it was more than a central place serving and supported by its surrounding agricultural hinterland. It commanded resources from a much wider area. Even though the first cities were city-states,

---

[18]V. Gordon Childe, *Man Makes Himself* (New York: New American Library, 1951), p. 124.

[19]J. N. Postgate, "The Temple in the Mesopotamian Secular Community," in Ucko *et al.*, eds., *Man, Settlement and Urbanism* (1972), especially pp. 813–820; the quotation is taken from p. 820. Parallels and contrasts between the roles of the temple in Mesopotamian and South Indian cities have been explored in Richard G. Fox and Allen Zagarell, "The Political Economy of Mesopotamian and South Indian Temples: The Formation and Reproduction of Urban Society," *Comparative Urban Research* 9:1 (1982), pp. 8–27.

rather than capitals of countries, they were the centers of political domination over neighbors and the controllers of a widely ranging trade that passed overland in great caravans or traversed the seas to distant ports.[20] Both by conquest and the collection of tribute and by control over trade, the original cities expanded the base from which they derived their wealth. They extracted the surplus not only from agriculturalists directly under their control but from the rest of the then-known "world."

Although the urban civilizations that appeared later (Egypt, then the Indus, China, and finally, much later, Central America) differed in detail from Mesopotamia, all shared these three characteristics. Egypt and China were both empire-oriented and organized on a grander scale than the city-states of Mesopotamia. This may have been because their central cities controlled more extensive river valley irrigation systems. In any event, both civilizations developed elaborate administrative apparatuses to oversee water distribution and to collect taxes. In contrast, long-distance trade seems to have played a more important role in the urban civilizations of Anatolia and the Indus Valley, with a commensurate elaboration of commercial regulations and import-export duties. Mesoamerican cities such as Teotihuacan seem to have originated, as did many Mesopotamian and Indus cities, as ceremonial centers, with their prime *raison d'être* their sacred role in religion. Thus, religious conquest or conversions were also routes to empire.

Regardless of the manner in which these early cities achieved their dominance, they shared some basic physical characteristics that reflected their social organization and their special relationship to their surroundings. All these early cities contained monumental temples, each with associated storerooms where wealth was kept. Equally universal were the elegant palaces of the rulers who were also heads of the religious hierarchy. Defensive walls were also typical, although not all early cities were fortified. (Even relatively small towns in Anatolia were walled, while the largest cities in Egypt apparently were not.)

Perhaps the most impressive walled city was Cheng-Chou near the Yellow River in China. Its wall, constructed around 1650 B.C., enclosed an area of some 3.2 square kilometers. Scholars have calculated that its construction would have required some 10,000 workers laboring 330 days per year for some eighteen years.[21] Equally impressive evidence that the early rulers were able to command limitless labor for the construction of monuments can be found in the pyramids of Egypt (the most famous of which are at Giza, with others scattered throughout the country) and the comparably ambitious pyramids in Mexico.

A further indication of the centralization of power and decision making in early empires was the fact that many of the major cities were carefully planned.

---

[20]See Robert Griffeth and Carol G. Thomas, eds., *The City-State in Five Cultures* (Santa Barbara, CA: ABC-Clio Press, 1981) for details on Sumerian city-states but also for a comparative view, presented especially in pp. 181–207.

[21]See Kwang-chih Chang, *The Archeology of Ancient China*, p. 234.

Cheng-Chou, like most Chinese cities, was laid out carefully according to the cardinal axes.[22] The towns of Mohenjo-Daro and Harappa in the Indus Valley demonstrate remarkable organization according to a gridiron pattern which could have been achieved only through central planning.[23]

Thus, both history and archaeological evidence from each of these urban civilizations point to the crucial importance of political centralization. Until it occurred, surplus could not be mobilized. And unless it was maintained, cities could not survive. A clear illustration of this principle is the Mayan civilization which rose and then fell in Central America. The institution of chiefdom was established throughout Mesoamerica between 600 B.C. and A.D. 300, at which point true cities appeared. The collapse of Mayan civilization in the ninth century A.D., which many scholars had previously attributed to a decline in population, has recently been explained in a more convincing fashion. The cities and the civilization that gave rise to them apparently came to an end because the class system broke down; surplus could no longer be mobilized.

But was a class system based upon "oriental despotism"[24] the only route to urbanization? Clearly this was not the case, for cities later developed in regions not bonded together through river valley irrigation systems, and in societies organized along more egalitarian lines. Empire can be achieved in many ways, as the European examples demonstrate.

EARLY EUROPEAN URBAN CIVILIZATIONS: GREECE AND ROME

Developments in Europe lagged far behind those in Asia and Africa, where great urban civilizations had flowered by the second millennium B.C. Significantly, European cities first began in areas geographically closest to the Middle East and were connected to it not only by the movement of goods and ideas but by the migrations of peoples. Europe's earliest cities appeared toward the end of the second millennium before the Christian Era, founded by the Mycenaean Greeks on mainland Greece and by the Minoans on the island of Crete. These two interrelated civilizations emerged between 2000 and 1500 B.C. Because Greek civilization is an important ancestor of our own, and because the Greek city-state or *polis* is close to the type of city that later developed in medieval Europe, the polis deserves careful examination.

---

[22]Paul Wheatley, *The Pivot of the Four Quarters: A Preliminary Inquiry into the Origins and Character of the Ancient Chinese City* (Chicago: Aldine, 1971).

[23]See C. P. Venkatarama Aiyar, *Town Planning in Ancient Dekkan* (Madras: Law Printing House, 1916), and the more recent book by Prabhakar Begde, *Ancient and Mediaeval Town-Planning in India* (New Delhi: Sagar Publications, 1978), pp. 15–17.

[24]The term and theory are from Karl Wittfogel, *Oriental Despotism: A Comparative Study of Total Power* (New Haven: Yale University Press, 1957).

The Greek Polis

Pounds calls the Greek *polis* "the best documented of all urban and quasi-urban institutions in the ancient world."[25] The documentation reveals that most of these city-states were quite small, having between 200 and 20,000 inhabitants each, in contrast to the much more populous centers in Asia. However, what they lacked in individual size they made up for in interurban organization. Literally hundreds of these small urban places were linked together through leagues and associations. Furthermore, mainland cities were linked to their colonies, that is, sister cities founded throughout Asia Minor by the surplus population from Greece. In some of these leagues there were dominant city-states; Athens became one such dominant polis by the fifth century B.C., living not only on the wealth produced in its small surrounding agricultural hinterland but on the proceeds from an active sea trade that ranged widely throughout the Mediterranean. Figure 2.6 shows the tribute colonies of the Greek city-states.

The Greek city-state illustrates an alternative path to urbanism, and yet the three basic prerequisites of the true city are present, albeit in modified form. Instead of gathering people together into a single large city, the Greeks apparently gained the critical population density required for urban life through political alliances among many decentralized settlements. Protected by the sea and masters of it by virtue of their sailing skills, they needed no walls to fend off potential invaders.

Social differentiation was extremely important in permitting the accumulation of surplus, but it was achieved in part by a differentiation in power among the city-states themselves, with a few dominant towns drawing tribute from client city-states within their league and from colonies planted in alien territorial footholds. Dependence upon a wide hinterland and its products was no less important to the Greek cities than to Cheng-Chou or Harappa, but in place of the great river overland caravan routes which were the lifelines of Asian cities, the Greeks had the sea lanes that crisscrossed the Mediterranean.

Internally, the inhabitants of the Greek city-states were highly differentiated by a system we seldom associate with classical ideals of freedom and democracy. First, there was a high degree of differentiation between men and women, and the beneficiaries of the system were almost exclusively male. Second, the surplus that permitted the construction of marble temples and marketplaces, the leisure time that allowed philosophers to ponder the nature of the universe and of good and evil, and the wealth that patronized the artistic creations of sculptors and dramatists, were either captured as tribute or produced by slaves.

Although slavery existed in the earlier Asian urban civilizations, it was a mixed category made up of a variety of types. "It was the Greek city-states that

---

[25]Norman J. C. Pounds, "The Urbanization of the Classical World," in *Annals of the Association of American Geographers* 59 (March 1969), p. 135. The description of the regional organization of Greek city-states is drawn from this source.

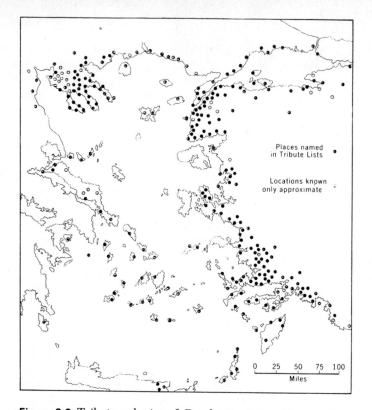

Places named
in Tribute Lists

Locations known
only approximate

0   25   50   75   100
Miles

Figure 2.6 Tribute colonies of Greek city-states. (*Source:* Norman Pounds, "The Urbanization of the Classical World," in *Annals of the Association of American Geographers.* Copyright 1969 by Association of American Geographers. Reprinted with permission.)

first rendered slavery absolute in form and dominant in extent."[26] The exact ratio of slaves to free persons in the Greek city-states cannot be known with precision. During the peak period of Athenian splendor in the fifth century B.C. it may have been as high as four slaves for every free person, although during later periods of decline it sank to a one-to-one ratio.[27] Thus, to the earlier ways of accumulating surplus to support cities the Greeks added two innovations: *slavery* for rural production and urban crafts, and *settler colonialism,* in which colonies were dependent upon a "mother city" or metropolis.

---

[26]Perry Anderson, *Passages from Antiquity to Feudalism* (London: NLB, 1974), especially Chapter 1. The quotation is from p. 19.

[27]Anderson's sources include M. I. Finley, "Between Slavery and Freedom," in *Comparative Studies in Society and History* VI (1963–1964), and his "Was Greek Civilization Based on Slave Labour?" in *Historia* 8 (1959). See also M. I. Finley, *The Ancient Economy* (Berkeley, Calif.: University of California Press, 1973), and *Ancient Slavery and Modern Ideology* (London: Chatto and Windus, 1980).

Rome

Both of these innovations were to be carried to even greater heights by Rome, which, by the second and third centuries A.D., had become the largest city ever known in the Western world and probably in the entire world up to that time. At its peak Rome may have had as many as one million inhabitants. Such a population could only have been supported through the perfection of previous means of extracting surplus and the innovation of new techniques to generate and concentrate wealth.

In the space of a few centuries, the imperial capital of Rome stood at the apex of a vast system of urban settlements. Some of those settlements were incorporated from preexisting urban civilizations (notably in the Middle East, North Africa, and Greece). Some were true colonies, established on virgin sites and populated by retired soldiers. And some were towns that had grown up around the military forts the Romans built to guard the frontiers of their expanding empire. Figure 2.7 shows only the European cities of the Roman Empire. There were equally numerous settlements in Asia Minor and North Africa.

Clearly, an empire of this size and complexity had never before been created. Innovations in methods of unification permitted this new scale. Religion was made more universal by incorporating a variety of tribal deities into

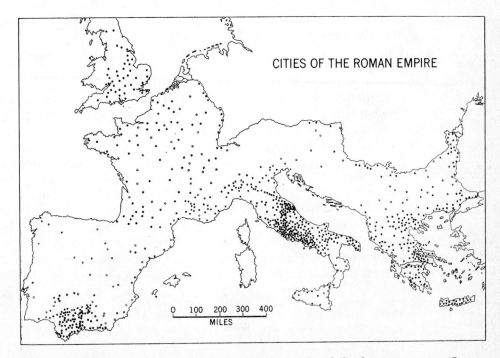

Figure 2.7 Cities of the Roman Empire in the second and third centuries A.D. (*Source:* Norman Pounds. "The Urbanization of the Classical World," in *Annals of the Association of American Geographers.* Copyright 1969 by Association of American Geographers. Reprinted with permission.)

the large array of Greek gods and goddesses. In early classical times, each group or tribe had its own deity. According to Fustel de Coulanges, early Greek cities were founded as "religious acts" and as sanctuaries for common worship, and each city had its own gods, corps of priests, dogmas, and ceremonies.[28] Unification of these separate cults via polytheism was a part of political unification. The same was true regarding law. One of the great contributions of Rome was its unified legal code, elements of which have been incorporated into contemporary legal principles and statutes.

Physical unification was no less important than symbolic and legal unification. As in Greek times, the empire was tied together primarily by the sea lanes that crisscrossed the Mediterranean. Rome commanded the key position in that sea and stood at the center of a web radiating in all directions. Grain and minerals were shipped from distant provinces to Rome, which served as both temple and storehouse. While sea traffic continued to be the cheapest mode of transport,[29] it was supplemented by land travel. The Romans produced one of the finest road systems ever built—a vast network of some 52,000 miles of well-maintained, well-policed highways that facilitated the free movement of goods and people throughout the empire. Many of these roads, duly repaired and reconstructed, still serve as the base for the major routes of Europe.

But it was in the political arena that Rome was most innovative. A relatively stable, broadly based system of social elites, combining centralized control at home with decentralized partial autonomy in the provinces, permitted Rome to retain its hegemony over an empire of tens of millions of inhabitants stretching over three continents and to maintain that power for over five centuries. Initially ruled by a relatively small traditional aristocracy, Rome adapted to the new demands of empire by gradually expanding the nobility to include clients and local rulers of incorporated provinces. Thus, provincial leaders were brought into the system itself, rather than allowed to form a threatening opposition hardened by exclusion. During the final stages of the empire the emperors themselves were being drawn from distant provinces.

One mechanism for ensuring the loyalty of local nobles was to give them large agricultural estates or *latifundia* and the slave labor needed to produce crops. Within Italy this concentration of land ownership in the hands of the nobility resulted in the impoverishment of small farmers who, once they lost their lands, were driven into Rome itself. There they became the working class periodically supplied through grain distributions (the proverbial "bread") and entertained by public spectacles ("circuses"). In place of small subsistence farms, a system of large-scale latifundia was introduced, farmed by slave labor. "The manpower for the enormous holdings which emerged from the late 3rd

---

[28]Numa Denis Fustel de Coulanges, *The Ancient City: A Study on the Religion, Laws, and Institutions of Greece and Rome*, trans. Willard Small (Garden City, NY: Doubleday Anchor, n.d.), see pp. 132–151.

[29]In the Diocletian Age it was cheaper to transport wheat by sea all the way from Syria to Spain than to cart it only 75 miles over land. See Perry Anderson, *Passages from Antiquity to Feudalism*, p. 20, citing A. H. M. Jones, *The Later Roman Empire*, vol. 2, pp. 841–2.

century [B.C.] onwards was supplied by the spectacular series of campaigns which won Rome its mastery of the Mediterranean world: the Punic, Macedonian, Jugurthine, Mithridatic and Gallic wars, which poured military captives into Italy to the profit of the Roman ruling class."[30] Conquest had always been one method for extracting a surplus, but never before had it been conducted on so grand a scale.

Maintaining this system depended, however, upon internal stability and military supremacy. Neither continued indefinitely. Internally, the system began to break down through conflicts among competing generals and emperors, each drawing strength from different areas of the empire. Rome itself was so overcrowded with residents dependent upon a steady infusion of food from outside that any interruption in supplies could ignite riots. So dense was the city that its buildings mounted to ten stories; and even though the mud and fired brick walls were reinforced by metal chains, the buildings often collapsed from overweight. Traffic was so heavy that eventually provision carts were allowed in only at night.[31] And in this demoralized atmosphere heretical religious movements preached a return to simple morality. Chief among them was the underground faith of Christianity, which eventually reached the rulers and became the official faith of the realm in the fourth century A.D.

The threats from outside also could no longer be repelled. Nomadic tribes moving across northern Europe continually tested the frontiers. Once the frontiers could no longer be defended by military might, the tribes broke through. The Roman Empire was subdivided into two parts, east and west. The Western Roman Empire gradually succumbed to the invader tribes, and its imperial city, Rome, regressed to a simple, straggling town. The provinces of Germany, France, and Spain were divided up among the tribal invaders, who even crossed the Strait of Gibraltar to preempt Rome's North African provinces.

THE PERSISTENCE OF URBAN CULTURE
IN THE MIDDLE EAST

The Eastern Roman Empire, with its capital city of Constantinople (now called Istanbul), continued to flourish. Its boundaries were pushed back only in the seventh century A.D. by nomadic invaders from the Arabian Peninsula. But whereas western urban life was eclipsed by the nomadic groups that had invaded Rome from the north (ushering Western Europe into the so-called Dark Ages), eastern urban life reached new heights in the civilization created by the Arabian nomads.

The contrast between the northern "barbarians" and the desert Arabs

---

[30]Anderson, *Passages*, Chapter 4, especially p. 60, from which the quotation has been taken.

[31]See Jerome Carcopino, *Daily Life in Ancient Rome*, trans. E. O. Lorimer (New Haven: Yale University Press, 1940) and Mason Hammond, *The City in the Ancient World* (Cambridge: Harvard University Press, 1972) for more details.

could not have been greater. The former had little need for the cities they found in their path, and their intertribal conflicts fragmented the vast domains previously unified under the Romans. The tribes of Arabia—newly galvanized by a universal monotheistic faith and familiar with sophisticated commercial centers such as Mecca and Medina—occupied the existing cities and used them as bases from which to unify the surrounding regions. The Arabs not only transformed existing Byzantine cities such as Damascus and Alexandria, but added their own regional capitals, such as Baghdad and Basra in Iraq, Cairo in Egypt, and Kairouan in Tunisia. By about A.D. 700, only a century or so after the birth of Muhammad, Islam had spread northward to encompass the Fertile Crescent and westward along the North African coast to reach the Atlantic. Eventually, its message would reach India, China, and Indonesia in the east, central Africa in the south, and Spain, Turkey, and the Balkans in the north. As in earlier cases of imperial expansion, religion played an important role in unification.

The heartland of urbanism thus shifted back to where it had originally begun, the triangle connecting Mesopotamia with Egypt and with the Indian subcontinent.[32] Once again the densest trade routes ran overland from the east to the Mediterranean, and once again the most heavily traveled seaways carried spices and fine goods from the Orient across the Indian Ocean. But the Islamic empire, while as vast in extent as the zone that had been politically unified under the Romans, was not as centralized. Instead of one major capital dominating the rest and drawing to itself the entire surplus of empire, many great cities coexisted, each the center of a somewhat autonomous dynasty. Some of these cities reached impressive levels of size and sophistication. Cairo, for example, contained a population in excess of half a million at its height in the fourteenth century, when Egypt held the monopoly over the east-west spice route.[33] Similar centers were sprinkled throughout the region—on the Indian subcontinent, in Persia, in the Fertile Crescent, in North Africa, and in Spain. With the rise to power of the Ottoman Turks, Istanbul (formerly Constantinople) became the prime empire city, containing almost a million inhabitants by the seventeenth century.

Islam not only kept alive the concept and practice of the city but preserved and further developed the science, philosophy, and learning of the Graeco-Roman world. In its universities and academies the works of Plato and Aristotle were translated, read, and expanded upon, and new ideas, introduced by such scholars as the fourteenth-century historian Ibn Khaldun, were later to influence the work of European thinkers such as Vico and Machiavelli. The Arab world thus served as a primary source for the Italian Renaissance, which began in the late fourteenth century A.D.

---

[32]It is this point which Hammond's otherwise excellent study misses.

[33]Janet Abu-Lughod, *Cairo: 1001 Years of the City Victorious* (Princeton: Princeton University Press, 1971).

POST-ROMAN URBANISM IN EUROPE

In contrast, the conquest of the Western Roman Empire by northern barbarians did cause a regression of urbanism on the European continent, but primarily in the northern zones, away from the Mediterranean coast. It is necessary to distinguish what happened to urbanism in France, Germany, and England during the so-called Dark Ages from conditions in Spain and Italy during the eight centuries (seventh to fifteenth) of Islamic hegemony.

Europe near the Mediterranean

Since commerce and long-distance trade continued to thrive in the eastern basin of the Mediterranean long after the "barbarians" presumably turned out the lights in western Europe, it should not surprise us that urban life remained vital in those portions of Europe tied to Mediterranean trade—in seafaring Venice, in Genoa, in southern France, and in Spain (which, until the thirteenth century, was largely under Muslim rule). Venice is the best proof that not all of Europe was "dark" in the Dark Ages.[34]

Venice originated in A.D. 568 when mainlanders, fleeing the invading Lombards, took refuge in the lagoons just offshore. By the seventh century, these people, whose only means of survival was the sea, gained political autonomy from the collapsed Western Roman Empire and affiliated themselves with the still vigorous Eastern Empire of Byzantium centered at Constantinople. This unique relationship made Venice the natural middleman for the east-west trade through the Mediterranean. Venice's population increased rapidly in the eighth and ninth centuries, and by the eleventh century the city virtually monopolized the east-west trade, which was intensifying as Europe's demand for spices increased and as the Islamic empires reached new heights of prosperity and power. By the fourteenth century, Venice's population approached 70,000 to 80,000, and by the beginning of the sixteenth century, 110,000.[35]

In summary, the Muslim expansion in the seventh century did not interrupt but actually helped to revive commerce in the Mediterranean Sea. The real change introduced by the new power was to relocate the core of the unified Mediterranean region from the west (Rome) to the east and south, that is, to

---

[34]It is strange that Henri Pirenne's famous book, *Medieval Cities* (Garden City, NY: Doubleday Anchor, 1956), should so often be cited to substantiate the myth that cities "died out" in the Dark Ages and were only revived much later through fairs and other periodic markets. Actually, he is quite explicit in emphasizing the persistence of southern European cities because of their sea-trading links to the eastern basin of the Mediterranean. See especially pp. 2–15.

[35]The most authoritative estimates of European urban populations were made by Beloch, a nineteenth-century German scholar whose material has been made available to us largely through the definitive compilation of J. C. Russell, *Late Ancient and Medieval Populations* (Philadelphia: American Philosophical Society, 1958). Most of the figures that appear in this section have been taken, unless otherwise noted, from various tables in the Russell monograph.

such places as Cairo, Baghdad, Fez, and Damascus. All of these cities began to grow rapidly in size as they, rather than European centers, drew on and accumulated the surplus of the world economy focused on the Mediterranean. The prosperity of Venice and other coastal cities in southern Europe was heavily dependent on their links to the eastern core. Their happy fate was in direct contrast to that of the rest of Europe.

Europe away from the Mediterranean

In areas away from the Mediterranean coast, the Germanic invasions of the sixth century caused a decline in population, a recession in urbanization, and an isolation from the rest of the world. This decline began to be reversed in the second half of the eighth century when the expanding Arab armies were turned back by Charles Martel at Poitiers (France) in A.D. 753. Charlemagne rose to power soon afterward and, in recognition of the vast conquests by his armies, was crowned Emperor of the Holy Roman Empire in 800. His attempts to reconstitute the old imperial system failed, however, since the region he controlled was essentially landlocked, cut off from international trade routes and therefore dependent upon a manorial system of economic self-sufficiency which could do little to sustain or encourage the growth of cities.

Charlemagne's attempts to reach the seas on Europe's north and thereby to link up with the Mediterranean core region by an alternative route were effectively blocked by the Vikings. These Scandinavian sailors controlled the northern seas, raiding the mainland and Britain for a period that lasted from 800 to about 1050. Their blockade undermined the centralized structure of Charlemagne's empire. By the end of the ninth century the empire had crumbled, leaving a system of decentralized feudalism as its only alternative.

Perry Anderson argues that the particular system of feudalism that began to appear by the early ninth century in the empire of Charlemagne was the specific result of a fusion between Roman and Germanic legacies. He sees the Roman Catholic Church as the "indispensable bridge" between the "imperial slave mode of production" characteristic of the late Roman Empire and the new mode of production called feudalism (in which local lords granted authority over land to their vassals in exchange for military service) which was to develop in medieval Europe.[36] The "retrenchment of local counts and landowners in the provinces, through the nascent fief system, and the consolidation of their manorial estates and their lordships over the peasantry, proved to be the bedrock of the feudalism that slowly solidified across Europe in the next few centuries."[37] It was at this time that fairs and periodic markets provided the chief outlets for commerce and that tiny settlements, inhabited by artisans and escaped serfs still under the protection of local princes, began to form as the

---

[36]Perry Anderson, *Passages*, pp. 128–140.

[37]Anderson, *Passages*, p. 142.

nuclei out of which northern and central European cities would once again emerge.[38]

The reemergence of cities depended on the same three key factors that had always accounted for urban growth, namely: population increase; political organization to institutionalize more complex inequality; and the capacity of certain core areas to amass surplus from a larger hinterland, either through military conquest or by control over long-distance trade. Northwestern Europe's long journey through the sixteenth century—the pivotal "moment" when it became the core of what Wallerstein has termed "the modern world-system"[39]—was marked by changes in all three conditions. The results of these changes became clearly visible in the expansion and proliferation of major cities on the continent and, eventually, in England.

Population growth was impressive. Europe's population had reached its lowest point between A.D. 543 and 950, but this was followed by a remarkable recovery and increase throughout the "high medieval period," from about 950 to the middle of the fourteenth century. By 950, internal peace had permitted the development of an overland route to link Germany, Flanders, and the Netherlands on the north with Italy, which commanded the routes to the Arab world and beyond, to the Oriental sources of spices. But because the overland route was tedious and expensive, trade was still limited. Once the Vikings no longer blockaded the North Sea, however, merchant towns on the North Sea and the Baltic rapidly became masters of the revived trade stretching between England and Russia.

In the late twelfth and early thirteenth centuries these merchant colonies established monopolies over the northern trade, forming *Hanses* (confederations) to connect their merchants at home and abroad. Northern European cities grew commensurately. In the fourteenth century, Bruges had a population of over 40,000; Brussels had reached 30,000; Ghent had perhaps 50,000 to 60,000, and Paris about as many. Other important towns were Hamburg, Strasbourg, and Cologne. While in comparison with the important cities of Italy and Spain these were all modest-sized towns, their

---

[38]These are the city forms described so fully in the classic book *Medieval Cities* written in 1925 by Henri Pirenne. It is important to recognize that these cities were very different from those which Max Weber singled out in his famous essay, *The City,* as examples of "the western medieval city." Weber draws his ideal type of occidental city from the city-states of medieval and Renaissance Italy which, as we have seen, had a different evolution.

[39]A *world system* is defined as an economically integrated large region characterized by a hierarchy of positions. The dominant sub-region is called the *core.* Integrated with the core, but through unequal exchange, is the *semi-periphery.* Even less integrated (and more exploited) are the *peripheral regions,* which give to but do not take from the core. The modern world system, with Europe as its core, began to form in the sixteenth century. See Immanuel Wallerstein, *The Modern World-System* vol. I (New York: Academic Press, 1974). It is important to recognize that there were world systems before that time, although they had a different structure. See Janet Abu-Lughod, *Before European Hegemony: The World System A.D. 1250–1350* (New York: Oxford University Press, 1989).

growth had been dramatically fast, clearly demonstrating the connection between trade and cities.

The upward trend in population was abruptly reversed in 1348–1350 by an epidemic of bubonic plague so devastating that it has been singled out from all others as the Black Death. This particularly virulent outbreak ravaged not only Europe but virtually all of the known world, killing off between a fifth and a half of the population wherever it struck. Ironically, mortalities were highest in those regions tied to the long-distance sea trade (since the lice that spread the infection were hosted by rats that were unwittingly transported to distant places on board cargo ships), and the disease took its highest toll in places that were densely settled, that is, in cities. To some extent, this differential impact helped to equalize the demographic positions of the thriving core region (the Arab-Venetian–controlled Mediterranean) and the more isolated and less densely populated periphery (continental Europe and the British Isles). Nevertheless, even in the latter places, the toll was heavy. It has been estimated that Europe lost between a fourth and a third of its total population during the Black Death, and that deaths on the continent alone may have amounted to 25 to 35 million persons.[40]

While recovery was slow and was periodically interrupted by plagues, Europe's population was again increasing rapidly by the end of the fifteenth century. This growth was clearly related to an intensification of trade and other contacts between peripheral northern and central Europe and the Mediterranean world, which remained, almost to the end of the sixteenth century, the core of the world economy. Trade and industry (especially textiles) were thriving, and a secondary sea route on the north was beginning to rival the one centered in the Mediterranean.

Continental Europe and England were dotted with towns and cities, and a centralized core of especially active and closely spaced towns was just emerging in southeastern England and the Low Countries, flanking the isthmus to the North Sea. The sequence of maps (Figures 2.8 through 2.11) reproduced from Chandler and Fox[41] shows the location of all European towns with 20,000 or more inhabitants between A.D. 800 and 1700. The first two maps make evident the revival of urbanism on the continent and the increasing importance of the northern coast, while the second set of maps shows the final shift to non-Mediterranean regions.

---

[40]See, for example, Warren Thompson and David T. Lewis, *Population Problems* (New York: McGraw-Hill, 1965), p. 397 for authoritative demographic estimates, and see Hans Zinsser, *Rats, Lice and History* (Boston: Little, Brown and Co., 1935) for a fascinating account of the impact of plagues on social history.

[41]A remarkable source of information on urbanization by continent and across time is Tertius Chandler and Gerald Fox, *3000 Years of Urban Growth* (New York: Academic Press, 1974). The authors have compiled the best estimates ever assembled on the sizes of cities at various points in time and by continent. This has recently been updated and corrected in a new edition by Tertius Chandler. See his *4000 Years of Urban Growth: An Historical Census* (Lewistown, NY: St. David's University Press, 1987).

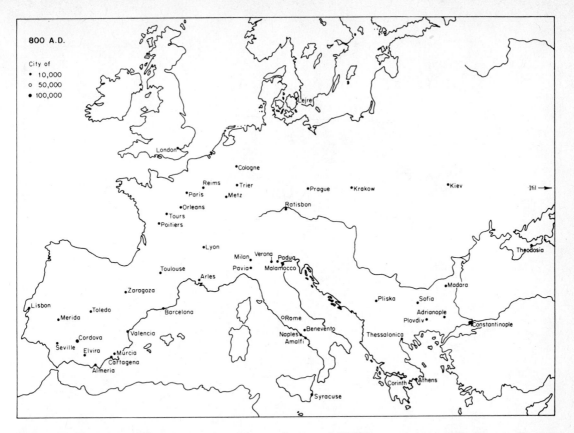

Figure 2.8 Locations of European cities with populations of 10,000 or more, A.D. 800. (*Source:* Tertius Chandler and Gerald Fox, *3000 Years of Urban Growth.* Copyright 1973 by Seminar Press. All rights reserved.)

THE CREATION OF A EUROPEAN-CENTERED WORLD SYSTEM

The two centuries following were to see the transformation of the entire world system through three important changes: (1) the subordination of the Mediterranean to the Atlantic, as Spain and Portugal, then Holland, and finally France and, especially, England, became the leading powers in a completely reorganized pattern of trade and conquest that was centered in Europe rather than in Asia; (2) the shift to the nation-state, which offered protection to merchant capital abroad; and (3) the accumulation of wealth and the capacity for productivity that would underlie the Industrial Revolution (which was as much a social invention as it was a technological breakthrough).

This industrial revolution in the eighteenth and nineteenth centuries completed the transformation of European cities and the societies that spawned them, thanks to population increases, the creation of new political and

Figure 2.9 Locations of European cities with populations of 10,000 or more, A.D. 1000. (*Source:* Tertius Chandler and Gerald Fox, *3000 Years of Urban Growth.* Copyright 1973 by Seminar Press. All rights reserved.)

economic systems that yielded a class structure quite different from what the world had previously known, and the partitioning of the entire globe into colonies and trading spheres of influence which permitted the core countries of Europe to rise to imperial heights, sustained by the resources and labor of the largest hinterland any urbanized core had ever commanded.

The story of this transformation must begin with the sixteenth century. It is true that historians date the Industrial Revolution from about 1750; but, like the first great revolution that brought humanity across the threshold into settled agriculture some 10,000 years ago, this second revolution that took place only some 250 years ago needed preparation. The prior reorganization of the social, economic, and political systems of the world was as important to the Industrial Revolution as the invention of the spinning jenny or the discovery of steam power. This reorganization began in the sixteenth century.

The Shift to the Atlantic

Any schoolchild remembers two dates: 1492, when Columbus was first discovered by Caribe Indians as he disembarked on their beach, eventually laying Spanish claim to a New (to him) World;[42] and 1498, when Vasco da Gama sailed his Portuguese ship along the coast of Africa to find a route to India that bypassed the Mediterranean and the Middle East. Simplistic as it may seem, and complicated as the actual struggle was, these events signaled the beginning of the end of Mediterranean supremacy. Although the results were not immediately apparent, from about 1580 on the world of the Mediterranean was "plunged into darkness" as other regions stole the limelight.[43] For a brief time these newly dominant regions were Spain and Portugal, but by the end of the next century they were clearly Holland, France, and even more so, England.

The complicated shift has been the subject of many detailed studies. While this process cannot be covered here,[44] its results must be, for they created the patterns of world urbanization that have evolved to this day, as well as the context within which American urban developments were to take place.

The Shift to the Nation-State

One of the most important transitions that occurred was from the city-state to the national or territorial state,[45] a change which began to occur when internal order was restored on the continent in the fifteenth century. As Wallerstein describes it, "from the sixteenth century on, the nation-states of western Europe sought to create relatively homogeneous national societies."[46] But why

---

[42]The irony is Jan Carew's. See his "The Origins of Racism in the Americas," in *African Themes,* ed. Ibrahim Abu-Lughod (Evanston, IL: Northwestern University, 1975).

[43]Fernand Braudel, *The Mediterranean and the Mediterranean World in the Age of Philip II,* trans. Siân Reynolds (New York: Harper & Row, 1972), vol. II, p. 1186.

[44]The discussion that follows depends heavily upon the positions, documented by the careful historical scholarship of many, set forth in three synthetic works: the voluminous two-volume study by Braudel, cited above; the three volumes thus far published by Immanuel Wallerstein on the evolution of the modern world system (vol. I, 1974; vol. II, 1980; vol. III, 1989); and Perry Anderson's *Lineages of the Absolutist State* (London: Humanities Press, 1974), which continues from his *Passages from Antiquity to Feudalism* (London: NLB, 1974). These sources represent a revised interpretation of modern history, taking the interrelated forces of economics and politics (called "political economy") as basic to an understanding of technical and cultural changes, and viewing national developments in the industrialized and underdeveloped worlds as comprehensible only in the context of international interdependence and transnational power. Viewing the process of urbanization from this vantage point leads one to reinterpret many well-known events and "facts" about the growth and distribution of cities.

[45]See Braudel, *The Mediterranean,* vol. I, p. 340, and Anderson, *Lineages of the Absolutist State,* p. 15.

[46]See Wallerstein, vol. I, p. 33.

was a unified national society so necessary for economic development and the industrial capitalism that it brought about?

We are so accustomed to thinking about industrial capitalism as "free enterprise" independent of state control that it is shocking to realize how much the development of both industry at home and imperialism abroad depended upon state power. Yet, in the sixteenth century, the centralized nation-state emerged "as the great collector and redistributor of revenue" and, whether intentionally or not, "became the principal entrepreneur."[47] Whereas the world had previously known empires, and indeed major cities had always been dependent upon them, these earlier empires had amassed surplus largely through tribute and protection money. In the sixteenth century state power was put to new uses, namely, to facilitate internal capital accumulation and to secure international monopoly rights over world trade.[48] The first of these permitted industrialization, the second, geographic expansion and colonization.

Population Growth and Wage Labor

By the sixteenth century industrial capitalists in western Europe were already harnessing the enlarged labor force at home through the "putting out" system, whereby merchants provided workers with raw materials and then bought back and marketed the finished products. This in itself was not new, for the commercial city-states of Italy and northern Europe had long been doing it. What was new was that labor was now more plentiful. Between 1500 and 1600 Europe's population nearly doubled; furthermore, as the demand for wool increased to serve the burgeoning textile industry, the shift from labor-intensive farming to sheep raising pushed many small farmers from their lands. These displaced workers offered their services to the industrialist-merchants. The higher productivity of larger-scale production in mechanized factories, however, required a regulated and secure market, a control that the newly powerful and regularized state machineries could provide. Wage labor began to develop domestically. Abroad, the institution of slave labor was being introduced to create more surpluses from the colonies in the New World.

Colonial Empires

Strong states could not only organize labor but also protect shipping and insure that their merchants received favorable terms of trade. It is no accident, then, that the European nation-states that successively served as the core for the newly developing modern world economy were the states that controlled the sea. While that had always been true, up to the sixteenth century the sea in question had been the Mediterranean. In the Age of Discovery, ushered in by

---

[47]Braudel, *The Mediterranean*, vol. I, p. 449. The reader is reminded that in the city-states of early Mesopotamia the temple served a similar function, albeit on a much smaller scale.

[48]Wallerstein, vol. I, p. 16.

the 1500s and really coming into its own by the 1600s, that sea became the Atlantic. Portugal, perfectly positioned geographically, was the first state to play a hegemonic role, largely because it was able to wrest control over the Indian Ocean and thereby monopolize the route to the East Indies. Spain's control over the New World similarly depended upon its control of the Atlantic routes. The English defeat of the Spanish Armada in 1588 clearly marked the end of Spain's monopoly, and by the seventeenth century, the Dutch and then the English had become the true masters of the Atlantic.

The rise to power of the "Protestant nations" (that is, the Netherlands and England) was related not only to their mastery of the sea but also to the Protestant Reformation in the middle of the sixteenth century. Max Weber argued, in his *The Protestant Ethic and the Spirit of Capitalism,* that this revolution in religious beliefs unleashed an enormous entrepreneurial spirit that carried northern Europe into the age of true capitalism and the Industrial Revolution. The effects upon urban developments of that shift in the locus of power can be seen clearly in the two maps, reproduced from Chandler and Fox, showing urban centers in Europe in 1600 and 1700 (Figures 2.10 and 2.11). The emergence of a core region, encompassing Holland and England, is clearly visible.

Population figures for selected cities confirm this shift. The population of Amsterdam quadrupled in the first half of the seventeenth century, rising from about 50,000 in 1600 to 200,000 by 1650, while the volume of Dutch shipping grew tenfold between 1500 and 1700.[49] The centralization of English power in London, plus the increased profits from international trade, led to an enormous growth in that city.[50] Whereas in 1605 some 75,000 persons were living in the medieval area within the walls and an additional 150,000 in London's suburbs (the population having roughly trebled since 1530), by 1660 the combined population of city and suburbs may have reached 500,000.[51]

Industrial growth accounted for part of this increase. Whereas in the beginning of the sixteenth century England had been industrially backward, taking second place to older textile centers in Italy, Germany, France, and Flanders, by the late seventeenth century it forged ahead. Particularly after 1669, as England increased its hegemonic edge, skilled Dutch workers migrated to England. With Holland finally worn out by separate wars with France and England, England emerged as the key power—both at home through industrial production, and abroad through mastery of the sea and, consequently, its possession of increasingly useful colonies in North America.

Even though the first permanent English settlement in the New World (Plymouth) was founded only in 1620, by 1700 England had between 350,000 and 400,000 subjects in the Western Hemisphere, in comparison with only

---

[49]Wallerstein, vol. II, p. 45.

[50]F. J. Fisher, "London as an 'Engine of Economic Growth,' " in *The Early Modern Town,* ed. Peter Clark (London: Longman Group, 1976), pp. 205–215.

[51]Subsequent to this, a plague in 1664, followed by the Great Fire of 1666, decimated London temporarily.

Figure 2.10 Locations of European cities with populations of 10,000 or more, A.D. 1600. (*Source: Tertius Chandler and Gerald Fox, 3000 Years of Urban Growth.* Copyright 1973 by Seminar Press. All rights reserved.)

70,000 for the French.[52] From 1660 onward the multiple New England and Middle Atlantic colonies became commercially integrated with Britain, serving eventually as an outlet for population and as a key link in the triangular trade that developed between Africa (the source of the slave labor that was to create such surpluses in the eighteenth century), the New World (the Caribbean and southern Atlantic colonies, which produced sugar, tobacco, and cotton, as well as the commercial and ship-building/rum-processing towns on the northern Atlantic coast) and England—truly the metropole for a growing portion of the globe by the eighteenth century.

All of these transformations had already occurred before the technological breakthroughs of the late eighteenth and early nineteenth centuries ushered in the era of mechanically powered industrialism. The shift to inanimate sources of energy produced a quantum jump in productivity, making it possible

---

[52]Wallerstein, vol. II, p. 102.

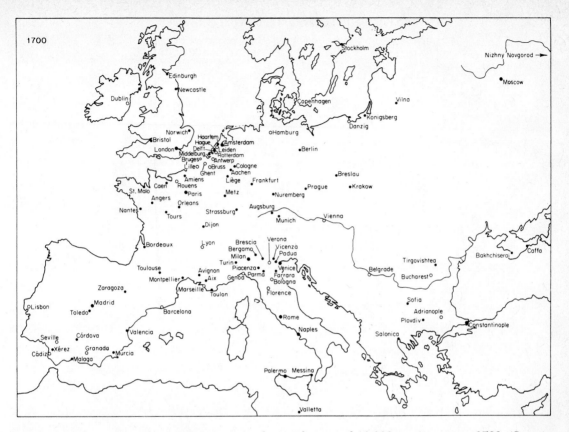

Figure 2.11 Locations of European cities with populations of 10,000 or more, A.D. 1700. (*Source:* Tertius Chandler and Gerald Fox, *3000 Years of Urban Growth.* Copyright 1973 by Seminar Press. All rights reserved.)

for world population to increase almost tenfold in the next few hundred years (see Figure 2.12), and for cities to become not merely the home of the favored few, as they had been from the time of their origin some 6000 years ago, but the natural habitat of humanity, containing in some case as many persons within a single metropolitan conurbation as had inhabited whole countries and regions in earlier times.

URBANISM UNLEASHED

It is to this amazing story we now turn. As Barbara Ward has noted, "In many ways, until the nineteenth century, the physical surface of human existence does not change much." Fourteenth-, even seventeenth- and eighteenth-century towns in Europe would not have been unfamiliar places to the inhabitants

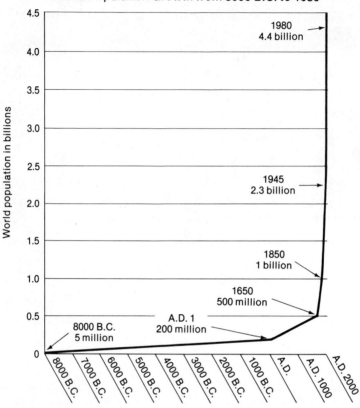

Figure 2.12 The exponential growth of world population from about 8000 B.C. to the year A.D. 2000.

of Babylon or of Cheng-Chou.[53] Gideon Sjoberg stresses these resemblances in his book, *The Preindustrial City,* which tries to generalize about the characteristics of all cities before the industrial age.[54] He notes that the modest-sized towns of the ancient and medieval worlds alike were ringed with defensive walls; that they ran on foot traffic or, at most, wheeled cart transport; that temples or churches were their central foci, with market squares nearby; that they contained tradespeople and artisans who produced primarily for local consumption and only secondarily for long-distance trade; and that they were ruled by a small elite which maintained military forces to protect themselves, to subjugate their neighbors, and to guard the transit of goods through their territories. He also notes that societies in the preindustrial era, no matter how

---

[53]Barbara Ward [Lady Jackson], *The Home of Man* (Toronto: McClelland and Stewart, 1976); quotation is from p. 21.

[54]Gideon Sjoberg, *The Preindustrial City: Past and Present* (Glencoe, IL: Free Press, 1960), *passim*.

powerful and centralized, were incapable of supporting urban populations that represented more than five or at most ten percent of the total population, since even slavery and the tribute of empires could not yield a higher surplus.

The new industrial cities that appeared by the nineteenth century were organized around very different principles. Once city-states became parts of nation-states, cities no longer needed protective walls. Instead, urbanism spread into the surrounding countryside, with the concentration of houses, markets, and workshops tapering off gradually, rather than ending abruptly. Links between urban centers grew stronger as complex urban systems were woven together, first by roads and by canals and other waterways, and then, after the 1830s, by railroads. Towns in the interior were thus linked to the rest of the world through ports that were in close contact with their counterparts throughout the world. Connections between rural and urban areas also strengthened as the dominance of the city extended itself to affect the day-to-day lives of farmers in hitherto isolated areas.

Internally, cities were physically transformed. Carriages and wide, wheeled carts, first pulled by draught horses but later powered by steam, electricity, and, eventually, internal combustion gasoline engines, speeded up the leisurely pace of street movement. These new means of transport required straight and wide streets to accommodate their size and speed. Temples or churches faded from center stage in the city, as did religion as the central organizing institution of society. Secular preoccupations took over, preempting central location. At the core of the new cities were the commercial enterprises, the administrative offices of the state, and the banks and financial institutions that stored money and credit (the new forms of surplus), much as the ancient temples had stored the surplus grain.

Underlying this new surplus was the productivity made possible by harnessing inanimate energy sources to the labor of men, women, and children who, displaced from the countryside, congregated in cities and had nothing to sell but their labor. Thus, a new factory system and a new form of capitalism completely replaced the guild system. The bifurcated class structure of capitalists and workers inside Europe was mirrored on the international level by a similar bifurcation between "have" and "have-not" nations. The "haves" had colonies from which they drew resources and labor power and to which they exported the larger and larger quantities of goods their factories were able to produce. The "have-nots" were the colonies, protectorates, spheres of trading interest, and otherwise subordinated regions of the world, from which resources were extracted and to which finished products were shipped.

The modern world system that began to be established in the sixteenth century reached its imperial phase by the end of the nineteenth century, creating urbanization in the core on a scale never before known, and producing cities for which no prior urban experience in the course of history was a precedent. This scale of urbanization and these cities are the immediate ancestors of our own world. The urban problems they experienced and the urban promises they made are still with us. In the next chapter we trace the spread of world urbanization and the creation of a world system of cities.

Chapter
3

The Urbanization of the World, 1800 to 2000

THE SPREAD OF CITIES

In 1800 fewer than three persons out of every hundred in the world lived in a settlement that, by any stretch of the imagination, could have been considered urban. At that time, London was the only city in the world, outside China, with a population approaching one million. Cities were truly exceptional environments for human beings. Of the close to one billion persons estimated to have been alive in 1800, less than 25 million experienced life in a place where at least 20,000 persons had settled together densely enough for their community to be considered a town or city.[1] Most people lived in the small-scale personalized

---

[1] How should one define an "urban" place? This question has puzzled many scholars and has no simple answer. A definition should be suited to the uses to which it will be put; it is not right or wrong, only more or less useful. For some purposes urban sociologists and statisticians use a "demographic definition": an urban place is a permanent settlement, having a single name and often a legal identity, which is densely settled by a certain minimum number of residents. Unfortunately, this minimum varies from country to country. In the United States, for example, a community need have only 2500 residents to be considered urban, whereas in other countries, 5000 or even 10,000 inhabitants must be assembled together for a place to be considered urban. Clearly, with such variability, comparisons between countries are difficult. To avoid this dilemma, the United Nations, following the lead of Kingsley Davis (see his 2-volume work, *World Urbanization 1950–1970*),

settings of the nomadic tribe, the isolated farmstead, or the tiny village; indeed, most had never even seen a big city, much less entertained the thought of adapting to life in one. Clearly, urbanization, as measured by the proportion of a region's population residing in cities or towns, remained at a very low level.[2]

In sharp contrast to this, by 1985 more than two out of every five persons in the world (2 billion out of 5 billion) lived in an urban place. *The number of city dwellers in 1985 was twice as great as the population of the entire world in 1800.* By 1990 there were approximately 250 cities in the world that had populations of a million or more, and the largest metropolises had in excess of 15 million inhabitants. (The Mexico City metropolitan region, the world's largest, now houses over 20 million, or almost as many people as had inhabited cities throughout the entire world in 1800.) Figure 3.1 shows the estimated populations of the world's largest cities for the year 2000.

For better or worse, cities have become our normal habitat. It is now a rare American who can imagine day-to-day life in an isolated village or on a farm, and even those living on farms or in villages are in daily communication with the ideas and the goods and services produced in cities. The trend toward universal urbanization shows no sign of abating. According to a United Nations projection, by the year 2025 some 62 percent of the world's 8.2 billion inhabitants will be living in urban places. By then, over 5 billion persons will be living in cities, while most of the rest will be affected by what goes on in them.[3]

---

recommends several size categories for urban places. UN Demographic Yearbooks accept the variable definitions of *urban* adopted by different countries, but use the minimum size of 20,000 to count urban populations internationally. United Nations demographers also distinguish "city populations" (those in places with 100,000 or more inhabitants) from "big city populations" (those in places with half a million or more). Metropolitan size may be even larger: a place of a million or more, according to Davis, or even 2.5 million, according to the United Nations. Throughout this chapter, unless otherwise noted, we use a minimum of 20,000 to define an urban place.

Clearly, the size of a settlement tells us very little about the quality of social life within it. Some of the earliest cities described in Chapter 2 never reached 20,000, even though in their time they represented the highest form of urban life and served as imperial capitals. On the other hand, today, given the increased scale of cities, a minimum size of 20,000 can easily be reached by many modest-sized suburbs and small towns lacking characteristics we would currently associate with city living. Additionally, in densely settled agrarian countries, the minimum size of 20,000 is often reached by agricultural villages in which no features of urban non-agricultural life are to be found. Clearly, then, demographic definitions have only limited sociological value.

The figures for 1800 have been based largely on the estimates made in the 1950s by Kingsley Davis and Hilda Hertz Golden. These have been incorporated in Hilda Golden, *Urbanization and Cities* (Lexington, MA: D. C. Heath, 1981), pp. 139, 145.

[2]The term *urbanization* has been used in many different ways, causing confusion. In this chapter we use the term in the following ways. The *process of urbanization* refers to the spread and increase of cities in a given society. The *level of urbanization* refers to the proportion of population that lives in cities, while the *rate of urbanization* is measured by changes in that proportion over time.

[3]The 1985 estimates are taken from Philip Hauser and Robert Gardner, "Urban Future: Trends and Prospects," in *Population and the Urban Future* (a document prepared by the United Nations Fund for Population Activities, International Conference on Population and the Urban Future in Rome, 1980), especially Table I. Their definition of "urban" was any place with 20,000 or more inhabitants. The authors of this article depended heavily on *The Growth of the World's Urban and Rural*

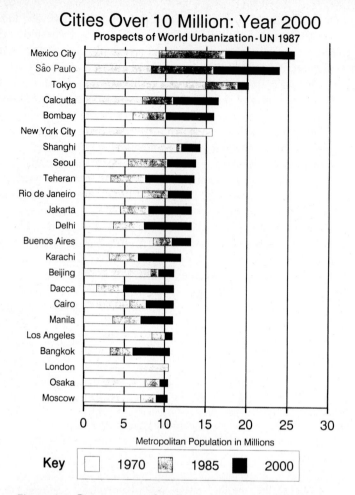

Figure 3.1 Cities expected to have populations of ten million or more by the year 2000, according to United Nations projections. (*Source:* Chart drafted by Janice Perlman's Megacity Project, used with permission. All rights reserved 1988.)

No prior transformation in human life has been as radical or as rapid as the urbanization that has occurred during the last two centuries. Are human beings

Population, 1920–2000 (United Nations, Population Studies No. 44, 1969), which was updated in *Patterns of Urban and Rural Population Growth* (United Nations, Population Studies No. 68, 1981). Newer estimates are included in Mattei Dogan and John Kasarda, eds., *The Metropolis Era,* vol. 1: *A World of Giant Cities* (Newbury Park, CA: Sage Publications, 1988), especially Chapter 1. By the year 2000, according to the UN report, *Estimates and Projections of Urban and Rural Population 1950–2025: 1982 Assessment* (New York: United Nations, 1985; esp. Table A-12), both Mexico City and São Paulo will have outstripped Tokyo as the world's largest metropolitan areas, and the largest "western" metropolitan region, New York–New Jersey, will have dropped to sixth place.

capable of living successfully in such large and densely settled environments? What dislocations to their existence have these changes caused? What social, economic, and political reorganizations have they required? What ways have been developed to cope with the enormous problems caused by such a transformation? Can we meet the challenges created by the urbanization of our planet?

It is fashionable nowadays to deplore urban conditions and to dream wistfully of a simpler life. Nostalgia for the small settlements that are believed to make possible a humane sense of community seems pervasive. Yet we do not have such a choice; the process of urbanization is not reversible at will. We have only one real choice—between cities that are increasingly degraded and full of problems and those that are humane and livable.

In order to exercise this choice, we need to understand the processes which led to the worldwide but as yet uneven phenomenon of urbanization. We need to understand the factors that have resulted in the kinds of cities we now have. And we need to trace back in time the causes of the problems so apparent in contemporary cities. This is our task in the next few chapters.

THE UNEVEN DISTRIBUTION OF URBANIZATION TODAY: A DIAGNOSTIC

While urbanization has indeed become a worldwide phenomenon in the past two centuries, today's cities are not spread uniformly over the globe. In fact, the most striking fact is their uneven distribution. This should not be surprising, given our earlier analysis of why cities first appeared and what economic and social transformations underlay their growth.

Countries that underwent industrialization early, that were at the original core of the modern world system (whose evolution was described at the end of Chapter 2), and that were rulers of colonial empires and beneficiaries of imperial trade, are still among the wealthiest nations in the world. They are the most "developed" and also the most urbanized, even though they may no longer be at the forefront of industrial development and even though almost all of their colonies have gained independence. In contrast, the least urbanized countries and regions of the world are those originally bypassed by the Industrial Revolution; most are located far from the core in western Europe, and many were formerly colonies.

These historical facts account for the correlation observed today between the wealth of a country (measured roughly by the value of its gross national product divided by the number of its inhabitants) and the level of its urbanization (measured by the proportion of its population living in urban places).[4]

---

[4]There have been many attempts to relate indicators of economic development to levels of urbanization. Some have used the amount of energy consumed per capita as a measure of "modernization," whereas others have used such indicators of social advancement as the infant mortality rate, the life expectancy at birth, and other measures of quality of life. The most commonly used measure of economic development, however, has been the sum of the value, at market prices, of all goods

Although the correlation is not perfect, it is high enough to prove the point. Table 3.1 shows some typical examples.[5] (Exceptions, such as larger recently rich oil states or tiny countries consisting of little more than a major city, have intentionally been omitted.) The table illustrates some of the connections between levels of urbanization, on the one hand, and the past and present position of countries in the international economy, on the other.

First, all the countries in the highest group except Japan were early industrializers, either located at the core or settled by persons from the core of the modern world system. These countries underwent their most dramatic periods of urban growth during the nineteenth century and have now begun to approach urban saturation. With between 74 and 92 percent of their inhabitants already living in cities, and with their total populations currently growing at low rates from natural increase (a small excess of births over deaths each year), these countries have already experienced their urban revolutions. Redistributions of their urban populations can be expected—both between regions and from one part to another of their urbanized centers—but the total proportion of their populations in cities should grow only modestly in the next few decades.

In contrast, the moderately developed countries whose industrial revolutions began only at the end of the nineteenth or early in the twentieth century now have between 59 and 77 percent of their populations living in cities. However, there is room for further urban growth as industrialization proceeds. Cities in these countries are growing at more than 1.5 percent per year, which suggests that by the end of the twentieth century they will have reached the level of urbanization presently typical among the early industrializers.

Countries that began to industrialize in the twentieth century are currently experiencing rapid spurts in urbanization, not only because of economic development but because of extremely high rates of urban natural increase. Presently, these countries have from 45 to 70 percent of their populations in cities. However, their cities are growing at rates that often exceed 3 percent annually. Cities in these developing nations are drawing migrants from the countryside in much the same way that urban areas in the developed world did in the nineteenth century, when the latter experienced their fastest rates of growth.

---

and services generated in a society within a given year, divided by the number of inhabitants. This is the gross national product per capita, the measure we use here. As with any other measure, the GNP/capita is imperfect. First, it excludes the goods and services that do not enter the marketplace. This means that unpaid services (housekeeping by family members, crops raised in subsistence farming, etc.), no matter how essential, are excluded from the calculation. Second, price is assumed to stand for value. Thus, the same product output in two different years will be given entirely different values, if the prices of items have gone up or down in the interim. (For example, the GNP of oil states has recently gone up drastically because of higher prices.) One should bear in mind these deficiencies in the measure when drawing conclusions from cross-national data.

[5]It should be noted that the data included in Table 3.1, selected from The World Bank, *World Development Report 1989* (New York: Oxford University Press, 1989), are not exactly comparable to those employed in United Nations reports. See our discussion of definitions in note 1.

Table 3.1 LEVEL OF WEALTH, LEVEL OF URBANIZATION, AND RATE OF URBAN GROWTH OF SELECTED COUNTRIES

Country	Gross national product/capita 1987 (in U.S. dollars)	Percent population in cities in 1987	Average annual urban growth rate, 1980–1987 (%)
Typical highly industrialized countries			
United States	18,530	74	1.0
Sweden	15,550	84	0.2
Japan	15,760	77	0.8
Germany (Fed. Rep.)	14,400	86	0.1
France	12,790	74	0.6
United Kingdom	10,420	92	0.3
Typical moderately industrialized countries			
Spain	6,010	77	1.4
Greece	4,020	61	1.4
Poland	1,930	61	1.5
Hungary	2,240	59	1.4
Typical industrializing countries			
Mexico	1,830	71	3.2
Peru	1,470	69	3.2
Turkey	1,210	47	3.4
Tunisia	1,180	54	2.9
Typical less developed countries			
Ghana	390	32	4.1
China	290	38	11.0
Indonesia	450	27	5.0
India	300	27	4.1
Pakistan	350	31	4.5
Burma	190 (for 1985)	24	2.3
Tanzania	180	29	11.3

Note: The figures in this table are not to be given detailed credence, although they do illustrate the general point. There are at least three sources of noncomparability. First, GNP is undercounted in socialist and subsistence economies, or put another way, is overcounted in capitalist economies. Second, country definitions of "urban" differ, as do their policies about annexation. And finally, the data themselves or for the intercensal date are almost all *estimates*.

Source: Selected from entries in tables 1 (pp. 164–165) and 31 (pp. 224–225) of The World Bank, *World Development Report 1989* (New York: Oxford University Press, 1989).

And finally, there are the large countries of Asia and Africa that are just beginning to industrialize during the second half of the twentieth century and still consist largely of agriculturalists. Some 25 to 40 percent of their populations have already settled in cities, some of which have grown to enormous size—both from high rates of natural increase and from high rates of outmigration from overcrowded rural areas. City life, however, is still atypical. These are the nations whose colonial past or dependent status delayed for a long time their entrance into modernity. But they include India and China, the world's demographic giants, which means that their expanding populations will be the major source of world and urban growth in the coming decades.

While the gross inequalities in levels of urbanization—so apparent in the nineteenth and early twentieth centuries—will not disappear by the year 2025, they will be considerably reduced. Table 3.2 shows the changes in levels of urbanization that occurred between 1920 and 1980 and projects these trends to the year 2025. In 1920 the level of urbanization in the more developed countries was almost five times as high as the level in the less developed countries. By 1980 the level of urbanization of developed countries was only a little more than twice that in the less developed world, and by 2025 that differential will be even less. Between 1920 and 1980, Europe, Oceana, and North America increased their urbanization levels by only one half. During the same period, however, the level of urbanization in Latin America tripled.

The continent where urbanization has been proceeding most rapidly is Africa. Although only seven percent of Africa's population lived in cities in 1920, the level of urbanization had more than quadrupled by 1980 (rising to

Table 3.2   THE PERCENTAGE OF POPULATION LIVING IN URBAN AREAS BY CONTINENT, 1920–2025

Region	Year					
	1920	1940	1960	1980	2000	2025 (projections)
World	19.4	24.5	33.9	41.3	48.2	62.5
More Developed	37.9	46.9	58.7	70.7	77.8	85.4
Less Developed	8.4	12.6	21.9	30.5	44.4	57.7
Europe	46.2	52.8	62.6	75.9	78.9	85.9
Oceana	47.1	54.6	66.2	75.7	73.1	78.4
N. America	51.9	58.9	67.1	73.7	78.0	85.7
S. America	22.4	30.8	49.4	64.8	76.6	84.2
USSR	16.1	30.8	48.8	64.8	74.3	83.4
Asia	8.8	12.9	20.8	27.4	35.7	53.7
Africa	7.0	10.4	18.2	28.9	42.2	58.3

Source: Philip M. Hauser and Robert Gardner, "Urban Future: Trends and Prospects," paper presented at the *International Conference on Population and the Urban Future* held in Rome, Italy (New York, 1980), Table 3. Update for 2000 and 2025 from A. S. Oberai, *Migration, Urbanisation and Development* (Geneva: International Labour Office, 1987), based on United Nations' projections.

almost 30 percent) and is expected to double again (to almost 60 percent) by 2025. The less developed regions appear to be recapitulating, even faster, the dramatic pace of urbanization previously experienced by the developed regions.

However, the processes whereby many underdeveloped areas are currently undergoing urbanization are not identical to those experienced by countries that went through their urban revolutions during the nineteenth century. For one thing, the recent developers find themselves in a world context markedly different from the past, and they are urbanizing under very different technological and economic conditions. Whereas the early industrializers/urbanizers could draw upon the resources of the entire world and could freely market their products in places where they faced little competition, today's late industrializers must break into a system already controlled by others. On the other hand, whereas the early industrializers had gradually to develop the technologies needed in order to increase productivity and make urban areas livable, the late developers have access to already existing technologies, albeit those which may not be best suited to their conditions.

Because of these and other variations, no single case of industrialization/ urbanization can perfectly represent all. At the minimum, several cases must be examined in detail, since the process of urbanization can only be understood in concrete situations. We therefore look first at England (and in passing, at other parts of western Europe) during the nineteenth century to demonstrate the advantages and problems of early industrialization/urbanization. We then turn to Egypt which, in similar fashion, illustrates many of the problems of aborted industrialization but explosive urbanization in the Third World.

We have chosen to look at England because in many ways it represents the "most favored" case, since population increase, comparative industrial advantage, and imperial power worked together to permit rapid transformation from an agrarian to an urban society. If the transition generated such large numbers of problems in even this "most favored" case, countries now accomplishing the same transformation can hardly be expected to have fewer.

There is a second reason for singling out the English and western European experiences. Most of the theories sociologists have developed to explain urban life, to predict what urban living implies for social relations, to characterize the differences between rural and urban societies, and so forth, were generated, implicitly or explicitly, from the European experience of the late nineteenth century. Many of the generalizations about urbanism as a way of life in urban sociology were drawn from this early western experience. We turn to these theories later in the chapter when we examine critically the consequences of urbanization on a global scale. At that time we will look at other, chiefly non-western, cases which raise questions about whether the theories developed in the West actually apply to other cultures—for urbanization does not everywhere and at every time have the same causes or consequences, nor do urbanites, everywhere and at all times, lead the same kinds of lives.

THE GROWTH OF CITIES IN EUROPE IN THE NINETEENTH CENTURY:[6] THE CASE OF ENGLAND

In Chapter 2 we saw how (1) the reshaping of the modern world system in the sixteenth century, (2) the reorganization of the state, commerce, and colonization in the seventeenth century, and (3) the technological innovations of the eighteenth century combined to make England, the Low Countries, and France the most powerful countries in the world. Given what we know about the causes of urban growth, it should not surprise us that population increase, a widening differentiation of social classes, and imperial expansion all accompanied the most rapid rise in the levels of urbanization the world had hitherto seen. England is both the clearest and best documented case, since fairly accurate censuses are available for England and Wales since 1801.

English Population Increase in the Nineteenth Century

In the three generations between 1801 and 1891, the population of England and Wales more than tripled, rising from under nine million in the early year to about 29 million by the later date. During this same period, the population living in cities with at least 20,000 inhabitants increased tenfold, from about 1.5 million in 1801 to over 15.5 million in 1891. The number of cities of that size increased twelvefold, from only 15 in 1801 to 185 by 1891, while the proportion of total population living in them rose from 17 percent to 53 percent of the total.

If one compares the figures shown in Table 3.3 with those for the world shown in Table 3.2, one can see that in the century-plus between 1920 and 2025, the world as a whole will have altered toward urbanization at about the same rate England did in the nineteenth century—but by a process that is quite different.

What caused the remarkable increase in England's population? Even though there was some increase in the birth rate, the primary cause was a sharp drop in the death rate. Accurate information on eighteenth-century death rates is hard to obtain; mortality rates for Sweden, because they go back farthest, are often used to estimate less known but similar cases. In Sweden between 1751 and 1770, only 620 out of every 1000 babies born lived to reach the age of 15, demonstrating how great a toll was taken of infants and children because of

---

[6]The single most significant source on urbanization in the nineteenth century is Adna Weber, *The Growth of Cities in the Nineteenth Century: A Study in Statistics.* This impressive compilation of information on early urbanization was a doctoral dissertation written for Columbia University and published in 1899 as vol. XI of *Studies in History, Economics and Public Law.* After decades of neglect it was finally reprinted in 1963 as part of Cornell Reprints in Urban Studies. The edition we use is the 1967 paperback edition from Cornell University Press. This basic source is indispensable for serious scholars; many of the early estimates produced by Kingsley Davis and Hilda Hertz Golden in the 1950s, in connection with the world urbanization project at Columbia University, are refinements of Weber's figures.

Table 3.3   TOTAL AND URBAN POPULATION OF ENGLAND AND WALES, 1801 TO 1891

Date	Total population	Population in cities of 20,000+	Percentage of total population	No. of cities of 20,000+
1801	8,892,536	1,506,176	17%	15
1851	17,927,609	6,265,011	35%	63
1891	29,002,525	15,563,834	53%	185

Source: Adapted from Table XVII, p. 43, of Adna Weber, *The Growth of Cities in the Nineteenth Century* (Ithaca, NY: Cornell University Press, 1967).

epidemics, intestinal disorders, uncertain food supplies, and the low level of medical knowledge and care. The crude death rate (the number of deaths occurring annually, divided by the total population $\times$ 1000) in that period for the most advanced regions of Europe was in the vicinity of 30 deaths per thousand per year. By 1850–60, in contrast, the crude death rate had fallen to about 20–21 per thousand per year. The major advances were achieved by protecting the lives of infants and children, always the most vulnerable group.[7]

The year 1798 is notable for two not unrelated events: first, the publication of Thomas Malthus's famous *Essay on the Principle of Population;* and second, Edward Jenner's successful use of cowpox serum to vaccinate against smallpox, one of the chief epidemic killers. The latter was to be credited with bringing about a major decline in death rates, ironically already the cause for the alarm being sounded by Malthus. Malthus warned that Europe's rapidly increasing population would soon outstrip the means of its support, leading to dire famine and disaster unless births could somehow be controlled. (He recommended moral restraint to control births.) In the short run, Malthus's worries were well founded. Europe's population grew by 50 percent in the next 50 years, even though the population of the rest of the world remained virtually constant because it did not benefit from the new controls over death. In the long run, however, Malthus was wrong in predicting imminent starvation, for innovations in technology and social organization and expansions in imperial control would make available to the burgeoning population of Europe resources far beyond his wildest dreams.

Technology and the Social Invention of the Factory

By the end of the eighteenth century, water power had already been harnessed to provide energy to run machines whose incremental advances were transforming methods of textile production. Steam engines were already being used

---

[7]An excellent critical source on early modern population growth is Warren Thompson and David Lewis, *Population Problems* (New York: McGraw-Hill, 1965), especially Chapter 15, pp. 401–417. The Swedish death rates appear on pp. 374–375, 394–396.

experimentally to propel wheeled carts. These provided the prototypes for motors that eventually would power the railways and turn the wheels of industrial production in the next century. Non-animal energy sources made it economical to take manufacturing out of the scattered homes to which the "putting out" system had decentralized it and to concentrate production in a new "social" invention, the factory.

Inanimate energy, by substituting water and then steam power for brute strength, also made it possible to harness the labor of the weak, a labor made more available through the reduction in infant and child mortality. As H. L. Beales, historian of the English industrial revolution, put it, the "rise of factories was a godsend to overseers [of workhouses for the poor who were] embarrassed with a swollen supply of pauper children."[8] The Hammonds, in their famous study, *The Town Labourer,* tell us how the first factory populations were assembled. "The mill-owners began by getting children from the workhouses, and this system of serf labour carried the mills over the first stages, until there was a settled population, able to provide women and children."[9]

The abuses were shocking, and activated early attempts to legislate, if not humanity, at least restraints on inhumanity. Thus, in 1802 the English Parliament passed an act governing the "Health and Morals of Apprentices" by which pauper apprentices were promised a shorter working day (only twelve hours!), an end to the night shift, one set of new clothes yearly, the separation of males from females in the dormitories, and not more than two sleepers to a bed.[10] But such laws were widely ignored. Thus, the Hammonds present data from a cotton mill in 1814–1815, where pauper children as young as seven years old worked 14 hours a day six days a week (with only a half hour for breakfast and another half hour for dinner), and, in addition, cleaned the machines between 6 A.M. and noon on Sundays, their day off![11]

These pauper children were eventually joined by immigrants from Ireland and by women and men forced off the land by the "second enclosures" that took place during the reign of George III (1738–1820), when "commons" land finally disappeared from village England. This eliminated forever "the possibility of squatting on unoccupied ground,"[12] and drove the landless into the towns that were growing up around factories.

> They were not so much towns as barracks: not the refuge of a civilization but the barracks of an industry. . . . [T]hese towns reflected the violent enterprise of an hour, the single passion that had thrown street on street in a frantic monotony of

---

[8]H. L. Beales, *The Industrial Revolution, 1750–1850: An Introductory Essay* (New York: Sentry Press, 1967; first published in 1928). The quotation is taken from p. 96. The swollen supply of children must be attributed to lowered infant mortality.

[9]J. L. Hammond and Barbara Hammond, *The Town Labourer: The New Civilization 1760–1832* (Garden City, NY: Doubleday Anchor, 1968), p. 10.

[10]Beales, *The Industrial Revolution,* p. 96.

[11]Hammond and Hammond, *The Town Labourer,* p. 128.

[12]Beales, *The Industrial Revolution,* p. 41.

disorder. . . . And these towns were precisely what they looked. They were settlements of great masses of people collected in a particular place because their fingers or their muscles were needed on the brink of a stream here or at the mouth of a furnace there.[13]

A new form of urbanism was taking shape, reflecting a social system that was creating industrial capitalism and was causing a growing gap between the rich and the poor. A contemporary observer, writing in the staid *Edinburgh Review* of 1813,[14] deplored the fact that, despite all the astonishing inventions and economic progress made in the late eighteenth and early nineteenth centuries, "the number of paupers in England had increased fourfold, and . . . the peace of the country is perpetually threatened by the outrages of famishing multitudes." Manufacturing, rather than bringing prosperity to all, had converted peasants into factory workers and factory workers into paupers.

Indeed, this was so. These conditions led Marx and Engels, writing from 1848 on, to their conclusion that capitalism was simplifying the class structure into two opposing camps: the capitalists (who owned the factories, the machines, the ships, and all the physical equipment whereby the new wealth was being produced) and the proletariat (the displaced yeomen, artisans, small shopkeepers, immigrants from Ireland, etc., who increasingly had nothing left to offer but their labor). Thanks to the population growth of the period and to the large "reserve" available in Ireland, there were so many of these potential workers that if some chose not to work for starvation wages, there were many more than willing to take their places.

Whether inequalities were the same as or greater than they had been before cannot be known with certainty. However, the poor were certainly dying off faster than the rich, as indicated by the comparative life expectancies reported in the famous 1842 *Report on the Sanitary Conditions of the Labouring Population of Great Britain.* The average age at death for professional persons, gentry, and members of their families was 38, whereas it was only 17 for mechanics, laborers, and their families.[15]

The novels of Dickens, written about this time, detail some of the effects of poverty on residents of London, but London was still civilized and refined in comparison with the more exclusively industrial towns where capitalism was brasher. The town of Manchester,[16] for example, was far more representative of the new social order than the more diversified commercial and governmental capital of London.

The Factory Town of Manchester   During the last quarter of the eighteenth century, the town of Manchester was utterly transformed by the

---

[13]Hammond and Hammond, *The Town Labourer,* p. 34.

[14]Quoted in Beales, *The Industrial Revolution,* p. 18.

[15]Asa Briggs, *Victorian Cities* (New York: Harper Colophon Books, 1970), p. 101.

[16]The setting of Dickens's *Hard Times.*

development there of the cotton industry. Between about 1770 and 1830 its population increased sixfold, as pauper children, displaced farmers, and Irish immigrants were pulled into factory labor. Urban historian Asa Briggs has drawn from early nineteenth-century literature on Manchester to paint a disturbing picture of the social transformations introduced by industrial capitalism. He notes that Manchester's "progress" was reflected not only in its new buildings but in its squalor, which was *"thought to be a necessary by-product of its increasing wealth."* In the 1780s, a growing gulf between rich and poor was noted, and by 1820 "it was a commonplace to attribute basic social and political differences to economic divisions of interest between mill owners and workers."[17] Indeed, one inhabitant, Canon Parkinson, wrote early in the nineteenth century:

> There is no town in the world where the distance between the rich and poor is so great, or the barrier between them so difficult to be crossed [as Manchester]. . . . The separation between the different classes, and the consequent ignorance of each other's habits and conditions, are far more complete in this place than in any country of the older nations of Europe, or the agricultural parts of our own kingdom. There is far less *personal* communication between the master cotton spinner and his workmen . . . than there is between the Duke of Wellington and the humblest labourer on his estate.[18]

The slum quarters of such new industrial centers as Manchester shocked the sensibilities of journalists, muckrakers, politicians, social reformers, and even industrialists. Various parliamentary investigations were conducted, and many public health officials, ministers, and social workers recorded their observations. These documents were available to Frederick Engels, Marx's collaborator, when in 1844 he wrote his scathing critique of *The Condition of the Working Class in England.*[19] After describing the dismal, entirely industrial quarters at the periphery of Manchester, Engels focused on the city itself, demonstrating how the city's land-use plan protected wealthy residents from even knowing how the working class lived. In many ways, his description of 150 years ago would fit some American cities today.

> There is a fairly large commercial district. . . . almost entirely given over to offices and warehouses. . . . [encircled by a belt of slums] occupied entirely by working class dwellings. . . . Beyond this belt . . . lie the districts inhabited by the middle and upper classes [and beyond them lie the homes of the plutocrats who] can travel from their houses to their places of business in the centre of town by the shortest routes, which run entirely through working class districts, without ever realizing how close they are to the misery and filth which lie on both sides of the road. This

---

[17]Briggs, *Victorian Cities*, p. 89; italics added.

[18]Quoted in Briggs, p. 114.

[19]The first publication of this work was in German in 1845. The edition we have used was translated by W. O. Henderson and W. H. Chaloner (New York: Macmillan Company, 1958). Engels depended not only on his own observations but upon contemporaneous newspaper exposés, parliamentary reports, and detailed social surveys just then being undertaken in selected slums.

is because the main streets which run from the Exchange in all directions out of the town are occupied almost uninterruptedly on both sides by shops, which are kept by members of the lower middle class.[20]

He suggested that shops were intentionally used to conceal the surrounding misery "to avoid offending the tender . . . eyes and . . . nerves" of the richer inhabitants.[21]

There was certainly much to conceal. The slum quarters ringing the central business district were incredibly overcrowded. There were basement dwellings; open privies; piles of filth, rubbish, and garbage; stagnant pools; even pigs, for "in this area, as in most of the working class districts of Manchester, pig breeders rent the courts and build sties there."[22] Manchester also boasted almost 300 common lodging houses accommodating perhaps five to six thousand residents. "In every room five or seven beds are made up on the floor and human beings of both sexes are packed into them indiscriminately."[23]

The newer quarters built especially for workers were even worse than the older converted quarters in the center of the city. New Town, also called "Irish Town," consisted of filthy deteriorated cottages, beneath which were "damp, dirty cellar dwellings." The unpaved lanes and alleys lacked drainage and "only in very dry weather . . . can one reach [the district] without sinking ankle-deep at every step."[24] The worst slum of all, however, was Little Ireland, in which four thousand persons, mostly Irish immigrants, lived crowded 20 persons per two-room dilapidated cottage. Each privy there was shared by an average of 120 persons.[25] It was little wonder that these districts were periodically ravaged by cholera or that the children growing up in the early industrial cities were wan and rickety.

The First Reformers   Engels was not alone in deploring such conditions. During the second half of the nineteenth century, the early "dislocations," originally considered to be the unintended consequences of overly rapid growth, became institutionalized into a class system which became increasingly polarized. During the remainder of the century, English reformers such as Charles Booth and his fellow parliamentarians devoted their efforts to chronicling the hardships introduced by the new capitalism, by the rampant urban growth that reduced older urban quarters to slums and generated new workingmen's quarters so jerry-built that they were slums before they were occupied, and by the in-migration of destitute farmers and refugees from England's most depressed internal colony, Ireland. By the end of the century, Mayhew

---

[20]Engels, *Condition of the Working Class,* pp. 54–55.

[21]*Ibid.,* p. 56.

[22]*Ibid.,* p. 63.

[23]*Ibid.,* p. 77.

[24]*Ibid.,* p. 65.

[25]*Ibid.,* pp. 71–73.

had written his vignettes of the life of street people in London,[26] Booth had conducted his massive study of the slums of London,[27] the settlement house movement had begun,[28] and philanthropists were beginning to become involved in subsidized housing, once it was recognized that the economy never would be able to provide decent affordable housing for the poor.[29]

England had passed through the first convulsions of industrialization into the modern age. So successful indeed was its industrial revolution in producing enormous quantities of goods that by the second half of the nineteenth century, England had both an insatiable demand for more raw materials to feed into the production line and a mounting problem of what to do with the products themselves. The need for both raw materials and markets was solved through imperial expansion.

The Sun Never Sets on the Empire

If the period of 1750–1850 was largely one in which the industrial and social machinery of modern capitalism was created, the period 1850–1900 was the period in which imperial expansion to secure raw materials and to capture markets became the central struggle. There is no doubt that the enormous expansion in the English economy and in English urbanism was linked to colonialism. Whereas earlier it had been enough to control shipping and trade, now it became necessary to secure these monopolies through force and political rule, especially as the later contenders—France, Germany, and even Belgium and Portugal—began to compete with England.

Table 3.4 shows the magnitude and timing of the colonial expansion into non-European regions between 1860 and 1900. During this period and up until World War I, England and France managed to parcel out much of the rest of the world between them, as can be seen from the figures presented in Table 3.5.

It is clear from these figures that the empire on which the sun never set was

---

[26]Henry Mayhew, *London Labour and the London Poor* (London: Griffin, Bohn and Company, 1861), originally entitled "A Cyclopedia of the Condition and Earnings of Those That Will Work, Those That Cannot Work and Those That Will Not Work."

[27]See Charles Booth, *Life and Labour of the People in London,* 17 volumes (London: Macmillan and Co., 1902–1903): the first series on *Poverty* (1902 in four volumes); the second series on *Industry* (in five volumes, 1903); the third series on *Religious Influences* (seven volumes, 1902–1903); and the final volume entitled *Notes on Social Influences and Conclusions* (1903). This was less anecdotal and far more scholarly than the earlier work by Mayhew. For bibliographic information and excerpts from his work, see *Charles Booth on the City: Physical Pattern and Social Structure,* ed. Harold Pfautz (Chicago: Phoenix Books, University of Chicago Press, 1967).

[28]The settlement house movement began in England at Toynbee Hall in 1884. It was there that Jane Addams, later to found Hull House in Chicago, first saw what a settlement house might do to alleviate the problems of the poor.

[29]See John Nelson Tarn, *Five Per Cent Philanthropy: An Account of Housing in Urban Areas Between 1840 and 1914* (London: Cambridge University Press, 1973), for a full and fascinating account of English attempts to subsidize housing for the urban poor.

Table 3.4   PERCENTAGE OF REGIONAL TERRITORY
BELONGING TO EUROPEAN COLONIAL POWERS
AND THE UNITED STATES, 1876–1900

Region	1876 %	1900 %	Increase/decrease %
Africa	10.8	90.4	+79.6
Polynesia	56.8	98.9	+42.1
Asia	51.5	56.6	+ 5.1
Australia	100.0	100.0	no change
America	27.5	27.2	− 0.3

Source: A. Supan as reproduced in Lenin, "Imperialism, the Highest Stage of Capitalism," *V. I. Lenin Selected Works,* vol. 1 (Moscow: Progress Publishers, 1970), p. 726.

Table 3.5   THE TWO LARGEST COLONIAL POWERS AND THE EXPANSION OF THEIR
EMPIRES DURING THE SECOND HALF OF THE NINETEENTH CENTURY

Year	Great Britain		France	
	Colonial area (sq. mi.)	Colonial inhabitants	Colonial area (sq. mi.)	Colonial inhabitants
1815–1830	?	126,400,000	20,000	500,000
1860	2,500,000	145,100,000	200,000	3,400,000
1880	7,700,000	267,900,000	700,000	7,500,000
1899	9,300,000	309,000,000	3,700,000	56,400,000
1914	11,500,000	393,500,000	3,640,000	55,500,000

Sources: Assembled and computed from Henry Morris, *The History of Colonisation* (New York: 1900), various tables; A. Supan, *Die territoriale Entwicklung des europäischen Kolonien* (1906), various tables; and presented in separate tables in Lenin's essay, "Imperialism, the Highest Stage of Capitalism."

the true hinterland upon which English urbanization in the nineteenth century depended. This phenomenon was also reflected in the urban growth rates of other European states that were beginning to catch up with England, in terms of both economic development and associated urban problems. Table 3.6 shows the changing levels of urbanization in these other countries during the second half of the nineteenth century. Clearly, Europe was already on its way to global urbanization.

The Sociological Analysis of the Great Transformation

It was at this time that social scientists began to explore the implications of these basic changes in the way people lived and to generate theories about what an urbanized society would be like. It is appropriate to stop here to examine those theories, in order to determine how they were related to the specific historic

Table 3.6 LEVELS OF URBANIZATION IN SELECTED EUROPEAN COUNTRIES DURING THE SECOND HALF OF THE NINETEENTH CENTURY

Country	Percentage of population living in cities*				
	Around 1850	Around 1860	Around 1870	Around 1880	Around 1890
England and Wales (1)	50	55	62	68	72
Belgium (2)	33	35	37	43	48
Prussia (3)	27	29	32	36	40
France (4)	25	29	31	35	37
Norway (5)	12	13	15	18	24
Hungary (6)	12	14	14	15	16
Sweden (7)	10	11	13	15	19
Denmark (8)	10	10	12	14	17
Switzerland (9)	9	11	13	15	17
Russia (10)	9	?	11	?	12

*Since the definition of urban varied from country to country, the data are not exactly comparable. However, they do show relative levels of urbanization over time.

Source: Adna Weber, *The Growth of Cities in the Nineteenth Century*, originally published in 1899 and based upon the available sources. Figures have been compiled from various tables. Page references are to the 1967 edition, as follows: (1) Table XVIII, p. 46, computations ours; (2) Table LXV, p. 116; (3) Table XLII, p. 82; (4) Table XXXIII, p. 68; (5) Table LXVI, p. 111; (6) Table LVII, p. 101; (7) Table LXIV, p. 110; (8) Table LXX, p. 113; (9) Unnumbered table, p. 117; (10) Table LXI, p. 107.

conditions in which they were generated and to determine the extent to which these conditions were generalizable to urban life, wherever it was to become pervasive.

The dislocations to social life experienced during Europe's "great transformation" included: (1) an increase in the scale of society through population growth and improved transportation and communication; (2) the full development of the centralized nation-state; (3) the heightened productivity made possible through harnessing poorly paid workers to machines powered by inanimate energy; (4) the increasing polarization of classes according to whether they owned land and machines (capital) or only labor; and (5) the wealth and glory, but also the uncertainties, introduced by the creation, through imperialism, of a world market.

It was natural that these would receive attention from social analysts. Within the newly developing fields of political economy, sociology, and anthropology, scholars clearly recognized that fundamental changes were taking place in the relationships between people, and that the connection between individuals and their society was undergoing important redefinition; given the revolutionary pace at which change was occurring, they could hardly have overlooked these facts. It was thus no accident that this period, from about 1850 to 1914, when Europe was undergoing wrenching change, was a remarkably fertile time for the development of theories of social change.

Some analysts, such as Karl Marx (1818–1883), focused on the economy and on the changing relations between the classes as capitalism became the dominant mode of production.[30] Others, such as Henry Maine (1822–1888), focused on the law, noting the decline of predetermined status bonds between persons, the growth of the individual as a legal entity, and the increased dependence on contracts that bound together specific actions of individuals without involving their total persons (as had been the case in slavery, indenture, or serfdom).[31] Still others, like Ferdinand Toennies (1855–1935), focused on the growth of the state and the transfer of many controls over the individual from the smaller communities of family and neighborhood (the *Gemeinschaft*) to the more impersonal and formal institutions in the larger public realm (the *Gesellschaft*).[32] And some, like Max Weber, exhaustively traced the institutional changes that facilitated and followed from such economic, legal, and political transformations.[33]

All these theorists recognized that in the modern world then emerging, kin and neighborhood, while still constituting basic anchors to social life, were being supplemented by new kinds of social relations to larger and more impersonal units—to the workplace, to the profession, and to such geographically extended units as the metropolis and the nation.

Obviously, at the same time these transformations were occurring, cities were proliferating and growing in size, as we have already seen. It was therefore perfectly natural that some thinkers should have drawn more explicit links between urbanization, per se, and the altering forms of social life. Two of these social analysts, Emile Durkheim (1858–1917) and Georg Simmel (1858–1918), were particularly influential in formulating theories that suggested that cities themselves were causing the changes in relationships that were being observed.

Durkheim, in his 1893 book, *The Division of Labor in Society,*[34] developed a complex argument to prove that the entire organization of society changed *because* increases in the number and density of inhabitants (by indirect inference: cities) *required* a greater division of labor and the development of a different type of social bond between people. No longer could "mechanical" solidarity, based upon what people had in common, hold society together; it had

---

[30]The simplest statement of his position is found in *The Communist Manifesto,* written in 1848 as a political tract. However, the serious student should also examine the fuller statements available in the larger corpus of work.

[31]Henry Maine, *Ancient Law* (London: John Murray, 1861).

[32]Ferdinand Toennies, *Gemeinschaft und Gesellschaft,* first published in Germany in 1887. It has been translated into English by Charles Loomis under the title *Community and Society* (East Lansing: Michigan State University Press, 1957).

[33]Like those of Marx, the works of Max Weber are voluminous. *The Theory of Social and Economic Organization,* trans. M. Henderson and Talcott Parsons (New York: Oxford University Press, 1947), is basic, but perhaps the most widely read and quoted of his essays is *The Protestant Ethic and the Spirit of Capitalism,* trans. Talcott Parsons (New York: Charles Scribner's Sons, 1958).

[34]Emile Durkheim, *De la division du travail social,* first published in French in 1893, and translated into English in 1933 by George Simpson under the title *The Division of Labor in Society* (New York: Macmillan, Free Press of Glencoe, 1964).

to be supplemented by a new type of bond he called *organic solidarity,* which grew out of an elaborate and interdependent division of labor. His description of the new larger-scale society was certainly accurate, as was his recognition that increased contacts and a greater division of labor (now on a global scale) create more mutual dependence. But his theory cannot be used to support the claim that big city life inevitably destroys the smaller communities of family and neighborhood. Durkheim has also been criticized, with more justification, for assuming that mutual dependence would naturally develop smoothly and be of mutual benefit to all parties, and for seeing conflicts and disorder as mere diseases to be cured, rather than as problems endemic to modern life.

Georg Simmel, particularly in his widely read essay, "The Metropolis and Mental Life," also seemed to be arguing that big city life, because it bombarded residents with too many diverse and unordered stimuli, actually required changes in the personality of urban dwellers to help them survive and adapt. He suggested that city people had to become less personal, more blasé, less "caring," in order to withstand the stress of city living. On the other hand, he also argued that only by disengaging from the full control of small communities of family and neighbors could the individual develop his or her personality to its highest form—and this quality he certainly admired. Elsewhere, he studied the nature of money as an influence even more important than urbanism in depersonalizing human relations. And in yet another of his essays, he examined the relationship between the development of personality and the structure of the social circles (networks, as they are now called) to which a person belonged, recognizing the connection between alternative identities and individuality.[35] His was certainly not a simpleminded theory making urbanism the cause of social disorder. (We shall return to his theory of social circles when we begin to develop our own theory of community in Chapters 10 through 12.)

It is important, therefore, to recognize that neither Durkheim nor Simmel deplored the new forms of social life that were emerging in cities, even though their theories have sometimes been invoked by opponents of urban growth to "prove" the inevitable dire consequences of urbanization. They, like the other social theorists noted above, described and tried to make sense out of the enormous changes Europe was going through. Theirs were not general theories of modernization and urbanization but specific theories linked to their own societies and the transformations of the nineteenth century.

It is well to bear this in mind in looking at urbanization and societal transfor-

---

[35]Simmel's brilliant essay, "The Metropolis and Mental Life," was translated into English by Kurt H. Wolff and reprinted in *The Sociology of Georg Simmel* (Glencoe, IL: Free Press, 1950), pp. 409–424. His *Philosophy of Money* (published originally in 1900 under the title *Philosophie des Geldes)* has recently been translated into English for the first time. See the translation by Tom Bottomore and David Frisby (London: Routledge & Kegan Paul, 1978). The lengthy essay in which he deals with networks, which he referred to in German as "social circles," is called, in English translation, *The Web of Group Affiliations* (1955). It appeared originally in 1922 and was one of Simmel's most mature works. The English translation by Reinhard Bendix appears in *Conflict and the Web of Group Affiliations* (Glencoe, IL: Free Press, 1955).

mations elsewhere. The United States, although part of Western culture, had a very different history of development than Europe and markedly different sources of urban population growth. Therefore, theories developed in Europe certainly needed to be revised to make them applicable to urban life in the United States. (Since we look at the American case in great detail in Chapters 4 through 6, we will not treat it here.) Countries in the nonwestern world are following different trajectories from either Europe or the United States, and thus need their own theoretical explanations of urban life.

To gain a true comparative perspective, we need to examine a markedly different case—one that illustrates the periphery. Just as England was used to represent urbanization at the core, even though its experience was not duplicated exactly by any other European country, Egypt can illustrate urbanization at the periphery, even though its experience was not identical to that of every other colonized nation. But if England represented the best possible scenario for early urbanization, Egypt represents one of the worst possible scenarios.

URBANIZATION AT THE PERIPHERY: THE CASE OF EGYPT

Egypt, like England, was virtually an island, although surrounded not by water but by desert. Unlike England, however, Egypt had been a state for thousands of years and had given rise to some of the world's earliest cities. By the time Europe was leaping toward statehood, industrialization, urbanization, and world conquest, however, Egypt had sunk to a decayed province of the declining Ottoman Empire. In 1798, the very year Malthus wrote his famous essay on population and Jenner published his success in vaccinating against smallpox, Napoleon's armies were marching from Alexandria upstream along the Nile to Cairo, and British and French naval forces were battling off the Egyptian coast. Egypt was about to be made a crucial peripheral region of Europe.

Egypt was not then very promising. Soon after the invasion, when Napoleon's scholars made their first estimates of Egypt's population and level of urbanization, they found that the country contained little more than 3 million inhabitants (one-third the number of inhabitants during medieval times), and that of these, perhaps ten percent lived in cities.[36] It would take the rest of the nineteenth century to restore Egypt's population to its medieval level, but by then it was neither the head of an empire nor a periphery irrelevant to the new core in Europe; rather, it was integrated as a dependent colony in the world system.

The French were forced to retreat in 1801, and soon afterward a semi-autonomous Egyptian dynasty was set up, but these political events were far less significant in the long run than the introduction of a new strain of long-staple cotton whose outlet was to be the textile mills of Lancashire. This shift

---

[36]*Description de l'Egypte: Etat Moderne* (Paris: Imprimerie Royale, 1822).

to export-oriented monoculture linked Egypt's fate to the core, making it an object of interest to overseas capitalists.[37]

At first, British and French interests in Egypt were chiefly strategic. Egypt was the land bridge between the Mediterranean Sea and the Indian Ocean and was therefore a key link between Great Britain and its commercial empire in India. This link was secured through the construction of the Suez Canal to join the Mediterranean with the Indian Ocean—a gigantic task undertaken with French and Egyptian capital and subsidized by conscripted Egyptian labor; the canal was opened to traffic in 1869.

By then, Egypt's economy had become closely integrated with England's, due to the shift to cotton growing. Particularly in the early 1860s, when American supplies of cotton were cut off because of the Civil War, Egypt became the major supplier to British mills. War-boom prices encouraged the Egyptians to undertake ambitious projects to transform Egypt from an exporter of raw materials to a processor of agricultural products (food processing, sugar refining, textile manufacture). However, when the sources of this capital dried up with the collapse of cotton prices in 1865, the schemes were continued by means of generous but extremely high-interest loans extended by European banks.

By 1875 bankruptcy was imminent and was only forestalled by the sale to Britain of all of Egypt's shares in the Suez Canal. The reprieve was brief. Soon afterward the state was placed in receivership and Britain and France entered to supervise its return to solvency. French and English competition was eventually resolved as part of a larger arrangement to divide up Africa. The French did not protest when Britain invaded Egypt in 1882, and from then until well into the twentieth century, Britain defended its economic interests (a certain supply of cotton) and its strategic interests (control over the Suez Canal), regardless of the effects on Egypt.

In the course of the nineteenth century, then, Egypt was transformed from a slightly irrelevant periphery to a colony, from a depressed subsistence economy to a monoculture supplying cotton to the world market, from Mamluk/Ottoman feudalism with little privately owned land to a capitalist state of large estates, bonded labor in the agricultural areas, wage labor in the factories, and residuals of medieval-type guilds in the traditional sector of the urban economy.

In the course of this transformation, both population and cities grew—but with consequences very different from those in Europe. Population tripled in the course of the century to regain its medieval peak of over nine million. Cities grew even faster. As in the case of the earlier English enclosures, the conversion of much communally owned agricultural land to private ownership drove peasants from the land into cities; but in this case, there was no industry to absorb them. By the end of the nineteenth century, about 15 percent of Egypt's larger

---

[37]E. Roger Owen, Jr., *Cotton and the Egyptian Economy, 1820–1914: A Study in Trade and Development* (Oxford: Clarendon Press, 1969).

population was living in towns and cities with 20,000 or more inhabitants. If one compares Table 3.3, showing English data, and Table 3.7, showing Egyptian, one finds a rough equivalence between the levels of population and urbanization of England and Wales in 1801 and Egypt in 1897. The countries seemed to be about one hundred years apart in their development.

But England and Egypt were light-years apart in terms of their roles in the world system, which led to very different patterns of urbanization. One was ruler, the other ruled; one was colonizer, the other colonized. One was the recipient of raw materials and the beneficiary of favorable terms of a trade that it controlled; the other was the source of raw materials at depressed prices and the recipient of manufactured goods that destroyed any possibility for internal development. During the course of the nineteenth and early twentieth centuries, Egypt "de-developed," despite an increase in population and a dramatic growth of cities.

It is clear from Table 3.7 that after very gradual change during the early decades of the present century, Egypt experienced a massive increase both in total population and in levels of urbanization, trends especially noticeable since the 1940s. This population increase, however, had causes and consequences

Table 3.7   CHANGES IN TOTAL POPULATION, NUMBER OF CITIES WITH 20,000 OR MORE INHABITANTS, PROPORTION OF POPULATION LIVING IN SUCH URBAN PLACES, EGYPT, 1897 TO 1980

Date	Total population	Number of cities with 20,000+	Percentage of population in cities 20,000+
1897	9,991,291	17	14.6
1907	11,135,610	20	14.4
1917	12,670,414	31	17.3
1927	14,083,276	38	20.7
1937	15,811,084	46	22.9
1947	18,805,826	57	29.2
1960	25,771,495	68	36.3
1966	29,720,423	80	40.0
1977	38,800,000	*	44.0
1980	42,126,000	*	44.0
1990**	53,000,000	*	46.4

*Information not available.

**medium projection

Sources: Processed data from 1897 through 1960 from Janet Abu-Lughod, "Urbanization in Egypt: Present State and Future Prospects," Economic Development and Cultural Change 13 (April, 1965): pp. 313–343. Post-1960 data from censuses of 1966 and 1976, the 1986 Demographic Yearbook, and our projections.

that were very different from those in Europe at an earlier time. In Europe, population growth had led to economic development, to the multiplication of generative urban centers, and to imperial conquests. In Egypt as in many other parts of the Third World, population growth had the reverse effect. Rather than serving as a trigger to economic development, population increase served as a barrier to economic growth because it weighted down an already troubled economy. It is this fact that makes the experiences of Third World countries so different from those of nineteenth-century Europe.

Some Comparisons to Rethink Theory

The introduction of DDT and antibiotics in the late 1940s led to significant drops in death rates throughout the world. The effects were most dramatic in Third World countries that had previously suffered from high mortality. The immediate effects were to drive natural increase rates substantially higher, even though commensurate economic growth did not necessarily follow. For the short run, at least, populations began to double every 30 years, even in places such as Egypt that were already overcrowded.

This paralleled, to some extent, the experience of Europe in the nineteenth century. However, emigration could not relieve the population pressure as it had for Europe, and opportunities for either self-propelled internal economic growth or external conquest were not available to the latecomers of the twentieth century. Economic stagnation in the countryside was met by emigration— but instead of seeking their fortunes in the New World, displaced farmers had only the city as their frontier.

The burgeoning populations of the largest cities in the Third World are consequences of this new condition. Cairo's metropolitan area, for example, grew from about 3.5 million in 1960 to over 10 million by 1987—not because there was a sudden demand from industry for a labor force, but because the rural areas could no longer contain or sustain the surplus population generated by population growth. Therefore, there is no comparison between London in 1880 and Cairo in 1980, nor any between Mahalla Al-Kubra (Egypt's major textile town) and Manchester in the early days of the Industrial Revolution. In many ways, poverty in Cairo today is less grinding than that suffered by the mill-hands of early English industrialization, but it is also less understandable, given our current capacity to provide decent housing and modern municipal services.

Nor is the cultural life of Cairo or the social behavior of Cairenes comparable to the European cases that gave rise to the theories linking urbanization with cultural change. Depersonalization is not a characteristic of Cairo urban life, nor have kin and neighbors been displaced by allegiance and relations to larger entities. Individualism is less important, and the social solidarity based upon similarities (Durkheim's mechanical solidarity) is still more vital in Cairo than in European cities. The *Gemeinschaft* still dominates the *Gesellschaft*, and status relations remain more important than contracts.

Thus, when we ask how well social theories developed by nineteenth-century European social scientists predict the nature of social life in contemporary Third World cities such as Cairo, Calcutta, or Shanghai, we must answer that they do not do very well at all.

WILL GLOBAL URBANIZATION CREATE HOMOGENEITY IN URBAN LIFE?

These comparative cases expose the culture-bound character of theories that seek to identify inevitable consequences of urbanization. They demonstrate how much the culture of given cities is tied to the overall culture of the country in which they are found, and how much this overall culture is shaped not only by history but by current economic arrangements and by the role a country plays in the international economy.

Cities of today are organized differently from cities in the historical past. Furthermore, contemporary cities in Asia, Africa, the Middle East, and Latin America all have their unique qualities related not only to the stage of history they have reached but to their political, economic, social, and cultural contexts. It could hardly be otherwise. True, within each culture and country there are marked differences between life in rural areas and life in cities, just as there are differences between the social classes within cities. True, these differences tend to be in the direction of greater impersonality, individualism, and inequality in urban areas. But one cannot conclude from these differences that size and density per se, or even improved communication and greater stimuli, have the same effects on social relations everywhere. We shall return to this point in the next chapters when we examine the American case to show how it, too, deviated in important ways from the theoretical expectations set forth by European observers analyzing their own cities in the late nineteenth century.

Thus, the urbanization of the world, while it has led to increased homogeneity when measured in terms of the level of urbanization (that is, the proportion of a country's population living in cities), has not necessarily led to homogeneity of urban life and culture. Diversity remains more striking than uniformity—especially when one compares cities in the early industrializing West (Europe and North America) with those in peripheral or non-western countries (in Asia, Latin America, and Africa). It is not possible simply to transfer what we know about contemporary large cities in our own society to all cities around the world. Countries and culture areas must still be studied individually to understand the nature of their cities, the ways of life that are urban, and the roles cities play in the nation.[38]

---

[38]The contrasts between Western urban processes and those now occurring in the rest of the world are emphasized in Janet Abu-Lughod and Richard Hay, Jr., eds., *Third World Urbanization* (New York: Methuen, 1979). See also Gerald Breese, ed., *The City in Newly Developing Countries* (Englewood Cliffs, NJ: Prentice-Hall, 1969); Philip Hauser and Leo Schnore, eds., *The Study of Urbanization* (1965); Stanley Brunn and Jack Williams, *Cities of the World* (New York: Harper & Row, 1983); and are especially well handled in Anthony King, *Urbanism, Colonialism, and the*

One form of homogenization does, however, seem to be occurring. As urbanization becomes more and more pervasive in a society, there is a tendency for the barriers between rural and urban areas to be broken down and for the contrasts between life in rural places and life in urban centers to be reduced. In the early days of urbanization, when cities constituted a minority way of life and increased their populations chiefly through the addition of rural migrants, they tended to take on many of the characteristics associated with rural communities. In the present period, as urbanism becomes more widespread, rural areas are increasingly affected by the metropolitanization of society in general. People in rural areas tend more and more to adopt patterns of behavior and beliefs we have traditionally called urban. This process is occurring in all countries where a majority of the population now lives in cities.

A clear illustration of this process is found in the United States, where, in the short history of the nation, the level of urbanization increased from a mere 5 percent to over 75 percent, the country's role shifted from colonized periphery to world power, and the functions of cities, as well as their appearance, social character, and role in the national economy, were totally transformed. In Chapters 4 through 6 we trace the growth and transformation of cities in the United States from their earliest to their most recent (and unprecedented) forms. These chapters are intended not only to give the reader concrete knowledge of how the cities we now live in came to be but also to illustrate many of the principles of urban growth and transformation laid out in Chapters 2 and 3.

To review, cities came into being not only when environment and technology permitted a shift to higher levels of population size and density, but also when socioeconomic and political reorganization made possible the harnessing of the society's surplus for a greater division of labor, heightened productivity, and increased social inequality. Such a reorganization occurred not only within a society but also in relation to its neighbors and trading partners. The factors of population growth, socioeconomic and political reorganization, and the changing relation to "empire" are as relevant to understanding the growth (and possible current decline) of cities in the United States as they are in accounting for the rise (and fall) of Ur, Babylon, Memphis, Manchester, and London.

World-Economy (London and New York: Routledge, 1990).

The Changing American City

Chapter
4

The Making of an Urban United States

*T*oward the end of the eighteenth century—about the time Jenner was developing his smallpox vaccine, Malthus was preparing his dismal predictions about population, and Napoleon was coming to power—the newly independent thirteen colonies, recently constituted as the United States, took their first official census. In the region east of the Mississippi were some three million white settlers and some three-quarters of a million persons of African origin, mostly slaves. Native Americans, whose number was subsequently estimated at about one million, were not included.

When this first census was taken in 1790, only two American cities had reached minimum "urban size" of 20,000: New York, with a population of about 33,000, and Philadelphia, with about 28,500. Boston, the third-largest city, fell just short of the urban mark with a population of some 18,000. If we measure the level of urbanization as the proportion of total population living in places with a minimum of 20,000 inhabitants, only 1.6 percent of the U.S. population was then urban, and the figure drops to 1.2 percent if native Americans are included. Even using the more generous U.S. legal definition of an urban place as any settlement having at least 2500 inhabitants, the level of urbanization in 1790 was only 5 percent, excluding Amerindians.[1]

In 1790 there was nothing to indicate that the United States would, in the course of 200 years, come to contain a population of some 250,000,000, of whom 75 percent would be living in metropolitan regions scattered from coast to coast, albeit occupying less than 16 percent of the total land area.[2]

In contrast to England and even Egypt, the cases presented in Chapter 3, the United States looked unpromising. By 1800, when London and suburbs boasted a population of close to a million and Cairo had some 260,000 inhabitants, cities in the United States were few and tiny, most of the continent remained unexplored and unsettled, and only 6 percent of all settlers lived in urban places with 2500 or more inhabitants.

The United States, then, offers one of the most dramatic instances ever recorded of transformation through industrialization and urbanization. Its development into an urban society was associated with several other causally linked transformations:

1. *Politically,* from a colony to a global power;
2. *Geographically,* from a coastal enclave to a continental network;
3. *Economically,* from a collector and exporter of raw materials, such as furs and timber, to the world's largest producer of industrial goods;
4. *Systemically,* from a periphery, tied to the European commercial core, to the core region of the modern world system; and
5. *Demographically,* from a relatively homogeneous population to a "melting pot" drawing upon increasingly diverse sources.

This chapter and the two that follow trace this remarkable transformation.

PHASES IN AMERICAN URBAN HISTORY[3]

Six phases can be distinguished, in which the regional spatial patterns of urbanization altered in fundamental ways and within which the forces that shaped urbanization (namely, population growth, social hierarchy, and relations to "empire") were essentially different. These are:

---

[1]Successive reports from the U.S. Census Office, as summarized in Blake McKelvey, *American Urbanization: A Comparative History* (Glenview, IL: Scott, Foresman & Company, 1973), especially Table 2, p. 24.

[2]U.S. Census of Population, Supplementary Reports, No. PC80-S1-5 (Washington, DC: Superintendent of Documents, October 1981), p. 1.

[3]It is somewhat arbitrary to divide the continuous stream of history into "phases." However, if the narrative is to be analytical, we must delineate phases that conform to the changing nature of American urbanism as it evolved from its origins in the tiny settlements at Jamestown (1609) and Plymouth (1620) to the present period in which urbanization has permeated the entire country. Periods A and B are covered in Chapter 4; Chapter 5 treats C(5), and the most recent phase, C(6), is explored in Chapter 6.

A. From Colonization to Decolonization, 1609–1830.
1. Cities as colonial outposts of the European core, 1609–1776.
2. Cities as cores of an increasingly independent American system, 1776–1830.
B. From Small-Scale to Large-Scale Industrialism, 1830–1920.
3. Cities as generative centers for their surrounding regions, 1830–1865.
4. Cities as components of a large-scale industrial system that becomes nationwide, 1865–1920.
C. Mature Metropolitan Consolidation and Transformation, 1920–present.
5. Cities expand into metropolitan complexes, 1920–1950s.
6. Urbanization becomes pervasive, contiguous, and dispersed, 1950s–present.

To some extent, the three major periods (A, B, and C) coincide with what economists refer to as the preindustrial, industrial, and postindustrial ages, but they were distinguished by more than their dominant methods of production. Technology was important, but equally significant were: (1) changes in the magnitude and sources of population growth; (2) changes in the forms of economic and political coordination and control; and (3) changes in the way American cities related both to their hinterlands and to the rest of the world. Thus, the same three factors that explained the origin and development of cities earlier and elsewhere also shaped the unique development of American cities.

FROM COLONIZATION TO DECOLONIZATION: 1609–1830

American urbanization was unique in a number of ways. First, the earliest coastal settlements that initiated urbanization were intended, planned, and communally organized. Second, these settlements were, from the start, designed to serve as bases for the extraction and collection of natural resources drawn from the new continent. And third, they were viewed, at least by the European countries issuing the charters and land grants, as vital outposts for an international system of commercial and mercantile expansion. These three characteristics established the nature of American cities between 1609 and 1776.

Cities as Colonial Outposts of the European Core, 1609–1776

The cities and towns that Dutch and English settlers established along the Atlantic coast during the seventeenth century were not preceded by conquering armies, nor were they unregulated zones of freedom to which European pioneers came as individuals. They were communally organized colonies for which charters had to be obtained, and they were created by organized groups of settlers, often bonded together by a "compact" or "covenant."[4]

Early settlements in New England provide the best illustrations. John Winthrop's colony of Boston, founded in 1630, was based upon a covenant which all citizens signed, promising to form a community that would become "as a city upon a hill."[5] Signers promised to serve God, and not only to love and support one another but also "faithfully to watch over one another's Souls."[6] Page Smith has argued that not only can the unique character of American cities be traced back to the intentioned covenant, but that the framers of the Constitution were, in fact, drafting a secular covenant, based on the earlier city model, when they established the republic.

Even when the new settlements were not "covenanted" in the literal sense, they were still planned and intentional. That was one reason why so many of them were designed according to the gridiron plan,[7] a characteristic they shared with the colonies implanted by the ancient Greeks in Asia Minor under similar circumstances. This parallel was not an accident, for the second fundamental characteristic of early settlements was that they were extensions of urban Europe, rather than central places growing up to serve their immediate hinterlands. Constance McLaughlin Green reminds us that "the forces that created [these early] . . . centers of an urban civilization on a nearly empty continent derived from the expansion of world trade during the seventeenth century under [the] English and Dutch."[8] Glaab and Brown put it another way when they stress that from the beginning towns were essential to colonial life. Towns "were not called into existence by an earlier development of farming, but rather constituted the necessary positions from which agriculture and other activities, such as the fur trade, could spread inland without losing connection with the great world."[9]

Because the first settlements were parts of an intended system of imperial trade, the important prerevolutionary towns were ports: Boston, founded in 1630; Newport, Rhode Island, founded in 1639; New York, founded in 1625; Philadelphia, founded in 1682; and Charles Town, South Carolina, founded in

---

[4]Max Weber's essay *The City*, trans. Don Martindale and Gertrud Neuwirth (Glencoe, IL: Free Press, 1958), makes much of the *conjuratio* in Italian city-states as a unique characteristic of western urbanism. It is important to note, however, that the *conjuratio* was an oath individuals swore to the "city," rather than an oath residents swore to each other.

[5]This provided the title for Page Smith's study of the early American town, *As a City upon a Hill: The Town in American History* (Cambridge, MA: MIT Press, 1966), which has been our major source on the role of the covenant in New England towns.

[6]Page Smith, *As a City upon a Hill*, p. 10. Here he quotes from the covenant of Hampton Falls, New Hampshire, which was not atypical.

[7]John Reps, in *The Making of Urban America: A History of City Planning in the United States* (Princeton, NJ: Princeton University Press, 1965) reproduces many of these plans, including one done by surveyor George Washington.

[8]Constance McLaughlin Green, *The Rise of Urban America* (New York: Harper Colophon Books, 1965), p. 2.

[9]Charles N. Glaab and A. Theodore Brown, *A History of Urban America* (New York: Macmillan Company, 1967). Quotation is from p. 3 of this edition.

1680. Carl Bridenbaugh, in his classic work entitled *Cities in the Wilderness*,[10] describes the economic base of these towns. Boston's economy rested upon shipbuilding, salted (preserved) fish, lumber, and turpentine (a tree resin). Newport's sea captains controlled the African slave trade. New York and Philadelphia shipped agricultural produce as well as furs and animal products brought in by trappers. Charles Town, thanks in part to an influx of planters from Barbados in the West Indies, controlled the Caribbean trade and shipped rice, indigo, and skins from its hinterlands. In exchange for these primary products the ports received goods manufactured in England. This was a classic case of colonial exchange designed to support the growth of European ports even more than those of the New World.[11]

Because it was easier to travel by ship than to go overland through a yet untamed American interior, the original ports were each linked more closely with Europe than with either their own immediate surroundings (hinterlands) or one another. Gradually, however, each of the towns came to dominate its own hinterland, which made local merchants and shippers increasingly resentful of the trade restrictions England imposed to guarantee English merchants control over the most profitable routes and products. The economic hardships created by these trade restrictions unified merchants in their struggle for freedom to trade where they chose and to avoid the stamp tax on imports, which they viewed as illegitimate "tribute." Linkages among the American port cities themselves helped forge the alliance that made the Revolutionary War possible.

Cities as Cores of an Increasingly Independent American System, 1776–1830

The Revolutionary War, while it led eventually to heightened urbanization, resulted in a temporary setback for cities. Not only were cities depopulated during the fighting,[12] but the rupture with England excluded American merchants and ports from imperial trade. No longer could they share the lucrative British exploitation of the West Indies or the profitable "long-haul" from those islands to England. Now they had to pay heavy duties on direct shipments to England[13] while their merchant ships were continually harassed on the high seas by their former comrades-in-empire—a situation that led directly to the

---

[10]The basic sources for the prerevolutionary period are Carl Bridenbaugh, *Cities in the Wilderness: The First Century of Urban Life in America, 1625–1742* (New York: Ronald Press, 1938), and its sequel, *Cities in Revolt: Urban Life in America, 1743–1776* (New York: Alfred Knopf, 1955).

[11]David Ward, *Cities and Immigrants: A Geography of Change in Nineteenth Century America* (New York: Oxford University Press, 2d printing 1972), p. 9. We have drawn heavily on this excellent work for the theoretical approach and the time periods utilized in this chapter.

[12]The major port cities are estimated to have lost about half of their populations between 1775 and 1776. See Green, *The Rise of Urban America*, pp. 51–52.

[13]*Ibid*. p. 53.

War of 1812. With independence, then, came the pressing need to rebuild the base upon which economic and urban growth rested.

Two developments restructured the economy, combining to create a more integrated national economy and the skeletal outlines of an *urban system* in which New York emerged as the dominant center.[14] The first was the wholesale conversion of the southern plantation system to the cultivation of cotton. The second was an intensified push into the "western" interior, at first via waterways and canals, but eventually by rail.

Despite its economic costs, political independence from England did not liberate the American economy from English needs. The United States continued its colonial role as a provider of raw materials. British textile mills were now demanding increased supplies of cotton. Thanks to technological innovations (including Katherine Greene's cotton gin, patented by Eli Whitney in 1793, which permitted easier separation of cotton fluff from seeds)[15] and in response to burgeoning demand, by 1810 "virtually all enterprising southerners were dedicating their energies to acquiring more land and more slaves to clear and plant it to cotton."[16] Barrington Moore contends that "between 1815 and 1860 the cotton trade exercised a decisive influence upon the growth of manufacturing" in the United States and that "the main impetus behind the growth of Northern capitalism itself through the 1830s came . . . from cotton."[17] However, only later was southern cotton fed into the mills of New England. At first it was directed almost exclusively toward Lancashire. New York merchants monopolized the shipping and eventually the financing of these crops, thus catapulting New York into prime position in the nation.

The second factor that led to New York's dominance in the newly integrated urban hierarchy was the creation, on the western "frontier," of a true periphery tied to the eastern seaboard. Especially in the early 1800s, western expansion took place along waterways. The Louisiana Purchase in 1803 had added New Orleans as a major port city, and the natural river system of the Mississippi and its tributaries served to draw the West and South closer together as trading partners. But it was northern canals that really opened the Midwest for settlement and that weaned it away from links to the South. Completion in 1825 of the Erie Canal (which linked New York City to the Great Lakes via the Hudson River) encouraged settlements in upper New York State and throughout northern Ohio. Not only did new cities such as Buffalo, the canal's farthest terminus, appear, but smaller towns along the way were ripe for developers.

---

[14]Glaab and Brown note that by about 1850 "it is in a broad way accurate to say that, with the . . . exception [of New England], the entire country was the hinterland of New York City, with Philadelphia and Baltimore competing for that business which New York was simply not big enough to handle." See Glaab and Brown, *A History of Urban America*, pp. 36–37.

[15]Eli Whitney's cotton gin was actually invented by a widow on whose southern plantation the young Whitney worked as tutor to the children. Since women were not eligible to take out patents, the credit went to the man in whose name the patent was granted.

[16]Green, *The Rise of Urban America*, pp. 60–61.

[17]Barrington Moore, Jr., *Social Origins of Dictatorship and Democracy: Lord and Peasant in the Making of the Modern World* (Boston: Beacon Press, 1966), pp. 116, 124.

Table 4.1 POPULATIONS OF PRINCIPAL U.S. CITIES, 1790 TO 1830

Cities	1790	1800	1810	1820	1830
New York	33,131	60,515	96,373	123,706	202,589
suburbs	—	—	4,402	7,175	39,689
total	—	—	100,775	130,881	242,278
Philadelphia	28,522	41,220	53,722	63,802	80,462
suburbs	15,574	20,339	33,581	45,007	80,809
total	44,096	61,559	87,303	108,809	161,271
Boston	18,320	24,937	33,787	43,298	61,392
suburbs	—	—	4,959	10,726	18,104
total	—	—	38,746	54,024	85,568
Baltimore	13,503	26,514	46,555	62,738	80,620
New Orleans	—	9,000	17,242	27,176	46,082
Cincinnati	—	750	2,540	9,642	24,831
Charleston	16,359	18,924	24,711	24,780	30,289
Albany	3,498	5,349	9,356	12,630	24,209
Washington	—	3,210	8,208	13,247	18,826
Providence	6,380	7,614	10,071	11,767	16,833
Pittsburgh	376	1,565	4,768	7,248	15,369
Richmond	3,761	5,737	9,735	12,067	16,060
Number of towns over 2500	24	33	46	61	90
Total residents in towns	202,000	322,000	525,000	693,000	1,127,000
Percent in towns over 2500	5.1	6.1	7.3	7.2	8.8
Total U.S. population	3,929,000	5,308,000	7,240,000	9,638,000	12,866,000

Source: Blake McKelvey, American Urbanization: A Comparative History (Glenview, IL: Scott Foresman and Company, 1973), p. 24.

New York City, the coastal "collector" for this system, became the undisputed commercial leader.[18]

The new cities of the Midwest were of two kinds. Some, like Cleveland, were established by New England townspeople who sought to reconstitute the values of community they thought were being eroded in their places of origin. Other settlements, however, were "promoted" as speculative ventures. In the 1820s and 1830s the pioneers for these "promoted" towns were often Irish

---

[18]See Green, The Rise of Urban America, p. 66; Ward, Cities and Immigrants, p. 25; Glaab and Brown, A History of Urban America, pp. 37–38. Throughout the 1830s and 1840s, canals continued to play a crucial role in linking the expanding western periphery with the prime port via the Great Lakes. By 1850, canals linked New York with the cities of Buffalo, Syracuse, Utica, Troy, and Albany (via the Hudson River and the Erie Canal), and less directly with Trenton, Harrisburg, Johnstown, and Binghamton through a southern and western route. Via the Great Lakes, other canal systems linked Pittsburgh, Erie, Cleveland, Columbus, Toledo, Louisville, St. Louis, and even Chicago into the New York system.

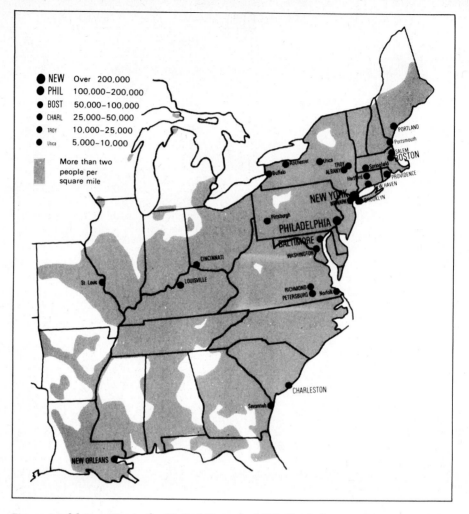

Figure 4.1 Major cities in the United States in 1830. Shaded zones show parts of the country where densities exceeded two persons per square mile. (*Source:* David Ward, *Cities and Immigrants: A Geography of Change in Nineteenth-Century America*, p. 27. Copyright © 1971 by Oxford University Press. Reprinted by permission.)

immigrants sent out to build the canals. Adventurous easterners followed, often encouraged by the canal companies that founded towns at critical junctures in the network. While not all towns were destined to succeed, when they did, many of their early settlers gained dramatically from judicious land investments, since land values skyrocketed.

The results of this phase of urban growth can be seen in the population totals of the country and its major cities. Between 1790 and 1830 the population of the United States increased from under 4 million to close to 13 million. By 1830 there were 90 towns with at least 2500 inhabitants, and their combined residents accounted for almost 9 percent of the total population of the country.

Table 4.1 shows the changes in the relative status of major American cities, the appearance of new cities at the periphery, and the dramatic growth in urban and overall population during these crucial forty years. Figure 4.1 shows the geographic pattern of these changes.

From Figure 4.1 it is clear that by about 1830 an urban system was coming into existence in the United States, one that would dominate developments for at least a century to come. The core cities, still concentrated on the New England–Middle Atlantic coast, not only continued to link the United States eastward across the Atlantic to world trade, but were becoming centers for their own periphery, which was spreading westward into the Mississippi River valley.[19]

By 1830 all the basic trends that were to be consolidated during the next few decades of growth had been established. Some small-scale industrialization had begun to appear in eastern cities. Immigration from depressed Ireland had begun to introduce a more rigidly stratified ethnicity into the American class system, although the period of great Celtic migration, with its political repercussions, lay ahead in the 1840s and 1850s.[20] Slums had already made their appearance in sections of the "older" cities, even though it was not until "the years of great urban growth and industrialization after 1830 [that] eastern seaboard cities rapidly acquired the characteristics associated with the manufacturing cities of Europe . . . [namely] misery, filth and overcrowding."[21] And the older system of town building according to communal organization was being replaced by an entrepreneurial model in which promoters, land speculators, and ambitious individuals lowered "the city upon a hill" down to the promoter's "town along the canal"—and later, the city along the rail line.[22] These changes were solidified during the next phase of American urbanization.

FROM SMALL-SCALE TO LARGE-SCALE INDUSTRIALIZATION

This lengthy period can be subdivided into two unequal parts: from 1830 to the Civil War of 1861–1865, during which industrial capitalism began to be established as the dominant trend of the future; and from about 1865 to 1910–1920, during which it became the pervasive pattern of the country. Clearly, the line between the two cannot be sharply drawn, because trends were cumulative and changes a matter of degree rather than kind. But at a certain point changes in scale, concentration, and pervasiveness do yield a change in quality. It is this that we shall try to capture in the sections that follow.

---

[19]The best account of the growth of the western periphery is Richard C. Wade, *The Urban Frontier: The Rise of the Western Cities, 1790–1830* (Cambridge, MA: Harvard University Press, 1959).

[20]See Marcus Lee Hansen, *The Atlantic Migration 1607–1860: A History of the Continuing Settlement of the United States* (New York: Harper & Row, 1940; reissued 1961), pp. 9, 84–120.

[21]Glaab and Brown, *A History of Urban America*, p. 84.

[22]Page Smith (*As a City upon a Hill*, Chapter 2) distinguishes two major types of American towns: those colonized by relatively homogeneous ethnic and religious groups, and those whose growth was cumulative and from diverse sources. He notes that by the time of the Civil War, "few communities based on the older forms of religious covenant were established" (p. 27), and that the cumulative towns, which came to predominate, were "notably lacking in community structure" (p. 31).

Cities as Generative Centers for Their Surrounding Regions, 1830–1865

Blake McKelvey, in his analysis of American urbanization, emphasizes that:

> The urbanization process in America began to acquire a faster beat in the 1830's. As the national population increased and migration into the West accelerated, the need for new and larger cities grew still more rapidly. . . . The urbanization of America first assumed the classic demographic format in the 1830's. Thus, while the nation's population increased 150 percent in the next three decades, that of its cities mounted three times as rapidly.[23]

Indeed, between 1830 and 1860 the number of urban places with at least 2500 inhabitants grew from 90 to 392, and the percentage of total population living in them grew from 8.8 percent to almost 20 percent. The number of cities with 100,000 or more inhabitants increased from one (New York) to nine, and their share of the total population rose from 1.6 to 8.4 percent (see Table 4.2).

There was, in short, an exponential rise in the scale of urbanization. In part this was a function of overall population, which grew from under 13 million in 1830 to close to 32 million by 1860, largely due to new patterns of international migration. In part it resulted from industrialization and associated forms of social stratification. (Industrialization was the creation of New England entrepreneurs, who were able to harness both water power and new immigrants to the factory.) And in part it was due to the fundamental reorganization of city-hinterland and interregional relations on the continent. Continental reorganization resulted from a political and economic realignment in which the West and the Northeast found common cause against the South. This realignment led to the Civil War, which ultimately consigned the defeated South to a rural existence, bypassed, until very recently, by the wave of urbanization that was to sweep over the nation.

Population Increases   The migration to America, which began in large numbers after 1830, must be seen as one "aspect of the growth and spread of the population of Atlantic Europe," for it was a direct outcome of the unprecedented population "explosion" in nineteenth-century Europe described in Chapter 3.[24] The introduction of the potato in eighteenth-century Europe had facilitated that explosion by expanding and stabilizing the food supply. The new crop could be raised by women and children, could withstand climate extremes, and most importantly, could be stored over the winter. In Hansen's phrase, the potato became to the poor of western Europe what rice was to China.[25] The peasants of Ireland and Germany became heavily dependent on it as the mainstay of their diet. However, it proved less dependable than had been anticipated.

---

[23]McKelvey, *American Urbanization,* p. 26.

[24]Hansen, *The Atlantic Migration,* p. 17.

[25]*Ibid.,* p. 20.

Table 4.2 POPULATIONS OF PRINCIPAL U.S. CITIES, 1830 TO 1860

Cities	1830	1840	1850	1860
New York	202,589	312,700	515,500	813,600
Philadelphia	161,271	220,400	340,000	565,529
Brooklyn	15,396	36,230	96,838	266,660
Baltimore	80,620	102,300	169,600	212,418
Boston	61,392	93,380	136,880	177,840
New Orleans	46,082	102,190	116,375	168,675
Cincinnati	24,831	46,338	115,435	161,044
St. Louis	5,852	14,470	77,860	160,773
Chicago	—	4,470	29,963	109,260
Buffalo	8,653	18,213	42,260	81,130
Newark	10,953	17,290	38,890	71,940
Louisville	10,340	21,210	43,194	68,033
Albany	24,209	33,721	50,763	62,367
Washington	18,826	23,364	40,001	61,122
San Francisco	—	—	34,776	56,802
Providence	16,833	23,171	41,573	50,666
Number of towns over 2500	90	131	236	392
Total residents in towns over 2500	1,127,000	1,845,000	3,543,700	6,216,500
Percent in towns over 2500	8.8	10.8	15.3	19.8
Total U.S. population	12,866,000	17,069,000	23,191,800	31,433,300

Source: Blake McKelvey, American Urbanization: A Comparative History (Glenview, IL: Scott, Foresman and Company, 1973), p. 37.

The year 1816, known as "the year without a summer," was so cold that even the potato crops failed. The ensuing famine drove many of the victims out of Europe. About 30,000 arrived annually in the United States between 1817 and 1819. At first these new immigrants were easily absorbed. They were either diffused to the expanding Midwest or snapped up in the building and shipping booms. However, an economic crash in 1819 in the United States made their absorption increasingly problematic. "In its report of December, 1819, the New York Society for the Prevention of Pauperism cited the jobless aliens as an important source of poverty in the city."[26]

The first potato blight appeared in Ireland in 1821–1822, foreshadowing the more devastating crop failures that were to come at mid-century. In the early 1820s, Irish emigrants forged a widening path along which a massive army would eventually move. In the 1830s not only they but hundreds of thousands of other Europeans emigrated in search of a better life,[27] taking employment

[26]Ibid., pp. 86–108; quotation from p. 108.

[27]Ibid., pp. 116, 178, 226.

in the new factories that were beginning to open, digging the canals that were infiltrating the West, or huddling together in their ports of entry.

The spirit with which they were greeted by earlier settlers was hardly generous. Their poverty was blamed not on economic conditions but on their "moral degeneracy." An 1834 article in *The New England Magazine* voiced an unconcealed racism against the Irish that would later find its political expression in the anti-foreigner Know-Nothing Party of the 1850s:

> [The Irish] almost invariably . . . will not assimilate with the rest of the inhabitants. They do not dispose themselves over our western savannahs . . . but they nest together in thickly-settled places, and constitute, with some praiseworthy exceptions, the most corrupt, the most debased, and the most brutally ignorant portion of the population of large cities.[28]

Despite such an inhospitable reception, many Irish soon had no alternative but to leave home. In October 1845 there was a severe potato blight in Ireland, and in 1846 the crops failed again. " 'If the crops fail us again,' declared a peasant, 'it will be the end of the world with us.' "[29] But in 1847 the crops were again lost, this time not only in Ireland but in Germany as well. Massive deaths from starvation and typhus epidemics drove survivors to the ships, to which they carried the disease; as many as a fifth of them died on their way to American ports, where the remainder were cruelly quarantined when they arrived. Between 1848 and 1850 there was heightened emigration from Ireland, following the 1848 potato crop failure, and from Germany, where economic ills were compounded by political repression.[30]

Between 1850 and 1860 more than 2.5 million "aliens poured into the country and the foreign-born inhabitants increased from 2,244,600 to well over 4,000,000. The number of Irish grew from 962,000 to 1,611,000, of Germans from 584,000 to 1,276,000, of English from 279,000 to 433,000."[31] Many concentrated in the cities; by 1860, some 40 percent (or 1.5 million) of the population of the fifty largest cities in the nation had been born abroad.[32] While their migration caused great hardships for them and severely overtaxed facilities in the urban areas into which they moved, it must be recognized that it was *their* increased numbers that propelled the rapidly accelerating rate of urbanization in the United States, and it was *their* work energy that was harnessed to the newly expanding industrial sector.

Industrialization and Increased Stratification The roots of industrialism in the United States were almost contemporaneous with those of Britain. The

---

[28]As quoted in Glaab and Brown, *A History of Urban American*, pp. 90–91.

[29]*Hansen, The Atlantic Migration*, p. 245.

[30]*Ibid.*, pp. 246–274.

[31]*Ibid.*, p. 280. Data taken from U.S. Immigration Commission, *Reports III—Statistical Review of Immigration, 1820–1910* (Washington, DC: 1911), p. 416.

[32]McKelvey, *American Urbanization*, p. 40.

first American textile mill, in Rhode Island, dated back to 1790,[33] and Eli Whitney's (or rather, Katherine Green's) cotton gins were from the beginning produced in a New Haven factory.[34] But operations were few, modest in size, and secondary to agriculture and the opening of new lands in accounting for economic growth and urban developments.

Some idea of the modest nature of early industrial ventures can be gained by contrasting the town of Manchester, Massachusetts, with the English city of Manchester described in Chapter 3. In New England's Manchester in 1837 there was one shoe factory in which 15 workers produced 3100 pairs of footwear a year, one tannery with three workers, and twelve carpentry shops employing 120. The community also produced a few thousand palm-leaf hats, some reed organs, a few fire engines, and four sailing ships.[35] This was a far cry from the mass drudgery and fast-paced machines of Manchester, England, deplored by Frederick Engels.

But even the more vigorous town of Holyoke, Massachusetts, reveals how underdeveloped American industrial capitalism was in contrast to England's. In 1832 the town's cotton textile mill was established with a labor force of several hundred, of whom perhaps half were locally recruited. The rest were immigrants.

> Irish immigrants were brought in by the company, and the farmers' daughters who had been willing to take jobs in the small-scale industries of the town were not inclined to work beside rough Irish laborers.[36] The native workers were thus gradually replaced by immigrants . . . [who came to constitute] a new social class—the proletariat.[37]

A few decades later, Holyoke had taken on many of the qualities of Manchester, England. The town's Board of Health reported in 1856 that there were "many families . . . huddled into low, damp and filthy cellars . . . and . . . attics . . . with scarcely a particle of what might be called air." Twenty years later the town had fire-trap tenements, an abysmal lack of sanitation, and open spaces covered with green slime, and was ravaged by epidemics of smallpox.[38] Such were the leveling effects of early industrialization.

It was on such suffering, however, that America's industrial might was built,

---

[33]Green, *The Rise of Urban America*, p. 60.

[34]McKelvey, *American Urbanization*, p. 32.

[35]Darius Lamson, *History of the Town of Manchester, Essex County, Massachusetts, 1645–1895*, as cited in Page Smith, *As a City upon a Hill*, p. 86.

[36]Barbara Berg has stressed the deterioration in the status of American women when they were displaced by immigrants in the labor force. See her *The Remembered Gate* (New York: Oxford University Press, 1978), especially Chapter 3.

[37]The information on Holyoke and the quotation are taken from Page Smith, *As a City upon a Hill*, pp. 92–93.

[38]*Ibid.*, pp. 93–94. His major source is Constance McLaughlin Green, *Holyoke, Massachusetts: A Case History of the Industrial Revolution in America* (New Haven, CT: Yale University Press, 1939).

and the fruits of this transformation were, like the sufferings, already evident during the period preceding the Civil War. As data presented by Ward indicate:

> Although the international industrial preeminence of the United States was established primarily after the Civil War, during the 1830's and more strikingly in the 1840's and 1850's, per capita productivity increased at a rate somewhat greater than that of the long-term trend of the nineteenth century . . . [T]he contribution of manufacturing to the total commercial product almost doubled between 1839 and 1859 to account for almost one third of the total at the latter date. . . . Between 1830 and 1870 the areas in and around the four major northeastern seaports and sections of southern New England, upstate New York, and southeastern Pennsylvania supported a sizeable industrial production and formed the center of the expanding American economy.[39]

The growth of this industrial core region could not have taken place at the rate it did without the infusions of population from across the Atlantic and without the heightened connections to the Midwest that were being forged by canals and railways.

Regional Reorganization of Center and Periphery   The canal system, designed to tie the cities of the Northeast with those proliferating in the interior, was virtually complete by the time of the Civil War. By 1860 some 4250 miles of canals were in place. But by that time railroads were already beginning to supplant canals as the major determiners of urban expansion.

The first interregional railway system was not constructed until the 1850s. Nevertheless, this development was so promising that by the outbreak of the Civil War, some 30,000 miles of track had been laid, and freight, which as recently as 1852 had been twice as dependent on canals as rail, was now being carried chiefly by rail.[40] Figure 4.2 shows the distribution of rail lines in 1860, while Figures 4.3 and 4.4 show the effects these improvements in transportation had on travel time. It was the canal and rail systems that forged the alliance between the West (i.e., the Midwest) and the North (i.e., the North Atlantic), an alliance that precipitated the Civil War;[41] and it was

---

[39]Ward, *Cities and Immigrants*, p. 32.

[40]*Ibid.*, p. 35.

[41]Barrington Moore, Jr., in *Social Origins of Dictatorship and Democracy*, calls the Civil War the dividing marker between the agrarian and industrial epochs in American history (p. 112). He notes that "by 1860 the United States had developed three quite different forms of society in different parts of the country: the cotton-growing South; the West, a land of free farmers; and the rapidly industrializing Northeast" (p. 115). While the Northeast was largely dependent upon southern cotton in the early phase of its industrial development, by the 1840s manufacturing had diversified and the newer plants of that region were more and more geared to providing the items needed by the agricultural West, which, in turn, sent more and more of its products eastward (p. 124). The southern farmers, who prior to 1850 had seen the western farmers as their "natural allies," increasingly began to see "the spread of independent farming as a threat to slavery and their own system" (p. 129). In short, it was the strengthening alliance between northern industrialists and western farmers that shaped the direction of the future and made inevitable the Civil War, a symptom of the breakdown of the prior alliance between the agrarian-slave South and northern capitalists.

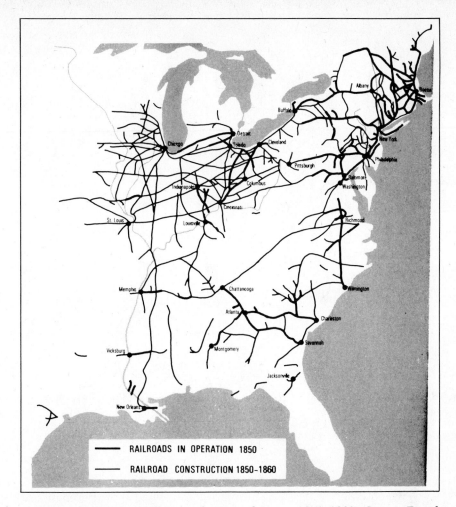

Figure 4.2 Railroad expansion in the United States, 1850–1860. (*Source:* David Ward, *Cities and Immigrants: A Geography of Change in Nineteenth-Century America,* p. 36. Copyright © 1971 by Oxford University Press. Reprinted by permission.)

these systems that catapulted Chicago from a handful of dwellings in 1834 to the country's fourth-largest city by 1870, with more than 250,000 inhabitants.

Chicago: The Prototypical New City   Chicago presents the clearest illustration of how dramatically regional linkages were realigned between 1830 and 1860 and how significant eastern capital and the great railroad venture were in forming the expanded core of industrialized urbanization. It also demonstrates the displacement of canals by railroads; the role of promoters, transpor-

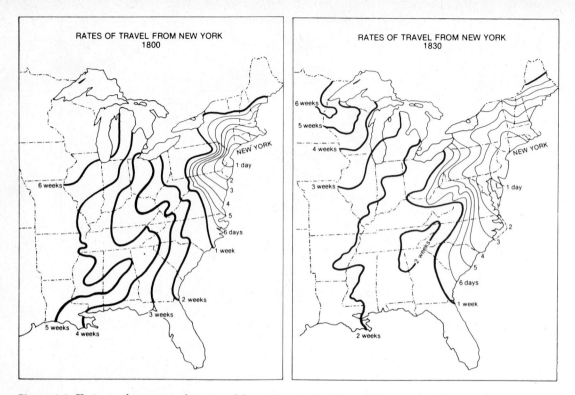

Figure 4.3 Estimated time it took to travel from New York to the Midwest in 1800 and in 1830. (*Source: Maps on p. 84 of Alfred Chandler, The Visible Hand, based upon Charles O. Paullin, Atlas of the Historical Geography of the United States.* Copyright 1932 by The Carnegie Institute, from whom permission to reprint has been obtained.)

tation companies, and land speculators in forming new cities; and the extent to which cities counted on immigration to swell their populations.[42]

While the origin of Chicago was clearly linked to a canal scheme, its rapid rise to dominance depended on the railroad. In 1829 the Illinois legislature appointed a canal commission to construct a water link between the Great Lakes and the Mississippi. One year later a large terminal city of Chicago was planned, even though the settlement then had only 50 inhabitants. A great boom in population and land values ensued, based entirely on the anticipation of future developments; in fact, work on the canal did not begin

[42]While the number of sources on this "Second City" are myriad, a few are particularly successful in presenting a synthetic view of the city's development. The massive illustrated work by Harold M. Mayer and Richard C. Wade, *Chicago: Growth of a Metropolis* (Chicago: University of Chicago Press, 1969), is the most comprehensive of these sources, but shorter works are also valuable. See Irving Cutler, *Chicago: Metropolis of the Mid-Continent*, 2d ed. (Dubuque, IA: Kendall/Hunt Publishing Company, 1976) for a well-written account of the earlier days of the city, and Brian Berry *et al.*, *Chicago: Transformations of an Urban System* (Cambridge, MA: Ballinger Publishing Company, 1976), which focuses primarily on developments in more recent years.

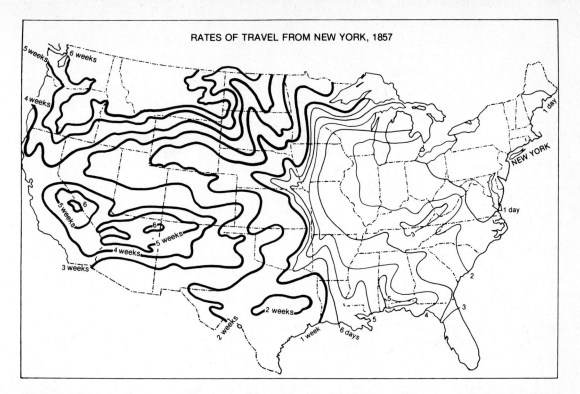

Figure 4.4 Estimated time it took to travel from New York to Midwest (shown in light lines) and the Far West (shown in heavy lines) in 1857, after the construction of rail lines. (*Source:* Map on p. 85 of Alfred Chandler, *The Visible Hand,* based upon Charles O. Paullin, *Atlas of the Historical Geography of the United States.* Copyright 1932 by The Carnegie Institute, from whom permission to reprint has been obtained.)

until 1836, and both work and the boom were cut short by the economic crash of 1837. Ten years later, when the canal had actually been constructed and was open to traffic, it was an idea whose time had come but also gone. By then it was obvious that railroads, not canals, would be the key to regional dominance.

In 1848, however, not a single line of track ran in the city, and it seemed that Galena, Illinois, rather than Chicago, might become the metropolis of the mid-continent. Wheeling and dealing by city promoters "captured" the railroad termini for Chicago, however, and by 1854 it had become the undisputed railroad capital for the West.[43] Two years later Chicago was at the center of a web of ten trunk lines linking almost 3000 miles of track.

Foreign immigration, industrial prowess, and the city's key role in connecting the financial headquarters in New York with the expanding frontier regions

---

[43]The early canal ventures are described in Mayer and Wade, *Chicago,* pp. 12–28. The shift to railroads is discussed on pp. 28ff, and their entire second chapter, pp. 35–166, describing the impact of the railroad on the city, is unequivocally entitled "Railroad Capital, 1851–1871."

of the far west and southwest, all underlay the incredibly fast growth of Chicago from 1837, the date of its first incorporation, to 1871, when most of the city, which by then housed some 300,000 inhabitants, burned down and had to be rebuilt. By then, more than half of the city's population was foreign-born (chiefly Irish and German), a considerable proportion of the city's productive base was coming from manufacturing, and the amount of freight that passed to and through Chicago was staggering.[44]

The urban system that was coming into focus by the Civil War thrust Chicago into the position of chief advance agent for eastern capitalism centered in New York. Once the South was defeated, this alliance allowed the two cities to dominate the final conquest of the continent. In Ward's opinion:

> By about 1870 . . . there were very few areas in the Middle West without effective rail connections to the Northeast. . . . Eastern capital not only financed the construction of railroads across Iowa, Missouri, Wisconsin and Minnesota but apparently was responsible for the development of . . . [Chicago] as marketing and exchange centers. The railroads were merely the instruments of a basic economic nexus which linked Chicago with New York and other sources of capital more closely than any other Middle Western city.[45]

The creation of the continental network of urbanization, which was virtually completed by World War I, followed from the framework that was established during the middle third of the nineteenth century.

Cities as Components in a Large-Scale Industrial System That Becomes Nationwide, 1865–1920

The fundamental nature of urbanization in the United States was revolutionized within the scant 50 years between the Civil War and the First World War. Almost every trend that still determines urban life in our day was set into motion during those critical decades. Most problems that still plague American cities began during that period, and many of the mechanisms for coping with large-scale society and industrial cities were first created in those fifty years.

Three broad trends characterized the period:

1. There was a demographic transformation as
   a) population increased very rapidly due to heightened immigration from abroad;
   b) urban populations became more heterogeneous because the sources of international migration shifted to include non–English-speaking groups from southern and eastern Europe; and
   c) there was considerable internal movement from east to west and from farm to city.

---

[44]Cutler, *Chicago*, p. 40 on immigration, pp. 73–77 on early industrial firms; Mayer and Wade, *Chicago*, Chapter 2, *passim*.

[45]Ward, *Cities and Immigrants*, pp. 36–37.

    2. There was regional reorganization as
        a) the "frontier" expanded all the way to the Pacific and finally closed;
        b) the nationwide urban system was completed; and
        c) the industrial belt of the Northeast and North Central emerged as the undisputed dominant core of the country, with other regions its periphery.
    3. Most importantly, there was a drastic reorganization of the socioeconomic and political system of the country, due to
        a) a shift to capital-intensive industrial production and to dependence upon inanimate sources of energy—notably steam—to run larger factories whose work processes were increasingly "rationalized";
        b) an increase in the scale of commercial and industrial enterprises, with growing centralization of decision making and professionalization of management, increased separation between the owners and the managers of firms, and an increased polarization between bosses and laborers; and finally,
        c) a growing involvement by the government in financing infrastructure, regulating the economy, and assuming responsibility for collective needs, city planning, and eventually, social welfare.

Obviously, all of these trends were interrelated, and it was their combined impact that transformed the urban system of the United States and created the cities whose character and problems are still familiar to us.

These cities, as they had evolved to the 1920s, became the objects of study for the new field of urban sociology. These cities also became the objects of control for the new field of urban planning that similarly had its origins around the turn of the century. Both the methods/theories developed by urban sociologists to study cities and the techniques/laws developed by city officials to plan them were adapted to the kinds of cities that had made their appearance by then. It should therefore not surprise us that both diagnoses and cures were time-bound. As American cities moved into their metropolitan and postindustrial phases after 1920, both the theories of analysis and the methods of control were to change.

Demographic Transformation In 1860 the entire population of the United States was only about 31.4 million, of whom some 6 million (about 20 percent) lived in places with at least 2500 inhabitants. Between then and 1920, some 28.3 million newcomers arrived from Europe, 23.5 million of them (or 83 percent) in 1880 or later. By 1920 the total United States population exceeded 105.7 million persons, of whom more than half (54 million) lived in communities with 2500 or more inhabitants. As can be seen from Table 4.3, almost 40 percent of the increase in U.S. population between 1860 and 1920 was directly due to immigration. And if the higher birth rates of immigrants are taken into account, probably half of the population growth during that period was actually due to immigration. Never again would the United States grow so rapidly from this source, since a series of laws passed between 1918 and 1924 closed the gates to free immigration, regulating a much smaller and "selected" flow into the country.

Table 4.3 TOTAL POPULATION, URBAN POPULATION, IMMIGRANTS, 1860–1920

Census year	Total population (000s)	Urban population (000s)	%	Immigrants who arrived in preceding decade	Immigrants as % net gain in decade
1860	31,443	6,217	19.8	(2,814,554)	—
1870	39,818	9,902	25.7	2,081,261	25%
1880	50,156	14,130	28.2	2,742,137	27%
1890	62,948	22,100	35.1	5,248,568	41%
1900	75,995	30,215	39.6	3,694,294	28%
1910	91,972	42,064	45.6	8,202,388	51%
1920	105,711	54,253	51.2	6,347,380	46%

	Cumulative population increase	Immigrants added	Immigrants as % of population increase
1860–1920	74,268,000	28,316,028	38%

Sources: Various reports of the U.S. Census; our calculations.

The period between 1870 and 1920 was also notable for the change in the places of origin of immigrants. Whereas between 1850 and 1870 most immigrants came from Ireland and Germany, after 1870 these two sources became relatively less important. Table 4.4 shows the new sources of immigration in southern and eastern Europe and demonstrates how these became the chief sending countries by 1890.

The destination of these new immigrants also diverged from the past. Earlier, white immigrants[46] had scattered and assimilated, for there were few activities to absorb them in the commercial cities of the time. Among the early immigrants, only the Irish tended to cluster in urban areas. Toward the latter part of the nineteenth century, however, the destination of immigrants became increasingly urban. After 1860 most immigrants entered the dominant port of New York. Many remained there or, if they moved, went to nearby cities where labor demands from new industrialization were high. They followed economic opportunities, many becoming unskilled and semi-skilled workers in the rapidly growing (larger) cities of the Northeast and North Central. By 1920, three-fourths of the foreign-born population were living in urban areas, in contrast to only half of the total population. Thus, foreign immigration contributed disproportionately to urban growth.

---

[46]We omit from this discussion and generalization the millions of African-Americans whose history was quite different. Until World War I, most remained in the rural South; therefore, their migration to cities will be discussed at length in the next chapter.

Table 4.4   DECENNIAL IMMIGRATION TO THE UNITED STATES

	Percentage from Country for Major Sources of Immigrants, 1860–1920					
	Percentage immigrants in decade from					
	1860–1869	1870–1879	1880–1889	1890–1899	1900–1909	1910–1919
Old sources						
Ireland	24.4	15.4	12.8	11.0	4.2	2.6
Germany	35.2	27.4	27.5	15.7	4.0	2.7
U. K.	14.9	21.1	15.5	8.9	5.7	5.8
Canada	4.9	11.8	9.4	0.1	1.5	11.2
New sources						
Russia	0.2	1.3	3.5	12.2	18.3	17.4
Austria-Hungary	0.2	2.2	6.0	14.5	24.4	18.2
Italy	0.5	1.7	5.1	16.3	23.5	19.4

Source: N. Carpenter, *Immigrants and Their Children*, U.S. Department of Commerce, Bureau of the Census, Monograph 7 (Washington, D.C.: Government Printing Office, 1927), pp. 324–325.

Immigration contributed more to large cities than to small, and more to cities of the North and North Central than to those of the West or South. Between 1860 and 1920 the number of urban places with 2500 or more inhabitants grew from about 400 to 2725, multiplying almost seven times, while places containing 100,000 or more persons increased eightfold from a total of 9 in 1860 to some 68 by 1920. Table 4.5 lists the major cities and shows how they grew between 1860 and 1910. Noteworthy is the fact that Chicago and Philadelphia joined New York on the list of cities with over a million inhabitants. The role immigration played in the "millionaire" status of these cities cannot be questioned.

Not all regions of the country absorbed an equal share of the immigrants.[47] In 1870 the Northeast hosted almost 47 percent of the foreign-born population, although it contained only 31 percent of the total population. By 1910, when its share of the total population had declined to 28 percent, its share of the foreign-born population remained high at almost 50 percent. The North Central also absorbed more than its share of immigrants. In 1870, when the region contained one-third of the population of the United States, it contained more than 42 percent of the immigrants; and even by 1910 there were somewhat disproportionate numbers of foreign-born in the region. In contrast, the South, vanquished in the Civil War and suffering the economic deprivations of defeat, was bypassed by the influx of immigrants; although it contained some 30 percent of the U.S. total population, it never had more than 5 to 7 percent of the

---

[47]The single best source on where immigrants settled is Ward's book, *Cities and Immigrants*.

foreign-born. The West, throughout the period in question, contained small proportions of both total and foreign-born populations.

Nor did foreign groups scatter at random. The Irish settled disproportionately in New England, while the Germans favored the Middle West. Russians and Italians concentrated in and around New York, while Poles and Slavic groups headed toward Chicago. Sometimes, mere accidents channeled the migrant chains, but more often the explanatory variable was the opportunity structure that existed in certain cities which were expanding very rapidly at the time an ethnic group was arriving. What jobs were available and where had more effect on what occupations immigrants would follow and where they would settle than did the cultural heritage and occupations they brought with them.

Migration to the cities, however, did not come exclusively from overseas; it also came from the farms. A striking demographic trend was the relative decline in farming between 1860 and 1920. In earlier times the overwhelming majority of Americans earned their livings in agriculture. At the time of the Civil War, some 60 percent of the working population still drew its income from farming. However, by 1920 this was no longer true. Fewer than 12 million Americans, or only 27 percent of the work force, were employed in agriculture by that time. Americans were becoming increasingly dependent upon industry, transportation, construction, and communication for their livelihoods. The concentration of population in cities was a natural consequence of this shift. The rate of urbanization would have been even higher had there not been a simultaneous population redistribution to the West in the final thrust to settle the continent.

Regional Reorganization and Completion of the Urban Network   Population continued to move westward into regions whose accessibility had been transformed by the railroad system. By 1857 the west coast was within a week's travel time from New York City by the fastest route, San Francisco was a thriving town, and all along the way railway companies, town promoters, and easterners seeking wider horizons were creating new settlements.

Table 4.5 POPULATION OF CITIES THAT REACHED 100,000 BY 1910*

Cities	1860	1870	1880	1890	1900	1910
Albany, N.Y.	62,367	69,422	90,758	94,923	94,151	100,253
Atlanta, Ga.	9,554	21,789	37,409	65,533	89,872	154,839
Baltimore, Md.	212,418	267,354	332,313	434,439	508,957	558,485
Birmingham, Ala.	—	—	3,086	26,178	38,415	132,685
Boston, Mass.	177,840	250,526	362,839	448,477	560,892	670,585
Bridgeport, Conn.	13,299[1]	18,969	27,643	48,866	70,996	102,054
Buffalo, N.Y.	81,129	117,714	155,134	255,664	352,387	423,715
Cambridge, Mass.	26,060	39,634	52,669	70,028	91,886	104,839
Chicago, Ill.	109,260	298,977	503,185	1,099,850	1,698,575	2,185,283
Cincinnati, Ohio	161,044	216,239	255,139	296,908	325,902	363,591
Cleveland, Ohio	43,417	92,829	160,146	261,353	381,768	560,663
Columbus, Ohio	18,554	31,274	51,647	88,150	125,560	181,511
Dayton, Ohio	20,081	30,473	38,678	61,220	85,333	116,577
Denver, Colo.	—	4,759	35,629	106,713	133,859	213,381
Detroit, Mich.	45,619	79,577	116,340	205,876	285,704	465,766
Fall River, Mass.	14,026	26,766	48,961	74,398	104,863	119,295
Grand Rapids, Mich.	8,085	16,507	32,016	60,278	87,565	112,571
Indianapolis, Ind.	18,611	48,244	75,056	105,436	169,164	233,650
Jersey City, N.J.	29,226	82,546	120,722	163,003	206,433	267,779
Kansas City, Mo.	4,418	32,260	55,785	132,716	163,752	248,381
Los Angeles, Cal.	4,385	5,728	11,183	50,395	102,479	319,198
Louisville, Ky.	68,033	100,753	123,758	161,129	204,731	223,928
Lowell, Mass.	36,827	40,928	59,475	77,696	94,969	106,294
Memphis, Tenn.	22,623	40,226	33,592	64,495	102,320	131,105
Milwaukee, Wis.	45,246	71,440	115,587	204,468	285,315	373,857
Minneapolis, Minn.	2,564	13,066	46,887	164,738	202,718	301,408
Nashville, Tenn.	16,988	25,865	43,350	76,168	80,865	110,364
New Haven, Conn.	39,267[1]	50,840[1]	62,882[1]	81,298	108,027	113,605
New Orleans, La.	168,675	191,418	216,090	242,039	287,104	339,075
New York, N.Y.[2]	1,174,779	1,478,103	1,911,698	2,507,414	3,437,202	4,766,883
Newark, N.J.	71,941	105,059	136,508	181,830	246,070	347,469
Oakland, Cal.	1,543	10,500	34,555	48,682	66,960	150,174
Omaha, Nebr.	1,883	16,083	30,518	140,452	102,555	124,096
Paterson, N.J.	19,586	33,579	51,031	78,347	105,171	125,600
Philadelphia, Pa.	565,529	674,022	847,170	1,046,964	1,293,697	1,549,008
Pittsburgh, Pa.[3]	77,923	139,256	235,071	343,904	451,512	533,905
Portland, Oreg.	2,874	8,293	17,577	46,385	90,426	207,214
Providence, R.I.	50,666	68,904	104,857	132,146	175,597	224,326
Richmond, Va.	37,910	51,038	63,600	81,388	85,050	127,628
Rochester, N.Y.	48,204	62,386	89,366	133,896	162,608	218,149
St. Louis, Mo.	160,773	310,864	350,518	451,770	575,238	687,029
St. Paul, Minn.	10,401	20,030	41,473	133,156	163,065	214,744
San Francisco, Cal.	56,802	149,473	233,959	298,997	342,782	416,912
Scranton, Pa.	9,223	35,092	45,850	72,215	102,026	129,867
Seattle, Wash.	—	1,107	3,533	42,837	80,671	237,194
Spokane, Wash.	—	—	—	19,922	36,848	104,402

(Continued)

Table 4.5 (*Continued*)

Cities	1860	1870	1880	1890	1900	1910
Syracuse, N.Y.	28,119	43,051	51,792	88,143	108,374	137,249
Toledo, Ohio	13,768	31,584	50,137	81,434	131,822	168,497
Washington, D.C.[4]	61,122	109,199	177,624	230,392	278,718	331,069
Worcester, Mass.	24,960	41,105	58,291	84,655	118,421	145,986

Notes:
1. Population of town; town and city not returned separately.
2. Population of New York and its boroughs as now constituted.
3. Includes population of Allegheny as follows: 1900, 129,896; 1890, 105,287; 1880, 78,682; 1870, 53,180; 1860, 28,702.
4. Population as returned from 1880 to 1910 is for the District of Columbia, with which the city is now coextensive.

*U.S. Bureau of the Census, *Thirteenth Census: 1910* (Washington, D.C.: U.S. Government Printing Office, 1913) 1, p. 80.

Source: Blake McKelvey, *American Urbanization: A Comparative History* (Glenview, IL: Scott Foresman, 1973), p. 73.

According to Glaab and Brown, during the period between 1860 and 1890 there emerged in the United States

> a national urban network—a complex, interrelated system of national and regional metropolises, specialized manufacturing cities, and hundreds of smaller subordinate cities of varying size and function. The rapid development of new regions of the country after 1860 created great opportunities in building new cities, but by 1890 this possibility was no longer open as the urban network had been substantially completed. . . . [*Most*] *cities destined to achieve even moderate size had been founded by 1890.*[48]

The date 1890 was not a capricious choice, for most scholars agree that by that time the frontier was beginning to close.[49] While towns continued to be founded to fill in the network, by 1910 they were no longer the bonanza they had been.[50] The conquest of the continent had been achieved. What remained was to consolidate and strengthen the system that had already emerged. In that new system, the industrializing Northeast and North Central regions of the country became the undisputed masters. Ward refers to the period between 1870 and 1910 as the time when the "core" of the United States was enlarged from the east coast to include the Midwest, and when the rest of the country became, more or less, its tributary empire.[51]

Given this secure economic dominance, it was not surprising that urbanization, while by then at least lightly sown across the continent, was most intensively cultivated in the core region. Within what came to be called the "manufacturing belt" (the Northeast plus the Great Lakes states), up to three-quarters

---

[48]Glaab and Brown, *A History of Urban America*, pp. 108–109; italics added.

[49]Green, *The Rise of Urban America*, p. 87.

[50]Glaab and Brown, *A History of Urban America*, p. 132. For full details on the role of railway companies and speculators in founding new towns, see pp. 112–131.

[51]Ward, *Cities and Immigrants*, pp. 39ff.

of the population lived in urban settlements, many of them in cities with a quarter of a million inhabitants or more. By 1910, this region contained 34 of the 50 cities in the nation with populations over 50,000, and 14 of the 19 cities in the country with populations over 250,000.[52] Therefore, when we discuss urbanization in the opening decades of the twentieth century and when we describe what cities were like, we are really talking about the cities of the "core" region, those which were being transformed through immigration from abroad and industrialization from within.

Socioeconomic and Political Reorganization We have noted how, over the course of 50 years, the proportion of American workers who derived their livelihoods from agriculture dropped precipitously, until by 1920 only about one in four workers was engaged in growing food for the rest. Conversely, industrial employment absorbed an increasing proportion of American workers, so that by 1920 some 40 percent earned their livings in manufacturing, construction, transportation, and communication; the remaining workers provided commercial and personal services.

Such urban activities had always existed, but they now took on new characteristics. What changed in the 50 years between 1870 and 1920 was not only a numerical expansion of non-farm activities, but also a revolution in how such activities were organized. The scale at which they were concentrated increased enormously. New forms of energy were introduced that, especially in heavy industry, boosted per-worker productivity (and wages) to hitherto unimagined levels. These changes required commensurate increases in capitalization and investment to create larger and more mechanized enterprises. And finally, the concentration of ownership and control over giant firms gave vast powers to a relatively small number of persons. Government, which had hitherto remained relatively aloof from business, was drawn more closely into the economy, largely as the provider of services and infrastructure, often as a facilitator but only occasionally as a regulator of business practices.

The other side of that increased concentration of power and its closer relationship with government was the creation in American cities of a working class made up not only of newly arrived immigrants but also of the native-born. While for some time to come the economy expanded so quickly that the appearance of this working class was partially concealed by seemingly unlimited opportunities for upward mobility, eventually the emerging class structure of American society was revealed in the urban centers, which became increasingly segregated by class.

Government was also called upon to provide the urban infrastructure needed by business and industry, as well as the amenities desired by leading citizens who, during this period, began to move farther out from the center into "suburbs" along trolley and rail commuter lines. Urban services, which hitherto

---

[52]Harvey Perloff *et al., Regions, Resources and Economic Growth* (Baltimore: Johns Hopkins Press, 1960), as cited in Ward.

had been provided largely on a volunteer cooperative basis, were gradually assigned to local governments. Given the motives and interests of business, which spearheaded the movement to have government provide such services, it should not surprise us that law and order were among the first demands, with preservation of property running close behind. Contagious diseases, which respected no class barriers, were also items for which government came to take responsibility. Only much later would government be called upon to take a similar interest in the priorities of the working class—namely, housing, public education, sanitation, wages, and welfare.

One measure of the increased importance of manufacturing in the national economy was the proliferation of industrial firms. According to an early study by Pratt,[53] in 1860 there were only some 4500 manufacturing "establishments" in Manhattan, and these employed only 90,000 workers. Forty years later Manhattan contained 27,000 manufacturing firms employing a labor force of close to 400,000 workers. But one should not visualize these establishments as large factories. Indeed, most establishments remained small, despite the fact that firms ranged from tiny artisan shops and home-type sweat shops all the way to large-scale and steam-powered factories of the type we more commonly associate with the industrial era.[54]

Mechanization, however, was increasing. One indicator of the extent to which inanimate energy sources were being substituted for human energy is the increased "horsepower" consumed per person between 1870 and 1920. In 1870, annual energy use was 43,000 horsepower per 100,000 population, a figure that doubled to 86,000 per 100,000 by 1900, increased to 151,000 by 1910, and stood at 492,000 per 100,000 by 1920.[55] Thus, within the 50 years in question, the horsepower at the disposal of the average American increased tenfold.

Not all industries shared equally in the switch to power-driven machines. But as early as 1880, in the factories of Philadelphia, which were quite representative, over 90 percent of all workers in shipbuilding, food refining, iron and steel, and fuel production worked in establishments whose machines were powered largely by steam, and the productivity of between 86 and 88 percent of all workers in textile, machine tool, hardware, and chemical firms was raised by the availability of steam power.[56]

---

[53]Edward Ewing Pratt, *Industrial Causes of Congestion of Population in New York City* (New York: Columbia University, Faculty of Political Science, 1911), as cited in Hilda H. Golden, *Urbanization and Cities* (Lexington, MA: D. C. Heath, 1981), p. 200.

[54]The coexistence within the same industrial era of artisan shops, sweat shops, hand tooling, factories of small and large size, and even the "putting out" system, is documented in fine detail for the city of Philadelphia. See Bruce Laurie and Mark Schmitz, "Manufacturing and Productivity: The Making of an Industrial Base, Philadelphia, 1850–1880," in Theodore Hershberg, ed., *Philadelphia: Work, Space, Family, and Group Experience in the 19th Century* (New York: Oxford University Press, 1981), pp. 43–92.

[55]See Golden, *Urbanization and Cities,* Table 8.3, p. 199.

[56]Laurie and Schmitz, "Manufacturing and Productivity," Table 3, p. 49. During the first half of the nineteenth century, two-thirds to three-fourths of all factory workers were women. Ironically,

Once the mines of western Pennsylvania were dug and railroads were available to transport the coal, steam power was increasingly substituted for the water power that had driven the machines in the early textile and shoe plants of New England. Steam power worked efficiently only when it did not have to be transmitted over a distance; this encouraged increases in plant size and the concentration of productive activities within the central zones of cities. The conversion to steam, which introduced what Patrick Geddes has called the "paleo-technic era,"[57] did much to create the congested and smoke-filled industrial cities associated with the late nineteenth century.

Steam power resulted in congestion in two ways. First, it only made sense in larger plants, which to some extent may account for the fact that in the course of the nineteenth century the average workplace employed larger and larger numbers of workers. In Philadelphia, for example, only 43 percent of industrial workers in 1850 were employed in plants that had more than fifty workers, but by 1880 almost two-thirds worked in such large plants.[58] And second, the larger and more concentrated the plants were, the more congested the residential areas around the plants became, for workers still walked to their jobs.

The increase in industrial scale led to organizational changes as well. Larger and more complexly mechanized industries required enormous capital outlays,[59] which in turn spelled the death of the informal business partnership that had been the major form of management during the eighteenth and early nineteenth centuries. New methods of organizing and financing production had to be developed. Alfred D. Chandler, Jr., who has written some of the finest case studies of the reorganization of American business enterprises,[60] argues

---

as industry became more mechanized, raising worker productivity and wages, women were excluded more and more from manufacturing jobs; they remained in the sweat shops. This led to an increasing divergence between the wages of men and women in manufacturing, and eventually, the rate of women's participation in manufacturing went down entirely. See Berg, *The Remembered Gate*, Chapter 5.

[57]See Patrick Geddes, *Cities in Evolution* (rev. ed., London: Williams and Norgate, 1949), pp. 60–108, for a fuller discussion of his distinction between the "paleo-technic" (steam) and "neo-technic" (electricity and gasoline) eras. Steam power intensified density, while electricity and gasoline reduced it. We come back to this in Chapter 5.

[58]Laurie and Schmitz, "Manufacturing and Productivity," Table 4, p. 50.

[59]Adna Weber, *The Growth of Cities in the Nineteenth Century* (Ithaca, NY: Cornell University Press, 1967), p. 27, presents some extremely interesting data on the increase in scale, capitalization, and value of manufactured product in American industry in the late nineteenth century. Between 1870 and 1880, the amount of capital invested went up 64 percent, while the average number of workers per firm increased by 32 percent. During the same period, the net value of manufactured product increased by 40 percent. In the following decade, these rates of increase doubled. Between 1880 and 1890, capital invested increased by 121 percent, the average number of employees per plant increased by 66 percent, and the net value of product went up by 107 percent. Clearly, the pace of industrialization was quickening.

[60]His classic early work was *Strategy and Structure: Chapters in the History of the American Industrial Enterprise* (Cambridge, MA: MIT Press, 1962), which contains detailed case studies of the evolution of General Motors, Du Pont, Standard Oil of New Jersey, and Sears, Roebuck.

convincingly that managerial innovations were first introduced within the rail-road industry and were later copied by firms involved in mass distribution and production.[61]

Chandler notes that the railroads, because they needed so much capital, were the first "big business" in America to separate ownership (stock) from management and to develop the role of salaried middle managers. Their needs for capital were so great that they required government subsidies, had to sell stock on the open market, and even had to go abroad for additional capital, thus involving government in business and introducing multinational financing. Furthermore, railroads were the first firms to form monopolies. By 1880, the railroads had been physically integrated into a single national network. How-ever, they were still owned and operated by separate firms whose prior at-tempts at informal "cooperation to control competition" were proving inade-quate and whose attempt to form a cartel had been blocked by government regulation. When informal cooperation and cartels failed, each firm sought to expand its own system to the largest possible size and to eliminate competition. These methods would be adopted by the commercial and manufacturing firms that became giants during the late nineteenth and early twentieth centuries.

The growth of giant corporations was significant because it allowed power-ful owners and managers to plan for and manipulate supply—that is, to substi-tute their *visible* hands for the invisible hand of the marketplace on which Adam Smith's economics had been predicated. The ability to plan and manipu-late led to the ability to join forces with government to obtain what was needed. On the national scene, the giant firms needed infrastructure and legal protec-tions. On the local scene, businesses needed protection of their property and a sizable supply of healthy and preferably docile workers. The latter two were not unrelated.

Public provision of services in local communities began in the period just before the Civil War, but only in the largest cities. "New York's finest" began with a force of 800 in 1844, but only in 1853 were they placed under the supervision of a board of police commissioners and literally forced to wear uniforms. Philadelphia established a central system of police in 1850, introduc-ing uniforms ten years later. Boston and Baltimore also set up police depart-ments in the 1850s. In the years that followed, particularly in those cities that received large numbers of immigrants, the police forces were increasingly used to discipline foreigners (an incredibly high percentage of arrests involved the foreign-born) and, by the time labor unrest rumbled through the industrial cities toward the end of the century, to discipline workers as well.[62]

---

[61]These new insights were incorporated into Chandler's later work, *The Visible Hand: The Manage-rial Revolution in American Business* (Cambridge, MA: Belknap Press, 1977), upon which we base our subsequent discussion.

[62]Labor organization, like "big business," began in the railway industry. There was a country-wide railway workers' strike in 1877, and in the depressed 1880s such events spread to other industries. "Chicago's Haymarket Riot in 1886 [occurred] when a bomb thrown at police dispersing protesting strikers from McCormick Reaper works [in Chicago] killed a policeman and spread hysteria

Protection of property against fire also assumed high priority, but again, public fire protection existed only in the largest cities. Cincinnati was the first community to introduce a paid municipal fire-fighting force (in 1853); its example was followed by many other major cities, including Chicago, Boston, New York, and Philadelphia.[63] Only gradually did smaller cities and towns follow, learning to pay public employees to do jobs private enterprise or volunteers had previously performed.

Sanitation and environmental controls were the last public services to be introduced, in part because it was not until the 1860s that causal relationships were uncovered between environmental conditions and certain diseases. (It was 1883 before the microorganism that caused cholera, a major urban killer, was isolated and traced to contaminated water supplies.) The New York Metropolitan Board of Health was established in 1866. Its first official act was to eliminate hogs from the city's streets.[64] Extension of sewer lines and supplies of potable water, the routine collection and disposal of garbage by municipalities, and other related health services were still to follow.

Despite these late starts and despite the fact that local governments were inadequately funded for the tasks being assigned to them, by the 1920s city governments were routinely policing the streets, putting out fires, and controlling infectious diseases, largely though environmental sanitation. They were also beginning to experiment with methods to regulate land uses within the community—a need which was related both to the spread of noxious factories and to the social structure that was evolving from the industrial system, a structure increasingly based upon class.

As Constance McLaughlin Green observed:

> Of the social changes attending this half century of industrial expansion, the most striking was the sharpened disparity of wealth between class and class in the cities. Pronounced differences in economic status had existed from the mid-seventeenth century onward, but the rise in the last quarter of the nineteenth century of great fortunes controlled by fewer than a half hundred families created a plutocracy that bore little resemblance to anything Americans had ever before known. Neither cultivated taste nor long-established social prestige mattered much in the new social order. Power, and with it social standing, now rested solely upon money, money acquired more often than not by pre-emption of water, oil, mineral and timber rights in the public domain, by manipulation of securities on the stock exchanges, or by exploitation of industrial wage earners. . . . As the work force at industrial plants rose into the thousands, the intimate relations that . . . had existed

---

through the city." By the early 1890s, labor unrest was frequently culminating in "pitched battles . . . between industrial workers and the police or strikebreakers hired by employers" (Green, *The Rise of Urban America*, pp. 103–104). Industrialists routinely blamed these problems on "outside agitators" (i.e., foreigners), but it was clear that industrialism was bringing to American cities the same kinds of exploitation known abroad, and therefore creating the same needs for reform.

[63]See Glaab and Brown, *A History of Urban America*, pp. 96–97; McKelvey, *American Urbanization*, pp. 43–44.

[64]Glaab and Brown, *A History of Urban America*, pp. 87–98.

between management and employees in the mills and factories of the 1850s vanished. . . . [O]perators, steel workers, and textile mill hands all too often became labor, a commodity to be handled like raw materials, bought as cheaply as the supply permitted and replaced when the purchase price threatened to cut into profits.[65]

The class distinctions that became more sharply etched toward the end of the nineteenth century were increasingly reflected in residential segregation. In the early nineteenth-century city, classes and white ethnic groups tended to mingle residentially, with economic variations within, more than between, neighborhoods.[66] In the city of Philadelphia, which has been studied in great detail, the period between 1870 and 1920 was characterized by increased residential segregation by income, occupation, and by the end of the nineteenth century, even ethnicity.[67]

To some extent, class segregation was a function of the journey to work. In general, because horse-drawn carriages were slow and expensive relative to workers' wages, poor people could spare neither the time nor the money to commute to work. A remarkably large number continued to walk to work, even early in the twentieth century. Low-income workers, therefore, lived huddled near the central industrial/warehouse/commercial zone, sifting and sorting themselves as best they could to be near relatives and co-ethnics, but never really able to separate themselves into homogeneous ethnic neighborhoods, because the areas were old and the vacancies, capricious. The introduction of street railways, electrified trolleys, and even interurban railroads that stopped along the way, made it possible for the wealthy to move out of the congested center. From the 1870s onward, "streetcar suburbs" began to be established at the ends of mass transit lines, but as yet these towns absorbed only a small proportion of the population.[68]

Most people, even the wealthy, continued to live within the city limits. If the rich were to insulate themselves from the poor and from the factories, they would have to do so within the framework of the local community. Thus, by the final years of the century there was a new interest on the part of the business communities of American cities and towns to improve the design of cities, to construct impressive buildings befitting an industrial nation, and to protect property values and their own residential zones through control over land uses

---

[65]Green, *The Rise of Urban America*, pp. 101–102.

[66]In Philadelphia, New York, and other northern cities, however, blacks, no matter how few in number, were usually found in only a few areas.

[67]See, for example, the pioneering work by Sam Bass Warner, Jr., *The Private City: Philadelphia in Three Periods of Growth* (Philadelphia: University of Pennsylvania Press, 1968); and the more complex follow-ups by the Philadelphia history group, especially Part II, entitled "Space," in Theodore Hershberg, ed., *Philadelphia*, pp. 121–232.

[68]See, for example, Sam Bass Warner, Jr.'s study of the evolution of Boston's trolley-line towns, *Streetcar Suburbs: The Process of Growth in Boston, 1870–1900* (Cambridge, MA: Harvard University Press and MIT Press, 1962). See also Joel Tarr, *Transportation Innovation and Changing Spatial Patterns in Pittsburgh, 1850–1934* (Chicago: Public Works Historical Society, 1978).

in the community. Out of these interests came the "city beautiful" movement, which reached its apogee in plans for the Chicago World's Fair of 1893 and the Burnham Plan for Chicago in 1907. Later, property values would also be protected through the application of local ordinances designed to regulate land use and to prevent the encroachment not only of businesses and industries but of tenements and other housing for the poor on those districts where the wealthy, and then the middle class, were progressively segregating themselves.[69]

THE CHANGED SHAPE OF THE CITY

By the time World War I broke out, the large American city had evolved into quite a different place than it had been at the time of the Civil War. First, its physical shape had become more defined and its internal organization more differentiated. At its center was a sharply visible central business district, distinguished from the immediately surrounding area by its high buildings—for skyscrapers began after 1890 (with the invention of steel-frame construction methods and the electrification of the Otis elevator) to push the vertical profile up sharply. Near the central business district was a zone specializing in warehousing, transport, and the pickup and delivery of long-distance goods. Railroads and watercourses determined the chief preferred sites for industrial establishments, which had grown both larger and dirtier. The noise, congestion, and smoke of these industrial zones were driving away the upper- and middle-class residents, who increasingly segregated themselves in districts farther from the city center, at distances that were roughly proportional to their ability to pay, in time and cost, for travel. The shape of the expanding city had changed from the relatively circular one of preindustrial times to the star pattern associated with fixed-track commutation. Urbanized zones elongated in narrow strips on either side of transport lines, leaving open lands and farms in the interstices. Left behind in the older sections of the city, near the center, were the workers whose numbers and density increased in proportion to the vitality of the economy.[70]

The social shape of the city had also changed. Extremes of wealth and poverty were now apparent. Counterbalancing the increasingly elegant, new, low-density and exclusively residential districts to which the upper and upper-middle classes had migrated were the walk-up tenements of the poor which, despite concern and attempts to regulate them, grew taller and more closely packed, cutting off light and air. Within these zones of high ethnic heterogeneity (since many of their residents were immigrants or the offspring of immigrants), small subsections formed over the years in which certain nationality

[69]For a brief history of the relationship between business interests and the city planning movement, see Christopher Tunnard, *The Modern American City* (Princeton, NJ: D. Van Nostrand Company, 1968), especially Chapters 4–6.

[70]See Ward, *Cities and Immigrants,* Chapters 3–5; Allan R. Pred, *The Spatial Dynamics of U.S. Urban-Industrial Growth, 1800–1914* (Cambridge, MA: MIT Press, 1966), *passim.*

groups dominated. Dominant groups provided themselves with shops selling their special foods, with newspapers in their native tongues, with churches and synagogues to conduct their particular religious services, and with other institutions designed to help mediate their difficult transition from Polish peasant, Italian farmer, or Jewish shtetl dweller, into American.[71]

The guiding metaphor in those days was the United States as a huge melting pot into which all nationalities were to be thrown—and assimilated. But the process was a slow and painful one. Many Americans of Anglo-Saxon stock looked with either disdain or sympathy upon the problems of the poor, attributing them to foreignness rather than to conditions spawned by the industrial era. That such foreignness merely compounded but did not cause their problems was evident from the fact that many of the same changes were occurring in English cities with far greater ethnic homogeneity. England, in fact, often served as the example from which Americans learned to diagnose their urban problems and to attempt solutions. Thus, investigations into the housing problem—tenements, overcrowding, lack of sanitation—followed the English model, and a Congressional inquiry in 1892 paralleled the earlier English Parliamentary investigations.[72] The so-called "new tenement" laws, designed to insure a modicum of light and air in the worker housing being built, were patterned after earlier English regulations. At the end of the 1880s a number of "settlement houses" were set up in American cities (including the Neighborhood Guild in New York, established by Stanton Coit in 1886, and Hull House in Chicago, established by Jane Addams and Ellen Gates Starr in 1889), all modeled on Toynbee Hall (founded in London in 1884), which had been visited by concerned Americans. Many of the first social surveys conducted in American cities—including the famous and voluminous Pittsburgh Survey, finally published in 1914[73]—were patterned after the work of Charles Booth in England.

---

[71]W. I. Thomas and his Polish collaborator, Florian Znaniecki, produced the definitive study of *The Polish Peasant in Europe and America,* in five volumes (Boston: Richard G. Badger, 1919–1920). For an overview of the adjustment of many immigrant groups, see Herbert Miller and Robert Park, *Old World Traits Transplanted* (New York: Harper and Brothers, 1921), which was actually written by W. I. Thomas who, for personal and professional reasons, was unable to publish this study under his own name.

[72]Under the direction of Carroll D. Wright, federal commissioner of labor, this "preliminary" investigation covered conditions in the worst slum areas of New York, Philadelphia, Baltimore, and Chicago.

[73]In 1905 a Charities Publication Committee, growing out of the settlement house movement and including Jacob Riis, the author of the famous New York exposé, *How the Other Half Lives: Studies Among the Tenements of New York* (1890; reissued New York: Hill and Wang, 1957) and Jane Addams, launched an enormous social survey of Pittsburgh, conducted by social workers. The findings, eventually published in six volumes between 1909 and 1914, covered crime, prostitution, housing, the family, child and woman labor, industrial working conditions, urban politics, etc. Earlier works that prepared the way included W. E. B. Dubois, *The Philadelphia Negro* (Philadelphia: Publisher for the University, 1899); Robert Woods, *The City Wilderness* (Boston: Houghton Mifflin, 1899), which dealt with Boston's slums; and Robert Hunter, *Tenement Conditions in Chicago* (Chicago: City Homes Association, 1901).

A THEORY OF URBAN LIFE FOR AMERICA

While the approaches of reformers were similar and many of the research findings were comparable, the American urban experience differed in fundamental ways from that of Europe. The "theories" of the city and of urban life that had been generated in Europe by Durkheim, Toennies, Simmel, and others could not be applied to America without modification. First, it was hard to talk about a transition from settled peasant life to large-scale modern urban life when the United States never had a peasantry and when there was no feudal "tradition" to which a hypothetically stable, premodern era could be anchored. Second, it was hard to attribute the unique character of urban life to heightened mobility, when Americans had been notorious for their footloose migrations long before cities had begun to grow so rapidly. In Europe, given ethnic homogeneity (or at least polyethnic stability), it was easy to recognize that many of the changes occurring in modern cities were due to the development of industrial capitalism. In the United States such developments occurred simultaneously with the great immigrations from eastern and southern Europe, and the effects of the former were often confused with those of the latter.

No sociological theory of the city, therefore, could be borrowed from Europe. A new one had to be developed indigenously. While this theory will be examined in greater detail in Chapters 7 and 10, at this point we simply note that it was set forth during the second and third decades of the twentieth century by a number of creative sociologists who collectively came to be called the Chicago School.[74] These sociologists—most of them farm boys or ministers' sons—took the heritage of European social theory and combined it with the methodologies of the British social survey and the social investigations of a group of women involved in social work and social amelioration in the city. Adding the theoretical assumptions of human "ecology" (a field just then being developed by geographers) and the mechanisms of urban land economics (also a new field), they developed a new theory and a research agenda for studying cities. For many decades to come, this theory and these methods defined the field of urban sociology, yielding rich new insights into the city and providing a consistent context according to which data and studies were interpreted.

It was a long time before the limitations of the Chicago School came to be recognized. The major limitations, of course, were that the theories and generalizations it developed made most sense when applied to the particular time and place where they had been generated. The brash, ethnically diverse, fast-growing city of Chicago, located on flat land where a century before there had been nothing but a garlic patch and a tiny fort, and growing up exclusively during the era of industrial capitalism, was an almost "ideal" example of the

---

[74]A number of "histories" of the Chicago School of urban sociology now exist. See Ernest Burgess and Donald Bogue, "Research in Urban Society: A Long View," in Burgess and Bogue, eds., *Contributions to Urban Sociology* (Chicago: University of Chicago Press, 1964), pp. 1–14; James F. Short, Jr., ed., *The Social Fabric of the Metropolis: Contributions of the Chicago School of Urban Sociology* (Chicago: University of Chicago Press, 1971); Robert E. Faris, Jr. *Chicago Sociology: 1920–1932* (Chicago: University of Chicago Press, 1970).

American city as it had evolved up to the First World War. The trouble was that it could neither "represent" the older cities of the east coast nor predict much about the metropolitan region—the new type of city that would evolve in the next historic epoch. Naturally, just as the theories of urban life generated in Europe were insufficient to account for American urban life, so the theories of urban life generated by the Chicago School of urban sociology would prove insufficient to explain the new type of urbanization that had already begun to appear by the time the theories were given their most mature expression in Louis Wirth's 1938 essay, "Urbanism as a Way of Life."[75]

There was another limitation to these theories which was perhaps even more serious. In general, they tended to gloss over the economics of production and the class structures generated by capitalism, and they ignored the role of the national government and of local political and legal structures in creating the American city they sought to understand. Taking for granted the primacy of the "invisible hand" of the marketplace in sifting and sorting populations and land uses in the urban environment, they failed to note the increasingly important role that the political system was playing in regulating land use, in distributing services differentially, and in shaping, through incentives and subsidies, the new urban environment that was already beginning to appear.

These criticisms are in no way intended to diminish the significance of the contribution of early urban sociologists. It would have been difficult in 1920 to predict the vast changes that lay ahead for American urban life. These included:

1. The restrictions on immigration from abroad and the mass out-migration of blacks from the rural South;
2. The role of the automobile in freeing urban developments from their attachment to fixed-path transportation systems and in opening up expansive peripheral zones for metropolitan growth;
3. The transformation of the economy from one devoted primarily to production to one devoted more and more to services; and
4. The emergence of the United States as a major world power with investments everywhere in the evolving world economy.

These developments and their impact on the American city are discussed in Chapter 5.

---

[75]Conventionally, the school's origin is dated from 1915, inaugurated by Robert Park's seminal article entitled "The City: Suggestions for the Investigation of Human Behavior in the City Environment," *American Journal of Sociology* 20 (March 1915), pp. 577–612. It is also recognized to have been "codified" by 1938 in one of the most widely read and reprinted of all the articles in the field, Louis Wirth's "Urbanism as a Way of Life," *American Journal of Sociology* 44 (July 1938), pp. 1–24.

Chapter
5

The Making of
Metropolitan America

*I*n the twentieth century, cities broke through the barriers that previously contained them. Like the medieval towns that preceded them, cities of the early nineteenth century had ended rather abruptly at open country, even though walls no longer marked their limits. Within the city, housing was dense, commerce centralized, and manufacturing increasingly concentrated; outside the built-up area were fields and farms. And although economic transactions between city and countryside were numerous and vital, the exchange that took place was between fairly distinct categories of people engaged in fairly distinctive sets of activities.

Even into the early years of the twentieth century, the distinction between city (urban) and countryside (rural) remained important. True, tentacles of the city already stretched out along trolley and rail lines, farmers increasingly depended upon what the town had to offer, and new means of communication (telephones, rapid mail delivery, newspapers, radios) extended urban influences farther into the hinterlands. But it was still meaningful to contrast urban and rural areas and to treat the "city" as a unique category of physical space, one that created a way of life different from that in small towns and hamlets, even those located close by.

By the second decade of the twentieth century, however, the relevant contrast was shifting. As metropolitan regions spread outward into the country-side, the hitherto useful distinction between urban and rural became increasingly imprecise. New concepts were needed to differentiate types of settlements; new terms were needed to refer to them. New measures were also required to estimate the impact of metropolitan centers on the regions around them and to trace the ways in which "urbanism" was beginning to penetrate even remote parts of American society. Although this urban transformation took place throughout the developed western world, it was particularly marked in the United States—in part because Americans had always been somewhat more mobile and ready to change the way they lived, in part because the vast areas of the still-undeveloped subcontinent allowed space in which radical adjustments could be made to shifts in technology and social organization.

The forces reshaping population distribution in the United States were particularly powerful and fundamental. Foremost among them was the rather sudden decline in the overall rate of population growth. The laws governing immigration were drastically revised in the early 1920s to restrict the number of newcomers and to set quotas for admission that favored the nationalities of those groups already in the country. In addition, growth from natural increase also declined, as birth control began to prevent involuntary childbearing.

The slower overall growth in the population meant that more and more, expansions in certain parts of the urban and national systems could occur only at the expense of others. Initially, this did not slow down the rates of *urban* growth, since there were still large numbers of persons in rural areas eager to leave their farms and massive numbers of African-Americans in the depressed post-Civil War South ready to move to northern cities. Eventually, however, American urbanization began to reach a saturation point, as did other industrialized countries. (See Figure 5.1 for the logistic curve of urban saturation.) As higher and higher percentages of the total population congregated in metropolitan areas, there were fewer and smaller pockets of nonurban areas from which newcomers to city life could be drawn.

With urban growth no longer fueled by immigration from abroad or fed from reserves left on the farms, the dramatic rates at which American cities had been growing began to level off. Population movements became largely redistributive. The redistributions that occurred in the twentieth century were: first, a *decentralization within metropolitan areas,* as cities expanded into the countrysides around them; and second, a *diffusion of metropolitan development to regions of the country outside the hegemonic manufacturing belt,* as cities in the "sunbelt" of the South and West absorbed greater shares of urban growth.

Several factors underlay the two types of urban deconcentration that occurred in the twentieth century. One was a fundamental revolution in the technologies of transport and communication, which reduced the "friction" of distance by allowing people and goods to circulate more rapidly, more cheaply, and in more directions than ever before, and which allowed contacts to be maintained and ideas to spread, even in the absence of face-to-face relations. These improvements permitted increased disengagement between physical proximity and interaction. Motor vehicles, by reducing travel time, expanded

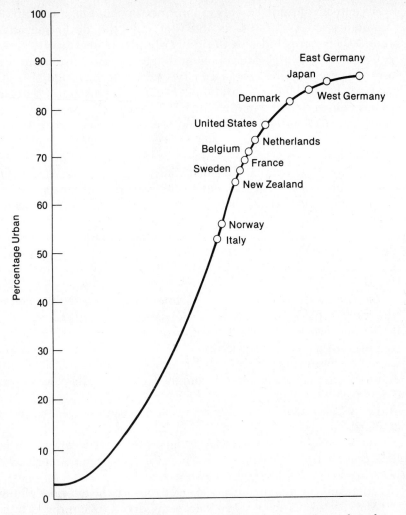

Figure 5.1 Logistic model of urban growth and percentage urban, by national definition, in 12 turnaround countries in 1970. (*Source:* John M. Wardwell, "Toward a Theory of Urban-Rural Migration in the Developed World" in Brown and Wardwell, *New Directions in Urban-Rural Migration.* Copyright 1980 by Academic Press. All rights reserved.)

the areas suitable for urban settlement; and because automobiles were free to move beyond the few and fixed paths of accessibility set by rail and trolley lines, they permitted development in the interstitial areas. Large peripheral zones suddenly became accessible to urban cores. The telegraph, telephone, and other newer means of communication, by freeing contact from proximity, were even more influential in permitting decongestion and a wider arena for transactions. All of these inventions permitted decentralization around existing metropolitan cores.

Eventually, improvements in intermetropolitan highways and even fuller communication systems facilitated not only the decentralization of cities around their cores but also the redistribution of metropolitan areas to new regions of the country. Metropolitan districts began to run into each other to form gigantic conurbations or co-cities to which the name of *megalopolis* or giant city has been given.[1] And those regions of the country that had formerly been dominated by the massive manufacturing belt (along the northeast coast and inland to Chicago) began to develop their own urban subsystems that increasingly competed for population. The westward movement of Americans continued as before, taking a slightly southerly direction after 1920, as the South, which had atrophied economically after the Civil War, finally began to recover and to share increasingly in the spread of urbanization.

A second factor that assisted in the process of urban deconcentration was nothing less than a reordering of the economic base of the society. We have earlier described how, during the nineteenth century, manufacturing gradually displaced agriculture as the chief source of wealth and the predominant activity of the American labor force. But during this early phase, which Geddes called the paleo-technic era, the centralizing force of steam was still the prime mover. By the twentieth century, however, America had entered the neo-technic era. Electricity replaced steam as the major source of energy for industry. Electricity made efficiencies possible even for small-scale factories, and permitted the decentralization of many operations, because electricity, unlike steam power, could be transmitted over long distances without loss of efficiency. In fact, once industrial production was freed from its need to huddle close to steam boilers, it was possible to spread out to the single-floor factory using the continuous assembly belt—a factory design that called for larger sites that were available at affordable cost only toward the outskirts of cities.

But even as industry was moving out of the central cities, more fundamental economic transformations were beginning to occur. America was entering what has been called the postindustrial era, during which services, rather than either farming or manufacturing, came to absorb the energies of most workers.

Manufacturing, even when efficiently served by improved transportation, is still tied to space. It still deals with bulky materials that must be moved physically from one place to another. Raw materials must be assembled at a single site; labor and machines must apply energy to transform the raw materials into products; and products themselves must be transported to the points where they are sold—either to enter manufacturing processes or to be used or consumed. Highway systems, container trucks, miniaturization, and automation can all help to loosen the geographic constraints upon manufacturing, but they cannot eliminate them entirely.

Services, in contrast, are inherently more flexibly located. Some, like the paperwork of vast bureaucracies, must still be concentrated, but not necessarily

---

[1]Jean Gottmann, *Megalopolis: The Urbanized Northeastern Seaboard of the United States* (Cambridge, MA: MIT Press, 1961).

near their clientele. Communicating words and numbers via airwaves, telephones, or computers is considerably freer from the friction of space than is the movement of coal or steel. Other services can be brought to consumers, especially when specialized facilities, only occasionally needed, can be called upon to supplement more routine procedures easily provided in numerous small offices. The shift to a service economy greatly facilitated the decentralization both of cities and of the urban system.

The communications revolution also blurred further the distinctions between city and country and between one region and another, thus reducing the advantages which early-developing centers and regions had in attracting additional enterprises. Similarly, the spread of crucial infrastructural prerequisites for modern life—hard-surfaced roads, electrification, adequate schools, and even television reception and computer terminals—broke the monopolistic hold of the largest metropolitan centers over the production of goods and services. This freed enterprises to seek out lower-priced labor (often not yet unionized), to search out new consumer markets, and even, once air-conditioning had made them more habitable, to migrate to pleasanter warm climates.

One cannot ignore the role that the federal government itself played in helping to equalize or reduce regional advantages. It was the federal government that built or financed the great interstate highway system which made hitherto isolated regions in the South and West accessible to developers. It was the federal government that, through its rural electrification program, brought power and television to the remotest rural areas. The federal government built the dams that freed vast areas from flooding and made water and electric power available to regions previously unable to support large populations. And it was the federal government that, through its taxation policy, made it attractive for companies to abandon old plants and build new ones. Furthermore, it was the system of government transfer payments that made it feasible for some individuals to abandon old homes and seek new communities in their old age. The expansion of government responsibilities during the New Deal, designed to rescue the United States from the deep depression of the 1930s, thus had important effects on urbanism.

These demographic, technological, economic, and political factors shaped the transformations in urbanism that have occurred since 1920. In this chapter and the next we track these changes more closely, distinguishing between two phases of the process. The first period, roughly between 1920 and 1960, was when cities spread outward from their centers to encompass vast suburban and exurban hinterlands, eventually generating the new form of localized saturation-urbanization we call "megalopolis." During the second phase, beginning in the 1960s, this process continued but was supplemented by a decentralization of the urban network itself; metropolitan developments spread outward from the highly urbanized regions of the so-called manufacturing belt to encompass larger and larger parts of the continent. Conurbations stretched from coast to coast. A new type of "city" society came into being in the United States.

CITIES EXPAND INTO METROPOLITAN COMPLEXES: 1920–1960

The origins of this new phenomenon appeared long before the trend was widespread enough to be recognized. Because expansion of the city could take place only in areas beyond the built-up zone, decentralization of a sort had been occurring for many decades, as cities increased in population and extent. It has been suggested, for example, that New York began its process of suburbanization by the middle of the nineteenth century, and that Philadelphia and Boston were not long in following.[2] However, in that early period, cities either still included vacant peripheral zones within their municipal boundaries or were able to annex their suburbs. Such suburbs were still functionally tied to their central cities because they were primarily dormitories for the wealthy. It was not until the period between 1920 and 1960 that suburbs became increasingly common, diversified, and politically autonomous, and that, therefore, they came into direct competition with central cities for economic bases and attendant fiscal solvency.

By 1910 the Bureau of the Census acknowledged that the old distinction between urban and rural no longer adequately captured the new phenomenon of the *metropolis,* that is, a unit including the central city and its adjacent and subordinate suburbs. In that year, statisticians introduced the category of "urbanized metropolitan area," singling out the 25 largest cities in the country (those with 200,000 or more inhabitants) and noting that an additional 19 cities (containing 100,000 or more in their central portions) were about to emerge as "metropolises." These 44 cities, together with their surrounding suburbs, already contained about 30 percent of the population of the United States.[3] The statisticians were adjusting their measures to a new development.

It is useful to distinguish between growth and development in an urban system. Growth refers to "those adaptations to environmental change *made within the context of established ways of behaving,"* while development "refers to adaptations to environmental change requiring *changes in the ways of doing things."*[4] Clearly, between 1910 and the 1920s the urban system in the United States was not merely growing larger, but was developing—that is, altering in character. A prerequisite for this transformation was the availability of additional population for urban residence. And, as had been true before, the sources of this population helped define the product—the new metropolitan communities.

---

[2]See Leo Schnore, *The Urban Scene* (New York: Free Press, 1959, reprinted 1965), as well as the work of Henry Binford and Sam Bass Warner, Jr., for Boston and Philadelphia.

[3]Blake McKelvey, *The Emergence of Metropolitan America, 1915–1966* (New Brunswick, NJ: Rutgers University Press, 1968), p. 4.

[4]This valuable distinction is taken from Edgar S. Dunn, Jr., *The Development of the U.S. Urban System,* vol. I (Baltimore and London: Johns Hopkins University Press, 1980), p. 14.

The Changing Sources of Urban Population

If the period between 1850 and 1910 was the time when American urban growth was fueled by immigration from abroad, the period between 1910 and 1960 was the time when the growth of metropolitan areas in the core industrial region of the United States was fueled chiefly by internal migration—from South to North and from farm to city. World War I (1914–1918) initiated this new trend, and many of the southern rural people who contributed to it were black.

The year 1914, when some 1.2 million foreign immigrants arrived, was the final year of the "Great Migration." After that, European immigration slowed to only a few hundred thousand a year, due first to the interruption caused by the war but later to legal restrictions established in 1917, 1920, 1922, and 1924. Quotas set in the latter year kept inflows to about 150,000 per year.

The economic boom generated by the war had created an insatiable need for labor—just at the time when it was no longer being provided through foreign immigration. Women and blacks were the most readily available substitutes. But while women were, in general, already in the places where they were needed, blacks were not. The war years stimulated the trek of this hitherto rural southern labor force to the industrial centers of the Northeast and North Central.

In 1910, some 90 percent of the slightly under 10 million African-Americans in the United States still lived in the South—a proportion that had remained remarkably stable since 1790. By 1960, in contrast, only 60 percent of them were still living in the South. Since the total number of blacks was by then approaching 19 million, this meant that a number equivalent to the total black population in 1910 was residing outside the South by 1960.

The urbanization of African-Americans during this 50-year period was even more dramatic than their regional redistribution.[5] Whereas in 1910 some 72 percent of all blacks lived in rural areas, by 1960, 72 percent were living in urban areas, particularly in the central cities of the nation's largest metropolitan areas. The major force behind this dramatic redistribution was the demand for additional workers initiated during World War I by industrial recruiters. Before 1914 blacks constituted less than 2 percent of the total population of New York City and similarly negligible proportions in other major northern cities. Between 1914 and 1920 these numbers trebled.

Because blacks, unlike the earlier immigrants, were forced into segregated

[5]Among the numerous sources that can be consulted, see Charles F. Peake, "Negro Occupation-Employment Participation in American Industry: Historical Perspective, Improvement during the 1960's and Recent Plateauing," *American Journal of Economics and Sociology* 34 (January, 1975); William Julius Wilson, *The Declining Significance of Race* (Chicago: University of Chicago Press, 1978); U.S. Bureau of the Census, "The Social and Economic Status of the Black Population of the United States: A Historical Review, 1790–1978," *Current Population Reports.* PC Series P-23, No. 80 (Washington, DC: Government Printing Office, November 1978); and John Moland, Jr., "The Black Population," in Amos Hawley and Sara Mazie, eds., *Nonmetropolitan America in Transition* (Chapel Hill, NC: University of North Carolina Press, 1981), pp. 464–501.

Table 5.1   THE URBANIZATION OF THE BLACK POPULATION, 1890–1988

| Year | Total black population (000s) | Urban black population (000s) | Percentage in urban areas | Percentage in rural areas | |
				Total	On farms
1890	7,489	1,498	20	80	na
1910	9,828	2,654	27	72	na
1940	12,866	6,304	49	51	35
1950	15,045	9,328	62	38	21
1960	18,849	13,760	72	27	8
1970	22,539	18,257	81	19	2
1980	26,488	21,720	82	18	< 1
1988	29,333	24,053	82	18	< 1

Sources: Data to 1970 in U.S. Bureau of the Census, "The Social and Economic Status of the Black Population in the United States: A Historical Review, 1790–1978," *Current Population Reports*, PC Series P-23, No. 80 (Washington, D.C.: Government Printing Office, 1978). Data for 1988 in U.S. Bureau of the Census, "The Black Population in the United States: March 1988." *Current Population Reports*, PC Series P-20, No. 442 (Washington, D.C.: Government Printing Office, 1989).

housing,[6] highly visible black communities began to appear in most northern industrial cities. In the 1919 economic recession that followed the end of the war, these ghetto nuclei "drew fire." Tensions erupted into race riots in such widely scattered locations as Chicago, Washington, D.C., and even Omaha, thus presaging future difficulties that were to beset American urban life. These difficulties had been foreseen neither by the European theorists of the city nor by the Chicago School urban sociologists who were just beginning to study "urbanism as a way of life."

The restored prosperity of the 1920s allowed blacks to make significant headway in finding urban employment, to enter many blue-collar occupations previously closed to them, and to continue to relocate to the North and to cities. The Depression of the 1930s slowed down this movement—as it did urban growth in general—but by 1940, as recovery and a new wave of migration began, about half of the close to 13 million blacks in the United States were living in urban areas (see Table 5.1).

The period of the Second World War replicated this earlier development but on a larger scale. Labor shortages again encouraged employers to recruit women and blacks, and again this resulted in a great uprooting of population from the rural South. The 1940s witnessed the migration of some three million

---

[6]Even as early as the nineteenth century, it was noted that African-American residents in northern cities were more segregated than white foreign immigrants. See, for example, the careful research on Philadelphia by Theodore Hershberg, *et al.*, "A Tale of Three Cities: Blacks and Immigrants in Philadelphia, 1850–1880, 1970," in *Race and Residence in American Cities*, special issue of the *Annals of the American Academy of Political and Social Science* 441 (January 1979). Fuller results are available in Hershberg, ed., *Philadelphia: Work, Space, Family and Group Experience in the 19th Century* (New York: Oxford University Press, 1981).

blacks from rural to urban areas. By 1950 only two out of every ten blacks still lived on a farm, while more than six out of ten lived in the large metropolitan centers of states in the Northeast and North Central regions. In that year, of 15 million African-Americans, close to 7 million were living in the central cities of large SMAs (standard metropolitan areas),[7] and another 2.2 million were in the fringes of SMAs beyond the central cities.

These trends continued into the 1950s. By 1960, less than one in ten blacks was still living on a farm, while over seven out of ten lived in urban areas, again mostly in central cities. Indeed, in some of the major industrial metropolitan centers, African-Americans had come to constitute a sizable minority of the center city population. Because white populations were suburbanizing on a massive scale at the same time blacks were heading toward the centers of SMSAs, American metropolitan areas were becoming increasingly segregated racially (see Tables 5.2 and 5.3).

Blacks were not the only subgroup within the United States to move to major metropolitan centers in the decades between 1920 and 1960. Even larger numbers of white farmers left the land for employment in cities. Their migration reflected completion of the first stage of the restructuring of the American economy, from agriculture to industry. We no longer needed farmers. At first, the number of farmers needed to grow food for the rest of the population stabilized, so farmers constituted a declining percentage of the still-expanding labor force. However, more recently we have been witnessing the disappearance of farming as a full-time occupation for all but a tiny fraction of Americans. Mechanization of agricultural production requires fewer and fewer hands to cultivate the same amount of land, while dramatic increases in yields permit the same amount of land to produce more food, sufficient not only to feed a larger domestic population but to supply grain and other agricultural products to the world market as well. Table 5.4 demonstrates the remarkable decline in the labor needed to produce certain agricultural commodities, while Table 5.5 shows the impact of this upon the absolute number of farm workers in the United States.

The major dislocations from farming first occurred between 1910 and 1920, and then between 1940 and 1960. In 1920, some 28 percent of all U.S. workers were still classified as farmers. Numbers changed little in the decades that followed, in part because the Depression interrupted the trend. Unemployment was so great in the cities that migration was discouraged, and there was even return migration to the countryside by those seeking to survive through subsistence farming. However, the decades beginning in 1940 saw a precipitous drop in the number of farm workers, even while the amount of land under cultivation continued to increase.

---

[7]Changing realities required reconceptualization in statistics. In 1950 the Bureau of the Census established a category called SMA, or standard metropolitan area, to designate major central cities together with their surrounding suburbs. By 1960 this measure was revised to set up standard metropolitan statistical areas (SMSAs). See the end of this chapter for a fuller discussion.

Table 5.2 PROPORTION OF BLACKS IN SELECTED CENTRAL CITIES, 1950 TO 1980, BY REGION

City	Percentage of center city residents who are black			
	1950	1960	1970	1980

Northeast/North Central Manufacturing Belt

City	1950	1960	1970	1980
Detroit	16	29	38	63
Newark	17	34	54	58
Baltimore	24	35	46	55
St. Louis	18	29	41	46
Cleveland	16	29	44	44
Chicago	14	23	33	40
Philadelphia	18	26	34	38
Cincinnati	16	22	28	34
Buffalo	6	13	20	27
New York	10	14	21	25
Pittsburgh	12	17	20	24
Milwaukee	3	8	15	23
Indianapolis	15	21	18*	22
Boston	5	9	16	22

South

City	1950	1960	1970	1980
Washington	35	54	71	70
Atlanta	37	38	51	67
New Orleans	32	37	45	55
Memphis	37	37	39	48
Dallas	13	19	25	29
Houston	21	23	26	28

West

City	1950	1960	1970	1980
Los Angeles	9	14	18	17
San Francisco	6	10	13	13
San Diego	5	6	8	9
San Antonio	7	7	8	7
Phoenix	5	5	5	5

*Results from boundary change annexing white suburban areas.

Source: Adapted from U.S. Census data compiled in Hilda Golden, *Urbanization and Cities* (Lexington, MA: D.C. Heath, 1981), Table 13.4, p. 334; we have computed 1980 data from U.S. Bureau of the Census, "Standard Metropolitan Statistical Areas and Standard Consolidated Statistical Areas: 1980," *1980 Census Supplementary Report PC80-S1-5* (Washington, D.C.: Government Printing Office October 1981).

Table 5.3 RACIAL CHANGES IN METROPOLITAN AREAS, 1920 TO 1960

Characteristic	1920	1930	1940	1950	1960
Number of metropolitan areas	112	143	150	191	212
Population in metropolitan areas (millions)	52.5	66.7	72.6	89.0	112.0
Percentage of metropolitan population that was white	92.6	91.2	90.1	87.2	82.4
Percentage of metropolitan population that was black	6.9	8.4	9.6	12.4	16.8
Percentage of whites in metropolitan areas living in central cities	65.9	63.9	61.6	56.6	47.8
Percentage of blacks in metropolitan areas living in central cities	67.2	72.8	74.6	77.2	79.6

Source: Derived from U.S. Census Office, *Eighteenth Census 1960*, (Washington, DC: Government Printing Office), as organized by Blake McKelvey, *American Urbanization: A Comparative History* (Glenview, IL: Scott Foresman & Company, 1973), Table 9, p. 129.

Table 5.4 CHANGES IN THE AVERAGE AMOUNT OF LABOR REQUIRED TO PRODUCE THREE BASIC CROPS IN THE UNITED STATES

Year	Man-hours per unit*		
	Corn used as grain	Wheat	Cotton
1800	344	373	601
1935–1939	108	67	209
1965–1969	7	11	30

*Per 100 bushels for corn and wheat; per bale for cotton.

Source: Office of the President, *Report on National Growth* (1972), p. 16, as reproduced in Gist and Fava, *Urban Society*, 6th ed., p. 74.

The very nature of agriculture changed in an irreversible manner. Agricultural production became not only mechanized but actually "industrialized," with the largest and most highly capitalized farms turning into big businesses. Between 1940 and 1974, for example, the average size of a farm rose from 175 acres to 440 acres.[8] Furthermore, the terms "farm resident" and "farmer" were no longer interchangeable. About ten percent of farm operators no longer lived on their farms, and over half of the income of households residing on farms no longer came from agriculture. Many farmers supplemented their incomes with

[8]See Olaf Larson, "Agriculture and the Community," in Hawley and Mazie, eds., *Nonmetropolitan America*, especially pp. 157, 164–165.

Table 5.5   THE DECLINE IN AGRICULTURAL LAND
AND LABOR FORCE BETWEEN 1920 AND
1980

Year	Number of farm workers (000's)	Farmland (000's of acres)
1920	11,390	1,494
1930	10,321	1,542
1940	8,995	1,658
1950	6,953	1,810
1960	4,219	1,839
1970	2,602	1,723
1980	2,250	1,042

Source: Data from Hilda Golden, *Urbanization and Cities* (Lexington, MA: D.C. Heath, 1981), Table 12.4, p. 308; corrected and updated by U.S. Department of Agriculture, *Agricultural Statistics* (Washington, DC, 1982), p. 385, and U.S. Department of Commerce, Bureau of the Census, *Statistical Abstract of the United States 1982–83* (Washington, DC, 1982), p. 386.

part-time or part-year employment in other occupations, while other members of their families entered nonfarming occupations.

Not only surplus farmers but also other primary workers from rural areas helped to swell the urban centers between 1920 and 1960. For example, when oil and gas began to be substituted for coal, mines in Appalachia, which had in any case been stripped of their more easily accessible veins, began to close down, leaving former workers with little choice but to move.

The results of all these population movements may be seen in Table 5.6, which shows the extent to which America became both urbanized and "metropolitanized" in the period in question. It should be borne in mind that "urban," as utilized in the census, refers to all places having at least 2500 inhabitants, while "metropolitan" refers to all residents in the census-delimited SMAs or SMSAs, even if they reside in places that are unincorporated. The data in Table 5.6 have been adjusted to take into account changing definitions.

We referred to the fact that the system itself was changing, developing rather than merely growing. It was developing in two apparently contradictory ways. First, it was concentrating, in terms of economic control and regional hegemony; but second, it was deconcentrating, in terms of the internal structure of the metropolitan centers, which gained increased control over the economy and the country. The first may be viewed as the expansion of "empire" and the heightened inequality that comes with large-scale social organization. The second was more clearly the result of greater internal social differentiation within cities and the translation of that differentiation into spatial segregation. Without social inventions such as credit, and without technical inventions such as improved communication and transport, such spatial segregation could not have taken the extreme form it did.

Table 5.6 ESTIMATED NUMBER OF URBAN AND METROPOLITAN
PLACES AND PERCENTAGE OF TOTAL POPULATION IN
THEM, 1920 TO 1960

	Urban places		Metropolitan areas	
Year	Number	Percent of population living in	Number*	Percent of population living in
1920	2,725	51.2	120	39.6
1930	3,179	56.1	142	51.2
1940	3,485	56.5	148	52.1
1950	4,077	59.6	168	56.1
		64.0†		
1960	6,041	63.0	212	66.7
		69.9†		

*The U.S. Bureau of the Census retro-estimated this number to earlier census dates before metropolitan areas were officially delimited.

†In 1950 the U.S. Bureau of the Census changed its definition of urban by including some residents of fringe areas outside large cities in something called "urbanized areas." These had formerly been classified as rural. The larger numbers include these persons.

Sources: Assembled from various census reports.

The Concentration of Economic and Political Power

We have seen how, beginning with railroads in the nineteenth century but moving on to industrial production, a few large nationwide firms came to control large segments of manufacturing. During the 1920s monopolies also breached the service and retail fields. As George Mowry pointed out, by 1930 "ten holding companies controlled over 70 per cent of the nation's electric power, branch banking had been so extended that 1 per cent of the nation's banks controlled 46 per cent of its banking resources, and chain stores were doing 37 per cent of the country's retail drug business, while similar figures in notions and groceries were even higher."[9] The extreme concentration of corporate power was documented by Adolph Berle and Gardiner Means, who described the new giant corporations within whose headquarters decisions were made that affected the nation. Although severely set back by the depression of the 1930s with its massive business failures, this trend toward giant corporations intensified after 1940, until by 1960 some 500 companies were accounting for two-thirds of the industrial production in the United States, while chain stores had virtually driven out local and smaller-scale firms.[10] Although the operations of these corporations were scattered coast to coast, the headquarters were

[9]George E. Mowry, *The Urban Nation, 1920–1960* (New York: Hill and Wang, 1965), p. 3.

[10]Adolph Berle, Jr., one of Roosevelt's advisors, was among the first scholars of this phenomenon. For an early evaluation, see A. Berle, Jr. and Gardiner Means, *The Modern Corporation and Private Property* (New York: Macmillan, 1933); for an even more critical view, see Adolph Berle, Jr., *Power Without Property* (New York: Harcourt, Brace, 1959).

increasingly centralized in a few of the largest cities, primarily New York City.

While the prosperity of the 1920s had encouraged centralization of private economic power, it took the depression of the 1930s to bring about a commensurate concentration of public power. It is hard for us today to appreciate the devastating character of the economic collapse that occurred in October 1929, when the stock market crashed, or to project ourselves into the circumstances that immobilized the productive capacity of the country, left millions victim to seemingly incurable unemployment, and revealed the impotence of government, as it was then constituted, to cope with the problems generated by economic crisis. As Constance McLaughlin Green described it:

> It was as if someone had turned a light switch and cut off the current. . . . [M]ortgage foreclosures cost farmers their land and city workmen their homes, savings evaporated, banks closed, and brokers jumped out of windows on Wall Street. Industrial giants slashed payrolls, reduced operations to a few hours a week, and sometimes shut down their plants altogether. The 6 million unemployed in 1930 rose with every passing month; an average of 100,000 workers were fired weekly during the next two years. In 1932 New York City alone had a million jobless, Chicago 660,000; 80 percent of Toledo's working people were unemployed, 60 percent of Akron's, 50 percent of Cleveland's.[11]

By the spring of 1932, one out of every three adults in Philadelphia and Pittsburgh was receiving charity, and by February 1932 Chicago had already spent all the money budgeted for relief for the entire year![12] Assistance was needed on a scale never before rendered; existing private charities and the small "welfare" funds in the hands of city governments proved totally inadequate to the task.

The election of Franklin D. Roosevelt in 1932 and the massive emergency reforms his new administration put into place within his first 100 days in office changed the character of American government by making the federal government responsible not only for regulating business practices to control dishonesty and abuses, but also for placing a variety of "safety nets" under citizens. Social security was instituted, the organization of labor unions was facilitated, and the federal government undertook massive infrastructural and construction projects throughout the United States, both to give employment to the unemployed and to provide facilities such as schools, highways, electricity, and flood control dams for citizens. Banking was reorganized, new credits were provided to permit refinancing of homes and farms as well as industrial reconstruction, and, when all else failed, direct relief was made available.

Although the New Deal appropriated many billions of dollars to assist rural areas and to finance relief projects in the countryside, in actual fact the bulk of the money was spent *in,* and the bulk of the construction projects were earmarked *for,* the cities—because it was in the major cities of the industrial Northeast and North Central that the ravages of the collapse were most

---

[11]Constance M. Green, *The Rise of Urban America* (New York: Harper & Row, 1965), p. 153.

[12]Mowry, *The Urban Nation,* pp. 76–77.

severely felt.[13] This collaboration between the federal government and the cities established precedents for the future fiscal dependence of urban governments upon federal funds. While federal subsidies allowed cities to take greater responsibility for their residents, cities were later left with these responsibilities, even when federal subsidies were withdrawn—one factor in the urban fiscal crises that would later arise.

The reforms of the New Deal also established the mechanisms that would facilitate a massive dispersion of metropolitan populations into the surrounding areas during the 1940s and 1950s (once war boom and recovery had occurred). The highways that were constructed and the subsidized home loans that were made available permitted and indeed made inevitable a massive suburbanization around metropolitan centers. This was the logical response of the building boom in the immediate post-World War II period, a boom heightened by the housing shortages that had built up during the Depression and World War II, coupled with an enormous spurt in the number of families formed and children born (the "baby boom") as delayed marriages finally occurred and as Americans withdrew into the security of home after many decades of insecurity.

The United States, having suffered none of the destruction that had been visited upon Europe during World War II, became the truly hegemonic power in the world in the late 1940s and early 1950s, able to provide its own population with unprecedented prosperity while still assisting in the recovery of the European economy. "By 1955 the American economy, with about 6 percent of the world's population, was producing almost 50 percent of the world's goods."[14] Such prosperity, attributable to America's unique position as the only industrial economy left intact after the war, could not have lasted; European and Japanese recovery were eventually to break the monopoly. But during those decades the tendencies toward deconcentration, first manifest in the 1920s but aborted by the Depression, finally received their full expression.

The Decentralization of the Physical City

While urbanites first equaled rural dwellers in number by 1920, suburbanites first equaled center city residents in the U.S. metropolitan population by 1960. Table 5.7 shows the changing relationship between cities and their suburban fringes in this period of increasing decentralization. As this table shows (even with all its inadequacies), whereas between 1910 and 1920 central cities were increasing in population at a greater rate than their suburban fringes, in every decade since 1920 the suburban ring has added population faster than the central cities. In fact, over the four decades in question, the difference between the two rates of growth increased. While the proportion of the total population of the United States living within the central cities of metropolitan regions remained remarkably constant at about one-third, the proportion living in

---

[13]*Ibid.*, Chapter 4, pp. 90–128.

[14]*Ibid.*, p. 203.

Table 5.7   SUBURBANIZATION OF U.S. CITIES, 1920 TO 1960

| Year | % of total U.S population in metropolitan areas | % in central cities of metropolitan areas | % in suburban rings of metropolitan areas | Metropolitan Population Distribution % increase in preceding decade | | |
				Central cities	Suburban rings	Difference
1920	50	33	17	25.6	21.5	− 4.1
1930	54	35	19	22.5	34.8	+12.3
1940	55	34	21	5.3	13.3	+ 8.0
1950	59	35	25	12.9	34.4	+22.5
1960	67	33	33	7.0	48.3	+41.3

Note: Two major problems enter into the measurement of the phenomenon of suburbanization. One is that metropolitan areas are constantly redefined, so that it is virtually impossible to reconstruct accurately the proportion of total population in them. We use the reconstruction by Irene Taeuber, "The Changing Population of the United States in the Twentieth Century," in vol. 5 of Commission Research Reports, *Population Distribution and Policy*, ed. Sara Mills Mazie, U.S. Commission on Population Growth and the American Future (Washington, DC: Government Printing Office, 1972), Table 19. A second is that between census dates, central cities may *annex* suburban areas formerly beyond their city limits. Therefore, some growth in *central* cities is actually suburban growth which has been "reclassified." Any corrections then will *reduce* the growth inside central cities and *increase* them outside. Intercensal growth rates for centers and peripheries have been taken from Hawley, as adapted by Hilda Golden, *Urbanization and Cities* (Lexington, MA: D.C. Heath, 1981), Table 13.1, p. 323.

suburban fringes of metropolitan areas actually doubled, from 17 percent in 1920 to 33 percent in 1960.

We have noted that American metropolitan regions became increasingly segregated by race during this phase of suburban expansion. As blacks continued to centralize, whites participated disproportionately in a "flight from the city" which, unfortunately, was in part a reaction to the growing number of blacks in central cities. Table 5.3 (p.123) demonstrated the cumulative effects of these two trends.

Accounting for Suburbanization   The introduction and democratization of the private passenger car was perhaps the single most important facilitator of suburbanization. In 1900 there were only 8000 cars registered in the entire country; the automobile was a novelty, a plaything for the rich. But by 1910 Henry Ford had revolutionized production methods and lowered costs of production for his new Model T, thus placing the car within reach of a wider market. The number of motor vehicles in circulation in 1905 was only 25,000, but by 1915 it had increased tenfold. By 1920, close to 10 million cars, taxis, buses, and trucks were on the roads, and this number rose to 74 million by 1960. The increase in the number of motor vehicles registered and in the surface of paved highways can be seen from Table 5.8. The newly paved roadways were concentrated in and around the major metropolitan centers of the country, which enhanced their competitive advantage *vis-à-vis* both rural areas and small cities and towns.

While the railroads continued to dominate the transport of goods, passen-

Table 5.8   THE SPREAD OF HIGHWAYS AND MOTOR VEHICLES BETWEEN
1920 AND 1960

Year	Surfaced highway miles (in thousands)	Motor vehicle registrations (in thousands)		
		Cars, taxis	Trucks, buses	Total
1920	369	8,131	1,108	9,239
1930	694	23,035	3,715	26,750
1940	1,367	27,466	4,987	32,453
1950	1,939	40,339	8,823	49,162
1960	2,557	61,682	12,186	73,868

Source: Hilda Golden, *Urbanization and Cities* (Lexington, MA: D.C. Heath, 1981), Table 12.6, p. 311.

gers increasingly depended upon roads and cars. Commutation to the center city for employment was no longer the exclusive prerogative of the wealthy. Particularly after World War II, the dormitory suburb became the natural habitat for the white middle-class population of metropolitan America. Such expansion would not have been physically feasible without the highways built and the automobiles produced, but equally important were the financial resources and credits made available, chiefly by the federal government. The construction of highways was financed by the government, while the purchase of automobiles was greatly facilitated by private consumer credit—a social invention of the 1920s.[15] And the building of vast residential estates, subdivisions, and new towns was made possible by an expansion of easy credit and subsidized mortgage loans, allowing millions of Americans to translate their rather remarkably constant preferences for the owned single-family home into reality. Even if consumers only sought to obtain the tax savings available through owning rather than renting their housing, buyers were virtually forced into single-family suburban houses, because apartment condominiums, which have recently become available in such enormous numbers, had not yet been "invented."

The rapid growth in fringe areas in the late 1940s and the 1950s was largely one of residences, but commercial facilities were not long in following their markets outward. The shopping center, designed for low-density residential zones and for communities served by the automobile, was another invention of the postwar period. Other services also decentralized, and office complexes began to cluster near shopping centers or in the downtowns of suburbs.

Manufacturing, which to some extent had been decentralizing since the

[15]Credit installment buying was "invented" in the 1920s, and by 1929 about three-quarters of all private cars and more than half of all major appliances were being bought on time payments. See Mowry, *The Urban Nation*, pp. 6–7.

design of the single-floor continuous assembly-line factory, intensified its move to the periphery of metropolitan centers after World War II. During the war a great deal of concern had been generated about the vulnerability to bombing of concentrated industrial districts. This potential vulnerability was vividly illustrated by the devastations that had occurred in Europe during the war. An ideology favoring decentralized plant locations, then, was in the air, and was translated into government policy. Incentives to abandon existing plants were created through federally sponsored fast tax write-offs, while corporations were encouraged to relocate on the periphery by suburban governments that competed with one another to offer the lowest real estate tax rates and to impose the least stringent regulations over building and environmental controls. The separation of manufacturing plants from central management was a further factor, and one that could not have occurred without improved means of communication, chief among them the telephone.

It is hard to evaluate the role played by the telephone in facilitating the decentralization that occurred around urban areas during the first half of the twentieth century. Ever since its invention in 1876, it had paradoxical effects on the city—facilitating both urban sprawl and the concentration of offices and administration in central business districts.[16] Unlike the automobile, the telephone served chiefly to organize interactions. Originally thought of as a toy whose chief functions would be recreational, the telephone proved most valuable for business, permitting the coordination of widely separated activities which previously had to be located near one another.[17] Jean Gottmann has suggested that the chief contribution of the telephone was to make locations more interchangeable with one another, to make space more fungible.

Clearly, this permitted (but did not in itself require) decentralization. Most students of office location agree, however, that the telephone was "the main factor which allowed geographic separation between office work and the other stages of business it administered, such as production, warehousing, and shipping of goods."[18] In short, the telephone made it possible to coordinate larger and more complex enterprises and to assemble the vast stores of information needed for day-to-day decision making without having to crowd all activities together in spatial proximity. Greater division of labor and the decentralization of plants into multiple locations were thus facilitated by the incredible telephone network that Cherry has called "by far the largest integrated machine in the world."[19]

---

[16]This is pointed out in a volume commemorating the hundredth anniversary of the invention of the telephone. See Ithiel de Sola Pool, ed., *The Social Impact of the Telephone* (Cambridge, MA: MIT Press, 1977).

[17]Colin Cherry, "The Telephone System: Creator of Mobility and Social Change," in de Sola Pool, *The Social Impact of the Telephone*, pp. 112–126.

[18]Jean Gottmann, "Megalopolis and Antipolis: The Telephone and the Structure of the City," in de Sola Pool, *The Social Impact of the Telephone*, pp. 303–317. Quotation is taken from p. 309.

[19]Cherry, "The Telephone System," p. 123.

The telephone not only facilitated decentralization around cities but also encouraged deconcentration of population and economic activities away from the older manufacturing belt of the United States to other parts of the country. It is quite remarkable how early the telephone network expanded and how its pattern of expansion not only reflected but actually shaped the metropolitan developments that occurred between 1920 and 1960. Figure 5.2 shows the expansion of the telephone network between 1890 and 1904.[20] The final map looks much like the distribution of SMSAs by the 1970s.

As residents and places of employment moved to the peripheries of major cities in the postwar period, the existing circulation systems of streets and highways required modification. Formerly, all roads "led to Rome," the central business district (CBD). Now, other major roads were needed to bypass the CBD and connect various parts of the periphery with each other. Commuting around the periphery reduced ridership on the radial mass transit systems that had been built since the turn of the century, undermining their financial solvency. Their deterioration encouraged further decentralization. Headquarters of firms relocated to suburban office buildings to be closer to their workers. And with larger populations both living and working in suburbs, the downtown stores were quick to recognize that they could recapture their best customers only by setting up branches in key growth zones on the outskirts.

The impact of the cumulative suburbanization of residences, commerce, and manufacturing was felt severely by the municipalities whose central cores supported these new edifices and made them possible. Annexation of the suburban fringes, however, was no longer as easy as it had been, and central cities saw their wealthiest citizens and their chief sources of tax revenues—business firms—deserting the areas of their taxing jurisdiction for greener pastures on the fringes. In the meantime, central cities were receiving large numbers of migrants from "backward" areas—the rural South, Appalachia, Mexico, Puerto Rico—whose skills were low and less and less in demand, but whose "safety-net" responsibilities the municipalities, aided by the federal government, had taken on since the reforms of the New Deal and its expansion.

Fears of the destruction of the tax base, at the very time demands upon the public purse were expanding, generated numerous proposals to revive center cities, largely through "regentrification" and urban renewal. The Housing/Urban Redevelopment Act of 1949, when it was first proposed, seemed to be an answer to the perplexing difficulties central cities were experiencing as a result of the postwar suburban building boom. So were later attempts to revive city centers by the construction of "golden triangles" and massive civic centers, and even later, to bring back manufacturing jobs through the creation of "urban enterprise zones."

The exodus of residents, commercial firms, and manufacturing plants from the centers of the nation's largest cities was perceived throughout the 1950s as

[20]Ronald Abler, "The Telephone and the Evolution of the American Metropolitan System," in de Sola Pool, *The Social Impact of the Telephone,* pp. 318–341.

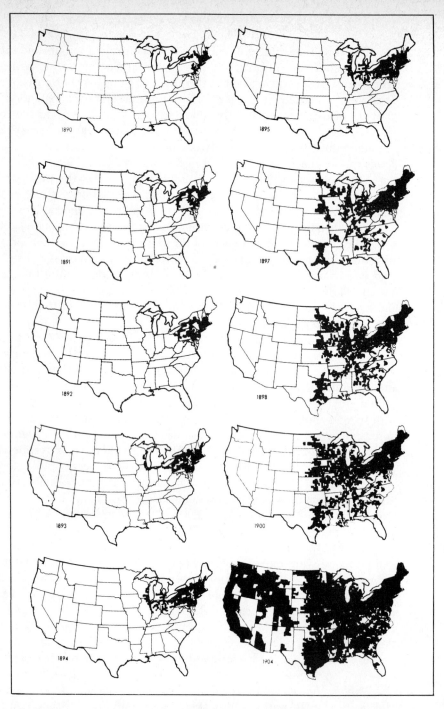

Figure 5.2 The expansion of AT&T's toll network, 1890–1904. (*Source:* Ronald Abler, "The Telephone and the Evolution of the American Metropolitan System," in I. de Sola Pool, ed., *The Social Impact of the Telephone,* p. 333. Copyright 1977 by MIT Press. All rights reserved.)

the most serious threat to the viability of existing metropolitan centers in the country. In fact, however, the older central cities of the manufacturing belt faced an even more threatening situation—one that would appear fully only in the ensuing phase of urban change in the United States: the regional redistribution of population and the urban system within which it was ordered.

The Regional Redistribution of Cities

From the earliest days, United States population movements had been from settled to unsettled areas, from east to west. However, massive immigration from abroad and internal migration from farms to industrializing centers served to counteract what otherwise would have been a steady decline in the population living on the east coast. As we have seen, some of those mitigating trends began to slow down in the 1920s, and by the early 1960s had virtually disappeared. Their disappearance unmasked the underlying trend toward a more equal distribution of population among the four major regions of the United States—a trend that would become clearer only in the 1960s and beyond.

In 1920, the shares of total population contained by the Northeast (including New England and the Middle Atlantic states), the North Central (both east and west), and the South (east and central) were still approximately equal (28, 32, and 31 percent of total population, respectively), as they had been from the time of the Civil War. Only the West (Mountain and Pacific states) still lagged behind, with some 9 percent of the total.

Between 1920 and 1960 the two most industrialized regions of the country, the Northeast and the North Central, grew only modestly, each increasing its population by about 50 percent. The loss of European immigration (in large part responsible for this poor showing) was only partially compensated for by the immigration of blacks from the South. Lower rates of natural increase and the out-migration of northerners toward the west coast also contributed to the slower growth of the northern regions.

During this same period, the South's population grew by 66 percent, since high rates of natural increase more than compensated for the out-migration of blacks headed for northern cities. However, the West was the major beneficiary of regional redistribution. Because the population was so low to begin with, it showed a 200 percent rate of growth in the four decades in question. This remarkable rate of growth was partially attributable to the Second World War, since U.S. involvement in the Pacific military arena encouraged the location there of war (including aerospace) industries and military installations. To some extent this growth also reflected changing sources of foreign immigration, for as Mexico began to be the chief sending country for foreign immigration, the port of entry for newcomers shifted from the east coast to the Southwest. But it is important to recognize that the growth basically reflected the continued westward march of the U.S. population that had been going on throughout the entire history of the country.

By 1960, then, the regional distribution of the U.S. population was quite changed. The share of population in the Northeast had dropped to 25 percent;

the North Central and the South held about 30 percent each; and the West contained some 16 percent of the total population. As can be seen from Figure 5.3, the long-term trend lines for regional distribution of population show few surprises for the period between the Civil War and the mid-1960s.

Between 1920 and 1960 the proportion of population living in urban areas continued to rise in all regions of the country, again as one might expect. However, also in accord with logic, the proportional changes in urban population were highest in those parts of the country where initial levels of urbanization had been lowest and where rates of total population increase were greatest. Figure 5.4 shows the percentage of each state's population that was classified as urban in 1920, while Figure 5.5 shows the figures for 1960. As these data demonstrate, during the 40-year interval virtually every state in the union experienced an increase in its level of urbanization. (The only exceptions were Massachusetts and Rhode Island, which by 1920 could be characterized as having reached the stage of "saturation urbanization.")

With the spread of population came greater equalization in the levels of urbanization throughout the country. In 1920, for example, Mississippi, the least urbanized state, had only 13 percent of its population in cities, as contrasted with 92 percent in Rhode Island. By 1960, some 38 percent of the population of Mississippi (still the least urbanized state) lived in cities, while close to 90 percent of the population of New Jersey (then the most urbanized state) resided in cities.

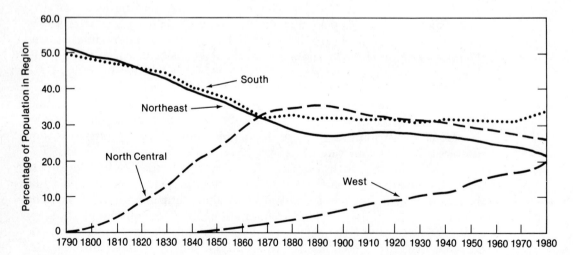

Figure 5.3 Percentage of U.S. population in Northeast, North Central, South, and West Regions, 1790–1980. (*Source:* John Long, "Population Deconcentration in the United States," *Special Demographic Analysis* CDS-81-5. U. S. Department of Commerce, Bureau of the Census, 1981.)

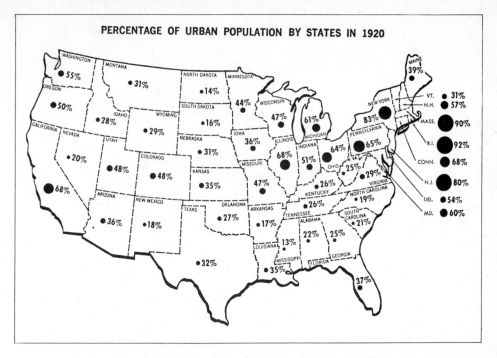

Figure 5.4 Percentage of urban population by states in 1920. (*Source:* George E. Mowry, *The Urban Nation 1920–1960.* Copyright © 1965 by George E. Mowry. Reprinted with the permission of Hill and Wang, a division of Farrar, Straus and Giroux, Inc.)

As urbanization levels rose, metropolitan areas, which had hitherto been concentrated in the Northeast and North Central regions of the country, began to appear and multiply in other regions. This came about as individual cities in the South and West increased in size and began to spill over into adjacent counties. Unfortunately, it is impossible to show how SMSAs would have been distributed in the United States in 1920 (since the term, concept, and system of presentation of data had not yet been invented) and to compare this with how they had come to be distributed later. In contrast with 1920, by 1960 all regions of the country contained large metropolitan areas, and the South and West, as well as the Northeast, were participating in a trend of growing conurbation. That trend has continued into the most recent period, but with a highly significant shift in scale and thus an apparent turnaround toward nonmetropolitan growth.

We shall examine these developments in the next chapter. But first it is important to describe the new statistical methods that were developed to capture the phenomenon of metropolitanization. Without understanding how metropolitan areas are delimited and measured, it is impossible to evaluate recent urban developments that seem to be initiating a new phase in the long history of cities in the United States.

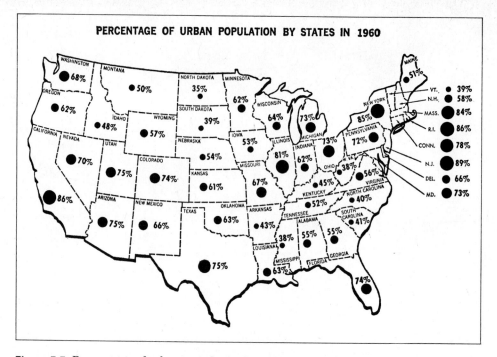

Figure 5.5 Percentage of urban population by states in 1960. (*Source:* George E. Mowry, *The Urban Nation 1920–1960.* Copyright © 1965 by George E. Mowry. Reprinted with the permission of Hill and Wang, a division of Farrar, Straus and Giroux, Inc.)

HOW WE MEASURE METROPOLITAN DEVELOPMENT

By 1950 it was evident that the postwar decentralization of cities in the United States was not being accurately measured by the older statistical unit hitherto used by the Bureau of the Census, namely, the "urbanized area." The metropolitan statistical area (MSA) was therefore devised to include, along with the urbanized area of a major city, the surrounding fringe region that, while not fully urban, was economically dominated by its central city. Given the fact that metropolitan areas were still thought of as enlarged cities, that is, relatively independent central places together with their "dependencies" beyond the city limits, this aggregate made sense. True, it was difficult to make comparisons between center city and suburban populations among various MSAs, because how much of an MSA was classified as center city and how much as fringe depended upon where political boundaries were located and on the ease with which a central city had been able to annex suburbs.[21] But the model of a

---

[21]The distinction between center city and suburban fringe was much more appropriate for the older-style cities in the manufacturing belt than it was for newer, spread-out and noncentered cities of the West, such as Los Angeles. Furthermore, older cities had ceased annexing their fringes after they encountered considerable resistance from the ring of wealthy suburbs that had already solidi-

single-centered metropolis, while of declining value in the heavily urbanized portions of the Northeast and North Central, still had reasonable congruence with the type of "metropolis" that was spreading throughout the United States.

By the time of the 1960 census, however, massive conurbations had already appeared and decentralization of urban population had reached such an extreme form that the assumptions underlying the MSA measure (namely, that there were single-centered metropolises that, along with their dependent fringes or suburbs, constituted "natural" or relatively self-contained regions of urbanization) were no longer tenable in many parts of the country. A new aggregate unit, the standard metropolitan statistical area (SMSA), was therefore adopted in that year by the U.S. Bureau of the Census to delimit larger zones around central cities that were functionally linked to the metropolitan economy. An SMSA was defined as an urbanized area including *at least* one center city having 50,000 or more inhabitants, together with all adjacent counties in which the *density* of settlement had reached a minimum level and from which a minimum specified *proportion* of the residents commuted daily to the center city. While this measure was more congruent with the changed spatial structure of metropolitan America, it retained the concept of discrete metropolitan areas, relatively independent of one another.

By that time it was also clear that, in those parts of the country where "saturation urbanization" had been reached—for example, BOSWASH (Boston to Washington) and CHI-GARY (Chicago to Gary, Indiana, the heartland of the Midwest)—even the enlarged SMSA was too small and simple a unit to capture the new forms of metropolitan interpenetration and multi-centeredness.

As urban saturation proceeded, the old model of self-contained metropolitan regions, no matter how complexly defined and no matter how broadly bounded, became less and less relevant. Another unit of measure was required to refer to a complex of metropolitan regions no longer distinct from one another but contiguous and interwoven. In 1960, therefore, the Bureau of the Census designated the conurbations of New York-Northwestern New Jersey and Chicago-Northwestern Indiana as standard consolidated areas, a classification repeated for these two regions in the 1970 census.

In 1970, the SMSA measure was kept intact, although due to the increase in the number of cities with at least 50,000 inhabitants and to the decentralization that had been occurring around almost all such cities, the Office of Management and Budget (the federal agency charged with identifying and adding SMSAs on the basis of provisional, interim, and decennial census returns) added 31 more SMSAs to the list of 212 they had named in 1960 and expanded the number of adjacent counties considered parts of existing SMSAs.

The census of 1980 (the findings of which will be discussed in the next chapter) took this process of redefinition a major step further. In addition to the

---

fied around them. On the other hand, newer cities in the West, whose fringes were still predominately rural and underserviced, were still considered desirable units for suburbs to attach themselves to.

SMSA unit, the 1980 census presented data on an expanded set of 17 supra-SMSA aggregates called standard consolidated statistical areas (SCSAs). These SCSAs consist of two or more adjacent SMSAs, at least one of which has a population of over one million persons. Data are available both for the SMSAs that make up SCSAs *and* for their populations as aggregated into SCSAs. The latter attempts to capture not the metropolis but the new megalopolis.

The Bureau of the Census, in its release of October 1981, presented the rationale for these new measures:

> Standard metropolitan statistical areas (SMSAs) and standard consolidated statistical areas (SCSAs) . . . are designated as [such] . . . by the Office of Management and Budget (OMB) to maintain geographic consistency in the presentation of data issued by Federal agencies. The general concept of an SMSA is one of a large population nucleus, together with adjacent communities which have a high degree of economic and social integration with that nucleus.
>
> . . . Each SMSA has one or more central counties containing the area's main population concentration—an urbanized area as defined by the Bureau of the Census, having at least 50,000 inhabitants. An SMSA may also include outlying counties which have close economic and social relationships with the central counties. The outlying counties must have a specified level of commuting to the central counties; they must also meet certain standards regarding metropolitan character, such as population density, urban population, and population growth.
> . . .
> The population living in SMSAs—the metropolitan population—is subdivided into "inside central city (or cities)" and "outside central city (or cities)."
>
> In some parts of the country, metropolitan development has progressed to the point that adjoining SMSAs are themselves socially and economically closely interrelated. These interrelated SMSAs are designated standard consolidated statistical areas (SCSAs) provided they meet the requirements of the official OMB standards.[22]

In June 1983, the Bureau of the Census made the first major redefinition of metropolitan areas since 1960. The single unit called a standard metropolitan statistical area was dropped entirely, and three new categories were put in its place:

1. The metropolitan statistical area (MSA), which refers to a free-standing metropolitan area, surrounded by nonmetropolitan counties and not closely associated with other metropolitan areas (the old idea of a metropolis!);
2. The primary metropolitan statistical area (PMSA), which is a metropolitan area closely connected to another;

---

[22]U.S. Department of Commerce, Bureau of the Census, *Standard Metropolitan Statistical Areas and Standard Consolidated Statistical Areas: 1980,* PC80-S1–5 (Washington, DC: Government Printing Office, October 1981), p. 4. In 1982 the Bureau of the Census began to reclassify urban metropolitan areas based upon 1980 commuting data. The boundaries of existing SMSAs were expanded to include new commuter counties and the designations of metropolitan statistical area (MSA), primary metropolitan statistical area (PMSA), and consolidated metropolitan statistical area (CMSA) were adopted.

3. Clusters of closely related PMSAs, which are grouped together, for reporting purposes, into a higher-level unit which supplants the old standard consolidated statistical area (SCSA) and is called a consolidated metropolitan statistical area (CMSA).

Also reflecting the changing reality of American cities and the scale to which conurbations have now grown, the various MSAs and PMSAs are grouped by size levels, into:

A. statistical areas with a million or more inhabitants;
B. those ranging in size between 250,000 and a million;
C. areas with 100,000 to 250,000 inhabitants; and
D. areas with over 50,000 but less than 100,000 inhabitants.

This new classification permits more detailed and controlled comparisons between types of metropolitan areas. In June 1983, the OMB issued a new list of various types of metropolitan areas and revised the county boundaries of many old ones, on the basis of the data from the 1980 census. It also added 38 more metropolitan statistical areas, almost all of them with 100,000 to 250,000 inhabitants.[23]

The redefinition by the Bureau of the Census of the units into which it aggregates population data is usually an indication that changes in the real world have recently outstripped our ability to measure them according to an older system. As we shall see in the next chapter, this has indeed happened. Truly revolutionary developments in American urbanization began to appear more clearly in American cities since the mid-1960s. If the period between 1920 and 1960 was the phase during which American cities were transformed into metropolitan regions, then the era that began sometime in the early 1960s was one in which metropolitan regions began to spread to encompass the entire society. Urbanization became so pervasive that, paradoxically, it seemed that cities were no longer growing. The only places left for them to expand into were the so-called nonmetropolitan regions.

The same was true with respect to socioeconomic forms of modern life. Urbanism as a way of life became so pervasive that it became virtually impossible to distinguish it from some other way of life. Urban occupations spread out into the countryside, blurring the distinction between urban and rural. Previous contrasts declined. It appeared that the congruence between cities as spatial containers for urban life and urban life itself was actually breaking apart. While we are still on the threshold of this revolutionary transformation of "the city," it is not too early to forecast the direction in which we appear to be moving. We turn to these developments in Chapter 6.

---

[23]Information contained in *The Number News* 3 (February 1983), pp. 1, 6–9; (April 1983), pp. 2, 6–7; *American Demographics* (June 1983). A list of the 38 new metropolitan statistical areas appears in John Herbers, "Major Cities Ringed by Suburbs Yielding to Sprawl of Small Metropolitan Areas," *New York Times,* July 8, 1983, p. 9. The Bureau of the Census retroactively reclassified U.S. 1980 population on the basis of its new definitions, which then raised the total population classified as metropolitan from 169,430,623 to 171,776,970, while dropping the number of nonmetropolitan residents from 57,115,182 to 54,768,835. More details will be presented in Chapter 6.

Chapter
6

The Urbanization of Everybody
All the United States a City

*I*n the depths of the 1930s depression two architects dreamed opposite visions of the city of the future.[1] One, a Swiss-born Parisian named Charles Edouard Jeanneret, better known as Le Corbusier, foresaw a forest of tall towers rising at regular intervals in a gardened landscape. Each tower was a veritable "vertical city" containing apartments and hotel rooms, schools, day-care centers, shops, offices, recreational facilities, communal eating halls, and laundries. Elevators linked floors, while underground rapid transit lines linked towers with one another and with manufacturing sites on the outskirts. Le Corbusier named this community the Radiant City (*La ville radieuse*). It was an architectural masterpiece constructed of steel and glass, organized politically according

---

[1]See Robert Fishman, *Urban Utopias in the Twentieth Century* (New York: Basic Books, 1977). This volume deals with Ebenezer Howard as well as with Le Corbusier and Wright. While we have not previously mentioned Howard, it is important to note that it was his vision, as expressed in *Garden Cities for To-Morrow* (London: Sonnenschein & Co., 1902), that predicted and indeed influenced the suburbs that were built all around American cities some 30 to 50 years later. In similar fashion, Le Corbusier and Wright, coming one generation after Howard, predicted and to some extent influenced at least parts of the contemporary city that is now taking shape before our eyes.

to occupational syndicates and organized socially around the communal facilities that were to be provided within each high-rise "neighborhood."[2]

A very different vision of the future city was projected by the American architect, Frank Lloyd Wright, noted founder of the "prairie school" of horizontal architecture. His image of the future was appropriately named Broadacre City,[3] because it spread sparsely over the landscape, maximizing each family's mobility and its access to communal facilities and open space. Each dwelling was to provide, on a small scale, almost all of the amenities of urban life, including home occupations and a wide range of informational services. A model of Broadacre City—ironically, displayed in Rockefeller Center—depicted a society that had been radically decentralized, not only physically but politically and socially as well. Wright expected large cities to disappear, along with large-scale businesses, which would no longer need cities. "In Wright's words, the city would have 'gone to the countryside.' "[4] Such radical decentralization would be made possible by technological change and miniaturization of production and would regenerate small-scale democracy.

Despite their differences, Le Corbusier and Wright both assumed that in the future, society would be totally urbanized, albeit according to very different patterns. In that they were quite correct. Chapter 5 demonstrated how, by 1960, American society was approaching the upper limits of a logarithmic curve for percentage of population in urban areas. We have called this terminal phase the point of "urban saturation."[5] Paradoxically, once most of the population already lives under urban conditions, the process of urbanization comes to an end.[6] Redistributions of urban population can occur. Cities themselves can

---

[2]Fishman, *Urban Utopias,* pp. 163–262. See also C. E. Jeanneret [Le Corbusier], *La ville radieuse* (Paris: Morance, 1931).

[3]Among the sources that can be consulted, in addition to Fishman's *Urban Utopias,* pp. 91–160, are Frank Lloyd Wright, "Broadacre City: A New Community Plan," in *Architectural Record* 77:4 (April 1935), pp. 243–254; and his earlier *The Disappearing City* (New York: W. F. Payson, 1932). Broadacre City is more fully developed in Wright's *When Democracy Builds* (Chicago: University of Chicago Press, 1945). The mature version is *The Living City* (New York: Horizon Press, 1958).

[4]Fishman, *Urban Utopias,* p. 91.

[5]Throughout most of human history, no more than 5–15 percent of the population could live in cities. Between 1830 and 1900 Europe and the Americas broke through the ceiling set by preindustrial conditions, and the remainder of the world is now following their example. But just as there was a lower limit in the preindustrial age, there appears to be an upper limit in the so-called postindustrial age. In large diversified countries in the postindustrial phase, the top limit appears to be about 80 percent in cities, although tiny "city-state" nations are even able to break through this ceiling.

[6]Discussing limits to urban growth, John Wardwell has pointed to the simple fact that since national urban growth tends to follow a logistic pattern (see our Figure 5.1 p. XXX above), "growth rates slow down and stabilize or even reverse as the asymptote, or upper limit, is approached." See his "Toward a Theory of Urban-Rural Migration in the Developed World," pp. 71–114 in David L. Brown and John Wardwell, eds., *New Directions in Urban-Rural Migration* (New York: Academic Press, 1980). Quotation taken from p. 74.

change in shape and form. But "deurbanization" is extremely unlikely, except in the event of a nuclear disaster that would destroy not only cities but civilization as we now know it.

This chapter discusses the current stage of urbanization in the United States. Even though society may now be almost completely urbanized, the patterns of city distribution in space and the form and organization of cities themselves continue to evolve. Interestingly enough, urban forms are now evolving simultaneously in the direction both of Radiant City (particularly in the centers of world cities such as New York, London, Paris, and Tokyo) and of Broadacre City, as miniaturization, automation, electronically wired "cottages" and mini-offices permit rapid decentralization of parts of the urban economy. Both of these changes have important consequences for urban life.

To comprehend the transformations that have been occurring especially rapidly since 1960, we must diagnose the extent to which saturation urbanization has occurred. To do this, we refer back to the same three factors used to explain the origin and development of earlier cities, namely: changes in population, alterations in politico-socioeconomic (hierarchical) organization, and the changing relation of cities to their "empires." As before, our analysis takes technological changes into account, not as determining factors but as elements that facilitate or constrain certain outcomes.

THE PHENOMENON OF SATURATION URBANIZATION: 1960 TO THE PRESENT

The phenomenon of saturation urbanization can be captured by two types of indicators. The first is statistical: Metropolitan areas in the United States now contain most of the population. The second is spatial: Metropolitan areas have expanded so widely that their "fields" increasingly overlap and merge, yielding virtually continuous, albeit not uniformly developed, urban regions.[7]

Statistical Measures

The high proportion of Americans who live in metropolitan areas results from two trends: first, over the years, many smaller cities have grown to minimum size or have so expanded their commuting radii that they have "turned into" metropolises; and second, existing metropolitan areas have expanded so dramatically that larger and larger stretches of their peripheries have been reclassified as metropolitan.

As can be seen from Table 6.1, which compares measures of SMSAs that

---

[7]In fact, Edgar Dunn, Jr. has subdivided the entire area of continental United States into 171 urban regions that differ from one another only in terms of size and density. See his *The Development of the U.S. Urban System*, vol. I (Baltimore and London: Johns Hopkins University Press, 1980), maps 1 and 3.

Table 6.1 DISTRIBUTION OF METROPOLITAN AND NONMETROPOLITAN POPULATION IN THE UNITED STATES, 1960 TO 1984, ACCORDING TO OLD AND NEW CENSUS DEFINITIONS OF METROPOLITAN BOUNDARIES

	Population in millions							
	Old definition (1)				New definition (2)			
	1960	1970	1980	1990*** (est.)	1960	1970	1980	1984 (est.)
United States	179.3	203.2	226.5	250.0	179.3	203.3	226.6	236.2
Outside SMSAs	66.4	63.8	57.1	56.3	46.6	47.8	54.6	56.4
Inside SMSAs	112.9	139.4	169.4	193.7	132.7	155.5	172.0	179.7
Central cities*	58.0	63.8	67.9	78.7				
Suburbs etc.*	54.9	75.6	101.5	115.0				
Central counties*					124.2	145.3	158.7	165.5
Outlying counties*					8.5	10.3	13.3	14.2
Number of SMSAs**	(212)	(243)	(318)					(277)

*Up to 1980, the Bureau of the Census made a distinction between "center city" and "outside center city" populations. Reflecting the spread of metropolitan regions and their increasingly complex structure (many MSAs now contain multiple "center cities"), the Bureau of the Census currently distinguishes between central and outlying counties in MSAs, rather than cities and suburbs.

**The number of SMSAs is as given at census time. The decline in the number of MSAs in 1984, contrasted with the number of SMSAs in the earlier periods, reflects the extent to which earlier metropolitan areas have now merged into conurbations.

***Author's projection, based on early returns for census of 1990.

Sources: (1) U.S. Department of Commerce, Bureau of the Census, Standard Metropolitan Statistical Areas and Standard Consolidated Statistical Areas, 1980, P80-S1-5, pp. 1–2. (2) U.S. Department of Commerce, Bureau of the Census, Patterns of Metropolitan Area and County Population Growth: 1980 to 1984, series P-25, no. 976, issued October 1985.

were used by the Bureau of the Census until 1982 with recalculations made using the bureau's new definitions of 1984, the percentage of population living in metropolitan areas either increased up to 1980 and then leveled off in 1980 (old definition), or remained remarkably constant since 1960 (new definition). This discrepancy warns us to use census reports with care.

Under the old method, the number of SMSAs designated by the Bureau of the Census increased from 212 to 318 between 1960 and 1980, while the population living in them rose from 112.9 million to 169.4 million. As can be seen from the second set of columns in Table 6.1, however, the new system of MSAs resulted in upward adjustments in all older metropolitan estimates. One effect of these recalculations was to reduce the size of the nonmetropolitan population in each census year, as rural counties were reclassified as parts of metropolitan regions. According to the revised 1980 census figures, ever since 1960 three-quarters of all Americans have been living in metropolitan areas. In the 1980s, according to preliminary returns of the 1990 census, the proportion of U.S. population in metropolitan areas climbed even higher, with an estimated 77 percent now living in cities and suburbs. Furthermore, as Table 6.2 shows, almost half of all Americans lived in the largest MSAs—those with more than a million inhabitants.

Table 6.2 PERCENTAGE DISTRIBUTION OF METROPOLITAN (BY SIZE) AND
NONMETROPOLITAN POPULATION IN THE UNITED STATES, 1960 TO 1990,
ACCORDING TO NEW CENSUS DEFINITIONS

	Percentage of total population				
	1960	1970	1980	1984	1990
United States	100.0	100.0	100.0	100.0	100.0
Outside metropolitan areas	26.0	23.5	24.1	23.9	22.5
Inside metropolitan areas*	74.0	76.5	75.9	76.1	77.5
By size					
million+	(47.0)	(49.2)	(47.6)	(47.5)	(50.2)
500,000–million	(9.8)	(10.0)	(10.3)	(10.4)	—
250,000–500,000	(8.3)	(8.4)	(8.7)	(8.8)	—
100,000–250,000	(7.6)	(7.7)	(8.2)	(8.2)	—
Under 100,000	(1.1)	(1.1)	(1.1)	(1.2)	—

*Different definitions have been used by William H. Frey and Alden Speare, Jr., in their definitive census mono-
graph, *Regional and Metropolitan Growth and Decline in the United States* (New York: Russell Sage Foundation,
1988). According to their Table 3.1 (p. 40), the percent of U.S. population residing in metropolitan areas rose
from 63.8 in 1960 to 75.4 in 1984.

Source: Our computations from Table 8, p. 57 of *Patterns of Metropolitan Area and County Population Growth:
1980 to 1984.* Series P-25, no. 976, issued October 1985, updated to 1988 by the Bureau of the Census;
preliminary returns, 1990, census of 2/20/91.

Most population increases in metropolitan areas have naturally taken place
beyond center city limits. Therefore, despite an increase in the number of
metropolitan areas, central cities account for a smaller share of the population.
According to recalculations by the Bureau of the Census, some 35 percent of
the U.S. population lived in the center cities of MSAs in 1970. This had declined
to 32 percent by 1980 and was only 31.3 percent by 1988. In contrast, the
percentage living in MSAs but outside center cities has risen steadily from 41
percent in 1970 to 44 percent in 1980, to 45 percent by 1984, and is currently
estimated at 46 percent. Suburban areas are now the most typical living environment for Americans.

Another way of tracing the same change can be found in Table 6.3. Notice
that in each of the decades since 1950, center cities increased their populations
at less than the rate of total population increase, whereas suburbs grew at rates
far above the national average. Finally, a new phenomenon made a brief appearance in the 1970s, namely, a heightened rate of growth in residual parts
of the country still considered "nonmetropolitan." Table 6.3 shows that
whereas in preceding decades the population in nonmetropolitan areas grew
much less rapidly than U.S. population as a whole, this was apparently reversed
in the 1970–1980 decade, when nonmetropolitan counties increased at rates
higher than central cities and only slightly less than suburbs. Recent revisions
made by the Bureau of the Census, however, cast doubt on what some scholars
had been calling "demetropolitanization," and the trend actually disappeared
in the 1980s. Preliminary findings from the 1990 census suggest that population
continued to decline in rural America in the most recent decade.

Table 6.3 AVERAGE ANNUAL PERCENTAGE INCREASE IN THE POPULATION OF THE UNITED STATES LIVING IN NONMETROPOLITAN AREAS AND IN CENTER CITIES AND SUBURBS OF METROPOLITAN AREAS, 1950–1990

	1950–1960 % increae	1960–1970 % increase	1970–1980 % increase	1980–1990 % increase
Total Population	1.8	1.3	1.1	1.0
Outside MSAs	.7	.7	1.4*	.4
Inside MSAs	2.6	1.6	1.0	1.2
Center cities	1.1	.6	.1	.6
Suburbs	4.7	2.3	1.7	1.3
MSAs by size				
million+			.8	1.0
250,000–million			1.5	1.2**
100,000–250,000			1.8	1.2**
Under 100,000			1.3	

*We believe that the apparent growth in nonmetropolitan areas between 1970 and 1980 was largely due to a measurement failure. See the arguments in Janet Abu-Lughod, "The Myth of Demetropolitanization," unpublished lecture, University of Cincinnati, 1981. Frey and Speare (1988) have recomputed figures from the 1980 census and concluded that at least one-third of the difference between nonmetropolitan and metropolitan growth rates between 1970 and 1980 disappeared when the MSA boundaries were redrawn on the basis of 1980 commuting data.

**MSA size categories for this period were: 500,000 to a million; and under 250,000.

Source: U.S. Department of Commerce, Bureau of the Census; for 1950–1980, see Report P80-S1-5, p. 2; for 1980–1984, *Patterns of Metropolitan Area and County Growth: 1980 to 1984*, Series P-25, no. 976, October 1985, p. 25; preliminary returns, 1990 census of 2/20/91.

Proponents of the demetropolitanization thesis suggested that the "age of the city" was coming to an end, and argued that Americans were abandoning metropolitan environments and their ways of life. As we shall see later, however, this apparent resurgence in nonmetropolitan areas largely reflected the changing form of metropolitan areas in the United States—a form that presages the physical, if not the social, appearance of Broadacre City.

Knowing that cities grow from the center to the outskirts, we should not be surprised to learn that central cities in many older urbanized portions of the country are no longer growing. Already built up and densely occupied, they can absorb more people only by replacing existing buildings with high-rises. In actual fact, however, most new skyscrapers are devoted to commercial uses. Because populations are recorded not where they are during the daytime but where they sleep,[8] residential densities actually decline in areas converted to nonresidential uses. Furthermore, given the changes in industrial location and

[8]One of the first scholars to call systematic attention to this phenomenon was Gerald Breese in his doctoral dissertation, later published as *The Daytime Population of the Central Business District of Chicago with Particular Reference to the Factors of Transportation* (Chicago: University of Chicago Press, 1949); a summary appears in his "The Daytime Population of the Central Business District," in Ernest W. Burgess and Donald J. Bogue, eds., *Contributions to Urban Sociology* (Chicago: University of Chicago Press, 1964), pp. 112–128.

in American housing patterns, many of the older dense slums that formerly surrounded centrally located places of employment have been cleared—either wholesale through urban renewal or piecemeal through abandonment. Gentrification (the rehabilitation of older residential units for middle- and upper-income occupants who live at lower in-dwelling densities than the poor) also contributes to population decline in older cities, as do expansions of parks, parking lots, universities, hospitals, and superhighways, all of which have absorbed larger proportions of central city land in recent decades.

Given these trends, it would be highly unlikely for central cities to grow much in population and extremely likely for them to lose population. Only newer or "overbounded" central cities would be expected to add residents, and these are found almost exclusively in the South and West (see Figure 6.1). Indeed, 96 of the 100 fastest growing MSAs in the country are located in these two newly urbanizing regions.

By contrast, suburban and exurban areas have increased in population very rapidly in the past 30 years. While these areas have not yet reached their "limits to growth," some parts are beginning to. The inner suburban rings are now almost as built up as the center cities they surround, and in some of these older communities whatever open land remains is being developed for nonresidential purposes. In addition, many suburbs are "protected" by exclusionary zoning (land use laws that specify unusually large lot sizes or elaborate dwellings), which leads developers to leap-frog over them to place new housing in unincorporated areas.[9] One can easily understand why exurban areas (including so-called nonmetropolitan areas not yet declared parts of census-delimited PMSAs and MSAs) might grow faster than inlying suburbs. Areas up to 60 miles or more from metropolitan "centers" have now become attractive sites for urban-linked housing, testifying to America's move into the phase of saturation urbanization.

Spatial Patterns

The spatial repercussions of saturation urbanization can be seen in Figure 6.2A, which shows the distribution of MSAs as of 1985. This map is remarkably similar to Figure 6.2B, prepared by Berry and Gillard, which shows "commuter fields" in 1970.[10] Both indicate the degree to which urban saturation has occurred.

---

[9]See Richard Babcock, "The Spatial Impact of Land-Use and Environmental Controls," pp. 264–287 in Arthur P. Solomon, ed., *The Prospective City: Economic, Population, Energy, and Environmental Developments Shaping Our Cities and Suburbs* (Cambridge, MA: MIT Press, 1980).

[10]Brian Berry and Quentin Gillard, *The Changing Shape of Metropolitan America: Commuting Patterns, Urban Fields and Decentralization Processes, 1960–1970* (Cambridge, MA: Ballinger Publication Co., 1977). Most of this volume consists of detailed maps of individual SMSAs and their commuting fields. The authors conclude that much of the country "is covered by a complex overlapping network of central city commuting fields, standing in sharp contrast to the limited extent of CBD[central business district]-oriented space . . . [which calls] into question the use of uni-centered (CBD-centered) urban models" (p. 46). Further, they note expansions in the commuting fields. Between 1960 and 1970, the "maximum commuting radius of central cities increased from an average of 58 to 64 miles, of counties from 64 to 72 miles, and of SMSAs from 66 to 76 miles" (p. 51), a figure anticipated to continue increasing.

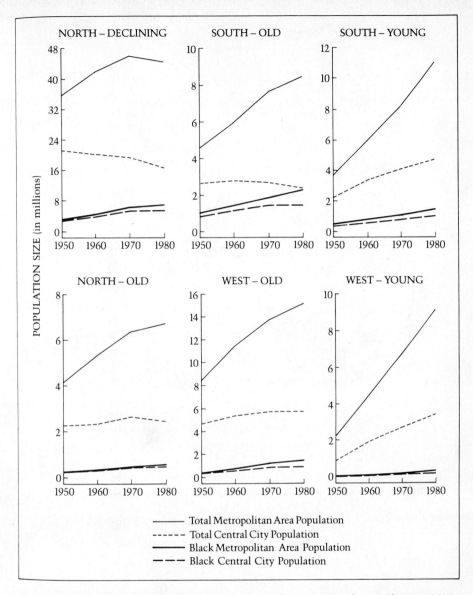

Figure 6.1 Population (total and black) in metropolitan areas and central cities, 1950–1980. Six different types of metropolitan-area groupings. (*Source:* William Frey and Alden Speare, Jr., *Regional and Metropolitan Growth and Decline in the United States.* Copyright © 1988 by The Russell Sage Foundation. Used with permission of the Russell Sage Foundation.)

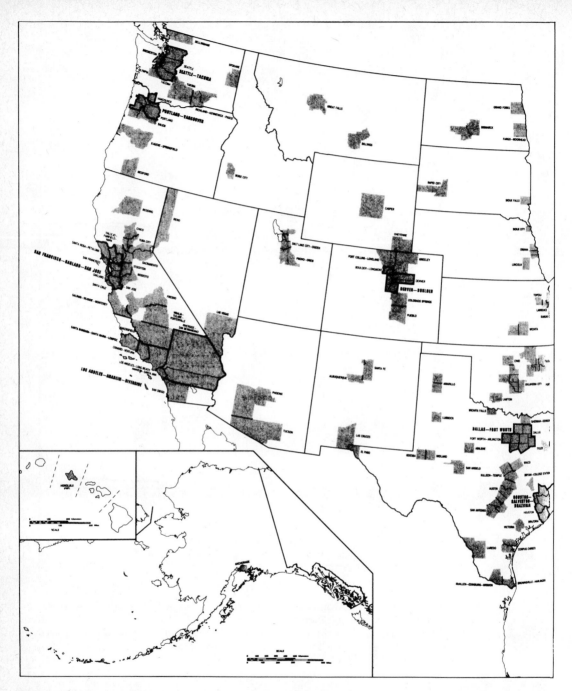

Figure 6.2A Metropolitan Statistical Areas (CMSAs, PMSAs, and MSAs) on June 30, 1985, as delimited by the U. S. Department of Commerce, Bureau of the Census. (*Source:* Bureau of the Census.)

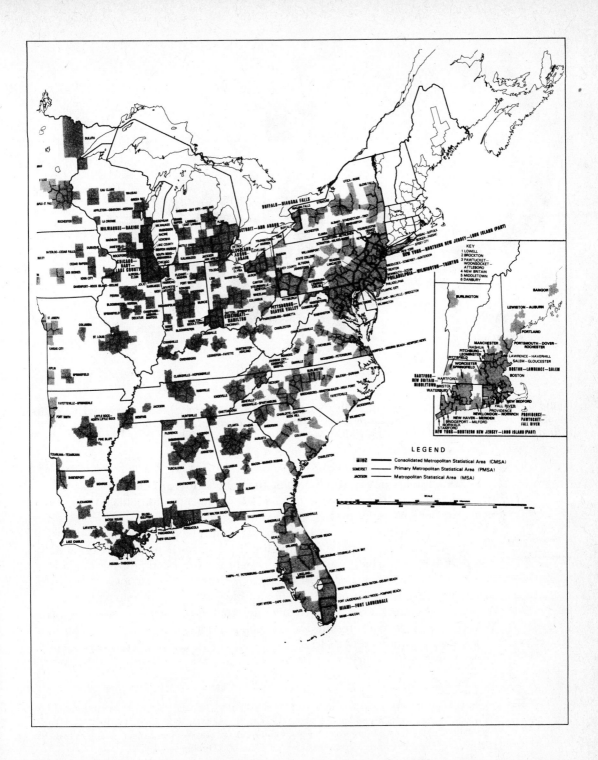

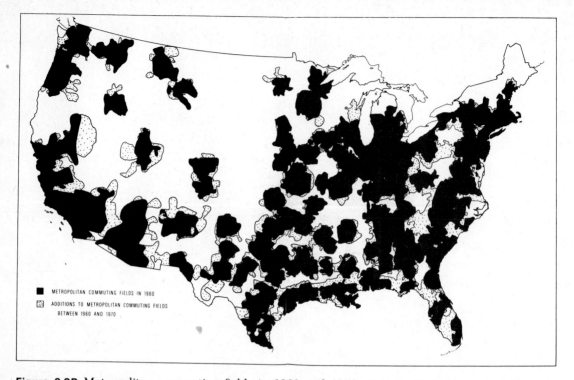

Figure 6.2B Metropolitan commuting fields in 1960 and 1970. (*Source:* Brian Berry and Quentin Gillard, *The Changing Shape of Metropolitan America: Commuting Patterns, Urban Fields and Decentralization Processes, 1960–1970.* Cambridge, MA: Ballinger Publishing Co., 1977.)

Such urban fields now virtually cover the subcontinent. Only the sparsely inhabited badlands, the Rockies, and the desert areas remain outside the dominance of the American metropolitan system.

While the map of MSAs as of 1985 offers impressive evidence of saturation urbanization, it fails to convey the full implications for everyday life created by this new form of urbanism, nor does it capture the changing texture of the landscape. David Meyer's *Urban Change in Central Connecticut: From Farm to Factory to Urban Pastoralism* offers a close-up view of one area literally enveloped by the saturation urbanization that now characterizes the BOS-WASH (Boston to Washington, DC) megalopolis, a conurbation first identified by Jean Gottmann in 1960.[11] In many ways, central Connecticut illustrates the changes in American urbanism described in the last two chapters. However, it

---

[11]Jean Gottmann, *Megalopolis* (Cambridge, MA: MIT Press, 1961); see also Jean Gottmann and Robert A. Harper, eds., *Metropolis on the Move: Geographers Look at Urban Sprawl* (New York: John Wiley, 1967). The phenomenon of giant conurbations was depicted even earlier in [Editors of *Fortune*], *The Exploding Metropolis* (Garden City, NY: Doubleday, 1958).

suggests a future foreseen by neither Le Corbusier nor Wright, containing a strange mixture of those two utopian dreams and revealing some of the problems concealed by their glowing visions.

Connecticut's colonial towns began as ports surrounded by agricultural hinterlands. In the early nineteenth century commerce was supplemented by water-powered industrialization, and in the second half of the nineteenth century the major towns became heavily industrialized, drawing their labor forces from the foreign immigrants who rapidly became the majority. These immigrants lived near the central factories, while the older-stock middle- and upper-class residents either moved farther west or suburbanized along streetcar lines. In the centers of the cities, densities increased and amenities declined as tenement housing went up.

With the decline of old-style industrialization in the twentieth century, the functions of central Connecticut changed again. Engulfed by megalopolis, the major cities became commercial, insurance, and service centers, while the rural areas became low-density residential districts serving the entire zone between Boston and New York City. In the process, central Connecticut lost its old urban character—and became, instead, an *amorphously urbanized* region without a center. In Meyer's words:

> There are no cores in central Connecticut. Rather there are specialized land use activities which the population makes use of. . . . In the six metropolitan areas [of Hartford, New Haven, New Britain, Waterbury, Bristol, and Meriden] . . . between 30 to 46 percent of the workers living in the central city commute to jobs outside it, and except for the New Haven area, fewer than 30 percent of the workers living outside central cities work in them. . . . [Since the development of shopping centers, retail activities largely ignore central cities.] In the metropolitan areas of . . . [the six metropolitan areas], central business district retail sales comprise less than 20 percent of metropolitan sales.[12]

The population of central Connecticut is growing very fast, but this growth is *not* occurring in its center cities. Rather, farming towns and villages are being transformed into residential estates whose occupants spread out in all directions each morning and reconvene in the evening to eat and sleep at home. Community, or "the sense of place," has fragmented, now that no single center attracts everyone.

Despite its prosperity and high growth, this combination of Radiant and Broadacre cities has hidden defects. Most serious are the racial polarizations that segregate darker-skinned city residents from suburban and exurban whites and the class polarizations that have exacerbated fiscal difficulties for the industrial cities inherited by blacks and Hispanics.[13] Meyer summarizes the dilemma: "In the twentieth century central Connecticut is seeing those who can afford

---

[12]David Meyer, *Urban Change in Central Connecticut: From Farm to Factory to Urban Pastoralism* (Cambridge, MA: Ballinger Publishing Co., 1976), extracted from pp. 31–33. Italics added.

[13]*Ibid*., p. 41.

it move to urban pastoral environments. The dynamos of the late nineteenth century—the industrial cities—have become the poor cousins of the twentieth century."[14]

One must ask how these economic and racial cleavages can be healed, and how the benefits of growth can be distributed according to some more equitable principle of social justice.[15] Can "community," the arena within which such disparities have traditionally been contested and negotiated, be reconstituted? Furthermore, one must ponder what it means to live in a society characterized by saturation urbanization, where three-quarters of the population live in metropolitan areas and 95 percent live within daily commuting distance of a city. We do not know the answers to these questions because never before in history have we faced them. Ours are conditions for which prior theories of urban life, premised on the contrast between urban and rural life, have little relevance.

The Need for New Concepts and Theories

Most inherited urban sociological theories focus on the unique cultural and social characteristics of city life, as contrasted with the "more natural" way of life in rural hamlets. The physical isolation of the latter was presumed to nurture "community," personal involvement, and social control, and to bridge class and ethnic barriers. In contrast, the "openness" of urban life was presumed not only to allow variations and deviations otherwise not permissible in a "small society" but also to cause the breakdown of community, the rise of impersonality, and the loss of deep involvement with others. Under conditions of saturation urbanization, however, territorial isolation no longer prevails anywhere. Even if we do not live in or commute to urban places, newspapers, telephones, radio, television, not to mention such newer techniques for bridging distance as computers and fax machines, bring us all within a common web of life whose chief cultural characteristics are urban.

While to some extent this has "homogenized" American life, to some extent it has merely moved the important and relevant contrasts to other levels. The crucial variable is no longer whether one lives in an urbanized region or not. Rather, differences in ways of life are related to:

1. Which *kind* of urbanized region one lives in—large or small, declining or growing, industrial or service-oriented;
2. Which *part* of an urbanized region one lives in—center city, outer city, suburb (old or new) or exurb;
3. How one *relates* to the metropolitanized economy—directly or indirectly, as a member of the dominant mobile elite or as a rejected member of the underclass; and

---

[14]*Ibid.*, p. 51.

[15]This is the key concept in an influential book by David Harvey, *Social Justice and the City* (Baltimore: Johns Hopkins University Press, 1973).

4. To what *extent* one can influence political decisions concerning policies that affect everyone's future.

We shall explore these issues in later sections of this book. But first we need to understand the forces that created urban saturation in the United States.

THE FORCES UNDERLYING THE NEW FORM OF URBANISM

We will examine three factors affecting modern urbanism. First, we explore the demographic changes that underlie both the size and the distribution of urban populations. Second, the changes in the political and economic structure of the United States as it enters the stage of late capitalism, sometimes called the postindustrial age, are examined critically. Finally, we trace how some of these recent changes are being generated, not only within metropolitan America but in the world. As the global system is restructured, American metropolitan areas are coming to perform very different functions in the international division of labor than they did in the past.

Population Changes

One reason American cities are no longer growing as dramatically as they did in the late nineteenth and early twentieth centuries is that U.S. population growth has itself become sluggish. The postwar "baby boom" temporarily masked the effects of the long-term downward trend in American fertility (see Figure 6.3). Just after World War II there was an explosion of marriages and births that had been postponed during wartime. There was a withdrawal into the bosom of the family and a retreat to conventional sex roles. Throughout the United States, the ideal family within the growing middle and upper working classes was an employed husband, a wife/mother at home, and two to four dependent children, preferably to be raised in a suburban single-family owned home. While obviously not all families achieved this ideal, perhaps a larger proportion of them did during the postwar period of prosperity than had earlier or would in the future. That aberration, however, was temporary.

Table 6.4 shows the "boom" and "bust" in fertility that occurred between 1947 and 1980. Fertility rates peaked in 1957, when close to 123 babies were born for every 1000 women in the childbearing years (15–44), and when some 4.3 million Americans were added to the population through births. Thereafter, fertility began to decline, reaching a low point in 1976 when only 65.8 babies were born per 1000 women in the childbearing ages and only 3.17 million Americans were added through births. Natural increase, therefore, no longer contributes much to metropolitan growth. Whereas in the 1960s metropolitan areas were growing at the rate of 1.1 percent per year from natural increase alone, during the early 1970s this had dropped to 0.8 percent and by 1980 stood at under 0.6 percent.

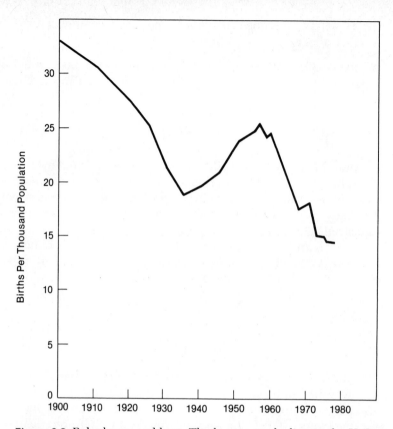

Figure 6.3 Baby boom and bust. The long-term decline in the U. S. birth rate between 1900 and 1980. (*Source:* Adapted from an article by William Alonso in Arthur Solomon, ed., *The Prospective City: Economic, Population, Energy, and Environmental Developments Shaping Our Cities and Suburbs* [Cambridge, MA: MIT Press, 1980]. Copyright 1980 by MIT Press. Used with permission.)

This new lower fertility is associated with some rather deep-seated social trends.[16] These trends were explored in *The Nation's Families: 1960–1990.*[17] The authors attribute the lowered fertility of today's families to the following factors:

1. The tendency for young people to marry later in life.
2. The tendency for couples, even when married, not to have children or, if having them, to bear fewer of them and to bear them later in life.

---

[16]See William Alonso, "The Population Factor and Urban Structure," in Arthur Solomon, ed., *The Prospective City*, pp. 32–51, especially p. 34. See also Edgar Rust's *No Growth: Impacts on Metropolitan Areas* (Lexington, MA: Lexington Books/D. C. Heath, 1975).

[17]George Masnick and Mary Jo Bane, *The Nation's Families: 1960–1990* (Boston: Auburn Publishing House for the Harvard-MIT Joint Center for Urban Studies, 1980).

3. The tendency toward divorce and the rearing of children in single-parent households.
4. The tendency for more women to enter the paid labor force, to remain there longer, and to be involved more in full-time and year-round employment.

Since few if any of these tendencies are likely to be reversed in the near future, natural increase is not likely to be a source of urban population increase, except in those newer cities especially attractive to young adults. The only counter-tendencies are an increase in births to unmarried women and the high fertility rate of some of the United States' most recent immigrants.

The age of population expansion through natural increase is therefore coming to an end. According to projections released by the Bureau of the Census in November 1982, ZPG (zero population growth, the sloganized goal of the ecology movement in the 1960s) may actually be around the corner. By the year 2050, according to census projections, the U.S. population will probably peak at about 310 million before stabilizing or actually beginning to decline. The vital rates that can yield ZPG have already appeared; it is only because our age structure still includes a large number of adults in the childbearing ages (the baby boomers grown up) that population will continue to increase from natural causes until 2050.

To a large extent, the recent stagnation in center city growth and the declines in some metropolitan centers can be attributed to the new low rate of natural increase. But against this negative factor are three compensating ones that will assure continued growth in certain parts of the metropolis and in cities

Table 6.4   THE BABY BOOM AND BUST: FERTILITY RATES AND NUMBER OF TOTAL BIRTHS IN THE UNITED STATES, 1947–1980, AT THREE-YEAR INTERVALS

Years of boom			Years of bust		
Year	Fertility rate*	Births (000's)	Year	Fertility rate*	Births (000's)
1947	113.3	3,817	1965	96.6	3,760
1950	106.2	3,632	1968	85.7	3,502
1953	115.2	3,965	1971	81.8	3,556
1956	121.2	4,218	1974	68.4	3,160
1959	118.8	4,245	1977	67.8	3,327**
1962	112.2	4,167	1980	69.2	3,598

*Number of live births in year per 1000 women aged 15–44. This number is the crucial one to watch, because it is independent of the size of the cohort having babies.

**Beginning of "shadow" baby boom. The increase in the number of babies born results entirely from the large number of "baby boom" girls who entered the childbearing ages in the late 1970s and early 1980s.

Source: Figures have been selected from those appearing in Table I of Bryant Robey, "A Guide to the Baby Boom," *American Demographics* 4 (September 1982), p. 18.

in certain regions of the country. First, urban expansion is affected more by the demand for housing units than by population per se, and such demand continues to spiral upward. Second, since the late 1960s, immigration from abroad has increased and has been directed almost exclusively toward cities. This new immigration, coming chiefly from Mexico and Asia, has changed the traditional urban ports of entry to favor the west coast and the Southwest. And third, as the metropolitan-dominated economy presses out into the countryside, a larger proportion of Americans will be incorporated into the "new form of the city" without changing residence.

Urban expansion is affected more by the demand for dwelling units than by increases in the number of inhabitants. Over the past decade, the number of households (one or more persons living together in a dwelling unit) has gone up much more rapidly than population. To put it another way, the average number of persons sharing a residential unit dropped from 3.11 to 2.75 between 1970 and 1980. The same factors that caused the decline in natural increase rates are responsible for this compensating phenomenon. The "graying" of America, as the population ages, and the greater tendency for older persons to remain in their own quarters rather than move in with children, have led to a disproportionate increase in the number of households. Other factors contributing to this trend are the tendency for young unmarried adults to set up independent households (either singly or with roommates), the tendency for divorced families to subdivide, splitting into two smaller households, and the tendency for the baby boom generation to start forming families.

Indeed, the proportion of households fitting the old ideal of a working father, a stay-at-home mother, and two to four dependent children represented only 9 percent of all households in 1968 and less than 4 percent by 1978, which has led sociologists to call this kind of family a "vanishing species."[18] The projections made by Masnick and Bane estimated that 20 million additional households would be formed between 1975 and 1990—even more than the 19.7 million households added between 1960 and 1975.[19] Therefore, despite the leveling off of the rate of population growth, metropolitan areas would continue to require additional housing and space.

The kinds of housing needed and the locations preferred, however, are considerably different from the past. Most *new* households consist of single men and women and previously married men and women with or without children. Their ability to maintain separate households is highly dependent upon the economy. If prosperity persists, they will undoubtedly continue to exercise their preference for independent households. However, any economic retrenchment could force them to "double up," thus wiping out the demand for expansion in the housing supply.

Locational preferences are easier to predict. Since by 1990 some 31 percent

---

[18]A. Wade Smith and Elsie Moore, paper presented to the American Sociological Association meetings, September 1982.

[19]Masnick and Bane, *The Nation's Families,* pp. 3–4.

Table 6.5   POPULATION TOTALS AND DISTRIBUTION IN STATES OF
            HIGHEST CONCENTRATION, FOR LARGEST NATIONALITY
            GROUPS OF "NEW IMMIGRANTS," 1980

| Group | U.S. total | Percentage distribution by state | | |
		First highest	Second highest	Third highest
Mexican	7,692,619	CA 44	TX 32	IL 5
Chinese	910,843	CA 43	NY 16	HI 10
Cuban	803,226	FL 59	NJ 10	NY 10
Filipino	795,255	CA 44	HI 18	IL 6
Korean	376,676	CA 27	NY 9	IL 6
Asian Indian	311,953	NY 18	CA 16	IL 10
Jamaican	253,268	NY 54	FL 10	NJ 6

Source: U.S. Census, as compiled and published in Jose Hernandez, "Improving the Data: A
Research Strategy for New Immigrants," in Urban Ethnicity in the United States: New Immi-
grants and Old Minorities, eds. Lionel Maldonado and Joan Moore. Vol. 29 of Urban Affairs
Annual Reviews (Beverly Hills, CA: Sage Publications, 1985), Table 4.1, p. 107.

of the households will be husband-and-wife families in which both work, while
another 26 percent will be working single or divorced persons (with or without
children), proximity to the workplace becomes increasingly significant. On the
other hand, only 14 percent of all households will be families in which only one
of the spouses works, while some growing percentage (28 percent) will be
families where no one works (retired, etc.). Only in these latter households
should the relationship between places of employment and residence be relatively unimportant.[20]

Because of the drop in natural increase, migration has become the major
variable affecting growth or decline in American urban areas. Two types of
migration must be distinguished: foreign immigration, which actually increases
total population, and internal migration, which merely shifts population from
one place to another.

With respect to immigration from abroad, the most striking trend has been
its changing source and destination. Whereas in the nineteenth century immigrants came from Europe and settled near their east coast ports of entry, today
immigration comes largely from the Caribbean, Central and South America,
and most recently, Asia, and the new immigrants are settling near their ports
of entry in the South, Southwest and West. Table 6.5 shows the nationalities of
the "new immigrants" and their tendency to concentrate in only a few states,
notably California, Texas, Florida, New York, and Illinois.

While proportionately the approximately 600,000 persons coming from
abroad annually does not match the great migrations of the nineteenth century,
foreign immigration is a leading source of overall national growth because

---

[20]Ibid., p. 5.

natural increase rates have dropped so precipitously. At lease one-third of all growth between 1980 and 1990 has been attributed to foreign immigration. Furthermore, since foreign immigrants are heavily concentrated in metropolitan areas and in only a few subregions of the country, their arrival contributes disproportionately to the expansion of certain regions and cities. This has been particularly true of Spanish-speaking immigrants.

Between 1970 and 1980, America's Hispanic population expanded by more than 60 percent to reach almost 15 million. By 1990, the Hispanic population will have increased to 18.4 million, and by 2000 to 20 million—at which point it will represent 8 percent of the total.[21] While the Hispanic population is quite diverse in origin, the largest proportion (over 60 percent) comes from Mexico. During World War II, at the same time southern blacks were actively recruited to northern industrial cities, Mexicans were recruited to provide cheap agricultural labor to the farms of the Southwest. By 1964, when the bracero program was officially terminated by the United States government, it had brought close to 5 million workers to the States. In addition to this legal program of migrant labor and to regular immigration, there was considerable illegal entry. The U.S. Immigration and Naturalization Service estimated that the number of "illegal" immigrants in the United States (most of these from Mexico) increased from about 162,000 in 1967 to over a million by 1977.[22] This, indeed, was one reason why in 1986 long-resident "illegal" immigrants lacking proper documents were given an opportunity to legalize their status.

Over the years, Chicanos (Mexican-Americans) have become less rural, more metropolitan. In the 1950s about two-thirds lived in metropolitan areas, but by 1970 this had risen to about 85 percent, where it has remained.[23] In addition to the 62.5 percent of Hispanics who are of Mexican origin, another 15 percent are from Puerto Rico, about 7 percent from Cuba, 7 percent from other parts of Central and South America, while the remainder are of diverse origin.[24]

---

[21]It is difficult to compare this figure with census totals for 1960 and 1970 because the census bureau changed its method of reporting Hispanic origin in the interim.

[22]See Alejandro Portes and John Walton, *Labor, Class and the International System* (New York: Academic Press, 1981), p. 47; Table 2.4, p. 53. Their source on the braceros is Julian Samora, *Los Mojados: The Wetback Story* (South Bend, IN: University of Notre Dame Press, 1971). Current estimates of illegal immigrants place this number considerable higher.

[23]See Marta Tienda, "The Mexican-American Population," pp. 502–548 in Amos Hawley and Sara Mills Mazie, eds., *Nonmetropolitan America in Transition* (Chapel Hill, NC: University of North Carolina Press, 1981). She notes (p. 506) that between the mid-1940s and the mid-1960s the Chicano population made the transition from agricultural foreign-born workers to a blue-collar, native-born population residing primarily in large metropolitan areas.

[24]Diverse reports from the 1980 census (especially PC80-S1–1, May 1981) as well as the results of a sample study on Hispanics conducted in 1979 by the Bureau of the Census. These have been updated in U.S. Bureau of the Census, "The Hispanic Population in the United States: March 1988," *Current Population Reports* Series P-20, no. 431 (August 1988), and in "Projections of the Hispanic Population: 1983–2080," *Current Population Reports* Series P-25, no. 995 (1985). The most recent book to consult for information on this population is Juan L. Gonzales, Jr., *Racial and Ethnic Groups in America* (Dubuque, IA: Kendall Hunt, 1990).

Hispanics are not distributed at random throughout the United States. Mexicans remain concentrated in California and the Southwest, Cubans have flocked to Miami, and Puerto Ricans still favor the Northeast. These tendencies account for the peculiar fact that almost three-fourths of all Hispanics are concentrated in only five states in the union: New York, Florida, Texas, California, and Illinois. Of the Hispanics concentrated in these few states, an overwhelming majority are located within major metropolitan areas, as Table 6.6 clearly shows. Obviously, some considerable amount of the growth of the Sunbelt cities can be attributed to the selective immigration of Hispanics and to their overwhelming tendency to settle in metropolitan areas. Table 6.7 gives

Table 6.6 POPULATION OF SPANISH ORIGIN BY REGION OF RESIDENCE AND BY LOCATION IN METROPOLITAN AND NONMETROPOLITAN AREAS, 1980

By region of residence	Number of Hispanics	Percent of All Hispanics
Northeast	2,604,261	18
New England	299,145	
Middle Atlantic*	2,305,116	
North Central	1,276,405	9
East North Central**	1,067,794	
West North Central	208,611	
South	4,473,172	31
South Atlantic†	1,193,823	
East South Central	119,315	
West South Central‡	3,160,034	
West	6,252,045	43
Pacific§	4,810,565	
Mountain	1,441,480	
All regions	14,605,883	100

By metropolitan status		
Inside SMSAs	12,800,000	87.6
Central cities	7,300,000	50.3
Outside central cities	5,440,000	37.3
Outside SMSAs	1,800,000	12.4
All	14,605,883	100.0

*Includes New York State with 1,659,245 Hispanics, mostly Puerto Rican.

**Includes Illinois with 635,525 Hispanics, diverse origins.

†Includes Florida with 857,898 Hispanics, many Cuban.

‡Includes Texas with 2,985,643 Hispanics, mostly Mexican.

§Includes California with 4,543,770 Hispanics, mostly Mexican.

Sources: Returns of the 1980 census.

Table 6.7 HISPANIC POPULATIONS IN METROPOLITAN AREAS HAVING MORE THAN 100,000 HISPANIC PERSONS, 1980

Metropolitan area	Total Hispanic population (000)	Inside central cities (000)	Outside central cities (000)	Inside central cities (%)	Outside central cities (%)
Los Angeles	2,066	867	1,199	42	58
New York–NJ	1,493	1,406	87	94	6
Miami	581	194	387	33	67
Chicago	581	422	159	73	27
San Antonio	482	422	60	88	12
Houston	425	281	144	66	34
San Francisco–Oakland	352	116	236	33	67
Riverside–San Bernardino, CA	290	82	208	28	72
Anaheim–Santa Ana, CA	286	145	141	51	49
San Diego	275	131	146	47	53
Dallas–Fort Worth	249	160	90	64	36
San Jose, CA	227	141	86	62	38
Phoenix	199	116	83	58	42
Denver–Boulder	173	95	78	55	45
Fresno, CA	151	51	99	34	66
Jersey City	145	42	103	29	71
Newark	132	61	71	46	54
Philadelphia (PA–NJ)	116	64	53	55	45
Oxnard–Ventura, CA	113	64	49	57	43
Tucson, AZ	111	82	29	74	26
Nassau–Suffolk countries, NY	102	—	102	—	100
Sacramento, CA	102	39	63	39	61

Source: Bureau of the Census.

the Hispanic population in selected MSAs with large communities. One might note the large number of Hispanics in cities on the west coast and in the South. It is also interesting that except in New York, the Hispanic population is less segregated and more suburbanized than the black population, which is concentrated in central cities.

Other foreign groups have also begun to enter the United States during the most recent period of easier immigration. Asians are still a relatively new and small group, but they are even more likely than Hispanics to settle in the MSAs of the nation. Table 6.8 gives the distribution of various racial groups in the United States in 1980 and compares their degree of "metropolitanization." As can be seen, with the exception of Amerindians, all racial minority groups are more likely to be living in MSAs than are whites. Asian immigration, therefore, has contributed disproportionately to metropolitan growth.

In contrast to the metropolitan growth that has been taking place due to

Table 6.8   DISTRIBUTION AND METROPOLITAN STATUS OF RACIAL GROUPS, UNITED STATES, 1980

	Total	White	Black	American Indian	Asian Pacific	Other
Inside SMSAs (%)	74.8	73.3	81.1	47.5	90.4	87.2
Inside Central Cities (%)	30.0	24.9	57.8	20.7	46.0	54.2
Outside Central Cities(%)	44.8	48.4	23.3	26.8	44.4	33.0
Outside SMSAs (%)	25.2	26.7	18.9	52.5	9.6	12.8
Number (in 000s)	226,505	188,341	26,488	1,418	3,501	6,757
Percentage of total U.S. population*	100.0	83.2	11.7	0.6	1.5	3.0

*Before rounding to 000s.

Source: 1980 Census of Population and Housing, Supplementary Report PC80-S1-1 (May 1981), p. 25.

foreign immigration, the oldest metropolitan centers no longer seem to be growing from internal migration. Rather, as the U.S. population redistributes itself regionally, the urban areas in the West and South and the zones beyond the existing MSAs are attracting population from the old manufacturing belt cities and their suburbs. African-Americans, who formerly contributed greatly to northern urban growth, are now remaining in the South or returning to it,[25] while other internal migrants who came from depressed regions may also be following suit. (Whether this situation was linked to the recessionary period of the late 1970s and early 1980s or indicates a longer-term trend cannot yet be determined.) Certainly, as the number of older retired persons living on transfer payments (pensions and social security) increases, more are free to move to warmer climates or lower-cost rural areas. And finally, as "the city moves to the countryside," to repeat Frank Lloyd Wright's only partially correct prediction, many people are able to remain where they are in nonmetropolitan areas, while increasingly benefiting from the decentralization of jobs, the expansion of commuting fields, and electronic "wiring" which permits widely separated persons to communicate with one another and even, increasingly, to tie into central systems without proximity. Melvin Webber, in a perspicacious article written in the early 1960s,[26] predicted a time when the dominant urban form would be "no place city," the point not of human physical interaction but of nodes in a complex system of information intersection.

Regardless of what has caused it, the fact is that net migration from

---

[25]See Thomas F. Pettigrew, "Racial Change and the Intrametropolitan Distribution of Black Americans," pp. 52–79 in Solomon, ed. *The Prospective City,* especially pp. 60–61 and 71–73. See also pp. 149–152 in William H. Frey and Alden Speare, Jr., *Regional and Metropolitan Growth and Decline in the United States* (New York: Russell Sage Foundation, 1988).

[26]Melvin Webber, "The Urban Place and the Nonplace Urban Realm," pp. 79–153, in Melvin Webber *et al.,* eds., *Explorations into Urban Social Structure* (Philadelphia: University of Pennsylvania Press, 1964). In this work, Webber anticipates some of the most advanced concepts in the field, *viz.,* Castells (1989) cited below.

nonmetropolitan areas no longer makes the contribution it formerly did to the growth of major metropolitan areas. It is this phenomenon that has led many analysts to talk about a return to the countryside or a renaissance in rural America.[27] We believe it would be a mistake, however, to interpret this trend as a devolution of urbanism. Rather, in the following section which describes recent changes in the economic organization of American business, we show how decentralization of production is going hand in hand with centralization of decision making. It is the former that gives to the newer pattern of settlement the appearance of Broadacre City, the "demetropolitanization" identified by these analysts. But it is the latter—namely the centralization of decision making, finance, and producers' services—that is also yielding, in the few cities of the nation that serve international functions, the appearance of Radiant City, within which tall towers compete with one another for space and light and multinational firms compete with the world for power.

Political and Economic Changes

The decades since World War II have revealed a major societal transformation[28] which many observers consider a "third wave"[29] as significant in scope as the first that brought forth the agricultural revolution or the second that led to the Industrial Revolution. The hallmark of this third revolution is the "production" and "distribution" of knowledge/information, originally identified as

---

[27]Calvin L. Beale, *The Revival of Population Growth in Nonmetropolitan America* (Economic Development Division, U.S. Department of Agriculture, ERS-605, 1975); Calvin L. Beale, "The Recent Shift in United States Population to Nonmetropolitan Areas, 1970–1975," *International Regional Science Review* 2 (1977), pp. 113–122; and Calvin L. Beale, "Internal Migration in the United States Since 1970," mimeographed statement before Select Committee on Population, U.S. House of Representatives, 1978. See also Brian Berry, ed., *Urbanization and Counter-Urbanization*, vol. 11 of *Urban Affairs Annual Reviews* (Beverly Hills, CA: Sage Publications, 1976); David L. Brown and John Wardwell, eds., *New Directions in Urban-Rural Migration: The Population Turnaround in Rural America* (New York: Academic Press, 1980), especially Wardwell's chapter, "Toward a Theory of Urban-Rural Migration in the Developed World," pp. 71–114; Amos Hawley and Sara Mills Mazie, eds., *Nonmetropolitan America in Transition* (Chapel Hill: University of North Carolina Press, 1981); Kevin McCarthy and Peter Morrison, *The Changing Demographic and Economic Structure of Nonmetropolitan Areas in the United States* (Santa Monica, CA: The Rand Corporation for U.S. Economic Development Administration, 1979); Peter Morrison and Judith Wheeler, "Rural Renaissance in America? The Revival of Population Growth in Remote Areas," *Population Bulletin* 31 (Population Reference Bureau, 1976); George Sternlieb and James Hughes, eds., *Post-Industrial America: Metropolitan Decline and Inter-Regional Job Shifts* (New Brunswick, NJ: The Center for Urban Policy Research, Rutgers University, 1975); Wilbur Zelinsky, "Is Nonmetropolitan America Being Repopulated? The Evidence from Pennsylvania's Minor Civil Divisions," *Demography* 15 (1978), pp. 13–39; James Zuiches, "Residential Preferences: Implications for Population Redistribution in Nonmetropolitan Areas," in Sara Mills Mazie, ed., *Population Distribution and Policy*, vol. 5 of Commission Research Reports (1972). See also Zuiches's articles in Brown and Wardwell; Hawley and Mazie.

[28]See Donald A. Hicks, ed., *Urban America in the Eighties: Perspectives and Prospects: Report of the Panel on Policies and Prospects for Metropolitan and Nonmetropolitan America* (New Brunswick, NJ: Transaction Books, 1982).

[29]Alvin Toffler, *The Third Wave* (New York: Bantam Books, 1980).

the cybernetic revolution. Two very different interpretations of this trend have been advanced. The first is Daniel Bell's, as expressed in his *The Coming of Post-Industrial Society.*[30] The second is the position of Ernest Mandel in his book entitled *Late Capitalism.*[31] These two views are well summarized by John Walton:

> In postindustrial society [as interpreted by Bell] the fulcrum of the economy shifts from manufacturing to the tertiary sector of commerce and services, the semi-skilled and engineering occupations are replaced by the professional and technical, technical skill comes to rival property as a basis of power, and the university replaces the business enterprise as the primary institution. Alternatively . . . [Mandel has] suggested that the advanced societies have moved to the stage of "late capitalism [which] far from representing a 'post-industrial society,' thus appears as the period in which all branches of the economy [including the service sector] are fully industrialized for the first time." Late capitalism follows on the era of monopoly capitalism and is made possible by the "third technological revolution" in which machines now produce raw materials and foodstuffs, automate industry, and invade the realm of circulation.[32]

Regardless of which interpretation one accepts, the basic facts are not in question. All acknowledge that the post-1960 American economy has been restructured.

Indications of this restructuring are found in labor force statistics. Just as in the Industrial Revolution agricultural employment gave way to manufacturing, so in the third revolution manufacturing has given way to services. To comprehend this change, one need only realize that some 90 percent of all jobs *added* between 1970 and 1980 were in services. By 1977, the service sector accounted for over two-thirds of all workers in the U.S. labor force, as can be seen from Table 6.9. Although somewhat differently computed, data from the 1980 census confirm the overwhelming significance of services. Of all employed persons 16 years of age and older in the United States in 1980, less than 4 percent still worked in the primary sector, while well over 60 percent were directly engaged in service-sector occupations.[33]

There are two remarkable facts that need to be emphasized in evaluating

---

[30]Daniel Bell, *The Coming of Post-Industrial Society: A Venture Towards Social Forecasting* (New York: Basic Books, 1973). The quotation included in the excerpt from Walton (see note 32) is cited as coming from p. 112 of Bell's book. A collection of essays that takes this perspective is Solomon, ed., *The Prospective City.* Manuel Castells, in *The Information City* (New York: Basil Blackwell, 1989), takes this approach further and treats infomation as a "new mode of develoment."

[31]Ernest Mandel, *Late Capitalism* (London: NLB, 1975). The quotation in the Walton excerpt is cited as p. 191.

[32]See Chapter 5 in Portes and Walton, *Labor, Class, and the International System,* especially p. 139, from which the quotation has been taken. Another formulation is described in Gary Gappert, "Future Urban America: Post-Affluent or Advanced Industrial Society," pp. 1–34 in G. Gappert and Richard Knight, eds., *Cities in the 21st Century,* vol. 23 of *Urban Affairs Annual Reviews* (Beverly Hills, CA: Sage Publications, 1982).

[33]Calculated from Table P-3 on "Labor Force Characteristics" of U.S. Department of Commerce, Bureau of the Census, *1980 Census of Population and Housing,* Supplementary Report PHC80-S1.

Table 6.9   EMPLOYMENT BY ECONOMIC SECTOR FOR METROPOLITAN AND
NONMETROPOLITAN AREAS, 1970 AND 1977

| | Thousands of employed persons 16+ years of age in | | | | | |
| | Metropolitan | | Nonmetropolitan | | Total | |
Sector	1970	1977	1970	1977	1970	1977
Primary Production:						
Agriculture, mining,						
forestry, fishing	1,051	1,149	2,379	2,601	3,431	3,751
Secondary Production:						
Manufacturing and						
construction	16,753	16,667	7,384	8,578	21,137	25,256
Tertiary Production:						
All services	35,316	42,854	12,378	16,360	47,694	59,214
All Sectors:						
Total employment	53,119	60,681	22,140	27,539	75,260	88,221
	Percentage of all employed persons 16+ years of age in					
Primary	1.97	1.89	10.75	9.44	4.56	4.25
Secondary	31.50	27.47	33.35	31.15	27.69	28.63
Tertiary	66.50	70.62	55.90	59.40	63.37	67.12
All	100.00	100.00	100.00	100.00	100.00	100.00

Note: Employees are classified by place of residence, not by place of employment. This table thus overestimates nonmetropolitan employment because many nonmetropolitan residents are employed in SMSAs, and many counties that were nonmetropolitan in 1970 have subsequently been reclassified as metropolitan by 1980.

Source: Various issues of *Current Population Reports,* as assembled in Table 6.1, pp. 234–235, of Mark David Menchik, "The Service Sector," in Hawley and Mazie, eds., *Nonmetropolitan America in Transition* (Chapel Hill, NC: University of North Carolina Press, 1981).

the so-called shift to service occupations. The first is that the expansion in services has been almost exclusively achieved by the increased labor-force participation rate of women. By 1985, 5 percent of male workers were in the primary sector (farming, forestry, and fishing), 41 percent worked in the secondary sector (chiefly industry and transport), while 53 percent were in the tertiary or service sector. This contrasts markedly with the distribution of the female labor force. Almost 88 percent of women work in the service sector, less than 12 percent in industry, and only 1 percent in the primary sector.[34]

The second important fact is that the occupations of persons living in metropolitan areas and those living in nonmetropolitan areas have grown increasingly alike, which supports our contention that saturation urbanization has really arrived. In contrast to the increasing duality of the labor market for males and females, a single labor market has replaced the dual spatial one in which

---

[34]United States Department of Commerce, Bureau of the Census, *Population Profile of the United States 1984/85* (1987), p. 31.

Table 6.10   PERCENTAGE DISTRIBUTION OF FULL-TIME EQUIVALENT EMPLOYMENT AND
CONTRIBUTION TO GROSS NATIONAL PRODUCT BY SECTOR, 1947–1977

Sector	Share of employment (%)			Share of GNP (%)		
	1947	1969	1977	1947	1969	1977
Agriculture	4.3	1.7	1.9	5.6	3.1	2.9
Extractive/Transformative						
(Manufacturing)	39.1	33.4	29.0	31.8	32.9	29.9
Services	56.6	64.9	68.4	62.7	64.0	66.1
Producer/Distributive	19.6	21.0	23.2	28.9	33.3	36.6
Nonprofit/Government	16.8	25.2	25.9	17.3	17.6	16.5
Retail and Consumer	20.2	18.8	19.2	16.5	13.1	13.0

Note: The categories are slightly different from those used in Table 6.9. Employed persons in Table 6.10 are measured in full-time equivalents, whereas in Table 6.9 the numbers refer to all employed persons, including part-time and part-year workers. Therefore, the figures in the two tables are not comparable.

Source: Table 2.1 of Thierry Noyelle and Thomas Stanback, Jr., *The Economic Transformation of American Cities* (Totowa, NJ: Allanheld, Osman, 1984), p. 17, modified for this text. Their table was generated from data available in U.S. Department of Commerce, Bureau of Economic Analysis, *The National Income and Product Accounts of the United States, 1929–74,* and *Survey of Current Business,* July 1978.

"rural" people worked in primary production while urbanites worked in the secondary (manufacturing) and tertiary (service) sectors. This change is demonstrated in Table 6.9.

Not captured in Table 6.9 are changes in the *kinds* of services or the differential rates at which these have been expanding. The problem is that "service sector" is too gross a category, including physicians and domestic servants, the President of the United States and shoe shine boys. Finer breakdowns are needed to evaluate the real shifts that have been occurring within the service sector. For this, the work of Thomas Stanback, Jr. and his associates is invaluable—particularly the book by Thierry Noyelle and Thomas Stanback, Jr., *The Economic Transformation of American Cities.* [35]

In this book the authors subdivide the service sector into six subtypes, each with a different history of growth. We have collapsed their six types into three: (1) services connected to the production or distribution of goods; (2) services that deal with customers or consumers; and (3) services offered by nonprofit or governmental organizations (health, education, etc.). When the employment in and the percentage of GNP contributed by each of these three subtypes are analyzed over time, the transformation in the American service economy becomes evident.

As can be seen from Table 6.10, since 1947 agricultural employment and

---

[35]Thierry Noyelle and Thomas Stanback, Jr., *The Economic Transformation of American Cities* (Totowa, NJ: Allanheld, Osmun, 1984). See also, for example, Thomas M. Stanback, Jr., Peter J. Bearse, Thierry Noyelle, and Robert Karasek, *Services/The New Economy* (Totowa, NJ: Allanheld, Osmun, 1981); and T. Stanback, Jr., *Understanding the Service Economy: Employment, Productivity, Location* (Baltimore: Johns Hopkins University Press, 1979).

the percentage of the gross national product (GNP) originating in the primary sector declined markedly. In contrast, manufacturing (the extractive/transformative category) continued to contribute almost as great a share to the GNP in 1977 as in 1947, but it did so with a smaller proportion of the labor force—the percentage of all jobs in manufacturing dropped from 39 percent in 1947 to 29 percent by 1977. The rise in service employment compensated for the declines in the agricultural and manufacturing sectors, but not all types of services expanded equally. Services involved in consumer contact actually declined, in terms of employment and in relative contribution to the GNP. It was only in the other two categories, producer/distributive services (to businesses and manufacturing) and services offered through government and nonprofit organizations, that increases were recorded. The former might more properly be thought of as part of production, while the latter reflects the expanding role of governmental "collective consumption."

The spatial implications of the shift to services are not the same for all three categories. Manufacturing and population have both been decentralizing.[36] The decentralization of population encourages a comparable decentralization of customer and consumer services. The same is not necessarily true with respect to either producer/distribution services or government/nonprofit services. In fact, both of these have actually been gravitating to the larger central cities of major metropolitan areas. Blue-collar and clerical/sales jobs may be declining in these cities, but jobs in the "new" services are definitely increasing.

This paradox is captured in J. Thomas Black's article on "The Changing Economic Role of Central Cities and Suburbs," which explains why, despite declines in residences, manufacturing, and even services of certain kinds, the largest cities are experiencing a heightened demand for downtown office space. The author notes:

> Central corporate offices, financial institutions, and the more specialized business and consumer services . . . all continue to value central locations because of the benefits of face to face contact among the professionals and managers and the economies of the agglomeration of different high-grade and specialized service and other business and financial activities.[37]

The expansion of these kinds of activities signals the restructuring of the American urban system into a more differentiated hierarchy of urban places. Both the decentralization of production and the centralization of administrative control reflect a basic reorganization of American business.

Firms have grown into larger, conglomerate, multilocational corporations whose centers of control are increasingly disengaged from the sites of their productive operations. Allan Pred notes that these kinds of firms have been

---

[36]See John F. Long, "Population Deconcentration in the United States," *Special Demographic Analyses* CDS-81–5, Department of Commerce, Bureau of the Census (Washington, DC: Government Printing Office, November 1981).

[37]J. Thomas Black, "The Changing Economic Role of Central Cities and Suburbs," in Solomon, ed., *The Prospective City*, pp. 80–123. Quotation from p. 108.

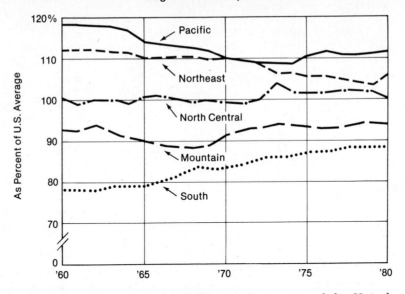

Figure 6.4 Decline in income differences by regions of the United States, 1960–1980. (*Source:* Based on U. S. Census reports.)

gaining an ever larger share of the economy and, therefore, of its jobs. Thus, "between 1960 and 1973 the number of domestic and foreign jobs controlled by the 500 largest multilocational industrial organizations in the United States grew from 9.2 to over 15.5 million." Pred concludes that "[t]he situation in the U.S., as well as in other advanced economies, has reached a stage where a clear majority of private sector employment is directly associated with domestically headquartered multilocational corporations and firms."[38]

The headquarters of these firms, which perform the control functions and which utilize specialized informational and financial services which they share with other large corporations, are located in only a few major metropolitan centers in the United States. The actual factories, warehouses, and sales outlets they control are increasingly dispersed to the exurbs or to low-labor-cost regions of the country, or even "shipped" overseas, as we shall see in the next section.

This disengagement is responsible for the paradoxes we observe in today's urban system. First, despite the spread of urban saturation and the greater regional income equality this has generated (see Figure 6.4 and Table 6.11), differences between urban places have grown more marked. Second, despite

---

[38]The essential source is Allan Pred, *City-Systems in Advanced Economies* (New York: John Wiley, 1977). Quotations are from pp. 98–99. Pred notes that "during the 1960s and early 1970s explicit and implicit locational decisions in the U.S . . . and other advanced economies led to a growing concentration of the most information-sensitive office employment in major metropolitan complexes at the same time as those places experienced absolute losses in manufacturing production-line employment" (p. 26).

Table 6.11 PER CAPITA INCOME INDEXED TO THE U.S. NATIONAL AVERAGE, BY REGIONS, 1840–1975

Year	New England	Mid-Atlantic	East North Central	West North Central	North Atlantic	East South Central	West South Central	Mountain	Pacific
1975	108	108	104	98	90	79	91	92	111
1970	108	113	105	95	86	74	85	90	110
1965	108	114	108	95	81	71	83	90	115
1960	109	116	107	93	77	67	83	95	118
1950	106	116	112	94	74	63	81	96	121
1940	121	124	112	84	69	55	70	92	138
1930	129	140	111	82	56	48	61	83	130
1920	124	134	108	87	59	52	72	100	135
1900	134	139	106	97	45	49	61	139	163
1880	141	141	102	90	45	51	70	168	204
1860	143	137	69	66	65	68	115	—	—
1840	132	136	67	75	70	73	144	—	—

Note: Index shows percentage above or below national average in that year. Note regional convergence.

Source: 1840–1970, *Historical Statistics of the United States, Colonial Times to 1970*, Washington, DC: Department of Commerce, 1975, p. 242; *Survey of Current Business*, vol. 56, August 1976, Table 2, p. 17. Reproduced from W. W. Rostow, "Regional Changes in the Fifth Kondratieff Upswing," in David Perry and Alfred Watkins, eds., *The Rise of the Sunbelt Cities* (Beverly Hills, CA: Sage Publications, 1977), p. 85.

productivity improvements and heightened profits to the large firms headquartered in major cities, inequalities within cities have been growing. In the same cities that serve as national headquarters for the largest firms, a high proportion of urban residents are unemployed and very poor, since the jobs controlled by these firms are either not located within the area or are in administrative, high-technology, or financial-specialized services, rather than in blue-collar or even clerical occupations.

The growing inequality among urban places has been documented by Noyelle and Stanback. Their analysis goes beyond the superficial distinction of cities in the Sunbelt versus cities in the Frostbelt and beyond the controversy over metropolitan versus nonmetropolitan growth. They find the key to recent developments in the American urban system in an increasing dichotomy between, on the one hand, nodal and specialized-service cities, and on the other hand, production centers and consumer-oriented service cities.

The nodal centers and the specialized-service cities serve as the locus for major economic decision-makers who determine where new investments will be located. In contrast, manufacturing centers and consumer-oriented service cities have become increasingly dependent on the broad economic directions mapped out by those decision-makers, and thus have increasingly lost control over their economic destinies.[39] Firms whose headquarters are in the handful

---

[39]Noyelle and Stanback, Jr., *The Economic Transformation of American Cities*, p. 10.

of national nodal MSAs are deciding to relocate industrial production to the Sunbelt, to nonmetropolitan areas, and now, increasingly, to Third World countries with even lower labor costs. Largely because the older cities in the North and North Central have aging economic infrastructures and are heavily unionized, newer (and faster-growing) industries are being relocated to nonmetropolitan areas or Sunbelt cities.[40]

Noyelle and Stanback classified the 140 largest SMSAs in the country on the basis of their economic "functions." At the top of the hierarchy were only four metropolitan regions—New York, Los Angeles, Chicago, and San Francisco—which they identified as national nodal centers. In the section that follows we show that these are also world cities, and that they serve not only to coordinate American internal economic activities but to articulate the American economy with the world economy. It is this latter function that ensures their hegemony in the U.S. urban system.

Beneath these four national (or rather, international) nodal centers are 19 regional nodal centers scattered throughout the country which, while not often containing national headquarters of major corporations, are the sites for their regional sales offices. In addition, they identify 16 other SMSAs, similarly scattered, that serve as subregional nodal centers. In general, all cities serving as diversified nodal centers are growing, in terms of both size and control over the economy.

In contrast, manufacturing centers are not growing or are even declining, because production has dropped or been decentralized. A disproportionate

---

[40]David C. Perry and Alfred J. Watkins, eds., *The Rise of the Sunbelt Cities,* vol. 14 of *Urban Affairs Annual Reviews* (Beverly Hills, CA: Sage, 1977) takes a somewhat different approach. We must ask why these firms decided to move their operations to the exurbs, to other regions of the country (including the Sunbelt), and even overseas. The answer is technological and financial.

First, automation of industrial production makes it possible to employ fewer and less skilled workers. Such workers can be obtained from a wider arena than the skilled workers formerly required for industrial production. Not only are they more generally available, but if they are recruited from areas with labor surplus or where unionization has not yet taken hold, they are considerably cheaper. Where labor intensive operations persist, the cheapest sources lie overseas, rather than in the United States.

Second, there are incentives to business to set up new firms in certain parts of the country or to internationalize their operations. Roger Vaughan ("The Impact of Federal Policies on Urban Economic Development," pp. 348–398 in Solomon, ed., *The Prospective City*) argues that "Federal policies have encouraged the movement of jobs from the Northeast toward the South and West and from central cities to suburbs and even nonmetropolitan areas. This consistent direction of influence has resulted largely from a favoring of new development over rehabilitation and repair. The bias runs through expenditure policies, the tax structure, and even through regulatory policies" (pp. 391–392). While federal policies have not been the root cause of decentralization, they have accentuated market forces such as technological change and changes in world trade patterns (p. 393). These points are underlined in George Peterson's article in this same book, "Federal Tax Policy and the Shaping of Urban Development," pp. 399–425; Peterson points out that federal subsidies have made it almost a foregone conclusion that the West and South and newer urban areas would be favored over older regions and cities. Finally, there is the question of internationalization. Here the advantages of multinational organization are enormous; it is easy to hide profits, transfer resources via bookkeeping to protect them from taxation, and so on.

Table 6.12   REGIONAL DISTRIBUTION OF MAJOR
TYPES OF SMSAs BY REGIONS, 1976

	Frostbelt	Sunbelt
Nodal Centers		
National Nodal	2	2
Regional Nodal	10	9
Subregional Nodal	3	13
Specialized Service Centers		
Functional Nodal	19	5
Government	7	8
Education	4	1
Consumer Oriented Centers		
Residential	2	1
Resort-Retirement	0	9
Production Centers		
Manufacturing	20	5
Industrial-Military	0	13
Mining-Industrial	2	5
Total	69	71

Source: Compiled and simplified from Thierry Noyelle and Thomas
Stanback, Jr., The Economic Transformation of American Cities
(Totowa, NJ: Allanheld, Osmun, 1984), Table 4.4, pp. 64–65.

number of these manufacturing cities are in the Frostbelt. Only two types of
specialized service or production centers have actually been experiencing
much growth: government and education centers, and industrial-military centers (the high-tech industries of weapons, aerospace, etc.). Both of these tend
to be located in the Sunbelt. Finally, Noyelle and Stanback identify a handful
of consumer-oriented SMSAs, most of which are resort-retirement centers.
Almost all of these are growing rapidly as older people flock to them, and almost
all are in the Sunbelt.

Thus, the differential growth rates of Frostbelt and Sunbelt cities are linked
to the restructuring of the American economy. Table 6.12 shows Noyelle and
Stanback's tally of the regional location of SMSAs by functional type; their text
explains the historical reasons why cities in these different regions are growing
at such different rates.

The restructuring of American corporations has not only caused increased
differentiation within the national urban system, but has also intensified cleavages within the major cities. It is perhaps significant that the New York CMSA,
which contains the corporate headquarters of 200 of the 500 largest firms in the
nation, also contains the highest proportion of families with incomes below the
poverty level among the major MSAs (according to 1980 census findings). For
an adequate explanation of this paradox of joblessness and poverty within the
context of corporate prosperity, one must look not only to the hierarchical
patterns of organization within the country but also to the evolving articulation
of the American economy with the world.

Relation of the United States to the World

The third factor that shapes urbanization is the relationship of cities to their empires. This could be seen quite clearly in the great early civilizations when "empire" was a tangible political entity whose boundaries were identified in terms of military vassalage and the payment of tribute. Even during the nineteenth century (when "empire" was defined as the right of a colonial power to extract surplus from a "backward" area), spheres of influence, protectorates, and direct rule identified the imperial domains of various powers. Today the nature of empire has changed as the world is increasingly brought within a single economic system. This system is harder to study because it is run not so much by states as by transnational corporations which, while centered in advanced nations, coordinate the economic activities of far-flung empires of firms, subsidiaries, contractors, and other agents located throughout the world.[41] The system has attracted growing attention from both world-system scholars[42] and more popular writers.[43]

New York, Chicago, Los Angeles, and San Francisco, the four cities that presently head the U.S. urban hierarchy, are essentially international or "empire" cities. When one examines the international context in which they operate, one discovers many other cities which have increasingly come to be linked in an international network of cities that controls the global economy (see Figure 6.5). The exploratory work of John Friedmann and Goetz Wolff is especially relevant to these points. In their article, "World City Formation: An Agenda for Research and Action,"[44] they describe an "emerging world system of production and markets" that is directed through a global network of cities. These world cities are all very large metropolitan areas, with five to 15 million inhabitants, that "play a vital part in the great capitalist undertaking to organize the world for the efficient extraction of surplus." Friedmann and Wolff argue:

> Since the second world war, the processes by which capitalist institutions have freed themselves from national constraints and have proceeded to organize global production and markets for their own intrinsic purposes have greatly accelerated. The actors principally responsible for reorganizing the economic map of the world are the transnational corporations. . . . The emerging global system of economic

[41]As usual, Jean Gottmann has been among the first to spot this new trend. See his edited book, *Centre and Periphery: Spatial Variations in Politics* (Beverly Hills, CA: Sage Publications, 1980), especially the article entitled "Organizing and Reorganizing Space," pp. 217–224. Interesting comparative work on imperial cities is being done by Christopher Chase-Dunn; see, for example, "The System of World Cities, 800–1975," in Michael Timberlake, ed., *Urbanization in the World-Economy* (Orlando, FL: Academic Press, 1985).

[42]See Terence K. Hopkins, Immanuel Wallerstein and associates, *World-Systems Analysis: Theory and Methodology* (Beverly Hills, CA: Sage Publications, 1982).

[43]Richard J. Barnet and Ronald E. Muller, *Global Reach: The Power of Multinational Corporations* (New York: Simon & Schuster, 1974).

[44]John Friedmann and Goetz Wolff, "World City Formation: An Agenda for Research and Action," *International Journal of Urban and Regional Research* 6 (1982), pp. 309–343.

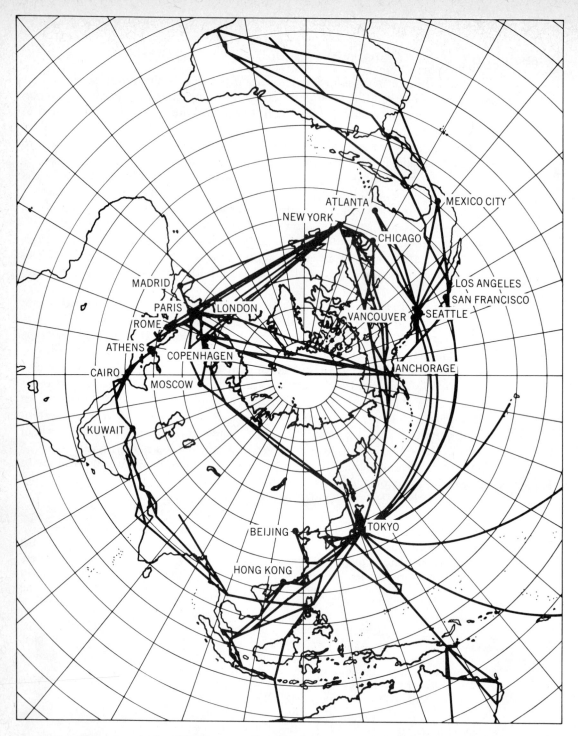

Figure 6.5 The network of world cities, seen from a polar projection. (*Source:* Based on a map originally prepared by John Friedmann and Goetz Wolff for their article on 'world cities' [*International Journal of Urban and Regional Research*] but not included in the published version.)

relations assumes its material form in particular, typically urban, localities. . . . At the apex of this hierarchy [of control] are found a small number of massive urban regions that we shall call world cities. Tightly interconnected with each other through decision-making and finance, they constitute a worldwide system of control over production and market expansion.[45]

These world cities, which include Tokyo, Los Angeles, San Francisco, New York, Miami, London, Paris, Frankfurt, Zurich, Singapore, Hong Kong, and Mexico City, are different from earlier imperial cities, because the system to which they are linked is worldwide in scope. Even Rome at its most imperial or London at the height of the British Empire never dominated more than a small fraction of the entire globe.[46]

What Noyelle and Stanback describe on the level of the American urban system, Friedmann and Wolff demonstrate on the international level. They note that as a shrinking number of giant multinational firms gain control over the world economy, decision making is increasingly disengaged spatially from the production lines. This disengagement, similar to what we have already seen on the U.S. urban system level, has been facilitated by many of the same technological and organizational shifts. As production becomes automated, it is increasingly feasible to locate factories in places with low labor skills and, especially, with low labor costs. As the income inequalities between regions in the United States decrease, the comparative advantage of moving westward or into the Sunbelt declines, while the attractiveness of Third World countries increases. But on the other hand, as technology becomes more refined, information processing represents a rising proportion of value-added.

Just as the few largest U.S. cities that attract corporate headquarters have become heavily specialized in producer services, so also "the core countries of capitalism are . . . assigned the role of research lab, control room, and financier, while the periphery produces."[47] This new international division of labor has recently attracted considerable attention from scholars, but few have traced how changes on the international level reflect back on the problems of American cities. The early exceptions are the article by Friedmann and Wolff (cited above), the anthology compiled by Dear and Scott,[48] various works by Bluestone and Harrison,[49] and the co-authored book by Portes and Walton (cited

---

[45]*Ibid.*, p. 310.

[46]*Ibid.*, p. 311.

[47]*Ibid.*, p. 316.

[48]Michael Dear and Allen J. Scott, eds., *Urbanization and Urban Planning in Capitalist Society* (New York: Methuen, 1981), especially the article by R. B. Cohen, "The New International Division of Labor, Multinational Corporations and Urban Hierarchy," pp. 287–315.

[49]See Barry Bluestone and Bennett Harrison, *Capital and Communities: The Causes and Consequences of Private Disinvestment* (Washington, DC: The Progressive Alliance, 1980); and their *The Deindustrialization of America* (New York: Basic Books, 1982). Even conservative publications acknowledge the influence of internationalization on the American urban economy. See, for example, *Cities in a Larger Context*, ed. Thomas W. Collins (Athens, GA: University of Georgia Press,

above). Among the more recent additions to this literature are books by Henderson and Castells, by Taylor and Thrift, by Saskia Sassen, and by Anthony King.[50] Edward Soja and his colleagues have also published an important article on Los Angeles.[51] These authors agree that one can understand neither the increased differentiation within the urban hierarchy in the United States nor the increased polarization of classes within nodal centers of the nation without reference to the changing world economy.

While it is easy to recognize that the international economy has an effect on cities in the United States, it is difficult to measure or trace this effect. Some estimate of the degree to which international trade contributes to the economy of certain urban centers in the United States is found in Table 6.13. Such trade has increased enormously within the last few decades. In 1960 the United States was a "closed" economy in which imports and exports represented only about 5 percent of what was produced and consumed. The American economy is now much more open, "with 20 percent of the goods it produces shipped abroad and something like 25 percent of the goods it consumes shipped in."[52] New York City is the major beneficiary of this new "imperial" system.

The negative side of the new international division of labor is the migration of certain jobs to overseas sites and the changing role of American cities from production to control/information/finance functions. These changes are partially responsible for the paradox of high unemployment rates in the midst of urban expansion. It is impossible to determine the precise number of jobs that have migrated overseas. One source suggests that it amounts to 17 percent of all manufacturing employment in the U.S. As William Neenan has pointed out, overseas employment has contributed significantly to the decline in jobs that occurred in most large cities of the United States in the 1960s.[53]

1980), and especially the article by Alvin Wolff, "Multinational Enterprise and Urbanism," pp. 76–96.

[50]One of the better recent collections connecting urban developments in core and Third World cities is Jeffrey Henderson and Manuel Castells, eds. *Global Restructuring and Territorial Development* (London: Sage Publications, 1987). See also M. J. Taylor and Nigel Thrift, eds., *Multinationals and the Restructuring of the World-Economy* (London: Croom Helm, 1986); Saskia Sassen[-Koob], *The Mobility of Labor and Capital: A Study in International Investment and Labor Flow* (Cambridge: Cambridge University Press, 1988); and Anthony King, *Global Cities: Post-Imperialism and the Internationalization of London* (London and New York: Routledge, 1990).

[51]Edward Soja, Rebecca Morales, and Goetz Wolff, "Urban Restructuring and Spatial Change in Los Angeles," *Economic Geography* 59 (1983), pp. 195–230. See also his article on Los Angeles in M. P. Smith and J. Feagin, eds., The *Capitalist City* (New York: Basil Blackwell, 1987), pp. 178–198.

[52]Portes and Walton, *Labor, Class and the International System,* pp. 145–146. Among the other sources that can be consulted on this issue are: Pegsy Musgrave, *Direct Investment Abroad and the Multinationals: Effects on the United States Economy* (Subcommittee on Multinational Corporations, Committee on Foreign Relations, U.S. Senate, 94th Congress, 1st Session; Washington, DC: GPO, August, 1975); Bluestone and Harrison, *Capital and Communities;* and Barnet and Muller, *Global Reach.*

[53]William B. Neenan, *The Political Economy of Urban Areas* (Chicago: Markham Publishing Co., 1972).

Table 6.13 MAJOR CENTERS OF INTERNATIONAL BUSINESS IN THE UNITED STATES BY 1974

SMSA	Foreign sales* Fortune 500 firms headquartered in SMSA ($ billions)	Share of total foreign sales (%)	Total sales Fortune 500 firms in SMSA ($ billions)	Share of sales of Fortune 500 sales (%)
New York	98.9	40.5	252.9	30.5
Detroit	21.5	8.8	76.0	9.1
Pittsburgh	15.2	6.2	40.1	4.9
San Francisco	13.1	5.4	25.5	3.2
Chicago	11.2	4.6	60.9	7.3
Los Angeles	9.3	3.8	38.4	4.6
Houston	6.7	2.8	17.4	2.1
Akron	4.2	1.7	12.6	1.5
Minneapolis	3.1	1.3	13.4	1.6
Paterson	2.9	1.2	10.1	1.2
St. Louis	2.9	1.2	17.3	2.1
Cleveland	2.7	1.1	17.2	2.1
Top 50 SMSAs	212.5	87.0	691.7	82.9

*Includes only the foreign sales of firms reporting them, or 255 of 386 corporations in the top 50 SMSAs.

Sources: Fortune, May 1975, and a survey of the foreign sales of U.S. corporations prepared from 10-K reports and prospectuses filed by corporations with the S.E.C. From Robert B. Cohen, "Multinational Corporations, International Finances, and the Sunbelt," pp. 211–226 in David Perry and Alfred Watkins, eds., The Rise of the Sunbelt Cities (Beverly Hills, CA: Sage Publications, 1977).

The most detailed estimates have been made not for the United States but for another advanced capitalist country, the Federal Republic of Germany. There, it has been estimated that "the number of workers directly employed by Federal German manufacturing corporations in foreign countries amounts to 20 percent of the total domestic labour force in . . . manufacturing."[54] While the United States may not yet have reached this figure, the trends in the two countries have been quite similar. In Germany, the number of foreign subsidiaries quadrupled between 1961 and 1976, with the largest increase occurring from the late 1960s on. That is certainly the period during which the American labor force underwent its most dramatic changes. Movement overseas of low-skill blue-collar manufacturing jobs has left underemployment and unemployment in American cities. To some extent, these losses are compensated for by an increase in the number of jobs in high-level technology, management, and

[54]Folker Frobel, Jurgen Heinrichs, and Otto Kreye, The New International Division of Labour, trans. Pete Burgess (Cambridge: Cambridge University Press, 1980), p. 20. The authors claim that this is an extremely conservative estimate, even though it is higher than that reached by other scholars. The care and detail of their study—unmatched by any comparable American study—give special credibility to their estimate.

producers' services; but the poor, the uneducated, and the unskilled (a large proportion of blacks and Hispanics) are unlikely to be helped by such expansions.

Interestingly enough, in the most recent period there has been some movement of low-paid employment back into American cities, but it is most often in the form of sweat-shop labor (largely Hispanic and Asian). The research of Saskia Sassen-Koob is particularly relevant here.[55] She suggests that, despite an overall decrease in manufacturing jobs in New York City, certain new industries began to grow in the 1970s, such as Chinatown's garment industry—involving not only sweat shops and piecework done at home, but larger factories as well. She attributes this to the influx of many Southeast Asian immigrants. "There is a growing awareness in the [garment] industry that wages in New York are increasingly competitive with those in the garment industry in Southeast Asia. And since a large share of production in Southeast Asia is for the United States, the availability of immigrant labor in New York City makes location of factories here increasingly profitable."[56] So the international system completes the circle, "importing" Third World workers into its core.

The polarization between center and periphery in the world system is thus mirrored within the various world cities whose spatial structure is increasingly bifurcated into the "citadel" and the "ghetto."[57] The citadel, with its tall gleaming skyscrapers housing the corporate headquarters and the informational and financial services that assist them in management, contains an elite with cross-national linkages whose job is to control their vast empires. This elite no longer has much connection with, nor does it feel responsibility towards, the occupants of the "ghetto" whose manufacturing jobs have been dispersed to other parts of the country and the world. The latter may be becoming a permanent underclass: members of the periphery living within the shadow of the core.[58]

---

[55]Saskia Sassen-Koob, "Recomposition and Peripheralization at the Core," in *The New Nomads: Immigration and Changes in the International Division of Labor* (special issue no. 5 of *Contemporary Marxism*, September 1982), pp. 88–100. Since that early article she has published increasingly significant work in this area. See, *inter alia*, her article in the excellent collection edited by Michael Peter Smith and Joe Feagin, *The Capitalist City* (New York: Basil Blackwell, 1988).

[56]Sassen-Koob, "Recomposition and Peripheralization at the Core," p. 93. Studies in Los Angeles reveal similar developments.

[57]Friedmann and Wolff, "World City Formation," p. 325.

[58]The concept of a permanent underclass (what Marx had called the *lumpenproletariat*) has recently received wide publicity. William J. Wilson, in his *The Truly Disadvantaged* (Chicago: University of Chicago Press, 1987), attributes the appearance of a permanent class of poor urban blacks to the lack of job opportunities for young men and the high fertility rates for young unmarried black women. He discusses neither international restructuring nor the disorganizing force of drugs.

All these changes have deep implications for American cities in the coming decades. They are the result primarily of the restructuring of the American economy to play a controlling (but not necessarily producing) role in the industrial system of late capitalism—the so-called postindustrial era. This new economy was facilitated by and has, in turn, intensified the "third revolution" symbolized by computers and improved communication. In the final section of this chapter we look at some of the technological changes that have helped bring into existence the new form of urbanization appropriate to this new era and the kinds of cities that we are likely to have, as the tendencies inherent in current trends are gradually translated into concrete form.

THE IMPACT OF TECHNOLOGY ON URBAN FORMS

Ernest Mandel's contention that the "postindustrial" era is really a period during which industrialization is spreading to services and information is supported by a look at how information transmission and processing have changed during the past few decades. Television and computers are obvious examples. Although the United States began its first television broadcasts in 1941, mass production did not make private sets readily available until 1946, after which use spread rapidly. The number of receivers in the United States increased from one million in 1949 to 10 million by 1951, to over 50 million by 1959; by now television is virtually universal. Television reception had originally been bound by line-of-sight transmission. In the decades of the 1960s and particularly the 1970s, the technologies of transmission became virtually free of the frictions of space. Today, satellites and cables allow transmission everywhere, while video cassettes provide packaged programs for home use. Microwave transmission and fiber optics technology continue to revolutionize communication.

The computer had a similar if less spectacular history. The first electronic computer, ENIAC, was built in 1946 (with 18,000 vacuum tubes!), but it was like a dinosaur—enormous but with a small brain. UNIVAC I, produced in 1951, represented a great improvement, but it too was so large and expensive that its main users remained the military and the government. The field was revolutionized when miniaturization by transistors and then silicon chips opened a mass market for tiny, efficient machines.

Originally, computers were accessible only at their massive centers. Now, simple telephone connections via modems can activate the link between a home processor and the vast memory cells of central computers. Software and other accessories have multiplied the use of small information and word processors in ordinary offices and homes and have made it possible for them to be linked into networks. Such links have been facilitated by changes in telecommunication. Local and long distance calls have become increasingly similar. Satellites permit random access networks, while digital computers control routings, making fax transmission of visual materials practical at last. These developments have led some to conclude that location is increasingly irrelevant in controlling access to information.[59]

Three effects of this information revolution have maximum real or potential impact on the city of the future. First, just as the machinery of the Industrial Revolution raised productivity and eventually reduced labor demand in manufacturing, so the new office machines are increasing productivity and may eventually reduce the demand for labor in the white-collar professions. Automation in production is being followed by automation in data processing. Second, just as the telephone disengaged production from management and permitted space to become more "fungible," so television and computers are permitting vast and wide-ranging networks of communication to be set up that are relatively independent of distance and density. And finally, because of their small size and flexible multidirectional linkages, the televisions and computers of today make possible for the first time a true reversal of the centralizing tendencies of modern life. The electronic "cottage" wired to other cottages and centers may be a dream of the future, but it is now technically feasible to radically decentralize offices—even into the homes of the workers.

Most changes in transportation have also facilitated decentralization. Just as the mass use of cars and trucks on an extensively reticulated highway system broke the hold of the railroads, so such innovations as "container" shipping have broken the monopoly of seaports and airports as exclusive break-in-bulk areas; containers can be packed and unpacked far from the terminals. Thus far the airplane has had mixed effects on urban patterns. While it has made many previously isolated areas accessible, it has paradoxically tended to concentrate traffic in a smaller number of key "hub" terminals, in a contemporary version of "death by dieselization."[60]

However, it is quite conceivable that all this may again change. Certainly, an era of mass private airborne transportation is not inconceivable. One can envisage what such a revolution would mean in reducing the time-cost of bridging distance and in homogenizing space. Should this come to pass, the future city may be unrecognizable. On the other hand, at least some have suggested that continuing energy shortfalls or rising costs of energy may slow down decentralization[61] or at least require increased substitution of communication for mobility.

---

[59]Ithiel de Sola Pool, "Communications Technology and Land Use," *The Annals of the American Academy of Political and Social Science* 451 (September 1980), pp. 1–12. David Burnham, *The Rise of the Computer State* (New York: Random House, 1980), emphasizes the negative side.

[60]A classic article by Leonard Cottrell, entitled "Death by Dieselization," pointed out that when railroads changed from coal to diesel oil, many small towns that previously provided water and coal were bypassed by trains and therefore shriveled. The same now appears to be happening in air travel.

[61]See Jon van Til, *Living with Energy Shortfall: A Future for American Cities and Towns* (Boulder, CO: Westview Press, 1982). A summary of his argument appears in his "New City Types in an Energy-Short World," pp 150–162 in Gappert and Knight, eds., *Cities in the 21st Century,* Vol. 23 of *Urban Affairs Annual Reviews,* 1982.

THE PHYSICAL AND SOCIAL FORMS OF THE EVOLVING PATTERN OF SATURATION URBANIZATION

In subsequent sections of this book we examine the evolving physical and social forms of the contemporary American city. Here we summarize the crucial trends that have given rise to them.

1. *Cities have been spreading over the landscape faster than population has increased within them.* This has led to much lower residential densities in urban regions and to a scattering of population over the land. In the process, contrasts between center city and outskirts have become increasingly blurred, except in the centers of the very largest metropolitan regions that play national and international roles.

2. *The shape of the "city" has been changing* in the process. No longer a uni-centered cone with densities highest in a CBD (central business district) that dominates the rest, the contemporary metropolitan region has become far more complexly organized. It often contains multiple centers serving different functions and is crisscrossed by interactional webs. The "cone" shape grows flatter (see Figure 6.6), and peaks of density at both center and periphery alternate with zones of low density.[62]

3. *There has been considerable equalization of the urbanization levels in various regions of the country, as saturation urbanization covers the continent.* The rapid growth of cities in the Sunbelt results from a process that has reduced the locational advantages of the older Northeast and North Central regions.

4. *The number of households in the United States has been increasing faster than the total population,* as families get smaller, as single-person households become more common, and as households split in two after divorce. Demands for space go up to accommodate these smaller households.

5. *There is at least the potential for a new wave of decentralization of workplaces,* as information processing joins manufacturing in moving to the countryside. Cottage work becomes a new possibility in the decentralized and low-density portions of our urbanized areas.[63]

---

[62]See Charles Leven, "Economic Maturity and the Metropolis' Evolving Form," pp. 21–44 in Gary A. Tobin, ed., *The Changing Structure of the City: What Happened to the Urban Crisis,* vol. 16 of *Urban Affairs Annual Reviews* (Beverly Hills, CA: Sage Publications, 1979).

[63]So far, this appears to be a fanciful possibility, but it cannot be discounted. It is estimated that about ten percent of American workers already work at home, and it is anticipated that this will be rising very rapidly in the years to come. Ronald Abler suggests that not only routine data processing but managerial functions will be decentralized to the home. "The high proportion of the national and metropolitan labor force working at information-processing jobs and advances in telecommunications will, by 1990, allow managerial, professional, and clerical personnel to work at home, substituting electrical communications for face-to-face contacts." See Ronald Abler, "The Telephone and the Evolution of the American Metropolitan System," in de Sola Pool, ed., *The Social*

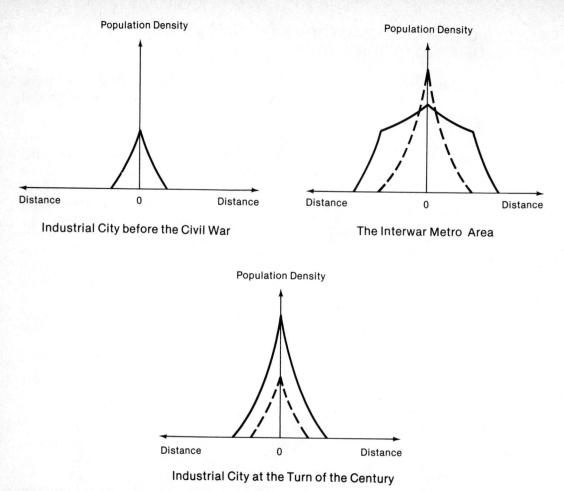

Figure 6.6 The changing height profile of typical U. S. cities before the Civil War, after industrialization at the turn of the twentieth century, and after early metropolitanization. (*Source:* Charles Leven, "Economic Maturity and the Metropolis' Evolving Form," in Gary Tobin, ed., *The Changing Structure of the City: What Happened to the Urban Crisis* [Beverly Hills, CA: Sage Publications, 1979], pp. 38–39. Copyright 1979 by Sage Publications.)

Impact of the Telephone (Cambridge, MA: MIT Press, 1977), p. 337. An uncritically enthusiastic argument that these new technological possibilities will transform urban life is Joseph F. Coates, "New Technologies and Their Urban Impact," pp. 177–195 in Gappert and Knight, eds., *Cities in the 21st Century,* especially pp. 181–183. An imaginative and widely reprinted account of what the office of the future may look like is S. B. Sutton, "Henry and Edward in the Office of the Future," *Harvard Magazine* (Nov.-Dec. 1982). One of the examples of successful office mechanization cited by Sutton was the Continental Illinois National Bank and Trust Company that in 1978 launched one of the first "work-at-home" programs. Ominously, that program closed down just after the article appeared.

6. *Remaining behind in the older-style cities that were built up under previous economic conditions are large masses of poor and unskilled persons, many of them belonging to racial or ethnic minorities.* They have been left behind in the whiplash of a major transformation of the American economy as it now enters the postindustrial era or the late stage of capitalism. If the city is not to become a holding pen for a permanent underclass bypassed by the "third wave revolution," some way must be found to integrate this domestic surplus.[64]

7. Finally, *as close neighbors become more distant through reductions in density, and as families become smaller through subdivision and reductions in fertility, the entire fabric of social life begins to change.* What new sources of social life will substitute for kin and place? Many decades ago, Emile Durkheim suggested that occupation (actually, the workplace) would compensate for the loss of cohesion previously provided by family and neighborhood.[65] But if workers are increasingly linked from their homes to their employers through machines, then what will offer the human contact we all need in order to live warmly and with conviction?

We have no firm answers to these questions, nor do we wish to join Frank Lloyd Wright and Le Corbusier in forecasting through a clouded crystal ball. But our task in the rest of this book will be to gain insight into American cities as they enter this new era of urbanism. In the process, many of the old theories about urban life will require revision and new approaches will be needed to evaluate the impact of cities on social life. We begin this task with a new definition of the city, one offered by Jean Gottmann:

> Central cities work like crossroads, rather than as castles at the top of the hill; they may be described as hinges working within networks.[66]

---

[64]Racial segregation in the nation's largest cities and rising unemployment rates for blacks remain the most pressing problems facing not only America's cities but the entire society. The prediction made by the Kerner Commission (appointed in 1968 to investigate the race riots that had recently erupted in numerous American cities), namely, that "our nation is moving toward two societies, one black, one white—separate and unequal," has been borne out by events. A restudy made in 1978 found conditions even more extreme than they had been ten years earlier. See the *Kerner Report of the National Advisory Commission on Civil Disorders,* February 29, 1968, for the earlier account, from which the quotation has been taken, and the special series, "Two Societies: America Since the Kerner Report," in *The New York Times* (March 1978) for the restudy. See also Gerald Jaynes and Robin Williams, Jr., *A Common Destiny: Blacks and American Society* (Washington, D.C.: National Academy Press, 1989). Desegregation at middle-class and higher levels has, according to Wilson (in *The Truly Disadvantaged*), ironically deprived the ghettos of their former leaders and models.

[65]Emile Durkheim, *The Division of Labor in Society,* trans. George Simpson (New York: Free Press, 1964), *passim,* but especially the preface to the third edition.

[66]Jean Gottmann, ed., *Centre and Periphery: Spatial Variations in Politics,* p. 223. This metaphor has been recast and given fuller meaning in the terms "nodes" and "flows" employed by Manuel Castells in *The Informational City* (New York: Basil Blackwell, 1989).

MOST OF THE FASTEST GROWING CITIES ARE LOCATED IN THE SUNBELT; MOST DECLINING CITIES WERE MANUFACTURING CENTERS.

Largest	1980	1990	Percentage change	Growing	Percentage change 1980–1990	Declining	Percentage change 1980–1990
1. New York	7,071,639	7,322,564	3.5%	1. Moreno Valley, CA*	319.6%	1. Gary, IN	−23.2%
2. Los Angeles	2,968,528	3,485,398	17.4%	2. Rancho Cucamonga, CA	83.5%	2. Newark	−16.4%
3. Chicago	3,005,072	2,783,726	−7.4%	3. Plano, TX	77.9%	3. Detroit	−14.6%
4. Houston	1,617,966	1,630,553	0.8%	4. Irvine, CA	77.6%	4. Pittsburgh	−12.8%
5. Philadelphia	1,688,210	1,585,577	−6.1%	5. Mesa, AZ	76.1%	5. St. Louis	−12.4%
6. San Diego	875,538	1,110,549	26.8%	6. Oceanside, CA	67.5%	6. Cleveland	−11.9%
7. Detroit	1,203,369	1,027,974	−14.6%	7. Santa Clarita, CA*	65.8%	7. Flint, MI	−11.8%
8. Dallas	905,751	1,006,877	11.2%	8. Escondido, CA	62.8%	8. New Orleans	−10.9%
9. Phoenix	790,183	983,403	24.5%	9. Arlington, TX	61.7%	9. Warren, MI	−10.1%
10. San Antonio	813,118	935,933	15.1%	10. Las Vegas, NV	56.3%	10. Chattanooga, TN	−10.1%
11. San Jose, CA	640,225	782,248	22.2%	11. Bakersfield, CA	54.4%	11. Louisville, KY	−9.9%
12. Indianapolis	700,974	741,952	5.8%	12. Mesquite, TX	51.3%	12. Peoria, IL	−9.1%
13. Baltimore	786,741	736,014	−6.4%	13. Glendale, AZ	50.5%	13. Macon, GA	−8.8%
14. San Francisco	678,974	723,959	6.6%	14. Ontario, CA	49.9%	14. Erie, PA	−8.7%
15. Jacksonville, FL	540,920	672,971	24.4%	15. Virginia Beach, VA	49.9%	15. Buffalo	−8.3%
16. Columbus, OH	565,021	632,910	12.0%	16. Modesto, CA	46.1%	16. Birmingham, AL	−7.7%
17. Milwaukee	636,298	628,088	−1.3%	17. Scottsdale, AZ	45.2%	17. Richmond	−7.4%
18. Memphis	646,170	610,337	−5.5%	18. Santa Ana, CA	44.0%	18. Chicago	−7.4%
19. Washington	638,432	606,900	−4.9%	19. Pomona, CA	42.0%	19. Atlanta	−7.3%
20. Boston	562,994	574,283	2.0%	20. Stockton, CA	41.0%	20. Kansas City, KS	−7.1%
21. Seattle	493,846	516,259	4.5%	21. Irving, TX	41.0%	21. Baltimore	−6.4%
22. El Paso	425,259	515,342	21.2%	22. Fresno, CA	40.5%	22. Akron, OH	−6.1%
23. Nashville	477,811	510,748	6.9%	23. Aurora, CO	40.1%	23. Toledo, OH	−6.1%
24. Cleveland	573,822	505,616	−11.9%	24. San Bernardino, CA	36.4%	24. Philadelphia	−6.1%
25. New Orleans	557,927	496,938	−10.9%	25. Vallejo, CA	36.0%	25. Dayton, OH	−5.9%
26. Denver	492,694	467,610	−5.1%	26. Overland Park, KS	35.5%	26. Knoxville, TN	−5.7%
27. Austin, TX	372,536	465,622	25.0%	27. Salinas, CA	35.2%	27. Memphis	−5.5%
28. Fort Worth	385,164	447,619	16.2%	28. Santa Rosa, CA	34.3%	28. Cincinnati	−5.5%
29. Oklahoma City	404,551	444,719	9.9%	29. Sacramento, CA	34.0%	29. Denver	−5.1%
30. Portland, OR	429,400	437,319	1.8%	30. Reno, NV	32.8%	30. Washington, DC	−4.9%

*Not incorporated in 1980.

Source: U.S. Census of Population and Housing, 1990, as released January 1991.

The City as Place

Chapter 7

The Form of the City and How to Discover It

*T*he most remarkable fact about cities is that the way buildings and people are arranged in space is not capricious. When one considers all the variation in urban forms at different times and in different cultures, one recognizes that the city is a *social product,* one that reflects society's values and social structure. Sociologists therefore study the physical structures of cities in order to better understand the societies that produce them. Ability to "read" the physical city for social clues is, indeed, one of the most important skills an urban sociologist must acquire. A few examples illustrate this point.

What occupies the center of a city often reveals what is most valued by a society. Thus, in medieval European cities the central location of the church or cathedral and the fact that it towered above the huddled huts of the workers testified to the central importance of religion. When such towns became the homes of important merchants engaged in long-distance trade, the cathedral on the square was joined by impressive guild halls. As the burghers took over the government of the town from the church hierarchy, the town hall took its proper place on the square. Thus, the evolution of European medieval towns clearly illustrates how spatial orders reflect changing social orders.

The relations among social groups within a city are often revealed by their physical distribution. For example, sixteenth-century Spanish towns in Latin

America, built according to plans specified in their charters, symbolized the social order the conquerors wished to establish. The aristocracy built their houses on large lots just adjacent to the main square, which was simultaneously the center of political, religious, and economic power. This plaza contained the governor's palace, the cathedral, the police station, the financial institutions, and main markets. The small homes of the poor were located far from the center of town. At first, Indians and, later, mestizo peasants were excluded from entering or settling in town. Only later, when their labor was needed for urban production, were these powerless groups permitted to settle at the fringes of the cities.[1] From this history arises the Latin American urban pattern of peripheral slums, so different from the pattern of central slums found in North American cities.

The initial exclusion of Indians from Latin American colonial towns tells us that ethnic and race relations may also be reflected (and intentionally maintained) in the urban pattern. For example, the colonial administration in South Africa instituted apartheid laws to segregate persons designated as White from those legally defined as Coloureds (persons of mixed racial origin), Asians (mostly East Indian), and Black Africans. Whites were assigned the best areas of town, which were developed at low densities and fully supplied with modern utilities. Blacks were either excluded entirely from the urban center or were relegated to undesirable peripheral locations (often on land unsuitable for residences) where even minimal services were lacking and where densities of development were very high. Asians and Coloureds, occupying the medium ranks of status in the society, also occupied intermediary positions in the spatial structure and enjoyed medium residential densities and amenities.

Racial segregation was part of the basic legal and economic system of colonial South African society, but elsewhere other means were used to achieve apartheid. For example, in North Africa, the French colonizers achieved their intended policy of segregating "natives" from Europeans largely through market mechanisms, zoning and building codes, and administrative discretion exercised by a bureaucracy committed to achieving "physical separation" between the "races" (e.g., French-European versus Moroccan).[2]

In the United States, racial segregation has had its own history. During the time of slavery, most African-Americans lived in southern rural areas. Those who lived in southern cities were not segregated into isolated areas; rather, the larger houses facing the streets were occupied by white owners, while their slaves lived in alley shacks. Initially, northern cities contained so few black freemen that they lived in scattered locations. A few cities may have contained nuclei of black concentrations, but there was nothing on the scale that was to appear later. Indeed, between 1860 and 1920 the dominant form of segregation

---

[1]See, *inter alia,* the selection by Alejandro Portes in *Third World Urbanization,* ed. by Janet Abu-Lughod and Richard Hay, Jr. (New York: Methuen, 1979), pp. 59–70.

[2]See Janet Abu-Lughod, *Rabat: Urban Apartheid in Morocco* (Princeton, NJ: Princeton University Press, 1980), *passim.*

found in American cities was not by race but by immigrant status, and these colonies of the foreign-born tended to disperse with time. It was expected that the small black ghettos, which formed during World War I, would follow a similar pattern of semi-voluntary segregation and then dispersal.

But as massive migration of blacks from rural areas in the South to major cities of the Northeast and North Central regions stepped up during World War II, it became painfully clear that white Americans did not view African-Americans as just another ethnic group, to remain in ghettos until acculturation had taken place, but rather as a lower "caste" to be separated residentially from whites. Private attempts were made to enforce residential apartheid through restrictive covenants. In northern cities, white owners of properties sold their land and houses, subject to a "restriction" on the deed which specified that the property could never be sold or rented to a black person. In 1948 the Supreme Court finally struck down the legal enforceability of these racial restrictive covenants, which meant that owners could no longer enforce such clauses through the courts.

But *de facto* segregation in northern cities had been achieved through mechanisms other than racial covenants. It therefore continued even after the latter were declared unenforceable. Real estate agents had been important actors in preserving the racial homogeneity of neighborhoods; they argued that if the races were mixed, land values and house prices would fall. Segregation was even assisted for a long time by the United States government in its capacity as underwriter of mortgage loans. In the 1930s, the Federal Housing Administration issued guidelines for mortgage-lending that declared racially mixed areas poor investment risks. This practice, later called "redlining," discouraged mortgage lenders from lending money on properties in sections of cities occupied by or soon to be occupied by blacks.

Even though the 1968 open housing laws prohibited racial "steering" and discrimination in showing, renting, and selling property to blacks, and redlining came under attack, informal practices of discrimination continue. While such practices are illegal, they are effective. African-Americans and black Hispanics remain the most segregated groups in American cities.

From even this brief discussion it should be obvious that urban spatial patterns do not occur in a vacuum. They are products of economic competition for space, of power and prejudice, and of political-economic decisions by banks and other nongovernmental organizations, as well as of formally adopted laws, informal administrative procedures, and even less visible tamperings with underlying processes. Furthermore, spatial patterns are the cumulative product of many past decisions and failures to decide. The spatial patterns at any point in time can be understood only with reference to the patterns in preceding periods.

Before one can analyze the processes whereby spatial patterns are created and transformed (a topic to be covered in Chapter 8), one must learn to discover, measure, and describe them. In Chapter 7, therefore, we introduce the methods that "classical" urban ecologists, urban land economists, urban geographers, and social area analysts have devised to uncover the spatial patterns of urban regions. Neither the findings nor the methods are "finished"—that is, they are not techniques or conclusions to be learned in a mechanical fashion. Rather, the student should recognize that urban sociology, like any other discipline, is the cumulative work of many scholars. Knowledge about the city and the repertoire of methods to study it are continually expanding and changing. In the section that follows, we show how these methods evolved in response to data and questions of immediate relevance. Such evolution continues to occur. A discussion of some of the innovative methods now being developed is reserved for Chapter 13, which focuses on the new research agenda.

CLASSICAL URBAN ECOLOGY

The approach to the spatial structure of the city that is almost synonymous with the field of urban sociology is called *human ecology* or *urban ecology*.[3] It seeks to describe patterns of land use and the residential distribution of people with different social characteristics. Urban ecology never deals with individuals; it is concerned only with collectivities as they exist in space. Since the data urban ecology uses are collective rather than individual, one cannot reason that simply because a relationship is found at the aggregate level, it will also be found among the individual units, nor can one reason that associations found at the individual level will also appear at the areal or collective level. To do so would be to commit the "ecological fallacy," that is, to confuse the general characteristics of an area with those of any given resident in it.

Some critics suggest that ecological analysis is unavoidably flawed by the "ecological fallacy" because of this discontinuity between levels of analysis.[4] However, this problem is not unique to ecological research, and can be dealt with simply by bearing in mind that since urban ecology's generalizations and correlations are about areal collectivities rather than about the specific individuals who live in them, its conclusions apply only to areas, not individuals. An example may help illustrate this point. Just because an upper-income zone has many whites and many servants, it does not follow that whites are necessarily the servants.

The Origins of Urban Ecology

Many of urban ecology's techniques developed from very crude beginnings when the field of urban sociology was first becoming established in the United

---

[3]As William Michelson has suggested, human ecology is both a method for analyzing spatial structure and a theory for explaining it. The former, he notes, still persists as a subspeciality, even after many of the early theoretical explanations have been rejected as incomplete or simply wrong. See his *Man and His Urban Environment: A Sociological Approach* (Reading, MA: Addison-Wesley, 1976), pp. 11–12.

[4]The classic critique is W. S. Robinson, "Ecological Correlations and the Behavior of Individuals," *American Sociological Review* 15 (June, 1950), pp. 351–357.

States. Thus, many of the questions originally posed by the field grew out of the time and place in which the methods were being sharpened. One must go back to the Chicago of 1910, by which time the city had grown to over two million from its modest beginnings in 1830. Physically the city had expanded very rapidly after the fire of 1871, absorbing successive waves of immigrants of successively less Anglo-Saxon origin. Like many rapidly growing cities, it suffered from housing shortages, overcrowded conditions, jerry-built structures, and an outmoded infrastructure that failed to keep pace with growth. The population was extremely diverse, and many newcomers were suffering from problems of cultural adaptation.

Philanthropists, ministers, and other social reformers were concerned with ameliorating the problems of slum housing, juvenile delinquency, social disorganization, disease, and high infant mortality that concentrated in poor immigrant quarters. Educators and social workers were concerned with expanding the school system, not only to train the young but to offer adult education (Americanization) to the many immigrants. Jane Addams and a number of other women who would eventually found the field of social work were actively engaged in working with these low-income immigrants, conducting housing surveys in their neighborhoods, extending social services through settlement houses, and pressuring for government assistance.

Faculty members of the recently organized Department of Sociology at the University of Chicago were also caught up in the ferment of the city. They sought not only to develop the theoretical underpinnings of their new field but to apply their knowledge to improve conditions around them. It was therefore not surprising that "the city" and its social "pathology" attracted their attention. By 1916 the faculty contained two scholars who left a lasting impact on the field of urban sociology: Robert Ezra Park and Ernest W. Burgess.[5] Together with their students and colleagues, they founded what has come to be called the Chicago School of urban sociology.

The earliest definition of the "problematic" of urban sociology was posed by Park in the path-breaking article he published in the March 1915 issue of a fairly new scholarly journal, *The American Journal of Sociology*. Few articles have had so strong an impact on any academic field, for in it, Park set the parameters of and the research agenda for the field of urban ecology for decades to come.

> [T]he city is rooted in the habits and customs of the people who inhabit it. The consequence is that the city possesses a moral as well as a physical organization, and these two mutually interact in characteristic ways to mold and modify one another. It is the structure of the city which impresses us by its visible vastness and

---

[5] Among the sources that can be consulted on Park, see Fred H. Matthews, *Quest for an American Sociology: Robert E. Park and the Chicago School* (Montreal: McGill-Queen's University Press, 1977); and Winifred Raushenbush, *Robert E. Park: Biography of a Sociologist* (Durham, NC: Duke University Press, 1979). A good overview of Burgess's work can be found in *The Basic Writings of Ernest W. Burgess,* ed. Donald J. Bogue (Chicago: Community and Family Study Center, University of Chicago, 1974).

complexity, but this structure has its basis, nevertheless, in human nature, of which it is the expression. On the other hand, this vast organization which has arisen in response to the needs of its inhabitants, once formed, impresses itself upon them as a crude external fact, and forms them, in turn, in accordance with the design and interests which it incorporates.[6]

This remains the crucial focus of human ecology[7]: namely, that people create their cities but then cities shape their lives.

Robert Park had been a newspaper reporter and later a publicist employed by Booker T. Washington. (Between these two experiences he had gone to Germany to take a belated doctorate in sociology.) W. I. Thomas recruited Park from Tuskegee Institute to the University of Chicago in 1913. By 1916 Park and his young office mate, Ernest Burgess, were giving the introductory-level sociology course. Their first collaborative effort was to compile a giant book of readings, *Introduction to the Science of Sociology.*[8] In addition to selections from Simmel and Darwin, among others, the book included a few selections on plant and animal ecology, reflecting Park's permanent fascination with the web of life and man's (and, unmentioned, woman's) place in it.

Park and Burgess also gave a joint fieldwork course on the city. Each brought his own perspective to that task. For Park, the city was a throbbing laboratory[9] for the study of human social behavior, filled with widely different

---

[6]Robert Park, "The City: Suggestions for the Investigation of Human Behavior in the City Environment," *American Journal of Sociology* 20 (March 1915), pp. 577–612. Quotation from p. 578.

[7]Park is often credited with inventing the term *human ecology.* However, when Park published this first article in 1915, he did not use the term. Not until the article was revised and reprinted in Park, Burgess, and McKenzie's *The City* (in 1925) was the term *human ecology* introduced. Park borrowed the nomenclature from a University of Chicago colleague. H. Barrows, a professor of geography at the University of Chicago, first used the term *human ecology* in his presidential address before the American Geographical Society in 1922. His essay was published in 1923. Even more significant is that the term "human ecology," as applied to urban sociology, appeared first not in the work of Park but in an article written by his student and future collaborator, Roderick D. McKenzie. This article, "The Ecological Approach to the Study of the Human Community," was originally printed in *Encyclopedia Americana* in 1923, reprinted in *American Journal of Sociology* 30 (November 1924) and finally reprinted in *The City,* ed. Robert Park, Ernest W. Burgess, and Roderick D. McKenzie (University of Chicago Heritage of Sociology Series, Chicago: University of Chicago Press, 1967; first published 1925). Although Park cites the piece by Barrows and acknowledges his intellectual indebtedness to him, he does not mention the work of McKenzie.

[8]The original version, published by the University of Chicago Press in 1921, ran well over a thousand pages and revealed Georg Simmel as one of the more important sources for many of the original concepts in sociology. For decades, this volume was known to graduate students of sociology as the "Green Bible," referring to both the color of its cover and its authority. An abridged student edition, running less than half the length of the original, was prepared by Morris Janowitz and published by the University of Chicago Press in 1969.

[9]While the phrase "the city as laboratory" is closely associated with Park's name, he was not the originator of this term. Indeed, as early as 1896, Albion Small, the first chair of the University of Chicago department of sociology, referred to Chicago as "a vast sociological laboratory." See his "Scholarship and Social Agitation," pp. 581–592 in the *first* issue of the *American Journal of*

"social types" and ethnic groups and exhibiting the kinds of problems his muck-raker newspaperman's soul ached to explore. For Burgess, whose major interest was social pathology, the city was the locus for social problems. In his course on social pathology he had begun to have students map the locations of diseases, crime cases, and so on. Burgess was later to reminisce:

> I had students in my course on Social Pathology making maps of all types of social problems for which we could get data. From this *began to emerge* the realization that there was a definite pattern and structure to the city, and that many types of social problems were correlated with one another.[10]

This statement is remarkable for its naïveté; such techniques of mapping social events had become well established in European scholarship during the late nineteenth century.[11] Nevertheless, his "insight" stimulated a long-term preoccupation in urban sociology with exploring the spatial order of the city.[12]

Burgess and the First Maps How was the spatial structure of the city to be discovered? At first, students in Burgess's courses mapped any information they could find—not only land use data but also social pathology events and rates, such as crime, insanity, and disease. (The very first map made in Burgess's class showed the home addresses of arrested juvenile delinquents.) Students prepared maps showing the locations of shoe stores, banks, and pawnbrokers, often transcribing them from telephone directories. Later, data were made available from court records, service agencies, and even surveys made by Illinois Bell Telephone. The work, however, was frustrating and capriciously confined to data that were readily available, not necessarily those most needed.

A proper model of sociological mapping already existed. The model, well known to Burgess, was the 1895 *Hull House Maps and Papers,* an ambitious social survey completed by Florence Kelley and the staff at Hull House. The two maps in this document were patterned on those Charles Booth had done for London. But whereas Booth's well-financed work had covered almost all of

---

Sociology (March 1896), as cited in Mary Jo Deegan, *Jane Addams and the Men of the Chicago School, 1892–1918* (New Brunswick, NJ: Transaction, Inc., 1988), pp. 37 and 51.

[10]See Ernest W. Burgess and Donald J. Bogue, "Research in Urban Society: A Long View," in *Contributions to Urban Sociology,* ed. Burgess and Bogue (Chicago: University of Chicago Press, 1964). Quotation taken from pp. 3–4, italics added.

[11]Adolphe Quételet, Charles Booth, etc. See the articles by Elmer, Levin and Lindsmith, and by L. D. Stamp, in *Urban Patterns: Studies in Human Ecology,* rev. ed. by George Theodorson (University Park, PA: Pennsylvania State University Press, 1982), pp. 8–19.

[12]Unfortunately, the temporal order was partially overlooked. Although time was introduced via the history of spatial orders, the study of how urbanites compete not only for space but for temporal priority was forgotten until very recently, when it was "rediscovered" by Kevin Lynch (*What Time is This Place?,* Cambridge, MA: MIT Press, 1972) and Murray Melbin ("Night as Frontier," *American Sociological Review* 43 (1978), pp. 3–22, and *Night as Frontier: Colonizing the World After Dark* (New York: Free Press, 1987). See also Edward Hall, *The Dance of Life: The Other Dimension of Time* (Garden City, NY: Doubleday Anchor, 1983); and Eviatar Zerubavel, *Hidden Rhythms* (Chicago: University of Chicago Press, 1981).

central London, the less adequately financed study at Hull House, with its small grant from the U.S. Department of Labor, could only survey the residents in the immediate neighborhood, a third of a square mile section on the near west side of Chicago.

The sociology students at the University of Chicago could not study the entire city by such tedious methods. Their chance to study the city as a whole had to await changes in the way the U.S. Census reported its findings. In 1910, under pressure from government officials and researchers, the Census Bureau subdivided New York City and eight other major communities, including Chicago, into census tracts (small subareas) and began to process its decennial data for these new districts.[13] Data from the census were arranged so that researchers and municipal officials could find out the characteristics of population and dwellings in each of these small subareas of the city. This opened up enormous possibilities for research. Rather than collecting their own data, researchers could now analyze data from the individual census tracts, already collected by the government, and could map the distribution of social characteristics and housing indicators to lay bare the spatial pattern of the city.

This did not take place immediately, however. Because at that time the Census Bureau did not publish its census tract data, research funds were needed for special tabulations. It was not until 1926 that such funds became available. Furthermore, analysis of census tract data required theory as well as money. The theory according to which many of the later analyses would be made was provided by Ernest Burgess in an article that was to become one of the most frequently cited in the field of urban spatial structure. Since its first publication in 1923, it guided a vast body of empirical research about urban spatial forms.

In this article, entitled "The Growth of the City: An Introduction to a Research Project,"[14] Burgess focused his attention on the phenomenon of urban expansion. He noted that cities grow outward, expanding from a central nucleus, the central business district. He posited that this expansion led to the development of successive rings of urban land use, each with its typical resident populations. That his schema was intended to apply to Chicago is given away by the fact that Burgess labeled the central business district the "Loop," a term used exclusively in Chicago. He also neatly superimposed his abstract schema on the semi-circular pattern of Chicago, as shown in Figure 7.1.

The five zones he distinguished were:[15]

---

[13]Walter Laidlaw, working with the New York Federation of Churches in the early 1900s, is credited with the idea that cities should be subdivided into small enumeration districts, later called census tracts.

[14]Originally published in 1923 in the *Proceedings of the American Sociological Society,* it was early reprinted in the 1925 edition of Park, Burgess, and McKenzie, *The City,* from which it is commonly cited. Reprinted numerous times, it is perhaps most accessible in George Theodorson's *Urban Patterns.*

[15]The following section outlining Burgess's zones draws heavily from the discussion in Noel Gist and Sylvia Fava, *Urban Society,* 6th ed. (New York: Thomas Y. Crowell, 1974), pp. 163–164, 167. Permission to incorporate it, in revised form, is gratefully acknowledged.

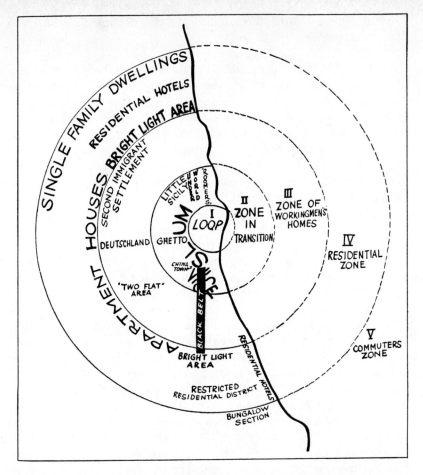

Figure 7.1 The schema of Burgess's theory of the growth of the city applied to Chicago. (*Source:* Ernest Burgess, "The Growth of the City," as reprinted in Park, Burgess and McKenzie, *The City* [Chicago: University of Chicago Press, 1925], p. 55. Copyright 1925 by University of Chicago Press. Reproduced with permission.)

1. *The central business district (CBD),* where skyscraper offices, department stores, cheap variety emporia, hotels, restaurants, and entertainment facilities were concentrated;
2. *The zone in transition* just around the CBD, where land was held in the hopes of speculative profits, and where properties had deteriorated into low-income slums;
3. *The zone of workingmen's homes,* modest apartments, two-flats and bungalows, just beyond the slums.
4. *The residential zone of middle-class homes,* whose apartments and houses contained the white-collar and semi-professional classes;

5. *The commuter zone,* a suburban ring occupied by the upper class at low densities.

In light of the transformation in the shape of the American metropolis that has occurred since the 1920s (traced in Chapters 5 and 6), we can see how time- and culture-bound his description is. Today, the central business district no longer monopolizes commercial and entertainment functions. Decentralized shopping districts, hotel and office complexes, and even manufacturing zones strung out along suburban ring roads have preempted many of the earlier functions of Zone 1 (CBD), and in newer cities of the West and Southwest, central business districts never did take on the appearance and functions that Burgess's theory anticipated for them.

Burgess had called the second zone, around the CBD, a "zone of transition," because it seemed to be in the immediate path of business and industrial expansion. At his time, it was densely occupied by low-income groups that included foreign immigrants and rural newcomers from the countryside, by unconventional artists or "Bohemians" gravitating to low rents and the company of other nonconformists, and by persons at the margins of legality or respectability (prostitutes, alcoholics, "criminal elements," etc.). The owners of the properties held them in the hope of future profits. In the 1920s, however, the entire dynamic of CBD expansion altered and speculators saw their dreams collapse. Instead of expanding outward, the CBD simply grew taller, thanks to elevators. Furthermore, immigration from abroad was cut off; eventually, these zones were inherited by the new proletariat, blacks from the rural South. The urban renewal legislation passed in 1949, designed to revive downtowns, subsidized the clearance of "transition zones" in many cities, and the recycling of them by developers for "better" (i.e., higher class) uses. This often brought city governments and real estate developers into conflict with powerless and poor minority residents whose homes and communities were being destroyed in the process.

The third area in Burgess's scheme was designated the "zone of working-men's homes." Superior in physical appearance to the area of transition but falling short of the residential districts occupied by the middle class, it was occupied by what we would now call "white ethnics," that is, the acculturated sons and daughters of those who had come as part of the great European migrations in the late nineteenth and earlier twentieth century. These areas— often adjacent to the earliest black ghettos that from the 1920s onward began to form in "zone of transition" slums—were later to become the embattled communities that at first violently resisted the entry of blacks into their neighborhoods (as ghettos expanded in the 1940s and 1950s), and that then moved, often *en masse,* to more "protected" neighborhoods in other quadrants of the city "off the path" of black expansion or farther out in the mass-produced suburbs built in the post–World War II period. None of this could have been anticipated by the Burgess theory, which was essentially insensitive to the problem of race relations in America.

Beyond the zone occupied by the working classes Burgess saw a broad band populated mainly by professional people, owners of small businesses, the managerial group, clerical and other white-collar workers, and the like. With large-scale suburbanization in the post–Second World War period, these groups deserted for greener pastures, their places frequently taken by the blue- and white-collar workers who abandoned the "zone of workingmen's homes" when it became contested turf in the 1950s and 1960s.

Burgess termed the outer periphery the "commuter's zone," an area beyond the political boundaries of the city, consisting of satellite towns and suburbs that exist in a dependent relationship with the metropolis. Some writers later dubbed these towns and hamlets "bedroom communities," because their (male) workers left them each day for city jobs. It is in this discussion that the time-bound character of the Burgess hypothesis is especially obvious. While he was accurately describing the new upper-middle-class suburbs typical of the streetcar and early automobile days, he assumed that cities would always be organized around a center—something which, as we have seen in Chapter 6, has become less and less true in the new postindustrial or late capitalism period. Such communities may remain "dormitories," but today more than half of their workers (male and female) commute to jobs in the suburbs, and many outlying communities contain full complements of business and commercial services.

Nonetheless, at the time Burgess was writing, his analysis was remarkably accurate for Chicago. He showed that in passing from the center of Chicago to the periphery, delinquency rates, sex ratios, and percentages of foreign-born persons tended to decrease, while home ownership rates increased.[16] In certain instances the gradients were uniformly continuous. These gradients were also observed by Shaw and McKay[17] in their ecological studies of delinquency and by Faris and Dunham[18] in a study of the ecology of insanity in Chicago.

Not only did Burgess believe he had captured the essential shape of the contemporary American city by his schema, but also that he had identified the process that brought it into being and could explain the mechanisms by which pathological urban conditions, such as slums, were produced. He hypothesized, for example, that as the central business district expanded to keep pace with increases in city size, the zones at the edge of the expanding CBD became ripe for real estate speculation. Owners, rather than repairing their structures there, merely held onto them, hoping to make windfall profits once the land was needed for commercial uses. When, due to the construction of skyscrapers, the land was not needed, the deteriorated properties became bad investments, to be milked rather than maintained. In this early article, Burgess showed a deep appreciation for the fact that the forces underlying change in the city were

---

[16]See Ernest Burgess, "The Determination of Gradients in the Growth of a City," *Publications of the American Sociological Society* 21 (1927), pp. 178–184.

[17]Clifford Shaw and Henry McKay, *Juvenile Delinquency and Urban Areas* (Chicago: University of Chicago Press, 1942).

[18]R. E. L. Faris and H. Warren Dunham, *Mental Disorders in Urban Areas: An Ecological Study of Schizophrenia and Other Psychoses* (Chicago: University of Chicago Press, 1939).

economic, not organic or "biotic." This insight, however, tended to be forgotten in the work of many later ecologists, who began to treat the growth of the city as if the city were an organism, rather than a machine for creating and distributing economic value under capitalism.[19]

Some of this misinterpretation of the forces underlying urban growth and change must be attributed to Robert Park. Over the years, the theory of human ecology had been maturing in Park's thinking, culminating in his 1936 article, "Human Ecology."[20] By that time, the idea that the city was an organism was entrenched in his thinking. He continued to posit two "orders" for human society: the "moral" order, including politics, economics, law, and culture; and the "subconsensual" or ecological order, in which populations adjusted spatially to one another and to their environment without conscious intent. Only the assumption that these orders came together within "natural areas" (neighborhoods) permitted the field to continue in the two somewhat different directions it had laid out: one, to use urban ecological data to delineate the spatial boundaries of these "natural areas"; and two, to conduct neighborhood studies, that is, to study the social communities that existed within these spatial units. We shall treat this issue in greater detail below, when we explore some of the problems this assumption caused. But here we need to return to our narrative.

The Local Community Fact Books   Once data from the U.S. census became available for the city of Chicago on the basis of small tracts, the mapping of social characteristics of the population took on renewed intensity. It had been obvious to the naked eyes of urban observers that, especially at that time, Chicago appeared to be a "mosaic of social worlds."[21] The problem was to "uncover" the boundaries between them so that planning and social services could be better carried out. Therefore, once funds were available after 1926, Burgess and his students began to work with census tract data from the 1920 census to delimit larger "service districts" in Chicago which would contain roughly homogeneous populations with particular planning needs. Some 75 "community areas" were delimited within Chicago, and data on population, housing, and other social and economic characteristics were processed and presented in the *District Fact Book,* a volume intended more as a handbook for civic and social agencies than as a sociological document.

This *District Fact Book* served as the model for a second and fuller edition which contained, in addition to data for the 75 community areas, sheets showing individual values for each component census tract. The new volume, published in 1938, was called *The Local Community Fact Book* and was prepared

---

[19]Harvey Molotch, "The City as a Growth Machine: Toward a Political Economy of Place," *American Journal of Sociology* 82 (September 1976), pp. 309–332.

[20]Robert Park, "Human Ecology," *American Journal of Sociology* 42 (July 1936), pp. 1–15.

[21]Louis Wirth, in his famous essay, "Urbanism as a Way of Life," *American Journal of Sociology* 44 (July 1938), is usually credited with this phrase, even though it was in common use by the time he published his article.

from 1930 census data by Louis Wirth with the assistance of Margaret Furez and Edward Burchard. As Louis Wirth noted in the introduction to the 1949 edition of the *Local Community Fact Book of Chicago* (which he also edited), the first fact book "became a model which was widely copied in other cities." The publication became serial, and issues were released covering the censuses of 1940, 1950, and 1960. Temporarily discontinued when an edition based on the 1970 census failed to appear, the series was resumed in 1980.[22]

In the 1920s what most clearly differentiated the social worlds described in the "fact books" was the ethnicity of neighborhoods. As immigrant groups poured in, each tended to settle in its own subarea of the city, in part because of common class position and the cost of housing, in part because newcomers had to fit in at about the same time and therefore clustered where vacant units were available, but also because people showed a decided preference for living with co-ethnics. Ethnicity, a variable certainly worth examining, was clearly related to space. It is interesting that although the number of blacks in Chicago had recently increased due to the influx during World War I, Burgess, in a 1928 article on racial segregation, contended that there was little difference between older ethnic ghettos and the Black Belt beginning to form on Chicago's south side.[23]

Class was also recognized as a major differentiator of the mosaic that made up the urban environment, although the relationship between classes was assumed rather than studied. From the 1860s onward, subareas in American cities had become increasingly differentiated by class. As the wealthier urbanites moved outward to new areas along streetcar lines, their places near the center were taken by workers in the industrial plants, many of whom were recent migrants from abroad. Burgess had captured this in his zonal hypothesis, and Park, in his 1915 article, had observed that American cities were beginning to become more segregated by class, following the lead of older European cities. The early urban sociologists noted the congruence of poverty and "social problems" and indeed hoped that the new science could be used to help solve such problems.

The Search for "Natural Areas"   Very early in their inquiries Park and Burgess were captivated by the idea that the city might, through its residential neighborhoods, give "community" to its residents. They thought of these

---

[22]Quotation from Louis Wirth and Eleanor H. Bernert, eds., *Local Community Fact Book of Chicago* (Chicago: University of Chicago Press, 1949), p. vii. The most recent volume is Chicago Factbook Consortium, *Local Community Fact Book: Chicago Metropolitan Area* (Chicago: Chicago Review Press, 1984), which covers suburbs as well as 77 community districts in the city.

[23]See Ernest W. Burgess, "Residential Segregation in American Cities," in *Annals of the American Academy of Political and Social Science* 40 (November 1928) as reprinted in *The Basic Writings of Ernest W. Burgess,* ed. Donald L. Bogue (Chicago: University of Chicago Press, 1974), pp. 117–123. The true differences were not revealed until St. Clair Drake and Horace Cayton published their two-volume classic on the Black Belt of Chicago, *Black Metropolis: A Study of Negro Life in a Northern City* (New York: Harcourt, Brace, 1945).

neighborhoods as "natural areas," a term derived from the biologists and geographers who had studied environmental niches in nature. They believed that if only the new science could help identify these natural spatial communities, then political and social service boundaries could be established that would utilize and strengthen the "natural" social units of the city. Thus, one of the early tasks of urban sociologists was to discover and delimit these subareas of the city—not only to help establish units for statistical data collection, but to set up neighborhood organizations to mediate between individuals and the presumed coldly impersonal character of city life.

Identifying natural areas or neighborhoods became a project of top priority, and urban sociologists assisted the census department in designing boundaries for census tracts and community areas. In fact, the assumptions that the city was subdivided into these natural areas and that such areas constituted neighborhoods or "communities" really underlay the rationale for delimiting census tracts in the first place.[24]

Perhaps the most explicit statement by the early urban ecologists on the place of natural areas in the organism of the growing city is found in a 1926 article written by one of Park and Burgess's best students, Harvey Zorbaugh (whose doctoral dissertation was the still classic *Gold Coast and the Slum,* a study of the near north side of Chicago).

> Now, in the intimate economic relationships in which all people are in the city, everyone is . . . in competition with everyone else . . . for position in the community. . . . In this competition for position the population is segregated over the natural areas of the city. Land values, characterizing the various natural areas, tend to sift and sort the population. . . . [All of this yields a city subdivided into dozens of natural areas which are both physical areas and cultural communities.] Natural areas and natural cultural groups tend to coincide. *A natural area is a geographical area characterized both by a physical individuality and by the cultural characteristics of the people who live in it.*[25]

Given this assumption that neighborhoods constitute natural areas, it was a reasonable next step to expand upon the work of social workers and settlement house personnel and do fieldwork in neighborhoods. Out of this came the great urban sociology tradition of the neighborhood study, to be explored in greater depth in Part IV. Long after urban sociologists had lost the conviction that there was anything "natural" about a segregated urban subarea, they continued to do studies of neighborhoods, many of which have become classic works in the field.

The assumptions that physical space and social space were coterminous and that neighborhoods were natural areas were soon to be overthrown. Perhaps

---

[24]See, for example, Calvin F. Schmid, "The Theory and Practice of Planning Census Tracts," *Sociology and Social Research* 22 (Jan.–Feb. 1938), pp. 228–238, as reprinted in Jack P. Gibbs, ed., *Urban Research Methods* (Princeton, NJ: Van Nostrand, 1961), pp. 166–175.

[25]Harvey Zorbaugh, "The Natural Areas of the City," *Publications of the American Sociological Society* 20 (1926), pp. 188–197, as reprinted in Theodorson, ed., *Urban Patterns,* pp. 50–54. Quotation from pp. 51–52; italics added for emphasis.

the most influential refutation was in Paul Hatt's brief article, entitled "The Concept of Natural Area."[26] Originally it had been assumed that natural areas with internal coherence *existed* in the city and that the task of the urban sociologist was really to "uncover" these natural areas. Hatt pointed out that the natural areas were actually "constructed" by the researcher and that many parts of the city defied such simple construction.

Continued Relevance of Census Tract Data   If census tracts do not identify or are not coterminous with natural areas, and if the city is not subdivided into mutually exclusive natural areas or communities that await discovery and field study, are the methods devised to study smaller areas of the city then useless? Can census tract information help researchers who plan to do sociological studies in various "neighborhoods" of the city? Of course. Urban sociologists have depended heavily on census tract information, long after they abandoned their search for natural areas.

One of the great assets of census tract information is that in many cities it has now been collected for the same units for 50 or more years. It is therefore possible to reconstruct the residential history of any subarea of the city by going back to earlier census tract returns, since the boundaries of census tracts remain relatively constant over time.[27] By computing the same indicators for each of the census years, one can reconstruct a fairly good development profile of the area.

Has population increased or decreased over the period? Has ethnic or racial composition changed radically over that period? What economic class or classes now live in the area? Has this changed over time? To answer this last question, one might want to trace the relative educational levels of residents of the area, and, if they are available, examine data on income and occupational distributions as well.

What about the age, sex, and marital characteristics of the population? Is the area one that is hospitable to young families, or to singles? Or does it contain an aging population that settled in the area a long time ago and has tended to grow old with the neighborhood? What is the ratio of the sexes in the area? It is possible to draw a population pyramid of the area which shows its special selective characteristics. Figure 7.2 shows some typical shapes of population pyramids for special kinds of subareas (skid rows, student areas, immigrant communities, areas catering to wealthy widows, new family-type suburbs, and the like).

The U.S. Census not only contains tables on population characteristics but

---

[26]In the *American Sociological Review* 11 (August 1946), pp. 423–427, reprinted also in Theodorson, ed., *Urban Patterns*, pp. 78–81.

[27]Occasionally the census department will subdivide an existing census tract when its population grows beyond the ideal limit of 5000 to 6000, but the boundaries of existing tracts are almost never adjusted at their edges. To test whether a given census tract has changed its boundary (or even if you are accumulating data for the same census tract over time), it is necessary to refer to the maps published with each census volume, which, in the case of large cities, will be with the appropriate SMSA volume.

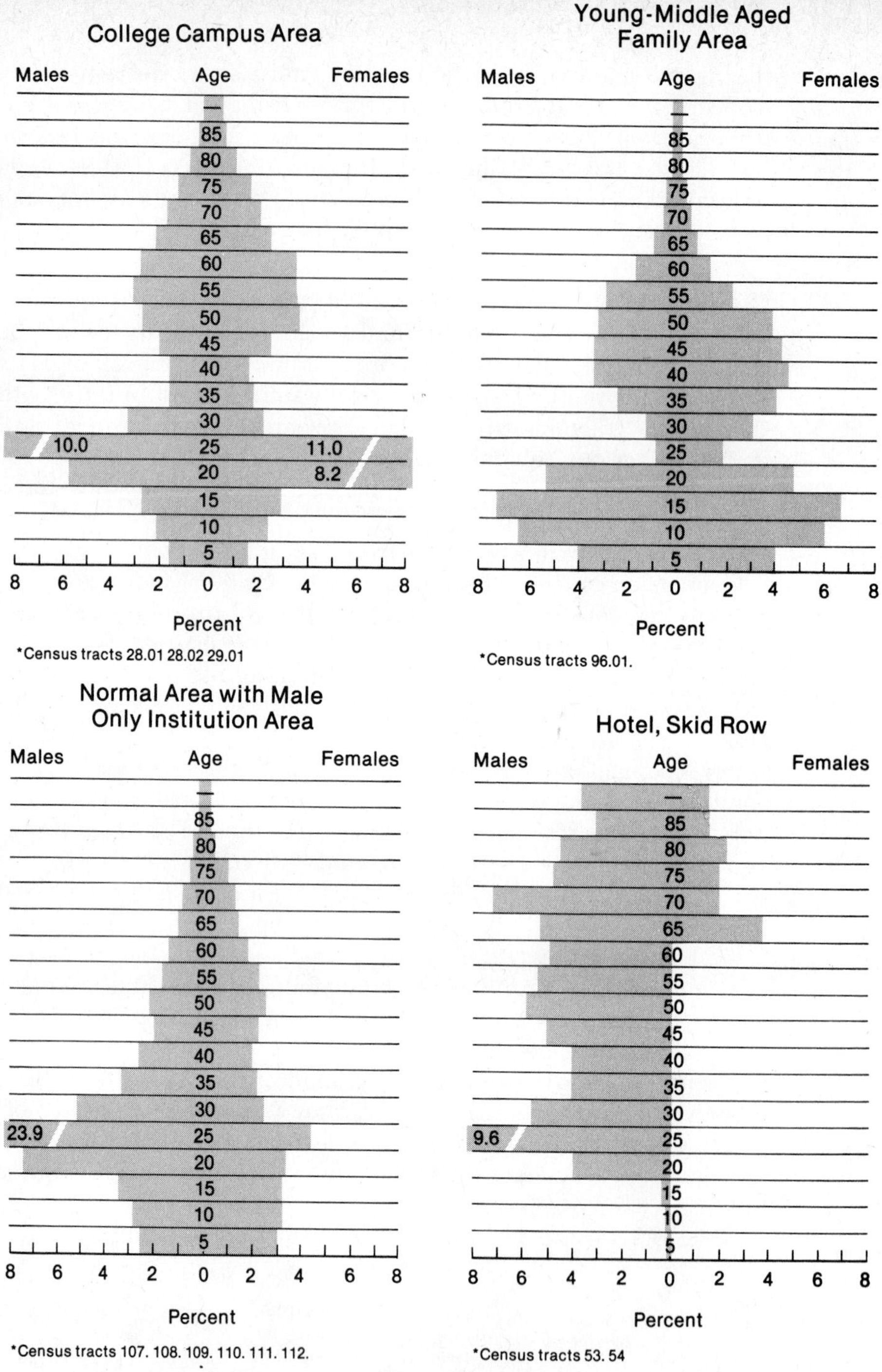

College Campus Area

Males   Age   Females

Males	Age	Females
	85	
	80	
	75	
	70	
	65	
	60	
	55	
	50	
	45	
	40	
	35	
	30	
10.0	25	11.0
	20	8.2
	15	
	10	
	5	

8 6 4 2 0 2 4 6 8

Percent

*Census tracts 28.01 28.02 29.01

Young-Middle Aged Family Area

Males	Age	Females
	85	
	80	
	75	
	70	
	65	
	60	
	55	
	50	
	45	
	40	
	35	
	30	
	25	
	20	
	15	
	10	
	5	

8 6 4 2 0 2 4 6 8

Percent

*Census tracts 96.01.

Normal Area with Male Only Institution Area

Males	Age	Females
	85	
	80	
	75	
	70	
	65	
	60	
	55	
	50	
	45	
	40	
	35	
	30	
23.9	25	
	20	
	15	
	10	
	5	

8 6 4 2 0 2 4 6 8

Percent

*Census tracts 107. 108. 109. 110. 111. 112.

Hotel, Skid Row

Males	Age	Females
	85	
	80	
	75	
	70	
	65	
	60	
	55	
	50	
	45	
	40	
	35	
	30	
9.6	25	
	20	
	15	
	10	
	5	

8 6 4 2 0 2 4 6 8

Percent

*Census tracts 53. 54

Figure 7.2 Sample population pyramids for census tracts with different types of resident populations. (*Source:* Social Science Research Laboratory, San Diego State University, prepared by Douglas Coe. Used by permission.)

has ones on housing. These constitute a rich source of information on subareas. One can, by looking at successive census returns for an area, tell when the buildings in the tract were constructed and how much rebuilding there has been. Information on the quality of housing can also be analyzed, including data on plumbing and cooking facilities as well as on the density of occupancy (number of persons per room)—a very sensitive indicator of housing quality and hence of the class position of occupants. In addition, the housing census contains information on the median rent of tenant-occupied dwelling units and the median value of owner-occupied units in the area. These, too, can serve as measures of the class of occupants over time.

It is clear that in many of these cases, absolute numbers will not be very valuable for comparison, since overall trends have altered the base values against which one would want to compare the census tract. Certainly, in historical urban studies, changes in the *relative* standing of the census tract are more significant than changes in the absolute values. This point is particularly relevant for rents and house values, because of inflation, but it is also relevant for educational levels and occupational distribution, since these too have altered in predictable ways over time. The best way to handle these secular trends is to compare the data for any census tract with those for the city as a whole or with an average of all tract values. Shifts in the relative position of a given tract over time will then become more apparent.[28]

Some questions have recently been raised concerning the value of census tract data, especially now that similar data are also available by block. Block data have an important advantage over census tract information, because blocks can be aggregated to conform to any desired larger area, such as a political ward, a school district, or a police precinct. This makes it possible, then, to collate data from the census with other routinely collected data that are reported for different kinds of districts (election results, school enrollments, crimes, licenses, etc.). The advantages of this approach were summarized as long ago as 1949 by Edward B. Olds, in his "The City Block as a Unit for Recording and Analyzing Urban Data."[29]

Now that it is easy to get block data and now that computers make it simpler to analyze such data, there is no great advantage to using census tracts. The major reason to continue analyzing data by census tracts is to be able to make historical comparisons, because the tract is the smallest unit for which data have been published over the past few decades. We do not know how long the Bureau of the Census will continue to publish data by census tracts. Since the 1980 census, block data have been available on computer tapes. Given that

---

[28]One must be careful, however, that the boundaries of the city have not changed in the interim. The entire urban area should be included, but if another city has been annexed between census dates the average will be distorted.

[29]*Journal of the American Statistical Association* 44 (December 1949), pp. 485–500, as reproduced in Gibbs, ed., *Urban Research Methods* (Princeton, NJ: Van Nostrand, 1961), pp. 148–166.

researchers can now purchase the tapes directly from the Census Bureau and analyze them in any desired manner, it will be hard to justify not creating one's own new "relatively homogeneous natural areas" by combining appropriate adjacent blocks.

The argument about natural areas and the social mosaic of the city continues. Today's proponents of the idea of "natural" neighborhoods stress that these areas keep changing in size and shape. They believe that more sensitive measures for smaller units (such as blocks) will facilitate the accurate delimitation of neighborhood units that also constitute social communities. Opponents, or at least doubters, of the idea of natural areas point out that the problem does not lie in an inability to find or measure these units, but rather in the fact that in the last analysis, these units are not real but, at best, statistical constructs. As such, they are only as good as the indices from which they have been constructed; and they are useful only if they are appropriate to the purposes for which they were designed. The debate continues, as does the development of techniques for uncovering the structure of cities.[30]

HOMER HOYT AND THE ECONOMIST'S VIEW

The classical methods developed by the Chicago School, using census tract data, were not the only or even the best ones to study the spatial structure of cities. It was an urban economist, analyzing very different kinds of data, who forced the first real reconsideration of the Burgess hypothesis, calling into question some basic assumptions and thereby advancing the field.

The first writings on human ecology, especially the articles by Roderick McKenzie, clearly acknowledged that the city was not a biological organism, but actually the result of competition for space and other resources. Among humans, such competition took place largely in the economic system by bidding up the price of land. Land values were, of course, the main interest of urban economists. Burgess was aware of the work of urban economists; indeed, in his theory on urban growth he cited the work of William Hurd, a contemporary land economist.

Urban land economics offered the theory from which Homer Hoyt developed his image of urban structure. Data on land values and rents were needed to test these propositions, however. In *One Hundred Years of Land Values in Chicago* (1933), Hoyt used data from the *Olcott Blue Book of Land Values*. However, just as census data supplanted the social survey of the early sociologists, offering a new and more sophisticated way to study urban structure, so

---

[30]A new problem in measurement has arisen, the result of the changing shape of metropolitan America. At the outer reaches of the metropolitan area, settlement is not dense enough to warrant subdivision into census tracts or any other subunits for data presentation. Incorporated towns or other compact settlements are treated as units for data presentation, but the open areas between them are all added together as unincorporated portions of the SMSA peripheral counties. This makes it difficult to pinpoint the spatial changes taking place in the outlying areas.

the "real property inventories" taken in 1934 offered a better way to study land values and rents in the city, providing the raw materials for Hoyt's famous study, *The Structure and Growth of Residential Neighborhoods in American Cities* (1939).

In 1934, during the Great Depression, real property inventories were made in 64 urban centers; the next year a number of other cities were added to the list. For every single building, information was collected on the type of structure; tenure of occupancy; length of time occupied by current resident; monthly rent; whether the dwelling was furnished or unfurnished; number of rooms; presence of running water, flush toilet, or bathtub; type of heating; number of stories in building; whether it had a basement; the year in which the structure was built; basic materials and type of construction; condition of the structure; sale value; type of lighting; cooking facilities; refrigeration; number and ages of all persons living in each dwelling unit; race of the household; whether there were roomers or extra households sharing the dwelling; and so on. As the extent of this enumeration indicates, the data were as complete as any that had ever been collected in a social survey. Not only were they superior in detail to data collected by the census, but they were transcribed, lot by lot, on to base maps of the community—so that there was no need to estimate the distribution of characteristics according to census tract.

One would have thought that by the mid-1930s there would have been fairly sophisticated comprehension of the structure of cities, without the naïveté shown by Burgess's comment in 1916. But Hoyt's incredibly rich study begins with much the same tentativeness about patterns. He asks:

> Is the American city an entity whose different types of land uses and residential neighborhoods are arrayed in definite patterns or is it a disorganized mass of structures scattered about in hit or miss fashion?[31]

The maps analyzed in this path-breaking study certainly revealed many patterns, as can be seen in Figures 7.3, 7.4, and 7.5. From these, Hoyt formulated his sector theory of urban development. Gist and Fava have concisely described this theory.

> Briefly, the theory holds that high-rent areas tend to be located on the outer fringes of one or more sectors or quadrants of the city, and that in some sectors the low-rent districts assume the shape of a cut of pie, extending from the center to the city's periphery. As cities grow in population, the high-rent areas move outward along one sector; districts thus abandoned by the upper-income groups . . . are inherited by people of lower economic status. Instead of forming a concentric zone around the periphery of the city, . . . the high-rent areas are ordinarily located on the outer edge of one or more sectors.[32]

---

[31]The quotation has been taken from p. 3 of Homer Hoyt, *The Structure and Growth of Residential Neighborhoods in American Cities* (Washington, DC: Federal Housing Administration, 1939). See Appendix I, "Data Used in the Analysis of City Structure," pp. 124–125, for the list of indicators.

[32]Noel Gist and Sylvia Fava, *Urban Society*, 6th ed., p. 164. Permission to reprint these comments here is gratefully acknowledged.

SHIFTS IN LOCATION OF FASHIONABLE RESIDENTIAL AREAS
IN SIX AMERICAN CITIES
1900 - 1936

FASHIONABLE RESIDENTIAL AREAS INDICATED BY SOLID BLACK

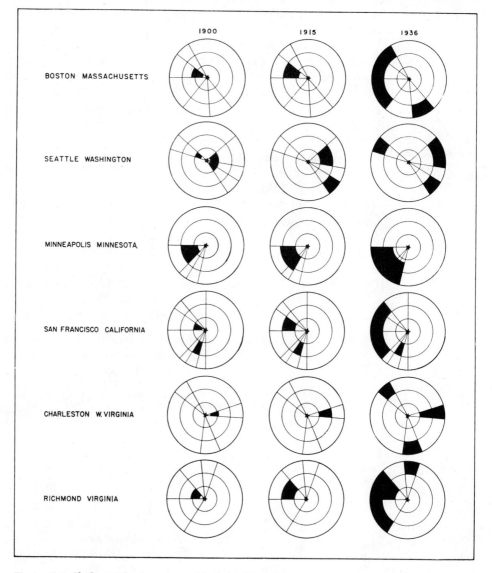

Figure 7.3 Shifts in the location of fashionable residential areas in six American cities between 1900 and 1936. (*Source:* Homer Hoyt, *The Structure and Growth of Residential Neighborhoods in American Cities* [Federal Housing Authority, Washington, D. C.: Government Printing Office, 1939], p. 115.)

GROWTH OF SETTLED AREAS
NEW YORK CITY
1800 – 1934

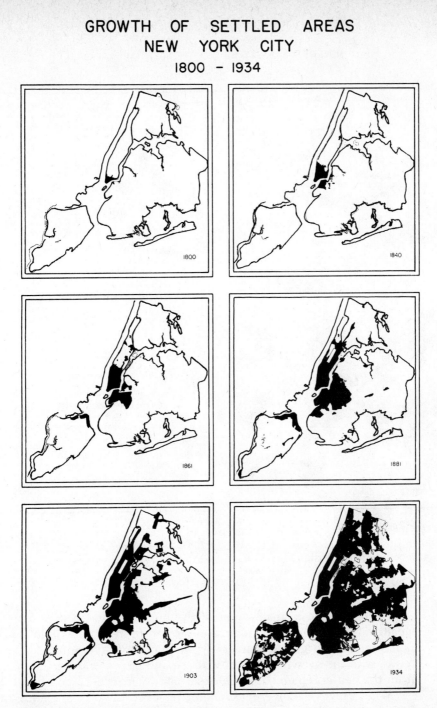

Figure 7.4 The expansion of settled areas of New York City between 1800 and 1934. (*Source:* Homer Hoyt, *The Structure and Growth of Residential Neighborhoods in American Cities* [Federal Housing Authority, Washington, D. C.: Government Printing Office, 1939], p. 157.)

MOVEMENT OF TYPES OF RESIDENTIAL AREAS

WASHINGTON D. C. 1904 - 1938

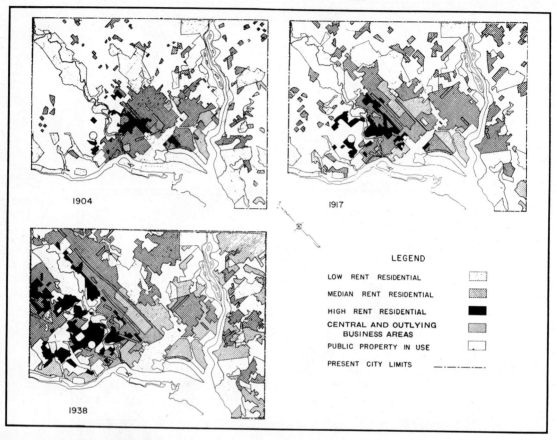

Figure 7.5 The movement of types of residential areas in Washington, D.C. between 1904 and 1938. (*Source:* Homer Hoyt, *The Structure and Growth of Residential Neighborhoods in American Cities* [Federal Housing Authority, Washington, D. C.: Government Printing Office, 1939], p. 169.)

In short, once a small sector of the inner city has been selected by the wealthy, this high-income area radiates outward into zones of newer construction when the city grows. Conversely, an inner-city sector inhabited by the poor tends, with the growth of the city, to expand outward along the major routes from the center, channeling the expansion of areas occupied by the poor.

While Hoyt's data were less adequate concerning racial ghettos, it is clear from his maps that small zones of black concentration in early years likewise tended to radiate outward from the early settlement. Furthermore, industrial areas were found to develop along river valleys, water courses, and railroad lines, instead of forming a concentric zone around the central business district as Burgess had assumed.

Hoyt likened the pattern of the American city to an octopus, with tentacles extending in various directions along transportation lines. At the time of his studies, this description was not inaccurate. However, the enormous expansion of cities into amorphous peripheral areas which contained preexistent settlements of various types, the "democratization" of the suburbs, and the loss of CBD dominance have rendered his astute generalizations somewhat less valuable today.

THE URBAN GEOGRAPHERS

The final strain out of which ecological analysis grew was urban geography, whose origins were almost coterminous with those of urban sociology. The first scientific study of a single city was published in France in 1911,[33] although a German book had appeared earlier describing the new field. The field did not really grow and become established until after World War II; when it did, it took over many of the preoccupations with urban physical structure that had fascinated urban sociologists and economists even earlier. Urban geographers contributed to the development of new and sophisticated techniques that permitted deeper insights into urban form—both for systems of cities and for the internal structure of the city. Modern urban sociologists need to master all methods for studying urban systems and internal city structures, whether these methods are now considered urban sociology or urban geography; when one studies an object as complex as a city, one can certainly not stop at disciplinary lines.

Regional Systems of Cities

Some of the earliest work on systems of cities and on the relationship between cities and their hinterlands was done by German economic geographers. The best known are Johann von Thunen (who published initially in 1826) and Walter Christaller (who first published his famous central place theory in 1933).[34] The discovery that cities were not isolated objects but were formed into constellations and systems which had predictable or at least describable characteristics was an important step forward in understanding the development of urbanization.

Theories about urban location and systems take as their starting point the function of cities in relation to other parts of the environment. These theories

---

[33]Raoul Blanchard's *Grenoble, étude de géographie urbaine,* cited in Harold Carter, *The Study of Urban Geography,* 3d ed. (London: Edward Arnold Publisher, 1981), p. 3.

[34]Walter Christaller, *Die Zentralen Orte in Suddeutschland,* first published in Jena by Gustav Fischer in 1933; available in English translation by C. W. Baskin, under the title *Central Places in Southern Germany* (Englewood Cliffs: Prentice-Hall, 1966). Johann Von Thunen's work is also available now in English translation; see his *Isolated State,* ed. Peter Hall (Oxford: Pergamon Press, 1966).

THE THEORETICAL PART

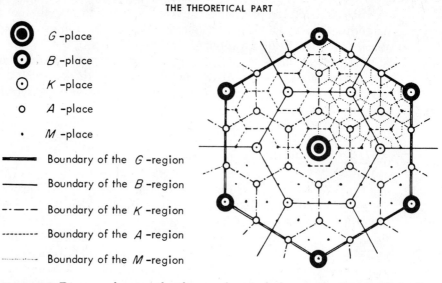

- ◎ *G* -place
- ◉ *B* -place
- ☉ *K* -place
- ○ *A* -place
- • *M* -place
- ▬▬▬ Boundary of the *G* -region
- ──── Boundary of the *B* -region
- ─·─·─ Boundary of the *K* -region
- ┄┄┄┄ Boundary of the *A* -region
- ┈┈┈┈ Boundary of the *M* -region

Figure 7.6 Diagram showing the theory of central place, according to Christaller. (*Source:* Walter Christaller, *Die Zentralen Orte in Suddeutschland* [published originally in Jena in 1933]. Reproduced from p. 66 of English trans. reprinted under the title, *Central Places in Southern Germany* [Englewood Cliffs, NJ: Prentice Hall, 1966].)

attempt to deduce consequences from abstract models. For urban geographers, the most important model is the one based upon a featureless (flat and empty) plain. Christaller examined the distribution of marketing towns in Germany and noted that each was surrounded by a service area which was roughly hexagonally shaped; he noted also that there appeared to be a hierarchy of such central places, with a number of marketing towns distributed around a larger and more important central place city which contained even more specialized services (see Figure 7.6). This basic theory has been refined and expanded into a more complex model by Brian Berry and William Garrison in their articles of 1958.[35] The Christaller model for market towns was expanded by Losch[36] into a more complex schema of sectors and rings, but the assumption was the same: namely, that it would be possible through mathematical modeling to devise law-like statements about the spatial structure of urban systems.

But clearly, not all cities functioned exclusively as marketing centers for surrounding areas. Many newer cities served chiefly manufacturing functions, and these might demonstrate a very different spatial patterning. The theory of

---

[35]See Berry and Garrison, "The Functional Bases of the Central Place Hierarchy," *Economic Geography* 34 (1958), pp. 145–154; and their "Recent Developments in Central Place Theory," *Papers and Proceedings of the Regional Science Association* 4 (1958), pp. 107–120.

[36]See A. Losch, *The Economics of Location* (New Haven: Yale University Press, 1954).

location for manufacturing centers goes back to the work of Alfred Weber.[37] The basic reasoning behind Weber's theory was that a manufacturing site would, *ceteris paribus,* be located at a point which minimized the transportation costs of all items that had to be assembled on a given site for production. Also to be taken into consideration was access to a given market for these products. Therefore, manufacturing cities would follow a different set of locational imperatives than would central place marketing centers (which minimized transportation costs of clients or consumers). Walter Isard refined this theory by expanding the locational model to take into account both minimizing costs of production and maximizing access to markets.[38]

Gradually, it came to be recognized that the distribution of managerial or service functions might deviate in significant ways from the distribution of commercial-retail functions and manufacturing functions. Presently, urban geography is attempting to develop the new theories required to explain the locational factors underlying this newest form of urban function. It should be recognized that spatial modeling, as now done by urban geographers, has become highly technical. The methods are not ones familiar to urban sociologists, and in many ways are not particularly helpful to them. Nevertheless, the particular analyses done by geographers can serve as useful background for urban sociologists trying to understand a given community.

The Internal Structure of Cities Revisited

Social Area Analysis   It is in the area of the internal organization of cities that the fields of urban geography and urban sociology converged. What began in urban sociology as the method of social area analysis eventually developed into the method of *factorial ecology,* now used primarily by urban geographers.

From the 1930s until 1950, the techniques of urban ecological analysis did not change much. As new data became available, these were added to the existing distributions, and as methods were refined, it became possible to map more data more elegantly. But in many ways, this successful proliferation of data brought about the downfall of the method itself. When urban ecologists had only a few pieces of information, they could assume that the pattern revealed through mapping actually stood for the pattern of the city itself.[39] But as more and more data became available, it became clear that such patterns were not entirely congruent. Furthermore, the existing method for testing congruence (namely, mapping each variable on a single transparent sheet and

---

[37]Published originally in German in 1909 but reissued in English translation by Carl J. Friedrich *Theory of the Location of Industries* (Chicago: University of Chicago Press, 1929, reissued 1957).

[38]Walter Isard, *Location and Space-Economy: A General Theory Relating Industrial Location, Market Areas, Land Use, Trade and Urban Structure* (New York: John Wiley, 1956).

[39]One sees this clearly in the article by Murray Leiffer, which was one of the first applications of Burgess's methods. See his "A Method for Determining Local Urban Community Boundaries," *Proceedings of the American Sociological Society* 26 (1933), pp. 137–143.

then overlaying the sheets to reach a common denominator!) became extremely unwieldy as more and more items of information became available. Both a theory that would aid in the selection of the "right" variables and a method for testing congruence based upon statistical rather than graphic congruency were needed.

The beginnings of this theory and method were developed by Eshref Shevky and Marilyn Williams in an early work, *The Social Areas of Los Angeles*, published in 1949.[40] It is perhaps significant that they were working on the city of Los Angeles, which, as Kevin Lynch put it, had a far less "imageable" pattern than Chicago. Whereas it might have been possible in the 1920s to get a vague sense of the physical structure of Chicago from wandering around in it, certainly such a procedure would not work for the sprawling region of Los Angeles in the late 1940s. If there *was* a spatial pattern to the city, more than the naked eye would be required to find it. The purpose of Williams and Shevky's study was, much like Burgess's, to use census data to subdivide the metropolis into "natural areas" suitable for planning health services.[41]

The analysts began with six census-tract indicators they hypothesized would fall on three separate dimensions of differentiation. Two were intended to capture the dimension of social class, three the dimension of life-style, especially with respect to family life, and the final, racial and ethnic segregation, with the intent of identifying those areas in which blacks or Hispanics were concentrated. Wendell Bell applied a similar method to arrive at the social areas of San Francisco,[42] and then Shevky and Bell published a small but very influential monograph in 1955, setting forth the details of the method in the context of a theory of social change.[43]

Shevky and Bell recommended analyzing data along three dimensions. The variables selected to measure social class were occupation (specifically, the proportion of males in blue-collar jobs) and education. The indicators of a second dimension they called "familism" (or its opposite, "urbanization") were the percentage of women in the labor force, the fertility ratio, and the proportion of single-family houses in the tract. The final dimension was race/ethnicity, for which the measure was the percentage of black and foreign-born in the population. A scoring system was devised so that each census tract received a value on each dimension—the value being expressed in terms of how much the tract deviated above or below the average of all tracts. Then, large natural areas were delimited for each of the three dimensions. When these were superim-

---

[40]Eshref Shevky and Marilyn Williams, *The Social Areas of Los Angeles: Analysis and Typology* (Los Angeles and Berkeley: University of California Press, 1949).

[41]This was, incidentally, the same function Howard Whipple Green had in mind in Cleveland when he made one of the first practical applications of census tract data analysis in the 1930s.

[42]Wendell Bell, "The Social Areas of the San Francisco Bay Region," *American Sociological Review* 18 (February 1953), pp. 39–47.

[43]See Eshref Shevky and Wendell Bell, *Social Area Analysis: Theory, Illustrative Application and Computational Procedures,* Stanford Series in Sociology, no. 1, 1955.

posed, what emerged was something called a *social area*, a subarea of the city that had a characteristic *combination* of values on the dimensions of class, ethnicity, and familism. The three dimensions, although inductively arrived at by Shevky and later theoretically rationalized by Bell, were originally only a good guess. It remained to test how good.

Wendell Bell attempted to test the theory through *factor analysis*.[44] He proved that the three dimensions could be separated by the method of factor analysis and, furthermore, that the variables which purported to measure them did indeed "load" onto the right dimensions. This opened the way for a new development—namely, the use of factor analysis as a method for mapping the structure of the city.

Factorial Ecology of American Cities In factor analysis, the procedure is the reverse of that followed in social area analysis. Instead of a few social indicators chosen on the basis of a priori hunches, factor analysis begins with a wide array of sociological indicators computed for each and every census tract. These variables are then subjected to factor analysis, a statistical method which reveals the latent patterns among them, as demonstrated by the matrix of their intercorrelations. Variables that fall together on a single factor (*vector* or *dimension of differentiation)* are then weighted to reach a combined standardized value for each census tract on the dimension. It is this set of combined weighted scores, rather than the values on separate variables, that is later mapped. A separate map is prepared for each vector or dimension (that is, factor); then, these maps can be overlaid to indicate social areas of the city, although this final step is often omitted.

The use of social area/factor analysis to determine the multiple spatial patterns of the city had some interesting results. For one, it suggested a possible resolution of the ongoing controversy between Burgess and Hoyt. In a crucial study, Theodore Anderson and Janice Egeland found that in four middle-sized American cities, instead of there being one and only one spatial pattern for the city, there were different spatial patterns for each of the factors or dimensions.[45] The socioeconomic dimension (which Hoyt had measured and mapped, using data on rents and values) tended to follow a sectoral pattern of distribution in space. On the other hand, the factor of familism (or rather, lack of familism) seemed to follow a concentric circle pattern, as Burgess had hypothesized. Ethnicity was a variable which was city-specific; no predictable spatial distributions were found, although minority areas were more likely to be central and poor and to lie adjacent to industrial zones.

Since the time of these first factorial ecologies, many studies of individual cities have been made. Recently, data from the 1980 census for a representative

---

[44]See Wendell Bell, "Economic, Family and Ethnic Status: An Empirical Test," *American Sociological Review* 20 (February, 1955), pp. 45–52.

[45]See Theodore Anderson and Janice Egeland, "Spatial Aspects of Social Area Analysis," *American Sociological Review* 26 (June 1961), pp. 392–298.

Percent White Collar Workers: 1980
San Antonio, Texas, SMSA by Census Tract

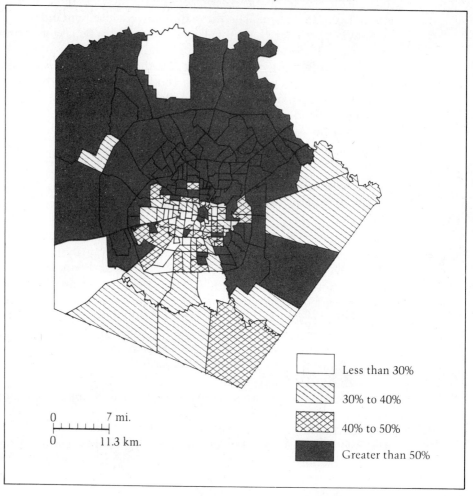

☐	Less than 30%
▨	30% to 40%
▨	40% to 50%
■	Greater than 50%

0 |—|—|—|—|—|—|— 7 mi.

0 —————————— 11.3 km.

Figure 7.7 Residential locations of white-collar workers in the San Antonio, Texas, SMSA in 1980, by census tracts. (*Source:* Michael White, *American Neighborhoods and Residential Differentiation* [New York: Russell Sage Foundation, 1987], p. 124. Copyright 1987, The Russell Sage Foundation. Used with permission of the Russell Sage Foundation.)

sample of 21 metropolitan areas have been elaborately processed by factor analysis by Michael J. White,[46] giving us our most convincing proof of the overall consistency of the three factors initially suggested by Shevky and Williams. This study reveals, as critics had intimated, that results are to some extent

---

[46]Michael J. White, *American Neighborhoods and Residential Differentiation* (New York: Russell Sage Foundation, 1987). It is impossible to do justice to this rich and detailed analysis in the short space allotted.

Average Household Size: 1980
San Antonio, Texas, SMSA by Census Tract

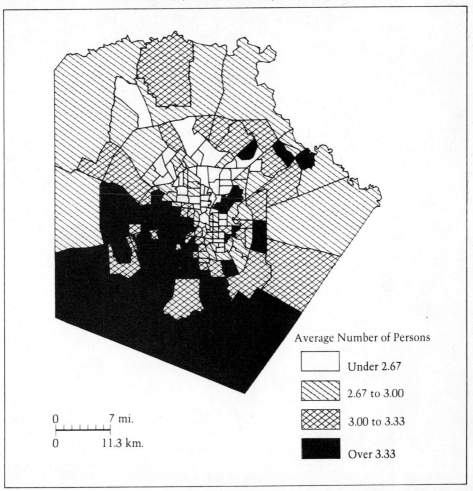

Average Number of Persons

	Under 2.67
	2.67 to 3.00
	3.00 to 3.33
	Over 3.33

Figure 7.8 Residential locations of average household sizes in the San Antonio, Texas, SMSA in 1980, by census tracts. (*Source:* Michael White, *American Neighborhoods and Residential Differentiation* [New York: Russell Sage Foundation, 1987], p. 127. Copyright 1987, The Russell Sage Foundation. Used with permission of the Russell Sage Foundation.)

dependent upon the variables included; but its chief contribution is to identify differences among metropolitan areas in terms of their factor structures.

Although socioeconomic status is a universally found dominant factor, there appear to be differences in the familism and race/ethnicity dimensions from city to city. Now that female participation in the labor force has become so common, fertility has plummeted, and the suburbs contain apartments suitable for atypical family types, the clear association between newly built suburban areas and familism has weakened, particularly in the new metropolitan areas

Percent Black Population: 1980
San Antonio, Texas, SMSA by Census Tract

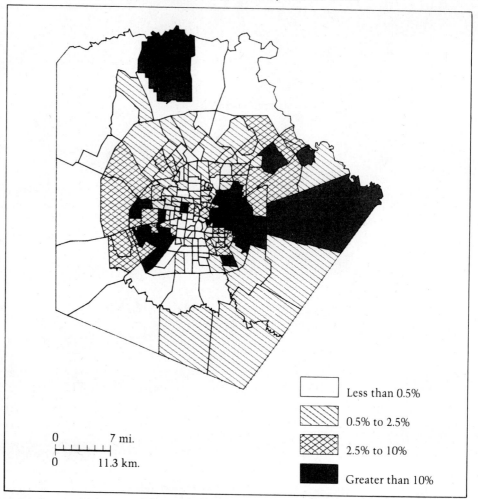

	Less than 0.5%
	0.5% to 2.5%
	2.5% to 10%
	Greater than 10%

0   7 mi.

0   11.3 km.

Figure 7.9 Percentage of black population in San Antonio, Texas, SMSA in 1980, by census tracts. (*Source:* Michael White, *American Neighborhoods and Residential Differentiation* [New York: Russell Sage Foundation, 1987], p. 130. Copyright 1987, The Russell Sage Foundation. Used with permission of the Russell Sage Foundation.)

of the South and West. Great diversity is found in the distribution of various ethnic and racial groups by region. Blacks are most concentrated, and there is a close connection between race, female-headed households, and poverty in metropolitan areas where African-Americans constitute the largest minority group. Asians are much less segregated (outside west coast cities), and Hispanics fall somewhere between. White suggests that Burgess's hypothesis about a concentric gradient for cities holds for socioeconomic status and, to some declining extent, for familism as well, whereas race and ethnicity show a polynucleated distribution. Figures 7.7, 7.8, and 7.9 show how class, family size, and minority status follow different patterns of distribution in San Antonio, Texas.

Comparative Factorial Ecologies   A number of studies have also been made outside the United States that are yielding the raw materials for a comparative study of urban spatial structure. At the beginning of this chapter it was seen how Latin American cities derived their characteristic spatial structures from a common origin and how colonial policies created dual cities in Morocco as well as in many other Third World countries with a colonial urban legacy. Such patterns tend to persist and constrain future uses of space. Nevertheless, modern technologies and industrialization introduce changes which modify existing patterns in a common direction.

One major difference between cities is whether they were substantially built up before or after the period of modern industrialism. As Gist and Fava pointed out,[47] studies made before factorial ecology was invented had already uncovered important contrasts between the typical spatial structures of preindustrial and industrial cities. For example, in cities whose major growth was in the preindustrial period, the city center still tends to be dominated by religious and governmental structures, although the major commercial markets are also present. Urban elites live next to the city core, whereas lower socioeconomic groups live progressively farther out. In contrast, cities whose major street patterns and public buildings were set down in the industrial period tend, as Burgess had predicted, to be centered on a "downtown" dominated by high-rise commercial enterprises that are surrounded by a decaying "zone in transition." Wealthier groups live far from the city center, generally progressively farther as socioeconomic level rises. In many cities, such as European capitals, where major developments took place in both the preindustrial and industrial periods, the ecological patterns tend to reflect a mix.[48] And, as we have seen, cities whose growth is taking place primarily in the postindustrial period (e.g., cities of the Southwest and west coast of the United States) tend to sprawl in more amorphous fashion.

Factorial ecology studies suggest that despite these great differences in the visible city, the same dimensions (or factors) may account for the principles by which their populations are distributed.[49] For example, a socioeconomic vector

---

[47]This paragraph draws heavily on the discussion in Gist and Fava, *Urban Society*, pp. 172–173; its incorporation here is acknowledged with permission and thanks.

[48]For Latin American cities, see Leo F. Schnore, "On the Spatial Structure of Cities in the Two Americas," in Philip M. Hauser and Leo F. Schnore, eds., *The Study of Urbanization* (New York: John Wiley, 1965); and Gideon Sjoberg, *The Preindustrial City* (Glencoe, IL: Free Press, 1960), Chapter 4. For descriptions of London, Paris, Vienna, and Stockholm, see Francis L. Hauser, "Ecological Patterns of European Cities," in Sylvia F. Fava, ed., *Urbanism in World Perspective: A Reader* (New York: Thomas Y. Crowell, 1968), pp. 193–216.

[49]The following discussion draws heavily on Janet Abu-Lughod, "Testing the Theory of Social Area Analysis: The Ecology of Cairo, Egypt" in *American Sociological Review* 4 (April 1969), pp. 198–

is the dominant factor in almost all urban factorial ecologies because, at least in the modern era, class is the single most important basis for distributing space in the city. In addition, most of the demographic measures that indicate differential fertility or family size are likely to cluster together in factorial ecologies in all societies. However, whereas demographic variables tend to fall on a different dimension than socioeconomic status in American cities, in cities within societies just beginning the demographic transition, where low fertility is highly associated with social class, such family-type measures tend to fall on the same dimension as class.[50] As might be expected, whether a race or ethnicity factor is found depends very much on the social cleavages in a given place.

It is impossible to generalize about the spatial structure of all cities, much less to expect these generalizations to apply to cities in the Third World. In addition to their cultural variations, some Third World cities have venerable histories, others were planned and built up during the colonial period, while many others contain both old and modern quarters. Below we will present information on two such complex cities: Calcutta, a relatively new city founded and planned by the British when they ruled India; and Cairo, a very old city that has undergone several successive "modernizations," first under indigenous (but French-influenced) rule, then under the British, and finally after independence. Neither city could be mistaken for an American urban center.

Berry and Rees,[51] working on Calcutta, and Abu-Lughod, simultaneously working on Cairo, formulated similar schemes of the various ways in which the underlying urban dimensions may be differentiated from one another. Their independent reviews of the factorial analyses of cities of varying cultural backgrounds and degree of industrialization indicate at least six combinations of the three dimensions: socioeconomic status, family status (labeled "stage-in-life cycle" or "urbanization" by some authors), and membership in minority groups.

The Factorial Ecology of Calcutta and Chicago[52]   Detailed study of Calcutta led Berry and Rees to view its ecological structure as exemplifying both preindustrial and industrial ecological features. Comparison of the social areas of Chicago and Calcutta, diagrammed in Figure 7.10, indicates that the cities

---

212. But see also Duncan Timms, *The Urban Mosaic: Towards a Theory of Residential Differentiation* (Cambridge: University Press, 1971), pp. 54–63 and Chapter 5; and R. J. Johnston, *Urban Residential Patterns: An Introductory Review* (London: Bell, 1971; New York: Praeger Publishers, 1972), pp. 330–353.

[50]In "Testing the Theory of Social Area Analysis," Abu-Lughod noted that in southern cities of the United States, where race, class, and fertility are tightly associated, the dimensions of family type and social class could not be separated factorially. Support for this position can be found in Maurice Van Arsdol, Jr., Santo Carmilleri, and Calvin Schmid, "The Generality of Urban Social Area Indexes," in *American Sociological Review* 23 (June 1958), pp. 277–284.

[51]See Brian J. L. Berry and Philip H. Rees, "The Factorial Ecology of Calcutta," *American Journal of Sociology* 74 (March 1969), pp. 445–491.

[52]The summary of Berry and Rees's work on Calcutta has been incorporated from pp. 174–175 of Gist and Fava, *Urban Society.*

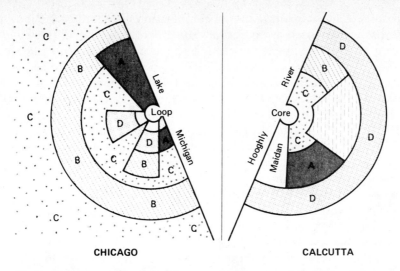

CHICAGO   CALCUTTA

Figure 7.10 Generalized social areas of Chicago and Calcutta. (*Source:* Brian Berry and Philip Rees, "The Factorial Ecology of Calcutta," *American Journal of Sociology* 74 [March 1969]. Copyright 1969 by University of Chicago Press which granted permission to reproduce.)

are similar in that socioeconomic status and family cycle are separate dimensions. Social areas of type "A" are those occupied by groups characterized by high socioeconomic status and low familism. In both cities such areas exist and are located fronting the special amenities—Lake Michigan in Chicago and the Maidan, a large park, in Calcutta. The distribution of the "D" social areas— those inhabited by groups combining lowest socioeconomic status with high familism (young age groups, many children)—clearly indicates the difference between preindustrial Calcutta and industrial Chicago. In Calcutta the "D" social areas encircle the periphery of the city; in Chicago they are found near the city center. Social area type "B" represents areas high in both socioeconomic status and familism. In Chicago these areas are located in a suburban ring, but not in Calcutta. Social area type "C" represents areas low in both familism and socioeconomic status; in Calcutta they are found near the central core, while in Chicago they are located in both a middle-city position and a vast belt beyond the suburbs. Figure 7.10 cannot portray adequately the much greater importance of the ethnic dimension of Calcutta, where ethnic origin and caste are strongly linked to occupation and other economic indicators. Berry and Rees note that in this regard Calcutta resembles the ecological model of cities of the American South.

The Factorial Ecology of Cairo   Abu-Lughod's 1966 factorial analysis of Cairo, Egypt,[53] demonstrates another way in which ecological factors may be

---

[53]This discussion is based on *Cairo: 1001 Years of the City Victorious* (Princeton, NJ: Princeton University Press, 1971) and "Testing the Theory of Social Area Analysis: The Ecology of Cairo,

related. Cairo exhibits a unique combination of preindustrial and modern patterns, because parts are very old while others are modern. However, only a few dimensions were needed to describe its ecological structure, and these dimensions were not greatly differentiated from one another. Abu-Lughod reduced the number of factors to three: life-style, settlements of unattached migrant males, and social pathology. Of these, the first factor explained more than half of the statistical variance among census tracts of Cairo in 1947 and again in 1960. This "life-style" factor measured more than socioeconomic class, however, since it included not only economic, but also family *and* ethnic variables. This overlap indicated an only partially decolonized and modernized society, one in which class and family patterns were still linked, and where "modern" areas contained many Europeans. High economic status was associated with a modern westernized life-style, including important changes in the role of women and in family size; low income status was associated with traditional family roles and high fertility.

Areas that scored highest on Factor I contained luxurious housing, which was occupied by well-educated persons served by resident domestic servants. Families in these districts had begun to follow more "modern" family patterns, sending their female children through school, marrying them off at later ages, and having fewer children altogether. Such areas were favored by the remaining European residents of the city. At the opposite extreme, in districts that scored lowest on Factor I, people were severely overcrowded in poor housing, most residents were illiterate, and females seldom attended school or had paid employment. Such traditional patterns of female exclusion from the educational and occupational systems went with marriage at a very young age and a post-nuptial life of high, sustained, and generally uncontrolled fertility.

On the basis of Factor I, life-style, Abu-Lughod delineated 13 major "subcities" of contemporary Cairo, each different in population characteristics, physical appearance, the kinds of housing and shopping facilities available, and even the way residents dressed and (probably) believed. These areas are shown in Figure 7.11.

Such areas exemplified three major ways of life in Cairo: the rural, the traditional urban, and the modern urban. The "rural" population of Cairo consisted not only of farmers but also of impoverished urban residents, many of them migrants to the city, whose way of life carried over much from their agricultural origins. This population, concentrated in a loose ring on the outskirts of Cairo in subcities III, VI, IX, and XIII, accounted for about 14 percent of the total population of Cairo in 1960. The traditional urban population, that is, those who tended to follow the economic activities, forms of social relationships, and systems of values which were more typical in Cairo generations ago, were concentrated in three inner city slum area (I, X, XII) that in 1960 accounted for 30 percent of Cairo's population. The modern urban (westernized)

Egypt." Both these sources summarize findings from her 1966 doctoral dissertation. We have drawn freely upon the summary formerly included in Gist and Fava, *Urban Society,* pp. 176–178.

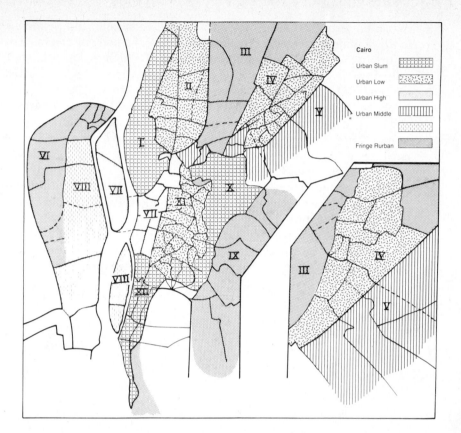

Figure 7.11 The thirteen subcities of Cairo, Egypt, in 1960, according to Factor I - Lifestyle. (*Source:* Janet Abu-Lughod, *Cairo: 1001 Years of the City Victorious* [Princeton: Princeton University Press, 1971], p. 187. Copyright 1971 by Princeton University Press.)

population was concentrated in one high-income area, VII, and one middle-income area, V, and in 1960 accounted for 9 percent of the population. The remainder of Cairo's population, about 46 percent, was found in areas II, IV, VII, and XI, which represented various low- and middle-income levels and various combinations of traditional and modern life-styles.

CONCLUSIONS

In this chapter we have traced the development of the methods urban sociologists use to analyze and describe the spatial structures of urban communities. As these methods have become more and more refined, they have led to an appreciation of the great variations which occur in urban spatial patterns and to comparative studies which attempt to explain these variations by relating spatial patterns to the technological, social, economic, and political conditions in the containing societies. By now an impressive body of comparative findings on urban spatial patterns has accumulated,[54] which makes it at least theoretically possible to develop a synthetic and generalizing theory of urban space in relation to the factors that shape it.

When sociologists were first learning to "see" the spatial patterns in cities and had just begun to develop their first crude techniques for "capturing" them in maps, not much theoretical sophistication could have been expected. But naïveté was due not only to primitive methods. Indeed, if anything, the "theory" of human ecology was cruder than the methods used to study it. In Chapter 8 we look at the changing theories set forth to explain why things and people are where they are in cities and that try to identify the crucial factors underlying shifts in locations. Over the past 20 years, more than an "evolution" in theory has taken place. Indeed, many claim that there has been a "scientific revolution" in how urban sociologists view the causes of urban spatial structure and evaluate the factors that lead to its transformation.

---

[54]For example, see Kent P. Schwirian, ed., *Comparative Urban Structure: Studies in the Ecology of Cities* (Lexington, MA: D. C. Heath, 1974); the 1982 edition of Theodorson, *Urban Patterns;* R. J. Johnston, *Urban Residential Patterns: An Introductory Review* (New York: Praeger Publishers, 1972); Brian J. L. Berry and John K. Kasarda, *Contemporary Urban Ecology* (New York: Macmillan Publishing Company, 1977); and Larry S. Bourne, ed., *Internal Structure of the City: Readings on Urban Form, Growth and Policy,* 2d ed. (New York and Oxford: Oxford University University Press, 1982).

Chapter
8

How Urban Spatial Structures Arise and Change

*E*xplaining *how* particular spatial structures of the city come into being and are maintained is far more complex than finding out *what* those spatial structures are. And it is here that, in contrast to the gradual developments that took place in the area of methodology, there have been fundamental changes in theory.

Current explanations for why cities exhibit the spatial patterns they do, and why people with various characteristics are found where they are in American cities, are quite different from those set forth in classical urban ecology. Indeed, a number of contemporary scholars have suggested that in the past two decades urban sociology has undergone a true "scientific revolution." In this chapter and the next we trace this revolution in understanding the *causes* of urban spatial structure. We show how these changes were related to (a) internal contradictions in the theory itself, (b) real changes in the nature of cities and in the economic and political systems that reproduce them, and (c) changes in the values of urban sociologists and their new sensitivity to deprived urban groups such as minorities and women.

HOW CLASSICAL ECOLOGY EXPLAINED URBAN FORM

Park, Burgess, McKenzie, and their followers thought of the city as the *organic* product of people living together. At the same time, they acknowledged that the city was held together and internally differentiated by an *economic market* in land values. Thus, from the start, the theory of urban ecological change had internal contradictions.

On the one hand, taking its initial model for urban communities from plant ecology, the theory saw "order" as the outcome of unconscious (even unintended) human actions more appropriate to scrub pines in dune succession than to human social behavior in complex societies.[1] It posited a subconscious human response to space and time that "adjusted" organisms to one another through turf sharing and temporal sequencing. In many ways, the recent efforts of Edward Hall to identify human subliminal responses to space and time address many of the early questions raised in human ecology.[2] But although Hall has certainly found *some* universals, his major emphasis has been upon the cultural variability of these responses, and such cultural variations refute any simple analogy to plant communities.

Even though the founders of urban ecology adopted terminology used by plant ecologists (segregation, invasion, competition, succession, dominance), seeking to explain changes in urban spatial structure in terms of them, they recognized that in human societies these processes were actually mediated through money and the market. They resolved this contradiction by assuming that the human analogy to competition and dominance in nature was economic competition in the marketplace (certainly a cultural process). That is, in place of the hidden forces of Darwinian "cruel nature," they substituted the "invisible hand" that guided Adam Smith's marketplace.

They could do this only because they accepted the classical economist's view of the market as the place where millions of individual transactions cumulate to express demand, regulate supply, set prices, and maximize the efficient distribution of goods and services. In this "Adam Smith marketplace," no single seller or buyer is able to influence price in a determining way. There are neither monopolies nor collusion among buyers or sellers. Government does not interfere to protect either the weak or the strong. Indeed, an invisible hand appears to guide collective outcomes that are not necessarily desired or intended by the individuals who participate in the market. It is this invisible hand that molds urban space through the mechanism of the market for land.

This idea—that population is "sifted and sorted" in a city by its ability to

---

[1]In Park and Burgess's *An Introduction to the Science of Sociology,* Park included an excerpt from a 1909 book, *Oecology of Plants,* by Eugenius Warming, which was concerned with symbiosis as the subliminal adjustment of different species to one another in a shared habitat. Park was later to apply this theory to urban coexistence.

[2]See Edward T. Hall, *The Hidden Dimension* (Garden City, NY: Doubleday Anchor, 1969) and *The Dance of Life: The Other Dimension of Time* (Garden City, NY: Doubleday Anchor, 1983).

pay and by its differential demands for various aspects of space and housing—fit well into the general ideology of the Chicago School. The founders of the Chicago School assumed that industrial and commercial interests were "dominant" in contemporary American cities, just as pine trees were dominant in scrub forests. They recognized that business interests could pay more for urban land than could most housing consumers, making commerce "the highest use." Next came industry, which was willing to pay a premium for locations that were advantageous to it in terms of production costs. Residential uses essentially "fit into" the residual spaces not sought by industry or commerce. Furthermore, they recognized that the rich, because they could afford to pay higher transportation costs, could move to the outskirts, while the poor needed central sites.

Unfortunately, while recognizing all these "facts" of urban sifting and sorting, they seem not to have recognized that the resulting configurations of space were not only a function of differential costs, technologies, preferences, and so on, but were *contingent on the capitalist system* with its freehold land market. Private ownership of land, however, was hardly a fact of nature; it was an institution created by a political system.

CRITICISMS OF THE CHICAGO SCHOOL

The first major criticism of the Chicago School attacked the analogy between cities and plant and animal communities. Alihan,[3] in a scathing critique of the work of classical urban ecologists, accused them of having drawn a false dichotomy between "society" (the socially organized parts of human interaction which Park had called "the moral order") and "community" (by which Park meant the biotic, subconsensual, territorially based symbiotic interactions that were analogous to plant and animal ecological environments). She contended that it was impossible to maintain the suggested distinction between the "social" and "biotic" communities, since the dominant influences in a contemporary city were clearly *social* institutions, devised by people.

Another set of criticisms, leveled slightly later, pointed out that the economic system, rather than being a natural mechanism for sifting and sorting, was a symbolic system expressive of interests, values, and (even more belatedly acknowledged) differential power. Land values, the economic mechanism that underlay the distribution of land uses and economic "housing classes" in the city, were not outcomes of impersonal "symbiotic" Darwinian competition but were actually products of Park's "moral order." Thus, William Form persuasively argued that land values were truly *values* that reflected social and cultural preferences, rather than impersonal automatic mechanisms.[4]

---

[3]Milla Alihan, *Social Ecology* (New York: Columbia University Press, 1938).

[4]See William Form, "The Place of Social Structure in the Determination of Land Use: Some Implications for a Theory of Urban Ecology," *Social Forces* 32 (May 1954), pp. 317–323.

Along these same lines was the important criticism raised by Walter Firey.[5] In his study of Boston's Beacon Hill, he pointed out that if Burgess's hypothesis were correct, this exclusive residential district close to downtown Boston should long since have deteriorated into a slum. In actual fact, one portion had, but the area of Louisburg Square continued to serve as an exclusive zone of upper-class residence because it retained its symbolic value to the Boston aristocracy. Firey suggested that human values, exercised through the social structure, were more important in shaping the urban environment than were such "organic" laws as invasion and succession that were posited by the classical urban ecologists.

Most recently, however, criticisms of the classical approach to urban ecology have come from a different source—political economy. Rather than attacking the "biotic" assumptions of early ecology, political economy critics attack the classical economic assumptions of a free market for land. They argue that the land market is deeply connected to monopoly capitalism and the political system.

What accounts for these changes in approach? To a certain extent, they result from changes in the way city space began to be allocated—changes which took place after the founders of the Chicago School of urban ecology had formulated their theories.

Real Changes in the Market for Land and Housing

Perhaps at the turn of the century Adam Smith's assumptions about the competitive market for land and real property were valid, but beginning in the 1910s and even more markedly in the 1920s and 1930s, a number of political changes were occurring in the United States that made these assumptions increasingly invalid. Among these changes were (1) the introduction of comprehensive zoning laws regulating land uses in cities; (2) enormous expansions in the governmental provision of public infrastructure (items of "collective consumption"); (3) direct government construction of subsidized public housing and interest and tax benefits subsidizing home ownership; and finally, (4) urban renewal and redevelopment programs which, among other things, involved government in setting urban land prices. Each of these political interventions significantly modified prices for land and real property in ways that "repealed" the laws of the market.

Zoning   A zoning ordinance is a set of local governmental regulations over the uses to which privately owned land can be put. The right of the city to zone is based on the "police power," that is, the power that allows local governments to pass laws to protect the health, safety, and welfare of residents. Attempts at piecemeal zoning began by the end of the nineteenth century. By the second decade of the twentieth century, following the model law passed in New York City in 1916, more comprehensive zoning laws became widespread in the

---

[5]Walter Firey, *Land Use in Central Boston* (Cambridge, MA: Harvard University Press, 1947).

United States. However, it was not until 1926 that the Supreme Court (in the definitive *Village of Euclid v. Ambler Realty* case) upheld zoning as a constitutional exercise of police power.[6]

Zoning regulations alter the rules according to which property values are established because, in essence, they serve to create *separate* and partially monopolistic markets for land within *each* of the different use districts. Given the fact that commercial firms are willing and able to pay higher prices for accessible land than are either industrial firms or residential property owners, the designation of only a limited amount of land for commercial use creates scarcity and, therefore, automatically increases prices—if not immediately, at least eventually. For example, rezoning a given piece of land from residential to commercial uses acts to *create* an increase in its value. Similarly, when parcels of land are protected as suitable only for upper-income residential uses, owners obtain an "unearned" increase in the value of those parcels. Conversely, low land costs are associated with the absence of regulations. Land on the outskirts of an urban community is often cheap not only because it is in plentiful supply but because it lies in unincorporated territories that have no local regulations or restrictions on its use; this is one reason industry prefers such locations.

In short, in place of an invisible hand regulating land prices and thus the distribution of land uses in the city (as assumed by the Chicago School), the hand of government was increasingly on the tiller. Regulations on land use imposed by local governments came to have an inordinate and quite visible influence on the evolving urban form. Since such regulations were first imposed at the time when urban ecological theory was explaining the evolution of past (prezoning) patterns, there was an understandable gap between the theory and the new realities.

Infrastructure and Collective Consumption   A second way the political system was having an increasingly important effect on land values and therefore on urban patterns was through government investment in infrastructure. When the early theories of urban ecology were first being formulated, such investments were still modest. However, in the decades that followed, municipal and state governments, and subsequently the federal government, became more and more involved in the provision of items of public consumption.

The connection between investments in infrastructure and the creation of land values is a clear one. It is well known that extensions of paved roads, of sewer lines, of municipal lighting, and of public services such as schools, have the direct effect of increasing the value of land in the immediate vicinity, just as the location of a municipal garbage dump depresses adjacent land values. (Economists refer to these effects as "externalities.") A substantial profit can be

---

[6]For a history of zoning in the United States, see Richard F. Babcock, *The Zoning Game* (Madison, WI: University of Wisconsin Press, 1966) and Seymour I. Zoll, *Zoned America* (New York: Grossman Publishers, 1969). A brilliant insight into the relationship between zoning categories and American cultural values is presented in Constance Perin, *Everything in Its Place: Social Order and Land Use in America* (Princeton, NJ: Princeton University Press, 1977).

made by someone who buys unimproved land at its "agricultural" price and then holds it until the municipality has installed the services that redefine the land as "suitable for urban uses." Therefore, having advance knowledge of *where* public investments are to be made can offer great profit to an investor. It is a small step beyond this to recognize that the ability to control the political system that decides *where* public funds are to be invested should be of considerable value to businesspeople, as a class.

None of this seems to have been recognized by the Chicago School theorists, who thought in terms of free competition. The city, it turned out, was not really much like the "five acres in a state of nature" posited by the early theorists. Rather, the city was an arena for the creation and re-creation of land values. Zoning, because it could create monopoly rights over land use, and public consumption investments, because they redistributed wealth and changed the value of land near them, were therefore important objects of interest and struggle for the various classes and ethnic groups competing for space and access in the city.

One example may help illustrate this last point: the political decision to invest in highways or in mass transit. Whereas in the classical ecological approach, this would have been defined as a technical question, today's political economists recognize it as a struggle for benefits. Wealthy individuals own cars and prefer to drive. When highways are improved and public parking facilities are constructed with public funds, owners of cars have the costs of their travel subsidized by the state. Conversely, the poor, the aged, and female heads of households are less likely to own cars and more likely to depend upon public transit facilities. Members of the latter group are the beneficiaries when public funds are allocated to improve public transit or to reduce fares, instead of being used to subsidize highway construction. In short, all decisions about the allocation of funds for public consumption are, in essence, decisions to redistribute wealth among the interest groups and classes that make up the population of the city.[7] Many of these macro-decisions are now made at the national rather than the municipal level.

In all fairness, one must recognize that at the time the classical theories of urban ecology were being formulated, the role of the federal government was still quite modest. That role has expanded dramatically in the past half century in ways that have radically altered how urban spatial structures evolve. One of the main areas in which the role of the federal government has expanded is in housing. And since the housing market is considered central in the sifting and sorting of populations in the city, any political-economic changes in how housing is made available differentially to the various competing groups in the city inevitably affects the spatial distribution of these groups. The two major ways that the federal government became involved in the housing market were by providing publicly subsidized housing for the poor, and by granting tax subsidies to higher-income buyers.

---

[7]That the situation can often be more complex than this is indicated in J. Allen Whitt's case study of BART, *Urban Elites and Mass Transportation* (Princeton, NJ: Princeton University Press, 1982).

Government Investments in and Subsidies for Housing   From the end of the nineteenth century to the early part of the twentieth, arguments were being made in England and the United States for philanthropic and public subsidies to provide adequate housing for the poor. One of the most influential books in this debate was written in 1919 by Edith Wood.[8] After reviewing the findings of the various urban commissions that had, since the turn of the century, investigated housing conditions of the poor in American cities, she concluded that *the poor would never be able to afford the cost of standard housing.* Various housing studies had set minimum adequate standards and had determined how much such standard dwellings would cost. Given these estimates and given the distribution of wages in American cities, Wood concluded that a substantial proportion of American workers were unlikely to be paid wages sufficient to allow them to buy or rent adequate housing units on the open market. The implication for policy was obvious. The state (or private philanthropy) would have to make up the difference between the cost of a standard dwelling and the ability of a poor family to pay for it, if all Americans were to be housed in standard dwellings.[9]

In addition to recommending public subsidies to provide housing for the poor, Wood also advocated regulations to set construction standards (building codes) and housing occupancy standards (housing codes); she believed that these regulations could prevent the construction and use of inadequate housing. The book ends with a strong plea that planning and zoning regulations be introduced into American municipalities, that model housing and building codes be adopted and enforced, that model housing estates be built through public or private subsidy, and that low-interest loans be made available through the government to enable poorly paid workers and their families to purchase decent housing.

Many of the policies advocated in this early report were subsequently adopted. They then began to affect the spatial organization of the city in ways not predicted by the early ecological theories. Especially after the federal government became directly involved in building public housing (in the mid-1930s) and particularly as government-backed and guaranteed low-interest home mortgage loans began to subsidize home purchase (and therefore, indirectly, home builders), it became increasingly difficult to talk about simple market mechanisms creating the urban pattern. Reforms often had unintended consequences.

Direct subsidies to build large public housing projects had the direct effect of concentrating poor people in inner city areas, because a sifting and sorting mechanism was built into the rules of housing eligibility (such as income ceilings, etc.). As these "islands of misery" became more clearly defined, middle-

---

[8]Edith Elmer Wood, *The Housing of the Unskilled Wage Earner: America's Next Problem* (New York: Macmillan Company, 1919).

[9]It is fascinating that in all these discussions, it is never suggested that wages be raised to permit workers to rent decent housing, although this was Frederick Engels's solution to "the housing question." Harvey and Stone, in arguments summarized on pp. 199–201, maintain that capitalism could not survive such a solution.

class home owners began to oppose the construction of such projects in their own neighborhoods, which marked the beginning of the NIMBY (not-in-my-backyard) response. Especially after World War II, when occupants of public housing projects began to be drawn increasingly from minority groups, it became almost impossible to find "acceptable" sites for new public housing projects, except in the predominantly black-occupied central slums. Finally, when the Supreme Court ruled that public housing authorities could not add to racial segregation by their site selection policies (which, in many cases, meant they could no longer build in the ghetto but had to find sites in white areas), many cities stopped constructing public housing altogether. Certainly, it would be hard to claim that the resulting spatial patterns, or the social conflicts they generated or perpetuated, were the effects of an "invisible hand." They were clearly the effects of governmental policy and the struggle for turf and advantage in the city.

The same must be said for the increased involvement of government in financing and guaranteeing mortgage loans or in offering tax benefits to home buyers. Edith Wood had advocated cheap mortgages to help working-class families buy their own homes. This policy was instituted in the 1920s and has subsequently been expanded many times. Such incentives to home ownership helped shape the evolving city in a variety of ways, chiefly by encouraging single-family home construction and attendant "urban sprawl." In addition, the federal government offered lending institutions guarantees on loans made available to certain "high-risk" or other special classes (such as veterans). And finally, tax incentives to home ownership were later built into the income tax laws. Home owners were permitted to exclude from taxable income not only the money they paid for local property taxes, but also the interest they paid on their mortgage and, later, their equity loans, whereas renters enjoyed none of these benefits.

These governmental policies created enormous, albeit somewhat inequitably distributed, incentives to American families to purchase their own homes. Such incentives (that is, subsidies), however, chiefly benefited "normal" families with stable middle to high incomes. The poor, widows, "atypical" female-headed families, minorities, and urban newcomers are all more likely to be renters because they cannot afford or do not need an owned home; ironically, these needy groups are ineligible for housing subsidies. Clearly, we cannot fault the founders of the Chicago School for failing to recognize how important these policies would be for shaping the city of the future and for sifting and sorting different populations into different parts of the metropolitan region. Few of the policies were even in existence at the time urban ecological theory was being written.

Urban Redevelopment and the Shape of the City   Urban renewal laws were another political influence on the spatial structure of the city. On the grounds that the war had generated a housing shortage, that cities were filled with slums needing to be cleared and rebuilt, and that subsidies were required to entice private real estate developers into renewing the centers of American cities, the federal government passed the Urban Redevelopment Law of 1949. This law helped municipal authorities condemn "blighted land" near the downtown districts, subsidized governmental authorities to purchase large parcels of land in prime locations at highly inflated "market value prices," and then helped cities pay to clear the land of its old and deteriorated structures. Once the land was cleared, the subsidies permitted cities to sell it back to private real estate developers at prices considerably below market value. Developers, in return for this subsidy and certain tax reductions as well, agreed to "redevelop" the land for "higher" uses (commerce or middle-class housing).

Recognizing that poor persons would be displaced by this "slum clearance" operation, the law required that relocation housing be found for them. However, the program did not add low-cost housing to the city's stock, nor did it provide rent subsidies to the displaced. Often, poor people were just crowded into the remaining low-rent areas, while more profitable new uses preempted their old locations.

While urban redevelopment may have been well intentioned, the practice left much to be desired. As had often been the case when governments uses incentives (subsidies) to cajole private enterprise into helping the poor or even the middle class, real estate developers managed to reap inordinate profits by siphoning off the public subsidies.[10]

To illustrate what happened all too often, we give a typical example from Chicago. A major real estate magnate in the city was able to purchase newly cleared land on the near north side of the city for a very low price.[11] This land, which was supposed to have been redeveloped for middle-income residents, actually ended up as a multi-block high-rise high-rental project catering to a newly affluent class of postwar urban residents, "swinging singles."[12] After many years of profit-taking, the developer finally converted the apartments into condominiums and sold them off at high prices. Thus, the developer benefited several times over from the public subsidies he received: first, through the unusually low price he paid for the cleared land; second, through the high rents he collected over the years, rents that excluded the middle class, who were to have benefited from urban renewal; and finally, by absorbing into the sale price the new higher value of the land, while unloading the apartments before costs of maintenance and repair threatened to reduce his profits.

Throughout the United States, similar ventures were undertaken in the

---

[10]Charles Abrams's book, *The City Is the Frontier* (New York: Harper & Row, 1965), is a cynical and sad summation of his lifetime in urban reform, in which he acknowledged that real estate interests always managed to subvert reforms and to profit from them. For a more current but equally cynical view, see Joe Feagin, *The Urban Real Estate Game* (Englewood Cliffs, NJ: Prentice-Hall, 1983).

[11]Actually, this land comprised the rooming house district described in Zorbaugh's *The Gold Coast and the Slum*—wedged between the Gold Coast along the lake front and "Little Sicily" (which subsequently served as the site of the infamous Cabrini Green public housing project).

[12]See Gerda Wekerle, "Vertical Village: The Social World of a Highrise Complex," Ph.D. dissertation (Department of Sociology, Northwestern University, Evanston, IL: 1974).

1950s and early 1960s. Not all, however, were as successful. In those cities where the government tried to prevent or reduce the kinds of windfall profits made in the Chicago project, developers stayed away in droves. The result was that in city after city, land that had been bought with federal subsidy and cleared by the municipality remained vacant, often turned into municipal parking lots, because developers were not interested in buying it back.

The deep flaws in the redevelopment approach were exposed by a number of critics in the mid-1960s, just before government policies moved on to other ways of "helping" the masses.[13] Our intent here is not to add yet another criticism to these early ones. Rather, it is to emphasize that federal legislation and direct or indirect investments in housing have had significant effects on the ecological structure of American cities and the changes that have taken place in them. None of these changes were, or could have been, predicted by the traditional Chicago School approach to urban ecology.

Housing Abandonment and Homelessness: Some Anomalies We conclude this section with some final examples which demonstrate graphically why the earlier theories of urban ecology have had to be reformulated; they simply could not provide an explanation for many of the urban problems that have accumulated in American cities in recent years. The classical urban ecological processes of segregation, invasion, and succession were unable to explain why sound housing in prime central locations was being abandoned at an unprecedented rate, or why homelessness has risen in recent years.

Over the past few decades, a relatively new phenomenon has been occurring in certain central portions of many older American cities. Apartment rental housing, even that in sound condition, is being abandoned by owners who stop paying taxes and try to evict residents. These buildings are left empty until vandalism or arson destroys their residual value. Owners collect insurance, and frequently, the land and building shells then become city-owned.[14]

Classical theory offers no explanation for the abandonment of housing. This is because abandonment is not due to a "natural" process of succession but rather, given the nature of capitalism, is a perfectly rational decision, based upon investment calculations, to disinvest in particular areas. In general, the housing that has been abandoned had long paid for itself through years of rental income; and yet, owners, reluctant to write off their investment, prefer to sell their properties for a final profit. Unfortunately, buyers with money may be uninterested, because more attractive alternative outlets for investment exist.

Sometimes, poorer buyers have wanted to invest but could not meet the down payment requirements; sometimes, they have been able to buy "on

---

[13]See Scott Greer, *Urban Renewal and American Cities* (New York: Bobbs-Merrill, 1965); and Martin Anderson, *The Federal Bulldozer: A Critical Analysis of Urban Renewal: 1949–1962* (Cambridge, MA: MIT Press, 1965).

[14]Although classical housing economics would have predicted that the worst-quality housing would be removed from the market in this way, in actual fact, abandoned housing was not necessarily of poor quality.

contract." This is a form of purchase where no down payment is required but where the seller holds the deed until *all* payments have been made, which means that the buyer builds no equity along the way and can lose credit for past payments, as well as the property itself, if a few payments are missed. Sometimes, purchasers with down payments have also had to buy on contract because they had difficulty borrowing the balance. Banks and other credit agencies may have "redlined" the zone (that is, declared it a high-risk area in which they will not loan funds). But whether or not the property can be marketed, property taxes must be paid and at least minimum maintenance and utilities must be provided. Should the city enforce building and housing codes, expensive repairs and renovations may be required.

Under these circumstances, an owner may decide to "abandon." The first steps are to stop paying taxes and to eliminate all repairs. Several years may pass before tax arrears force a sale of the property, and so many building code violations may pile up that the building is condemned (and therefore cannot be legally rented to tenants). However, condemnation simply prevents the structure from being legally occupied; the owner is not required to remove the building, and in fact, it may continue to be occupied by squatters. The main goal of the owner now becomes to divest himself of ownership while recouping what he can on his investment. Occasionally, arson-for-profit occurs, when the owner manages to have his building burn down and to collect insurance money. If he is less lucky, the city takes over the property and either fixes it up or pays the cost of tearing it down, while the owner takes a final tax benefit for his "loss."

We have not attempted a full explanation of the phenomenon of housing abandonment. But from even the brief scenario described here it should be evident that none of this could have been predicted from the urban ecological theories of invasion, succession, dominance, and natural areas. Housing abandonment is not an organic process in which old houses die and are removed from the housing market. Housing abandonment is a byproduct of the fact that overvalued inner-city housing is no longer an attractive outlet for capital investment; it must be decapitalized before it can be "recycled" through gentrification.

This suggests an explanation for the surge in homelessness in American cities in the 1980s which is quite different from the one offered by classical urban ecology. The removal of affordable housing from the market through arson and abandonment, and in certain cities with housing shortages, through "warehousing" (the accumulation by owners of vacant apartments in buildings slated for future gentrification), significantly reduced the housing stock available to low-income persons. In the same decade, the number of poor persons needing such housing actually increased because of economic restructuring. At the same time, government policy changed. There was a complete cessation in the construction of new public housing projects that might otherwise have accommodated the very poorest. The alleged substitute for new public housing, Section 8 housing (housing for which the government made up the difference between what a poor family could pay in rent and what a landlord demanded), added no new housing units but merely redistributed existing housing. It is not difficult, therefore, to see why the number of persons unable to find affordable housing units increased dramatically over the decade. Political policies and economic changes, both in the larger economy and in the calculus of housing investment and returns, are the new elements that have compounded the problem of homelessness.

The Political Economy Critique of Classical Ecology

From the foregoing it is clear that the economic system has proven to be much more important than the symbiotic siftings and sortings posited by classical urban ecology theory in accounting for the spatial structure of the American city. In recent years, more and more urbanists have been taking a critical view of classical ecology and have been putting forward an alternative explanation for urban spatial structure termed *political economy,*[15] because it stresses both the political *and* economic reasons for city structure.

In general, today's political economists begin with the assumption that the allocation of space (a scarce resource) in the city is a matter primarily of power—economic and political—rather than one of economic competition in a free market. They note that differential values are *created* in the marketplace not only by free and open competition but through governmental regulations of land use, governmental patterns of taxation, and the operation of banks and mortgage companies, many of which are regulated or guided by government. They note that, more and more, the chief determinants of differential land values are selective investments in collective consumption (infrastructure in roads, utilities, etc., as well as government services of a welfare type) which enhance values for owners of certain properties while reducing those of others. This analysis is so basic to the field that it represents a virtual reformulation of urban theory.

PARADIGMATIC CHANGE

Thomas Kuhn[16] suggested that in any scientific field there are some periods during which "normal" science is conducted, as scholars elaborate and refine the basic propositions and accepted knowledge in the field. At such times it is possible to speak of a common model, exemplar, or paradigm for the science— one that guides the work of most researchers. There are other times, however, when basic shifts occur in the very definition of what is true and what kinds of research can be considered relevant. These he calls "scientific revolutions."

Although Kuhn concentrated chiefly on the so-called "hard" sciences, con-

---

[15]This nineteenth-century term originally referred to all of the social sciences before subfields (sociology, political science, and economics) were created. Political economy includes Marxism but is not confined to it. Adam Smith was a political economist.

[16]*The Structure of Scientific Revolutions* (Chicago: University of Chicago Press, 1962).

tending that most social sciences were still in the pre-paradigmatic phase of development, we believe that even in the social sciences there have been deep scientific revolutions in certain fields. Urban sociology is one of these. In his 1973 book,[17] David Harvey called attention to the paradigmatic shift that was occurring in urban geography. A similar trend was occurring in urban sociology, although it was not specifically recognized and acknowledged until somewhat later.[18] In place of "normal science," urban sociology entered a phase of revolutionary questioning and reformulation.

Two changes are often found to precede such shifts in the way scientific fields conceptualize their objects. First, within the scientific field itself, anomalous findings begin to accumulate—findings that cannot be adequately explained according to existing theories. While in the "hard" sciences these new anomalous findings may arise because things which were always there are suddenly seen for the first time, in the social sciences the world itself may change, thus creating new "facts" not taken into consideration by the old theories. In the preceding section we have described some of the anomalies that arose out of increased governmental regulations and interventions in the market and out of a political and racial climate that interfered significantly with the operation of pure competition—the paradigm which was supposed to "explain" them.

A second source of paradigmatic change, especially in the social sciences, is the cultural climate of ideas and values, not just in the science but in the outside society. These values affect how scientists "see" the objects of their study. Certainly, a number of changes were occurring in the late 1960s. In many cities in the United States the 1960s were characterized by large-scale urban unrest and rioting. These coincided with the era of student rebellions, not only in the United States but throughout Europe. At the same time, social scientists were finally being drawn from groups which had previously been relatively excluded from academe, namely, blacks and women. Since both these groups were questioning their former subordinate positions and were playing a more active role in revising how "science" viewed them and their needs, it is not surprising that some of the major changes in the paradigm of urban sociology have come in areas dealing with race and gender in the city.

Thus, in the 1970s and 1980s, both scientific "anomalies" and larger social

---

[17]David Harvey, *Social Justice and the City* (London: Edward Arnold, 1973; republished by the Center for Metropolitan Planning and Research, Baltimore: Johns Hopkins University Press, 1975).

[18]See, for example, the secondary accounts in Michael P. Smith, *The City and Social Theory* (New York: St. Martin's Press, 1979) and Peter Saunders, *Social Theory and the Urban Question* (New York: Holmes and Meier, 1981), which describe the shift in detail. John Walton has made this point explicit in his "The New Urban Sociology," *International Social Science Journal* 32 (1981), pp. 374–390; as have Janet Abu-Lughod, in her review essay, "Marxist Urban Sociology," *Contemporary Sociology* 8 (March 1979), pp. 192–196, and Sharon Zukin, in "A Decade of the New Urban Sociology," *Theory and Society* 9 (1980), pp. 575–602. Most recently, this shift has been described in Mark Gottdiener and Joe Feagin, "The Paradigm Shift in Urban Sociology," *Urban Affairs Quarterly* 24 (December 1988), pp. 163–187.

changes caused a scientific revolution in sociology in general, and in urban sociology in particular. Earlier, the dominant paradigm in sociology (associated with Talcott Parsons) emphasized societal integration and balance, gradual change, voluntary action, and "systemness." This basic approach was compatible not only with classical urban ecology but with neoclassical theoretical refinements set forth by Amos Hawley,[19] Otis Dudley Duncan, and Leo Schnore.[20] This compatibility was not accidental, since in many ways the rather benign functionalist theories of Durkheim had contributed to both. The violent events of the 1960s cast doubt on these theories of social integration in a conflict-free universe.

In place of functionalism and social system theory, then, many theorists began to see conflict, even class struggle. In place of voluntaristic action, influenced but not determined by culture, many of the new theorists began to emphasize structural contradictions growing out of the material conditions of society and the forms of production in the economic system. It is striking that for the first time in mainstream American sociology, the nineteenth-century theories of Karl Marx began to be openly discussed and debated, rather than dismissed out of hand.[21]

In the field of sociology this led to greater openness and a willingness to at least examine competing paradigms. In the field of urban sociology in particular, it led to a serious critique of existing theory and research practice. This critique addressed itself both to the relevance of the questions being asked by urban sociology and to the scientific objectivity of the answers provided by existing theory. Both in general sociology and in urban sociology, conflict theory, Marxist analysis, political economy, a concern with the world system of capitalism, and an interest in the role played by the state in advanced capitalist societies became new issues to be explored. This paradigmatic change, even if it is later superseded by other paradigms, has radically restructured the way we study cities and how we explain their spatial structures.

In his 1981 article on changes in urban sociology, Walton identified five characteristics of the new approach.[22] First, scholars are now preoccupied with

---

[19]See especially Hawley's brilliant volume, based at least in part upon notes left by Roderick McKenzie, *Human Ecology* (New York: Roland Press, 1950). Hawley has summed up a reasoned account of ecological theory in his *Human Ecology: A Theoretical Essay* (Chicago: University of Chicago Press, 1986).

[20]O. D. Duncan and Leo Schnore, "Cultural, Behavioral and Ecological Perspectives in the Study of Social Organization," *American Journal of Sociology* 65 (1959), pp. 132–146; O. D. Duncan, "Human Ecology and Population Studies," in Philip Hauser and O. D. Duncan, eds., *The Study of Population* (Chicago: University of Chicago Press, 1959).

[21]It is interesting in this context to note that in the over 1000 pages of Park and Burgess's 1921 text, there are only six references to Marx, and these either mention him in passing or dismiss his ideas as irrelevant or wrong.

[22]Walton, "The New Urban Sociology," p. 376, but see also Walton, "Discipline, Method, and Community Power," *American Sociological Review* 31 (1966). pp. 684–689.

proving (or disproving) that urbanism and urbanization are "theoretical" objects for study. Second, scholars assume that urbanism and urbanization can be understood only by examining the interplay between relations of production, consumption, exchange, and the structure of state power. Third, the new paradigm holds that urban processes (e.g., ecological patterns, community organization, economic activities, class and ethnic politics, local government) can only be understood in terms of structural variables. Fourth, social change is viewed as growing chiefly out of conflicts and contradictions between classes. And finally, critics stress that alternative positions on urban analysis and policy need to be understood in terms of their normative (ideological and distributive) implications.

In the process, many of the propositions and assumptions in classical urban ecology have been undergoing revision, and a good many of them have been rejected entirely. It is still too early to predict what the ultimate effect of the new paradigm in urban sociology will be or how the findings derived from the new critical approach can be integrated with the knowledge that has accumulated in the 75 years urban sociologists have been studying the city. But Kuhn emphasized that controversy is healthy and necessary for scientific advance. If he is correct, then urban sociology will be considerably strengthened by its recent rethinking of "the urban question."

Two authors, David Harvey and Manuel Castells, led the way to the new paradigm. Both attacked classical urban ecology from a neo-Marxist perspective. Because their work was both early and influential, we cover their contributions in some detail.

David Harvey's Criticism

In 1973, David Harvey, a British geographer, published his book *Social Justice and the City*. Few works in recent scholarship have had such strong repercussions in urban studies. The format of the book previewed the changes urban sociology would go through in the next decade. The first chapters posed the conventional human ecology question of how physical space affects human behavior and presented a critique of ecological determinism essentially based on cognitive psychology. Harvey argued that space is not "out there" waiting to be experienced, but is relevant only when it is perceived by human beings and given a cultural interpretation. Space, contended Harvey, is therefore always socially defined. But neither cognitive psychology nor cultural semiotics can explain how a given ecological pattern comes into existence. How populations and uses are distributed in urban space is determined not by symbols but by the distribution of real economic and political resources in society. Space in the city is a scarce resource; it is distributed not according to subconsensual symbiosis but according to economic-political competition and conflict.

In his third chapter Harvey went on to ask whether the resulting distribution was "just." Concluding that it was not, he changed the focus of his book to injustice. Chapter Four examined the question of poor ghettos, asking why they occupy high-value land in the centers of major cities. The author rejected the traditional explanation offered by classical urban ecology, not because it was wrong but because it viewed the process as both inevitable and benign.

> Park and Burgess both appeared to regard the city as a sort of man-produced, ecological complex within which the processes of social adaptation, specialization of function and of life style, competition for living space, and so on acted to produce a coherent spatial structure, the whole being held together by some culturally derived form of social solidarity which Park . . . called "the moral order." The various groups and activities within the city system were essentially bound together by this moral order, and they merely jockeyed for position (both social and spatial) within the constraints imposed by the moral order. The main focus of attention was to find out who ended up where and what conditions were like when they got there. . . . It is curious to note, however, that Park and Burgess did not pay a great deal of attention to the kind of social solidarity generated through the workings of the economic system nor to the social and economic relationships which derive from economic considerations. . . . As a result, the urban land-use theory which they developed has a critical flaw when it is used to explain the ghetto.[23]

Harvey pointed out that many decades before Burgess formulated his theory of concentric circles, Frederick Engels had already observed the same phenomenon in Manchester, England. The difference between the two was not *what* they described but *how* they accounted for what they observed and what they proposed to *do* about it. In similar fashion, Harvey observed that using explanations drawn from standard land economics, one can predict *where* ghetto slums will be located. Indeed, two well-regarded regional land-use theorists, Alonso and Muth, used such theories to explain why slums and ghettos end up toward the centers of American cities (on high-value land). An analysis of competitive bidding in the capitalist land market leads to the prediction, in fact, "that poor groups must, of necessity, live where they can least afford to live."[24] But, asked Harvey, once we know this, what should we do about it?

It is here that Harvey made a radical break with academic urban geographers and sociologists. Whereas urban sociologists and geographers have usually stopped their analysis once they discover that ghettos are the logical outcome of the workings of the economic system, Harvey went on to advocate changes in the economic system to prevent undesired outcomes. He argued:

> Our objective is to eliminate ghettos. Therefore, the only valid policy with respect to this objective is to eliminate the conditions which give rise to the truth of the theory. . . . The simplest approach here is to eliminate those mechanisms which serve to generate the theory . . . [namely,] competitive bidding for the use of land. . . . This . . . [suggests that we could eliminate ghettos by supplanting] competitive bidding with a socially controlled urban land market and socialized control of the housing sector. Under such a system, the . . . theory (which is a normative theory

---

[23]Harvey, *Social Justice and the City,* pp. 131–132.

[24]*Ibid.,* p. 137.

anyway) would become empirically irrelevant to our understanding of the spatial structure of residential land use.[25]

Thus, while urban land values and rents are seen by classical and neoclassical theorists as "explaining" or bringing into being the particular spatial form of American cities, Harvey, as a proponent of radical change in the economic system underlying this outcome, recommended that the "basic rules" for determining land values and rents be altered through political decisions. He argued that since political decisions have created our economic system, we have the political right to change that system if we are not pleased with its outcomes.

Since reaching this position, Harvey has devoted his attention to tracing exactly how the economic system works and how it brings about so many consequences that he believes are unjust and destructive of social welfare. Among the more interesting of his empirical investigations are those that trace housing abandonment in the central slums of Baltimore, that examine the effects of macroeconomic housing cycles on western economies, and that examine the historical connections between capitalism and cities.[26] Even more important than the empirical research he has done, Harvey's reconceptualizing the "benign competition for niches" assumed by the Chicago School of urban ecology as, instead, class struggle and conflict has influenced the field drastically.[27]

Manuel Castells and Urban Social Movements

Class conflict and the idea that the city is an arena for social movements which attempt to modify the rules of the system to yield outcomes more favorable to their interests underlie the thinking of another urbanist who has been similarly influential in redefining the field of urban sociology. Manuel Castells is an international figure. Born in Catalan, Spain, and having taught in Paris during the student rebellion period of the late 1960s, he became a professor at the University of California, Berkeley, and an international planning

---

[25]*Ibid.*, p. 137.

[26]See David Harvey, "The Political Economy of Urbanization in Advanced Capitalist Societies: The Case of the United States," in *The Social Economy of Cities*, ed. by Gary Gappert and Harold M. Rose, vol. 9 of *Urban Affairs Annual Reviews* (Beverly Hills, CA: Sage Publications, 1975), pp. 119–163; David Harvey, "Government Policies, Financial Institutions and Neighborhood Change in United States Cities," in *Captive Cities*, ed. Michael Harloe (London: John Wiley, 1977); and a series of pieces of Marxist analysis of investment and rents which have appeared in the radical geography journal, *Antipode*. Harvey's *The Limits to Capital* (Chicago: University of Chicago Press, 1982) explores housing investment cycles in the United States and Great Britain, while his two-volume study, supra-titled *Studies in the History and Theory of Capitalist Urbanization* (Baltimore: Johns Hopkins Press, 1985), not only addresses theoretical issues but includes a case study of the development of Paris within his framework.

[27]Perhaps the clearest statement of this position appears in David Harvey, "Labor, Capital, and Class Struggle Around the Built Environment in Advanced Capitalist Societies," in *Urbanization and Conflict in Market Societies*, ed. Kevin Cox (Chicago: Maaroufa Press, 1978; London: Methuen, 1978).

consultant. The first of his books to come to the attention of American scholars was *La question urbaine,* published in France in 1972.[28] Particularly after it was translated into English five years later, it caused a great stir in the discipline and generated a fairly extensive literature, some of it quite independent of his influence.[29]

The Urban Question began with a dramatic declaration: "This book was born out of astonishment." Astonishment at what? At the fact that in 1968, "although waves of anti-imperialist struggle are sweeping across the world . . . , movements of revolt are bursting out at the very heart of advanced capitalism, . . . [and] the revival of working class action is creating a new political situation in Europe," no one recognizes that the theories which are guiding government intervention into urban problems on an unprecedented scale are, in fact, *ideologies* which serve the interests of the ruling classes, rather than true scientific theories.[30]

The first seven chapters of the book document the pressing urban problems and deliver a scathing critique of previous research on the city. Castells is particularly harsh in his treatment of the Chicago School. These chapters serve to introduce Chapters 8–10, which deal with "The Urban Structure." In an oblique criticism of classical ecology in general, and Brian Berry in particular, Castells begins Chapter 8 by arguing that "to consider the city as the projection of society on space is both an indisputable starting point and *too elementary an approach.*" Following a Marxist approach, he then defines space as:

> a material product, in relation with other material elements—among others, men, who themselves enter into particular social relations, which give to space (and to the other elements of the combination) a form, a function, a social signification. It is not, therefore, a mere occasion for the deployment of the social structure, but a concrete expression of each historical ensemble in which a society is specified. It is a question, then, of establishing . . . the structural and conjunctural laws that govern its existence and transformation. . . . *This means that there is no theory of space that is not an integral part of a general social theory.*[31]

This recognition, that one's theory of space is related to one's general theory of society, allows Castells to criticize the Chicago School's theory of space as ideological, because it rested upon a false analogy with natural phenomena, posited a benign, nonconflictual set of relationships among individuals (not classes) which have inevitable outcomes, and indeed, reflected the dominant ideology of capitalism.

---

[28]French edition published by François Maspero. It was not published in English translation until 1977, and then, in a much transformed and modified edition. See Manuel Castells, *The Urban Question: A Marxist Approach,* trans. Alan Sheridan (London: Edward Arnold, 1977).

[29]Among these sources, one should consult C. G. Pickvance, ed., *Urban Sociology: Critical Essays* (New York: St. Martin's Press, 1976), which includes some early translated articles by Castells; and Manuel Castells, *City, Class and Power,* translated from the French by Elizabeth Lebas (New York: St. Martin's Press, 1978).

[30]Castells, *The Urban Question,* pp. 1–2.

[31]*Ibid.,* p. 115, italics added.

Moving beyond this, Castells asks how the specific forms of social space can be understood using the fundamental concepts of historical materialism. His answer is that urban form is created by the "historical articulation of several modes of production" at any point in a city's life. Thus, "[t]o analyse space as an expression of the social structure amounts, therefore, to studying its shaping by elements of the economic system, the political system and the ideological system, and by their combinations and the social practices that derive from them."[32]

Castells does this in a 1983 book, *The City and the Grassroots*, which contains case studies of urban space as affected by urban social movements.[33] Drawing on a variety of historical materials (e.g., on sixteenth-century Castile; the 1871 Commune of Paris; early twentieth-century Glasgow; Veracruz, Mexico in 1922; the urban ghetto revolts in American cities in the late 1960s), he tries to demonstrate continuities in the "production of urban meaning." Other long case studies deal with such diverse topics as mass housing on the outskirts of Paris, the Chicano and gay populations in San Francisco, squatter settlements in Latin America, and the citizens' movement in Madrid that helped bring down the Franco regime. In these studies he demonstrated his new approach to urban sociology.

Other Political Economists

American urbanists of Marxist persuasion had already begun to follow Castells's prescriptions by the late 1970s, as demonstrated in the collected volume entitled *Marxism and the Metropolis*, edited by Tabb and Sawers. In this book David Gordon presented a theory of the evolution of American cities based upon shifts in the dominant modes of production.[34] He posited three stages of the urban form in the United States, each related to the mode of production that dominated the period. The first, the Commercial City, was formed by merchant capital accumulation. The second, the Industrial City, was formed by industrial capitalism. The third (and present stage), the Corporate City, is dominated by corporate headquarters and finance capital. Each mode of production is associated with a different pattern of spatial organization.

Among the other articles in this same book are two that attempt political-economy analyses of dominant themes in urban ecology, namely, urban organization and the "housing question." Both illustrate a sharp break with the previous paradigm of urban sociology and move in the direction advocated by Castells. In the conclusion to his article on "The Postwar Politics of Urban Development," John H. Mollenkopf distinguished his work from older analyses.

---

[32]*Ibid.*, pp. 125–126.

[33]Manuel Castells, *The City and the Grassroots* (Berkeley and Los Angeles: University of California Press, 1983), based primarily on work by his students.

[34]See David Gordon, "Capitalist Development and the History of American Cities," in *Marxism and the Metropolis: New Perspectives in Urban Political Economy*, ed. William K. Tabb and Larry Sawers (New York: Oxford University Press, 1978), pp. 25–63.

Orthodox political science and economics have attempted to explain metropolitan decentralization and the content of urban politics with what are in essence market models. For both economists and political scientists, departure for the suburbs simply constituted a choice individuals made about lifestyles, given a range of means and opportunities. . . .

[We reject] such views on two counts: first, market explanations remain essentially circular unless the context in which the market operates is specified. In this case, markets function in the midst of a basic conflict over the direction and purpose of urban life, namely the conflict between urban form for human purposes and urban form for efficient capitalist production. . . .

Second, market explanations deny or obscure the central yet contradictory role of the state. . . . Land-use patterns are inherently collective, public matters. They cannot be set up without government actions ranging from roads and sewers to police and fire protection to government constraints on how owners use their property. As a result, land use questions . . . inevitably tend to become political. How the politics of land use are organized, and therefore contained, provides the central theme of U.S. political history.[35]

Note how well his argument addresses, in direct fashion, the anomalies described earlier in this chapter.

Another article from the same volume, by Michael Stone,[36] addresses a second question raised earlier, namely, whether capitalism can ever provide adequate housing for the poor. Using the same reasoning Edith Wood followed 60 years earlier, Stone concluded that, despite the tremendous economic development that has taken place in the interim, a large proportion of American families still cannot afford decent housing. Unlike Wood, however, he argued that this problem can *never* be solved within the framework of capitalism:

The problem is partly caused by the extremely high cost of housing. . . . But it is also the result of the extremely unequal distribution of income produced by the labor market. *Capitalism cannot solve the problem of incomes and housing costs* because the required reduction in housing costs would lead to the collapse of the housing market.

Following the same method as Wood, Stone used the relatively conservative estimates of the Joint Center for Urban Studies of MIT/Harvard to establish the fact that at least one out of every five Americans is inadequately housed. (Actually, Stone believes the percentage is one out of four.) Examining income data for American families and rent/house cost data for adequate housing, he concluded that built into the American capitalist system is the fact that a large number of American families will never earn enough to "demand" a standard dwelling unit in the market at the prices being asked for such dwellings.

---

[35]John Mollenkopf, "The Postwar Politics of Urban Development," in Tabb and Sawers, eds., *Marxism and the Metropolis*, pp. 117–152. Quotation taken from pp. 147–148. See also John Mollenkopf, *The Contested City* (Princeton, NJ: Princeton University Press, 1983).

[36]Michael E. Stone, "Housing, Mortgage Lending and the Contradictions of Capitalism," in Tabb and Sawers, eds., *Marxism and the Metropolis*, pp. 179–207. Quotation taken from pp. 179–180, emphasis added.

Whereas Edith Wood took the view that the government or private philanthropy would be able to subsidize the difference, Stone reached a more tragic conclusion:

> *There is no way that capitalism can resolve the conflict between the labor market and the housing market.* In order to eliminate shelter poverty and prop up the housing market, every household would have to be guaranteed an income at least equal to the BLS [Bureau of Labor Statistics] lower budget. . . . [But if this occurred,] labor would then take a bigger share of the nation's productive output: profits would decline, leading to reduced investment and reduced production. . . . [W]ith no unemployment and no low-wage jobs, capital would lose its power over labor. The working class could no longer be maintained in a subordinate position. . . . This solution would lead to the collapse of the labor market. . . .
>
> On the other hand, if a large proportion of American families continue to have insufficient incomes, the housing market will collapse, as it already has in many urban neighborhoods where housing stands abandoned. . . . [T]o eliminate shelter poverty without disturbing the labor market, the price of housing would have to . . . be driven down, in some cases to zero. Property values would collapse, and private investment in housing would cease. Mortgage payments would stop on many buildings, leading to collapse of the mortgage system, and with it much of the financial structure of capitalism. . . .
>
> Shelter poverty is thus more than a social problem incidental to the basic functioning of the economic system. *It will not be eliminated simply through growth in the capitalist economy or modest government assistance.* Rather, it must be recognized as *an inherent contradiction* between some of the most basic institutions of capitalism—*a contradiction which the system cannot resolve without bringing about the demise of capitalism itself.*[37]

Stone suggests that it was in order to stave off this collapse that the government became deeply involved in housing programs. The principal strategy was to finance low-interest loans to encourage home ownership among the upper levels of the working class. A second strategy was to construct subsidized public housing for the poorest group or, more recently under the Section 8 program, to subsidize their rents by making up the difference between the 25 percent of their income they can afford to pay for housing and the market cost of adequate housing. But this has still left a large number of the working poor[38] for whom additional subsidies are required. Thus, despite the fact that we have put into place all the policies recommended in 1919 by Edith Wood, the issue of "Housing the Poor: The Case for Heroism"[39] continues to challenge urbanists, critics, and government planners.

We have presented some of the criticisms of classical urban ecology that have come recently from political economists of the Marxist camp. The student might well ask at this juncture whether Marxism is an essential part of the

---

[37]*Ibid.*, pp. 184–185. Italics added for emphasis.

[38]Note that questions of unemployment and homelessness are ignored in this discussion.

[39]The title of a provocative volume exploring public subsidies for housing: Alexander Polikoff, *Housing the Poor: The Case for Heroism* (Cambridge, MA: Ballinger Publishing, 1978).

criticism or whether it is possible to follow a political economy analysis of cities without necessarily being a Marxist. Although the political economy critique came first from persons who labeled themselves Marxists, the new approach they introduced is being used by persons from a wider range of political persuasions. If the theory gives a credible explanation for what is going on in cities, then the political position of the analysts should neither validate nor discredit the conclusions. Tabb and Sawers themselves suggest this:

> The various arguments to be found in this book concerning the political economy of housing, urban renewal, spatial patterning and racism do not stand or fall on the acceptance or rejection of capitalism as an economic system. It is possible for readers to agree with much of what is said and still find American capitalism the best possible system, even given all its problems.[40]

In fact, in recent years the new paradigm introduced by Marxists has become "mainstream," as evidenced by the publication of three important books: the 1982 volume of the *Urban Affairs Annual Reviews* that contained a wide variety of articles by non-Marxist social scientists who employ a political economy perspective in their work; Logan and Molotch's highly acclaimed *Urban Fortunes* (1987), which takes for granted many of the premises just discussed; and a 1988 collection of articles, *Business Elites and Urban Development*, which spells out in case after case how the imperatives of capitalism and the interests of business investors drive growth policies in American cities.[41]

Some of the most original contributions to the field, however, continue to come from urban land specialists who take a more radical perspective on how the economy creates land values. Among these we might single out François Lamarche and Allen J. Scott. Lamarche, in a 1972 article in French, traced the creation of land values in the city of Montreal in a brilliant *tour de force* which can serve as an exemplar to the new paradigm.[42] Scott's 1980 book, *The Urban Land Nexus and the State*,[43] also represents a step beyond the criticisms then current in the field and points to how the new paradigm can offer a different set of insights into the creation and transformation of spatial patterns in the city. Interestingly enough, it is this most advanced radical critique of urban ecology that also offers a way to integrate the new thinking with the old.

The core of Scott's book is found in Chapters 6 through 8, where he discussed how space for production and reproduction is allocated, and how the state intervenes to guide these urban land allocations. He saw contemporary North American and West European cities as perfect reflections of the logic of

---

[40]Tabb and Sawers, *Marxism and the Metropolis*, p. 17.

[41]See Norman I. Fainstein and Susan S. Fainstein, eds., *Urban Policy Under Capitalism*, vol. 22 of *Urban Affairs Annual Reviews* (Beverly Hills, CA: Sage Publications, 1982); John Logan and Harvey Molotch, *Urban Fortunes: The Political Economy of Place* (Berkeley, CA: University of California Press, 1987); and Scott Cummings, ed., *Business Elites and Urban Development* (Albany, NY: State University of New York Press, 1988).

[42]François Lamarche, "Property Development and the Economic Foundations of the Urban Question," translated into English and published in C. G. Pickvance, ed., *Urban Sociology: Critical Essays*, pp. 85–118.

[43]Allen J. Scott, *The Urban Land Nexus and the State* (London: Pion, 1980).

advanced capitalism, in which cities have become "vast machine[s] for the production, circulation and consumption of commodities." Despite the efforts of early utopian industrialists to coordinate work (production) and life (reproduction) in the human community, this "dichotomy . . . has, if anything, tended to become more and more pronounced with the passage of time."

According to Scott, it was the search for profit in the modern industrial era that led businesses, seeking cheap land and low-cost labor, to desert the urban cores, which in turn caused such inner city problems as unemployment, fiscal austerity, and the decay of social services. Thus, Scott agrees with other Marxist critics that it was not the technology of production but the economics of profit, assisted by the state, that caused the contemporary "slash and burn" desertion by industrialists of center city employment sites.[44]

Turning to space for reproduction, Scott examined the issue of residentially differentiated neighborhoods, asking on what basis they are differentiated and how this differentiation relates to capitalism. Scott noted that descriptive *factorial ecologies* (explained in our Chapter 7 above) have shown over and over again that "out of the apparent sociocultural chaos of the North American city there emerge three basic dimensions of variation (or factors) representing the dominant pattern of urban society," namely social rank, ethnicity, and familism, of which the first accounts for most of the variance. He takes these descriptive categories, however, and translates them into tools of analysis.

> It is possible . . . to go beyond the restricted empiricist interpretations of urban factorial ecology, and on the basis of the theory of modes of production . . . show that the factors of social rank, ethnicity and familism . . . are essentially intermediated expressions of fundamental capitalist social and property relations. . . . [T]he empirical patterns observed by factorial ecologies are (both) outcomes of the division of labour as established within the system of commodity production, and . . . reflections of the innate logic of reproductive processes that are specific to capitalist society. . . .
>
> These three main social dimensions . . . are thus reflections of the global functions and purposes of capitalist society. . . . Once determined within the broad structure of society, they are cast out, as it were, into urban space where they coalesce out into distinctive geographic entities. In other words, these factors, so far from being chaotically intermingled throughout the urban land nexus, have a marked spatial as well as sociological expression.[45]

BEYOND POLITICAL ECONOMY: RACE AND GENDER

Because the political economy critique began from a Marxist perspective, it stressed such issues as the relations of production, the class system generated from the mode of production, and the role of the state in allocating privileges, with respect both to collective consumption and to the private market for land. These processes account directly for the spatial patterns observed in land uses and for the residential segregation by social rank found in American cities.

---

[44]*Ibid.*, quoted from p. 86; see also p. 109.

[45]*Ibid.*, quoted from pp. 119–121.

As Scott reminds us, however, social rank is only one, albeit the dominant, factor or dimension found in factorial ecologies. The other two factors are ethnicity (which in the U.S. context generally means race) and familism (which in essence means gender roles). As has been proven through factorial ecologies, the spatial distributions of race and gender role characteristics are *not the same* as the pattern of spatial differentiation by class, although clearly they are not unrelated. (For example, certain racial characteristics and certain gender roles are associated with low class position in contemporary American society.) Therefore, it is necessary to go beyond the political economy critique to explore the special disabilities in the city that arise from being black or female (or both).

Recall that changes in the urban ecology paradigm came not only from real changes in the world and a greater openness to Marxist perspectives in sociology but from social protest movements (for black and female liberation) and the integration into the field of minority scholars who had a greater sensitivity to the special plight of blacks and women in the city than did the white males who founded the Chicago School of urban ecology. The inclusion of these scholars has also transformed the paradigm.

Both classical ecology *and* the political economy alternative tended to ignore or failed to predict many of the problems women faced in the city. Women urban sociologists and planners were the first to recognize the special needs of women and were the first to point out certain blind spots in the classical ecologist's model of residential choice. Noting that the ecology model assumed a traditional family consisting of a working father, a stay-at-home mother, and dependent children, these critics pointed out that women were increasingly playing new roles and therefore had sets of needs in the city which were quite different from those assumed by social analysts and urban planners. The vector of familism revealed in the various factorial ecologies seemed to be tapping these variations in female roles with respect to the bearing and rearing of children.

The classical ecology and political economy models also proved insufficient with respect to race. Particularly in the United States, they failed to predict ethnic and racial cleavages in the employment and housing markets—cleavages based on emotions that seemed to go well beyond economic rationality and the profit motive of capitalism. Especially after the race riots and urban protests of the 1960s, urban sociologists were forced to look more closely at the causes of what the Kerner Report of 1968 referred to as the creation in the United States of two societies—not just separate but very unequal. These two societies were being allocated not only very different positions in the class structure, but also very different spaces in the city, with major implications for the urban pattern.

Therefore, in addition to the corrections made to classical ecological theory from the political economy perspective, there have been other corrections made from the standpoint of blacks and women in the city. These perspectives, too, are now being integrated into the theories of spatial structure. While the subjects of gender and race are too complex to cover in detail, in the next chapter we propose to discuss, albeit superficially, some of the main changes in theory that have resulted from the awareness of these issues.

Chapter 9

The "New" Variables: Gender and Race

Chapter 7 described some of the recurring findings of social area analysis and factorial ecologies, namely, that the spatial distribution of population in cities could be summarized parsimoniously in terms of three somewhat independent dimensions or vectors of social characteristics: class position, stage in the family cycle, and race/ethnicity.

The most important determinant of spatial organization in modern industrialized cities is class. The financial, educational, and occupational levels of housing consumers yield differences in life-styles, providing, differentially, the incomes available to realize them. Since spatial segregation by class has consistently appeared in factorial ecology analyses conducted for cities in many cultures, we must conclude that it is, to some degree, found in all societies. Spatial segregation by class is not difficult to explain. Given that income is unequally distributed in any society, that such inequalities are translated into differential ability to pay for housing, and that, at least within modern industrialized market societies, high-income consumers exhibit a marked preference for living among others of similar status, class segregation is usually achieved through the market mechanisms stressed by the theorists of the Chicago School and measured by classical urban land economists. This vector was explored in the preceding chapter.

In this chapter we examine the other two vectors, which appear to be less stable over time and space: family type and race. These factors, also identified in social area analysis, have not been found so consistently in factorial ecologies elsewhere, nor have they proven so easy to explain. And within the United States, their role in creating the spatial patterning of cities has changed over time, reflecting changes in gender roles and in the racial and ethnic composition of urbanites. As factors of spatial differentiation, both urbanism/familism and ethnicity appear to be more culturally specific than class is. One would therefore anticipate that changes in social values and behavior concerning them would be reflected in the changing urban pattern of their distributions.

Neither gender nor racial minority status is fully independent of class position, as might be anticipated. Being a career woman in a dual-income childless marriage, a single mother, or a housewife-mother with an income-earning husband, are more than family role differences; they not only alter the priorities accorded in housing preferences but are usually linked to economic class as well. Being an African-American (woman or man), and thus the victim of discrimination in education, jobs, and housing, is more than an ethnic status; it is usually a prescription for low income. Indeed, black single mothers are the most disadvantaged group with the least choice in housing. Thus, gender and race are not independent of class position. Rather, they constitute additional *socially defined* forms of status disability or powerlessness.

However, the spatial distributions by family type and by race/ethnicity operate in distinctly different ways. Whereas racial and ethnic differences can (but need not) be translated into spatial segregation, it is rarely the case that males and females occupy separate spaces in the city. If there *is* spatial segregation according to gender roles, it is most likely to be explained by the characteristics of the men and women themselves: whether they are married, single, widowed, or divorced; whether they are parents or childless; whether they are employed or out of the paid labor force; and whether they are young or old. It is only in this sense that we may speak of gender, or more precisely, family roles, as a force shaping the ecology of the city.[1]

WOMEN IN THE CITY

Of the three dimensions identified by social area analysis, the one Shevky had called "urbanism" and Wendell Bell had renamed "familism" was the least convincingly conceptualized. The three variables used to indicate this dimen-

---

[1] It should be pointed out that "gender" (i.e., the social roles associated with the biological category of sex) is, of course, not the same as "family role." It has always been assumed that the household is the decision-making unit that maximizes its collective welfare by its selection of a dwelling. Ann Markusen, among others, has pointed out that this is not necessarily a valid assumption in patriarchal societies where the male "head" exercises his preferences, with the wife's needs coming only secondarily. See, for example, Ann Markusen, "City Spatial Structure, Women's Work, and National Urban Policy," pp. S23-S44 in the special issue of *Signs* on *Women and the American City* (Spring 1980) ed. by Catherine Stimpson *et al.*

sion were the percentage of women in the labor force, the fertility ratio (that is, the number of young children per 1000 women in the childbearing ages), and the percentage of all dwellings that were single-family owned houses. To be high on the familism end of this continuum, an area had to contain a large proportion of women who were not in the paid labor force, a preponderance of large families, and a high proportion of owner-occupied single-family homes. Conversely, to be high on its opposite end, that of urbanism, an area had to contain many employed women, few children, and a high proportion of rented apartment dwellings. It is evident from this description that areas high in familism would be found chiefly in suburban residential zones occupied by middle- to upper-class families where male family heads commuted to employment, whether in the city or, increasingly, in other parts of the suburban ring, whereas high urbanism zones would contain singles and young working couples without children and would more likely be concentrated in areas containing small rental apartments near the center of town. Thus, when these measures are examined more closely, it is easy to see that the analysis was highly specific to a particular moment in history. One can also identify the groups to which the analysis does not apply.

Clearly, the syndrome that social area analysis called "familism" was essentially postwar American conventional middle-class family life, in which gender roles were rigidly distinguished and the "baby boom" had made childrearing the exclusive preoccupation of many women. Within this class, marriage was then early and virtually universal. Wives were seldom in the paid labor force because their husbands were earning a family wage and because discrimination and gender-based wage differentials, as well as ideology, discouraged women from seeking jobs. The ideal female role was, in clear contrast, the full-time task of reproducing the population, that is, bearing and rearing children and caring for the "house as haven" (to use Lasch's felicitous phrase),[2] within which the strength and spirit of the wage earner could be restored. The housing arrangement considered most suitable for this class and family type was, of course, the self-contained and preferably owned single-family home, most readily available on the outskirts of the city or in the suburbs.

Feminists were later to question this arrangement, arguing that it was not given by nature but, rather, resulted from the defeat of what Dolores Hayden referred to as *The Grand Domestic Revolution*,[3] that is, housing reforms that nineteenth- and early twentieth-century feminists had advocated to relieve

---

[2]Christopher Lasch, *Haven in a Heartless World* (New York: Basic Books, 1977).

[3]Dolores Hayden, *The Grand Domestic Revolution: A History of Feminist Designs for American Homes, Neighborhoods, and Cities* (Cambridge, MA: MIT Press, 1981). This book describes a long tradition of feminist reform opposing the individualization of responsibilities for housework and child care, which they saw as the major impediment to the emancipation of women. When feminists designed utopian communities, they most commonly communalized such functions as cooking, cleaning, laundry, and, of course, child care. To some extent, we are now witnessing such collectivization, but instead of being generated by housing reformers, it seems to be coming from commercial demand, driven by women's increased participation in the paid labor force.

women of some of their domestic responsibilities. In retrospect, many feminists viewed this triumph of the American Dream (the concentration of children and dependent wives in self-contained suburban homes) as a regression to patriarchy, facilitated by the exclusion of females from the paid labor force and by society's failure to provide families with more collectivized domestic and child-care services. While this family type peaked several times in modern western history, most notably in the Victorian era, in the United States it reached an apogee in both public visibility and prevalence in the period immediately following World War II. This was the period during which social area analysts were defining the vector of familism.

It is important, therefore, to recognize that "familism" had a specific cultural referent, one that corresponded to a particular gender role and a particular definition of "the family" which applied most accurately to the white middle class. It did not apply to everyone, or indeed, to most. The presence of children in a subarea did not in itself qualify the district as "familistic" because, among the poor, the presence of children had never precluded female participation in the labor force. African-American women had many children as well as an extremely high rate of labor force participation; what many lacked was a husband who earned a family wage. Nor was the combined presence of many children and of women not in the paid labor force sufficient to give a subarea a high score on familism. Areas in which many female heads of households received welfare assistance for their children were not considered to be highly familistic, because such clients were too poor to qualify for home ownership. Areas of high familism, then, were well-to-do districts that contained high proportions of the "ideal American family" with its stereotypic sex roles.

As American household characteristics began to change in the 1970s and 1980s, however, this narrow definition of the type of environment women (i.e., families!) needed began to be less applicable, even to the middle class. With advances in the usual age of marriage, an increase in the percentage of women remaining single or childless, a decline in age-specific fertility even among women who married, and a dramatic rise in the number of female-headed households, there were more and more women whose housing choices were somewhat independent of male preferences or had to be exercised without the financial assistance of men. Indeed, by 1985, less than 28 percent of all families in the United States consisted of a married couple and their dependent children, while almost as high a proportion were headed by females.[4] Indeed, less than one in six families met the ideal criteria of a working husband, a stay-at-home wageless wife, and one or more dependent children. Clearly, modeling the urban housing supply according to the presumed needs of this small minority of households was becoming less and less realistic.

Furthermore, as family structure changed and as the "family wage" proved inadequate to support all dependents, women's participation in the labor force

---

[4]U.S. Department of Commerce, Bureau of the Census, *Population Profile of the United States, 1984/85.* Current Population Reports series P-23, no. 150 (April 1987), p. 20. Note that "families" are not the same as "households."

soared. Between 1950 (the peak of "familism") and 1985, the percentage of women in the paid labor force increased from about 35 percent to 55 percent, while men's dropped from 87 percent to 77 percent. Most dramatic was the increased tendency of mothers to hold jobs. By 1985, almost half of the women who had given birth to a child within the preceding year were working for pay.[5] Combining domestic and child-care responsibilities with paid employment outside the home generated a very different set of housing and locational needs for working mothers, needs best served by a more concentrated neighborhood, sufficient nearby facilities for child care, and a convenient and inexpensive public transportation system.

Even before these changes had appeared so clearly in the statistics, however, women scholars had begun to criticize the phallocentric view of traditional urban planners, who were planning cities for a form of family that was rapidly disappearing. They accused the planning profession of viewing women and their needs from an exclusively male and middle-class perspective.[6]

Since the early 1970s, a veritable avalanche of specialized literature has appeared, most of it produced by and circulating primarily among women scholars.[7] In addition to her early book, in 1984 Dolores Hayden published a seminal critique of gender and housing.[8] Numerous anthologies have also appeared, of which the special 1980 issue of *Signs,* and the collections edited by Suzanne Keller, by Gerda Wekerle *et al.,* and by Eugenie Birch are particularly significant.[9] Also relevant to rethinking the relationship between women and

---

[5]*Ibid.,* p. 30 for female labor force participation rates; p. 9 for labor force participation of new mothers.

[6]The earliest critique of middle-class male biases in city planning that I have been able to find is a paper delivered by Pat McCormick, "Notes from a Woman Planner," at the 1971 meetings of the American Institute of Planners. The earliest coherent criticism was lodged in 1973 at a conference on women and the city, co-sponsored by the American Society of Planning Officials and the Housing and Urban Development Office of the U.S. government. The papers from this conference have been collected and edited by Karen Hapgood and Judith Getzels, *Planning, Women and Change* (Chicago: American Society of Planning Officials, 1974). See especially Janet Abu-Lughod, "Designing a City for All," which was a keynote address for this conference.

[7]A notable exception is William Michelson, who examined time and space budgets for a sizable sample of Toronto households; his empirical research demonstrates the impact of employment upon mothers' domestic needs. See *From Sun to Sun* (Totowa, NJ: Rowman and Allanheld, 1985).

[8]Dolores Hayden, *Redesigning the American Dream: The Future of Housing, Work, and Family Life* (New York: W. W. Norton, 1984).

[9]Catherine Stimpson *et al.,* eds., *Women and the American City.* Special issue of *Signs* 5:3 (Spring 1980); Suzanne Keller, ed., *Building for Women* (Lexington, MA: Lexington Books, 1981); Gerda Wekerle, David Morley, and Rebecca Peterson, eds., *New Space for Women* (Boulder, CO: Westview Press, 1980); and Eugenie Ladner Birch, *The Unsheltered Woman: Women and Housing in the 1980s* (New Brunswick, NJ: Transaction Books, 1985). See also Suzanne MacKenzie, "Gender Restructuring and Urban Restructuring," in R. Peet and N. Thrift, eds., *Geography: The Political Economy Perspective* (Boston: Unwin Hyman 1989). For a good bibliography on the subject, see Deborah Husted, *Women and Urban America: A Selected and Multidisciplinary Bibliography of Materials Since 1960* (Monticello, IL: No. P2440 of Vance Bibliographies, 1988). A new case study of women's attempts to solve their housing problems is Susan Saegert and Jacqueline Leavitt, *From*

the city is the fairly large literature now generating on the changing American family.

Reformulations of urban ecology have been required for at least three reasons. First, as we have noted, women scholars in particular have called attention to how poorly present-day cities meet the needs of women.[10] While the suburban dream may have suited their husbands, in women it very often caused depression and what has been termed "suburban sadness," a syndrome quite similar to stimulus deprivation. (Betty Friedan, in her book *The Feminine Mystique,* called housewife isolation "the sickness without a name."[11]) Second, as the nature of gender roles and family life began to change, the urban pattern which perhaps had been appropriate for the older generation became increasingly ill-suited to the new. Third, the growing number of female-headed households was correlated with rising rates of single motherhood, divorce, and desertion, which made children in such households the fastest growing and largest proportion of the "new" poor. Not only did such families have special needs that went unfulfilled in the city—in particular, the need for more "joint" households and cooperative living arrangements—but they were severely handicapped in their search for solutions by their very low incomes.

Among the special problems of women that can be singled out for special attention are:

Logistics   As women join the labor force in greater numbers, their problems of getting to work are intensified. Even in the growing number of "nontraditional" families, women still tend to bear the ultimate responsibility for childcare arrangements and the double burden of work and house care, which means that they cannot afford to spend much time on their "journey to work." Furthermore, in dual-earner families, the husband usually has priority in using the family car, so that when the wife joins the labor force, a transportation crisis often results. When only one car is available, the wife is frequently dependent upon public transportation (in short supply in most suburbs and virtually nonexistent for commuting between suburbs). As studies in Sweden and North America have shown, wives often take lower-paying jobs in the neighborhood, in order to avoid the extra time and cost of getting to work.[12] It has even been suggested that large offices have been relocating to the suburbs to take advan-

---

Abandonment to Hope: Community Households in Harlem (New York: Columbia University Press, 1990).

[10]A critical evaluation of how cities might be redesigned to fit women's needs appears in Eugenie Ladner Birch, ed., *The Unsheltered Woman.* See also Matrix Collective, *Making Space: Women and the Man Made Environment* (London: Pluto Press, 1984).

[11]Betty Friedan, *The Feminine Mystique* (New York: W. W. Norton, 1963).

[12]Susan Hanson and Ibipo Johnston, "Gender Differences in Work-Trip Length: Explanations and Implications," *Urban Geography* 6 (1985), p. 193–219; Susan Hanson and G. Pratt, "Spatial Dimensions of the Gender Division of Labor in a Local Labor Market," *Urban Geography* 9 (1988), pp. 173–193; Brent Rutherford and Gerda Wekerle, "Captive Rider, Captive Labor: Spatial Constraints and Women's Employment," *Urban Geography* 9 (1988), pp. 116–137.

tage of this "trapped" labor force of educated white mothers now available for work.

Some degree of de-suburbanization, or what has been called the "return to the city," may in fact be due to the increased participation of married women in the labor force, although, given the relocation of service jobs to the suburbs, this may prove to be only a temporary phenomenon. The revival of cottage industries, the increased number of small businesses run by women, and the ubiquitous "home work" facilitated by, among other things, computers, suggest that jobs have followed people. If the conflicts between work and family responsibilities are to be solved for suburban women, they will have to be resolved in the suburbs where more than half of all urbanites now live.

Female-headed Households   As previously noted, the high divorce rate, the tendency for marriages to be delayed, and the rise in the number of widows, have all resulted in an increase in the proportion of female-headed households. Suburban residence, as it is now available, is often ill-suited to these housing consumers, even though the expansion of multi-family dwellings in outlying locations has loosened the tight link between location and house type. Some widows and divorced mothers of dependent children would like to remain in the home formerly shared with their husbands. However, it is often legally and economically difficult for them to do so. Suburban zoning ordinances, which often specify single-family occupancy, prohibit the doubling up of partial families who wish to share costs and child-care responsibilities. They also often prohibit in-law apartments and the subdividing of homes, which makes it difficult for widows to supplement their incomes by renting out rooms or subdividing a home too large for their needs and too expensive for their means. Group housing for the aged, increasingly needed as the number of very old (over 80) goes up, has also been blocked by zoning regulations.

Furthermore, traditional suburban neighborhoods are often ill-suited to the needs of single women. Single mothers need the services and housing types that are more likely to be found in multi-family districts in the city; however, such areas often present "safety" problems for such women.

Research is being done to examine how women actually use the city, to identify the special facilities women require but do not now have access to, and to specify the types of housing and neighborhoods best designed to facilitate the multiple roles they play. Women architects and planners have begun to address these issues and to design experimental arrangements, but until demand can be translated into supply and zoning laws are changed to allow such experimental units to be built, we are unlikely to see much segregation of women with varying needs into separate zones of the urban fabric; thus far, only the aged (mostly widows) appear to be segregated into special quarters such as retirement communities.

Finally, although most single mothers are not black, an increasing proportion of African-American families are headed by women. Such families face a double handicap in locating appropriate housing. Research on the housing needs of these households is still in its infancy. A number of recent studies have begun to examine the special characteristics and needs of black women, although such books have seldom focused on how such needs can best be fulfilled in cities.[13]

The Aged   The aging of the population has increased the number of female-headed households, due to the growing number of widows who live alone. Too little serious attention has been paid to the needs of aged females in the city. Two levels need to be distinguished: the old, and the very old (i.e., those over 80). Whereas the able-bodied younger aged are still able to live alone, it is probable that some form of modified group housing offers the best solution for the aged infirm.[14] Much has recently been written on the new burden middle-aged women bear in caring for their parents, the onset of which often dovetails with the maturation of their children and conflicts with labor force participation. We are a long way from finding adequate solutions for the problems of the aged (and their daughters).

Homelessness   A final problem is created by the recent increase in the number of homeless women, either alone or with dependent children. Until fairly recently, the homeless in American cities were typically males who had disengaged from family life and were unemployed or working only sporadically. The skid rows in American cities were primarily occupied by this male population. However, in the 1980s, with the decline of direct investment in publicly subsidized housing at the same time that poor female-headed and single female-parent households were increasing in numbers, a new phenomenon began to appear—women with young children, who had no other home but converted hotel rooms, shelters, or even the street. Coupled with early, and largely unsupervised, dismissals of mental patients from institutions, this has led to the emergence of a new group of homeless, namely, women and children. Society has not even begun to address this pressing problem.[15]

Although adding women, in considering the special groups that inhabit the city, has required a number of basic modifications in urban theory, it has not required a radical reformulation of the basic ecological propositions concerning the creation and maintenance of the urban pattern. On the other hand, exploring the influence of racial cleavages on the urban pattern has. Indeed, in no other area have the earlier theories proven so wrong.

---

[13]See, for example, Harriette Pipes McAdoo, ed., *Black Families,* 2nd ed. (Newbury Park, CA: Sage Publications, 1988), and Harriette Pipes McAdoo and John McAdoo, eds., *Black Children* (Newbury Park, CA: Sage Publications, 1985), as well as Margaret Simms and Julianne Malveaux, eds., *Slipping Through the Cracks: The Status of Black Women* (New Brunsick, NJ: Transaction Book, 1986).

[14]See G. Streib *et al., Old Homes—New Families: Shared Living for the Elderly* (New York: Columbia University Press, 1984), especially pp. 239–243.

[15]See, for example, Peter Rossi, *Without Shelter: Homelessness in the 1980s* (New York: Priority Press Publications, 1989).

RACE AND HOUSING

The Trickle-Down System

The classical approach to urban ecology took for granted that there would always exist differences in income; it anticipated that these income differences, mediated through consumer preferences and different propensities to spend a proportion of that income on housing, would yield a finely graded set of housing consumers. Some housing consumers would be wealthy and motivated enough to demand fine new accommodations; others would have to make do with "hand-me-downs."

The "trickle-down" mechanism was how such adjustments in the allocation of housing were expected to take place. Presumably, the wealthiest bidders would move to the highest-quality new housing, thereby vacating units of somewhat lesser quality which would, in turn, be inherited by families with lower incomes. This process would continue all the way down to the housing consumers in the weakest market position, who would have to settle for the residual housing no one else wanted. In this model, only ability to pay (and not racial or other extraneous characteristics) mattered.

The analogue to this individual housing process was the "trickle-down" theory of neighborhood succession, in which wealthier and more urban-acclimated groups would desert older neighborhoods for new, leaving them (and the poorer quality housing they contained) for less powerful groups to inherit. As ethnic groups assimilated and moved up the social hierarchy, they would spread out to areas of "second settlement," thus making room for newcomers to the city. These new groups would, in turn, follow a similar progression.

There were a number of problems with the trickle-down housing theory. First, the theory assumed that the number of households would not expand faster than the number of units added to the housing stock, because if it did, there still would not be enough housing to go around, much less to trickle down to the very poorest consumers. Obviously, it also assumed that when the additions to the housing stock exceeded the increase in the number of households, filtering down would continue until the worst units were emptied out and removed entirely from the housing market. Neither of these expectations has materialized. Given the drop in average household size, the need for dwelling units has continued to rise in many places, even in center cities where population is actually declining. And although housing units are frequently removed from the housing market through abandonment, it is by no means the case that the units lost are the most dilapidated.

Second, the trickle-down housing theory assumed that there would be no extraneous restrictions to prevent the housing stock from moving smoothly from one set of consumers to another; that is, no characteristics of housing consumers except the prices they were willing and able to pay would influence the distribution of dwelling units. However, the race and ethnicity of housing consumers have proven to be major barriers to the transfer of the housing stock.

The same defects were found in the theories of neighborhood succession. Trickle-down neighborhood theories were premised on several assumptions. First, they assumed that there would always be new groups at the bottom to take the place of earlier groups: No group would remain permanently at the end of the queue for housing and neighborhoods. Second, the theories assumed that no extraneous restrictions would prevent the smooth transition of neighborhoods from one group of occupants to the next. Despite their somewhat militant sound, the terms "invasion" and "succession" were used by urban ecologists to refer to a peaceful and gradual process.

In the United States, however, race has been a major distorter in the process of housing and neighborhood succession. Racial prejudice has interfered with the smooth movement of white and black populations in the city—by creating both an unnatural shortage of housing for blacks during the early period of ghetto expansion, and unnatural vacuums and surpluses during later periods of stabilized population growth and white flight. The changes in the labor market, described in Chapter 6, dampened the demand for blue-collar workers in central cities just at the time that African-Americans, as the "most recent immigrants" (albeit from the rural South rather than abroad), were ready to use such jobs as the first rungs in the ladder of upward mobility. Finally, with the end of massive migration to the United States, only a few groups of newcomers came into American cities after the blacks: Hispanics, chiefly, and then Asians. Neither of these groups, however, had to contend with quite the same degree of prejudice as have native blacks. Therefore, rather than pushing African-Americans "up," such groups have tended to move ahead of them in the pecking order of U.S. ethnic groups. Hispanics, for example, have tended to settle in buffer zones between areas of black and white settlement, while most Asian newcomers have been absorbed into the polyethnic, mostly white, communities that in most cities are located a distance from the central slums. Blacks, then, have been left "holding the bag" of central slums.

The Dual Housing Market   Both the "trickle-down" theory of housing and the "neighborhood succession" process upon which many of the predictions of classical urban ecology were premised were, therefore, essentially undermined by the "race problem" in American cities. Racial segregation created a dual housing market in which two separate and unequal housing markets existed—one for blacks, the other for whites.[16]

At the time of the great migrations from the rural South to northern cities, the amount of housing available to blacks in northern cities was greatly restricted by discrimination. Because of these restrictions, buildings in areas open to black residents tended to be occupied at densities higher than those in white areas; families had to double up, and apartments and houses were subdivided to create additional dwelling units. Because demand exceeded supply, rents for

---

[16]A good exposition of the dual housing market can be found in articles contained in Gary Tobin, ed., *Divided Neighborhoods: Changing Patterns of Racial Segregation*, vol. 32 of *Urban Affairs Annual Reviews* (Newbury Park, CA: Sage Publications, 1987).

these smaller and deteriorating units were even higher than those for better dwellings located in areas not open to black occupancy. One can see how these socially generated restrictions on the supply of housing open to African-Americans meant that (1) owners did not need to repair or maintain the structures, since renters could be found even for units of the worst quality, and (2) doubling up and high densities of occupancy led to higher rent returns but faster deterioration. Thus, the dual housing market was profitable for owners of black-occupied units, much as they may have complained.

The dual housing market was also profitable for real estate agents and absentee investors who were involved in the process of expanding the residential zones open to blacks. Because of pent-up demand in the so-called "black belts" and ghettos of the nation, properties just adjacent to these zones were in high demand. The burgeoning demand for additional units in the black housing market meant that blacks had to pay excessive prices for scarce housing, even if this required a higher percentage of their incomes. Blockbusting real estate agents and speculative investors could therefore make an enormous profit by manipulating whites and blacks. They played on the fears of white residents to motivate them to sell their homes at prices below their actual values. Spreading rumors that owners would lose their investments when blacks moved into the neighborhood, they encouraged panic selling by white owners. Speculators then purchased these buildings at abnormally low prices, changed their occupancy to black, and then saw the values of the properties not only recover but move to even higher levels. Many would then sell off the bargain properties at a good profit and would reinvest their money in new areas along the path of ghetto expansion.

The profits to be made in the dual housing market, however, were predicated on continued expansion of black demand, continued segregation in the housing market, and continued strong demand by whites for center city housing. All of these variables changed in recent decades and, in the process, led to the phenomenon of black suburbanization and contributed to inner-city housing abandonment.

The Vacuum Created by White Flight In the 1950s and 1960s, "white flight" from the center cities of those SMSAs having large black populations stepped up. It was white families who took maximum advantage of the burgeoning opportunities for home ownership and suburban residence that were facilitated by government tax subsidies and mortgage incentives. The Open Housing Law of 1968 made it illegal to discriminate on the basis of race when renting or selling apartments and houses. While this did not eliminate prejudice or do away completely with the dual housing market, in combination with the white flight that was reducing the white population of the central city faster than their places could be taken by black or Hispanic newcomers, it did much to undermine the barriers that for so long had interfered with smooth racial transitions.

By the 1970s, African-American outmigration from the South was tapering off; in addition, there was some black suburbanization as middle-class blacks were no longer confined to ghetto residences.[17] Therefore, black demand for central city residences did not grow as fast as it had before. Whites, on the other hand, suburbanized much faster than blacks, to some extent speeding up their flight because they feared school desegregation (mandated by *Brown v. Board of Education*) and later the "threat" of busing. The white groups that remained in the city became increasingly vocal (and sometimes violent) in defending their "turf."

Increasingly, then, the populations of central cities—especially in the large urban centers of the North and Northeast Central—shifted toward minority groups. This perpetuated de facto segregation, even though the law ostensibly forbade it. And yet, the number of African-Americans and Hispanics did not increase as fast as the number of housing units that were changing from restricted white to open occupancy. In place of the artificial shortage of black housing created by the dual housing market, there was sometimes a "surplus" of housing—no longer wanted by whites but not demanded by blacks, at least by blacks willing and able to pay what was asked. In many ways, this new imbalance in the housing market, caused by an inversion of the dual housing market of earlier times, accounted for some of the housing abandonment that occurred in center cities in the 1970s.[18]

Black Poverty: The Cause of Insufficient Economic Demand?

Housing abandonment, as we have shown, does not occur because no one needs the housing, but rather because those who do need it will not or cannot pay what landlords want. While to some extent the rapid expansion of housing available in the "black housing market" created an unwillingness on the part of middle-class blacks to pay the segregation premium that had formerly been demanded, this was compounded by an inability of low-income black consumers to pay the going rate. Only if there were truly "open housing" (no discrimination) *and* if there were no differences between the distributions of white and black incomes could the housing stock be moved from one housing market to the other without causing major dislocations. The incomes of blacks and whites, however, are not equal. In fact, the discrepancy between white and black incomes in American cities is wide, which intensifies the segregation that comes

---

[17]See Wade Clark Roof, ed., *Race and Residence in American Cities,* special issue of *Annals of the American Academy of Political and Social Science* 441 (January 1979). In the 1970s, and even more in the 1980s, black suburbanization has continued to expand, although not at the rates that might have been expected from income alone. Black suburbanization has not necessarily resulted in greater racial desegregation. Rather, inlying suburbs in the path of black-zone expansion seem to have absorbed most of the growth, with racial mixing being a temporary event on the way to resegregation. See Thomas A. Clark, "The Suburbanization Process and Residential Segregation," in Gary Tobin, ed., *Divided Neighborhoods,* pp. 115–137.

[18]While there are many case studies now of disinvestment and abandonment, one of the more detailed studies has been done by Robert Giloth, "Disinvestment in South Shore's Large Rental Properties," conducted by the Center for Urban Economic Development at University of Illinois, Chicago Circle (mimeograph, March 1981).

from discrimination in the housing market.[19] Thus, ethnic/racial segregation in housing is facilitated, at least in part, by racial inequities in the job market.

African-Americans are discriminated against not only in housing but in employment as well. Such discrimination, coupled with recent changes in the demand for labor, affects the prevalence of poverty and helps to create the largest class of the poor—women who head their own households, of whom many are black. Thus we find that social rank (class), familism (the position of women), and ethnicity (racial segregation) are interconnected.

It should be noted that while in absolute numbers, most poor people in the United States are white, that is only because over 85 percent of Americans are white. The absolute number of the poor is not to be confused with the relative probability of being poor. In 1982, according to estimates made by the U.S. Bureau of the Census from a sample study, close to 35 million Americans (about 15 percent of the total population) were poor, that is, had per capita incomes below the "poverty line." Minority status was highly correlated with poverty. Although among whites the poverty rate was only 12 percent, among Hispanics the rate was close to 30 percent, and among black Americans it was almost 36 percent. Thus, even though blacks made up only 12 percent of the total population, they accounted for 28 percent of the poor. Furthermore, since the black population is now heavily concentrated in the center cities of the largest metropolitan areas, blacks constitute a disproportionate percentage of the inner city poor.[20]

Why are blacks so poor? Originally, the explanation given by urban sociologists was that having only recently migrated from backward rural areas, blacks had not yet made the adaptation to urban life that earlier immigrants had made. Presumably, as African-Americans remained longer in the city and as they received more and better education, they would, like the foreign immigrants who had preceded them, reduce the educational gap between themselves and their white neighbors and would, in the process, reduce the income gap as well. The situation has turned out to be far more complex, as is evident from a 1983 study on black poverty.[21]

According to this study, the income gap between whites and blacks in the United States has remaind as great as it was in 1960, despite enormous strides

[19]At least this was the major finding of a careful study of changes in poverty and segregation between the censuses of 1970 and 1980. This study found that both racial segregation *and* economic segregation interacted to account for the change. See Douglas Massey and Mitchell Eggers, "The Ecology of Inequality: Minorities and the Concentration of Poverty, 1970–1980," in *American Journal of Sociology* 95 (March 1990), pp. 1153–1188. See also Douglas S. Massey, "American Apartheid: Segregation and the Making of the Underclass," *American Journal of Sociology* 96 (Sept. 1990), pp. 329–357.

[20]Data were presented in a news conference by Gordon W. Green, Jr. of the U.S. Bureau of the Census on August 2, 1983, and reported in *The New York Times,* August 3, 1983, pp. 1 and 9.

[21]"A Dream Deferred: The Economic Status of Black Americans. A Working Paper" (mimeographed report issued by the Center for the Study of Social Policy, Washington, DC, 1983). Findings were summarized in *The New York Times,* July 18, 1983.

in the education of blacks that virtually closed the education gap and despite the growth of a sizable black middle class. Black poverty can no longer be blamed on rural residence or recency of migration (blacks are now more urbanized than whites), or on illiteracy (educational levels of blacks and whites are now virtually the same), or on any of the usual explanations given in urban sociology.

Rather, black poverty seems to be due to two facts. First, blacks are paid lower wages than whites, even when they have the same education: black college graduates earn about the same as white high school graduates. Second, black males have very low rates of labor-force participation, because they are very likely to be involuntarily unemployed or discouraged from seeking work in the first place. This situation has evidently been growing worse, as the restructured American economy eliminates entry-level jobs except in dead-end services, and as the discrepancy between where jobs are located and where blacks can live grows greater. (See Tables 9.1 and 9.2.)

Because African-American men suffer from such high rates of unemployment and discouragement, they are likely to absent themselves from their families, which has led to the dramatic increase in the proportion of black families headed by women. The 1983 study concluded, therefore, that the individual gains made by black middle-class families since the 1960s were wiped out, at the global level, by an increase in the black male unemployment rate and the enormous increase in black female-headed households (which have the highest probability of being poor).[22]

The proportion of black males over 16 years of age who were not working doubled between 1960 and 1980, from about 25 percent in the former year to close to 50 percent by 1980.[23] While it is likely that simple discrimination played some part in this exclusion of black males from the economy, there is no reason to attribute it exclusively to racism. (In fact, most public opinion polls report a drop in direct racist views, or at least in their expression to poll-takers.) What is more likely is that the increased unemployment of blacks is attributable to recent declines in the demand for labor in American industry, especially in inner city locations. As some have suggested, black males have become supernumerary to the economy. Faced with such poor prospects, they often become

---

[22]As a number of observers have pointed out, this had led to a bifurcation in the black community itself between the middle class (made up of "normal" families, often with working wives, which have experienced the most dramatic increases in family income and have closed the gap to whites of comparable status) and what some are referring to as an almost permanent "underclass" consisting of poor blacks unable to find work and thrown on welfare. See, for example, Reynolds Farley and Suzanne M. Bianchi, "The Growing Gap Between Blacks," *American Demographics* 5 (July 1983), pp. 15–18, as well as the new census monograph by Reynolds Farley and Walter Allen, *The Color Line and the Quality of Life in America* (New York: Russell Sage Foundation, 1987). The fullest descriptive study of black disabilities in America is Gerald D. Jaynes and Robin M. Williams, Jr., *A Common Destiny: Blacks and American Society* (Washington, DC: National Academy Press, 1989).

[23]The discrepancy between this figure and the first line in Table 9.1 is caused by the exclusion from this table of males who are so discouraged that they are no longer looking for work in the formal legal economy.

Table 9.1 UNEMPLOYMENT RATES OF CENTER CITY MALES, AGED 16–64, BY RACE AND YEARS OF SCHOOL COMPLETED, 1969, 1977, 1982

	White			Black		
Schooling	1969	1977	1982	1969	1977	1982
Did not complete high school	4.3	12.2	17.7	6.6	19.8	29.7
Completed high school	1.7	8.0	11.0	4.1	16.2	23.5
Attended 1+ Years College	1.6	4.7	4.4	3.7	10.7	16.1
All Levels	2.6	7.7	9.5	5.4	16.5	23.4

Source: John D. Kasarda, "Urban Change and Minority Opportunities," in Paul E. Peterson, ed., *The New Urban Reality* (Washington, D.C.: The Brookings Institute, 1985), p. 57, as reproduced in William H. Frey and Alden Speare, Jr., *Regional and Metropolitan Growth and Decline in the United States* (New York: Russell Sage Foundation, 1988), p. 416.

Table 9.2 PERCENTAGE NOT AT WORK OF OUT-OF-SCHOOL CENTER CITY AND SUBURBAN BLACK MALE RESIDENTS, AGED 16–64, WHO HAVE NOT COMPLETED 12 YEARS OF EDUCATION, 1969–1987

Region of the U.S. and metropolitan residence	1969	1977	1982	1987
All Regions				
central city	18.8	38.3	49.5	49.5
suburban ring	16.3	31.4	38.2	33.4
Northeast				
central city	21.1	42.8	44.8	44.0
suburban ring	15.1	27.0	34.4	30.8
Midwest				
central city	19.5	42.6	54.3	55.5
suburban ring	8.0	44.3	43.6	41.3
South				
central city	15.4	32.0	47.3	45.8
suburban ring	15.9	24.9	37.9	32.1
West				
central city	27.4	42.3	60.4	60.8
suburban ring	38.9	44.2	37.7	34.2

Source: John D. Kasarda, "Urban Industrial Transition and the Underclass," in *Annals of the American Academy of Political and Social Science* 501 (January 1989), pp. 26–47. Taken from Table 8, p. 42.

so discouraged that they stop looking for work, finding incomes, where possible, in the illegitimate economy.[24] When they are unemployed, their ability to

---

[24]See Terry Williams and William Kornblum, *Growing Up Poor* (Lexington, MA: D. C. Heath, 1985) for a graphic description of the "choice" young black males from poor neighborhoods must exer-

support a family drops precipitously—hence the increase in the proportion of black households headed by women.

The proportion of black families headed by women more than doubled between 1960 and 1980, a sixfold increase since 1950. In 1950 only 8 percent of black families with children lacked a male head. By 1960 this proportion had risen to 21, and by 1980 it stood at 47 percent. Since female-headed households are twice as likely to be poor as other types of families, the relationships between the class system, ethnicity, and family type are clear.

There is a vicious circle that ties the three together in the case of African-Americans. Changes in the basic economy seem to have "surplused" a large number of black males. Unable to find work, they withdraw from the labor force. They are unable to support families, which means that households become matricentered. Such households are often poor and, because fathers are absent, are eligible for dependent child payments and for subsidized housing. Thus, they also tend to become segregated racially in public housing projects or central slums. Ever since the United States stopped expanding its supply of public housing, the number of mother-children families who are without homes has grown dramatically.

Segregation: Cause or Effect?

The degree of racial segregation in U.S. cities is often attributed to the poverty of urban blacks. However, this is not the entire explanation. Because there are also so many poor whites in American cities (numerically, if not proportionately), income segregation is not incompatible with racial desegregation. In fact, scholars have estimated that only about 10 percent of the residential racial segregation observed in American cities can be attributed to economic causes;[25] the remainder is due to racial attitudes which in the United States have continued to distort the spatial structure of American cities. Even though middle-class blacks have become more numerous in recent years, and many have moved to the suburbs, they still tend to be concentrated in segregated suburbs, or to integrate (temporarily) suburbs that are really extensions of existing ghettos.

Does segregation make a difference? And in what ways? Segregation must be considered central to the question of equal access to public goods. Residential segregation potentially permits highly differentiated (and inferior) public services and facilities in all-black areas, whereas in integrated areas, such items of collective consumption would presumably have to be distributed more equit-

cise—between very bad neighborhood jobs or none at all, and better "opportunities" in illegal activities such as drug dealing. Failure to include these activities, and the incomes derived from them, in employment and income statistics leads analysts to underestimate economic conditions in American ghetto communities.

[25]A. Sorenson, K. Taeuber, and J. Hollingsworth, "Indexes of Racial Residential Segregation for 109 Cities in the United States, 1940 to 1970," *Sociological Focus* (April 1975).

ably, because blacks and whites would be served by the same facilities. Urban sociologists have developed careful techniques for measuring segregation and for determining whether it is increasing or decreasing. This close attention to segregation comes in part because they believe that segregation *does* make a difference, not only in how the housing market works, but in how racial groups are socially created, interact, and view one another. Before we look at what difference segregation makes, we need to digress a bit to explain how segregation is measured.

How Much Racial Segregation Is There?   A great deal of research effort has focused on answering two interrelated questions. First, how much residential segregation is there in cities in the United States? And second, has racial segregation increased or decreased over time? A final, but often subsidiary, question is: What factors in a city lead to greater or lesser segregation?

Perhaps the earliest, and certainly the most careful, attempt to measure racial segregation in American cities was done by Karl and Alma Taeuber; the methods they developed to measure segregation during the 1940s and 1950s have been adopted (and adapted) by all later scholars, and their findings have been the benchmark by which subsequent desegregation has been evaluated.[26] Demographic studies of segregation all utilize some kind of "segregation index" to measure the degree to which blacks and whites live separately in cities. Because the results depend at least in part upon which segregation measure is used, variations in this index need to be understood.

The residential segregation index in most general use is the *index of dissimilarity.* It measures *the distribution of white and nonwhite* (that is, mostly "black") *households among census blocks.* Scores on this index range from 0 to 100, with higher values indicating higher levels of residential segregation. This index asks: What percentage of a group would have to move to another location (in this case, another block) in order to achieve a distribution of races within each block (or census tract, if that is the areal unit used) that is the same as their representation in the city as a whole?[27]

---

[26]See Karl Taeuber and Alma Taeuber, *Negroes in Cities* (Chicago: Aldine Publishing Company, 1965) for the benchmark study from which all later trends are measured.

[27]The formula for the index of dissimilarity (D) is

$$D = \frac{1}{2} \Sigma \left[\frac{x_k}{x_t} - \frac{y_k}{y_t} \right]$$

where x_k and y_k represent the number of black and white persons who reside in a subarea; x_t and y_t are the total number of blacks and whites in the city. One objection to segregation indexes of all kinds is that the measures are extremely sensitive to the size of the areal unit within which segregation is being measured. In general, the smaller the unit (e.g., the block instead of the census tract), the greater its potential for homogeneity and therefore, *ceteris paribus,* the higher its level of segregation. Because of this, one should never compare a segregation index based on census tracts with one based on blocks.

A distinction needs to be made between absolute and relative measures of segregation. The index of dissimilarity measures the *absolute* segregation within a city; it quantifies the discrepancy between the spatial patterns that actually exist within a city and those that would exist, if the races were randomly intermixed. It is therefore partially affected by the relative sizes of the two groups studied. Whereas two cities may have the same scores or indexes of dissimilarity, the nature of segregation and its consequences may be qualitatively different in a city where one-third of the population is black than in one in which only 2 percent is black. A black who lives inside a large, highly segregated community is much less likely to interact with whites during the day than an equally "segregated" black who lives in a tiny and therefore not self-sufficient black community.

To capture this reality of exposure to segregation, the *index of dominance* (which is a measure of *relative* rather than absolute segregation) is often used. The index of dominance does not look at the city-wide distribution of racial or ethnic groups; rather, it measures the racial or ethnic composition of a *given areal unit.* Not only does it take into account the actual size of the group whose segregation is being measured, but it is sensitive to the size of the area. Thus, the number of areal units into which the city is subdivided for this computation has an effect on the level of segregation found.

The index of dominance asks: What proportion of the population in an individual's residential area is composed of others who have the same ethnic or racial characteristic?[28] This measure thus tells us something about how much exposure blacks and whites have to each other, and thus the extent to which racial mixing might be expected to increase knowledge about and comprehension of the life experiences of others. Because neither measure captures the full phenomenon, studies often compute both measures of racial segregation.

The results of neither method give cause for complacency. By any measure, segregation remains high. Furthermore, successive studies do not allow us to conclude that racial segregation is disappearing from American cities. While racial segregation has declined somewhat since the Taeubers began to measure it in 1940, by 1970 little had changed, and only recently has segregation begun to drop—albeit very slowly.[29]

---

[28]The formula for the index of dominance (D) is:

$$D = \frac{1}{\Sigma N(G \times g_i / P_i)};$$

where
G = Total population of the group whose residential pattern is being examined;
g_i = The population of that group residing in the ith areal unit;
P_i = The total population of the ith areal unit; and
N = The total number of areal units.

[29]Among the more important works to be consulted, see Reynolds Farley and Walter R. Allen, *The Color Line and the Quality of Life in America* (New York: Russell Sage Foundation, 1987).

Consequences of Segregation Does it matter in practical terms how segregated black and white populations are from one another in the city? While, theoretically, segregation should not make a practical difference, in actual fact it almost always does. Certainly, it has been substantiated that all-black areas in cities do not receive their fair share of public services and facilities.

In one sample analysis in Chicago, for example, clear evidence of discriminatory city servicing was found between white and black areas in the city.[30] In 1977, white police districts averaged 17 persons per police officer, whereas black and black-Latino districts averaged 26 and 27 persons per police officer, respectively. This was true despite the fact that crime rates were considerably higher in black and black-Hispanic areas than they were in white districts.

With respect to fire protection, the distribution of personnel was somewhat more equitable—but not when relative risk was taken into account. In predominantly white fire districts of the city there were 7.9 fire fighters per 10,000 persons to handle some 26.8 structural fires per 10,000 persons. In predominantly black areas, where fires were far more common, the average number of structural fires per 10,000 persons was 64, while the number of firemen to handle them was only 11.5 per 10,000.

With respect to neighborhood facilities provided by the Chicago Park District, similar inequities were found, with disproportionately more facilities, programs, and staff being channeled to white wards. The report concluded that the odds were stacked against Chicago's black and Latino branch libraries and that the regional transit authority subsidized wealthy rail passengers on commuter routes while the poor (largely minority) users of the Chicago Transit Authority facilities were required to pay higher fares.

These data were gathered before the 1982 election of Harold Washington as Chicago's first black mayor. The discriminatory services reported in this study were a major issue in the election, and many of the black and Hispanic voters, who gave overwhelming support to Washington at the polls, expected political gains to be translated into a new set of priorities in urban services for their districts. But such a consequence is never assured. There are now black mayors in a large number of American cities that contain substantial numbers of black residents; their pluralities, however, are often associated with declining resources and heightened demands, which may signal a pyrrhic victory.[31]

The question of the relationship between racial segregation and school quality is another that has engaged researchers. The Supreme Court, reasoning

---

[30]See Tom Brune, ed., *Neglected Neighborhoods: Patterns of Discrimination in Chicago City Services* (pamphlet reprinted from *The Chicago Reporter,* published by the Community Renewal Society, 1981; reprinted from articles published 1977–1980).

[31]See Robert Staples, *The Urban Plantation: Racism and Colonialism in the Post–Civil Rights Era* (Oakland, CA: Black Scholar Press, 1987).

that separate schools could *not* be equal, ruled (in *Brown v. Board of Education*) that the provision of "separate but equal" school facilities violated the Constitution, and ordered schools to be integrated. But it was difficult for many cities to integrate schools without doing away with the neighborhood school because residential segregation was so extreme. In those cities with especially high segregation indexes and very large proportions of black school-aged children, it was literally impossible to achieve balanced racial composition in the schools without sending inner-city blacks to suburban schools in the metropolitan region, a strategy which could not be used because of the political structure of home rule and school district boundaries. Of course, integration is not necessarily the goal of all blacks, nor does it guarantee that they will receive high-quality education.

The case of quality housing is simpler. Segregated housing is almost invariably associated with low quality and high prices. This is because segregated housing creates a dual housing market. Since historically, supply exceeded demand within the white housing market while demand exceeded supply in the black market, segregation was largely responsible for the higher rents and prices that urban blacks paid for poorer housing.

As we have already seen, the recent high rate of abandonment and arson in districts occupied by blacks results in part from the fact that the black population is no longer forced to pay high rents for badly deteriorated housing because (1) black population increase has in many cases leveled off, and (2) middle-class blacks have benefited from the open housing legislation and have been able to escape from the central ghettos. But low-income blacks are often still trapped in inner city slums. For them, discrimination in the workplace is more serious than discrimination in the housing market. Black male unemployment rates have recently soared, encouraging the growth in number of female-headed households, since only if the father is absent can a mother collect welfare. William Julius Wilson has stressed not that race does not matter, but that *class* within the black community *is now more important than race* per se in setting differential life chances.[32] He notes that there is a growing gap between the black middle class, which has benefited from affirmative action, enhanced opportunities for education, and better jobs, and the large *lumpenproletariat* among the inner city urban blacks and poor rural sharecropper blacks whose positions (and hopes) have eroded. The marginalization of the black male from the economy and the feminization of black poverty are the results of large-scale societal factors that are only partly due to discrimination. Nevertheless, they cannot be corrected and improved without very systematic attention to the goal of providing more and better jobs to African-Americans—both male and female. Residential segregation, while it does not cause unemployment, makes it harder for African-Americans to compete for the jobs that do exist.

---

[32]See his *The Declining Significance of Race,* especially the epilogue to the 1981 second edition of the book (Chicago: University of Chicago Press, 1981). See also his *The Truly Disadvantaged* (Chicago, University of Chicago Press, 1987).

SPACE HAS CONSEQUENCES

In our discussion of racial segregation we noted that one of the reasons residential segregation and school segregation are viewed as having discriminatory effects is that spatial patterns have real social consequences. The physical isolation of a group causes or reinforces its social isolation; proximity is required for easy social interaction, and "body mixing" is at least a prerequisite for more social forms of mixing. Thus far, however, we have only a kind of commonsensical set of assumptions on which to go.

We know that, other things being equal, it is more probable that someone will marry a neighbor than a stranger, provided gender, age, class, religion, and so on are "right." Sociologists have actually been able to quantify this common-sense understanding in a series of studies on assortive mating, in which they find an association between proximity and marriage partner selection.[33] This association is well known to nonsociologist parents who try to control their children's friends by moving to a neighborhood or sending their children to schools where they are likely to meet "the right kind of people," or "people like ourselves." In fact, this everyday world rule (namely, that making birds of a feather flock together is easier when birds of a feather are already flocked together) is one which underlies many of the studies urban sociologists have made into the relationship between physical space and social interactions.

Commonsense knowledge also tells us that our spatial environment affects our behavior, often in subtle and sometimes in not-so-subtle ways. Crowd behavior is certainly one not-so-subtle influence. (It is perhaps significant that Robert Park's dissertation dealt in part with "the crowd.") Being in a crowded football stadium cheering for one's team in the company of other excited fans is intrinsically different than viewing a game at home on television. Listening to rock music at home is not the same as hearing it in a collective rite such as Woodstock. Private experiences lack the synergistic intensity that comes from communal participation. In fact, sociologists believe that occasional collective rituals, which permit such synergistic intensity, are essential to the tightening of preexisting social bonds or the formation of new ones.

But not all spatial influences have consequences as clear as those associated with being in a crowd. Edward Hall has explored how spatial arrangements may have subtle influences on our behavior.[34] He observed, for example, that birds and animals tend to "space" themselves (that is, set distances between themselves and others which indicate quite accurately the context of the interaction—fight or flight, intimacy, threat, etc.); human behavior exhibits many of these same patterns, but with a difference. Humans do not respond to space and distance in universal ways that are genetically programmed, but in ways that

---

[33]See J. Bossard, "Residential Propinquity as a Factor in Marriage Selection," *American Sociological Review* 38 (1932), pp. 219–224; Rose J. Kennedy, "Premarital Propinquity and Ethnic Endogamy," *American Journal of Sociology* 48 (1943), pp. 580–584.

[34]See especially his *The Hidden Dimension* (Garden City, NY: Doubleday Anchor, 1969).

have been learned in their cultures. Hall found that "intimate distance" ranges from very close (for Latin Americans and Arabs, for example) to quite far (for Anglo-Saxons), but is always shorter than formal distance.

Thus, it follows that spatial arrangements "cue" certain kinds of behaviors, particularly within a given culture. The way office furniture is arranged, for example, has been found to influence the types of egalitarian or hierarchical interactions that take place. Most executives know this intuitively. Sitting behind an imposing desk, or keeping a visitor standing and at a distance, increases the "social distance" between the host and guest and thus enhances the host's authority. On the other hand, if the executive rises, greets the guest near the door, and then steers the visitor to another part of the office with couches or chairs set more equally and informally, the "social distance" between the two has been successfully bridged.[35] Other social psychologists have learned what the best interior decorators (and many untrained homemakers) have always known: that certain settings can either intensify discomfort and "dis-ease" or put people at their ease and make them relax. Some of these studies have been applied in the design of public institutions (doctor's waiting rooms, hospitals, etc.) to help manipulate the client population.[36]

In short, the "person on the street" and the Gestalt psychologist agree that the spatial arrangements of the built environment (and of the individuals with whom such arrangements make it most probable for us to interact) have a decided effect on social life. In the next chapter we will look at how urban sociologists took these insights and tried to fashion a theory that made a logical connection between the *physical space* of the city and the type of *social space* (social interactional patterns) that could be expected. While the original formulation may have been overly simplistic and therefore flawed, it did begin a search which has yielded more specific propositions on how and when physical space affects social space, and has led to the development of methods to study the interactional connections between social and physical space.

---

[35]See many of the selections in Harold Proshansky, William Ittelson, and Leanne Rivlin, eds., *Environmental Psychology: Man and His Physical Setting* (New York: Holt, Rinehart and Winston, 1970).

[36]See Robert Sommer, *Personal Space: The Behavioral Basis of Design* (Englewood Cliffs, NJ: Prentice-Hall, 1969).

Studying Community— Not Necessarily a Place

Chapter
10

The End of Ecological Determinism

URBANISM AS A WAY OF LIFE: ONE OR MANY

When the field of urban sociology was first being established in the 1920s and its domain and subject matter were being delimited, a second area (that received as much attention as urban ecology) was the study of *community* in city life. The concept of community occupies a privileged place in the romantic symbolic lexicon of America, as significant as mother, apple pie, and democracy. Robert Nisbet's definition is typical for both its content and poeticism:

> By community, I mean something that goes far beyond mere local community. The word . . . encompasses all forms of relationships which are characterized by a high degree of personal intimacy, emotional depth, moral commitment, social cohesion, and continuity in time. Community is founded on man conceived in his wholeness rather than in one or another of the roles, taken separately, that he may hold in the social order.
>
> It draws its psychological strength from levels of motivation deeper than those of mere volition, or interest, and it achieves its fulfillment in a submergence of individual will that is not possible in unions of mere convenience or rational assent. Community is a fusion of feeling and thought, of identity and commitment,

of membership and volition, It may be found in, or given symbolic expression by, locality, religion, nation, race, occupation or crusade.[1]

One sees immediately the deep connection between this definition of community and the nineteenth-century discourse of Ferdinand Toennies.

American urban sociology, from its inception, shared Toennies's pessimistic obsession with *The Eclipse of Community*,[2] as the title of Maurice Stein's famous book put it. Indeed, underlying the preoccupation of early Chicago School founders with the differences between urban and rural ways of life was a concern that city life would destroy the foundations of community. This preoccupation perhaps received its clearest expression in Louis Wirth's essay, "Urbanism as a Way of Life"[3] which, for many years after its publication in 1938, was considered *the* definitive "theory" of urban sociology. It addressed the question of whether community was possible in large cities and set forth a logical set of theoretical propositions which seemed to give a negative answer to that question.

Defining the city as a large and permanent settlement, densely inhabited by a heterogeneous population, Wirth deduced from these ecological characteristics the cultural and social nature of "urbanism as a way of life." He argued that increases in the size, density, and heterogeneity of settlements would, inevitably and automatically, lead to a *loss* of community, in the *Gemeinschaft* sense of the term. Table 10.1 shows graphically the structure of Wirth's argument.

Size and complexity were the crucial independent variables. Following the anthropological theories of Herbert Spencer and Emile Durkheim, Wirth reasoned that any increase in the size and density of human settlements would lead quite naturally to greater social complexity and diversity. These ecological factors—characteristic of cities—led, he claimed, to the special forms of social life found in cities, as distinguished from rural areas:

1. A tendency toward secondary relationships, where individuals interact largely in terms of their roles rather than in terms of their whole personalities;
2. Relative anonymity (made possible because people can "get lost" in the crowd); and

---

[1]Robert Nisbet, *The Sociological Tradition* (New York: Basic Books, 1966), as quoted in E. Digby Baltzell, ed., *The Search for Community in Modern America* (New York: Harper & Row, 1968), p. 2. One of the best sources on the concept of community is Jessie Bernard's small gem, *The Sociology of Community* (Glenview, IL: Scott, Foresman & Company, 1973).

[2]Maurice Stein, *The Eclipse of Community: An Interpretation of American Studies* (Princeton, NJ: Princeton University Press, 1960; paperback edition, 1971).

[3]Louis Wirth, "Urbanism as a Way of Life" (*American Journal of Sociology* 44 [July 1938]), pp. 1–24, but reprinted in most urban sociology anthologies). Wirth's independent variables seem to have been taken from Durkheim's *The Division of Labor in Society*, written originally in 1898 as a doctoral dissertation. His dependent variables were drawn in large measure from Simmel's essay on "The Metropolis and Mental Life,"written originally in 1902–1903.

Table 10.1 LOUIS WIRTH'S SOCIOLOGICAL DEFINITION OF THE CITY IN RELATION TO SIZE, DENSITY, AND HETEROGENEITY

	A schematic version
PERMANENCE	Greater the number of people interacting, greater the potential differentiation
	Dependence upon a greater number of people, lesser dependence on particular persons
SIZE An increase in the number of inhabitants of a settlement beyond a certain limit brings about changes in the relations of people and changes in the character of the community	Association with more people, knowledge of a smaller proportion, and of these, less intimate knowledge
	More secondary rather than primary contacts; that is, increase in contacts which are face to face, yet impersonal, superficial, transitory, and segmental
	More freedom from the personal and emotional control of intimate groups
	Association in a large number of groups, no individual allegiance to a single group
DENSITY Reinforces the effect of size in diversifying men and their activities, and in increasing the structural complexity of the society	Tendency to differentiation and specialization
	Separation of residence from work place
	Functional specialization of areas—segregation of functions
	Segregation of people: city becomes a mosaic of social worlds
HETEROGENEITY Cities products of migration of peoples of diverse origin Heterogeneity of origin matched by heterogeneity of occupations Differentiation and specialization reinforces heterogeneity	Without common background and common activities premium is placed on visual recognition: the uniform becomes symbolic of the role
	No common set of values, no common ethical system to sustain them: money tends to become measure of all things for which there are no common standards
	Formal controls as opposed to informal controls. Necessity for adhering to predictable routines. Clock and the traffic signal symbolic of the basis of the social order
	Economic basis: mass production of goods, possible only with the standardization of processes and products
	Standardization of goods and facilities in terms of the average
	Adjustment of educational, recreational, and cultural services to mass requirements
	In politics success of mass appeals—growth of mass movements

Source: Eshref Shevky and Wendell Bell, *Social Area Analysis,* Stanford Sociological Series #1 (Stanford, CA, Stanford University Press, 1955), pp. 7–8. As reproduced in Noel Gist and Sylvia Fava, *Urban Society,* 6th ed. (New York: Thomas Y. Crowell, 1974).

3. More formal types of social organization (i.e., a dependence upon voluntary organizations rather than the more "natural" groups of kin and neighbors).

In short, it appeared from this essay that *urbanization per se* leads inevitably to a loss of community.

WAS IT URBANISM OR MODERNITY?[4]

Many of the social consequences of urban ecology that Wirth identified had already been described by Georg Simmel, who attributed them to "modern" life, rather than to the city *per se*. Indeed, the major problem with Wirth's essay was that it vacillated between describing a *general* phenomenon called "urbanism as a way of life" and a much more specific cultural form, "American industrial capitalism as a way of life."

His own presentation was somewhat ambiguous. In certain passages he acknowledged that he was describing the specific urban culture found in western industrial societies in the early twentieth century. However, if his description was related to a specific historical case, then how could these characteristics be deduced from the universal characteristics of "the city" as a large, permanent, dense settlement of heterogeneous inhabitants?

In fact, they could not. While, other things being equal, an increase in the size, density, and heterogeneity of *a given city at a given historical moment* might be likely to have social consequences in the predicted direction, only a very limited theory of human behavior in cities could be generated directly from Wirth's variables. At the minimum, a combination of sociocultural and ecological factors had to be taken into account.

Early on, Wirth's theory was critiqued for its tendency to overgeneralize. Certainly, such grand propositions as his could not account for the very wide variations in city life that were evident even among American cities under industrial capitalism. Wirth himself had actually acknowledged this, since in the very same article he described the American city as a mosaic of social worlds *with different ways of life,* and noted that *Gemeinschaft* tended to live on even in large cities, particularly in ethnic quarters such as "the ghetto" (referring to the topic of his doctoral dissertation, the Jewish community of Chicago).

Many critics pointed out that in American cities, class and occupation, ethnic identity, and life cycle stage (at the minimum) were intervening factors affecting how residents differentially experienced and reacted to their environments. When new suburbs were constructed after World War II, for example, transplanted urbanites behaved quite differently once they were in the smaller communities. While at first it seemed that their intense social life confirmed the

---

[4]Much of the following discussion is based on Janet Abu-Lughod, *The City is Dead—Long Live the City: Some Thoughts on Urbanity* (Monograph 12, Berkeley, CA: Center for Planning and Development Research of the University of California, 1969).

Wirth hypotheses (by confirming their converse), in actual fact further studies revealed that it was not only that residents were all in the early stage of the family cycle (when neighborliness is common), but that the "pioneering" character of the new environment itself led to the intense level of sociability found in the new suburbs.

In contrast, Bennett Berger's investigation of a working-class suburb inhabited by former city dwellers found little socializing and much loneliness,[5] while Young and Willmott found a similar reduction in neighborhood-centered socializing when working-class East Londoners were relocated from a dense slum to a low-density housing estate outside London.[6] In both cases, the working-class subjects were accustomed to organizing their social life around relatives who lived near them; they had little preparation for (or interest in) socializing with "strangers" who happened to be neighbors. In fact, both these subject groups seem to have been relocated from what Herbert Gans, in his path-breaking study of an Italian community in Boston, had called an "urban village."[7]

As investigators looked further, they found other anomalies. They found small, low-density areas occupied by homogeneous populations that exhibited few of the so-called "rural virtues" of social intimacy and interlocking social networks.[8] They found quarters in large, densely settled heterogeneous metropolises which were essentially village-like (as Gans had described) in the degree to which many residents' lives revolved around the local community. These studies made it increasingly clear that, at the very minimum, the variables of class, ethnicity, and gender/family cycle stage had to be controlled if the effects of ecological factors on social behavior were to be isolated.

Studies from other societies tended to reinforce the refutations of Wirth that were coming from American and English subcommunities and subcultures. The two dimensions of "size" and "degree of urbanity" were finally disengaged analytically in the late 1950s.[9] By that time, sociologists were able to point to large, densely settled, heterogeneous cities in Asia and Africa that showed few of the negative characteristics previously assumed to follow inevitably from increased size and density. There was little anonymity in these cities. Indeed, individuals were often enmeshed in extensive primary networks that involved far greater numbers of persons than theory had ever thought possible.

---

[5]See Bennett M. Berger, *Working Class Suburb: A Study of Auto Workers in Suburbia* (Berkeley, CA: University of California Press, 1960).

[6]Michael Young and Peter Willmott, *Family and Kinship in East London* (London: Routledge & Kegan Paul, 1957).

[7]See Herbert J. Gans, *The Urban Villagers: Group and Class in the Life of Italian-Americans* (New York: Free Press of Glencoe, 1962, reissued Macmillan, 1983).

[8]John Seeley *et al.*, *Crestwood Heights: A Study of the Culture of Suburban Life* (New York: Basic Books, 1956), a study of an upper-middle-class suburb of Toronto.

[9]The first formal graph separating these two dimensions appeared in Richard Dewey, "The Rural-Urban Continuum: Real but Relatively Unimportant," in *American Journal of Sociology* 66 (July 1960), pp. 60–66.

Moreover, strong kinship and para-kinship relationships permeated institutions which, by definition, would have been secondary and associational in western culture. Miner's study of an African city[10] was perhaps the first to criticize Wirth, but many other authors have subsequently proved, beyond a shadow of doubt, that *ecological variables operate through the social structure and the cultural values of urban residents,* which makes their social consequences always less than determinate.[11]

Within a given culture or subculture, variations in size, density, heterogeneity, and the newly rediscovered ecological variable of mobility might produce differences in behavior. Nevertheless, one could scarcely predict from one culture to another, much less assume universal determinants and consequences. Two cities of different size within the same society would be more like one another than two cities of the same size from two very different cultures. Furthermore, within each city and society, the factors of class and family, and possibly ethnic background, would be likely to create additional congruencies, independent of ecological differences. In short, rather than there being one "urban way of life," there were varieties of urban life that required empirical study and a far more complex theory of explanation that focused on the causes of these differences.

Once the comforting premises that had sustained urban theory were rudely undermined by these refutations, the field began to fragment. It subdivided into three—at times antagonistic—camps. Each sought its own answer to the perplexing question of how the characteristics of an urban area interact with the characteristics of their residents to yield particular forms of social behavior in the city and particular types and degrees of "community." The first, who we may call the *neoclassical ecologists,* have sought to refine the propositions linking physical and social space and to specify the conditions under which particular spatial arrangements might be expected to have predictable social consequences. The second group, the *culturalists,* have emphasized that it is "way of life" or subculture that determine how people use and shape their physical space; they have tended to minimize the influence of physical space on behavior. Most recently, a third approach has been added, which expresses the cultural view but in terms of structural characteristics: *urban network analysis.* (We will discuss this third approach in Chapter 12.)

To a remarkable extent, the political economists have tended to ignore the entire question of how city characteristics affect community, on the grounds that class relations predict social and interactional patterns better than do spatial arrangements. Only Logan and Molotch, in their recent book, *Urban*

---

[10]See Horace M. Miner, *The Primitive City of Timbuctoo* (Princeton, NJ: Princeton University Press, 1953).

[11]Janet Abu-Lughod, in a widely cited and reprinted article, "Migrant Adjustment to City Life: The Egyptian Case," *American Journal of Sociology* 67 (July 1961), pp. 22–32, refuted Wirth's argument point by point, using evidence from Cairo.

Fortunes,[12] have attempted to relate the two by exploring the political economy of place as socially inhabited. They show how localities develop common stakes in political outcomes.

EXTENSIONS OF CLASSICAL ECOLOGY

The classical position of urban ecologists was that the spatial arrangements of things and people in one's environment have independent effects on one's behavior. Since they believed that humans shared with plants and animals the subtle capacity to respond to the environment, we should not be surprised to find that the work of ethologists (scholars who study animal behavior) and animal psychologists looms rather large in neoclassical ecology. Studies of territoriality and turf, the meaning of distance and spacing and how they signal emotional predisposition and intended response, and the connections between high density and antisocial acts are central to this subfield.

Territoriality

One of the major interests of students of animal behavior has been the idea of territoriality.[13] It has been repeatedly observed that various species tend to mark out and defend their turf.[14] Indeed, Robert Ardrey has gone so far as to suggest that the human institutions of private property and even the nation-state have their origins in the *territorial imperative* which man shares with other species. Ardrey has alleged:

> Man . . . is as much a territorial animal as is a mockingbird. . . . We act as we do for reasons of our evolutionary past, not our cultural present. . . . If we defend the title to our land or the sovereignty of our country, we do it for reasons no different, no less innate, no less ineradicable, than do lower animals. The dog barking at you from behind his master's fence acts for a motive indistinguishable from that of his master when the fence was built.[15]

---

[12]John Logan and Harvey Molotch, *Urban Fortunes: The Political Economy of Place* (Berkeley, CA: University of California Press, 1987).

[13]An excellent summary of the literature on spatial aspects of animal behavior and their application to humans can be found in Mark La Gory and John Pipkin, *Urban Social Space* (Belmont, CA: Wadsworth Publishing Company, 1981). A good critique of this literature can be found in Chapters 5–7 of Gerald D. Suttles, *The Social Construction of Communities* (Chicago: University of Chicago Press, 1972), pp. 111–188.

[14]One of the earliest of such studies was E. Howard's *Territory in Bird Life* (New York: Dutton, 1920), but since that time the importance of territoriality in most other species has been confirmed.

[15]Robert Ardrey, *The Territorial Imperative: A Personal Inquiry into the Animal Origins of Property and Nations* (New York: Atheneum, 1966), p. 5. Like many sociobiologists, Ardrey overstates the case for genetic imprinting; but in his more measured presentation of data, he proves that animals, like humans, modify territoriality not only when environments change but when cultural

One need not go as far as Ardrey, however, to recognize that in cities, where diverse populations push up against one another, cultural patterns do develop that emphasize space as a boundary marker and that utilize access to particular spaces as an indicator of "belonging." One of the most sensitive accounts of how Americans signal social distance and handle space in public places is Lyn Lofland's *A World of Strangers: Order and Action in Urban Public Space*. [16]

Every urban sociologist who has done participant observation in a city comes to recognize spatial markers. For example, a field researcher may enter a restaurant, store, or bar, thinking he or she is in public space, only to be stared down as a stranger; it becomes uncomfortably clear that the bar or other meeting place is *not* public space but is part of the territory of a local group. Every student of boys' gangs knows the importance of turf and the dangers of not respecting the defensive boundaries of the gangs' territoriality. Even in our homes we make rather important territorial distinctions between "onstage" and "offstage," with only intimate guests permitted to see the messy kitchen and the steamy role of cook, which lie offstage when the self is being presented at a formal dinner party. Americans formerly used territory to signify social distance, as when the Sunday parlor was used to entertain high-status visitors, including the minister, whereas family members and intimates gathered around the kitchen table. [17]

No one, therefore, would deny that humans are territorial animals, or that the spatial arrangements we create have consequences—whether intended or not. Most analysts refuse to go as far as Ardrey, however. The most sophisticated position now taken by students of territoriality is that social structure, culture, and psychology always mediate territoriality in humans (see Figure 10.1). They acknowledge that the same physical setting may have quite different effects on different people, depending upon what the individuals bring with them to the setting.

Numbers or Size

It was Georg Simmel who astutely recognized how much the size of a group affects social interactions within it. He teased out the implications of the size of groups, from the two-person group (the dyad) whose very existence is threatened by the loss of only one member; to the three-person group (the triad),

---

substitutes for conflict are found. Like the sociobiologists, also, Ardrey suffers from a male bias which makes him trace the territorial instinct to the male of the species (because he is interested in preserving his sexual access to females)—a projection, onto the animal kingdom and onto other cultures, of his own ethnocentric set of values as a western male in the twentieth century.

[16] Lyn Lofland, *A World of Strangers: Order and Action in Urban Public Space* (New York: Basic Books, 1973). William H. Whyte, in his *City: Rediscovering the Center* (New York: Doubleday, 1988), has recently done some fine observational studies in pubic space.

[17] See Erving Goffman, *The Presentation of Self in Everyday Life* (Garden City, NY: Doubleday Anchor, 1959).

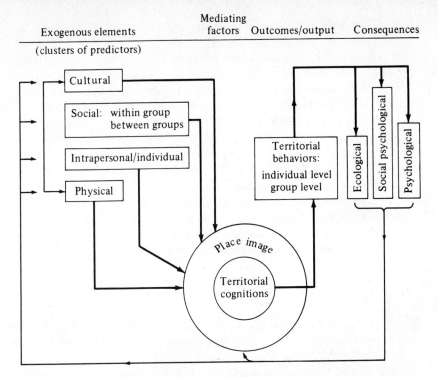

Figure 10.1 Conceptual model of human territorial functioning. (*Source: Ralph B. Taylor, Human Territorial Functioning: An Empirical Evolutionary Perspective on Individual and Small Group Territorial Cognitions, Behaviors, and Consequences* [Cambridge: Cambridge University Press, 1988], p. 92. Copyright 1988 by Cambridge University Press. Used with permission.)

inherently unstable, he claimed, because it lends itself to divide-and-rule and to the two-against-one coalition; to the "party," which requires a larger number of participants to achieve the desired level of conviviality. He suggested that gathering together *very* large numbers of persons (such as the residents of a big city) actually causes interactions to become more superficial and less invested with emotion.[18]

Ever since his provocative essays, sociologists have been exploring the influence of group size upon social relations. However, what many studies have failed to consider is that it is not just the size but the *composition* of the group that affects interactions. In addition, they have failed to note that the theoretical size of the group may be larger than its actual face-to-face size, because absent

---

[18]See *The Sociology of Georg Simmel,* ed. and trans. Kurt H. Wolff (Glencoe, IL: Free Press, 1950), especially "On the Significance of Numbers for Social Life," pp. 87–104; "The Quantitative Determination of Group Divisions and of Certain Groups," pp. 105–117; "The Isolated Individual and the Dyad," pp. 118–144; "The Triad," pp. 145–169.

members might still be taken into consideration. Boundaries might also be ambiguous.

This becomes clearer when we consider *how* the size of an urban place can possibly affect human behavior. The size of a city, for example, is especially difficult to measure when the boundaries are no longer sharply defined, as they were in medieval times when the city ended at its surrounding wall. With the saturation urbanization now prevalent in the United States, the boundaries within which size is to be calculated have become increasingly arbitrary. Are we to consider the political limits of the city or suburb? The entire metropolitan area? The urban "field" or commuter zone? Because size is no longer unambiguous, a number of analysts of American urbanism have recommended that the concept of scale be substituted for that of size.[19] The idea of scale fits well with the approach of network analysis, since it is not the number of people in the surrounding environment but the number and extent of our network connections to them that influence how we behave.

Density

Density was the second independent variable isolated by Wirth. It has attracted even more interest than size. Ever since Durkheim, social scientists have attempted to isolate the special influence of density on social relations. Durkheim made a conceptual distinction between *physical density* (population concentration) and *moral density* (the rate of interaction). He argued that an increase in moral density caused the shift in social relations found under conditions of urbanization. Examining the societies of his time, Durkheim complacently concluded that if the technology remained constant, an increase in the physical density of settlement would lead, *ceteris paribus,* to an increase in the number of social interactions. This somewhat uncertain leap from physical to moral density was the logical flaw in Durkheim's argument in *The Division of Labor in Society,* a flaw which led analysts astray in more than one way.

Certainly, higher density does yield a higher *potential* for interaction, as Table 10.2, showing the number of persons living within a ten-mile radius of one another under different densities, demonstrates.[20] A density of one person per square mile is equivalent to that of American Indians when Europeans first arrived on the continent. The higher densities of 17,000 and 25,000 persons per

---

[19]This suggestion came first from the social area analysts and appeared in the 1955 publication by Eshref Shevky and Wendell Bell, *Social Area Analysis: Theory, Illustrative Application and Computational Procedures* (Stanford University Series in Sociology no. 1, Stanford, CA: Stanford University Press). They drew upon the theory of social change put forth by Godfrey and Monica Wilson in *The Analysis of Social Change, Based on Observations in Central Africa* (Cambridge: Cambridge University Press, 1945). Scott Greer was probably the originator of the idea, and certainly the most cogent presentation of the theory appears in his *The Emerging City: Myth and Reality* (New York: Free Press of Glencoe, 1962).

[20]See Philip Hauser "Statistics and Society," *Journal of the American Statistical Association* 58 (1935).

Table 10.2   THE NUMBER OF PERSONS LIVING
WITHIN A 10-MILE RADIUS OF
ONE ANOTHER AT VARYING
CONDITIONS OF DENSITY

Population density	Number of persons within a 10-mile radius
1 person /sq. mi.	314
50 persons/sq. mi.	15,700
8,000 persons/sq. mi.	2,512,000
17,000 persons/sq. mi.	5,338,000
25,000 persons/sq. mi.	7,850,000

Source: Philip Hauser, "Statistics and Society," Journal of
the American Statistical Association 58 (1935), p. 301.

square mile are equivalent to residential densities in Chicago and New York City, respectively.

While this table proves that higher densities *make possible* more interactions, there is no reason to believe that the number of *actual* social interactions would be the same as the number of *possible* interactions. Groups occupying an environment at densities of about one person per square mile are hunting and gathering communities. Therefore, we would expect that almost all 314 individuals within a 10-mile radius might be aware of, if not in contact with, one another. On the other hand, densities of 25,000 persons per square mile exist only under conditions of urban living. Such densities permit a complex division of labor and a duplication of land uses, making it extremely unlikely that the 7.8 million inhabitants within a 10-mile radius would ever be in contact with, or even aware of, all others.

The one likely social consequence of high density (and therefore large numbers) would be that the ratio of strangers to known persons goes up as density increases. That is, if personal movement were the same in two areas 10 miles in radius but with different population densities, we would predict that in the area of higher density, one would encounter more persons and, within limits, would be more likely not to know at least some of those encountered. This is why when we meet friends where we usually see them (in the neighborhood, at work), we take their presence for granted, whereas if we meet them "accidentally" in another setting, we are surprised.

It was from this phenomenon that Wirth reasoned that anonymity would be greater in large and densely settled cities. Certainly, one of the characteristics of cities is that they do bring us into at least fleeting contact with many more strangers than we would meet in a small town or village. This need not, however, cause the kind of "social disorganization" hypothesized by theorists of the Chicago School, since, as Lyn Lofland illustrates so well in *A World of Strangers*, even interactions with strangers can be regulated and ordered.

Despite this, a number of sociologists have suggested that density *per se* has a negative influence on social behavior.[21] They have depended in part upon animal experiments, perhaps the most famous of which were conducted by J. B. Calhoun on Norway rats.[22] Calhoun allowed wild rats to breed within the close confines of laboratory pens until they were visibly overcrowded. Once high densities were reached, the rats entered a "behavioral sink," that is, their behavior deteriorated and became "antisocial." Male rats exhibited heightened aggression, and a few dominant males caused the rest to cower or to become impotent or homosexual; female rats were reluctant to breed, and when they did, their normal nest-making activities were haphazard. Occasionally they even devoured their young.

The reason why Calhoun's data became instantly famous is that they fit so well into the urban theory that had blamed high density and poor housing for the ills of urban society. At least since the 1930s, advocates of subsidized housing had stressed the connection between poor housing and the poor physical and mental health and social pathology (crime, alcoholism, gangs, etc.) of its occupants. Many of the early studies by Chicago School sociologists had tried to draw a causal connection between the physical character of a neighborhood (including its density) and rates of insanity, crime, gangs, and the like. These findings were used to justify public expenditures to improve housing quality. However, the simple connection between density and these socially undesirable characteristics has never been proven. (More likely, poor housing and crowding are associated with poverty, which is also associated with the measures of pathology.)

First, it is necessary to make a distinction between business and residential density. The daytime densities in central business districts are higher than nighttime residential densities, and yet the former are seldom blamed for causing "social disorganization." Second, with respect to residential density, one must distinguish between ground density and in-dwelling density. Ground density measures the number of persons per square mile (or any other area), regardless of how high the buildings are or how much actual residential space is available per person. In-dwelling density measures some average amount of either floor area or cubic space available per person, or (more commonly, as in the census) is measured by the number of persons per room of dwelling space.

Clearly, each of these kinds of density should be expected to have a different effect. Business district density affects the rate of stimulation, jostling, and

---

[21]See especially Jonathan Freedman, *Crowding and Behavior* (New York: Viking Press, 1975). For good reviews of the literature on this topic, see Omer R. Galle and Walter R. Gove, "Overcrowding, Isolation, and Human Behavior: Exploring the Extremes in Population Distribution," in *Social Demography,* ed. Karl E. Taeuber, Larry Bumpass, and James Sweet (New York: Academic Press, 1978), pp. 95–132; and Chapters 1 and 2 of Walter R. Gove and Michael Hughes, *Overcrowding in the Household: An Analysis of Determinants and Effects* (New York: Academic Press, 1983), pp. 1–44.

[22]See, for example, J. B. Calhoun, "Population Density and Social Pathology," *Scientific American* 206 (1962), pp. 139–148.

probably the proportion of strangers encountered. It *may* lead to some of the immunity to stimulus identified by Simmel and, later, by Milgrim and Meier.[23] Ground density affects the total number of potential contacts that could be made in the vicinity. In-dwelling density (especially overcrowding) may affect interpersonal relationships within the family or household and heighten stress, but cross-cultural evidence suggests that the results are definitely mediated by expectations and cultural patterns.[24]

In short, neither large numbers nor high density, in themselves, have the inevitable effects posited by Wirth's theory of "urbanism as a way of life." Does this mean that numbers and density have no effects? Hardly. It simply means that the theory linking the ecological characteristics of cities with behavioral consequences of those characteristics must be far more complex than had previously been assumed.

Position in Space

A third area of great interest to neoclassical ecologists is the relationship between the disposition of people in space and the probabilities of their interaction. Chapter 9 included a discussion of racial segregation and suggested that one of the consequences of racial segregation in our society has been reduced interaction between blacks and whites. In that analysis we assumed that low opportunities for interaction have inhibited mutual understanding and thus have made it harder to overcome the gap created by prejudice. To what extent is this accurate?

An important study done in the late 1940s on interracial housing concluded that residential proximity did increase interactions between and did reduce negative stereotypes among black and white residents in low-rent housing projects.[25] The study was conducted in four public housing projects occupied by blacks and whites. In two of the projects, families were assigned to apartments as units became available, independent of race. In the other two, the projects were subdivided into white and black subareas, and apartments were assigned by race. In the attitude and behavior survey taken when tenants first

---

[23]In his essay "The Metropolis and Mental Life," trans. Kurt H. Wolff, (*The Sociology of George Simmel,* pp. 409–424), Simmel claimed that urbanites developed a blasé attitude to protect themselves against too many and too frequent stimuli. This same argument is developed by Richard Meier in his *A Communications Theory of Urban Growth* (Cambridge, MA: MIT Press, 1962). Meier uses communication theory to show that stress comes from excessive and random stimuli; the organism handles such stress by blocking many messages and responding to others without feelings. Stanley Milgrim ("The Experience of Living in Cities," *Science* 167 [1970], pp. 1461–1468) has used this to build up a whole theory to explain why Americans in New York seem to be immune to the sufferings of others, blaming indifference on density. We doubt his conclusion.

[24]See Robert C. Schmitt, "Implications of Density in Hong Kong," *Journal of the American Institute of Planners* 24 (August 1963), pp. 210–217.

[25]Morton Deutsch and Mary Evans Collins, *Interracial Housing: A Psychological Evaluation of a Social Experiment* (Minneapolis: University of Minnesota Press, 1951).

moved in, there were few differences between whites who moved into the segregated projects and those who moved into the integrated ones. However, when tenants were resurveyed after living in either segregated or integrated housing, it was found that those whites who lived together with blacks had changed their behavior considerably and interacted with their black neighbors, while those whites who lived in the segregated projects remained as aloof and prejudiced as before. In this study, the tenants were all drawn from the same economic class; such economic homogeneity enabled proximity to affect behavior.

Social homogeneity was also present in a second study that found significant effects on interaction and friendship patterns due to the spatial layout of residences.[26] In this case, researchers studied two residential projects that had been constructed on a university campus to house returning veterans and their families. One project consisted of row houses, the second of low-rise apartment buildings. Not only were the occupants observed and interviewed to see who their friends were, but rumors were floated to trace the paths of information transfer via friendships. The study uncovered a strong influence of space on interactions. Persons whose apartments were centrally located knew more people and tended to be better informed than those living in end units. In the low-rise apartment buildings, residents whose apartments were near the stairwell were more socially central than those whose apartments were midway between the two stairwells. Here again, however, the occupants were relatively homogeneous in age and family-cycle stage and in their temporary occupation, student. Furthermore, all had entered at roughly the same time, so that previous relationships did not predetermine present ones. Under those conditions, the influence of proximity, pure and simple, was found to operate.

That such an influence could also be found among middle-class professionals was proven by William H. Whyte, who studied "the men in gray flannel suits" in the newly constructed Chicago suburb of Park Forest.[27] He found that within the new neighborhoods, friendships followed paths and overlapping space. Neighbors got to know one another when they took out the garbage, parked their cars in common courts, or supervised the outdoor play of their children. People who lived in houses near the center of the courts had more social interactions than those in peripherally located houses. Here again, social homogeneity permitted space to have an impact.

The question is: To what extent can spatial proximity overcome social distance? Where individuals of diverse class and culture are placed in close proximity to one another, will they become friends? On this we have much less evidence. It is unlikely that physical proximity alone can overcome great social differences. Physical space influences but does not determine social relations.

---

[26]See Leon Festinger, S. Schachter, and Kurt Back, *Social Pressures in Informal Groups: A Study of Human Factors in Housing* (Stanford, CA: Stanford University Press, 1950). Chapter 8 in William Michelson, *Man and His Urban Environment: A Sociological Approach, with Revisions* (Reading, MA: Addison-Wesley, revised 1976), pp. 168–190, reviews these and other studies.

[27]William H. Whyte, *The Organization Man* (New York: Simon & Schuster, 1956).

This is particularly crucial, since Wirth's definition of a city had also included heterogeneity. This should have alerted him to expect not just one urban way of life but many.

THE CULTURALISTS: VARIETIES OF URBAN EXPERIENCES

Perhaps as a reaction against the overdeterminism of the classical ecological approach, some scholars have questioned whether the environment has much impact on social relations and cultural patterns. Oscar Lewis, for example, has argued that since "social life . . . occurs for the most part in small groups . . . , the variables of number, density and heterogeneity . . . are not crucial determinants of social life or personality."[28] He suggested that the nature of social interactions is conditioned more by social class, ethnicity, and age-gender-family role than by the physical setting in which people live.

Herbert Gans has perhaps made the strongest case for this position. Especially in his article "Urbanism and Suburbanism as Ways of Life,"[29] he argued that the social characteristics of any group of persons are far more important than the physical communities in which they live, in determining the way they relate to others. In Gans's community study of Levittown, a middle-class suburb of Philadelphia, he seemed to prove his point by showing that the same setting yielded quite different life-styles, depending upon the social characteristics of residents.[30] To some extent his study of Italian-Americans in an urban quarter of Boston, *The Urban Villagers,* offered similar evidence for the primacy of culture over space.

The culturalists acknowledge that different subareas of the city exhibit somewhat different patterns of life, but they contend that the segregation of persons by family cycle stage, by class, by ethnicity and the like, and the differential locations of these types in the city are sufficient to explain the congruence between location and life-style. They argue that there is a great deal of self-selection into areas where social patterns are congruent with needs and values. Suzanne Keller, in her book, *The Urban Neighborhood,*[31] stresses that the definition of a good neighbor is not always and everywhere the same. In some subareas of the city, a good neighbor is someone who helps, lends

---

[28]Oscar Lewis, "Further Observations on the Folk-Urban Continuum and Urbanization," in Philip Hauser and Leo Schnore, eds., *The Study of Urbanization* (New York: John Wiley, 1965); quotation from p. 497. Abu-Lughod has also argued for the intervening variable of culture. See her "Migrant Adjustment to Urban Life: The Egyptian Case," *American Journal of Sociology* 67 (July 1961), pp. 22–32.

[29]In A. M. Rose, ed., *Human Behavior and Social Processes* (Boston: Houghton Mifflin, 1962), pp. 625–648.

[30]Herbert J. Gans, *The Levittowners: Ways of Life and Politics in a New Suburban Community* (New York: Pantheon Books, 1967).

[31]Suzanne Keller, *The Urban Neighborhood: A Sociological Perspective* (New York: Random House, 1968).

things, and is friendly; in other subareas, the best neighbors mind their own business and do not interfere. Sylvia Fleis Fava found quite different definitions of neighboring in urban and suburban areas.[32] Presumably, individuals gravitate to those areas of the city that best suit them. Some of the neighborhood studies that have documented the wide variations in urban ways of life will be discussed in Chapter 11.

Claude Fischer, in *The Urban Experience,* has referred to one form of the culturalist view as *compositionalist.* He paraphrased their argument as follows:

> In compositionalist terms, the dynamics of social life depend largely on the nonecological factors of social class, ethnicity, and stage in the life-cycle. Individuals' behavior is determined by their economic position, cultural characteristics, and by their marital and family status. The same attributes also determine who their associates are and what social worlds they live in. It is these attributes—not the size of the community or its density—that shape social and psychological experience.[33]

While Fischer would not classify himself as a compositionalist, in his early empirical work the major variables he used to account for different types of social networks within cities were the personal attributes of the subjects, not the areas in which they lived.[34] Because his sample included only city dwellers, however, Fischer could not test his hypothesis that cities permit the development of specialized subcultures held together through personal networks, and that this, rather than "urbanism as a way of life," is what makes urban culture different from rural. A test of this hypothesis could not be done until he undertook the research described in *To Dwell Among Friends.*[35]

Because this work depends upon an understanding of network analysis, we shall reserve it to Chapter 12 in which we present promising new ways to untangle the complicated (and loose) relationships between the ecological setting and the forms of community life they can contain. But first, we need to look more closely at the variety of ways of urban life and at "community" in the city, as these have been described in the second great tradition of urban sociology, the community study.

---

[32]See Sylvia F. Fava, "Contrasts in Neighboring: New York City and a Suburban County," in W. M. Dobriner, ed., *The Suburban Community* (New York: Putnam, 1958), pp. 122–130.

[33]Claude S. Fischer, *The Urban Experience* (New York: Harcourt Brace Jovanovich, 1976), pp. 34–35.

[34]Not only that reported in *The Urban Experience* but also in the collected work by Fischer and others, entitled *Networks and Places: Social Relations in the Urban Setting* (New York: Free Press, Macmillan, 1977). Fischer (as well as this author) would classify himself as a combination of the two.

[35]See Claude S. Fischer, *To Dwell Among Friends: Personal Networks in Town and City* (Chicago: University of Chicago Press, 1982).

Chapter
11

Community and Neighborhood Studies

*C*ommunity studies have a long history in urban sociology. They differ from ecological investigations in their approach and methods. In general, community studies utilize anthropological field research methods, thus making them the shared domain of sociologists and anthropologists. Central to the methodology, which is sometimes called ethnography, is that researchers immerse themselves for relatively long periods of time (a year or more) in the social life of a group of people who share a given residential environment. The researchers generally live in the locality, engage in and observe its day-to-day routines, form friendly relations with a wide variety of people, participate in as many ways as possible in the community's formal and informal institutions, and are in constant attendance at meetings and social events of local groups and organizations. They may conduct more formal interviews, but in general the community study does not depend upon questionnaires or other quantitative techniques, except to supplement what can be learned through observation. Full observational notes, which are recorded daily, eventually become the raw material from which the analysis is written up.

Given this demanding approach, it is clearly impossible for a single individual or even a research team to study simultaneously *all* the ways of life that coexist in the sprawling megalopolitan regions that our urban arenas have become. From the beginning, less ambitious goals have been set for community studies. In the handful of cases where an entire urban community has been studied, the size of the selected town has been relatively small. And as we shall see, the usual community study adopts a far less ambitious agenda: namely, to study life in a subarea of a city, usually a neighborhood that is presumed to constitute a relatively homogeneous or at least coherent community occupying a discrete physical space.

STUDYING A WHOLE CITY: THE IMPOSSIBLE DREAM

The model for a community study of a whole city remains the remarkable two-volume work produced by Robert and Helen Lynd, who studied Muncie, Indiana, in the 1920s and again in the 1930s.[1] They called their city "Middletown" because they believed it to be quite representative of other modest-sized American communities. The enormous scope of their study can be conveyed through its table of contents, which reveals that almost every aspect of urban social organization came within their purview. It is not surprising that this ambitious project has never really been duplicated, although several volumes of a restudy of Middletown by Theodore Caplow and associates have now appeared.[2]

A second major attempt to study a whole town was made by anthropologist William Lloyd Warner and his associates, who spent many years investigating the relatively small town of Newburyport, Massachusetts. They published several volumes, each dealing with a specific aspect of that community.[3] Warner and his associates called their community "Yankee City," even though by the time they studied it, the true Yankees were far outnumbered by immigrant industrial laborers and their descendants.

The avowed purpose of the Yankee City series, however, was not to understand urban life per se, but rather to develop research techniques and to gain insight into changes in the American system of social stratification. Indeed,

---

[1]Robert S. Lynd and Helen M. Lynd, *Middletown: A Study in Contemporary American Culture* (New York: Harcourt, Brace and Co., 1929). The restudy, designed to trace how the Depression had affected the community, was entitled *Middletown in Transition: A Study in Cultural Conflicts* (New York: Harcourt, Brace and Co., 1936).

[2]See Theodore Caplow, Howard Bahr, Bruce Chadwick, Reuben Hill, and Margaret Williamson, *Middletown Families: Fifty Years of Change and Continuity* (Minneapolis: University of Minnesota Press, 1982); Caplow, Bahr, and Chadwick, *All Faithful People: Change and Continuity in Middletowns's Religion* (Minneapolis: University of Minnesota Press, 1983); and Caplow and Chadwick, "Inequality and Life Styles in Middletown, 1920–1978," *Social Science Quarterly* 60 (1979), pp. 367–386.

[3]William Lloyd Warner, *Yankee City* (New Haven: Yale University Press, 1963); Warner and Paul S. Lunt, *The Social Life of a Modern Community* (New Haven: Yale University Press, 1941); Warner and Lunt, *The Status System of a Modern Community* (New Haven: Yale University Press, 1942); Warner and J. O. Low, *The Social System of a Modern Factory* (New Haven: Yale University Press, 1947); Warner and Leo Srole, *The Social Systems of American Ethnic Groups* (New Haven: Yale University Press, 1945).

Warner had selected the town just because it was small enough to facilitate his investigations. One innovation in Warner's study of the class structure of Yankee City was the conceptualization of classes not as congeries of "objective" indicators but as functioning groups of individuals and families, with network ties and envalued boundaries that were established and maintained through behavior. In this, Warner anticipated much of what network analysts would eventually seek to diagram and measure. A second innovation was the treatment of ethnicity, which placed such groups in the evolving opportunity structure set by changes in the economy.

Even as they studied the town, however, external influences on it were growing stronger, which Warner and his associates had not anticipated. Whereas formerly the town was relatively self-contained and the elite drawn from its stock of original residents, as the dominant industries came more and more under the managerial control of firms from outside, Newburyport ceased to be the closed system the researchers had hoped it would be.

Other sociologists and anthropologists focused on more specialized problematics, utilizing entire small communities as their study sites. Some of the best known of these studies are John Dollard's *Caste and Class in a Southern Town;*[4] James West's (pseudonym for Carl Withers) study of the perceived class structure of a farming town he called Plainville;[5] Arensberg and Kimball's perceptive study of family and community in an Irish village;[6] and August Hollingshead's analysis of the cliques and life-styles of young people, in *Elmtown's Youth.*[7]

Several studies of entire communities that focused specifically on political structure and decision making were also attempted. Analysts developed two quite different methods for uncovering the structure and process of community power in two exemplary case studies that came to markedly different conclusions. Robert Dahl studied decision making in New Haven, Connecticut, by examining the resolution of specific community controversies. On the basis of these, he concluded that New Haven was governed by a shifting coalition of interest groups. No single elite structure could be found in the city, although certain actors (e.g., Yale University, real estate interests) could be singled out as consistently important.[8]

---

[4]John Dollard, *Caste and Class in a Southern Town* (New Haven: Yale University Press, 1937).

[5]James West (pseud. for Carl Withers), *Plainville, U.S.A.* (New York: Columbia University Press, 1945). A restudy was made by Art Gallaher, Jr. See his *Plainville Fifteen Years Later* (New York: Columbia University Press, 1961).

[6]Conrad M. Arensberg and Solon T. Kimball, *Culture and Community* (New York: Harcourt, Brace and World, 1965).

[7]August Hollingshead, *Elmtown's Youth: The Impact of Social Classes on Adolescents* (New York: John Wiley, 1949). For an evaluation of early community studies and a discussion of their methods, see Hollingshead, "Community Research: Development and Present Condition," *American Sociological Review* 13 (April 1948), pp. 126–146.

[8]See Robert Dahl, *Who Governs?* (New Haven: Yale University Press, 1961). It is interesting that a later analysis of New Haven, focusing on community controversies over urban redevelopment, seemed to confirm Dahl's diagnosis of interest coalitions and the role of Yale University in affecting

Floyd Hunter, studying the power structure of Atlanta, Georgia, came to a different set of conclusions. He interviewed a snowball sample of community leaders, expanding his list of important people by asking various community actors to name other "influentials" in the city. This method yielded a different picture of the power structure—one more akin to that found in Newburyport by Warner and his associates, who had followed a similar method, than the one Dahl had uncovered in New Haven. The elite of Atlanta seemed to be made up of a set of interlocking networks of people who may have had somewhat different interests but who participated in a common social order. One of the unresolved questions in studies of community power is whether the differences between Dahl's and Hunter's findings arose because they studied different cities or because they used different methods. Research continues to search for an answer to this question.[9]

Virtually the last exemplary community study of an entire town, albeit a tiny one, was conducted by Arthur Vidich and Joseph Bensman in Candor, New York (near Ithaca).[10] This community had once been relatively self-contained. The main theme of the study, *Small Town in Mass Society,* was that, as in Yankee City, the larger world was impinging and reshaping the class structure and culture of Candor, as it was drawn into the web of metropolitan culture. This same issue is developed in one of the most recent studies of entire communities—although in this case, one could not even call them "towns." In her sensitive study, *Fisher Folk,*[11] Carolyn Ellis compared two small rural communities on Chesapeake Bay, developing the theme of how life has changed as residents become more integrated into the wider society.

---

community decisions. See the article by Norman and Susan Fainstein, "New Haven: The Limits of the Local State," pp. 27–79 in Susan Fainstein *et al., Restructuring the City: The Political Economy of Urban Redevelopment* (London and New York: Longman, 1983.)

[9]Floyd Hunter, *Community Power Structure: A Study of Decision Makers* (Chapel Hill: University of North Carolina Press, 1953). A later study of Atlanta reached quite different conclusions. See Clarence Stone, *Regime Politics: Governing Atlanta.* (Lawrence, KS: University Press of Kansas, 1989). The troubling question is whether disparate findings are merely an artifact of the methods employed. This hypothesis was explored by John Walton in his "Discipline, Method, and Community Power: A Note on the Sociology of Knowledge," *American Sociological Review* 31 (1966), pp. 684–689; Walton has critiqued community power studies in "Community Power and the Retreat from Politics," reprinted in *New Perspectives on the American Community,* ed. Roland Warren and Larry Lyon (Homewood, IL: Dorsey Press, 1983). See also Nelson Polsby, *Community Power and Political Theory* (New Haven, CT: Yale University Press, 1963). A recent book, *Community Power: Directions for Future Research,* ed. Robert J. Waste (Newbury Park, CA: Sage Publications, 1986), includes a reconsideration of New Haven politics by Robert Dahl, as well as a new piece by G. William Domhoff, "The Growth Machine and the Power Elite." Mark Gottdiener, in *The Decline of Urban Politics* (Newbury Park, CA: Sage Publications, 1987) suggests that as decisions of real importance to cities are moved up the ladder to the federal government or are shunted laterally to corporations, the value of focusing on local politics *per se* has declined to irrelevance.

[10]Arthur Vidich and Joseph Bensman, *Small Town in Mass Society: Class, Power, and Religion in a Rural Community* (Princeton, NJ: Princeton University Press, 1958; reissued Doubleday Anchor, 1960).

[11]Carolyn Ellis, *Fisher Folk: Two Communities on Chesapeake Bay* (Lexington, KY: University of Kentucky Press, 1986).

Given this trend, in which cities, towns, and even rural settlements have lost their "boundaries" and cannot be studied in isolation, the advantages of studying an entire community, over studying a small portion of it, have begun to disappear. In light of the enormous tactical difficulties involved in studying "whole" communities, the field has retreated to a more modest agenda. Most community studies in an earlier era had been conducted in subareas of large cities. Today, these are the almost exclusive focus of the declining number of community studies that are still being conducted.

STUDIES OF RESIDENTIAL NEIGHBORHOODS

Robert Park's early essay, "The City," sowed the seed for the study of locality-based communities that shared both a spatial site in the city (a common location in physical space) and a set of common social characteristics such as class and ethnicity (a common "location" in social space). Park had singled out the densely packed urban slum of East London and various Italian immigrant quarters in American cities as examples of small "communities" where people of the same class and/or ethnic position occupied distinctive quarters in the city and where, therefore, *Gemeinschaft*-like relations persisted. If, indeed, the city was a "mosaic" of social worlds, then what could be more natural than to study these "worlds"? When this idea was combined with the concept of the "natural area," it was inevitable that the neighborhood study would develop into one of the mainstays of urban sociology.

Neighborhoods that constituted "natural areas" were, to use our more contemporary terms, urban subareas where "small" sociocultural space and "small" physical space occurred in combination. It is significant that almost every community study focused on an urban subarea where this was still true. This left increasingly large portions of metropolitan areas completely unstudied, as we shall see.

Besides being a residential district that appeared to have some basis for local "community," the ideal site for a community study was a residential district to which the researcher could gain entry. Eliminated at the outset, then, were exclusive enclaves of the wealthy, which set up insurmountable monetary and social barriers to entry. Eliminated, in addition, were those portions of the urban environment that had almost no local institutions or social life, since a researcher cannot penetrate a community that is not "there." Researchers were also attracted by the "exotic," leading them to study groups less well known to white middle-class Americans. The result was a highly distorted sample of "urban ways of life."

It should not surprise us then, to learn that successful community studies have concentrated disproportionately on poor rather than rich communities, on ethnically or racially segregated rather than diversified communities, on locally ordered rather than diffuse or externally oriented communities, and on homogeneous rather than mixed residential quarters. One need merely enumerate the most renowned community studies from urban sociological literature to confirm this. (See Figure 12.1, p. 303, which demonstrates the concentration of neighborhood studies in the cell of small physical and small social space.)

Studies of Inner-City Ethnic Neighborhoods

Ethnic neighborhoods were among the earliest to attract sociological investigation. This tradition was well established even before the Chicago School codified the genre of the neighborhood study; members of settlement houses dealing with ethnic communities had already pioneered in this area. Of the neighborhoods studied, those occupied by Italians have received the fullest treatment.

Italians   Harvey Zorbaugh's study in the 1920s in Chicago, *The Gold Coast and the Slum,*[12] had examined three contiguous districts on the near north side of the city. The economic status of each district was related to its distance from Lake Michigan. Along the easternmost lakefront lived the elite of the city. Behind this "gold coast" lay the world of furnished rooms—inexpensive housing occupied by artists, persons following a bohemian life-style, and relatively poor transient whites. The westernmost swath was a notorious quarter called Little Sicily, where Italian immigrants lived lives almost entirely encapsulated by their relations to compatriots. This overcrowded tenement district had much in common with, for example, the Lower East Side of Manhattan, whose appalling housing conditions had earlier been documented by Jacob Riis.[13]

Gradually, the Italian communities in American cities began to assimilate, although enclaves of Italians remained somewhat segregated from the rest of the city. In Boston, for example, there were two major urban neighborhoods whose residents were primarily of Italian descent. William F. Whyte studied one of them in his *Street Corner Society: The Social Structure of an Italian Slum,* which has become a classic community study, even though it concentrated almost exclusively on young, mostly unmarried, males involved in a social club.[14] Later, Herbert Gans lived in another Italian neighborhood that was slated for urban renewal, recording his observations in *The Urban Villagers: Group and Class in the Life of Italian-Americans.*[15] His study was both broader and more detached than Whyte's had been. By living for several years in the neighborhood, he came into contact with a variety of "ways of life" in a community that outsiders might have seen as homogeneous, and thus tried to classify residents by their life-styles and approaches to experience.

---

[12]Harvey Zorbaugh, *The Gold Coast and the Slum* (Chicago: University of Chicago Press, 1929).

[13]Jacob Riis, *How the Other Half Lives: Studies Among the Tenements of New York* (reissued New York: Hill and Wang, 1957).

[14]William Foote Whyte, *Street Corner Society: The Social Structure of an Italian Slum* (Chicago: University of Chicago Press, 1955). See also his "The Slum: The Evolution of Street Corner Society," in *Reflections on Community Studies,* ed. Arthur Vidich, Joseph Bensman, and Maurice Stein (New York: John Wiley, 1964).

[15]Herbert J. Gans, *The Urban Villagers* (New York: Free Press, 1962).

Two later studies examined the reactions of second- and third-generation Italian communities to undesired "invasions" and alterations in their formerly stable ethnic neighborhoods. Gerald Suttles studied the reactions, in a large Italian neighborhood on the near west side of Chicago, to the construction of a university campus in the neighborhood. He also investigated the way four ethnic groups (Italians, Puerto Ricans, Chicanos, and African-Americans from a large public housing project) coexisted in what had formerly been an exclusively Italian area, dividing up the territory by space and temporal succession.[16] Ethnic succession and the tensions it entails have also been chronicled in Jonathan Rieder's recent study of Canarsie, a neighborhood in Brooklyn that has been the site of a high degree of racial tension between the earlier Italian and Jewish residents and the black newcomers.[17]

Jews Jews were a second group that originally occupied segregated quarters in American cities and thus attracted the attention of urban sociologists. Louis Wirth's doctoral dissertation, later published as *The Ghetto,*[18] dealt with this subgroup in Chicago, showing how assimilation affected the community. The original settlement on the near west side was the port of entry for new immigrants, but as children moved up in class position they tended to move to a neighborhood of "second settlement," formerly dominated by the higher status German Jews. The process of selective dispersal has continued. Most recently, an area of "third settlement" has formed in the suburbs. Goldstein and Goldscheider also studied this generational change in their book on suburban Jewish-Americans[19], but by the time of their study it was hard to use the methods of community participant observation, since ethnicity no longer corresponded to class and locality.

Only three ethno-racial minorities remain for which community study methods continue to be employed, and it is no accident that these constitute the three most visible and segregated groups in American cities today. They are the Hispanics, the Asians, and the African-Americans.

Hispanics Surprisingly, this large and diverse ethnic group has been insufficiently studied from a community perspective. The area in New York called the Barrio, to which Puerto Rican immigrants flocked in the postwar period, was described in early works by Elena Padilla and David Wakefield.[20] Mexican-

---

[16]Gerald Suttles, *The Social Order of the Slum* (Chicago: University of Chicago Press, 1968).

[17]Jonathan Rieder, *Canarsie: The Jews and Italians of Brooklyn Against Liberalism* (Cambridge, MA: Harvard University Press, 1985).

[18]Louis Wirth, *The Ghetto* (Chicago: University of Chicago Press, 1928).

[19]Sidney Goldstein and Calvin Goldscheider, *Jewish-Americans: Three Generations of a Jewish Community* (Englewood Cliffs, NJ: Prentice-Hall, 1968).

[20]D. Wakefield, *Island in the City: Puerto Ricans in New York* (New York: Citadel Press, 1960); Elena Padilla, *Up from Puerto Rico* (New York: Columbia University Press, 1958). See also Patricia Sexton, *Spanish Harlem: An Anatomy of Poverty* (New York: Harper & Row, 1965); and the somewhat narrow study by Lloyd Rogler, *Migrant in the City: The Life of a Puerto Rican Action Group* (New York: Basic Books, 1972).

American boys' gangs in Los Angeles have been described by James Vigil,[21] while Ruth Horowitz has made a perceptive study of Hispanic girl gang members on the near west side of Chicago.[22] But most other works on Hispanics have focused on the ethnic subgroups in various cities (e.g., Portes on the Cubans of Miami, and others on the Dominicans of New York City[23]), without producing a traditional ethnographic study of an Hispanic neighborhood.

Asians   Unlike Hispanic communities, Chinatowns in American cities have from the start attracted attention as exotic encapsulated communities cut off from the larger society by physical segregation and linguistic and cultural differences (although intersecting with the larger urban community through restaurants and other services). Because of these barriers, however, most if not all of the sociologists who have written about Chinese neighborhoods have themselves been Chinese.

Perhaps the first account of American Chinatowns was written by Rose Hum Lee,[24] but her work was not a neighborhood study. Most early studies of Chinatown have little relevance today, now that such communities have increased dramatically in size and have achieved a balanced age distribution and sex ratio, thanks to the post-1965 immigration. Furthermore, as the sources of Chinese immigration have diversified, the former "small social space" of Chinatowns (predominantly males from Canton) has enlarged and become more differentiated to include old timers and recent migrants, immigrants from Hong Kong and Taiwan as well as mainland China, women and children as well as men, professionals and wealthy capitalists as well as peasants. This diversification, coupled with a rapid drop in the formerly strong prejudice against Orientals, has led to a dispersal into outlying areas of city and suburbs of many persons of Chinese origin or descent, not only into secondary mini-Chinatowns but into areas without spatial concentration. On the other hand, central Chinatowns have been infused with Vietnamese and Cambodian refugees, concerning whom studies are now only beginning to be made.[25]

----

[21]See James Diego Vigil, *Barrio Gangs: Street Life and Identity in Southern California* (Austin: University of Texas Press, 1988).

[22]See Ruth Horowitz, *Honor and the American Dream* (New Brunswick, NJ: Rutgers University Press, 1983).

[23]Glenn Hendricks, *The Dominican Diaspora: From the Dominican Republic to New York City— Villagers in Transition* (New York: Teachers College Press, Columbia, 1974). Separate articles on various new immigrant groups from Latin America and the Caribbean can be found in Nancy Foner, ed. *New Immigrants in New York City* (New York: Columbia University Press, 1987).

[24]Rose Hum Lee, *The Chinese in the United States of America* (Hong Kong: Hong Kong University Press, 1960).

[25]For example, see Bernard Wong, *Chinatown: Economic Adaptation and Ethnic Identity of the Chinese* (New York: Holt, Rinehart and Winston, 1982) and *Patronage, Brokerage, Entrepreneurship and the Chinese Community of New York City* (New York: AMS Press, 1988). See also Peter Kwong, *The New Chinatown* (New York: Hill and Wang, 1987). Ivan Light is among the few who

The Japanese have undergone even greater changes in status and location than the Chinese. Before the Second World War, most persons of Japanese origin who lived in the United States were agriculturalists concentrated on the west coast. Many were interned in concentration camps during the war and afterwards were dispersed to other parts of the country, settling primarily in urban areas. However, with the rapid rise of Japan to industrial power during the past few decades, a new form of Japanese colony has been forming in various suburbs, where businessmen and their families, on temporary assignment to international business capitals in the United States, have tended to congregate. Their "chain migration" is often facilitated by their companies. No community studies exist for this group.

A final Asian subgroup has arrived only recently in the United States: the Koreans. Most have congregated in such world cities as New York, Los Angeles, and Chicago; and at least in New York, many have entered a special economic niche, the small family-run grocery convenience store. Because their places of business are scattered throughout the city and their residences, when not in or near Chinatown, are similarly scattered, this immigrant group cannot be studied through the neighborhood. Testimony to how much ethnicity has shifted from consumer to producer roles is the study by Ilsoo Kim on Koreans grocers in New York. Because this community is organized into nonspatially concentrated social (and supply) networks rather than residential neighborhoods, Kim had to devise new ways to study this ethnic "community."[26]

African-Americans of Various Origins One of the first studies of a black urban community was Drake and Cayton's *Black Metropolis,* which used Chicago School methods to study the Chicago "Black Belt" (really a city within the city), the large sector of black residence that stretched southward from the Loop.[27] The authors traced a gradient of status as one moved away from the CBD, analyzed the role of institutions (churches, burial societies) and economic enterprises (insurance agencies, small business, the "numbers" racket) in organizing the community into subunits, and tried to place the growth of

have explored the new refugee groups. Although some studies are now appearing on Hmong, Laotians, Vietnamese, and Cambodian newcomers, none is a true "community study."

[26]Ilsoo Kim, *New Urban Immigrants: The Korean Community in New York* (Princeton, NJ: Princeton University Press, 1981). In contrast to New York City, Los Angeles has developed a core area, called "Koreatown," in which Korean business firms have congregated. While this Korean community has been studied, the focus was on entrepreneurs, rather than on residential neighborhoods. See Ivan Light and Edna Bonacich, *Immigrant Entrepreneurs: Koreans in Los Angeles, 1965–1982* (Berkeley, CA: University of California Press, 1988).

[27]St. Clair Drake and Horace Cayton, *Black Metropolis: A Study of Negro Life in a Northern City* (New York: Harcourt, Brace and Co., 1945), in two volumes. An earlier study by W. E. B. DuBois, *The Philadelphia Negro* (Philadelphia: University of Pennsylvania Press, 1899), was more an analysis of status and life-styles in the black community than a neighborhood study in the strict sense of the term.

the community within the historical context of the mass move up from the South.

Since that seminal study, sociologists and anthropologists have examined lifeways within various black communities. Perhaps the best of these was Ulf Hannerz's participant observation in an African-American area of Washington, D.C. Entitled *Soulside*,[28] the study distinguished many ways of life in what outsiders might view as a homogeneous community—everything from mainstreamers to true action seekers, and to "marginals" (such as corner men and the female-headed households to which they are loosely attached). A closer view of the latter subgroup can be found in Elliot Liebow's *Tally's Corner*, which described the life of a small number of men frequenting a corner and participating only desultorily in the day-work job market, and in Eli Anderson, whose *A Place on the Corner* chronicled social interaction within a group of young black males who hung around a take-out liquor store on Chicago's southside.[29] The networks of support and sharing developed by black women on welfare in St. Louis were analyzed by Carol Stack in her sensitive study, *All Our Kin*.[30]

Far fewer studies of mainstream black culture can be found. Despite the recent suburbanization of many members of the growing black middle class, only one relatively thin study exists: Sternlieb and Beaton's *The Zone of Emergence: A Case Study of Plainfield, New Jersey*.[31] Other studies on predominantly black public housing projects exist, such as Moore's *Vertical Ghetto*[32] and Clare Cooper's *Easter Hill Village*[33]—although the housing project described by Cooper was not exclusively black. While we have small-scale investigations of single streets where drugs play a role, and a few studies of gangs, we have no community studies that systematically detail the impact of drugs on

---

[28]See Ulf Hannerz, *Soulside: Inquiries into Ghetto Culture and Community* (New York: Columbia University Press, 1969). Hannerz is a Swedish anthropologist who achieved remarkable acceptance in the black ghetto in which he lived for his study. He attributes his success to the fact that as a foreigner presumed not to share American prejudices, he was able to have nondefensive interactions.

[29]Elliot Liebow, *Tally's Corner: A Study of Negro Streetcorner Men* (Boston: Little Brown, 1967). Eli Anderson did a deeper participant observation study of a small group of similar men who congregated near a local liquor store in Chicago. See his *A Place on the Corner* (Chicago: University of Chicago Press, 1978). Anderson's newest contribution is *Streetwise: Race, Class and Change in an Urban Community* (Chicago: University of Chicago Press, 1990), on Philadelphia.

[30]Carol Stack, *All Our Kin: Strategies for Survival in a Black Community* (New York: Harper & Row, 1974).

[31]George Sternlieb and W. Patrick Beaton, *The Zone of Emergence: A Case Study of Plainfield, New Jersey* (New Brunswick, NJ: Transaction Books, 1972).

[32]William Moore, *Vertical Ghetto: Everyday Life in an Urban Project* (New York: Random House, 1969), which studied life in the infamous Pruitt-Igoe project of St. Louis, subsequently destroyed on the grounds that it was unlivable.

[33]Clare Cooper, *Easter Hill Village: Some Social Implications of Design* (New York: Free Press, 1975).

what is now called the "black underclass," although some work is currently being done on this group by Terry Williams, among others.

Studies of White Working-Class Zones and Middle-Class Suburbs

With the exception of a few studies of white lower-class neighborhoods, principally occupied by Appalachians who have been treated as an "indigenous" ethnic group,[34] hardly any community studies exist on very poor white neighborhoods in the United States, even though most poor persons in the United States are white. Instead, the neighborhood studies of whites are largely confined to working-class districts outside the centrally located slums or, more typically, in middle-class suburbs.

White Working-Class Zones   In general, sociologists have found it difficult to focus their studies of the "working class" on the neighborhoods in which the members of that group reside; instead, they have often begun with the workplace itself. While these are not, strictly speaking, "community studies," they do shed light on how home and work are connected, showing how dependent the social life of males, at least, is upon their workplace. By far the best community study of working-class urban culture is William Kornblum's *Blue Collar Community*, which described how life for these workers (who were primarily second-generation eastern Europeans) in the steel mills south of Chicago was organized—on the job, in the bars, and in local politics.[35] This study chronicled a stable community that would soon lose its way of life when the steel mills closed, leaving most of the men unemployed. David Halle's *America's Working Man: Home, Work, and Politics Among Blue Collar Property Owners*[36] also began with the workplace, a chemical factory in New Jersey, around which many social relations formed. One of the defects of studies done in this manner is that women and children are somewhat peripheral to the analysis.

In contrast, Young and Willmott's study of the dock area of East London[37] focused more strictly on the neighborhood itself and stressed the importance

---

[34]See, for example, Todd Gitlin and Nanci Hollander, *Uptown: Poor Whites in Chicago* (New York: Harper & Row, 1970). An exception to this rule is Ida Susser's *Norman Street: Poverty and Politics in an Urban Neighborhood* (New York: Oxford University Press, 1982), which deals with a Brooklyn, predominantly Italian, neighborhood.

[35]William Kornblum, *Blue Collar Community* (Chicago: University of Chicago Press, 1974). A sad sequel to this study is David Bensman and Roberta Lynch's *Rusted Dreams: Hard Times in a Steel Community* (New York: McGraw-Hill, 1987; and Berkeley: University of California Press, 1988), which describes the unemployment, hardships, and destruction of this work-related community that followed the closing of the South Chicago steel mills in 1980.

[36]David Halle, *America's Working Man: Home, Work, and Politics Among Blue-Collar Property Owners* (Chicago: University of Chicago Press, 1982).

[37]Michael Young and Peter Willmott, *Family and Kinship in East London* (London: Routledge & Kegan Paul, 1957).

of kinship (especially the mother-daughter bond) in structuring English working-class culture. Indeed, when these low-income families were moved to better housing conditions in a distant housing estate, the families lost their bearings; the close relationship between adult mothers and their daughters (also mothers), which had been the glue of community, was lost when the nuclear family relocated. A parallel study in the United States was Bennett Berger's *Working Class Suburb*,[38] which detailed how life changed for a set of working-class workers and their families when the aircraft factory in which the men worked relocated far outside Los Angeles. Required to move to an unfamiliar suburb, and deprived of the kinship circles around which much of their social life had been organized, they seemed unable to substitute neighbors for their lost family connections.

In general, however, our survey of community studies reveals a paucity of works that tell us about life in those working- and lower-middle-class areas of center cities where life is not organized around ethnicity or race. And there are virtually no studies made in the vast "gray areas" of two flats and small apartment buildings in the outer city, occupied by middle-class white-collar workers, owners of small businesses, bureaucrats, and so on. These groups remain *terrae incognitae* in the field of urban sociology, even though they represent a very large proportion of urban residents.

White Middle-Class Suburbs If studies of the inner city have concentrated almost exclusively on poor areas occupied by immigrants and minority groups, community studies of the suburbs have tended to focus exclusively on white middle-class (and mostly "new") communities. In the immediate postwar period, when these areas were burgeoning on the outskirts of every major metropolis, the stereotype, generated largely in the mass media but perpetuated in sociological writings, was of a community of enormous homogeneity. The contempt that scholars felt for the "ticky-tacky boxes" of the new suburbs and for the "cookie-cutter people" who presumably lived in them was ill-disguised. It took some time before it was recognized that diversity was to be found not only in cities but in the suburbs that were coming to contain the majority of urbanites.

The earliest community studies done of the new suburbs were those of John Seeley, R. A. Sim, and E. W. Loosley, who studied an upper-income suburb of Toronto they called Crestwood Heights,[39] William H. Whyte, who studied the "men in the gray flannel suits" who had settled in the new suburb of Park Forest, south of Chicago,[40] and Herbert Gans, who studied residents in a more middle-class "new town" built by the Levitt Brothers just outside Philadel-

---

[38]Bennett Berger, *Working Class Suburb: A Study of Auto Workers in Suburbia* (Berkeley: University of California Press, 1960).

[39]John Seeley, R. A. Sim, and E. W. Loosley, *Crestwood Heights* (New York: Basic Books, 1956).

[40]William Holly Whyte, *The Organization Man* (New York: Simon & Schuster, 1956).

phia.[41] These studies have become classics. However, because they focus on dormitory suburbs, they suffer from a deficiency opposite to the one noted with respect to studies of blue-collar workers; they contain much information on the lives of women and children and on leisure-time activities and community organizations, but they tell us little about paid employment and how it shapes life in the neighborhood.

More recently, the new town of Columbia, built outside Washington, D.C., has attracted sociological attention, including studies by Brooks[42] and Burkhart,[43] who have tried to evaluate the implications of life in a planned multiclass town designed for work as well as residence. In general, however, the studies of suburban life have not kept pace with the growing significance of this form of urban environment and its effects on family life.[44]

Special Communities

Most of the neighborhood studies we have surveyed so far delimit the residential community by class, race, ethnicity, or some combination of these dimensions of social space. There have been far fewer community studies that examined neighborhoods characterized by special age, sex, or life-style dimensions. Among these are studies of retirement communities and of "counter-culture" enclaves.

Retirement Communities   Given the aging of the American population and its increased tendency toward residential segregation in retirement communities, it should not surprise us to find that sociologists have also investigated "urban" life in such subareas. Rather than the isolation of "urbanism as a way of life" that Wirth's theory predicted, at least some investigators have found considerable "community." Barbara Myerhoff studied the intense social relations and organization among older Jews in a California town,[45] while Arlie Hochschild reported a similar phenomenon in *The Unexpected Community*.[46] Somewhat less romantic portraits were painted by Sheila Johnson in her study

---

[41]Herbert J. Gans, *The Levittowners: Ways of Life and Politics in a New Suburban Community* (New York: Vintage Books, 1967).

[42]Richard O. Brooks, *New Town and Communal Values: A Case Study of Columbia, Maryland* (New York: Praeger, 1974).

[43]Lynne Connolly Burkhart, *Old Values in a New Town: The Politics of Race and Class in Columbia, Maryland* (New York: Praeger, 1981).

[44]Sylvia Fava, "Women's Place in the New Suburbia," in *New Space for Women*, ed. Gerda Wekerle *et al.* (Boulder, CO: Westview Press, 1980).

[45]See Barbara G. Myerhoff, *Number Our Days: A Triumph of Continuity and Culture Among Jewish Old People in an Urban Ghetto* (New York: Simon & Schuster, 1978).

[46]*The Unexpected Community: Portrait of an Old Age Subculture* (Berkeley: University of California Press, 1973).

of a trailer-camp retirement community in California where many of the residents were isolated from family and neighbors and developed emotional attachments to TV as a substitute, and by Maria Vesperi, who studied old people in St. Petersburg, Florida.[47]

Cultural Enclaves   Only a few of the many "deviant subcultures" that coexist in cities have been the subject of community studies. Among these, "bohemian" artist colonies have attracted a disproportionate amount of attention. Greenwich Village in New York was the subject of an early study by Caroline Ware,[48] and nearby SoHo, to which artists priced out of Greenwich Village later moved, has been studied by no less than three analysts: Charles Simpson,[49] James Hudson,[50] and Sharon Zukin.[51] Zukin's book, *Loft Living,* is probably the best community study to be done from a political economy perspective, since she not only describes how residents live, but reveals the entire process of investment and politics that transformed this previously nonresidential zone of loft factories (no longer demanded in the postindustrial economy) into a "trendy" quarter for artists and yuppies seeking alternative life-styles.

Another attempt to capture the type of community generated by alternative life-styles is Bennett Berger's study of hippie communes,[52] although these are primarily rural. The gay community of San Francisco has been the subject of several shorter studies, including one reported in Castells's *The City and the Grassroots.*[53]

Surprisingly absent from the roster of urban community studies are those that document the life-styles of a "new" group, the young urban professionals ("yuppies"), whose existence has been widely publicized in the press, and whose preference for center city living has been credited with fueling the gentrification that has been occurring in many central city inlying areas, often displacing poor and minority residents from affordable housing. Gerda We-

---

[47]See Sheila Johnson, *Idle Haven: Community Building Among the Working-Class Retired* (Berkeley: University of California Press, 1971). Retirees and their impact upon St. Petersburg's "image" are the subjects of Maria D. Vesperi, *City of Green Benches: Growing Old in a New Downtown* (Ithaca, NY: Cornell University Press, 1985).

[48]Caroline Ware, *Greenwich Village, 1920–1930: A Comment on American Civilization in the Postwar Years* (Boston: Houghton Mifflin, 1935).

[49]Charles Simpson, *SoHo: The Artist in the City* (Chicago: University of Chicago Press, 1980).

[50]James Hudson, *The Unanticipated City: Loft Conversions in Lower Manhattan* (Amherst: University of Massachusetts Press, 1987).

[51]Sharon Zukin, *Loft Living: Culture and Capital in Urban Change* (Baltimore: Johns Hopkins Press, 1982).

[52]Bennett Berger, *The Survival of a Counterculture: Ideological Work and Everyday Life Among Rural Communards* (Berkeley: University of California Press, 1981).

[53]"Cultural Identity, Sexual Liberation and Urban Structure: The Gay Community of San Francisco," pp. 138–170 (based on the dissertation of Karen Murphy) in Manuel Castells, *The City and the Grassroots* (Berkeley: University of California Press, 1983).

kerle's perceptive study of life in Carl Sandburg Village (a set of new high-rise apartment structures near downtown Chicago) is one of the few done on this group.[54]

What We Know and Don't Know from Community Studies

As we have seen, in spite of the work of so many scholars done over a period of some 50 years, it is remarkable how little we know about life in American cities, and how distorted is the sample of cases we have accumulated. For the most part, we know a great deal about small local communities that occupy "small physical space" and "small social space"—that is, encapsulated neighborhoods whose special characteristics have isolated them, so to speak, from the rest of the city. (See Chapters 12 through 14 for fuller explanations of these terms.) Best studied have been "urban villages" (to use Gans's not quite accurate phrase) in older eastern and midwestern cities. Many of these can be characterized as "natural areas," as this term was originally used by members of the Chicago School. Yet even in such small areas, analysts found much more diversity than the concept of a "mosaic" of social worlds would have predicted, and the boundaries of even encapsulated communities have turned out to be far more open than the stereotypes suggested.

To some extent, the concentration of researchers on these increasingly atypical areas has been an artifact of the methods they used. It is perhaps only in defenseless urban villages organized around a local focus that a researcher can enter a community, get to know its members through their dense networks of interactions that occur largely in local space, and attend events and meetings in institutions and organizations that are directed to local concerns and that involve local persons. As urban life changes, however, a smaller and smaller percentage of metropolitan dwellers live in these types of communities. Thus, the methods of study yield their own blinders and biases.

Seldom does a researcher select a neighborhood which contains a wide range of social types and which, therefore, is likely to experience struggles among different groups over the disposition and use of an area. Gerald Suttles's *Social Order of the Slum* stands out as one of the few examples of this type of neighborhood study. He recognized that coexisting in a small portion of the near west side of Chicago were several ethnic groups from the lower-middle to lower class: Hispanics, blacks, Italians, as well as the newcomers introduced when the new university campus was constructed—the students and professionals. Even the high skills of Suttles, however, could not gain him equal access to all these subcommunities. Whereas Italian youth are treated in great detail, blacks and Hispanics are viewed "from the outside," while students and professionals are taken for granted. Nevertheless, Suttles's work sensitizes us to the need for very different kinds of methods to trace the "differential association"

---

[54]Gerda Wekerle, *Vertical Village* (Ph.D. dissertation in sociology, Northwestern University, 1974).

of groups in the same neighborhood. As we shall see in the next chapter, network analysis offers just such a technique for studying complex and open-ended communities.

NONSPATIAL COMMUNITIES

As indicated in the quotation by Nisbet that opened Chapter 10 (pp. 269–270), not every community is spatially separated or locality anchored. In fact, the very earliest field research studies done in urban sociology under the direction of Robert Park focused on communities that shared social, but not necessarily physical, space. The Jack Roller (an occupational type that lived by preying on drunks),[55] the Taxi Hall Dancer (a woman who was a partner-for-hire at dance halls),[56] and the Hobo (a nomad who lived in the unseen interstices of the physical world),[57] for example, were primarily social types occupying unique niches in the urban community and generating their own cultural rules and "moral order." A community, conceived in this way, was closer to an occupational group in an elaborate division of labor than to the *Gemeinschaft* territorial community we call a neighborhood, even though it may occupy specific sites in the physical space of the urban community.

The older methods worked out for community studies have not proven very useful for studying these interactions within social groupings. (See Chapter 14 for a fuller discussion of nonspatial communities.) Nor are such methods appropriate to study the communities of contemporary America which have, to some extent, been freed from many physical and locational constraints by the automobile, the airplane, the telephone, the computer, and the fax machine. For those communities that have transcended, relatively speaking, the limitations of physical space, new research methods are needed to uncover and map "community."

THE NEED FOR NEW WAYS TO STUDY COMMUNITY IN THE CITY

When cities consisted of small bounded districts, when relationships could only be maintained by face-to-face interactions, and when simple transport technology made this difficult if not impossible over long distances, then the local community *was* the community in which most people lived out their lives. As we have seen in the chapters on the transformation of American urbanization, and especially in Chapter 6 on contemporary or "postindustrial" urban forms of metropolitan existence, this has ceased to be true for most urbanites.

---

[55]Clifford Shaw, *The Jack-roller: A Delinquent Boy's Own Story* (Chicago: University of Chicago Press, 1930).

[56]Paul Cressey, *The Taxi Dance Hall* (Chicago: University of Chicago Press, 1932).

[57]Nels Anderson, *The Hobo* (Chicago: University of Chicago Press, 1923).

The theory of "urbanism as a way of life" posited that once the small, relatively homogeneous face-to-face groupings broke up, due to larger size, interactional density, and differentiation (and, we would add, mobility), community or *Gemeinschaft* would disappear. It would live on only in the residual "urban villages" so nostalgically studied by urban sociologists.

That has certainly not turned out to be the case. Rather, communities continue to exist in metropolitan America, but they are often different kinds of communities, whose existence and characteristics can no longer be captured through the traditional methods devised by the field. Fortunately, new theories and methods are now being developed to explore the range and diversity of communities that still organize our lives. It is to these that we turn in the next chapter.

Chapter
12

Networks in Social Space and Paths Through Physical Space
New Ways to Study Community

As we have seen in Chapter 11, in the field of community studies only small-scale, relatively homogeneous and encapsulated neighborhoods were really accessible or appropriate to study via the anthropological methods of participant observation, thus limiting the approach. If we conceptualize the entire matrix of possible forms of social interaction (Figure 12.1), we can see immediately that the neighborhood studies described in Chapter 11 are concentrated in the cell of small physical and small social space, whereas most studies of whole communities have taken as their problematic how an increase in the range of physical space (the incursion of the outside world) affects social interactions within the smaller physical unit. (These terms are defined in Figure 12.1 and will be more fully discussed in Chapter 14, which synthesizes the conclusions of Chapters 10–13.)

Social interactions within groups that occupy large physical space but small social space, or in groups that occupy small physical space but range widely in social space, remain relatively unstudied. An example of the former would be the so-called jet setters, who continually meet one another in far-flung, albeit highly selective points around the globe; they maintain their social community despite its spatial fragmentation. An example of the latter would be small urban neighborhoods that house very different social groups which may share the same physical setting but have little else in common. A neighborhood such as the East Village of Lower Manhattan—which contains homeless people in its park, squatters in abandoned buildings, drug dealers in "crack houses," aged Ukrainians left over from an earlier urban village, anarchists and undocumented aliens avoiding governmental surveillance, struggling students and experimental artists seeking cheap rents, in addition to Puerto Ricans, blacks, and the well-to-do young urban professionals who entered when the area began to be gentrified—cannot be investigated by the usual methods devised for community participation studies.

It is not surprising, then, to find that the neighborhood studies that have been done tend to refute Wirth's theory of "urbanism as a way of life." But this is largely because they have dealt almost exclusively with bounded and inwardly focused localities which, for reasons of marginal ethnicity, minority status, or old age (all elements of low power), remain somewhat isolated from the rest of the urban environment. They constitute small distinctive "cells" in an increasingly amorphous urban landscape. Such research sites have become increasingly hard to locate, however, except in ports of entry for new immigrant groups or in residual enclaves left over from a previous way of life. This "loss of object" may be one reason why community studies, as they have traditionally been conducted in urban sociology, seem now to be dying out as a genre.

Such bounded zones are clearly of declining importance in the new metropolitan regions of saturation urbanization, where transportation and communication innovations are freeing social interactions from mere spatial proximity and where social differentiation among urbanites is coming to be based less upon what someone was born with, and more upon the life-style an individual

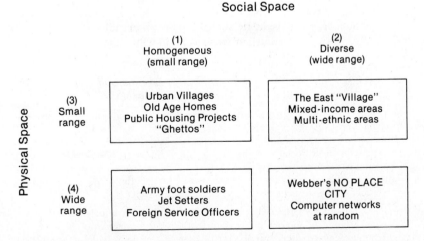

Figure 12.1 Community studies in the matrix of scale and social and physical space (*Source:* Original with author.)

selects from a wide array of alternatives. (Admittedly, the *degree* of choice is still contingent, in large measure, on constraints imposed by class, race, ethnicity, gender, and stage in the life cycle.[1])

In this new type of urban life, social relations are no longer necessarily coterminous with spatial relations.[2] One does not necessarily socialize with one's neighbors because they are handy, nor does distance, in itself, preclude the maintenance of important social ties. And out of the wider array of individuals from which one *could* select one's friends and associates, one has at least the potential to become more choosy, finding those with whom one shares highly specialized interests, rather than those with whom one shares residence or even kinship ties. In short, individuals can build their own networks of significant others.

Simple observation is sufficient to indicate that Americans, even though most no longer live in villages—rural *or* urban—are not therefore automatically cut adrift from society. The predicted loss of community that was to have followed inevitably and tragically from the growth of cities has not occurred for most people, even though some individuals and even subgroups may suffer from what Durkheim termed *anomie* (literally, normlessness).[3]

The challenging task of urban sociology, then, is nothing less than to reconceptualize how social life is actually lived, and to reach a new and much more sophisticated theoretical understanding about the relationship between people and their environments. In this new conceptualization, people must be seen as active makers of their social lives, not passive responders to determining ecological factors. This revision requires new theories about social life in cities that diverge drastically from those of the neoclassical ecologists. To understand why a new approach is needed, we must return to the idea of the "natural area." Saunders put the matter particularly well:

> The significance of the concept of natural areas for the Chicago School's human ecology is twofold. First, it overcomes the empirical problem associated with the biotic-cultural division by specifying an observable object—the ghetto, the red light district, the suburb or whatever—in which these two aspects of human orga-

---

[1] See Janet Abu-Lughod, *The City is Dead—Long Live the City* (Monograph 12, Berkeley, CA: Center for Planning and Development of the University of California, 1969).

[2] Mel Webber, "Order in Diversity: Community Without Propinquity," reprinted in *Neighborhood, City, and Metropolis,* ed. R. Gutman and D. Popenoe (New York: Random House, 1970). An early distinction between social and physical space can be found in Arnold Feldman and Charles Tilly, "The Interaction of Social and Physical Space," *American Sociological Review* 25 (1960), pp. 877–884. We concur in our conceptualization of physical space. However, we believe that their use of the term *social space* is already contaminated by geography. As will become clear in Chapter 14, we believe the two should be kept analytically distinct.

[3] Emile Durkheim, the originator of this term, used it in two different works. In his first book, *The Division of Labor in Society,* he stressed that *anomie* is a condition of society that arises when regulation and peaceful coexistence break down. Later, in *Suicide,* he used the term in a more individualistic and psychological sense to refer to the distress that comes from not having a clear sense of society's norms, which can come from social isolation.

nization have become fused. *A natural area . . . is also a cultural area.* It is on the one hand an area characterized by division of labour and competitive cooperation, while on the other hand it is a moral area characterized by consensus and communication. It therefore . . . *can be studied both ecologically and sociologically,* as a natural unit or as a social unit.[4]

Social area analysis, by showing that spatial differentiation is not unidimensional, refutes the idea of an unambiguously demarcated "natural area," isolated from other spatial subareas of the city. Network analysis, by demonstrating that proximity is an important but by no means *the most* important basis for social relations, refutes the idea that the residential neighborhood is necessarily also a social or moral community.

NETWORK ANALYSIS: A NEW TOOL FOR URBAN SOCIOLOGICAL RESEARCH ON SOCIAL SPACE

The theoretical roots of network analysis can be traced back to Georg Simmel, who presented his ideas in a long essay entitled "Social Circles" that was published in German in the early twentieth century but was not available in English translation until 1955.[5] In it, Simmel specified the relationship between urbanization-modernization and the types of networks people could be expected to have. Simmel suggested that modern urban life was distinguished from rural or premodern urban life by the structural characteristics of people's "social circles," or what we would now call *networks*.

In premodern life, the identities of individuals and the social groups to which they belong are consistent with each other and are thus not in conflict. A person belongs to a family, which in turn is part of a larger kinship grouping, which in turn inhabits a given territory. Under such structural conditions, social identity is, in Simmel's word, "overdetermined" and is, to that extent, involuntary. There can be very little individuality in such a society because the "social coordinates" that identify individuals and locate them in social space are ascribed to them and are held in common with many others.

Simmel considered that what was truly unique about modern life was that individuals could belong to a variety of social circles which did not necessarily overlap. In addition to being a member of a family, an individual might play in a band with nonrelatives, belong to a chess team with nonmusicians, and have friends at work who are involved with neither music nor chess. Because of the multiplicity of social circles a person might belong to, and because of the almost infinite number of ways these circles could be combined, no two persons

---

[4]Peter Saunders, *Social Theory and the Urban Question* (New York: Holmes and Meier, 1981), pp. 60–61; emphasis added.

[5]*Die Kreuzung sozialer Kreise* [literally, social circle], trans. by Reinhard Bendix under the title, "The Web of Group-Affiliations," and first published in English in Kurt Wolff and Reinhard Bendix, eds. and trans., *Conflict and the Web of Group-Affiliations* (Glencoe, IL: Free Press, 1955).

would ever share the exact same "coordinates in social space." Thus, each would be a uniquely defined individual. Simmel attributed personal freedom to this new form of social affiliation and considered it to be the essence of modern society.

Some Applications of Network Analysis

Simmel had used the term "social circles" as a metaphor, rather than as an operational tool for social research. A generation was to go by before network analysis was applied in research, and even then, the first applications came not from sociologists but from epidemiologists, mathematical psychologists, and social anthropologists. As Berkowitz points out in his excellent history of the development of network analysis,[6] in the early 1950s Anatol Rapoport began to construct formal mathematical models of diffusion along network structures; at the same time, social anthropologists began to map the social networks of groups of people.

The Contributions of Social Anthropologists In 1954, John Arundel Barnes published his famous "Class and Committees in a Norwegian Island Parish,"[7] which summarized a larger study of networks of social relations within this relatively closed rural society. Three years later, Elizabeth Bott published her study of the differences between the social networks of 20 married couples in the working and middle classes of England.[8] This pilot study suggested that whereas middle-class couples were likely to share networks (that is, to engage in social relationships as a couple), the networks of working-class husbands and wives rarely overlapped. Here was perhaps the first evidence of observable structural differences between the social networks of different classes.

Anthropologists continued to develop these techniques for mapping networks. Particularly active were the British structural anthropologists from the University of Manchester—a number of whom were involved in research in African urban areas. In 1969, the book that expressed the culmination of this research tradition appeared and was widely read by sociologists struggling with similar research questions.[9]

In the studies by anthropologists, however, networks were viewed from the standpoint of the individual (and thus were called "egocentric networks"). Figure 12.2 shows some sample diagrams. It was therefore difficult to aggregate

---

[6]See S. D. Berkowitz, *An Introduction to Structural Analysis: The Network Approach to Social Research* (Toronto: Butterworths, 1982), pp. 2–3.

[7]John A. Barnes, "Class and Committees in a Norwegian Island Parish," *Human Relations* 7 (1954), pp. 39–58.

[8]Elizabeth Bott, *Family and Social Network* (London: Tavistock Publications, 1957).

[9]J. Clyde Mitchell, ed., *Social Networks in Urban Situations: Analysis of Personal Relationships in Central African Towns* (Manchester: Manchester University Press, 1969).

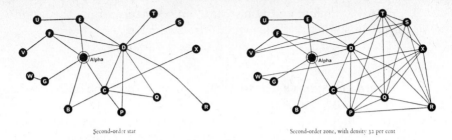

Figure 12.2 Social networks of low density (on left) and high density (on right). (*Source:* J. A. Barnes, "Networks and Political Process," in J. Clyde Mitchell, ed., *Social Networks in Urban Situations* [Manchester: University of Manchester Press, 1971], pp. 60–61.)

these networks, and therefore to generalize about the kinds of networks different types of people (varying by age, sex, class, marital status, ethnicity, etc.) would be likely to have in different physical settings (center cities, suburbs, small towns, rural areas, etc.). Thus it was hard to use the networks mapped by urban anthropologists to test propositions in urban sociology.

In the 1960s, however, sociologists were working independently on this problem and were developing a different approach to networks. During the mid-1960s, the mathematical advances in graph and diffusion theory were brought together with the descriptive mapping of social anthropologists, giving rise to what Barry Wellman has referred to as the "social network concept."

> Reversing the conventionally accepted logic of inquiry in social science, structuralists came to argue that social categories (e.g., classes, strata) and bounded groups (e.g., biochemists) could best be discovered by examining the relations between and among social actors or institutions. Rather than beginning with an *a priori* classification of the observable world into discrete sets of categories, then, they postulated the opposite: *begin with a set of relations and from them derive a typology and map of the structure of groups.*[10]

Without methodological improvements, however, this concept of networks, while powerful, could not be operationalized.

Berkowitz describes two breakthroughs in network analysis that began to translate the metaphor into a research tool: one on structural equivalence by Harrison White and his associates,[11] the other on multidimensional scaling by

---

[10]Quoted from S. D. Berkowitz, *An Introduction to Structural Analysis,* p. 3, emphasis added. Note how this conceptual and methodological shift parallels the shift from "uncovering" to "constructing" the spatial structure of the city, as described in Chapter 7 above. Note also the return to the methodology W. Lloyd Warner had attempted in his Yankee City studies.

[11]See Harrison White *et al.,* "Structural Equivalence of Individuals in Social Networks," *Journal of Mathematical Sociology* 1 (1971), pp. 49–80.

Edward Laumann and Louis Guttman.[12] Of these, only the latter was applied to urban studies and thus will be treated here.

Edward Laumann's Contribution   Laumann's 1966 book, *Prestige and Association in an Urban Community,*[13] began to explore the relationship in contemporary American urban society between personal/social characteristics and the degree to which friends were selected from among persons with the same characteristics. Unfortunately, this first study included only 422 white adult male residents of Cambridge and Belmont, Massachusetts. The restricted sample made it impossible for Laumann to compare the networks of groups differing in gender, stage in the family cycle, or race. Furthermore, although he was able to compare networks of Catholics and Protestants (there were too few Jews in the sample to permit generalization) and of persons of different ethnic ancestry, he did so only to test whether these variables affected the degree to which friendships were restricted to members of the same socioeconomic class. In addition, because his sample only included men who lived in small suburban towns, he could not investigate how different physical environments might affect the nature of people's networks. He could not say whether the networks of urbanites, for example, differed systematically from those of rural people or of residents in isolated small towns.

Despite these limitations, the study made a number of major contributions, particularly in the realm of methodology. Respondents were asked to give the occupations and kinship relation (if any) of their three closest friends. On the basis of this "differential association," Laumann was able to calculate the social distance between occupations in social space (for a simplified graph based on his complex three-dimensional analysis, see Figure 12.3). He found that members of occupational groups at the highest and lowest levels of prestige were quite encapsulated, having a disproportionate number of associations with others within their occupation, whereas those in the middle-ranking occupations had relationships that crossed occupational boundaries. Having kin for friends was most common among respondents from the lower middle class, rather than among people in the lower class, which he had expected. And finally, even though ethnicity was not a crucial variable in this first study, some differences were found between assimilated persons of Anglo-Saxon origin and those of more recent immigration.

---

[12]Berkowitz is slightly inaccurate here, since he claims on p. 6 that the Laumann-Guttman application of smallest-space multi-dimensional scaling to this problem occurred in 1971–1972, whereas it actually dates back to Laumann and Guttman's article in *American Sociological Review* 3 (April 1966), pp. 169–178, which was reproduced in modified form as Chapter 6 of Edward O. Laumann, *Prestige and Association in an Urban Community: An Analysis of an Urban Stratification System* (Indianapolis: Bobbs-Merrill Company, 1966), pp. 89–104.

[13]Edward O. Laumann, *Prestige and Association in an Urban Community* (Indianapolis: Bobbs-Merrill Company, 1966).

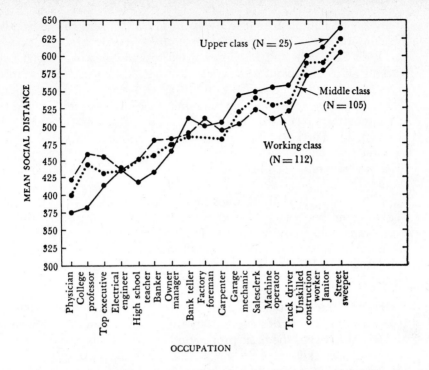

(The reader should note that the relatively good linear fit in this figure for the three sets of means is in part due to ordering the occupations in terms of their average social distance scores for the sample as a whole. The regression analysis discussed below, however, is based on an independently derived measure of occupational prestige.)

Figure 12.3 Mean social distance by self-identified class, for seventeen occupational stimuli. (*Source:* Edward O. Laumann, *Social Prestige and Association in an Urban Community: An Analysis of an Urban Stratification System* [Indianapolis: Bobbs-Merrill Co., 1966], p. 44. Copyright 1966 by Bobbs-Merrill.)

In Laumann's later study, *The Bonds of Pluralism: The Form and Substance of Urban Social Networks*,[14] ethnicity became a central variable, along with class. What had been only implicit in the Massachusetts study was made explicit and refined in this study of the social circles of 985 native-born adult white males living in the Detroit SMSA in 1965–1966. Among other things, the respondents were asked to identify their three closest male friends (including relatives, if they so chose) and to provide information on each regarding occupation, ethnicity, religion, and so on. The data gathered in this manner were

---

[14]*The Bonds of Pluralism: The Form and Substance of Urban Social Networks* (New York: John Wiley, 1973).

analyzed by Laumann in *The Bonds of Pluralism* and reanalyzed by Claude Fischer and his associates in *Networks and Places.*[15]

Both Laumann and Fischer wanted to know how the social networks of various kinds of urbanites differed. However, they were limited in that their sample excluded women, children, the aged, blacks, and persons born abroad. Therefore, they were only able to examine the effects of religion, ethnicity, and class (measured by educational level and occupation) on the social networks of white males. Furthermore, because their sample came from a single undifferentiated metropolitan area, they could not test whether the type of residential area in which one lived had any influence on the types of social networks one would develop.

Only later could these questions be investigated: in the work of Barry Wellman on the social networks of residents in a subarea of Toronto; and in a very large-scale study by Claude Fischer on the social networks of men and women in center-city, suburban, small-town, and semi-rural locations in northern California. It is to these studies that we now turn.

Barry Wellman's Contribution   Barry Wellman conducted one of the first true network studies designed to investigate the nature of modern urban life and to test whether the basic proposition in urban theory—namely, that urbanism led to a breakdown of the social order—was, in fact, correct.[16] Wellman and his associates interviewed 845 adult residents of East York (an upper-working-class, lower-middle-class neighborhood) in Toronto. For the first time, women as well as men were interviewed. Respondents were asked to give detailed information about the six persons outside the home to whom they felt closest.

On the basis of their answers, Wellman concluded that most urbanites were embedded in intimate social networks. Contrary to the "social breakdown" or "community lost" theory, which posited that urbanites were members of a lonely crowd, subsisting on a meager diet of secondary, unfeeling, and fleeting social relations, he found that only 2 percent of his sample could not list at least one social intimate, and 61 percent could list five or more persons in their social network of intimates. Given Laumann's findings that lower-middle-class urbanites had strong friendship relations with blood relatives, it should not surprise us that about half of all intimates were kinfolk; the remainder were non-kin, mostly identified as friends. The closest ties were to immediate kin, followed by friends. In comparison, ties to neighbors and coworkers were comparatively weak.

Although Wellman's urban respondents were thus linked socially to others, their linkages were clearly different in structure from those one might find in a rural place. Only 13 percent of the persons who were named as social inti-

---

[15]Claude Fischer *et al.*, eds., *Networks and Places: Social Relations in the Urban Setting* (New York: Free Press, 1977).

[16]Barry Wellman, "The Community Question: The Intimate Networks of East Yorkers," in *American Journal of Sociology* 84 (1979), pp. 1201–1231.

mates actually lived within the respondents' neighborhoods. Most did live in Toronto, which suggests that proximity was not totally irrelevant, but a substantial number (especially kin) lived quite far away. Telephone calls and occasional visits substituted for daily or weekly face-to-face contact. Because of this geographic dispersion, the networks, except for kin, were not dense. That is, one's friends were not likely also to be friends of one another. Presumably, in a smaller community where proximity could become the basis of contact, one's friends would also be known to one another.

On the basis of these results, Wellman argued for a theory of community which he called "liberated." It is close to Simmel's idea of multiple social circles under conditions of social modernity. Wellman suggested that first, the modern separation of home, work, and kin "involves urbanites in multiple social circles with weak solidary attachments." Second, however, the existence of cheap means of transportation and communication makes it possible for urbanites to maintain contact with primary ties, despite their geographic dispersion. Third, the scale, density, and diversity of the city and nation-state create the possibility for individuals to participate in a variety of only loosely bonded multiple social circles. Finally, "spatial dispersion of primary ties and heterogeneity of the city make it less likely that those to whom an urbanite is linked will themselves be densely knit into solidary communities." Table 12.1 shows how Wellman's findings about the social networks of East Yorkers support his "community liberated" theory better than either what he calls the "community lost" theory (that

Table 12.1   THE COMMUNITY QUESTION: LOST, SAVED, AND LIBERATED ARGUMENTS COMPARED WITH EAST YORK FINDINGS

Argument	Community lost	Community saved	Community liberated	East York findings (main tendencies)
Basis of intimacy				
Availability	Rare	Abundant	Abundant	5+ intimates
Relational	Formal role	Kin, neighborhood	Friendship, work	Kin, friendship
Spatial	Local	Local	Metropolitan, national	Metropolitan
Mode of contact	In person	In person	In person, telephone	Telephone, in person
Communal structure				
Density	Sparse	Dense	Sparse	Sparse
Reciprocity	No	Yes	Uneven	Uneven
Boundedness	Ramified	Tight	Ramified	Ramified
Basis of assistance				
Prevalence	Minimal	Abundant	Moderate	Moderate
Relational source	Formal ties	Kin, neighborhood	Friendship, work	Parent/child, work
Residential basis	Local*	Local	Metropolitan, national	Metropolitan
Density	Dense*	Dense	Sparse	N.S.
Structural source	Secondary	Solidary group	Network ties	Network ties

*To the extent to which primary ties exist.

Source: Barry Wellman, "East Yorkers and the Community Question," *American Journal of Sociology* 84 (1979), p. 1224.

cities cause social disorganization and loneliness) or the "community saved" theory (that older forms of close-knit neighborhood communities persist in the contemporary city).

To summarize, from the mid-1960s onward, a few investigators began to examine the social networks of urban residents, although neither the personal characteristics of these residents (such as their class, age, sex, family stage, ethnicity, race) nor the types of residential communities in which they lived (center city, outer city, suburb, exurb, nonmetropolitan small town) were as yet systematically linked to the structural characteristics of their social networks. The agenda behind these studies was clearer and better linked to urban sociological theory than were the preliminary findings. The kinds of questions that were being asked were inherited not only from classical ecological theory but from the even earlier European theorists whose works had set the parameters for the field of sociology. We might review these questions here.

1. In what way does life in modern large-scale societies differ from that in preindustrial times?
2. In what way does life in the modern city differ from life in preindustrial cities and in rural areas?
3. What variations are found in the "ways of life" within the modern city, and to what can these variations be attributed?
4. How does proximity affect human interactions and social relations? For whom is proximity still important? Which kinds of persons have social ties to communities that transcend the local neighborhood?

These are questions that could be answered only speculatively before the development of the social network method of inquiry and analysis. While urban sociologists have not yet fully answered them, substantial strides are currently being made to understand how modern urban social life differs from that in earlier times and in nonurban places. The answers we are getting suggest great variation and complexity.

Claude Fischer's Study of Urban Networks A second generation of network studies is now coming into existence, of which Claude S. Fischer's *To Dwell Among Friends: Personal Networks in Town and City*[17] perhaps represents a turning point. In 1977–1978 Fischer and his associates interviewed 1050 English-speaking adults (males and females) in 50 northern California communities that varied from highly urbanized quarters in central San Francisco to isolated small towns some 200 miles away. The sample was stratified to permit valid comparisons on the basis of both personal characteristics (age, family cycle stage, gender, occupation, and level of education) and type of residential community (center city, suburban metropolitan, independent small town, and semi-rural area). Unfortunately, Hispanic and African-American areas were avoided, persons who could not speak English were not interviewed, and no attempts were made to interview in rural areas.

---

[17]Claude S. Fischer, *To Dwell Among Friends* (Chicago: University of Chicago Press, 1982).

A methodology was carefully designed to separate the influence of an individual's social characteristics (location in social space) from the influence of the residential community in which he or she lived (location in physical space) in tracing the effects on an individual's social network. This was essential because of the close association between personal characteristics and residential location, due to selective sifting and sorting. Therefore, in addition to presenting aggregated information on the nature of social networks in each of the different residential settings, the study controlled for social characteristics (occupation, education, class, marital status, age, and ethnicity) in order to measure the residual effects of physical space on network formation. This was a critical step in disengaging the influence of social space (what we might call a person's "coordinates in social space," such as his or her occupation, education, marital status, age, ethnicity, and so forth) from that of "physical space" (where a person lives).

Methodologically, the Fischer study was substantially more sophisticated than the earlier network studies that had only gathered information about three or six associates (a somewhat arbitrary limit). Instead, respondents were asked to name as many persons as they wished in each of the following categories: persons who cared for their home when they were out of town; persons with whom they discussed work-related decisions; individuals with whom they had engaged in recent social activities; those with whom they discussed leisure interests; individuals they dated or were engaged to (if unmarried); those with whom they discussed personal worries or to whom they went for advice on important matters; and persons from whom they might be able to borrow a large sum of money. After all these names were compiled, respondents were asked to add the names of anyone else who was important to them. Most respondents named between 12 and 24 "associates" through this procedure.

The interviewer then asked the genders of the associates, how the respondent knew them, to whom respondents felt closest, which ones lived within five minutes' drive of home, which ones within an hour's drive, which persons were in the "same line of work" (including homemakers), which persons were of the same religious and ethnic background, which persons shared the respondent's favorite pastime, and so on. Even more detailed information was obtained regarding three to five of the person's closest associates. Fischer used these answers to build up fairly detailed pictures of the social worlds of various types of respondents who lived in different ecological locations.[18]

Two kinds of conclusions relevant to an understanding of urbanism as a way (or ways) of life were reached in this study. The first kind describes the relationship between the personal/social characteristics of people and the types of social networks they have. Significantly, the relevant personal/social characteristics fall into the three categories always found in social area analyses and factorial ecologies, namely, class, ethnicity, and family status. The second set of conclusions has to do with the relationship between the kinds of physical

---

[18]*Ibid.*, pp. 35–38.

communities people live in and the kinds of social networks they have, independent of their social characteristics.

Class (as measured by educational level and income) had a marked effect on the size and complexity of social networks. In general, the more educated the respondents, the more social activities they engaged in, the larger their personal networks, and the greater the companionship and intimacy available from them. Both high education and high income were associated with a proportionate decline in the number of relatives respondents listed as part of their network. Among all respondents kin remained important sources of assistance, especially monetary, but the wealthy and educated were more likely to depend on friends as confidants and leisure-time companions.

While better educated and richer respondents had more varied and larger social networks than respondents in lower classes, their networks were more spread out geographically and less socially dense[19] than the networks of other groups. Fischer concluded, "In general, affluent respondents seemed less hampered by constraints and better able to take advantage of far-flung social opportunities than were the less affluent respondents." Here is certainly evidence of a decline in the importance of ascribed characteristics of kinship and locality in shaping social networks. This decline was most marked among the rich, who could best afford to choose their associates.

Age, gender, and stage in the family cycle were also found to affect the kinds of social networks respondents developed. Older respondents tended to engage in fewer social activities, to have smaller networks (and especially to have fewer non-kin in their networks), to have their contacts more spatially circumscribed, and to be less intensely related to others than were younger respondents. Men and women were affected differently by age, however. Whereas older men tended to become quite isolated socially, middle-aged women were described as "unusually sociable." Marriage tended to increase the social ties respondents had with people in their neighborhood and with their kin; marriage especially restricted the non-kin and non-neighborhood contacts of women. Married men "reported fewer confidants than did never-married men, which was not so for women. It appears that men tended to fully satisfy their needs for a confidant by turning to their wives, while wives drew on intimates besides their husbands."[20] The presence of children at home restricted the social networks of parents and particularly of mothers. Women with children at home engaged in fewer social activities, and had less social support and more localized social networks than other respondents. Other things being equal, women were more involved with kin than were men. Thus, just as wealthier respondents were better able to sustain wide-ranging, large and diversified networks because they had fewer constraints on their choices, so persons less tied down to home and children tended to have networks that were less confined to kin and neighborhood.

---

[19]The social density of a network is measured by the number of persons known to a respondent who are also known to one another.

[20]Claude Fischer, *To Dwell Among Friends,* p. 253.

Finally, although sample selection did not really permit a detailed study of network variations by religion, race, and ethnicity, "it appeared that blacks and Chicanos had smaller, less supportive, and more culturally encapsulated networks than did comparable Anglos."[21] This conclusion, however, must be regarded cautiously. The blacks and Chicanos included in Fischer's sample were living in predominantly white areas, where they may have been unusually isolated. Community studies of ethnic enclaves, such as Gans's *The Urban Villagers,* and of poor blacks, such as Carol Stack's *All Our Kin,*[22] suggest that networks for these groups are generally large, geographically concentrated, and socially dense. Additional studies are definitely called for to test these propositions.

Fischer asked what factors accounted for the observed differences in the social networks of his respondents. He granted that, to some extent, personality must have been responsible, but far more important were variations in opportunities and constraints, due to people's positions in social space:

> People's positions in the social structure—their educational and financial resources, status in the labor force, ethnic memberships, family commitments, residential locations, and so on—expose them to varying opportunities for forming personal relations and provide them with varying means for taking advantage of these opportunities.[23]

Just as opportunities and constraints were provided by social and personal characteristics, so they were also created by one's physical environment.

The second set of conclusions from Fischer's study related networks to places of residence, holding social characteristics constant. Fischer contended that urban/rural differences had not yet disappeared, despite saturation urbanization. Selective migration continued to bring young and better educated people into urban areas and to move older persons out to less urbanized areas. In addition to this sifting and sorting, however, Fischer believed that his data indicated residual effects of the physical environment itself on social life. When he controlled for the differences in social characteristics of urban, metropolitan, small-town, and semi-rural residents, he still found many differences which he believes were due to the physical setting. Thus, "urban residence apparently discourages involvement with kin, especially with extended kin," or at least leads residents to be more selective about which kin they will continue to see. "Urbanism seemed to . . . discourage involvement and encourage selectivity with neighbors" as well. "Urban residents were definitely involved more with 'just friends' . . . than were small-town respondents." He concluded:

> Urbanism clearly reduced . . . involvements with people drawn from the "traditional" complex of kin, neighborhood, and church and slightly increased their

---

[21]*Ibid.,* p. 254.

[22]Carol B. Stack's *All Our Kin: Strategies for Survival in a Black Community* (New York: Harper & Row, 1974) indicates the extent to which poor blacks in St. Louis built up a dense network of kin-like relations for mutual aid and support.

[23]Claude Fischer, *To Dwell Among Friends,* p. 254.

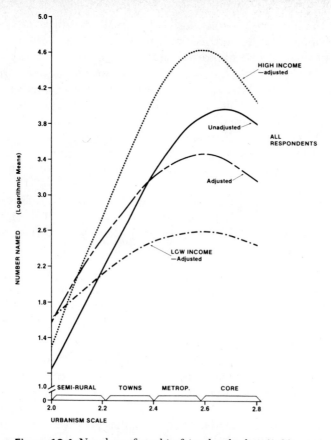

Figure 12.4 Number of nonkin friends who live 5–60 minutes' drive away from respondents, by urbanism of place of residence in northern California (semi-rural fringe, separate town, San Francisco metropolitan district, or central core of San Francisco). (*Source:* Claude S. Fischer. *To Dwell Among Friends* [Chicago: University of Chicago Press, 1982], p. 168. Copyright 1982 by University of Chicago Press.)

involvements with people drawn from more modern and more voluntary contexts of work, secular associations, and footloose friendship.[24]

Complementing the findings of Barry Wellman, he found that the social networks of city dwellers tended to be more geographically dispersed and less socially dense than those of persons living in smaller places. The relationship between type of residential community and the degree to which networks were socially encapsulated was less clear. The effect depended upon whether one had social characteristics which were "in the majority" or "in the minority." In

---

[24]*Ibid.*, p. 258.

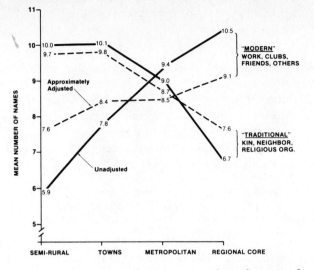

Figure 12.5 Number of names given by urbanism of place of residence, according to a traditional/modern distinction among primary social contexts, northern California. (*Source:* Claude S. Fischer. *To Dwell Among Friends* [Chicago: University of Chicago Press, 1982], p. 119. Copyright 1982 by University of Chicago Press.)

small towns, for example, the social networks of persons who were in the majority were far more homogeneous than those of similar people who lived in the city. The reverse was true for persons with minority characteristics. In small towns, such persons had heterogeneous networks, whereas in cities their networks included more persons like themselves.

The explanation for the apparent contradiction in these findings was simple and supported Fischer's basic thesis. The size and density that define the city make possible social heterogeneity, not only because cities attract variety but because deviant individuals can find others who share their characteristics. This permits the formation of subcultures which then intensify and solidify their distinctiveness. In small towns, persons with minority characteristics must adapt to the majority; in large cities, they are freer to be themselves. Conversely, urban areas expose persons with majority characteristics to a large number of "different" kinds of people, contributing to greater heterogeneity in their social networks.

As can be seen from this account, urbanism is associated with some differences in social life, independent of the personal and social characteristics of respondents (see Figures 12.4 and 12.5). While there may not be only one urban way of life, there are certainly some forms of social life that are distinctive to modern cities and that result, at least in part, from the numbers and density present in the physical environment.

ACTIVITY PATTERNS: A NEW TOOL TO STUDY PATHS IN PHYSICAL SPACE

If social networks can be thought of as the paths through which people move in social space, activity patterns can be thought of as the paths through which people move over time through geographic space. (See Chapter 14 for a fuller explanation.) It is interesting that urban sociologists, despite their preoccupation with the ecological variables of space and time, have tended to ignore the important connections between these two variables. The main methodological innovations have come, instead, from urban geographers and city planners.

The Work of Chapin and Associates

In the mid-1960s, when social network analysis was just beginning to make important strides, the first of a series of studies of "human activity patterns" in the city was being conducted by F. Stuart Chapin, Jr. and Henry Hightower on a sample of residents in Durham, North Carolina.[25] The experimental methods developed there were later applied to an analysis of activity systems in Washington, D.C., using data that had been collected at the SMSA level in 1968, supplemented by more detailed information collected from two selected neighborhoods, one predominantly black, the other predominantly white.[26]

This work revived an old technique in the social sciences which had virtually been abandoned since the 1930s, when Pitrim Sorokin had tried it: the time budget, a daily log recording how people spent their time. Chapin combined this, however, with a space budget, a comparable log recording where people were at various times of day, modeled after the origin-destination traffic studies that planners had been making since the 1940s. Chapin acknowledged his indebtedness to the Swedish geographer, Torsten Hagerstrand,[27] for many of the methods used in his study of activity systems.

Chapin was interested in systematic differences in the ways persons of differing family status, economic class, and race used their time and interacted spatially with the metropolis. But instead of asking respondents directly, he analyzed the time/space budgets that had been recorded by a sample of household heads and their spouses for a typical weekday and a Saturday or Sunday.

---

[25]See F. Stuart Chapin, Jr. and Henry C. Hightower, *Household Activity Systems—A Pilot Investigation* (Chapel Hill: Center for Urban and Regional Studies, Institute for Research in Social Science, University of North Carolina, 1966).

[26]See F. Stuart Chapin, Jr., *Human Activity Patterns in the City: Things People Do in Time and Space* (New York: John Wiley, 1974).

[27]Torsten Hagerstrand, "What About People in Urban Science," in *Papers of the Regional Science Association* 24 (1969–1970), pp. 7–21. See his later "Survival and Arena," in T. Carlstein *et al.*, eds., *Timing Space and Spacing Time*, vol. 2, entitled *Human Activity and Time Geography* (London: Edward Arnold, 1978).

From these data he was able to reconstruct "average" time and space budgets for various subgroups of respondents. Some of the findings from Chapin's study are quite consistent with those found in network studies.

First, activity patterns were found to vary significantly by gender and family status. On a weekday, males spent an average of 7.35 hours (including travel time) at their jobs and a little more than an hour in shopping, homemaking, and home maintenance. In contrast, females averaged 3.26 hours at paid employment and about 5 hours shopping and taking care of the home.[28] Respondents under 35 with no children spent the most (average spousal) time at work and the least in home care. The maximum time spent on home care was in households containing children under 13 years of age. Children interfered drastically with "discretionary" time available for socializing, watching television, participating in organizations, or engaging in leisure-time activities. Young household heads with no children had a daily average of 6.27 hours of discretionary time. When there were young children present, this dropped to 5.4 hours. The heads of childless households spent more than two hours a day socializing or enjoying non-TV recreations. In contrast, the most overloaded group, parents of young children, averaged only about one hour a day in such activities. Older householders spent their time quite differently. Retirement was common when the head was over 65 and there were no children in the home. Therefore, the average spousal time spent in paid employment was only 1.26 hours, while discretionary time, commensurately larger, was spent on television viewing (2.4 hours per day), on socializing, in organizational activities, and on other recreations.

Thus, the stage in the family cycle largely determined the degree to which time constraints were placed on social activities, especially out of the home. Other things being equal, young adults with no children were more likely to be in the labor force, were freer to travel farther for their leisure activities, and were more likely to maintain a large and wide-ranging circle of friends. Older persons stayed closer to home, and families with young children had severe time constraints in socializing. These findings are consistent with those of Wellman and Fischer. However, since neither Wellman nor Fischer had interviewed nonwhites, they were unable to say whether their findings also applied to blacks or to test for any systematic differences by race. The Chapin study made such comparisons possible.

Race was found to relate significantly to the use of time and space. In general, black respondents averaged more time at work than white respondents. Because of their longer work hours,[29] blacks had less discretionary time than whites. Furthermore, what spare time they had, they spent at home

---

[28]It should be remembered that female labor force participation rates were considerably lower in 1968 than they are now.

[29]It will be recalled, however, that this was measured as an average of spousal time; the higher labor force participation rates of black females probably accounted for much of this difference.

watching TV (2.4 hours daily in comparison to 1.4 hours in the white sample). And when they did go out of the house, their movements were more restricted. The mean sum of the distances from home to out-of-house activities was 12 miles for blacks, as contrasted with 15 miles for whites. The greater spatial encapsulation of blacks is evident in Figure 12.6, reproduced from the Chapin

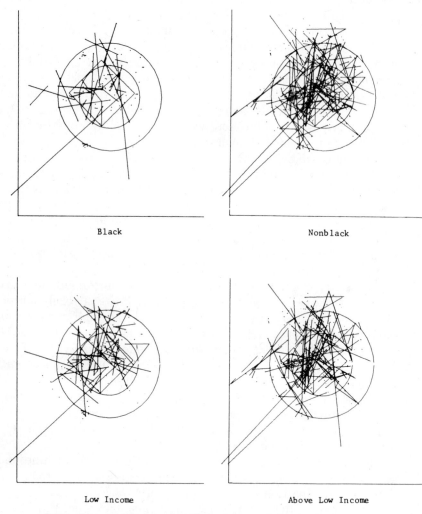

Black

Nonblack

Low Income

Above Low Income

Note: Dots signify home locations where activity is done at home; the radius of inner ring is seven miles from the Washington Monument, and the outer ring 12 miles.

Figure 12.6 Urban paths through the Washington, D.C. metropolitan area for socializing, by income level and race, 1968. (*Source:* F. Stuart Chapin, Jr., *Human Activity Patterns in the City: Things People Do in Time and Space* [New York: John Wiley, 1974], p. 140. Copyright 1974 by John Wiley.)

study. To some extent, the racial differences can be explained by income/class differences, but even after these were controlled, there were residual differences that can only be explained by racial segregation and the fact that blacks used a smaller proportion of the metropolitan area than did whites.

Class explained many of the racial differences that were found. Poorer, less educated whites spent their leisure time watching television, whereas better educated blacks had out-of-the-home uses of discretionary time that were more like their white counterparts. Other differences, notably the average spousal time spent in paid employment, could be explained by differential labor force participation rates rather than by ethnic or cultural differences *per se*.

One of the major limitations in the Chapin study was that family type could not be controlled by race or class. Therefore, it was impossible to tell whether the time and space constraints of poorer persons and of blacks were due not to race or class per se, but rather to differences in their family characteristics.

Another limitation of the Chapin study was that little attention was paid to locational differences. Do urbanites, suburbanites, and small-town residents differ in the amounts of time they allocate to different activities and in the spatial range of their activities? While Chapin was able to make some comparisons of time allocations in different types of places, using data from a 1969 SMSA sample survey, in these analyses he did not control for race, class, or family type, a procedure that would have been necessary to determine whether location made a residual difference.

Nevertheless, it is striking how few and relatively small the differences by location were, although all were in the expected direction. Clearly, most of the differences in work-time could be accounted for by the shorter travel distances between home and work for those living in small cities. That suburbanites spent less (average spousal) time at work and more in home care could be explained largely by the prevalence of young children in such households. Differences in the use of leisure time were explicable largely by class and race differences. Inner-city residents spent more time watching television, whereas suburban and fringe residents concentrated more on family activities, organizations, and socializing. Obviously, finer grained studies are needed if we are to judge the effects of various urban and nonurban environments on the space and time budgets of residents.

The group whose activities were subject to the greatest constraints (and who therefore should be most affected by poor location and environmental defects) were working mothers, as might be expected from our discussion in Chapter 9. The time and space budgets of families with employed mothers, as contrasted with families where the mother did not work outside the home, were compared in a path-breaking study by William Michelson.

Michelson's Study

Michelson reported his findings in *From Sun to Sun: Daily Obligations and Community Structure in the Lives of Employed Women and Their Fami-*

lies. [30] In this study, Michelson selected his sample of families with children in two separate stages. First, census tracts were systematically sampled to be representative of metropolitan Toronto, and then dwellings within them were randomly sampled to find families with the required characteristics. In some families the mother was employed; in others she was at home. Time and space budgets were collected from mothers, spouses if present, and older children. The study illustrates in dramatic fashion the time and space pressures on the most harassed segment of contemporary urbanites, employed women with children. (One fascinating finding was that their lives were even more heavily burdened when their spouses were present than when they were absent!)

The Michelson study added two significant innovations to earlier work. First, it collected data not only on adults but on children, whose patterns of urban living up to then had never been studied, and who still remain a largely unknown group. And second, it took a sophisticated view of space. Michelson paid special attention to the linkages among the trips individuals made, showing that what is important is not just time/cost from home for each errand, but also how easily errands can be combined in a single outing. Thus, the location of babysitters or day care centers *on the way to work* reduced travel time, as did shopping facilities on the way to other errands.

This alerts us to the fact that the convenience of paths through the city is as important as (if not more important than) the simple distance from place to place. Some new techniques for mapping linked activity patterns have recently been developed, and these appear quite promising for future research. *Point pattern analysis* [31] identifies patterns of clustering or regularities in sets of geographic locations. To my knowledge, urban sociologists have not yet applied these methods in their studies of paths through physical space.

THE ECOLOGY QUESTION REVISITED

In Part IV we have reviewed some of the research that has been undertaken to determine how life in cities differs from life in other spatial settings. We have tried to evaluate the extent to which ecological characteristics of the urban environment, such as size, density, and heterogeneity, influence the nature of social life and the kinds of human relationships in the city.

From the preceding chapters it is clear that the field of urban sociology has come a long way from the somewhat ambiguous formulation of the problem presented by Louis Wirth in 1938. His formulation was not necessarily incorrect, but it was incomplete and oversimplified. The question: "What is the effect of a particular environment on human behavior?" is, in the last analysis, unan-

---

[30] William Michelson, *From Sun to Sun: Daily Obligations and Community Structure in the Lives of Employed Women and Their Families* (Totowa, NJ: Rowman and Allanheld, 1985).

[31] Barry Boots and Arthur Getis, *Point Pattern Analysis*, Scientific Geography Series, vol. 8 (Newbury Park, CA: Sage Publications, 1988).

swerable. It depends on who is being affected. The reasonable question for urban sociologists to ask is: "How are physical and social space related—both to each other and to the social behavior that flows from and in turn helps to modify them?"

To assume that there is a simple and unidirectional causal connection between the physical environment and social behavior is to take an unwarranted and indeed misleading shortcut. Both the physical and social environments act as independent variables; and while they are undoubtedly connected, the relationship between them is not necessarily tight. Each may vary within limits to create an independent effect. Furthermore, cognitive and subjective interpretations always intervene between any environment—whether social or physical—and the responses it elicits from social actors. The thrust of our argument is that people who live in the same city may, in fact, be inhabiting very different worlds, not only because cities contain a variety of physical and social settings within their boundaries but also because people perceive and interact with these settings in significantly different ways—they "inhabit" different cities.

In Chapter 13 we reexamine the question of diversity within our metropolitan regions, introducing some new ways to classify particular configurations of social and physical space. We make recommendations for how these might be used to revive in meaningful and productive ways the now largely discredited "neighborhood case study." In Chapter 14 we reexamine the question of how physical and social space actually interact and suggest ways to study how different types of urban residents perceive their cities and how they actually use different parts of the urban environment. Note that we have altered the basic question from: "Is there an urban way of life?" to "What accounts for the variety of urban ways of life?"

The City Is Dead—Long Live the City

13

Changing Theories and the Research Agenda

W_e have seen in the preceding chapters how older theories and methods in urban sociology have been simultaneously undermined by changes in the *object of study* (that is, cities themselves have changed, both physically and in terms of the political economy of their production) and by changes in *the way people relate to city life,* now that urbanism has become so pervasive in American society. The appearance of saturation urbanization, documented in Chapter 6, has required a rethinking of many of the concepts that have previously guided theoretical and empirical work in urban sociology. Chief among the concepts that must be discarded is the urban-rural contrast.

THE DECLINING IMPORTANCE OF THE URBAN-RURAL CONTRAST

Less and less useful to us in our research is the hardy urban-rural continuum which, ever since the late nineteenth century, had provided the fundamental theoretical underpinning for the field. The neat and formerly powerful contrast between rural and urban ways of life has become increasingly blurred, as urbanism has spread into the farther reaches of the countryside and country, and as isolated rural farming places all but disappear in the process.

Furthermore, the different physical settings that were implied by the terms "urban "and "rural" (physical settings that were presumed to "cause" different life-styles) have increasingly become scrambled spatially and have actually been *internalized* within the diversified environments that our metropolitan regions now encompass. These different physical forms of settlement have been transposed to *within* complex metropolitan regions[1] which now contain:

1. *City centers,* with their dense slums, abandoned sections, ethnic enclaves, racial ghettos, "ports of entry" for new immigrants, guarded "citadels" of big business, and their associated apartment "castles" for the wealthy.

2. *Outer-city and older inlying suburban areas,* with their moderate-density apartment-house quarters for middle- and working-class tenants, their low-density single-family zones within the city proper, and a variety of types of suburban districts that now range across much of the class and family-type spectrum.[2] These also contain new forms of commercial, administrative, and industrial complexes, for the most part located along the outer edges of an earlier commutation band and concentrated at highway intersections.

3. *New outlying suburban and exurban zones* loosely tied to the metropolitan economy. While these quarters sometimes bear a superficial resemblance to rural settings, they may actually contain upper-income "second homes" and "gentleman farmer" estates, together with the people who offer services to the upper class; they also contain workers employed in decentralized factories, and, increasingly, in the back offices of firms whose headquarters remain in center cities, plus a sprinkling of retirees and part-time farmers.

4. *Special function towns and cities,* such as rurally located industrial and mining places, high-tech (mostly military) development and production centers, universities and research parks, retirement communities, and the like, where ways of life are not so much "small town" as they are scaled-down versions of the modern metropolis or its quarters.

Given this change in the nature of "cities" in the United States, we need to find new ways to categorize and describe the types of communities into which our population has been sifted and sorted.

---

[1]Jack Meltzer has termed these "metroplexes." See his *Metropolis to Metroplex: The Social and Spatial Planning of Cities* (Baltimore: Johns Hopkins University Press, 1984).

[2]See the work of Mark Baldassare for the variety of suburban types and the problems they face. His study of Orange County, California, exposes the complexities and problems in even the best of them. See *Trouble in Paradise: The Suburban Transformation in America* (New York: Columbia University Press, 1984).

NEW WAYS TO DESCRIBE SOCIAL AND PHYSICAL SPACE

With this new diversification of living environments has come a need for concepts more precise than such broad terms as rural, urban, suburban, or even exurban. How many terms we shall need, of course, will depend upon our purposes. Some promising methodological advances have recently been made, however, which point the way to a new approach to an old question.

Claritas, a market research firm, has recently developed a system that transcribes, onto maps of zip-code areas, data that have been drawn from census reports, consumer preference surveys, analyses of sales data, and studies of past voting behavior.[3] Using *cluster analysis* (a method very similar to factor analysis), they have reduced these data to delimit *40 distinguishably different types of urban and rural and small-town residential zones* which they claim exhaust the major variations. Each type has its own characteristic mix of residents (along the three dimensions that factorial ecologies had so clearly separated: class, family, and ethnicity) and its own life-style patterns.

Table 13.1 gives a thumbnail description of these 40 types of residential environments and estimates the proportion of U.S. households that were living in them in 1987. We have regrouped the Claritas types in a rough manner, sorting them by their physical settings (center city, suburban, exurban, midsized town, small town, or rural) and by the salient economic, family-cycle stage, and ethnic/racial characteristics of their inhabitants.

These 40 types of residential communities presumably differentiate (or predict) quite different ways of life that reflect not only differential economic power but particular sets of needs, attitudes, consumer preferences, and even interactional behavior. To some extent, we might say that Claritas, which collated data from many more sources than have been available to urban ecologists and which applied the method of cluster analysis to reduce the data, has solved one of the methodological problems originally set in urban ecology. Although Weiss's report on their findings frequently falls victim to the ecological fallacy, Claritas has apparently succeeded in delimiting something close to the "natural areas" envisaged in urban sociology when the field just began, and has applied this concept not only to city neighborhoods alone but to the entire country.

The purposes of their work were, admittedly, quite different from those of urban sociology. They wanted (1) to guide businesses in deciding exactly where to locate outlets and what goods to carry in them; (2) to help designers of marketing and advertising campaigns fine-tune the sales appeals they will make through direct mailings; and even (3) to assist political strategists in planning which issues candidates for political office should stress in areas with different types of constituents. These purposes are explicitly related not to social scientific ends but to other "more practical" ones. However, the study does provide social scientists with possibilities for reaching a new level of understanding of how ways of life and characteristics of residents vary systematically in different

---

[3]Michael Weiss, *The Clustering of America* (New York: Harper & Row, Tilden Press, 1988).

Table 13.1 THE 40 CLUSTERS OF LIFE-STYLES FOUND BY CLARITAS CORPORATION IN ITS ZIP-CODE ZONE ANALYSIS

Cluster name	Thumbnail description of characteristics	Percentage of U.S. households in cluster*
Upper income, mostly white, mostly suburban		
1. Blue-blood Estates	America's wealthiest neighborhoods, includes suburban homes	1.1
2. Furs and Station Wagons	New money in metropolitan bedroom suburbs	3.2
3. Pools and Patios	Older, upper-middle-class suburban communities	3.4
4. Gray Power	Upper-middle-class retirement communities	2.9
High income, mostly white center city		
5. Urban Gold Coast	Upscale urban high-rise zones	0.5
6. Money and Brains	Posh big-city enclaves of town houses, condos, and apartments	0.9
Subtotal (1–6)		**12.0**
Comfortable income, some ethnics, mostly suburban or exurban		
7. Black Enterprise	Predominantly black middle- and upper-middle-class neighborhoods	0.8
8. Two More Rungs	Comfortable multi-ethnic suburbs	0.7
9. Blue-Chip Blues	The wealthiest blue-collar suburbs	6.0
10. Young Suburbia	Child-rearing outlying suburbs	5.3
11. Blue-Collar Nursery	Middle-class child-rearing towns	2.2
12. God's Country	Upscale frontier boomtowns	2.7
13. New Homesteaders	Exurban boom towns of young, midscale families	4.2
Comfortable income, mostly single or without children		
14. Young Influentials	Yuppie, fringe-city condo, and apartment developments	2.9
15. Bohemian Mix	Inner-city Bohemian enclaves like Greenwich Village, N.Y.C.	1.1
16. New Beginnings	Fringe-city areas of singles complexes, garden apartments, and trim bungalows	4.3
Heterogeneous midsized towns		
17. Towns and Gowns	America's college towns	1.2
18. Middle America	Midscale, midsize towns	3.2
Subtotal (7–18)		**34.6**

Table 13.1 (*Continued*)

Cluster name	Thumbnail description of characteristics	Percentage of U.S. households in cluster*
	Working-class, mostly suburban	
19. Levittown, U.S.A.	Aging post–World War II tract suburbs	3.1
20. Rank and File	Older blue-collar industrial suburbs	1.4
21. Norma Rae–Ville	Lower-middle-class milltowns and industrial suburbs, primarily in South	2.3
	Working-class, mostly urban	
22. Old Yankee Rows	Working-class rowhouse districts	1.6
23. New Melting Pot	New immigrant neighborhoods, primarily in the nation's port cities	0.9
24. Emergent Minorities	Predominantly black, working-class city neighborhoods	1.7
25. Heavy Industry	Lower working-class districts in the nation's older industrial cities	2.8
26. Single City Blues	Downscale, urban, singles districts	3.3
27. Smalltown Downtown	Inner-city districts of small industrial cities	2.5
	Small, lower-income mixed towns and villages	
28. Coalburg and Corntown	Small towns based on light industry and farming	2.0
29. Agribusiness	Small towns surrounded by large-scale farms and ranches	2.1
30. Shotguns and Pickups	Crossroads villages serving the nation's lumber and breadbasket needs	1.9
31. Golden Ponds	Rustic cottage communities located near coasts, mountains, lakes	5.2
32. Mines and Mills	Struggling steeltowns and mining villages	2.8
Subtotal (19–32)		**33.6**
	Urban poverty areas, largely minority	
33. Downtown Dixie-Style	Aging, predominantly black neighborhoods, typically in southern cities	3.4
34. Hispanic Mix	America's Barrios	1.9
35. Public Assistance	America's inner-city ghettos	3.1

(*Continued*)

Table 13.1 (*Continued*)

Cluster name	Thumbnail description of characteristics	Percentage of U.S. households in cluster*
Rural poverty areas, mixed ethnic/race		
36. Grain Belt**	The nation's most sparsely populated rural communities	1.3
37. Back-Country	Remote, downscale farm towns	3.4
38. Share Croppers	Primarily southern hamlets	4.0
39. Tobacco Roads	Predominantly black farm communities throughout the South	1.2
40. Hard Scrabble	The nation's poorest rural settlements	1.5
Subtotal (33–40)		19.8
Total U.S. Households		100.0

*It is not legitimate to use these percentages to generalize to the class structure of the United States. First, the percentages refer to households, not people, and poorer households tend to be larger, on average, than wealthier ones. Therefore, zones that contain the richest Americans account for a smaller percentage of the total population than the table suggests, whereas zones in which the poorest Americans are concentrated actually account for a higher percentage of the total population than indicated in the table. Second, the totals refer to *all* households residing in the 40 different types of communities. Not every household in each zip-code area, however, has the characteristics of the area's average. Indeed, even small zip-code areas may harbor highly diverse populations. Readers must therefore beware of the notorious "ecological fallacy," especially in the middle ranks of status.

**May not be classifiable with poverty areas.

Source: Michael J. Weiss, *The Clustering of America* (New York: Harper & Row, 1988), pp. 4–5. We have regrouped their 40 clusters into class, family, and ethnicity/race types, have sorted them as city, suburb, small town, and rural, and have subtotaled categories kept separate in the original study.

physical settings. It is tragic that the modest funding hitherto available for scholarly urban research never permitted it to conduct the same kind of comprehensive investigation of urban differentiation that Claritas has done. Comparable funding could have made it possible to answer the important questions the field posed from the beginning but which it could not answer from the limited data available.

Better funded, Claritas found a way to combine information on the social characteristics of residents—their class position, their family status, and their race/ethnicity—with information on the physical characteristics of the places in which they live—center city, suburban or rural, densely settled apartment districts, sparsely settled areas of single-family homes—and to crosscut both of these with the regional locations and economic functions of the communities themselves. All of this makes great intuitive sense, given what we know about contemporary American communities. Furthermore, their ability to demonstrate a predictive connection between these syndromes of characteristics of people and place and actual behavior—even if it is, thus far, only what brand of catsup is preferred (to unkindly satirize their important work)—offers great promise. Urban sociologists should be able to use their categories to study behaviors they deem more relevant.

One very important finding from the Claritas analysis—and one with significant implications for urban sociology—is that there is no clear correspondence between the life-styles they distinguish and any simple locational distinction among urban, suburban, and nonmetropolitan areas. While each cluster of consumers tends to exercise a "typical" preference for certain locations and living environments, a far more fine-grained system of sifting and sorting has evidently gone on, one which is increasingly contingent on choice. (We will return to this point later.)

Another clear and important conclusion is that although the 40 different types of districts are certainly not distributed at random throughout the various regions of the United States (see Figures 13.1–13.3 for examples of regional distribution), the ways of life within districts of each type, even though they may be widely separated in terms of geographic region, have more in common with one another than they have with ways of life in other types of zones in their immediate vicinity. This is striking evidence of the nationalization of culture in the United States.

These congruencies suggest one way to overcome the problem of insufficient funding for social science research. A large (but not enormous) number of detailed ethnographic community studies, conducted in a carefully selected set of small areas (possibly chosen to represent sharply contrasting "clusters" identified through the Claritas method), could be used to unravel the complexity of causation and even to resolve the debate between the ecological and compositionalist hypotheses, identified in Chapter 10.

Such studies would need to collect *comparable data* on values, attitudes, perceptions, and specific behavior (e.g., social networks and time and space budgets) from residents who vary by age, sex, marital status, family responsibilities, discretionary monetary and time resources, ethnic backgrounds, subcultural life-styles, and the like, in each of the different types of zones. Studies that investigate why particular types of people have chosen particular locations and types of housing, the constraints under which they operated in making such choices, the ways these individuals conceptualize the urban environment and the attitudes they hold toward specific parts of it, and their behavior, both within and beyond their own districts, might reveal how social and physical space are really related.

Of course, the Claritas methodology does not solve all problems. As in earlier ecological research, the power of the Claritas categories to predict social behavior remains contingent upon the relative homogeneity within their sub-areas. It is not possible to escape from this problem, which has plagued urban ecology since the field first began. Relatively homogeneous zip-code areas, like relatively homogeneous census tracts, are easier to study than mixed areas. But we know from Chapter 11 that there are many physical portions of the metropolitan region that bring together populations that are not homogeneous in their social and demographic characteristics. This is especially the case in those

Figure 13.1 National distribution of "Young Suburbia" (top) and "Urban Gold Coast" (bottom) zip code zones, according to Claritas. (*Source:* Michael J. Weiss, *The Clustering of America* [New York: Tilden Press, 1988], p. 7. Copyright © 1988 by Michael J. Weiss. Reprinted by permission of Harper & Row, Publishers, Inc.)

center city districts (and now, even in inlying suburbs) that are undergoing rapid change. In such cases—when an area in being "gentrified," when occupancy is changing from white to black, when an ethnic ghetto such as Chinatown is expanding into adjacent zones, and the like—several population subgroups (or Claritas "types") coexist within a census tract or zip-code zone.

Important questions for urban sociologists are raised by such diversity and coexistence, which cannot be answered by any typology. In these cases, what we really want to know is not what the average characteristics of an area are, but rather: What are the interactional patterns among residents of very diverse kinds? What are the conflicts such diversity generates, and how are they resolved? How does life in diversely composed neighborhoods differ from that in more homogeneously constituted neighborhoods?

ZQ 37: HISPANIC MIX

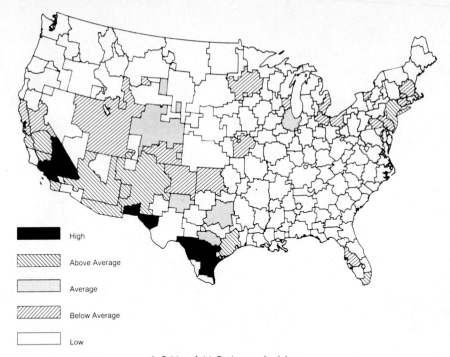

High

Above Average

Average

Below Average

Low

1.9% of U.S. households
Primary age range: 18–34
Median household income: $16,270
Median home value: $49,533

Thumbnail Demographics
poor inner-city enclaves
multi-unit housing
predominantly Hispanic singles and families
grade-school educations
blue-collar jobs

Politics
Predominant ideology: moderate
1984 presidential vote: Reagan (51%)
Key issues: social programs, foreign-policy doves

Sample Neighborhoods
West San Antonio, Texas (78207)
East Los Angeles, California (90022)
Bushwick, Brooklyn, New York (11232)
Pilsen, Chicago, Illinois (60608)
Riverside, Miami, Florida (33135)
Hoboken, New Jersey (07030)

Figure 13.2 National distribution of "Hispanic Mix" zip code zones, according to Claritas. (*Source:* Michael J. Weiss, *The Clustering of America* [New York: Tilden Press, 1988], p. 380. Copyright © 1988 by Michael J. Weiss. Reprinted by permission of Harper & Row, Publishers, Inc.)

ZQ 40: PUBLIC ASSISTANCE

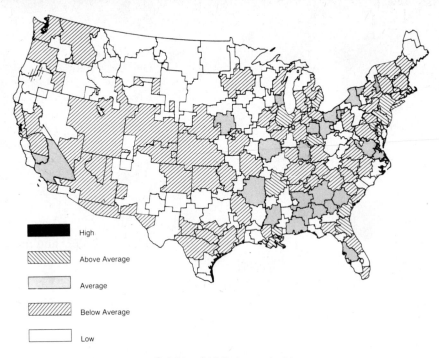

■	High
▨	Above Average
▨	Average
▨	Below Average
□	Low

3.1% of U.S. households
Primary age groups: 18–24 and 65+
Median household income: $10,804
Median home value: $28,340

Thumbnail Demographics
inner-city ghettos
multi-unit housing
predominantly black singles and one-parent families
grade-school educations
mixed blue-collar and service jobs

Politics
Predominant ideology: moderate
1984 presidential vote: Mondale (83%)
Key issues: poverty, jobs

Sample Neighborhoods
West Philadelphia, Pennsylvania (19122)
Watts, Los Angeles, California (90002)
Fox Creek, Detroit, Michigan (48215)
Hyde Park, Chicago, Illinois (60653)
Downtown Louisville, Kentucky (40202)
Morrisania, South Bronx, New York (10456)

Figure 13.3 National distribution of "Public Assistance" zip code zones, according to Claritas. (*Source:* Michael J. Weiss, *The Clustering of America* [New York: Tilden Press, 1988], p. 390. Copyright © 1988 by Michael J. Weiss. Reprinted by permission of Harper & Row, Publishers, Inc.)

We still lack methods to study such communities, even though they appear to be increasing in our large cities. Clearly, this issue remains high on any new research agenda. This is why network analysis appears to offer so promising a method. Particularly where residents with very different social characteristics share the same physical space, it is essential to "unpack" the multiple communities that coexist and that on occasion come into conflict with one another within a given area. Rather than assuming that residents constitute a "community," we must learn to trace the actual interactions that occur selectively, both within the common physical space and between subgroups in the neighborhood and their counterparts in other neighborhoods.

Furthermore, in order to select the neighborhoods that are to be systematically compared and to identify the types of data that need to be collected, a far more sophisticated model for the relationship between social and physical space is absolutely essential. Once we have given up the easy assumptions of ecological determinancy, we must develop new concepts and methods appropriate to the study of how space affects human behavior. In Chapter 14, therefore, we set forth such a model, relating the model's concepts to specific research methods appropriate for studying them. One reason why such new methods and approaches are needed is that the correlations between physical and social space, which could perhaps have been taken for granted when urban sociology just began as a field, have broken down. The new megalopolitan arenas now contain mixes and diversities that were formerly more segregated in space.

NEW BASES FOR DIVERSIFICATION

Social space, like physical space, is now more diverse and less rigidly segregated. Take, for example, one of the major desiderata of "urbanism as a way of life," namely, cultural heterogeneity. Whereas formerly, the causes of social differentiation could be attributed largely to certain objective characteristics that residents *had*—their places of origin (ethnic descent, rural or urban place of birth), their ascribed social characteristics (race, age, gender), their partially achieved status (occupation, education, class position)—today, differences in social behavior are increasingly linked to *life-style choices* that are only in part dependent upon preexisting categories. Choice operates to diversify the effects of many of these differences. Knowing whether a respondent is a man or a woman no longer tells you whether or not the person works for pay. Knowing that someone is a lawyer does not tell you how he or she will dress or behave. Knowing the ethnicity of an individual does not allow you to predict values or beliefs. There has been diversification *within* those categories.

Decisions about whether or when to marry and whether to stay married, whether or not to have children, decisions about the type and degree of urbanity one seeks and the trade-offs in amenities one is willing to make, decisions about housing tenure (to buy or to rent) and about living in an apartment or in some other kind of building, even decisions about the people one wishes to associate with (kin, friends, or work associates) have become the true differentiators *within* categories of persons who may have the same objective social characteristics. While it is still clearly the case that those with the most economic and political power are best situated to exercise those choices, and that such freedom of choice may be highly constrained for those with few economic and political resources, even members of the "underclass" exhibit variations in life-style that go beyond docile acceptance of powerlessness. Some deprived youngsters grow up to become drug peddlers and petty thieves, while others become bank tellers or even sociologists.

Even so simple an analytic unit as "the neighborhood" turns out to be less uniform and "objective" than we formerly thought. For some people, a neighborhood is a mere block-face or single apartment building, where relations can range from very intimate (dependent upon a dense network of mutual assistance and heavy social pressure to ensure conformity) to highly impersonal and formal (as when relative strangers organize to patrol at night, or to pay for a guard or for janitorial services). For some, the neighborhood may be the few blocks surrounding the residence they have occupied for a long time, building up networks of association and support through locally oriented shops, schools, churches, and social or political organizations. For others, the neighborhood may consist merely of the vicinity around their own dwelling units, which is "used" for convenience but concerning which residents make minimal demands for relative safety and accessibility and invest neither time nor emotion.

For some "locals," the larger neighborhood or even the city can take on an important symbolic and social meaning, serving as a source of identity ("I come from Grosse Pointe"), an outlet for energy ("I serve on the zoning board"), or even an arena in which to form "intimate secondary relationships," which Peggy Wireman suggests now characterize many of the ways Americans relate to one another in "communities of limited liability."[4] At the opposite extreme are those itinerant cosmopolitans whose homes are mere "pads" from which

---

[4]See Peggy Wireman, *Urban Neighborhoods, Networks, and Families: New Forms for Old Values* (Lexington, MA: D. C. Heath, 1984). According to Wireman, intimate secondary relationships are those in which there is "intense involvement, warmth, intimacy, sense of belonging, and rapport; mutual knowledge of character; minimal sharing of personal information; minimal socializing; involvement of the individual rather than the family; a commitment that is limited in time and scope and with a relatively low cost of withdrawal; a focus on specific rather than diffuse purposes; consideration of public rather than private matters; and a preference for public meeting places" (p. 3). Many local boards, booster associations, PTAs, Little Leagues, and urban gardening groups may exhibit such qualities, and may offer a gratifying sense of community, at least for the few who play active roles in them. In his early book on the local press, Morris Janowitz called these "communities of limited liability." See his *The Community Press in an Urban Setting: The Social Elements of Urbanism*, 2d ed. (Chicago: University of Chicago Press, 1967). Albert Hunter and Gerald Suttles developed this concept in greater depth in their jointly authored chapter, "The Expanding Community of Limited Liability," pp. 44–81 in Gerald Suttles, *The Social Construction of Communities* (Chicago: University of Chicago Press, 1972).

they make their connections to a wider world, without connecting to their immediate surroundings.

Furthermore, the "communities" that have real significance to people need not be locality-based. Perhaps the most extreme example of intimate secondary relations can be found in a midwestern group organized around medieval jousting. It has only periodic existence, as when members gather to celebrate King Richard's Fair outside Chicago. The participants adopt fictitious personae, taking on invented names, genealogies, medieval places of origin, and occupations. They sew or purchase clothing to dress their parts, donning the empire gowns or suits of metal or tunics appropriate to their imagined stations. Participants are not allowed to use their own names; must conceal their real identities, backgrounds, or occupations; and are cautioned not to socialize with one another in the everyday world. And yet, the enormous commitments of time, energy, and money that go into creating this fantasy world are obviously compensated for by satisfaction.[5] Somewhat less extreme are athletic teams and theatrical or dance groups, where intra-group status may be quite incommensurate with "real world" position.

For many, the workplace serves the function of providing intimate secondary relationships. This has always been true for male blue-collar "career" workers, as evidenced in studies that have been made in such workplaces as factories and steel mills,[6] but it also seems true for women workers. The office sociability of white-collar women is readily acknowledged; but when Patricia Zavella interviewed Chicanas about their part-time and intermittent employment in a California canning factory (certainly unpleasant work), the women repeatedly responded that they liked working not merely for the income but for the social contacts their workplace provided.[7] At the opposite end of the class spectrum are the upper-class women volunteer workers who were studied by Arlene Daniels.[8] These women have made careers out of unpaid philanthropic work that involves planning and participating in social activities. Intimate secondary relationships also exist in groups with less social legitimacy; occupational networks exist among drug dealers, as is evidenced by a unique study done by Patricia Adler.[9]

Communities, therefore, may be spatial or nonspatial. They may be residential, occupational, or interest-oriented. They may be linked to a given locale or

---

[5] As describe in an unpublished research paper written in 1986 by Joan Vitek, then a graduate student at Northwestern University.

[6] See, for example, William Kornblum, *Blue Collar Community* (Chicago: University of Chicago Press, 1974), and David Halle, *America's Working Man: Home, Work, and Politics Among Blue Collar Property Owners* (Chicago: University of Chicago Press, 1982).

[7] See Patricia Zavella, *Women's Work and Chicano Families: Cannery Workers of the Santa Clara Valley* (Ithaca, NY: Cornell University Press, 1987).

[8] Arlene Daniels, *Invisible Careers* (Chicago: University of Chicago Press, 1988).

[9] Patricia Adler, *Wheeling and Dealing: An Ethnography of an Upper Level Drug Dealing and Smuggling Community* (New York: Columbia University Press, 1985).

they may range widely across state and even national borders. The major point to be recognized is that they are not *given* to us in mechanical fashion by the neighborhoods in which we reside. Rather, the communities in which our significant lives take place are socially *constructed* by differential association, even though their construction is clearly constrained. These communities are, in Georg Simmel's pregnant phrase, social circles that may or may not overlap. Individuals and groups *shape and bound* these communities in highly diverse and individualistic ways that may bear much or little relationship to the way urban space is arranged. This, indeed, is why network analysis has proven so necessary a research tool for urban sociologists.

What is true of the social environment is even truer of the physical or built environment. Since a second crucial development in the new megalopolitan areas appearing in the United States is the diffuseness of their physical boundaries, there is less and less congruence between these units and either how social relations are organized or the way economic and political institutions are structured.[10]

Such localities as the neighborhood, the city, the suburb, the metropolitan area, the county, the state, even the federal government, are no longer closed systems, nor are these administrative units coterminous with the forces that govern our lives. This has led to a true crisis in governance. It should therefore not be surprising that official statistical, administrative, or electoral boundaries fail not only to conform to "natural" boundaries, but even to delimit comparable zones for governmental purposes. Many years ago, Robert Wood studied the 1400 administrative "governments" of the New York metropolitan area.[11] These included everything from police precincts, school districts, and other mini-units, to metropolitan-wide mosquito abatement agencies and even organizations whose jurisdictional charge crossed state borders—demonstrating how impossible it would be to coordinate their activities and plans, even if a metropolitan government were established.

Moreover, many of the factors one would like to control and coordinate are no longer within the hands of local governments, even if they were to become metropolitan-wide and coherent units. Decisions to invest or disinvest in certain states and regions, to move plants from one place to another, to create jobs or to destroy them, to feed some taxing localities and starve others, lie not with government planners but with large conglomerate firms (often with overseas operations as well). Local initiatives to create incentives may serve to reallocate some individual plants, but only when no other more overriding considerations are at stake.

---

[10]This is a particularly serious issue because, as Ira Katznelson has so astutely observed, politics in the United States has generally been organized around localities of residence, rather than around the class interests that are the dominant organizing principle of, for example, European political struggles. See his *City Trenches: Urban Politics and the Patterning of Class in the United States* (Chicago: University of Chicago Press, 1981).

[11]Robert Wood, *1400 Governments: The Political Economy of the New York Metropolitan Region* (Cambridge, MA: Harvard University Press, 1961).

Local units now share their powers with counties, states, and increasingly, with the federal government.[12] As we have shown in Chapter 8, the involvement of the federal government in regulating the tax structure for individuals and businesses, in manipulating interest rates and the money supply, in redistributing wealth through tax incentives and welfare functions, and in helping to provide such collective goods and services as highways, hospitals, housing, and schools, have all tended to reduce local self-sufficiency and autonomy. Since these subventions usually come earmarked for specific purposes, local capital budgeting consists of plugging gaps and bearing costs of upkeep for items generated at higher levels of the system.

But even at the national level, there is only vague correspondence between boundaries and the forces that determine what goes on within them. In today's global economy, the big investments cross frontiers, and in today's global politics, alliances—military and otherwise—transcend the borders of political units, leading some to speak of the "decline of the nation-state."

All these changes have created environments for which older theories and research agendas have proven increasingly inadequate and even deceptive, because they point us in wrong directions. New sources of data must be tapped and new theoretical frameworks must be devised to address the two basic problematics of urban sociology, which remain:

1. *The city as a consumed environment:* How is it consumed and with what consequences? This is the problematic of how the built environment, in all its complexity, affects people having different psychological, social, and cultural characteristics.
2. *The city as a produced environment:* What produces it? This is the problematic of the political economy of space and the built environment.

Chapter 14 attempts to build upon the knowledge already presented to develop some theoretical concepts that could, if duly researched, move the field of urban sociology to a new level of synthesis and understanding with respect to the first question. It focuses on ways to study how space in the city is *consumed,* and how the consumers actively participate in the psychosociological *creation* of the physical and social environments that influence their behavior.

Chapter 15 examines in greater detail how the built environment is actually *produced,* exploring the roles played by various interacting agents—builders, investors, political actors, businessmen and industrialists of different types, urban planners, legal structures, local, state, and federal programs, and so on—in creating our urban environments. It poses, although clearly cannot answer, the crucial question of how we can get the kinds of cities we want.

---

[12]See Mark Gottdiener's *The Decline of Urban Politics: Political Theory and the Crisis of the Local State* (Newbury Park, CA: Sage Publications, 1987).

Chapter
14

A Paradigm for Studying Environment and Behavior in the City

*I*n Chapter 10, three alternative explanations were set forth, each claiming to account for the wide variation in ways of life that appear in different urban settings. The first of these is the somewhat deterministic explanation offered by traditional or neoclassical urban ecology, which suggests that differences in the size, density, and heterogeneity of settlements account for differences in forms of social interaction. The causal structure of this explanation is that certain objectively quantifiable aspects of the *physical* environment lead directly to specific forms of human behavior, almost as a reflex. The second, somewhat less deterministic explanation is that offered by pure *culturalists,* who argue that differences in social behavior are better explained by reference to the objective cultural characteristics of the actors themselves than by reference to the physical settings in which they find themselves. In this explanation, social norms and patterns of interacting in space are seen as relatively independent of the way space is arranged. The causal line moves from cultural norms to behavior, with physical space only a minor intervening variable.

The third explanation, called *compositionalist,* puts these two models together, arguing that populations with various characteristics (including cultural traits) select, insofar as feasible, physical environments which suit their needs, and that their behavior is then modified by the characteristic life-styles of those around them. Thus, both the physical and the social environments in which

342

people live modify how they use space. This more sophisticated causal model moves from cultural and individual characteristics to choices of physical environment and then to social behavior, which depends on the characteristics of their co-residents.

As Claude Fischer has shown in *To Dwell Among Friends*, the compositionalist approach is very promising. It needs, however, to be taken further than Fischer has done in his important work. It has the potential to allow us to integrate findings from factorial and cluster analyses (such as the 40 neighborhood types identified by Claritas and described in Chapter 13) with those from network analysis and activity systems, treated in Chapter 12. However, because it continues to examine the actions of *individuals* rather than social *groups*, it leaves unexplored the *process* whereby space is or is not perceived and utilized in the construction of community. While we shall not be able to describe this complicated process here, the purpose of Chapter 14 is to lay out some concepts and associated methodologies which, if pursued in future research, might yield valuable insights into it.

At the end of Chapter 12 we argued that the question asked by traditional urban ecology, namely, "What are the effects on human behavior of particular physical environments?" was remarkably naive and unanswerable. We recommended a far more general and less deterministic formulation, namely, "How are physical and social space related, both to each other and to behavior?" Now we propose to look at the specific variables needed to explore the very complex interrelationship between social and physical spaces. What types of data are required? And how should they be analyzed to yield meaningful answers to the basic question of the relationship between physical-social space and social behavior? To answer these questions, a far more complex model will be required than the one traditional urban ecology provided.[1]

A MODEL FOR STUDYING SOCIAL AND PHYSICAL SPACE

Figure 14.1 presents such a model. The circular arrangement in the diagram is intended to show the continuous feedback between elements in the physical and the social environments, with neither considered fully independent. The concentric rings are arranged from the most general causes (the outside rings) to their most specific and action-connected effects (the inner circle). However, causality moves in both directions. Reading the rings from outside to inside, one traces the complex process through which the environment shapes behavior. Reading the rings from the center to the outside, however, one sees the effect that experience has on perceptions and cognitions and thus upon the general environment itself. The new terms used in this model are defined in Table 14.1 and will be explained further in the section that follows.

---

[1]A preliminary version of the present chapter appeared earlier in Janet Abu-Lughod, "A Paradigm for Studying Environment and Behavior in the City," pp. 268–287 in Lenore Borzak, ed., *Field Study: A Sourcebook for Experiential Learning* (Beverly Hills, CA: Sage Publications, 1981).

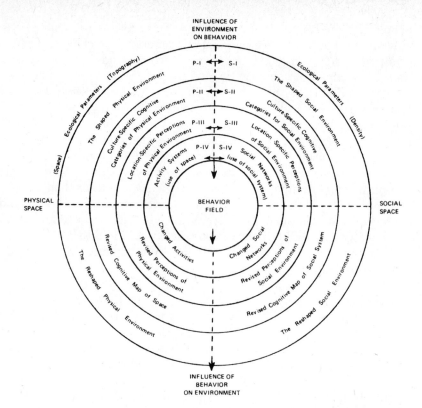

Figure 14.1 Model of the relationship between the social and physical environments and human behavior. (*Source:* Original with author but has appeared in Janet Abu-Lughod, "A Paradigm for Studying Environment and Behavior," in Lenore Borzak, ed., *Field Studies: A Sourcebook of Experiential Learning* [Beverly Hills, CA: Sage Publications, 1981], p. 270. Copyright 1981 by Sage Publications, Inc. Reprinted with the permission of the publisher.)

In Table 14.1 we distinguish at least four levels of analysis along two different dimensions. First, we distinguish conceptually the physical environment from the social environment, while recognizing that the two will be interrelated in a manner which is always a matter for empirical investigation. Second, within each of these dimensions we distinguish four levels of increasing specificity of influence upon individual behavior. Here we define each of these terms more precisely.

Level I: Objective Space

The most general influence, in the sense that it imposes ultimate constraining limitations upon human behavior, is the objective environment, including not

Table 14.1 TYPES OF SPACE AND APPROPRIATE METHODS FOR STUDYING THEM

Level of analysis	Type of space	Appropriate method
Level I Objective map of social and physical space as shaped by culture and technology	Real Space Generalized	Physical space mapped by time-cost, accessibility, etc. Social structure space mapped by macro-sociological methods
Level II Cognitive maps of social and physical space as shaped by culture and subculture	Awareness or Exposure Space	Concepts and categories used for placement of physical environment stimulus and concepts and categories used for social placement
Level III Perceptual maps of social and physical space as affected by location of perceiver in physical and social space		Mental maps of the physical environment; subjective maps of the social system
Level IV Behavior maps in physical and social space	Participation Space	Activity systems in physical space; social networks in social space

only nonhuman features of the landscape, both natural and man-made, but human and social features as well. If there is a real world, it is described at this level of analysis. The legitimate starting point for such a description, however, would never be nature in the abstract, but rather, environment (both social and physical) as shaped by people. While this is occasionally referred to in the literature as the "built environment," that term carries too limiting a meaning. We prefer to refer to the "shaped environment."

Objective Physical Space   For any group of persons exposed to it, objective physical space is the physical environment of that group as it has been molded and modified by culture, including but not confined to technology. Thus, climate, temperature, and prevailing winds are less important than differences in climate, temperature, and air quality created through differential modification—heating plants, air conditioning, atmospheric pollution, and the like. Except in societies existing under the most primitive technologies, the question "What is the effect of climate on human irritability?" is somewhat inappropriate, if that climate is differentially modified before it exercises its influence. Hot, humid temperatures may have one effect in a poverty area, another in the air-conditioned Pentagon. Whether or not climate is a significant variable depends upon the research problem; it cannot be judged a priori.

Similarly, whereas terrain and topography are certainly important variables in objective physical space, except among primitive hunting bands it makes more sense to study the work required to overcome frictions of topography at present levels of technology. The same is true for distance. It is not absolute distance in feet or miles, but accessibility in time and cost in the shaped physical environment that is the legitimate variable to be studied, at least in societies where transportation and communication advances have significantly distorted linear space.

Ecologists have focused on the natural physical environment and have sought causal connections between it and human behavior. Yet, our society has reshaped the natural environment so drastically, especially in cities, that it is only the shaped physical environment that impinges upon human actors. Therefore, the old maps of physical space drawn by geographers—with contour lines and distances marked in Euclidian space—no longer reflect the physical environment to which we are exposed. It should scarcely surprise us, then, that only weak and tenuous correlations have been found between these grossly inaccurate "reconstructions" of the physical environment and either the social environment or interpersonal behavior. The first challenge—and one increasingly met by the "new geography"—is to provide better maps of the physical environment that will capture its transformed character. The "principle of the least effort," as conceptualized by George Zipf, still applies in the physical world; we have simply lost our ability to test it by failing to measure and map distance realistically.

Objective Social Space   Objective social space for any group of people is the social environment of that group, as it has been molded and indeed created by culture. As is true for objective physical space, our maps of the social environment need to reflect this. The traditional urban ecology variables of numbers, density, and heterogeneity do not directly cause social behavior. It is not the number of persons per se that constitutes the social environment, but rather their distribution by type and their differences in organization. It is not physical density per se that affects behavior; it is the density of interactions, and who it is that interacts, with what frequency, and with what degree of organization.

It is true that the distribution of persons and the organization of their roles and interactions are not natural "ecological" variables, any more than a transportation system is a natural feature of physical space. Like transportation, social organization is necessarily a part of the *shaped* environment—this time, the shaped *social* environment. This is inevitable. Except in the hypothetical case of a horde with a totally undifferentiated social structure, the question "What is the effect of numbers or density upon human irritability and the probability of a behavioral sink?" is, if not totally inappropriate, at least of extremely limited significance. Numbers have one effect when individuals have only unstructured or unstable social organization to program their interactions (as in a mob), another where interactions are structurally and normatively integrated (as in schools, a Fourth of July pageant, or a church meeting). Distance in social space, like that in physical space, is also a product not of natural features so much as cultural features. Like numbers, social distance must be studied in terms of social meanings if it is to reflect accurately the constraints and limitations of the "objective" world.

Sociology has some highly appropriate tools and concepts for the measurement of objective social space. Chief among these is the concept of *social distance.* Interestingly enough, this concept has been operationalized in such a way that it actually measures the accessibility of various groups to one another with respect to social interactions of increasing intimacy. Two groups are considered socially close if little work would be required to overcome the social space between them—that is, if members of these groups put up little resistance to interaction. Groups that are considered socially distant are those for which considerable work would be required to overcome the resistance they feel toward one another. The reader will immediately recognize the similarity between this conceptualization and that of physical distance described earlier.

Social distance is not the only measure available for mapping social space. Actually, all attempts by social scientists to describe the social structure of given groups or societies, to identify pecking orders and hierarchies, to develop the categories into which individuals and groups are classified by a society, to identify the institutionalized channels of recurring interaction—in short, much of the ongoing activity of social scientists—is directly addressed to mapping shaped social space. And it is always this shaped social environment that impinges upon us and influences our behavior.

The old maps drawn by ecological determinists—with points for people and the physical distance between the points denoting social density—fail miserably as reflections of the social environment to which persons are exposed and to which they react. Social distance, rather than physical distance, has become the most potent determiner of differential interaction. Where choice is limited by physical isolation, human interactions cross social lines inadvertently and involuntarily; as scale increases, so do choice and volition. Just as in the area of physical space we recognized the need for new maps which reflect the transformed physical environment, so in social space we need more accurate reconstructions of the effective social environment. We need maps of a nongeographic kind—tables, diagrams, network charts—that capture the transformed character of social space.

In Table 14.1 we have used the term "objective" in relation to the social and physical environments to be analyzed on Level I because their reconstruction is relatively independent of any particular subjective vantage point.[2] At this level we are talking about the generalized environment, or, to put it more

---

[2]It is patently impossible to design maps of the social and physical environments of a society without using some conceptual symbols and categories as given by language and culture. In that respect, no map is ever objective in the sense of being perspective-free. Cognitive and perceptual categories are unavoidably involved in the objective maps of physical and social space drawn by geographers and social scientists. Presumably, however, the categories and perceptions they use are generally applicable across wide ranges of cultural and physical conditions. Thus, kinship categories can be used to map social space in both an American city and the Australian bush, even though kinship has different patterns and meanings in each culture. The same is true with respect to land use categories of physical space.

accurately, about an intellectual reconstruction of the environment as projected from outside the environment and at a considerable "distance" from it. In that sense, the reconstruction is merely a particular kind of map well known to cartographers, a bird's-eye view, with perspective distortions held to a minimum. By "objective," then, we mean the opposite of perspective-specific, rather than the opposite of either emotional or imaginary. In this way, objective space is radically different from awareness space.

Awareness Space

We recognize that persons living in a given social and physical environment are only vaguely and incompletely aware of that objective environment. All persons—even social scientists, when they are not actually analyzing macrodata—operate with maps of their physical and social surroundings that are less complete and more perspective-specific than those described on Level I. We have called these *cognitive and perceptual maps,* and the reality to which they conform is referred to as *awareness space.* Levels II and III are placed within this more subjective realm and are distinguished on the basis of their increasing specificity.

Other scholars have made parallel distinctions, often using the term "psychological environment" to encompass awareness space. We prefer not to use the term "psychological" to refer to both the culture-specific differences in cognition, analyzed on Level II, and the location-specific differences in experience, analyzed on Level III. Conceptual awareness and perceptual awareness are related but still distinguishable aspects of what Kurt Lewin has collapsed together into the "psychological environment."[3]

Level II: Cognitive Maps   No two individuals in the world can ever experience exactly the same social or physical environment. This is true because of

---

[3]Kurt Lewin has distinguished between the "objective environment," or what he calls the "foreign hull of the Life Space," and the "psychological environment," by which he means the environment as it is selectively attended and interpreted by the individual. In *Theory and Problems in Social Psychology* (New York: McGraw-Hill, 1948, p. 38), D. Krech and R. S. Crutchfield paraphrase this view:

> The real environment is . . . [what] would be described by an objective observer; the psychological environment is . . . [what] would be described by the experiencing person himself. . . . The very same physical environment can result in radically different psychological environments for two different persons.

Anthropologists have been particularly sensitive to the role of culture in shaping perceptions of space. For example, A. Irving Hallowell wrote early and extensively on this topic. See, for example, his "Cultural Factors in the Structuralization of Perception," pp. 164–195 in J. H. Rohrer and M. Sherif, eds., *Social Psychology at the Cross Roads* (New York: Harper & Row, 1951), as well as his book, *Culture and Experience* (Philadelphia: University of Pennsylvania Press, 1955), especially Chapters 4 and 9. The work of the philosopher Ernest Cassirer is also relevant here.

two basic realities. First, no two persons *occupy exactly the same location* in social or physical space; and second, no two individuals *carry exactly the same internalized image,* or *cognitive map,* [4] of the social and physical environment against which new stimuli are placed for comparison, interpretation, and evaluation. This is because no two persons have had exactly the same set of previous experiences—including culturally learned or indirect experiences—with the world. Lack of congruence in location implies differential exposure, which in turn should lead to the construction of different perceptual maps of the physical and social milieus. Lack of congruence in past experience should lead to different cognitive maps of the physical and social environments. Both of these sources of variation can be expected to result in major discrepancies between how an objective social scientist or human geographer might map the social and physical environments and how any given individual might subjectively experience, and then react to, those environments.

All science must cope with the task of making classes out of unique cases. If we unable to move beyond the unique—if we are unwilling to assume that groups of individuals, by virtue of similar social placement or proximity in physical space, share a more or less common exposure to common sets of stimuli, and if we refuse to concede that similarly socialized individuals share a common definition of the meanings of those stimuli by virtue of their shared culture, then no social science is possible. For those of us who accept the possibility (though with difficulty) of a "science" of human groups, the problem is not whether it is legitimate to move beyond the unique, but rather, how best to establish categories and the criteria to assign objects to categories (classification) that will allow us to predict and understand certain uniformities in behavior.

The concept of culture offers one way of categorizing commonness or similarity in perception, meaning, and interpretation. Individuals are said to share a common culture when they hold roughly similar cognitive maps of the social and physical environments external to them. By this we mean that they have learned and internalized certain categories for experience, that they tend

---

[4] Edward C. Tolman, a psychologist experimenting with maze-running rats, used the term "cognitive map" to refer to the internalized and generalized image of the physical environment that is built up in the "mind" of an experimental animal on the basis of experience. He distinguished between "broad" and "narrow" cognitive maps. Rats with broad cognitive maps were more experienced with different kinds of mazes and were thus able to run them rapidly; rats with narrow cognitive maps tended to follow old solutions or to revert to time-consuming trial-and-error methods. It is intriguing to consider human parallels. Persons with diversified experiences in the spatial and social worlds may develop broad cognitive maps that enhance their adaptability, whereas isolates may have narrow maps that prevent easy negotiations in strange surroundings. See Edward C. Tolman, "Cognitive Maps in Rats and Men," originally in *Psychological Review* (July 1948), as reproduced in Edward C. Tolman, *Collected Papers in Psychology* (Berkeley, CA: University of California Press, 1951), pp. 241–264. In another experiment, this time performed by observing Indian monkeys, it was found that in solving environmental puzzles, urban monkeys were considerably more resourceful and devious than rural monkeys; the analyst hypothesized that the greater number of varied stimuli and challenges in the urban environment led to this difference.

to share interpretations of and reactions to the various stimuli that reach them from their social and physical environments, and that they entertain similar beliefs concerning the ways in which elements of the "outside world" are significantly related and how they are to be evaluated. Subcultures are usefully distinguished when, although they may share with other groups within the larger culture a similar *Weltanschauung* (that is, the same general view of what constitutes reality), they have cognitive maps that deviate in significant ways from those more commonly held.

Obviously, these cognitive maps are not independent of the "objective" reality on which they are based and against which they are continually tested and, when found wanting, modified. They are internalized guides to experience, not arbitrary substitutes for it. And yet, they have a force and continuity of their own, even when objective circumstances are somewhat altered. For example, within contemporary American culture the cognitive mapping of kinship is usually shallow and restricted, largely because social placement according to descent is less useful than other methods of placement, such as consumption styles, occupation, and appearance. Kinship as a criterion for social placement is considered to have only weak predictive value and hence is poorly developed in the cognitive maps of social space most Americans carry within them.

However, among certain subcultures, significant deviations from this rule can be found. Among ardent members of the Daughters of the American Revolution, kin descent has high salience, and placement by region and family may be more important than placement according to present status in the economy. Similarly, Kentucky mountaineers utilize an internalized cognitive map almost exclusively structured according to kinship; it is only after they migrate to cities like Chicago or Cincinnati that they begin to supplement this cognitive map, hitherto quite satisfactory and functional, with other maps to the social terrain. Interestingly enough, urban middle-class Jews apparently work with kinship maps as complex as those internalized by proper Bostonians or Kentucky mountain folk. Kinship and its extension, ethnicity, constitute critical coordinates for the initiation and extension of social relationships.

Cognitive maps are also important in spatial orientation, as anyone who has gotten lost in a foreign city knows. Physical environments give clues to land use, direction, and place that are internalized generically. Cultural uniformities yield cognitive maps to physical space to which those outside a culture and its experience are not privy. A desert nomad who can negotiate his way over what appears to a New Yorker as trackless wastes of sand is operating with a culturally learned sensitivity not to a particular place but to environmental cues, such as the depth and shape of the dried river beds, the direction of the wind, the position of the sun and stars, and the presence of vegetation. This same bedouin, transported to New York, would in turn marvel at the subliminal ability of an American urbanite (even one who has never been in New York before) to navigate the city, guided by street signs, land uses and building types, and the presence of trucks and other traffic. Urban Americans can "find" a downtown because internalized from their previous learning are cues to the order of the physical environment. Placed in Peking or Cairo, they may face great difficulties, however, and will gradually have to modify their cognitive maps to comprehend the different spatial arrangements of their environment.

Cognitive maps based upon territoriality are of variable quality. Although territoriality per se is perhaps no longer as important in contemporary America as it formerly was, certain subcultures still place heavy stress upon it, both for physical and social placement. Kentucky mountaineers divide the world into specific ridges and hollows, urban gangs divide the city into "turfs," and certain class and ethnic subcultures place heavy stress upon locality in their cognitive maps of the world. They all have a strong sense of who belongs in an area and who doesn't. Beacon Hill may merely be steep terrain to the motorcyclist who guns his motor to ascend it, but it is sacred turf (on only one side) in the cognitive map of an upper-class Bostonian.

Level III: Perceptual Maps *Perceptual maps* are somewhat more specific than cognitive maps, in that they use the categories and generalized concepts of cognitive maps in order to interpret those portions of the social and physical environment which fall within the individual's or group's experiential world. Perceptual maps are not only culture-specific but are also location-specific. Although geographers will immediately recognize that this is the level on which Peter Gould's mental maps belong,[5] a somewhat more detailed explanation may be required for other readers.

Perceptual maps are the view of the environment with the self at center and with the laws of perspective operating to enlarge what is close and important and to telescope or even eliminate distant or unimportant items (see Figure 14.2 for an amusing example). Perceptual maps differ from objective maps in being narrower in scope, more selective in "attention," and heavily distorted by vantage point. Again, however, if one is to move beyond the problem of uniqueness, one must assume that individuals who occupy common locations in social and physical space are probably exposed to roughly similar sets of experiences which, when interpreted according to similar cognitive maps, give them a similar perspective on both the social and physical worlds.[6]

What is meant by "common location"? Few conceptual problems are presented by physical space. People who share a common situs (location in physical space) are said to share a common location. Except for differences in sensory

---

[5]Peter Gould and Rodney White, *Mental Maps* (New York: Penguin, 1974).

[6]This is, of course, not strictly accurate. Since human beings are capable of moving around, their geographic coordinates cannot be fixed; their situs, in reality, can only be described by the shape and circumference of their movements through space and time. We have reserved this more accurate definition of location for analysis on Level IV.

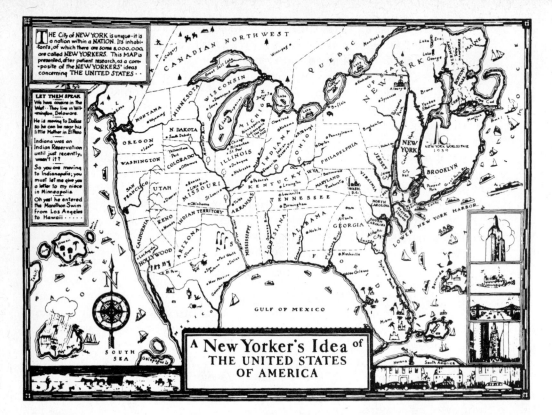

Figure 14.2 A New Yorker's mental map of the United States, distorted by perspective. (*Source:* F. V. Thierfeldt and Company, Books and Maps. Copyright by Florence Thierfeldt. Reproduced with permission.)

abilities, they are presumably exposed to roughly the same set of stimuli. At Level III, common location in physical space may be assumed when individuals share a common "starting point" for their movements—that is, when they share a residential location or a destination point. When we analyze or dissect a physical environment, our goal is to distinguish contiguous areas of physical similarity (cities, neighborhoods, regions, business districts, shopping centers, industrial zones) and to classify them. Then we can hypothesize that individuals within those physical spaces are exposed to roughly common sets of stimuli emanating from the surrounding physical space (for example, visual images and impressions, noise levels, degrees of crowding, temperatures, opportunities to participate in certain activities).

Since groups of individuals who share a common location in the physical environment are, by virtue of that location, exposed to only a *portion* of the entire objective physical environment, it is to be expected that their mental reconstructions of that environment will be basically different from the reconstructions a human geographer might generate at a distance. In mental maps, there exists a prevailing principle of greater detail and accuracy in the foreground (closest to the person "making" the map), and fuzziness, telescoping, and downright "mistakes" toward the peripheries of both knowledge and salience. A mental map is what an environment looks like to an individual who is experiencing it and is therefore behaving accordingly. It is the "definition of the situation" in physical terms.

Much empirical research has already been done on mental maps of the physical environment. Perhaps the first explorations were conducted by Kevin Lynch and reported in his early but still unsurpassed book, *The Image of the City.* [7] The questions he posed were: How do individuals visualize their physical environments? How much of those environments are they actually aware of, and therefore take into account, when negotiating their way through them? Some of his findings are quite suggestive. First, he found that individuals vary widely in terms of the mental maps they have of the same surroundings. Highly mobile people who are exposed to many parts of the urban environment have better and broader maps, while persons who lead highly circumscribed lives tend to blur details rapidly beyond their turf and are easily disoriented in new surroundings.

Second, he found that all respondents, regardless of the width of their respective maps, tend to "blow up in scale" those portions of the surrounding territory that are closest to them and to compress both distant and dull portions of the urbanscape. Distortions based upon salience and values are also found. Important and highly valued parts of the environment appear very large in an individual's mental map; distasteful or unused portions of the environment tend to be compressed or vanish altogether.[8]

Third, Lynch found that maps are distorted not only because people in different locations have different perspectives, but also because certain locations themselves offer more stimuli by their very character (were, in Lynch's terminology, more "imageable" or "legible"). Thus, in general and regardless of specific location, interesting environments with varied and easily symbolized and distinguishable landmarks are routinely reproduced in people's maps of physical space. On the other hand, dull, confusing, or undifferentiated urbanscapes remain blurred and poorly reproduced, even by residents with intimate and long-term exposure to them.

Why are mental maps important, and why should sociologists be concerned with them? Mental maps are sensitive indicators of the environment *as it is actually experienced and interpreted by social actors.* Mental maps reveal the

---

[7]Kevin Lynch, *The Image of the City* (Cambridge, MA: MIT Press, 1960).

[8]There are obvious parallels here to well-verified principles in the social psychology of perception. Recall the classic experiment which found that poor children consistently overestimated the size of a dime. Individuals routinely enlarge the size of important (salient) objects.

differential awareness people have of their surroundings, which reflects the differential exposure they have had to it in the past and which strongly determines their future experience. The uses which a person makes of his or her physical environment and the responses it generates are radically circumscribed not only by the nature of the environment but by the person's perceptions of it. Therefore, mental maps are projective "tests" from which values can be inferred, as well as direct measures of the highly selective and creatively organized environments that actually operate upon a person and that thereby influence his or her behavior.

If mental maps are good measures of location-specific physical space, what would be the analogous measures for social space? In order to answer that question, we must first specify what location in social space means. Think of an individual as being located in social space according to "coordinates" that place him or her in the society's "social structure." The task of the social scientist is to determine the most significant dimensions in this social space, according to which persons are "located." These dimensions may vary from culture to culture, but some are virtually universal.

Undoubtedly, one critical dimension in any social structure is class. When social scientists attempt to describe the class structure of a given society, their goal is to classify together those individuals who share enough of a common location in social space that they are exposed to a common set of stimuli emanating from the surrounding social environment (that is, derogation from those "above" them, adulation, or at least deference, from those "below").

A second universal dimension of social structure is classification based upon age and sex, since roles, responsibilities, and prerogatives are assigned according to specific "locations" in the age and sex gradings of the social structure. Persons who share a common location in the age-sex structure are differentially exposed to the remainder of society and are differentially treated by others. Children, for example, have a predetermined relationship to adults in most societies and might, therefore, be expected to share certain common perspectives. Adolescents in our own society have gradually evolved a particular vantage point from which to relate to other age groups and have, to some extent, developed a common perception of the social order. In most societies, males and females occupy distinguishable positions in the social structure, positions which are further distinguished according to family life and maturation cycles.

In addition to these two universal dimensions of social space, particular societies may utilize other criteria. In contemporary American society, for example, race, and to a lesser extent, ethnicity, are particularly important dimensions of social space, since members of certain racial or ethnic groups are exposed to the society and are treated by others in a manner that is directly related to their "position" on these dimensions. In other societies religion may operate as the critical dimension of social placement. In still other places, dimensions such as linguistic groups, castes, place of origin (rural migrants versus city-born, etc.) may be significant. Because societies differ in their social organization, researchers always have to select the locational coordinates most predictive of differential exposure to the social environment and therefore of different perceptions of it in any given setting.

We take the position that individuals perceive the social environment around them in a manner that is as location-specific as their perceptions of the physical environment. That is, we assume that individuals sharing a common location in social space develop fairly common mental maps of the social structure that are heavily influenced by their perspective in the social system. These mental maps have been found to deviate in fairly predictable ways from those generated at a distance by the macrosociologist or anthropologist. The mental maps of the class system, as held by persons at the top of the class hierarchy, are somewhat different from those held by persons at the bottom, and both differ from the structure described by social scientists on the basis of overall data. Prestige-rankings of occupations are different for high-ranking persons and for those at unskilled ranks, even though, as in Lynch's mental maps, some occupations such as medicine and law are so "imageable" that they consistently appear at the top.

Thus far we know much less about the mental maps of the social environment held by persons of different ages or by men versus women. This appears to be an area deserving of research. Similarly, while we are often painfully aware that the social system of the United States looks quite different to blacks, white working-class Catholics, middle-class Jews, and WASPs, the research that would delineate the special mental maps of the surrounding social environment held by members of these subgroups is still in its infant stage.

In summary, perceptual (or mental) maps of the physical and social environments indicate how aware individuals (at different locations in physical and social space) are of their environments and how they attend selectively to those environments to which they are exposed. Presumably, if one wished to understand or predict what given individuals will do with a particular environment, how they will respond to a given social or physical milieu, one would need to know how that environment is perceived by them. It is likely that behavior will be governed more by what they believe that environment to be than by what it "actually" is.[9]

Just as behavior is in part guided by mental maps, so mental maps, in the last analysis, are merely the generalized product of the recurring behavior of those who hold them. They are built up gradually over time through the storage

---

[9]Some of the important work done on this can be found in the area of the perception of crime or the fear of rape. Men and women have very different perceptions of urban dangers, with the higher fears of women related to rape. Almost half of the women in the urban samples queried by Margaret Gordon and her colleagues reported feeling unsafe alone in their neighborhoods at night, in contrast to only 7.5 percent of the men. See Margaret Gordon et al., "Crime, Women and the Quality of Urban Life," *Signs: Journal of Women in Culture and Society* 5 (1980) Supplement, pp. S144–160. There is an obvious discrepancy, however, between what women fear most and where the "objective" dangers lie. Women believe that their risks of rape are greatest from an unknown male of a different race whom they meet on a deserted dark street in a strange neighborhood. Therefore, they restrict their movements accordingly. In contrast, however, the perpetrator of rape is more likely to be a male of their own race and class, probably known to them, and the rape will most probably occur in a setting they usually do not fear (at home or on a date). One can see, therefore, how "definitions of situations" override statistical probabilities in determining behavior. See Margaret Gordon and Stephanie Riger, *The Female Fear* (New York: Free Press, 1989).

and organization of interpreted sense data, which is one reason they are so much more finely reticulated in the "zones close to home"—that is, in the zones of maximal experience. This brings us to Level IV. If Level I is "real" and broad space, and Levels II and III are "awareness" space, then Level IV is "action" space; it focuses upon the movement or "behavior" of persons in restricted fields of both physical and social space.

Level IV: Behavior Space

Just as objective space—physical and social—is far broader than any one individual or group can conceptualize, so that portion of social and physical space which any one individual or group experiences regularly is usually only a small fraction of the space of which they are aware. That sample, however, is extremely crucial: first, because it is on the basis of limited aggregated experience that perceptual and cognitive maps are gradually refined, expanded, and modified; and second, because if physical and social environments can be expected to exercise any direct effect upon human behavior, it must be assumed that, in the last analysis, the effect is exercised through experience. Only that portion of the environment in *direct* contact with the social actor "causes" a behavioral effect, even though the impact of the effect is conditioned *indirectly* by both the objective structure of the larger system and the symbolic and conceptual meanings attributed to experience.

It is an irrelevant question to ask how the density of Chicago's Loop affects an individual who never goes there. Whatever effect it has is, at most, indirect, either because those with whom the individual interacts are edgy when *they* return from it, or because the individual orients himself or herself with respect to it and its values without experiencing it directly. These indirect influences, however, are not ecological in the sense that they represent an impact of the environment upon behavior. The physical and social morphologies of the Loop do not impinge directly. When we ask the question "What is the effect of a given social or physical environment upon social behavior and upon the 'mentality' of the actor?" we are asking an ecological question that must be answered on its own terms. The other questions are interesting but not germane.

Directly experienced physical and social space are what we here call *action* or *behavior space.* Until recently, behavior space was treated almost as a stepchild in ecological research on urban areas. Rather than being given top priority in the formulation of research designs on life in cities, it was at best treated as a dependent variable to be deduced from the physical environment. Researchers did not recognize that it constitutes the critical and proper level at which to initiate inquiries into the independent variables that do or do not lead to "urbanism as a way of life." It is the argument of this chapter that only through studying behavior in social and physical space can we ever develop a typology for comprehending and predicting the nature of social life in cities.

What is behavior space? *Behavior space in the physical environment* is the path through physical space followed by any social actor as he or she goes about the business of living. Behavior space for a three-year-old boy consists of his circuit through the neighborhood and his occasional supervised forays into the wider world. By tracking him, as he desultorily ambles through the alley, stopping to watch an ant here or a sidewalk game there, as he takes his dime to the candy store or accompanies his sister to her friend's house, one begins to build an empirical description of his physical environment, its paths and connections, and of his selective contact with the surrounding physical space. In short, one builds a model of the experiential world which influences his behavior. If the elevator is forbidden territory to him, the existence of facilities on the tenth floor is irrelevant to his actions, even though it might be included in a geographer's objective map of his physical world. If he cannot cross the busy street in front of his home, his physical world truncates there. If he finds the fence behind his home too high to even see over, his physical environment effectively terminates there. And if we, as social researchers, insist on asking how the residential density of his census tract (ten square blocks, which far exceeds his experiential world) affects his behavior, we deserve all the wrong answers we shall undoubtedly get.

On the other hand, his father travels 20 miles to work each day and, in addition, often attends a baseball game in another part of town, shops at a distant discount center, and visits friends scattered throughout the metropolitan area. Only by tracing his path through physical space over time and by identifying his physical connections and selective contacts with surrounding physical space can we build some description of the physical environment that effectively influences *his* behavior. We can no sooner predict his attitudes from a knowledge of his census tract's density than we can his three-year-old son's. We might come somewhat closer in predicting his wife's attitudes, particularly if she is kept fairly close to home by domestic responsibilities. While her experiential world is far broader and more detailed than her son's, it is probably narrower than her husband's. Indeed, if "neighborhood," as it has conventionally been viewed by city planners, has any validity as a category for physical exposure, it is more likely to apply to the housewife than to other family members. But, even here, we cannot presume in advance that we know her physical environment until we observe her and collect data on her physical movements through space; she may be the queen of England or the director of HUD!

In this illustration we have pointed to one fairly common correlation between a particular location in social space (in this case, age-sex attribute space) and a physical behavior pattern with social interaction and attitudinal consequences. As we have argued, other dimensions of social location may also be significantly correlated with differences in behavior space. Social class, for example, is probably a social space locational variable with high predictability concerning physical mobility and the dimensions of behavior in space. Race and ethnicity may also be found to relate to environmental exposure. State of health, level of education, and other hypothesized independent variables may need to be investigated before we can demonstrate empirically a relevant connection between placement in objective social space and elements of the physical environment which are directly experienced and which thus influence attitudes and actions. Are there cross-cultural similarities? How strong are they? What is the influence of cultural differences upon the shape, scope, and content of differently experienced physical behavior space? Methods for analyzing, describing, summarizing, and aggregating people's paths through physical space are needed if we are ever to answer such questions.

As already mentioned in Chapter 12, one somewhat tedious method of studying paths through physical space consists of collecting information on daily, weekly, and other cyclical movements for various purposes by persons with different social characteristics. The data are collected through conventional time budgets and origin-destination home surveys. This very old method has been further facilitated by computer technologies. The uses to which these data are put and the kinds of questions which are being asked of the data are, however, quite original.

It will be realized from Chapter 12 that the term applied to this method by the researchers at the University of North Carolina who developed it is the *household activity system.* [10] The data compiled for household activity systems permit the mapping in physical space of the network paths of a wide variety of individuals; furthermore, they permit some summary statistical measures of the geographic extent, connectedness, and "density" of various physical networks. If persons who occupy significantly similar positions in social space actually have similar activity patterns in physical space, then we should be able to classify subgroups in the society in a way that allows us to make real predictions concerning the effects of ecological variables on their social life.

If the household activity system offers a method for investigating and summarizing behavior in physical space, what method can be used to study behavior in social space? Again, we are already familiar with this from Chapter 12. Utilized first by anthropologists, social network analysis is now being adapted for use by urban sociologists, although much remains to be done to devise simple and easily aggregated measures. Social network analysis is designed to plot the extent, connectedness, and density of the social relationships of individuals and groups.

A person's social network may be thought of as the "path" through social space that is followed by an individual as he or she goes about the business of contacting and interacting with selected "significant others" in the social environment. And just as an individual's activity system in physical space can be mapped with reference to geographical coordinates in the spatial world, so an individual's *social network* or *interaction system* can be mapped with reference to coordinates in social space. Some groups of persons interact only with "similars"; they are said to be socially "encapsulated." Others interact with a wide range of persons who differ from themselves in age, sex, class, or ethnicity; they are said to be socially "cosmopolitan." Some individuals interact selectively on the basis of kinship; others, on the basis of common interests and even political views.

---

[10]F. Stuart Chapin, Jr., *Human Activity Patterns in the City: Things People Do in Time and Space* (New York: John Wiley, 1974); see our Chapter 12 above for a fuller exposition.

Plotting social networks (that is, mapping interactions in the social environment) offers many possibilities for comparative urban analysis. Do members of certain subcultures have typically arranged social networks? Do these differ systematically from the typical networks of other groups? Are there high correlations between common location in social space and the types of social networks that are evolved to relate to the outside social environment? Are there typical networks according to class position, occupation, or age and sex within a given culture or subculture?

REPHRASING URBAN SOCIOLOGY'S BASIC QUESTION

We are now ready to return to the questions that urban ecology has always asked, namely: Do certain types of physical arrangements facilitate or inhibit the development of certain types of social interactions? Within the parameters set by a culture or subculture, could cities and neighborhoods within the city be designed to encourage the kinds of social networks that might give a heightened sense of security and community to urban residents?

These questions differ greatly from the simple one of how to manipulate (abstract) physical space to change (abstract) human behavior. And yet they are questions we can ask and begin to answer if we use the more complex model and paradigm of multileveled social and physical space suggested in this chapter. They pose a new agenda for research into urban life which, if imaginatively pursued, could make urban sociological research one of the most vital subfields of the discipline. We appear to be at the beginning of an exciting quest—to understand finally how humans interact with each other and with their environments. And, as we have shown, this relationship is far more complex than was originally believed when the field of urban sociology first began.

Why is this question important? The answer is simple. If we wish to design cities that will encourage healthy human relations, we must understand how specific urban environments contribute to or detract from that goal. Our quest is nothing less than a search for guidelines to create a "good city."

Chapter
15

Changing Cities—Can Their Future Be Planned?

*I*mplicit throughout this book has been the idea of the "good city"—which has never been defined. There is a large literature about [e]utopias [eu=good + topia=place] which is devoted to specifying the kinds of urban environments that would facilitate happy and productive lives for their residents. Perhaps the most imaginative of these attempts is the small provocative book by Paul and Percival Goodman, entitled *Communitas*. [1] In this book the authors begin with values. They set out three paradigms (really definitions) for the "good city," each with its own dominant value or goal. The Goodmans then systematically deduce the kind of built environment that could best achieve each goal.

Paradigm 1 is called the "city of efficient consumption" or "The Metropolis as a Department Store." To maximize efficiency in consumption the Goodmans design a city with a dominant market-carnival center, while spreading out the residences into rings of lower and lower density. They suggest that this model is currently the preferred one in the United States.

Paradigm 3 makes "efficient production," not consumption, its central

---

[1] See Paul and Percival Goodman, *Communitas: Means of Livelihood and Ways of Life* (New York: Random House, 1947; reissued New York: Columbia University Press, 1990).

value. To maximize the goals of efficient production, they rigidly separate industrialized workplaces from residences and recommend investing heavily in the former while keeping investments in the latter to minimum standards. They suggest that this model is most appropriate for poor countries whose most pressing needs are for economic development.

The Goodmans themselves strongly advocate Paradigm 2 (the happy medium!), in which production and consumption goals are both seen as integral parts of a happy life. They advocate a city design that integrates smaller workplaces with clustered housing so as to minimize the length of the journey to work and to reduce the potential conflict between the demands of production-time and of family-time. These ends can be achieved, they suggest, through "small-grained" settlements in which land uses are intermixed. From even this brief exposition it is clear that the judgment about what constitutes a "good" city is not independent of the goals people set for their society.

There is a second way, however, to judge how "good" cities are, and that is to ask those who live in them how satisfied they are with their environments, and what they would like to see changed. Given the diversity of life-styles, which reveals the coexistence in the same society of different values, this is probably a fairer approach in a democracy. To some extent, we can say that people "vote with their feet" by moving to those environments that best fulfill the goals they prefer. However, many are not free to exercise their choices, either because the environment they would really prefer does not yet exist, or, more commonly, because they are constrained in their choices by a lack of economic and political power.[2] Therefore, where people actually live is only an imperfect guide to where they would like to live.

While we therefore cannot define precisely what constitutes an ideal city, we can say one thing: at the minimum, a good city is one about which a majority of residents express satisfaction. In these terms, we would have to acknowledge that American cities fall far short of the ideal. Americans are not very happy with their cities, if the results of a poll conducted by Louis Harris and Associates for the U.S. Department of Housing and Urban Development are reliable.[3]

In 1978, a large, nationally representative sample of Americans was asked: "If you could live anywhere you wanted, which one of the kinds of places listed below would be your first choice?" Respondents were asked to select among six types, ranging from large cities to small and middle-sized towns, from suburbs to freestanding communities and rural areas. Table 15.1 shows their responses.

If we contrast where people want to live (as indicated in this survey) with where they actually do live (as reported in Chapter 6), the discrepancy is marked. Far more Americans want to live in communities having less than

---

[2]See Nelson Foote, Janet Abu-Lughod, Louis Winnick, and Mary Mix Foley, *Housing Choices and Housing Constraints* (New York: McGraw-Hill, 1960).

[3]I am indebted to Sylvia Fava for allowing me to incorporate here the material on the Harris Poll which she originally prepared for the book we planned to co-author. See Louis Harris Associates for Department of Housing and Urban Development, *A Survey of Citizens' Views and Concerns About Urban Life: Final Report* (Washington, DC: U.S. Government Printing Office, 1978).

Table 15.1   IF YOU COULD LIVE ANYWHERE YOU WANTED TO
Which One of the Kinds of Places Listed Below Would Be Your Very First
Choice?

Type of location	Preference of each race-ethnicity (%)			
	Total	White	Black	Hispanic
(1) Large city (250,000 +)	16.1	13.0	38.1	31.6
(2) Medium-size city near a large center (50,000–250,000)	11.2	10.8	10.1	14.9
(3) Medium-size city *not* in suburbs	8.3	8.0	9.8	10.0
(4) Small city, town, or village (under 50,000) near a large center	15.4	16.0	11.0	12.8
(5) Small city, town, or village *not* in the suburbs	22.7	24.5	12.7	16.9
(6) Rural area	24.7	26.3	15.6	10.6
Not sure	1.5	1.3	2.7	3.2
All places	100.0	100.0	100.0	100.0

Source: Louis Harris Survey for the Department of Housing and Urban Development, 1978. Adapted from data in vol. 1, pp. 91–92 and vol. 2, p. 558.

250,000 inhabitants than in any other type of setting, and more want to live in rural areas than in cities with 250,000 or more inhabitants. Not only big cities but even suburbs seem to be rejected in this survey, with almost a third of the sample preferring medium-sized or small towns that are not suburbs!

These preferences predominantly reflect the views of the white subsample which, of course, accounted for most respondents; in contrast, members of minority groups who, as we have earlier shown, are most likely to live in center cities of metropolitan areas, expressed a strong preference for urban life. Of the black and Hispanic respondents, almost half chose cities (small and large), a fourth chose small or large suburbs while only a small minority (15.6 percent of blacks and 10.6 percent of Hispanics) said they preferred rural areas, whose depressed and depressing state many had probably experienced! However, while prior experience had both positive and negative effects on preferences, the stereotypes and attitudes held by all were remarkably similar.

Respondents expressed a stereotype of big-city life that was decidedly negative. Some 92 percent thought that large cities had the most crime, and 82 percent thought they were the worst places in which to raise children. Some 62 percent believed that large cities had the worst schools, and an equal number thought they offered the worst housing. No wonder so few wanted to live in them.

On the other hand, large cities were valued for their amenities and services, with 87 percent acknowledging that large cities had the best plays and cultural activities, 75 percent agreeing that they had the best public transportation systems, 69 percent saying they had the best restaurants, and about 60 percent crediting them with the best employment opportunities and health care facilities.

Whereas the objective realities may in fact be quite different from the beliefs respondents expressed, these were in fact the "definitions of the situation" to which most Americans subscribed in 1978. There is no reason to believe that attitudes toward "the city" have become more favorable in the years since 1978. Indeed, they seem to have become even more negative. In a Gallup Poll taken in 1989, only 19 percent of the respondents preferred to live in a city, while another 24 percent selected a suburb. In contrast, 34 percent favored small towns (not suburban), while the remaining 22 percent said they really wanted to live on a farm. (Four out of five respondents actually lived in metropolitan areas.)

It has been said that we get the kinds of cities we deserve. This appears to be a cruel judgment. And yet, who are we to blame for our large cities, which so many Americans believe are filled with problems and from which they dream of escape? As stressed throughout this book, cities always reflect the societies of which they are a part. This is universally true, regardless of whether we examine cities of different historical epochs, in very different regions and cultures, or at wide ranges of technological and economic sophistication. Why should American cities, as we approach the twentieth-first century, be any different?

Certainly, money alone does not guarantee livable cities. Many countries whose per capita incomes are lower than in the United States seem to have cities with less crime, more efficient transportation systems, fewer slums, and more generous and more equitably distributed urban services (including health, schools, and housing). And public opinion polls in Scandinavia, for example, reveal that urban residents have a much higher level of contentment with their living environments than we have in the United States.[4] Something else must be operative.

Recently, it has even become fashionable to compare some of the largest cities in the United States not with the great capitals of the developed world, but with the teeming problem-ridden giant cities of the Third World, with their massive unsolved problems.[5] This should give Americans pause. Do we really have the cities we deserve? And if so, how can we deserve better ones? Given our wealth, why are we not doing better?

In the introduction to this book we stressed our belief that values cannot be excluded from science. Now this point must be made more explicit. The relationship between values—as expressed in the priorities set for the urban and national agenda—and the society and cities that follow from them, must be of central concern to social scientists. Classical urban sociology was not value-free. Rather, its values were concealed in its premises, which assumed the workings of a free market, saw sifting and sorting as the process by which individual consumers maximized their utilities through their housing and location choices, and viewed

---

[4]David Popenoe, *Private Pleasures, Public Plight* (New Brunswick, NJ: Transaction Books, 1985).

[5]Within the past few years a number of urbanists and planners (as well as the press) have begun to talk about New York as a "Third World city." See the work of Saskia Sassen, Matthew Edel, Arthur Paris, and especially Janet Abu-Lughod, "New York and Cairo: A View from Street Level," *International Social Science Journal*, No. 125 (August, 1990), pp. 307–318.

the location choices made by businesses and housing investors, exercised through competitive bidding on location, as maximizing efficiency.

As we have noted earlier, the validity of these premises is not at all self-evident, nor do the premises accurately reflect the way decisions are made in American cities in the twentieth century. Ever since the end of the nineteenth century, when planning first began and when political agendas and decisions began to exercise an expanding influence on social, economic, and spatial competition in our urban areas, the assumptions of classical urban sociology have become less and less accurate as reflections of reality. And although the tools of planning have grown in scope and complexity and the involvement of government in provisioning and exercising control over our cities has expanded enormously over the past century, these interventions have brought us no closer to our avowed goals of coping with urban problems and producing cities liked by their residents.

Can it be that the forces that are creating cities we reject are not subject to planning? Or are cities being planned, but by agents and organizations not subject to democratic political processes? Alternatively, are those very political processes giving us not the kinds of cities we say we want, but the kinds from which at least some of us benefit?

These are deep questions whose answers are not easily provided. But they are questions worth pondering. In this chapter we do not propose to answer them. Rather, we set a less ambitious agenda, namely, to describe the efforts that have been made to plan our cities, to demonstrate that such efforts have often failed to reach their avowed goals, and to distinguish among the types of explanations scholars have offered to account for these failures. We end with some prescriptions for ways to understand the processes that create our cities and some thoughts about how we can change them, if not into eutopias, at least into cities that satisfy more of us more of the time.

EARLY EFFORTS TO PLAN THE SOCIAL AND PHYSICAL SPACE OF CITIES

Physical Planning

History provides many examples of cities that were intentionally planned. These examples, however, have disproportionately been new towns implanted by dominant political authorities—for example, colonies implanted overseas by imperial powers, defensive fortified towns in alien territories, and palace cities designed to house the entourages of rulers and to symbolize their power.[6] In the United States, the most notable example of a planned new city was Wash-

---

[6]For examples drawn from European history, see Wolfgang Braunfels, *Urban Design in Western Europe: Regime and Architecture, 900–1900* (Chicago: University of Chicago Press, 1988).

ington, D.C., whose open site was selected because it would permit an independent capital, free of the already entrenched economic and political interests of preexisting cities.[7]

Most cities in the United States, however, were not planned by governmental authorities, although certainly, surveyors and developers exercised some foresight in the laying out of roads and lots.[8] Most American cities developed in response to the demands of the economy and, as we have seen, grew increasingly crowded and degraded with the shift to industrialism. It was then that urban environments were first judged deficient and that political efforts were begun to improve them.

At the local level, planning began to be advocated in the second half of the nineteenth century to make American cities both more beautiful and more efficient. At that time, however, planning was viewed as a way to gain rational control over the physical environment and was directed largely towards esthetic ends. Christopher Tunnard's small classic, *The Modern American City*, chronicles some of this early history.[9] During the second half of the nineteenth century, periodic "international expositions" were held in Europe and later the United States, in which western nations vied with one another to display their accomplishments (and wares).[10] The first American exposition was held in Philadelphia in 1876, and beaux arts architect Richard Morris Hunt's reaction to European sophistication in architecture and planning was one of shame and envy; he urged American cities to follow the example of Baron von Haussmann's Paris plan, which had opened broad boulevards in dense areas and had introduced vistas and wondrous focal buildings into that crowded city. Von Haussmann's definition of the role of planning was to prevail for the next 25 years, a period during which the "City Beautiful" movement flourished.[11]

---

[7]See Elizabeth Kite, *L'Enfant and Washington, 1791–1792* (Baltimore: Johns Hopkins University Press, 1929). American history offers even earlier examples, such as William Penn's Philadelphia, as well as Savannah, Georgia, and Annapolis, Maryland. New towns, however, were usually laid out by surveyors. George Washington was originally one such surveyor, and some of his town plans are reproduced in John Reps, *The Making of Urban America* (Princeton, NJ: Princeton University Press, 1965).

[8]Very often, the last goal sought in such planning was livability and resident satisfaction. More important, in such early planning attempts, was a maximization of sales and profits. The gridiron plan of narrow rectangular blocks imposed on Manhattan Island in 1811 at the behest of real estate developers was intended to facilitate land development and property sales. See Edward K. Spann, "The Greatest Grid: The New York Plan of 1811," pp. 11–39 in *Two Centuries of American Planning*, ed. Daniel Schaffer (Baltimore: Johns Hopkins University Press, 1988).

[9]Christopher Tunnard, *The Modern American City* (Princeton, NJ: Van Nostrand, 1968).

[10]Non-European countries were also represented at these fairs, but through the stereotypes of them held by westerners. See Timothy Mitchell, *Colonising Egypt* (Cambridge: Cambridge University Press, 1988) for a sensitive account of how the "Orient" was represented in 19th century international expositions, and what that presentation implied in terms of power to define reality.

[11]Tunnard, *The Modern American City*, pp. 36–46.

The fruits of that movement could be seen in the Columbian Exposition of 1893 in Chicago, where the director of works for the exposition, architect Daniel Burnham, not only oversaw the planning of "imperial" buildings and grounds in Jackson Park, but eventually, with the backing and support of the Chicago Commercial Club (which enrolled everybody who was anybody in Chicago industry and commerce), developed the Chicago Plan of 1909. What was happening in Chicago was paralleled in other major cities, as landscape architects like Frederick Olmsted and major site planners and architects like Mead and White played important roles in sprucing up the front yards of American cities. The backyards were left to the settlement house movement and the nascent field of social work.

The Split Between Physical and Social Planning

From the beginning of planning, there was a curious split. *Physical planning* emphasized appearance and facade, while *social reform* emphasized the needs of poor people and saw urban social problems as rooted in the economic system. The two approaches competed with one another to mobilize local governmental resources to advance their chosen ends. Thus, politics and economics were, from the start, involved in these two visions of urban reform, but from different vantage points and with very different priorities and agendas.

On one side were the captains of industry and commerce who sponsored the elaborate public works designed by architects and landscape architects (for there were as yet no city planners) to create an image for their cities that they could be proud of, and who used their considerable economic power to bypass or bribe the political machines, such as New York's Tammany Hall, that were becoming entrenched in local governments. Control over the city halls of most major American cities was by then in the hands of "bosses" ("Boss" Tweed in New York, "Bath House" John and "Big Bill" Thompson in Chicago) whose political power depended on their ability to distribute, in return for electoral loyalties, patronage jobs which increased in direct proportion to the expansion of local services such as the police, municipal transport, schools, street cleaning, and fire protection.[12] The political bosses were non-aristocrats (to put it mildly) whose strength came from the overwhelming voting power of mostly poor (and "ethnic") immigrants. It was a strange political coalition, to say the least!

On the other side were muckrakers, reformers like Jane Addams, supporters of the growing labor union movement, and others working in different ways with the poor immigrant communities of the cities. They tended to see "social planning" as their goal, and viewed the problems of cities in class terms. While they fought for better housing, more parks, better schools, and other amenities that were part of the physical environment, they never forgot that it was wages

---

[12]This might be considered an early precursor to what Harvey Molotch has referred to as "the growth machine," which now dominates local politics. An even earlier example, of course, was the role of new town promoters in the settling of the Midwest and West.

and working conditions, as well as other "social" inequalities and instabilities, that were the root causes of the misery they saw around them.[13] They sought a "class alliance" with the political machines. However, the reforms they advocated, such as substituting civil service appointments for patronage jobs and replacing pork-barrel deals with "scientific planning," would have ultimately undermined the power of local machines, a message not lost on the astute bosses.

The split between these two approaches was completed by the early decades of the twentieth century. In the battle between them, planning as social reform lost out to planning as physical reform. The assumption of urban ecologists—that changing the physical environment would alter social life—was used as a justification for the almost exclusive emphasis on physical planning. It took the Great Depression of the 1930s to overturn this resolution of the conflict.

The Birth of the Welfare State

As we have seen in Chapter 5, the crisis generated by the depression that began in 1929 was so great that it overwhelmed all prior divisions of labor between local, state, and federal governments, and the social dislocations were so devastating that it was obvious that physical planning alone could not "fix" them. Socioeconomic planning (and a lot of money) would be required to get the system moving again. Only the federal government could command sufficient power and financial resources to prod civil society into recovery. Nevertheless, local and states' rights were not completely ignored; rather, an attempt was made to establish a partnership between the federal government and units at lower levels of the governmental system. Hence, federal funds began to be filtered through local governments to subsidize federally initiated (but locally agreed to) reforms. Public housing began on a noticeable scale in the 1930s as just such a collaborative effort.

It is not possible to say whether or not the New Deal succeeded in pulling the United States out of the depression, since by the end of the 1930s, the demand for munitions and other products in connection with World War II led to rapid economic recovery. The diversion of resources to war, however, left many urban and housing needs neglected. In the postwar period, these were turned to via the established partnership between local and federal governmental units, and it appeared that the rift between social and physical planning had been healed. Socioeconomic planning took its place next to physical city planning, two aspects of a single approach to solving urban problems.[14] The two parts did not necessarily work well together.

---

[13]See Ira Katznelson, *City Trenches: Urban Politics and the Patterning of Class in the United States* (New York: Pantheon, 1981).

[14]A useful collection of articles on this can be found in Daniel Schaffer, ed., *Two Centuries of American Planning* (Baltimore: Johns Hopkins University Press, 1988).

Redesigning cities to accommodate automobiles (highways, cloverleafs, downtown bypass routes, parking lots and garages) became a major preoccupation of physical planners, while socioeconomic planners worried primarily about how to provide an adequate supply of decent housing. The Urban Redevelopment Act of 1949 was intended to serve both goals. The federal government contributed much of the financing for urban improvements and subsidized housing. In return, local governments, which had the option of participating, had to provide some matching funds and had to use their local legal powers (their police powers and their powers of eminent domain)[15] to gain control over large parcels of privately owned land that were needed for the improvements.

The two forms of planning that were supposed to work together actually worked, perhaps unintentionally, at cross-purposes. The work of the transportation planners facilitated a massive outmigration from U.S. center cities by bringing distant rural areas within commuting range. Spreading suburbanization was the result. Furthermore, the increased highway commuting on the new highways generated an insatiable demand for additional parking space in center cities.

The social planners and housers focused their activities on the center city, where the (1930s) goal of clearing slums was combined with the (1950s) goal of revitalizing center cities through gentrification. New apartment housing for the middle class ran into conflict with replacement housing for the poor. The result of these efforts was a net destruction of affordable housing in center cities.[16] Significant amounts of slum land were cleared, but what was not used to provide space for highways and middle-income housing or to make room for institutional expansions (of hospitals, universities, civic centers, etc.) went to meet the growing demands of commuters for places to put their cars.

At first, some new subsidized housing for the poor was also located on this cleared land. However, with the growth of an association between "poor" and "black" (see Chapter 9), such housing tended to be located in areas already occupied by minorities. This strategy was eliminated by the Gautreaux and similar cases, which ruled that public housing could not be located in ways that would intensify the existing segregation of the races. Unfortunately, the unintended consequence of these legal decisions was to remove local governments' motivation to construct public housing. Almost no public housing, except that designed to accommodate the poor elderly (still mostly white), was subsequently built.

---

[15]The power of *eminent domain* resides chiefly in the local government, which can take privately owned real property for a public purpose; it must pay a just compensation at a mutually agreed upon price or, failing that, one determined in a court of law. The *police power* grants to local governments the right to take private property from owners through condemnation, when such private property constitutes a threat to the life, safety, or welfare of citizens. No compensation need be paid.

[16]Martin Anderson's *The Federal Bulldozer* (Cambridge, MA: MIT Press, 1964) was perhaps the most scathing of many critiques.

The Urban Redevelopment Act, even after amendments, continued to come under attack from both the left and the right of the political spectrum. The left accused it of destroying the homes of the poor and minorities to help the rich; the right attacked public housing (from which the privileged did not benefit) as "socialist" and began to advocate privatization of public housing, a policy later instituted via Section 8. The latter program offered a public subsidy to owners of privately held housing who were willing to rent to poor people; it gave landlords the difference between what they said they could rent their apartments for on the open market, and what qualified low-income residents could afford to pay.[17] But we are ahead of our story.

The Rebirth of Social Planning

By the mid-1960s, if not before, it was becoming evident that the high hopes entertained about planning, both physical and social, in the immediate postwar period were collapsing. Neither type was solving the social problems of the poor and especially the minority poor, whose patience was at an end. When city after city experienced violent and often self-punishing destruction in the urban riots of the mid-1960s, federal policy took a new tack.

The Johnson administration, prodded by urban "unrest," declared "war on poverty," a somewhat hyperbolic term. A large number of new programs were instituted in the social realm. The intent was to decentralize power over planning to neighborhoods where local needs and priorities were to be set by residents. Furthermore, social planning was expanded to encompass—at long last—the issue of jobs (through CETA). Federal grants for local facilities, job training, community development, and the like were available to urban neighborhoods, if they could organize themselves to fill out the complex applications required.[18] (The Reagan administration later terminated most of these programs.)

The Johnson administration eventually admitted that training people for jobs that did not exist in the local community could not help poor people much. Thus, priorities shifted to expanding the economic base of inner-city neighborhoods by creating "urban enterprise zones."[19] The social planning idea behind this approach was a partnership between public and private actors (e.g., what in Figure 15.2 [see p. 376] we call that domain of political economy initiated

---

[17]One of the best surveys of successive federal housing policies is Allen Hays, *The Federal Government & Urban Housing: Ideology and Change in Public Policy* (Albany: State University of New York Press, 1985). The scandals that rocked the U.S. Department of Housing and Urban Development (HUD) in 1989–1990, in the immediate post-Reagan era, were associated either with Section 8 housing or the resale (without forwarding the proceeds to the government) of properties in HUD ownership.

[18]This gave an opportunity for "advocate planners" to offer their services, but also tended to give an advantage to communities with well-educated or savvy residents who could take advantage of programs intended for the disadvantaged. Some scandals resulted from these programs.

[19]The idea had been tried in England, where it proved no more successful.

by government but executed by private enterprise). Private investors were offered financial incentives to open businesses in certain poor urban areas designated as enterprise zones. In return, the benefiting investors had to promise that the jobs their companies created would go to local residents. Again, the anticipated results often failed to materialize. Unemployed local residents were deemed unsuitable, and some firms, after taking advantage of the subsidies, departed because their operations still proved unprofitable.[20]

The End of Planning

Under the Reagan administration, however, funding for all sorts of urban social programs dried up, and urban planners—physical and social—fell on hard times. The loss of faith in the ability of planners to solve urban problems appeared to be matched by a loss of will to address them. All public housing construction virtually stopped, and gradually most housing subsidies were eliminated as well. Furthermore, some cities began to tear down older low-income housing projects where these developments occupied centrally located sites that were newly demanded by an expanding corporate sector. Suggestions were also made to "privatize" existing projects by selling off the units. It is little wonder that in the 1980s the number of homeless in major cities (and even small towns) rose precipitously, and that in addition to the older forms of homelessness (men in skid rows and hobo "jungles"), women and dependent children joined their ranks.

Few programs have been restored since then, as attention shifted to the "war on drugs" that was adopted as the favored program of the Bush administration. In this new "war," city planners have had no role to play. Stricter law enforcement, combined with social and medico-social work directed chiefly toward giving preventive information and re-educating addicts, have been the dominant strategies advocated.

WHY PLANNING FAILED

Thus, despite the high hopes held out for it, city planning, even when independent, well-intentioned, and competent,[21] has proven disappointing. There is considerable disagreement, however, about why city planning has failed to ameliorate urban problems. The various diagnoses of the causes of planning failure are related to theories about how cities are actually produced, which are in turn related to the kinds of policies critics advocate to produce better ones. We have classified the explanations for the failure of planning into three main

---

[20]An example of a typical scandal attached to this program was that involving the Wedtech Company in New York City's South Bronx, where collusive cheating by politicians and industrial investors was subsequently revealed and the information widely disseminated in the press. Other cases occurred but went undetected or unpublicized.

[21]Karl Mannheim's criteria for good planning; see his *Freedom, Power, and Democratic Planning* (London: Routledge & Kegan Paul, 1951).

types, together with their variations, and have ordered them by how fundamental to their assumptions is the idea that the basic social priorities of America need to change.

1. *Better or different planning is needed.*
   a. The mildest critics claim that we have not yet succeeded in producing good cities because we are not yet good enough at planning. Given improved information, more professional planners, better laws, more money, and concerted will, we can do better.[22] A variation of this critique is that planning has failed because it has been in the hands of distant and "technical" professionals who are insensitive to local needs. Greater involvement of citizens in the planning process, the mobilization of local talent, and a system of decentralized control and local empowerment could make planning more adapted to people's wishes.[23]
   b. A somewhat harsher view focuses on differential power. It suggests that planners have always served the interests of those citizens well-endowed with economic and political power better than they have served the interests of the poor and weak.[24] Critics taking this position support the training of "advocate planners" (those who will work for, rather than against the poor), and champion grassroots movements to empower classes and groups whose voices have hitherto been silent or silenced.[25]
2. *Planners have not been given powers commensurate with their responsibilities.*
   a. A second line of criticism attributes failure to the fact that the

---

[22]To some extent, this is implicit in Matthew Crenson's argument in *Neighborhood Politics* (Cambridge, MA: Harvard University Press, 1983), although he advocates a greater role for local citizens in planning.

[23]Saul Alinsky was one of the first to advocate local goal setting and local action initiatives. See his *Reveille for Radicals* (Chicago: University of Chicago Press, 1946) which for a long time was considered the bible of community organizers. Indeed, he ran a school to train activists in his techniques of community mobilization. See Milton Kotler, *Neighborhood Government: The Local Foundations of Political Life* (Indianapolis: Bobbs-Merrill, 1969) for a review of earlier attempts at community organizing. A more sophisticated approach is evident in Jeffrey Henig's *Neighborhood Mobilization: Redevelopment and Response* (New Brunswick, NJ: Rutgers University Press, 1982), which stresses the extent to which variables at higher levels of the system (national and international) intervene in neighborhood futures. See also the wise (and early) article by Richard Applebaum, "The Future Is Made, Not Predicted," *Society* 14 (1977), pp. 49–53.

[24]Perhaps the strongest statement of this position can be found in (former) planner Robert Goodman's very bitter diatribe, *After the Planners* (New York: Simon & Schuster, 1971).

[25]Manuel Castells, in his *The City and the Grassroots* (Berkeley and Los Angeles: University of California Press, 1983), is today's most ardent advocate of this position. However, local empowerment is not without its costs. Local area citizens often have preferences that go against the law or the public interest, as evidenced by the NIMBY ("not in my backyard") position, the wide support in certain urban areas for excluding blacks, and by some of the scandals that have resulted (in New York at least) from abuses by the new local school boards. See Ira Katznelson, *Schooling for All: Class, Race and the Decline of the Democratic Ideal* (New York: Basic Books, 1985).

organizations and agents who *really* make the decisions which shape our cities are not planners at all—or certainly not city planners. The mildest form of this position is that city planners are employees of city governments that follow policies intended to advance the interests of an extra-governmental business elite.[26] Most urban policies adopted will therefore favor a "growth imperative" that is as gratifying to local boosters (and to government officials) as it is profitable to developers, real estate investors, and other businessmen who gain from expanding the market demand for their goods.[27] Thus, planners tend to work for growth—for personal, political, and economic reasons.

b. A harsher version of this critique is almost conspiratorial in tone, suggesting that government is a mere pawn in the hands of unscrupulous capitalists who manipulate urban policies, as they do all other policies, to maximize their profits and to immobilize any counter force that might come from worker organization.[28]

c. More sophisticated is the (so-called) neo-Marxist position taken by, for example, Henri Lefebvre[29] and David Harvey,[30] who note that in the complex circuits of capitalism, the built environment and governmental investments in it and in associated research and development and infrastructure, serve to resolve the periodic crises of over-accumulation that are an integral part of capitalism as a form of economic organization. In their view, the built environment under capitalism is *not intended to serve people's needs*, except incidentally. Rather, it serves as an outlet for excess investment

---

[26]See, for example, the collection of essays in Scott Cummings, ed., *Business Elites and Urban Development* (Albany: State University of New York Press, 1988). See also Roger Friedland and Donald Palmer, "Park Place and Main Street: Business and the Urban Power Structure," *Annual Review of Sociology* 10 (1984), pp. 393–416; Robert Alford and Roger Friedland, "Political Participation and Public Policy, *Annual Review of Sociology* 1 (1975), pp. 429–479; and Richard Child Hill, "Separate and Unequal: Governmental Inequality in the Metropolis," *American Political Science Review* 68 (1974), pp. 1557–1568.

[27]Harvey Molotch has put this position most cogently. See his classic article, "The City as a Growth Machine," also incorporated into John Logan and Harvey Molotch's *Urban Fortunes* (Berkeley: University of California Press, 1987). A very measured evaluation of many of the positions that have been taken, relating politics to economic interests, can be found in John Mollenkopf's review essay, "Who (or What) Runs Cities, and How?" in *Sociological Forum* 4 (1989), pp. 119–137.

[28]Many of the articles contained in, for example, Tabb and Sawers's collection, *Marxism and the Metropolis* (New York: Oxford University Press, 1978), border on this conspiratorial tone.

[29]Henri Lefebvre is the most important thinker in this regard. Unfortunately, his works have remained, with a single and unimportant exception, untranslated into English. Serious students must consult his most important work in its French original. See *La production de l'espace* (Paris: Editions Anthropos, 1974; 2nd ed. 1981).

[30]According to Mark Gottdiener, in his *The Social Production of Urban Space* (Austin: University of Texas Press, 1985), David Harvey has drawn heavily on Lefebvre's thought for his analysis of the three circuits of capitalist investment, as shown in Figure 15.1.

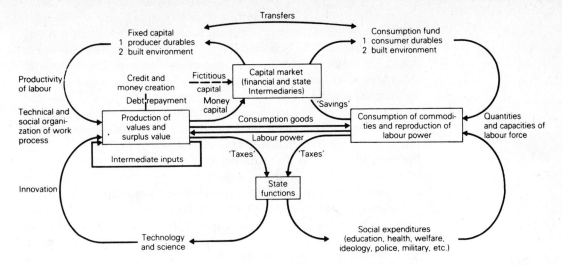

Figure 15.1 Relations among the primary, secondary and tertiary circuits of capital, according to David Harvey. (*Source:* Variously reprinted in many of David Harvey's books. Copyright 1985 by Johns Hopkins University Press. Reprinted with permission.)

capital and as a "bank" for the temporary storage of excess production (see Figure 15.1 from Harvey). These critics note that "capitalists" do not constitute a monolithic class; rather, the interests of capitalists whose profits come from rents (so-called *rentier* capitalists) are often at odds with those of capitalists whose profits come from production and who therefore seek low rents in addition to low labor and materials costs.[31]

3. *Since urban problems are not locally caused, they cannot be solved through local planning.*

   a. None of the preceding positions directly addresses the question of *level* of decision making, although theorists in each camp may also acknowledge that *local* planning often fails because the *real* decisions about the future of any given locality lie far beyond the control of local elites, businessmen, real estate investors and speculators, politicians—and especially, planners![32] They argue that local

---

[31]Rather than viewing capitalists as constituting a unified ruling class, a number of conflict theorists have concentrated on dissecting divisions and contradictions within the elite. The most famous study in this tradition is C. Wright Mill's *The Power Elite* (New York: Oxford University Press, 1956), but such an approach is also implicit in the work of John Mollenkopf—for example, *The Contested City* (Princeton, NJ: Princeton University Press, 1983) and "Who (or What) Runs Cities, and How?" in *Sociological Forum* 4 (1989), pp. 119–137. See also the excellent collection edited by Kevin R. Cox, *Urbanization and Conflict in Market Societies* (Chicago: Maaroufa Press, 1978).

[32]There is now a large and growing literature on this. For example, Thierry Noyelle and Thomas Stanback, Jr., in *The Economic Transformation of American Cities* (Totowa, NJ: Allanheld, Osmun,

planners cannot control whether population will grow or decline, whether the local economy will prosper or wither, whether a city will be selected as a hub city by an airline or will be bypassed in direct air service, whether it will receive massive investments in federal expenditures for weaponry (including research and development, production, or testing) or a disproportionate share of state and federal funds for other more humane facilities such as hospitals, universities, flood control, or irrigation. It is these factors, rather than local planning, that determine a city's fate.

b. Focusing on business investments, many critics have pointed to the growing scale of capitalism, which now encircles the globe. The increase in the importance of transnational corporations, the flow of American capital overseas, the selection of a few American cities as investment outlets for foreign capital,[33] and the informalization of labor processes in the advanced capitalist world, as off-shore operations (runaway shops) return to the centers of world cities to employ imported laborers in sweatshops,[34] all make a mockery of local efforts to plan.

c. A more subtle point is that whereas at least *some* of the decisions made at these higher levels of the system may have been intended, local areas (and their residents) are also at the mercy of the *unintended* (and often powerful) *consequences* of policies adopted elsewhere for very different ends. Planning not only fails because it does not control the real levers of decision making, but because even the best laid plans can be undermined and reversed by national and even international events with no "designs" on the local area. The so-called energy shortage of the early 1970s is a good case in point.

1984), point to the importance to the growth of Atlanta and Miami of their selection as international airline hub cities. The work of Ann R. Markusen, Peter Hall, and Amy Glasmeier, *High Tech in America: The What, How, Where and Why of the Sunrise Industries* (Boston: Allen & Unwin, 1986), includes shocking proof of the connection between what is termed "high tech" and the world of military weapons research and production, so liberally funded by the federal government.

[33]Joe Feagin's *Free Enterprise City: Houston in Political-Economic Perspective* (New Brunswick, NJ: Rutgers University Press, 1988) analyzes the impact of international events on that city's development. See also the works of Saskia Sassen, cited in Chapter 6, and her forthcoming book, *Global Cities* (Princeton, NJ: Princeton University Press, 1991). Foreign investment in the United States, directed largely to growing southern and western cities (Atlanta, Seattle, etc.), is substantial. A recent article by Peter Applebome, "The Dutch Find New Treats in America," *(New York Times Business Supplement,* September 24, 1989), presented data from the U.S. Department of Commerce, noting that between 1984 and 1988 direct foreign investment in the United States grew from about $150 billion to about $325 billion. In 1988, Britain was the largest investor (about $100 billion), followed by the Netherlands and the Netherlands Antilles (some $60 billion in combined investments); Japan ran third, with a total of some $53 billion invested in the United States.

[34]For example, see Alejandro Portes's 1989 collection on *The Informal Economy* and Saskia Sassen's *The Mobility of Labor and Capital,* both of which discuss the growing informal sector in "first world" major metropolises. Sassen's forthcoming book, *Global Cities,* explores this phenomenon which she claims is occurring not only in New York, but in Paris, London, and even Tokyo!

The rapid increases in the price of oil were not motivated to cause changes in cities in the United States; and yet, such rises did inhibit, temporarily, the spreading out of the cities.[35] Less extreme examples are Congress-initiated changes in U.S. tax laws or adjustments by the Federal Reserve Bank in the discount rate (which sets other interest rates for borrowed money).[36] The former are intended to raise revenues for government without dampening the "business climate" for investment, while the latter are intended to stabilize gradually rising prices and thus to smooth out economic cycles. One important unintended effect of both of these interventions is a reactive fluctuation in the number of building starts (the number of new houses and apartments that will be built), which in turn affects the overall supply and therefore the cost of housing.

A MODEL FOR ANALYZING HOW CITIES ARE ACTUALLY PRODUCED

If we are to design policies that could shape our cities into better places, if we are to gain greater control over the "urban outcomes" that are our cities, we will clearly need a better understanding of the forces that create them. Each of the critics whose ideas have just been outlined has a "hidden" model for how cities are actually produced—a model that makes certain variables central and discounts others. The different approaches are, in part, ideological. However, the disagreements cannot be resolved at the level of ideology. Clearly, better studies are needed.

The research agenda we are calling for would systematically examine specific urban outcomes to trace the complex decision-making paths that "caused" them. If, as shown in Figure 15.2, local government planners are involved in only a very tiny proportion of the decisions that yield urban outcomes, it should certainly not be surprising that local government planning is often ineffectual, and ironically, that when it is effective, its results are often disastrous for the poor and for minorities. Planning *is* going on, but the actors in this planning are not necessarily those people called "planners."

Figure 15.2 presents a rough model of the forces that affect urban outcomes (i.e., the production and reproduction of the form of the city). A few words of explanation are required to make this diagram intelligible. In the diamond at

---

[35]See, for example, Jon van Til, *Living with Energy Shortfall: A Future for American Cities and Towns* (Boulder, CO: Westview Press, 1982), and his "New City Types in an Energy-Short World," pp. 150–162 in vol. 23 of *Urban Affairs Annual Reviews,* ed. Gary Gappert and Richard Knight (Beverly Hills, CA: Sage Publications, 1982). There is a voluminous literature on the relationship between forms of transportation and city structure. A replay of oil-price boosts had begun by August 1990.

[36]See, for a recent critique along these lines, Michael Peter Smith, *City, State, Market: The Political Economy of Urban Society* (New York: Basil Blackwell, 1988), especially Chapter 1.

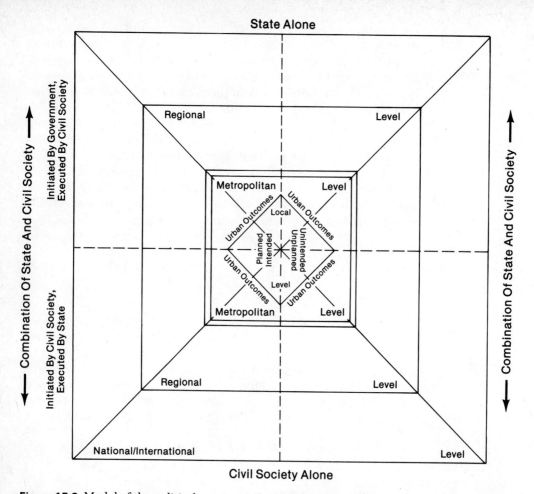

Figure 15.2 Model of the political economy of urban decision making. (*Source:* Original with the author.)

the very center of the diagram we place URBAN OUTCOMES, that is, the effects on urban areas of the forces that are shown in the rest of the model. Of these urban outcomes, some are intended (someone tried to achieve them or planned for them), whereas the rest (how many remains an empirical question) can be considered unplanned, resulting either from the accidental combination of the separate utility curves of individual actors (Adam Smith's marketplace?)[37] or as

---

[37]To take only one example, no one would claim that the goal of real estate speculators' "turning over" property rapidly for a quick return, or holding land out of the marketplace unduly in order to "make a killing" later, fits well with the marginal utility model of classical urban land economists or the "consumer is sovereign" assumption of classical housing demand theorists. For a particularly

the unintended consequences of planning for goals that did not have cities as their primary, or even acknowledged, object.

In the top and bottom triangles we have placed two main categories of actors: (1) the "state," in the widest sense of that term; and (2) "civil society," or the non-state system. The "state," placed at the upper part of the diagram, includes the formal and administrative apparatus of government. Actors in this apparatus include all elected and appointed government officials charged with setting policy goals—policy-makers. Civil society, placed at the lower part of the diagram, includes all those who function exclusively in organizations not considered a part of the formal governmental structure, although voting citizens are also placed in this category. These include persons working in private businesses and industries (the "non-governmental" economy), as well as consumers selecting their own housing, deciding among alternative types of transportation, and making all sorts of other choices concerning investment, location, and consumption patterns.

Clearly, the categories of civil society and the state are not rigidly separated. Civil society and the state cooperate in many decisions that relate to cities (as well as to almost everything else). Indeed, the term "political economy" is intended to convey this overlapping area in which state and civil society come together. The triangles to the left and right, therefore, represent such areas of interaction. The top halves of the side triangles refer to those parts of political economy in which government initiates programs (with planned or unintended urban consequences or outcomes) and then employs elements in civil society to execute them, offering whatever legal and economic incentives (tax exemptions, deregulation, subsidies, etc.) are deemed necessary to achieve ends set primarily by government. The so-called "privatization" of what were formerly viewed as direct governmental responsibilities (e.g., providing garbage pickups or even publicly constructed low-income housing) would come into our model here.[38]

---

trenchant (even acerbic) account of the "distortions" to the market and the impediments to rational planning created by urban real estate speculation, see Joe Feagin, "Urban Real Estate Speculation in the United States: Implications for Social Science and Urban Planning," *International Journal of Urban and Regional Research* 6 (1982), pp. 35–59. Kenneth Newton has argued that the filtering-down process in housing has led to poor housing; see his "Feeble Governments and Private Power: Urban Politics and Policies in the United States," pp. 37–58 in Louis Masotti and Robert Lineberry, eds., *The New Urban Politics* (Cambridge, MA: Ballinger, 1976). Some interesting points on the overlapping membership of the elite on governing boards of industrial firms and of banks making mortgage loans are made by Richard E. Ratcliff in "Banks and the Command of Capital Flows: An Analysis of Capitalist Class Structure and Mortgage Disinvestment in a Metropolitan Area," pp. 129–159 in Maurice Zeitlin, ed., *Classes, Class Conflict and the State* (Cambridge, MA: Winthrop, 1979).

[38]Not all arguments for the privatization of public housing are ill-intentioned or without reason. For example, see Irving Welfeld, *Where We Live: The American Home and the Social, Political, and Economic Landscape, from Slums to Suburbs* (New York: Simon & Schuster, 1990), which makes a very different diagnosis of American housing problems and recommends very different policies to solve them than do, for example, the more critical writings in the anthology edited by Rachael Bratt, Chester Hartman, and Ann Meyerson, *Critical Perspectives on Housing* (Philadel-

The bottom halves of the side triangles refer to policies (some intended to have consequences in urban areas, others not directed or planned in terms of their urban consequences) that are undertaken by government in response to initiatives and pressures generated in civil society. These can be activities initiated by the powerful ("What's good for General Motors is good for the country," an official once suggested),[39] or they can be "stimulated" by the less powerful—as when urban riots in Watts and other minority areas of American cities in the 1960s forced the federal government to pay more attention, albeit only briefly, to the problems of urban poverty. President Johnson's "war on poverty," as well as the gains made by many "urban social movements," would be classified here.

Finally, the nested squares are intended to represent the various scales or levels of operation in both systems. The outermost square focuses on decisions and actions that take place on the most geographically extended level of global and national policy, whether such policies are made by multinational firms (in civil society) or by NATO, Congress, or the Pentagon, for example (in state society). At a somewhat lower level of the system are those policies that are largely regional in scope (affecting the South, the Northeast, etc.) or even only statewide. Inside this is an even smaller square that refers to the specific metropolitan areas affected by the governmental and civil society decision-makers operating at that scale. We could imagine a still smaller square for specific cities within metropolitan regions, or particular urban subareas which are the arenas for very local organizations within state or civil society.

AFTER THE PLANNERS

Much work remains to study how specific urban outcomes result from the interaction of all the various types of influences that are brought to bear on cities. Rather than being too critical of planning failures, perhaps we need to apply ourselves seriously to the study of how things actually work. Too much was expected of planners, and too little control over the key forces shaping our cities was theirs to command. Since, as we have seen, local planners can seldom even influence many of the powerful forces operating in civil society, much less control those that are generated at state, national, and, increasingly, at international levels of the system, how can we expect planning, as it is now done, to change cities in fundamental ways? The problems that generate urban prob-

---

phia: Temple University Press, 1986). See the glowing reactions of housing economist Louis Winnick, in his review of Welfeld's book, in "To House a Nation," *The Public Interest* (Winter 1989), pp. 137–141.

[39]Recently there has been much debate on whether the state can be so easily dismissed as a mere "tool" of elites in civil society, as C. Wright Mills came close to doing in *The Power Elite*, or whether the state needs to be conceptualized as a somewhat more autonomous actor, pursuing its own interests. Many, including the writers in Theda Skocpol *et al.*, eds., *Bringing the State Back In* (New York: Cambridge University Press, 1985), have argued for the latter position.

lems grow organically out of the society itself, and nothing less than attention to the problems of society will solve them.

If we are to get better cities, if we are to deserve better cities, then we cannot wait patiently for a technological or administrative "fix." We must find out what really creates our cities, both physically and socially. We must reach a deeper understanding of the forces and processes that have shaped them— that have caused them to become what they are now and that daily and continually reproduce and modify them. Such forces are well beyond the control of planners and administrators, although they are the collective outcomes of all our attitudes, institutions, and social structures. To get changed cities—to *change* our cities into a better image of our society—we must change the society itself.

Knowing the causes of the urban outcomes we do not like, and then working to change the conditions that lead to them—that is our task as social scientists and as citizens. There is no hiding place. Today, as before, middle- and upper-class people try to run away from the city or to barricade themselves against the city (whether figuratively, through suburban exclusion zoning, or literally, through such policed "private" grounds as Bel Aire). Max Weber defined a "true city" as a place that *walled out the non-city.* In an ironic reversal of this, our efforts are now more often directed to *walling the city out of our lives.*

But especially in today's global-village-city-metropolis, walls constitute even less of a solution than they did in the Middle Ages. The cities erupt periodically, disease spreads, the disenfranchised turn in despair or blocked ambition to drugs and worse. Walls will not save us, nor will flight. Abraham Lincoln said a society could not survive half free and half slave. Were he to look at our cities today, he might have rephrased this to refer to the intractable inequities in our cities. The title of David Harvey's book, *Social Justice and the City,* may be either epitaph or moral guide to American cities which need social justice as never before. Urban sociology alone cannot bring about social justice. But knowing what cities are and how they evolve and change may assist us in achieving a just society. Such a society will have cities we love and are proud to live in.

Bibliography

Abler, Ronald. "The Telephone and the Evolution of the American Metropolitan System." In *The Social Impact of the Telephone,* ed. Ithiel de Sola Pool. Cambridge, MA: MIT Press, 1977.

Abrams, Charles. *The City Is the Frontier.* New York: Harper & Row, 1965.

Abu-Lughod, Janet. *Before European Hegemony: The World System* A.D. *1250–1350.* New York and London: Oxford University Press, 1989.

Abu-Lughod, Janet. *Cairo: 1001 Years of the City Victorious.* Princeton, NJ: Princeton University Press, 1971.

Abu-Lughod, Janet. *The City Is Dead—Long Live the City: Some Thoughts on Urbanity.* Monograph 12. Berkeley, CA: Center for Planning and Development of University of California, 1969.

Abu-Lughod, Janet. "Designing a City for All." *Planning, Women and Change,* ed. Karen Hapgood and Judith Getzels. Chicago: American Society of Planning Officials, 1974. Reprinted in *The Internal Structure of the City,* ed. Larry Bourne. New York: Oxford University Press, 1982.

Abu-Lughod, Janet. "Marxist Urban Sociology." *Contemporary Sociology* 8 (March 1979), pp. 192–196.

Abu-Lughod, Janet. "Migrant Adjustment to City Life: The Egyptian Case." *American Journal of Sociology* 67 (July 1961), pp. 22–32.

Abu-Lughod, Janet. "New York and Cairo: A View from Street Level." *International Social Science Journal,* No. 126 (August 1990), pp. 307–318.

Abu-Lughod, Janet. "A Paradigm for Studying Environment and Behavior in the City." *Field Study: A Sourcebook for Experiential Learning,* ed. Lenore Borzak, pp. 268–287. Beverly Hills, CA: Sage Publications, 1981.

Abu-Lughod, Janet. *Rabat: Urban Apartheid in Morocco.* Princeton, NJ: Princeton University Press, 1980.

Abu-Lughod, Janet. "Testing the Theory of Social Area Analysis: The Ecology of Cairo, Egypt." *American Sociological Review* 34 (April 1969), pp. 198–212.

Abu-Lughod, Janet. "Urbanization in Egypt: Present State and Future Prospects." *Economic Development and Cultural Change* 13 (April 1965), pp. 313–343.

Abu-Lughod, Janet and Richard Hay, Jr., eds. *Third World Urbanization.* 2d ed. New York: Methuen, 1979.

Adams, Robert McC. *The Evolution of Urban Society: Early Mesopotamia and Prehispanic Mexico.* Chicago: Aldine Publishing Company, 1966.

Adams, Robert McC. *Land Behind Baghdad: A History of Settlement on the Diyala Plains.* Chicago: University of Chicago Press, 1965.

Adams, William R. *Nubia: Corridor to Africa.* Princeton, NJ: Princeton University Press, 1977.

Addams, Jane *et al. Hull-House Maps and Papers. A Presentation of Nationalities and Wages in a Congested District of Chicago, by Residents of Hull House, a Social Settlement.* No. 5 of the Library of Economics and Politics, ed. Richard T. Ely. New York: Thomas Y. Crowell, 1895.

Adler, Patricia. *Wheeling and Dealing: An Ethnography of an Upper Level Drug Dealing and Smuggling Community.* New York: Columbia University Press, 1985.

Aiken, Michael T. and Paul E. Mott, eds. *The Structure of Community Power.* New York: Random House, 1970.

Alford, Robert and Roger Friedland. "Political Participation and Public Policy." *Annual Review of Sociology* 1 (1975), pp. 429–479.

Alihan, Milla. *Social Ecology.* New York: Columbia University Press, 1938.

Alinsky, Saul. *Reveille for Radicals.* Chicago: University of Chicago Press, 1946.

Alkim, U. Bahadir. *Anatolia from the Beginnings to the End of the 2nd Millennium.* Trans. James Hogarth. Cleveland, OH: World Publishing Co., 1968.

Altman, Irwin. *The Environment and Social Behavior: Privacy, Personal Space, Territory and Crowding.* Monterey, CA: Brooks/Cole Publishing Co., 1975.

Altman, Irwin and Abraham Wandersman, eds. *Neighborhood and Community Environments: Human Behavior and Environment.* New York: Plenum Press, 1987.

Anderson, Elijah. *A Place on the Corner.* Chicago: University of Chicago Press, 1978.

Anderson, Elijah. *Streetwise: Race, Class and Change in an Urban Community.* Chicago: University of Chicago Press, 1990.

Anderson, Martin. *The Federal Bulldozer: A Critical Analysis of Urban Renewal: 1949–1962.* Cambridge, MA: MIT Press, 1965.

Anderson, Nels. *The Hobo.* Chicago: University of Chicago Press, 1923.

Anderson, Perry. *Lineages of the Absolutist State.* London: Humanities Press, 1974.

Anderson, Perry. *Passages from Antiquity to Feudalism.* London: NLB, 1974.

Anderson, Theodore and Janice A. Egeland. "Spatial Aspects of Social Area Analysis." *American Sociological Review* 26 (June 1961), pp. 392–398.

Applebaum, Richard P. "The Future Is Made, Not Predicted—Technocratic Planners vs. Public Interests." *Society* 14 (1977), pp. 49–53.

Ardrey, Robert. *The Territorial Imperative: A Personal Inquiry into the Animal Origins of Property and Nations.* New York: Atheneum, 1966.

Arensberg, Conrad M. and Solon T. Kimball. *Culture and Community.* New York: Harcourt, Brace and World, 1965.

Armstrong, Warwick and T. G. McGee. *Theatres of Accumulation: Studies in Asian and Latin American Urbanization.* London and New York: Methuen, 1985.

Babcock, Richard F. *The Zoning Game: Municipal Practices and Policies.* Madison, WI: University of Wisconsin Press, 1966.

Baldassare, Mark. *Trouble in Paradise: The Suburban Transformation in America.* New York: Columbia University Press, 1986.

Ball, D. *Microecology: Social Situations and Intimate Space.* Indianapolis: Bobbs-Merrill, 1973.

Baltzell, E. Digby, ed. *The Search for Community in Modern America.* New York: Harper & Row, 1968.

Barnes, John A. "Class and Committees in a Norwegian Island Parish." *Human Relations* 7 (1954), pp. 39–58.

Barnet, Richard J. and Ronald E. Muller. *Global Reach: The Power of Multinational Corporations.* New York: Simon & Schuster, 1974.

Beach, Mark. *Desegregated Housing and Interracial Neighborhoods: A Bibliographic Guide.* Philadelphia: National Neighbors, 1975.

Beale, Calvin L. "The Recent Shift in United States Population to Nonmetropolitan Areas, 1970–1975." *International Regional Science Review* 2 (1977), pp. 113–122.

Beale, Calvin L. *The Revival of Population Growth in Nonmetropolitan America.* Washington, DC: U.S. Department of Agriculture, Economic Development Division, 1975.

Beales, H. L. *The Industrial Revolution, 1750–1850: An Introductory Essay.* New York: Sentry Press, 1967.

Beauregard, R., ed. *Economic Restructuring and Political Response.* Vol. 34 of *Urban Affairs Annual Reviews.* Newbury Park, CA: Sage Publications, 1989.

Becchieri, M. G., ed. *Hunters and Gatherers Today.* New York: Holt, Rinehart & Winston, 1972.

Bell, Daniel. *The Coming of Post-Industrial Society: A Venture Towards Social Forecasting.* New York: Basic Books, 1973.

Bell, Wendell. "Economic, Family and Ethnic Status: An Empirical Test." *American Sociological Review* 20 (February 1955), pp. 45–52.

Bell, Wendell. "The Social Areas of the San Francisco Bay Region." *American Sociological Review* 18 (February 1953), pp. 39–47.

Bensman, David and Roberta Lynch. *Rusted Dreams: Hard Times in a Steel Community.* Berkeley: University of California Press, 1988.

Berg, Barbara J. *The Remembered Gate: Origins of American Feminism: The Woman and the City, 1800–1860.* New York: Oxford University Press, 1978.

Berger, Bennett. *The Survival of a Counterculture: Ideological Work and Everyday Life Among Rural Communards.* Berkeley, CA: University of California Press, 1981.

Berger, Bennett. *Working Class Suburb: A Study of Auto Workers in Suburbia.* Berkeley, CA: University of California Press, 1960.

Berkowitz, S. D. *An Introduction to Structural Analysis: The Network Approach to Social Research.* Toronto: Butterworths, 1982.

Berle, Adolph A., Jr. *Power Without Property.* New York: Harcourt, Brace, 1959.

Berle, Adolph A., Jr. and Gardiner Means. *The Modern Corporation and Private Property.* New York: Macmillan, 1933.

Bernard, Jessie. *The Sociology of Community.* Glenview, IL: Scott, Foresman & Company, 1973.

Berry, Brian J. L., ed. *Urbanization and Counter-Urbanization.* Volume 11 of *Urban Affairs Annual Reviews.* Beverly Hills, CA: Sage Publications, 1976.

Berry, Brian J. *et al. Chicago: Transformations of an Urban System.* Cambridge, MA: Ballinger Publishing Co., 1976.

Berry, Brian J. L. and William Garrison. "The Functional Bases of the Central Place Hierarchy." *Economic Geography* 34 (1958), pp. 145–154.

Berry, Brian J. L. and William Garrison. "Recent Developments in Central Place Theory." *Papers and Proceedings of the Regional Science Association* 4 (1958), pp. 107–120.

Berry, Brian and Quentin Gillard. *The Changing Shape of Metropolitan America: Commuting Patterns, Urban Fields and Decentralization Processes, 1960–1970.* Cambridge, MA: Ballinger Publication Co., 1977.

Berry, Brian J. L. and John D. Kasarda. *Contemporary Urban Ecology.* New York: Macmillan Publishing, 1977.

Berry, Brian and Philip H. Rees. "The Factorial Ecology of Calcutta." *American Journal of Sociology* 74 (March 1969), pp. 445–491.

Beshers, James and Edward O. Laumann. "Social Distance: A Network Approach." *American Sociological Review* 32 (1967), pp. 225–236.

Betz, D. Michael. "The City as a System Generating Income Inequality." *Social Forces* 51 (1972), pp. 192–198.

Bibby, Geoffrey. *Looking for Dilmun.* New York: Knopf, 1970.

Binford, Henry. *The First Suburbs: Residential Communities on the Boston Periphery: 1815–1860.* Chicago: University of Chicago Press, 1985.

Bingham, Richard D., Roy Green, and Sammis White, eds. *The Homeless in Contemporary Society.* Newbury Park, CA: Sage Publications, 1987.

Birch, Eugenie Ladner, ed. *The Unsheltered Woman: Women and Housing in the 1980s.* New Brunswick, NJ: Center for Urban Policy Research, Rutgers University, 1985.

Blakely, Edward, ed. *Planning Local Economic Development.* Newbury Park, CA: Sage Publications, 1989.

Bluestone, Barry and Bennett Harrison. *Capital and Communities: The Causes and Consequences of Private Disinvestment.* Washington, DC: The Progressive Alliance, 1980.

Bluestone, Barry and Bennett Harrison. *The Deindustrialization of America: Plant Closings, Community Abandonment, and the Dismantling of Basic Industry.* New York: Basic Books, 1982.

Booth, Alan and J. Edwards. "Crowding and Family Relations." *American Sociological Review* 41 (1976), pp. 308–321.

Booth, Charles. *Life and Labour of the People in London.* 17 volumes. London: Macmillan and Company, 1902–1903.

Boots, Barry N. and Arthur Getis. *Point Pattern Analysis.* Vol. 8 of Scientific Geography Series. Newbury Park, CA: Sage Publications, 1988.

Bott, Elizabeth. *Family and Social Network.* London: Tavistock Publications, 1957.

Bourne, Larry S., ed. *The Internal Structure of the City.* 2d ed. New York: Oxford University Press, 1982.

Braidwood, Robert. "The Agricultural Revolution." *Scientific American* 203 (September 1960), pp. 130–152.

Braidwood, Robert and Gordon Willey, eds. *Courses Toward Urban Life.* Chicago: Aldine Publishing Company, 1962.

Bratt, Rachael G., Chester Hartman, and Ann Meyerson, eds. *Critical Perspectives on Housing.* Philadelphia: Temple University Press, 1986.

Braudel, Fernand. *The Mediterranean and the Mediterranean World in the Age of Philip II.* Two volumes. New York: Harper & Row, 1972 (English trans.). Originally published in French in 1949.

Braudel, Fernand. "Pre-modern Towns." As condensed and translated in *The Early Modern Town,* ed. Peter Clark, pp. 53–90. London: Longman, 1976.

Braunfels, Wolfgang. *Urban Design in Western Europe: Regime and Architecture, 900–1900.* Chicago: University of Chicago Press, 1988.

Breese, Gerald, ed. *The City in Newly Developing Countries.* Englewood Cliffs, NJ: Prentice-Hall, 1969.

Breese, Gerald. *The Daytime Population of the Central Business District of Chicago with Particular Reference to the Factors of Transportation.* Chicago: University of Chicago Press, 1949.

Bridenbaugh, Carl. *Cities in Revolt: Urban Life in America, 1743–1776.* New York: Alfred Knopf, 1955.

Bridenbaugh, Carl. *Cities in the Wilderness: The First Century of Urban Life in America, 1625–1742.* New York: Ronald Press, 1938.

Briggs, Asa. *Victorian Cities.* New York: Harper Colophon Books, 1970.

Brooks, Richard O. *New Town and Communal Values: A Case Study of Columbia, Maryland.* New York: Praeger, 1974.

Brown, David L. and John Wardwell, eds. *New Directions in Urban-Rural Migration: The Population Turnaround in Rural America.* New York: Academic Press, 1980.

Brune, Tom, ed. *Neglected Neighborhoods: Patterns of Discrimination in Chicago City Services.* Reprinted from *The Chicago Reporter,* articles published between 1977 and 1980. Chicago: The Community Renewal Society, 1981.

Brunn, Stanley D. and Jack Williams. *Cities of the World.* New York: Harper & Row, 1983.

Bulmer, Martin. *The Chicago School of Sociology: Institutionalization, Diversity, and the Rise of Sociological Research.* Chicago: University of Chicago Press, 1984.

Burgess, Ernest W. *The Basic Writings of Ernest W. Burgess,* ed. Donald J. Bogue. Chicago: Community and Family Study Center, University of Chicago, 1974.

Burgess, Ernest W. "The Determination of Gradients in the Growth of a City." *Publications of the American Sociological Society* 21 (1927), pp. 178–184.

Burgess, Ernest W. "The Growth of the City: An Introduction to a Research Project." *Proceedings of the American Sociological Society* 18 (1923), pp. 85–97.

Burgess, Ernest W. and Donald J. Bogue, eds. *Contributions to Urban Sociology.* Chicago: University of Chicago Press, 1964.

Burkhart, Lynne Connolly. *Old Values in a New Town: The Politics of Race and Class in Columbia, Maryland.* New York: Praeger, 1981.

Burnam, David. *The Rise of the Computer State.* New York: Random House, 1980.

Byerts, Thomas *et al.,* eds. *Environmental Context of Aging: Lifestyles, Environmental Quality and Living Arrangements.* New York: STPM Press, 1979.

Calhoun, J. B. "Population Density and Social Pathology." *Scientific American* 206 (1962), pp. 139–148.

Calhoun, J. B. "The Role of Space in Animal Sociology." *Journal of Social Issues* 22 (1966), pp. 46–58.

Caplow, Theodore and Bruce Chadwick. "Inequality and Life Styles in Middletown, 1920–1978." *Social Science Quarterly* 60 (1979), pp. 367–386.

Caplow, Theodore, Howard Bahr, and Bruce Chadwick. *All Faithful People: Change and Continuity in Middletown's Religion.* Minneapolis: University of Minnesota Press, 1983.

Caplow, Theodore, Howard Bahr, Bruce Chadwick, Reuben Hill, and Margaret Williamson. *Middletown Families: Fifty Years of Change and Continuity.* Minneapolis: University of Minnesota Press, 1982.

Carcopino, James. *Daily Life in Ancient Rome.* New Haven: Yale University Press, 1940.

Caro, Robert A. *The Power Broker: Robert Moses and the Fall of New York.* New York: Knopf, 1974.

Castells, Manuel. *City, Class and Power.* Trans. Elizabeth Lebas. New York: St. Martin's Press, 1978.

Castells, Manuel. *The City and the Grassroots.* Berkeley and Los Angeles: University of California Press, 1983.

Castells, Manuel. *The Urban Question: A Marxist Approach.* Trans. Alan Sheridan. London: Edward Arnold, and Cambridge, MA: MIT Press, 1977. Originally published as *La question urbaine.* Paris: Maspero, 1972.

Castells, Manuel. *The Informational City: Information Technology, Economic Restructuring and the Urban-Regional Process.* New York: Basil Blackwell, 1989.

Catanese, Anthony James. *The Politics of Planning and Development.* Beverly Hills, CA: Sage Publications, 1984.

Center for the Study of Social Policy. "A Dream Deferred: The Economic Status of Black Americans. A Working Paper." Washington, DC: Center for the Study of Social Policy, 1983 (mimeographed report).

Chandler, Alfred D., Jr. *Strategy and Structure: Chapters in the History of the American Industrial Enterprise.* Cambridge, MA: MIT Press, 1962.

Chandler, Alfred D., Jr. *The Visible Hand: The Managerial Revolution in American Business.* Cambridge, MA: Belknap Press, 1977.

Chandler, Tertius. *4000 Years of Urban Growth: An Historical Census.* Lewistown, NY: St. David's University Press, 1987.

Chandler, Tertius and Gerald Fox. *3000 Years of Urban Growth.* New York: Academic Press, 1973.

Chang, Kwang-chih. *The Archaeology of Ancient China.* New Haven: Yale University Press, 1977.

Chapin, F. Stuart, Jr. *Human Activity Patterns in the City: Things People Do in Time and Space.* New York: John Wiley, 1974.

Chapin, F. Stuart, Jr. and Henry C. Hightower. *Household Activity Systems: A Pilot Investigation.* Chapel Hill: University of North Carolina, Center for Urban and Regional Studies, Institute for Research in Social Science, 1966.

Chicago Factbook Consortium. *Local Community Factbook: Chicago Metropolitan Area.* Chicago: Chicago Review Press, 1984.

Childe, V. Gordon. *Man Makes Himself.* New York: New American Library, 1951.

Childe, V. Gordon. *New Light on the Most Ancient Middle East.* 4th ed. London: Routledge & Kegan Paul, 1964.

Childe, V. Gordon. "The Urban Revolution." *Town Planning Review* 21 (April 1950), pp. 3–17.

Christaller, Walter. *Central Places in Southern Germany.* Trans. C. W. Baskin. Englewood Cliffs, NJ: Prentice-Hall, 1966. Originally published as *Die Zentralen Orte in Suddeutschland.* Jena: Gustav Fischer, 1933.

Clark, Peter, ed. *The Early Modern Town.* London: Longman Group, 1976.

Clark, Terry Nichols and Lorna C. Ferguson. *City Money: Political Processes, Fiscal Strain, and Retrenchment.* New York: Columbia University Press, 1983.

Clarke, Graham and Stuart Piggot. *Prehistoric Societies.* New York: Knopf, 1965.

Coates, Joseph F. "New Technologies and Their Urban Impact." In Gappert and Knight, eds., *Cities in the 21st Century,* pp. 177–195. Vol. 23 of *Urban Affairs Annual Reviews.* Beverly Hills, CA: Sage Publications, 1982.

Cohen, R. B. "The New International Division of Labor, Multinational Corporations and Urban Hierarchy." In Michael Dear and Allan Scott, eds. *Urbanization and Urban Planning in Capitalist Society,* pp. 287–315. New York and London: Methuen, 1981.

Collins, Thomas W., ed. *Cities in a Larger Context.* Athens, GA: The University of Georgia Press, 1980.

Cooper, Clare. *Easter Hill Village: Some Social Implications of Design.* New York: Free Press, 1975.

Cox, Kevin R., ed. *Urbanization and Conflict in Market Societies.* Chicago: Maaroufa Press, 1978; London: Methuen, 1978.

Crenson, Matthew. *Neighborhood Politics.* Cambridge, MA: Harvard University Press, 1983.

Cressey, Paul. *The Taxi Dance Hall.* Chicago: University of Chicago Press, 1932.

Cummings, Scott, ed. *Business Elites and Urban Development.* Albany, NY: State University of New York Press, 1988.

Cutler, Irving. *Chicago: Metropolis of the Mid-Continent.* Dubuque, IA: Kendall/Hunt Publishing Co., 1976.

Dahl, Robert. *Who Governs?* New Haven: Yale University Press, 1961.

Dahlberg, Frances, ed. *Woman, the Gatherer.* New Haven: Yale University Press, 1981.

Daniels, Arlene Kaplan. *Invisible Careers.* Chicago: University of Chicago Press, 1988.

Danielson, Michael. *The Politics of Exclusion.* New York: Columbia University Press, 1976.

Davis, Kingsley, ed. *Cities: Their Origin, Growth, and Human Impact.* Republished from *Scientific American.* San Francisco, CA: W. H. Freeman, 1973.

Davis, Kingsley. *World Urbanization 1950–1970.* Vol. I: *Basic Data for Cities, Countries, and Regions,* Population Monograph Series 4, 1969. Vol. II: *Analysis of Trends, Relationships, and Development,* Population Monograph Series 9, 1972. Berkeley, California: University of California Institute of International Studies.

Dear, Michael and Allen J. Scott, eds. *Urbanization and Urban Planning in Capitalist Society.* New York and London: Methuen, 1981.

Deegan, Mary Jo. *Jane Addams and the Men of the Chicago School, 1892–1918.* New Brunswick, NJ: Transaction Books, 1988.

Deutsch, Morton and Mary Evans Collins. *Interracial Housing: A Psychological Evaluation of a Social Experiment.* Minneapolis: University of Minnesota Press, 1951.

Dewey, Richard. "The Rural-Urban Continuum: Real but Relatively Unimportant." *American Journal of Sociology* 66 (July 1960), pp. 60–66.

Dogan, Mattei and John Kasarda, eds. *The Metropolis Era.* Vol. I: *A World of Giant Cities.* Vol. II: *Mega-Cities.* Newbury Park, CA: Sage Publications, 1988.

Dollard, John. *Caste and Class in a Southern Town.* New Haven: Yale University Press, 1937.

Domhoff, G. William. "The Growth Machine and the Power Elite: A Challenge to Pluralists and Marxists Alike." In *Community Power: Directions for Future Research,* ed. Robert Waste. Newbury Park, CA: Sage Publications, 1986.

Domhoff, G. William. *Who Really Rules: New Haven Community Power Re-examined.* Santa Monica, CA: Goodyear, 1978.

Drake, St. Clair and Horace Cayton. *Black Metropolis: A Study of Negro Life in a Northern City.* New York: Harcourt, Brace and Co., 1945.

DuBois, W. E. B. *The Philadelphia Negro.* Philadelphia: University of Pennsylvania Press, 1899.

Duncan, Beverly and Otis Dudley Duncan. "Residential Distribution and Occupational Stratification." *American Journal of Sociology* 60 (March 1955), pp. 493–503.

Duncan, Otis Dudley, Ray P. Cuzzort, and Beverly Duncan. *Statistical Geography.* Glencoe, IL: Free Press, 1961.

Duncan, Otis Dudley and Leo Schnore, "Cultural, Behavioral and Ecological Perspectives in the Study of Social Organization." *American Journal of Sociology* 65 (1959), pp. 132–145.

Dunn, Edgar S., Jr. *The Development of the U.S. Urban System.* Vol. I: *Concepts, Structures, Regional Shifts.* Baltimore and London: Johns Hopkins University Press, 1980. Vol. II: *Industrial Shifts, Implications.* Baltimore: Johns Hopkins University Press, 1983.

Durkheim, Emile. *The Division of Labor in Society.* Trans. George Simpson. New York: Macmillan Free Press, 1964.

Eisler, Riane. *The Chalice & the Blade.* San Francisco: Harper & Row, 1987.

Ellis, Caroline. *Fisher Folk: Two Communities on Chesapeake Bay.* Lexington, KY: University of Kentucky Press, 1986.

Engels, Frederick [Friedrich]. *The Condition of the Working Class in England.* Trans. W. O. Henderson and W. H. Chaloner. New York: Macmillan Company, 1958.

Fainstein, Norman I. and Susan S. Fainstein, eds. *Urban Policy Under Capitalism.* Vol. 22 of *Urban Affairs Annual Reviews.* Beverly Hills, CA: Sage Publications, 1982.

Fainstein, Susan S. and Norman I. Fainstein, eds. *Restructuring the City: The Political Economy of Urban Redevelopment.* London and New York: Longman, 1983.

Faris, Robert E. *Chicago Sociology: 1920–1932.* Chicago: University of Chicago Press, 1970.

Faris, R. E. L. and H. Warren Dunham. *Mental Disorders in Urban Areas: An Ecological Study of Schizophrenia and Other Psychoses.* Chicago: University of Chicago Press, 1939.

Farley, Reynolds and Walter R. Allen. *The Color Line and the Quality of Life in America.* New York: Russell Sage Foundation, 1987.

Fava, Sylvia, ed. *Urbanism in World Perspective: A Reader.* New York: Thomas Y. Crowell, 1968.

Fava, Sylvia F. "Contrasts in Neighboring: New York City and a Suburban County." In *The Suburban Community,* ed. W. M. Dobriner, pp. 122–130. New York: Putnam, 1958.

Feagin, Joe. *Free Enterprise City: Houston in Political-Economic Perspective.* New Brunswick, NJ: Rutgers University Press, 1988.

Feagin, Joe. *The Urban Real Estate Game: Playing Monopoly with Real Money.* Englewood Cliffs, NJ: Prentice-Hall, 1983.

Feagin, Joe. "Urban Real Estate Speculation in the United States: Implications for Social Science and Urban Planning." *International Journal of Urban and Regional Research* 6 (March 1982), pp. 35–59.

Feldman, Arnold and Charles Tilly. "The Interaction of Social and Physical Space." *American Sociological Review* 25 (1960), pp. 877–884.

Festinger, Leon, S. Schachter, and K. Back. *Social Pressures in Informal Groups: A Study of Human Factors in Housing.* Stanford, CA: Stanford University Press, 1950.

Finley, M. I. *The Ancient Economy.* Berkeley, CA: University of California Press, 1973.

Finley, M. I. *Ancient Slavery and Modern Ideology.* London: Chatto and Windus, 1980.

Finley, M. I. "Between Slavery and Freedom." *Comparative Studies in Society and History* 6 (1963–1964).

Finley, M. I. "Was Greek Civilization Based on Slave Labour?" *Historia* 8 (1959).

Firey, Walter. *Land Use in Central Boston.* Cambridge, MA: Harvard University Press, 1947.

Fischer, Claude S. *To Dwell Among Friends: Personal Networks in Town and City.* Chicago: University of Chicago Press, 1982.

Fischer, Claude S. *et al.*, eds. *Networks and Places: Social Relations in the Urban Setting.* New York: Free Press, 1977.

Fischer, Claude S. *The Urban Experience.* New York: Harcourt Brace Jovanovich, 1976.

Fishman, Robert. *Urban Utopias in the Twentieth Century.* New York: Basic Books, 1977.

Foner, Nancy, ed. *New Immigrants in New York City.* New York: Columbia University Press, 1987.

Foote, Nelson, Janet Abu-Lughod, Louis Winnick, and Mary Mix Foley. *Housing Choices and Housing Constraints.* New York: McGraw-Hill, 1960.

Forbes, Dean and Nigel Thrift, eds. *The Socialist Third World: Urban Development and Territorial Planning.* Oxford: Basil Blackwell, 1987.

Form, William. "The Place of Social Structure in the Determination of Land Use: Some Implications for a Theory of Urban Ecology." *Social Forces* 32 (May 1954), pp. 317–323.

Fox, M. B. "Working Women and Travel: The Access of Women to Work and Community Facilities," *American Planning Association Journal* (Spring 1983), pp. 156–170.

Fox, Richard and Allen Zagarell. "The Political Economy of Mesopotamian and South Indian Temples." *Comparative Urban Research* 9:1 (1982), pp. 8–27.

Freedman, Jonathan. *Crowding and Behavior: The Psychology of High Density Living.* New York: Viking Press, 1975.

Frey, William H. "Metropolitan America: Beyond the Transition." *Population Bulletin* 45 (July 1990), pp. 1–50.

Frey, William H. and Alden Speare, Jr. *Regional and Metropolitan Growth and Decline in the United States.* New York: Russell Sage Foundation, 1988.

Friedan, Betty. *The Feminine Mystique.* New York: W. W. Norton, 1963.

Friedland, Roger and Donald Palmer. "Park Place and Main Street: Business and the Urban Power Structure." *Annual Review of Sociology* 10 (1984), pp. 393–416.

Friedmann, John and Goetz Wolff. "World City Formation: An Agenda for Research and Action." *International Journal of Urban and Regional Research* 6 (1982), pp. 309–343.

Fröbel, Folker, Jurgen Heinrichs, and Otto Kreye. *The New International Division of Labour.* Trans. Pete Burgess. London: Cambridge University Press, 1980.

Fusfield, Daniel R. and Timothy Bates. *The Political Economy of the Urban Ghetto.* Carbondale, IL: Southern Illinois University Press, 1984.

Fustel de Coulanges, Numa Denis. *The Ancient City: A Study on the Religion, Laws, and Institutions of Greece and Rome.* Garden City, NY: Doubleday Anchor Books, no date.

Galaskiewicz, Joseph. *Exchange Networks and Community Politics.* Beverly Hills, CA: Sage Publications, 1979.

Galaskiewicz, Joseph. *The Social Organization of an Urban Grants Economy.* New York: Academic Press, 1985.

Gallaher, Art, Jr. *Plainville Fifteen Years Later.* New York: Columbia University Press, 1961.

Gans, Herbert J. *The Levittowners: Ways of Life and Politics in a New Suburban Community.* New York: Pantheon Books, 1967.

Gans, Herbert J. "Urbanism and Suburbanism as Ways of Life." In *Human Behavior and Social Processes,* ed. A. M. Rose, pp. 625–648. Boston: Houghton Mifflin, 1962.

Gans, Herbert J. *The Urban Villagers: Group and Class in the Life of Italian-Americans.* New York: The Free Press of Glencoe, 1962; reissued New York: Macmillan, 1983.

Gappert, Gary and Richard Knight, eds. *Cities in the 21st Century.* Vol. 23 of *Urban Affairs Annual Reviews.* Beverly Hills, CA: Sage Publications, 1982.

Geddes, Patrick. *Cities in Evolution.* London: Williams and Norgate, 1949.

Gibbs, Jack P., ed. *Urban Research Methods.* Princeton, NJ: Van Nostrand, 1961.

Gist, Noel and Sylvia Fava. *Urban Society.* 6th ed. New York: Thomas Y. Crowell, 1974.

Gitlin, Todd and Nanci Hollander. *Uptown: Poor Whites in Chicago.* New York: Harper & Row, 1970.

Glaab, Charles N. and A. Theodore Brown. *A History of Urban America.* New York: Macmillan Company, 1967. Second edition of 1976 is shorter and less scholarly.

Goffman, Erving. *The Presentation of Self in Everyday Life.* Garden City, NY: Doubleday Anchor, 1959.

Golden, Hilda. *Urbanization and Cities.* Lexington, MA: D. C. Heath, 1981.

Goldfield, David R. and Blaine A. Brownell. *Urban America: From Downtown to No Town.* Boston: Houghton Mifflin, 1979.

Goldstein, Sidney and Calvin Goldscheider. *Jewish-Americans: Three Generations of a Jewish Community.* Englewood Cliffs, NJ: Prentice-Hall, 1968.

Gonzalez, Juan, Jr. *Racial and Ethnic Groups in America.* Dubuque, IA: Kendall Hunt, 1990.

Goodman, Paul and Percival Goodman. *Communitas: Means of Livelihood and Ways of Life.* New York: Random House, 1947. Reprinted New York: Vintage Books, 1960; New York: Columbia University Press, 1990.

Goodman, Robert. *After the Planners.* New York: Simon & Schuster, 1971.

Gordon, David. "Capitalist Development and the History of American Cities." In *Marxism and the Metropolis,* ed. William K. Tabb and Larry Sawers, pp. 25–63. New York: Oxford University Press, 1978. Reissued in 1984.

Gordon, David. "Class Struggle and the State of American Urban Development." In *The Rise of the Sunbelt Cities,* ed. David Perry and Alfred Watkins, pp. 55–82. Beverly Hills, CA: Sage Publications, 1977.

Gordon, Margaret *et al.* "Crime, Women and the Quality of Urban Life." *Signs: Journal of Women in Culture and Society* 5 (1980) Supplement, pp. S144–160.

Gordon, Margaret and Stephanie Riger. *The Female Fear.* New York: Free Press, 1989.

Gottdiener, Mark. *The Decline of Urban Politics: Political Theory and the Crisis of the Local State.* Newbury Park, CA: Sage Publications, 1987.

Gottdiener, Mark. *The Social Production of Urban Space.* Austin, TX: University of Texas Press, 1985.

Gottdiener, Mark. "Space as a Force of Production." *International Journal of Urban and Regional Research* 11:3 (1987), pp. 404–416.

Gottdiener, Mark. and Joe Feagin. "The Paradigm Shift in Urban Sociology." *Urban Affairs Quarterly* 24 (December 1988), pp. 163–187.

Gottdiener, Mark and A. Lagopoulos. *The City and the Sign.* New York: Columbia University Press, 1986.

Gottmann, Jean, ed. *Centre and Periphery: Spatial Variations in Politics.* Beverly Hills, CA: Sage Publications, 1980.

Gottmann, Jean. *Megalopolis: The Urbanized Northeastern Seaboard of the United States.* Cambridge, MA: MIT Press, 1961.

Gottmann, Jean and Robert A. Harper, eds. *Metropolis on the Move: Geographers Look at Urban Sprawl.* New York: John Wiley, 1967.

Gould, Peter and Rodney White. *Mental Maps.* New York: Penguin, 1974.

Gove, Walter R. and Michael Hughes. *Overcrowding in the Household: An Analysis of Determinants and Effects.* New York: Academic Press, 1983.

Granovetter, Mark. "The Strength of Weak Ties." *American Journal of Sociology* 78 (1973), pp. 1360–1380.

Green, Charles and Basil Wilson. *The Struggle for Empowerment in New York City.* New York: Praeger, 1989.

Green, Constance McLaughlin. *The Rise of Urban America.* New York: Harper Colophon Books, 1965.

Greer, Scott. *The Emerging City: Myth and Reality.* New York: Free Press of Glencoe, 1962.

Greer, Scott. *Urban Renewal and American Cities.* Indianapolis: Bobbs-Merrill, 1965.

Griffeth, Robert and Carol G. Thomas, eds. *The City-State in Five Cultures.* Santa Barbara, CA.: ABC-Clio, Inc., 1981.

Gugler, Josef, ed. *Urbanization in the Third World.* New York: Oxford University Press, 1988.

Gurkatnak, H. R. and W. A. LeCompte, eds. *Human Consequences of Crowding.* New York: Plenum Press in coordination with NATO Scientific Affairs Division, 1979.

Gutman, Robert, ed. *People and Buildings.* New York: Basic Books, 1972.

Gutman, Robert and David Popenoe, eds. *Neighborhood, City, and Metropolis.* New York: Random House, 1970.

Hagerstrand, Torsten. "Survival and Arena." In *Timing Space and Spacing Time,* ed. T. Carlstein *et al.* Vol. 2, entitled *Human Activity and Time Geography.* London: Edward Arnold, 1978.

Hagerstrand, Torsten. "What About People in Urban Science." *Papers of the Regional Science Association* 24 (1969–1970), pp. 7–21.

Hall, Edward T. *The Dance of Life: The Other Dimension of Time.* Garden City, NY: Doubleday Anchor, 1983.

Hall, Edward T. *The Hidden Dimension: An Anthropologist Examines Man's Use of Space in Public and Private.* Garden City, NY: Doubleday Anchor, 1969.

Halle, David. *America's Working Man: Home, Work, and Politics Among Blue-Collar Property Owners.* Chicago: University of Chicago Press, 1982.

Hallman, Howard W. *Neighborhoods: Their Place in Urban Life.* Beverly Hills, CA: Sage Publications, 1984.

Hallowell, A. Irving. "Cultural Factors in the Structuralization of Perception." In *Social Psychology at the Cross Roads,* ed. J. H. Rohrer and M. Sherif, pp. 164–195. New York: Harper & Row, 1951.

Hallowell, A. Irving. *Culture and Experience.* Philadelphia: University of Pennsylvania Press, 1955.

Hammond, J. L. and Barbara Hammond. *The Town Labourer: The New Civilization 1760–1832.* Garden City, NY: Doubleday Anchor, 1968.

Hammond, Mason. *The City in the Ancient World.* Cambridge, MA: Harvard University Press, 1972.

Hannerz, Ulf. *Exploring the City: Inquiries Toward an Urban Anthropology.* New York: Columbia University Press, 1980.

Hannerz, Ulf. *Soulside: Inquiries into Ghetto Culture and Community.* New York: Columbia University Press, 1969.

Hansen, Marcus Lee. *The Atlantic Migration 1607–1860: A History of the Continuing Settlement of the United States.* New York: Harper & Row, 1940.

Hanson, Susan and Ibipo Johnston. "Gender Differences in Work-Trip Length: Explanations and Implications." *Urban Geography* 6 (1985), pp. 193–219.

Hanson, Susan and G. Pratt. "Spatial Dimensions of the Gender Division of Labor in a Local Labor Market." *Urban Geography* 9 (1988), pp. 180–202.

Hapgood, Karen and Judith Getzels, eds. *Planning, Women and Change.* Chicago: American Society of Planning Officials, 1974.

Harloe, Michael, ed. *Captive Cities.* London: John Wiley, 1977.

Harris, David. "New Light on Plant Domestication and the Origins of Agriculture: A Review." *Geographical Review* 57 (January 1967), pp. 90–107.

Harvey, David. "Government Policies, Financial Institutions and Neighborhood Change in United States Cities." In *Captive Cities,* ed. Michael Harloe. London: John Wiley, 1977.

Harvey, David. "Labor, Capital, and Class Struggle Around the Built Environment in Advanced Capitalist Societies." In *Urbanization and Conflict in Market Societies,* ed. Kevin Cox. Chicago: Maaroufa; London: Methuen, 1978.

Harvey, David. *The Limits to Capital.* Chicago: University of Chicago Press, 1982.

Harvey, David. "The Political Economy of Urbanization in Advanced Capitalist Societies: The Case of the United States." In *The Social Economy of Cities,* ed. Gary Gappert and Harold M. Rose. Vol. 9 of *Urban Affairs Annual Reviews.* Beverly Hills, CA: Sage Publications, 1975.

Harvey, David. *Social Justice and the City.* London: Edward Arnold, 1973; republished Baltimore: Johns Hopkins University Press, 1975.

Harvey, David. *The Urbanization of Capital* and *Consciousness and the Urban Experience,* which constitute the two volumes of *Studies in the History and Theory of Capitalist Urbanization.* Baltimore: Johns Hopkins University Press, 1985.

Hatt, Paul. "The Concept of Natural Area." *American Sociological Review* 11 (August 1946), pp. 423–427. Reprinted in *Urban Patterns,* ed. George A. Theodorson. Rev. ed. University Park, PA: Pennsylvania State University Press, 1982.

Hauser, Francis L. "Ecological Patterns of European Cities." In *Urbanism in World Perspective: A Reader,* ed. Sylvia F. Fava, pp. 193–216. New York: Thomas Y. Crowell, 1968.

Hauser, Philip. "Observations on the Urban-Folk and Urban-Rural Dichotomies as Forms of Western Ethnocentrism." In *The Study of Urbanization,* ed. Philip Hauser and Leo Schnore. New York: John Wiley, 1965.

Hauser, Philip and Robert Gardner. "Urban Future: Trends and Prospects." *International Conference on Population and the Urban Future.* New York: United Nations Fund for Population Activities, 1980, pp. 7–77.

Hauser, Philip and Leo Schnore, eds. *The Study of Urbanization.* New York: John Wiley, 1965.

Hawley, Amos. *Human Ecology: A Theoretical Essay.* Chicago: University of Chicago Press, 1986.

Hawley, Amos. *Human Ecology: A Theory of Community Structure.* New York: Ronald Press, 1950.

Hawley, Amos and Sara Mills Mazie, eds. *Nonmetropolitan America in Transition.* Chapel Hill, NC: University of North Carolina Press, 1981.

Hayden, Dolores. *The Grand Domestic Revolution: A History of Feminist Designs for American Homes, Neighborhoods, and Cities.* Cambridge, MA: MIT Press, 1981.

Hayden, Dolores. *Redesigning the American Dream: The Future of Housing, Work and Family Life.* New York: W. W. Norton, 1984.

Hays, R. Allen. *The Federal Government & Urban Housing: Ideology and Change in Public Policy.* Albany: State University of New York Press, 1985.

Henderson, Jeffrey and Manuel Castells, eds. *Global Restructuring and Territorial Development.* London: Sage Publications, 1987.

Hendricks, Glenn. *The Dominican Diaspora: From the Dominican Republic to New York City—Villagers in Transition.* New York: Teachers College Press, Columbia, 1974.

Henig, Jeffrey R. *Neighborhood Mobilization: Redevelopment and Response.* New Brunswick, NJ: Rutgers University Press, 1982.

Hershberg, Theodore, ed. *Philadelphia: Work, Space, Family, and Group Experience in the 19th Century.* New York: Oxford University Press, 1981.

Hershberg, Theodore *et al.* "A Tale of Three Cities: Blacks and Immigrants in Philadelphia, 1850–1880, and 1970." In special issue of *Annals of the American Academy of Political and Social Science* 441 (January 1979) entitled *Race and Residence in American Cities,* pp. 55–81.

Hicks, Donald A., ed. *Urban America in the Eighties: Perspectives and Prospects. Report of the Panel on Politics and Prospects for Metropolitan and Nonmetropolitan America.* New Brunswick, NJ: Transaction Books, 1982.

Hill, Richard Child. "Separate and Unequal: Governmental Inequality in the Metropolis." *American Political Science Review* 68 (1974), pp. 1557–1568.

Hochschild, Arlie. *The Unexpected Community: Portrait of an Old Age Subculture.* Berkeley: University of California Press, 1973.

Hollingshead, August. "Community Research: Development and Present Condition." *American Sociological Review* 13 (April 1948), pp. 126–146.

Hollingshead, August. *Elmtown's Youth: The Impact of Social Classes on Adolescents.* New York: John Wiley, 1949.

Hopkins, Terence K., Immanuel Wallerstein and Associates. *World-Systems Analysis: Theory and Methodology.* Beverly Hills, CA: Sage Publications, 1982.

Horowitz, Ruth. *Honor and the American Dream.* New Brunswick, NJ: Rutgers University Press, 1983.

Howard, Ebenezer. *Garden Cities for To-Morrow.* London: Sonnenschein & Co., 1902.

Hoyt, Homer. *One Hundred Years of Land Values in Chicago.* Chicago: University of Chicago Press, 1933.

Hoyt, Homer. *The Structure and Growth of Residential Neighborhoods in American Cities.* Washington, DC: Federal Housing Administration, 1939.

Hudson, James. *The Unanticipated City: Loft Conversions in Lower Manhattan.* Amherst, MA: University of Massachusetts Press, 1987.

Hunter, Albert. *Symbolic Communities.* Chicago: University of Chicago Press, 1974.

Hunter, Albert and Gerald Suttles. "The Expanding Community of Limited Liability." In Gerald Suttles, *The Social Construction of Communities,* pp. 44–91. Chicago: University of Chicago Press, 1972.

Hunter, Floyd. *Community Power Structure: A Study of Decision Makers.* Chapel Hill: University of North Carolina Press, 1953.

Hunter, Robert. *Tenement Conditions in Chicago: Report by the Investigating Committee of the City Homes Association.* Chicago: City Homes Association, 1901.

Husted, Deborah. *Women and Urban America: A Selected and Multidisciplinary Bibliography of Materials Since 1960.* No. P2440. Monticello, IL: Vance Bibliographies, 1988.

Isard, Walter. *Location and Space-Economy: A General Theory Relating Industrial Location, Market Areas, Land Use, Trade and Urban Structure.* New York: John Wiley, 1956.

Jacobs, Jane. *The Death and Life of Great American Cities.* New York: Random House, 1961.

Jacobs, Jane. *The Economy of Cities.* New York: Random House, 1969.

Janowitz, Morris. *The Community Press in an Urban Setting: The Social Elements of Urbanism.* 2d ed. Chicago: University of Chicago Press, 1967.

Jaynes, Gerald D. and Robin Williams, eds. *A Common Destiny.* Washington, DC: National Academy Press, 1989.

Jeanneret, Charles Edouard [Le Corbusier]. *La ville radieuse.* Paris: Morance, 1931.

Johnson, Sheila K. *Idle Haven: Community Building Among the Working-Class Retired.* Berkeley: University of California Press, 1971.

Johnston, R. J. *The American Urban System: A Geographical Perspective.* New York: St. Martin's Press, 1982.

Johnston, R. J. *Urban Residential Patterns: An Introductory Review.* London: G. Bell and Sons, 1971. Reprinted New York: Praeger Publishers, 1972.

Kadushin, Charles and Delmos J. Jones. "To Him Who Hath Shall Be Given: The Social Consequences of Network Support in a Tough City." Paper presented at the annual meetings of the American Sociological Association, August 1989 (mimeograph).

Kasarda, John D. "Jobs, Migration, and Emerging Urban Mismatches." In *Urban Change and Poverty,* ed. G. H. McGeary and Laurence Lynn, Jr. Washington, DC: National Academy Press, 1988.

Kasarda, John D. "Urban Change and Minority Opportunities." In *The New Urban Reality,* ed. Paul Peterson. Washington, DC: Brookings Institute, 1985.

Kasarda, John D. "Urban Industrial Transition and the Underclass." *Annals of the American Academy of Political and Social Science* 501 (January 1989), pp. 26–47.

Katznelson, Ira. *City Trenches: Urban Politics and the Patterning of Class in the United States.* New York: Pantheon, 1981.

Katznelson, Ira. *Schooling for All: Class, Race and the Decline of the Democratic Ideal.* New York: Basic Books, 1985.

Keller, Suzanne, ed. *Building for Women.* Lexington, MA: D. C. Heath, 1981.

Keller, Suzanne. *The Urban Neighborhood: A Sociological Perspective.* New York: Random House, 1968.

Kerner, Otto J., Jr. *et al. Report of the National Commission on Civil Disorders.* Washington, DC, 1968. For update, see the special series, "Two Societies: America Since the Kerner Report," in *The New York Times* (March 1978).

Kim, Ilsoo. *New Urban Immigrants: The Korean Community in New York.* Princeton, NJ: Princeton University Press, 1981.

King, Anthony. *Global Cities: Post-Imperialism and the Internationalization of London.* New York and London: Routledge, 1990.

King, Anthony. *Urbanism, Colonialism, and the World-Economy.* New York and London: Routledge, 1990.

Kite, Elizabeth. *L'Enfant and Washington, 1791–1792.* Baltimore: Johns Hopkins University Press, 1929.

Knight, Richard V. and Gary Gappert, eds. *Cities in Global Society.* Newbury Park, CA: Sage Publications, forthcoming.

Kornblum, William. *Blue Collar Community.* Chicago: University of Chicago Press, 1974.

Kotler, Milton. *Neighborhood Government: The Local Foundations of Political Life.* Indianapolis: Bobbs-Merrill, 1969.

Krech, D. and R. S. Crutchfield. *Theory and Problems in Social Psychology.* New York: McGraw-Hill, 1948.

Kuhn, Thomas. *The Structure of Scientific Revolutions.* Chicago: University of Chicago Press, 1962.

Kwong, Peter. *The New Chinatown.* New York: Hill and Wang, 1987.

La Gory, Mark and John Pipkin. *Urban Social Space.* Belmont, CA: Wadsworth, 1981.

Lake, Robert, ed. *Readings in Urban Analysis: Perspectives on Urban Form and Structure.* New Brunswick, NJ: Rutgers University Center for Urban Research, 1983.

Lamarche, François. "Property Development and the Economic Foundations of the Urban Question." In *Urban Sociology: Critical Essays,* ed. C. C. Pickvance, pp. 85–118. New York: St. Martin's Press, 1976.

Lamberg-Karlovsky, C. C. and Martha Lamberg-Karlovsky. "An Early City in Iran." In *Cities: Their Origin, Growth and Human Impact,* ed. Kingsley Davis, pp. 28–37. San Francisco: W. H. Freeman, 1973.

Larson, Lawrence H. *The Urban West at the End of the Frontier.* Lawrence, KS: The Regents Press of Kansas, 1978.

Larson, Olaf. "Agriculture and the Community." In *Nonmetropolitan America in Transition,* ed. Amos Hawley and Sara Mazie, pp. 147–193. Chapel Hill, NC: University of North Carolina Press, 1981.

Lasch, Christopher. *Haven in a Heartless World.* New York: Basic Books, 1977.

Laumann, Edward O. *Bonds of Pluralism: The Form and Substance of Urban Social Networks.* New York: John Wiley, 1973.

Laumann, Edward O. *Prestige and Association in an Urban Community. An Analysis of an Urban Stratification System.* Indianapolis: Bobbs-Merrill Company, 1966.

Laurenti, Luigi. *Property Values and Race: Studies in Seven Cities.* Berkeley, CA: University of California Press, 1960.

Laurie, Bruce and Mark Schmitz. "Manufacturing and Productivity: The Making of an Industrial Base, Philadelphia, 1850–1880." In *Philadelphia: Work, Space, Family, and Group Experience in the 19th Century,* ed. Theodore Hershberg. Oxford: Oxford University Press, 1981.

Lee, Rose Hum. *The Chinese in the United States of America.* Hong Kong: Hong Kong University Press, 1960.

Lefebvre, Henri. *La production de l'espace.* Paris: Editions Anthropos, 1974; 2nd ed. 1981.

Lefebvre, Henri. *La revolution urbaine.* Paris: Gallimard, 1970.

Leiffer, Murray. "A Method for Determining Local Urban Community Boundaries." *Proceedings of the American Sociological Society* 26 (1933), pp. 137–143.

Lembcke, Jerry and Ray Hutchinson, eds. *Research in Urban Sociology: A Research Annual.* Vol. I: *Race, Class, and Urban Change.* Greenwich, CT: JAI Press, 1989.

Lenin, Vladimir. "Imperialism, the Highest Stage of Capitalism." In *Lenin: Selected Works,* vol. I (no translator shown), pp. 667–768. Moscow: Progress Publishers, 1970.

Leven, Charles. "Economic Maturity and the Metropolis' Evolving Form." In *The Changing Structure of the City: What Happened to the Urban Crisis,* ed. Gary A. Tobin, pp. 21–44. Vol. 16 of *Urban Affairs Annual Reviews.* Beverly Hills, CA: Sage Publications, 1979.

Lewin, Kurt. *A Dynamic Theory of Personality.* Trans. D. K. Adams and K. E. Zener. New York: McGraw-Hill, 1935.

Lewis, Oscar. "Further Observations on the Folk-Urban Continuum and Urbanization." In *The Study of Urbanization,* ed. Philip Hauser and Leo Schnore. New York: John Wiley, 1965.

Lieberson, Stanley. "The Impact of Residential Segregation on Ethnic Assimilation." *Social Forces* 40 (1961), pp. 52–57.

Liebow, Elliot. *Tally's Corner.* Boston: Little, Brown, 1967.

Light, Ivan and Edna Bonacich. *Immigrant Entrepreneurs: Koreans in Los Angeles, 1965–1982.* Berkeley, CA: University of California Press, 1988.

Local Community Fact Book of Chicago. Series, see under different editors.

Lofland, Lyn. "The 'Thereness' of Women: A Selective Review of Urban Sociology." In *Another Voice: Feminist Perspectives on Social Life and Social Science,* ed. Marcia Millman and Rosabeth Kanter. Garden City, NY: Doubleday, 1975.

Lofland, Lyn. *A World of Strangers: Order and Action in Urban Public Space.* New York: Basic Books, 1973.

Logan, John and Harvey Molotch. *Urban Fortunes: The Political Economy of Place.* Berkeley, CA: University of California Press, 1987.

Logan, John R. "The Disappearance of Communities from National Urban Policy." *Urban Affairs Quarterly* 19 (1983), pp. 75–90.

Long, John F. "Population Deconcentration in the United States." *Special Demographic Analyses* CDS-8105. U.S. Department of Commerce, Bureau of the Census. Washington, DC: Government Printing Office, November 1981.

Long, Norton E. "The Local Community as an Ecology of Games." *American Journal of Sociology* 64 (1958).

Losch, A. *The Economics of Location.* New Haven, CT: Yale University Press, 1954.

Lynch, Kevin. *The Image of the City.* Cambridge, MA: MIT Press, 1960.

Lynch, Kevin. *What Time Is This Place?* Cambridge, MA: MIT Press, 1972.

Lynd, Robert S. and Helen M. Lynd. *Middletown.* New York: Harcourt, Brace and Co., 1929.

Lynd, Robert S. and Helen M. Lynd. *Middletown in Transition: A Study in Cultural Conflicts.* New York: Harcourt, Brace and Co., 1936.

Madden, J. F. "Why Women Work Closer to Home." *Urban Studies* 18 (1981), pp. 181–194.

Maine, Henry. *Ancient Law.* London: John Murray, 1861.

Maldonado, Lionel and Joan Moore, eds. *Urban Ethnicity in the United States: New Immigrants and Old Minorities.* Vol. 29 of *Urban Affairs Annual Reviews.* Beverly Hills, CA: Sage Publications, 1985.

Malthus, Thomas. *An Essay on the Principle of Population As It Affects the Future Improvement of Society.* London: J. Johnson in St. Paul's Church-Yard, 1798 (available in numerous reprints).

Mandel, Ernest. *Late Capitalism.* London: NLB, 1975.

Mannheim, Karl. *Freedom, Power, and Democratic Planning.* London: Routledge & Kegan Paul, 1951.

Marcuse, Peter. "Abandonment, Gentrification and Displacement: the Linkages in New York City." In *Gentrification of the City,* ed. Neil Smith and Peter Williams. Boston: Allen and Unwin, 1986.

Markusen, Ann R. "City Spatial Structure, Woman's Work, and National Urban Policy." Special issue of *Signs,* ed. Catherine Stimpson *et al.* on "Women and the American City," Spring 1980, pp. SS524–544.

Markusen, Ann R., Peter Hall, and Amy Glasmeier. *High Tech America: The What, How, Where, and Why of the Sunrise Industries.* Boston: Allen & Unwin, 1986.

Marx, Karl and Frederick Engels. *The Communist Manifesto.* Variously printed.

Masnick, George and Mary Jo Bane. *The Nation's Families: 1960–1990.* Boston: Auburn Publishing House for the MIT-Harvard Joint Center, 1980.

Massey, Doreen. *Spatial Divisions of Labor: Social Structures and the Geography of Production.* New York: Methuen, 1984.

Massey Douglas S. "American Apartheid: Segregation and the Making of the Underclass." *American Journal of Sociology* 96 (September 1990), pp. 329–357.

Massey, Douglas and Mitchell Eggers. "The Ecology of Inequality: Minorities and the Concentration of Poverty, 1970–1980." *American Journal of Sociology* 95 (March 1990), pp. 1153–1188.

Matthews, Fred H. *Quest for an American Sociology: Robert E. Park and the Chicago School.* Montreal: McGill-Queen's University Press, 1977.

Matthiae, Paolo. *Ebla: An Empire Rediscovered.* Trans. Christopher Holme. Garden City, NY: Doubleday, 1981.

Matrix Collective. *Making Space: Women and the Man Made Environment.* London: Pluto Press, 1984.

Mayer, Harold M. and Richard C. Wade. *Chicago: Growth of a Metropolis.* Chicago: University of Chicago Press, 1969.

Mayhew, Henry. *London Labour and the London Poor.* Three vols. in two. London: Griffin Bohn and Company, 1861.

McAdoo, Harriette Pipes, ed. *Black Families,* 2d ed. Newbury Park, CA: Sage Publications, 1988.

McAdoo, Harriette Pipes and John McAdoo, eds. *Black Children.* Newbury Park, CA: Sage Publications, 1985.

McCarthy, Kevin and Peter Morrison. *The Changing Demographic and Economic Structure of Nonmetropolitan Areas in the United States.* Santa Monica, CA: The Rand Corporation for the U.S. Economic Development Administration, 1979.

McKelvey, Blake. *American Urbanization: A Comparative History.* Glenview, IL: Scott, Foresman & Company, 1973.

McKelvey, Blake. *The Emergence of Metropolitan America, 1915–1966.* New Brunswick, NJ: Rutgers University Press, 1968.

McKenzie, Roderick D. "The Ecological Approach to the Study of the Human Community." *American Journal of Sociology* 30 (November 1924). Reprinted in *The City,* ed. Robert Park, Ernest W. Burgess, and Roderick D. McKenzie. Chicago: University of Chicago Press, 1925.

Meggers, Betty. "The Transpacific Origin of Mesoamerican Civilization: A Preliminary Review of the Evidence and Its Theoretical Implication." *American Anthropologist* 77 (March 1975), pp. 1–23.

Meier, Richard L. *A Communications Theory of Urban Growth.* Cambridge, MA: MIT Press, 1962.

Melbin, Murray. *Night as Frontier: Colonizing the World After Dark.* New York: Free Press, 1987.

Mellaart, James. *The Archaeology of Ancient Turkey.* London: Bodley Head, 1978.

Mellaart, James. *Catal Huyuk: A Neolithic Town in Anatolia.* New York: McGraw-Hill, 1967.

Mellaart, James. *Earliest Civilizations of the Near East.* London: Thames and Hudson, 1965.

Meltzer, Jack. *Metropolis to Metroplex: The Social and Spatial Planning of Cities.* Baltimore: Johns Hopkins University Press, 1984.

Meyer, David. *Urban Change in Central Connecticut: From Farm to Factory to Urban Pastoralism.* Cambridge, MA: Ballinger Publication Co., 1976.

Michelson, William. *Man and His Urban Environment: A Sociological Approach.* Rev. ed. Reading, MA: Addison-Wesley, 1976.

Michelson, William. *From Sun to Sun: Daily Obligations and Community Structure in the Lives of Employed Women and Their Families.* Totowa, NJ: Rowman and Allanheld, 1985.

Michelson, William, Saul V. Levine, and Anna Rose. *The Child in the City.* Toronto: Toronto University Press, 1979.

Milgrim, Stanley. "The Experience of Living in Cities." *Science* 167 (1970), pp. 1461–1468.

"Miller, Herbert" and "Robert Park" [written anonymously by W. I. Thomas]. *Old World Traits Transplanted.* New York: Harper and Brothers, 1921.

Mills, C. Wright. *The Power Elite.* New York: Oxford University Press, 1956.

Miner, Horace M. *The Primitive City of Timbuctoo.* Princeton, NJ: Princeton University Press, 1953.

Mitchell, J. Clyde, ed. *Social Networks in Urban Situations: Analysis of Personal Relationships in Central African Towns.* Manchester: Manchester University Press, 1969.

Moland, John, Jr. "The Black Population." In *Nonmetropolitan America in Transition,* ed. Amos Hawley and Sara Mazie, pp. 464–501. Chapel Hill, NC: University of North Carolina Press, 1981.

Mollenkopf, John H. *The Contested City.* Princeton, NJ: Princeton University Press, 1983.

Mollenkopf, John H. "The Postwar Politics of Urban Development." In *Marxism and the Metropolis,* ed. William K. Tabb and Larry Sawers, pp. 117–152. New York: Oxford University Press, 1978.

Mollenkopf, John. "Who (or What) Runs Cities, and How?" *Sociological Forum* 4 (1989), pp. 119–137.

Molotch, Harvey. "Capital and Neighborhood in the United States." *Urban Affairs Quarterly* 14 (1979), pp. 289–312.

Molotch, Harvey. "The City as a Growth Machine: Toward a Political Economy of Place." *American Journal of Sociology* 82 (September 1976), pp. 309–330.

Monkkonen, Eric H. *America Becomes Urban: The Development of U.S. Cities and Towns 1780–1980.* Berkeley and Los Angeles: University of California Press, 1988.

Moore, Barrington, Jr. *Social Origins of Dictatorship and Democracy: Lord and Peasant in the Making of the Modern World.* Boston: Beacon Press, 1966.

Moore, William. *Vertical Ghetto: Everyday Life in an Urban Project.* New York: Random House, 1969.

Mowry, George E. *The Urban Nation, 1920–1960.* New York: Hill and Wang, 1965.

Mumford, Lewis. *The City in History: Its Origins, Its Transformations, and Its Prospects.* New York: Harcourt, Brace and World, 1961.

Myerhoff, Barbara. *Number Our Days: A Triumph of Continuity and Culture Among Jewish Old People in an Urban Ghetto.* New York: Simon & Schuster, 1978.

Neenan, William B. *The Political Economy of Urban Areas.* Chicago: Markham Publishing Co., 1972.

Nelson, Kathryn P. *Gentrification and Distressed Cities: An Assessment of Trends in Intrametropolitan Migration.* Madison: University of Wisconsin Press, 1988.

Newton, Kenneth. "Feeble Governments and Private Power: Urban Politics and Policies in the United States." In *The New Urban Politics,* ed. Louis Masotti and Robert Lineberry, pp. 37–58. Cambridge, MA: Ballinger, 1976.

Nisbet, Robert. *The Sociological Tradition.* New York: Basic Books, 1966.

Noyelle, Thierry and Thomas Stanback, Jr. *The Economic Transformation of American Cities.* Totowa, NJ: Allanheld, Osmun, 1984.

Oberai, A. S. *Migration, Urbanisation and Development.* Geneva: International Labour Office, 1987.

Olds, Edward B. "The City as a Unit for Recording and Analyzing Urban Data." *Journal of the American Statistical Association* 44 (December 1949), pp. 485–500.

Owen, E. Roger, Jr. *Cotton and the Egyptian Economy, 1820–1914: A Study in Trade and Development.* Oxford: Oxford University Press, 1969.

Padilla, Elena. *Up from Puerto Rico.* New York: Columbia University Press, 1958.

Palen, John and Bruce London, eds. *Gentrification, Displacement and Neighborhood Revitalization.* Albany: State University of New York Press, 1984.

Park, Robert. "The City: Suggestions for the Investigation of Human Behavior in the City Environment." *American Journal of Sociology* 20 (March 1915), pp. 577–612. (Incorrectly cited as 1916 by many authors and somewhat different from the 1925 version reproduced in Park, Burgess, and McKenzie, *The City.*)

Park, Robert. "Human Ecology." *American Journal of Sociology* 42 (July 1936), pp. 1–15.

Park, Robert and Ernest W. Burgess, eds. *An Introduction to the Science of Sociology.* Chicago: University of Chicago Press, 1921. 2d ed. 1924. Student (abridged) edition by Morris Janowitz. Chicago: University of Chicago Press, 1969.

Park, Robert, Ernest W. Burgess, and Roderick D. McKenzie, eds. *The City.* University of Chicago Heritage of Sociology Series. Chicago: University of Chicago Press, 1967. First pub. 1925.

Peake, Charles F. "Negro Occupation-Employment Participation in American Industry: Historical Perspective, Improvement During the 1960's and Recent Plateauing." *American Journal of Economics and Sociology* 34 (January 1975).

Peet, Richard. *International Capitalism and Industrial Restructuring.* Boston: Allen & Unwin, 1987.

Peet, Richard and Nigel Thrift, eds. *Geography, The Political Economy Perspective.* Boston: Unwin Hyman, 1989.

Perin, Constance. *Everything in its Place: Social Order and Land Use in America.* Princeton, NJ: Princeton University Press, 1977.

Perry, David C. and Alfred J. Watkins, eds. *The Rise of the Sunbelt Cities.* Vol. 14 of *Urban Affairs Annual Reviews.* Beverly Hills, CA: Sage Publications, 1977.

Peterson, George. "Federal Tax Policy and the Shaping of Urban Development." In *The Prospective City,* ed. Arthur P. Solomon, pp. 399–425. Cambridge, MA: MIT Press, 1980.

Peterson, Paul. ed. *The New Urban Reality*. Washington, DC: Brookings Institute, 1985.

Peterson, Paul E. *City Limits*. Chicago: University of Chicago Press, 1981.

Pfautz, Harold, ed. *Charles Booth on the City: Physical Pattern and Social Structure*. Chicago: University of Chicago Press, 1967.

Pickvance, Christopher G., ed. *Urban Sociology: Critical Essays*. New York: St. Martin's Press, 1976.

Pirenne, Henri. *Medieval Cities*. Garden City, NY: Doubleday Anchor, 1956. Lectures given originally in 1925.

Piven, Frances Fox and Richard A. Cloward. *Regulating the Poor: The Functions of Social Welfare*. New York: Pantheon, 1971.

Plotkin, Sidney. *Keep Out: The Struggle for Land Use Control*. Berkeley: University of California Press, 1987.

Polikoff, Alexander. *Housing the Poor: The Case for Heroism*. Cambridge, MA: Ballinger Publishing, 1978.

Polsby, Nelson. *Community Power and Political Theory*. New Haven, CT: Yale University Press, 1963.

Pool, Ithiel de Sola, ed. *The Social Impact of the Telephone*. Cambridge, MA: MIT Press, 1977.

Portes, Alejandro. *The Informal Economy: Studies in Advanced, and Less Developed Countries*. Baltimore: Johns Hopkins University Press, 1989.

Portes, Alejandro. "Urban Latin America." In *Third World Urbanization,* ed. Janet Abu-Lughod and Richard Hay, Jr., pp. 59–70. London and New York: Methuen, 1979.

Portes, Alejandro and John Walton. *Labor, Class and the International System*. New York: Academic Press, 1981.

Postgate, J. N. "The Temple in the Mesopotamian Secular Community." In *Man, Settlement and Urbanization,* ed. Ucko *et al.,* pp. 813–820. Cambridge, MA: Schenkman Publishing Co., 1972.

Pounds, Norman J. C. "The Urbanization of the Classical World." *Annals of the Association of American Geographers* 59 (March 1969), pp. 135–157.

Pratt, Edward Ewing. *Industrial Causes of Congestion of Population in New York City*. New York: Columbia University Faculty of Political Science, 1911.

Pred, Allan R. *City-Systems in Advanced Economies*. New York: John Wiley, 1977.

Pred, Allan R. *The Spatial Dynamics of U.S. Urban-Industrial Growth, 1800–1914*. Cambridge, MA: MIT Press, 1966.

Pred, Allan R. *Urban Growth and the Circulation of Information: The United States System of Cities, 1790–1840*. Cambridge, MA: Harvard University Press, 1973.

Proshansky, M., W. Ittelson, and L. Rivlin, eds. *Environmental Psychology: Man and His Physical Setting*. New York: Holt, Rinehart and Winston, 1970.

Ratcliff, Richard E. "Banks and the Command of Capital Flows: An Analysis of Capitalist Class Structure and Mortgage Disinvestment in a Metropolitan Area." In *Classes, Class Conflict and the State,* ed. Maurice Zeitlin, pp. 129–159. Cambridge, MA: Winthrop, 1980.

Ratcliff, Richard E. "Declining Cities and Capitalist Class Structure." In *Power Structure Research,* ed. G. William Domhoff, pp. 115–138. Beverly Hills, CA: Sage Publications, 1980.

Raushenbush, Winifred. *Robert E. Park: Biography of a Sociologist.* Durham, NC: Duke University Press, 1979.

Reps, John. *The Making of Urban America: A History of City Planning in the United States.* Princeton, NJ: Princeton University Press, 1965.

Rieder, Jonathan. *Canarsie: The Jews and Italians of Brooklyn Against Liberalism.* Cambridge, MA: Harvard University Press, 1985.

Riis, Jacob. *How the Other Half Lives: Studies Among the Tenements of New York.* New York: Hill and Wang, 1957; published originally in 1890.

Robey, Bryant. "A Guide to the Baby Boom." *American Demographics* 4 (September 1982), pp. 16–19.

Robinson, W. S. "Ecological Correlations and the Behavior of Individuals." *American Sociological Review* 15 (June 1950), pp. 351–357.

Rodgers-Rose, La Frances, ed. *The Black Woman.* Beverly Hills, CA: Sage Publications, 1980.

Rogler, Lloyd. *Migrant in the City: The Life of a Puerto Rican Action Group.* New York: Basic Books, 1972.

Roof, Wade Clark, ed. *Race and Residence in American Cities.* Special issue of *Annals of the American Academy of Political and Social Science* 441 (January 1979).

Rosenthal, Donald B. *Urban Housing and Neighborhood Revitalization: Turning a Federal Program into Local Projects.* New York and Westport, CT: Greenwood Press, 1988.

Rosenthal, Donald B., ed. *Urban Revitalization.* Beverly Hills, CA: Sage Publications, 1980.

Rossi, Peter. *Without Shelter: Homelessness in the 1980s.* New York: Priority Press Publications, 1989.

Rossi, Peter H. and Robert A. Dentler. *The Politics of Urban Renewal.* Glencoe, IL: Free Press, 1961.

Rothblatt, Donald, Donald Garr, and Jo Sprague. *The Suburban Environment and Women.* New York: Praeger, 1979.

Russell, J. C. *Late Ancient and Medieval Populations.* Special issue of *Transactions of the American Philosophical Society.* New series, vol. 48 (June 1958). Philadelphia: American Philosophical Society.

Rust, Edgar. *No Growth: Impacts on Metropolitan Areas.* Lexington, MA: Lexington Books/D. C. Heath, 1975.

Rutherford, Brent and Gerda Wekerle. "Captive Rider, Captive Labor: Spatial Constraints and Women's Employment." *Urban Geography* 9 (1988), pp. 116–137.

Rutherford, Brent and Gerda Wekerle. "Single Parents in the Suburbs: Journey-to-work and Access to Transportation." *Transportation Planning and Practice* 3 (1989).

Saegert, Susan. "The Androgynous City: From Critique to Practice." In *Handbook of Housing and the Built Environment in the United States,* ed. Willem Van Vliet and Elizabeth D. Huttman, pp. 23–37. New York: Greenwood Press, 1988.

Saegert, Susan and Jacqueline Leavitt. *From Abandonment to Hope: Community Households in Harlem.* New York: Columbia University Press, 1990.

Sahlins, Marshall. *Stone Age Economics.* Chicago: Aldine, 1972.

Salerno, Roger. *Louis Wirth: A Bio-Bibliography.* Westport, CT: Greenwood Press, 1987.

Sanders, William and Deborah Nichols. "Ecological Theory and Cultural Evolution in the Valley of Oaxaca." *Current Anthropology* 29 (Feb. 1988), pp. 33–80.

Sassen, Saskia. *Global Cities.* Princeton, NJ: Princeton University Press, forthcoming 1991.

Sassen-Koob, Saskia. "Growth and Informalization at the Core: A Preliminary Report on New York City." In *The Capitalist City,* ed. Michael Peter Smith and Joe Feagin, pp. 138–154. New York: Basil Blackwell, 1988.

Sassen[-Koob], Saskia. *The Mobility of Labor and Capital: A Study in International Investment and Labor Flow.* Cambridge: Cambridge University Press, 1988.

Sassen-Koob, Saskia. "Recomposition and Peripheralization of the Core." In *The New Nomads,* special issue of *Contemporary Marxism* 5 (Sept. 1982), pp. 88–100.

Saunders, Peter. *Social Theory and the Urban Question.* New York: Holmes and Meier, 1981.

Sawhill, Isabel and John Palmer. *The Reagan Record: An Assessment of America's Changing Domestic Priorities.* Washington, DC: The Urban Land Institute, 1984. Also Cambridge, MA: Ballinger Publishing Co., 1984.

Schaffer, Daniel, ed. *Two Centuries of American Planning.* Baltimore: Johns Hopkins University Press, 1988.

Schmid, Calvin F. "The Theory and Practice of Planning Census Tracts." *Sociology and Social Research* 22 (Jan.–Feb. 1938). Reprinted in *Urban Research Methods,* ed. Jack P. Gibbs. Princeton, NJ: Van Nostrand, 1961.

Schmitt, Robert C. "Implications of Density in Hong Kong," *Journal of the American Institute of Planners* 24 (August 1963), pp. 210–217.

Schwirian, Kent P., ed. *Comparative Urban Structure: Studies in the Ecology of Cities.* Lexington, MA: D. C. Heath, 1974.

Scott, Allen J. *The Urban Land Nexus and the State.* London: Pion, 1980.

Scott, Allen J. and Michael Storper. *Production, Work, Territory.* Boston: Allen & Unwin, 1986.

Seele, Keith C. and Bruce Williams, "Ancient Nubian Artifacts Yield Evidence of Earliest Monarchy," *New York Times,* March 1, 1979.

Seeley, John, R. A. Sim, and E. W. Loosley. *Crestwood Heights: A Study of the Culture of Suburban Life.* New York: Basic Books, 1956.

Selznick, Philip. *TVA and the Grass Roots.* Berkeley and Los Angeles: University of California Press, 1949.

Sennett, Richard, ed. *Classic Essays on the Culture of Cities.* New York: Appleton-Century-Crofts, 1969.

Sexton, Patricia. *Spanish Harlem.* New York: Harper & Row, 1965.

Shaw, Clifford. *The Jack-Roller: A Delinquent Boy's Own Story.* Chicago: University of Chicago Press, 1930.

Shaw, Clifford and Henry McKay. *Juvenile Delinquency and Urban Areas.* Chicago: University of Chicago Press, 1942.

Shevky, Eshref and Wendell Bell. *Social Area Analysis: Theory, Illustrative Application and Computational Procedures.* Stanford University Series in Sociology No. 1. Stanford, CA: Stanford University Press, 1955.

Shevky, Eshref and Marilyn Williams. *The Social Areas of Los Angeles: Analysis and Typology.* Los Angeles and Berkeley: University of California Press, 1949.

Short, James F., Jr., ed. *The Social Fabric of the Metropolis: Contributions of the Chicago School of Urban Sociology.* Chicago: University of Chicago Press, 1971.

Simmel, Georg. *Conflict and the Web of Group Affiliations.* Two essays translated by Kurt Wolff and Reinhard Bendix. Glencoe, IL: Free Press, 1955.

Simmel, Georg. "The Metropolis and Mental Life." In *The Sociology of Georg Simmel,* trans. Kurt H. Wolff, pp. 409–424. Glencoe, IL: Free Press, 1950.

Simmel, Georg. *Philosophy of Money.* Trans. Tom Bottomore and David Frisby. London: Routledge & Kegan Paul, 1978.

Simmel, Georg. *The Sociology of Georg Simmel,* ed. and trans. Kurt Wolff. Glencoe, IL: Free Press, 1950.

Simmel, Georg. "The Web of Group-Affiliations." In *Conflict and the Web of Group-Affiliations,* ed. and trans. Kurt Wolff and Reinhard Bendix. Glencoe, IL: Free Press, 1955.

Simms, Margaret and Julianne Malveaux, eds. *Slipping Through the Cracks: The Status of Black Women.* New Brunswick, NJ: Transaction Books, 1986.

Simpson, Charles. *SoHo: The Artist in the City.* Chicago: University of Chicago Press, 1980.

Sjoberg, Gideon. "The Origin and Evolution of Cities." *Scientific American* (1965).

Sjoberg, Gideon. *The Preindustrial City: Past and Present.* Glencoe, IL: Free Press, 1960.

Small, Albion. "Scholarship and Social Agitation." *American Journal of Sociology* 1 (March 1896), pp. 581–592.

Smith, Michael Peter. *The City and Social Theory.* New York: St. Martin's Press, 1979.

Smith, Michael Peter. *City, State, and Market: The Political Economy of Urban Society.* New York: Basil Blackwell, 1988.

Smith, Michael Peter and Joe Feagin, eds. *The Capitalist City.* New York: Basil Blackwell, 1988.

Smith, Neil. *Uneven Development: Nature, Capital and the Production of Space.* New York: Basil Blackwell, 1984.

Smith, Neil and Peter Williams, eds. *Gentrification of the City.* Boston: Allen & Unwin, 1986.

Smith, Page. *As a City upon a Hill: The Town in American History.* Cambridge, MA: MIT Press, 1966.

Soja, Edward, Rebecca Morales, and Goetz Wolff. "Urban Restructuring: An Analysis of Social and Spatial Change in Los Angeles." *Economic Geography* 59 (April 1983), pp. 195–230.

Solomon, Arthur P., ed. *The Prospective City: Economic, Population, Energy, and Environmental Developments Shaping Our Cities and Suburbs.* Cambridge, MA: MIT Press, 1980.

Solomon, Arthur P. and Kerry D. Vandell. "Alternative Perspectives on Neighborhood Decline." *Journal of the American Planning Association* 48 (1982), pp. 81–98.

Sommer, Robert. *Personal Space: The Behavioral Basis of Design.* Englewood Cliffs, NJ: Prentice-Hall, 1969.

Sorenson, A., K. Taeuber, and J. Hollingsworth. "Indexes of Racial Residential Segregation for 109 Cities in the United States, 1940 to 1970." *Sociological Focus,* April 1975.

Spann, Edward K. "The Greatest Grid: The New York Plan of 1811." In *Two Centuries of American Planning,* ed. Daniel Schaffer, pp. 11–39. Baltimore: Johns Hopkins University Press, 1988.

Stack, Carol. *All Our Kin: Strategies for Survival in a Black Community.* New York: Harper & Row, 1974.

Staples, Robert. *The Urban Plantation: Racism and Colonialism in the Post Civil Rights Era.* Oakland, CA: The Black Scholar Press, 1987.

Stein, Maurice. *The Eclipse of Community: An Interpretation of American Studies.* Princeton, NJ: Princeton University Press, 1960; paperback 1971.

Stephen, Elizabeth H. "1980 Census Geography." *American Demographics* (January 1982), pp. 31–35.

Sternlieb, George and W. Patrick Beaton. *The Zone of Emergence: A Case Study of Plainfield, New Jersey.* New Brunswick, NJ: Transaction Books, 1972.

Sternlieb, George and James Hughes, eds. *Post-Industrial America: Metropolitan Decline and Inter-Regional Job Shifts.* New Brunswick, NJ: The Center for Urban Policy Research, Rutgers University, 1975.

Stimpson, Catherine *et al.,* eds. *Women and the American City.* Special issue of *Signs.* Supplement 5:3 (Spring 1980).

Stone, Clarence. *Economic Growth and Neighborhood Discontent: System Bias in the Urban Renewal Program of Atlanta.* Chapel Hill, NC: University of North Carolina Press, 1976.

Stone, Clarence. *Regime Politics: Governing Atlanta.* Lawrence, KS: University Press of Kansas, 1989.

Streib, G., W. E. Folts, and M. Hilker. *Old Homes—New Families: Shared Living for the Elderly.* New York: Columbia University Press, 1984.

Summers, Gene F., E. M. Beck and Jon Minkoff. *Industrial Invasion of Nonmetropolitan America: A Quarter Century of Experience.* New York: Praeger Publishers, 1976.

Susser, Ida. *Norman Street: Poverty and Politics in an Urban Neighborhood.* New York: Oxford University Press, 1982.

Suttles, Gerald D. *The Social Construction of Communities.* Chicago: University of Chicago Press, 1972.

Suttles, Gerald D. *The Social Order of the Slum.* Chicago: University of Chicago Press, 1968.

Szelenyi, Ivan. *Urban Inequalities Under State Socialism.* New York: Oxford University Press, 1983.

Tabb, William K. and Larry Sawers, eds. *Marxism and the Metropolis: New Perspectives in Urban Political Economy*. New York: Oxford University Press, 1978. 2d ed., 1984.

Taeuber, Karl I. and Alma F. Taeuber. *Negroes in Cities*. Chicago: Aldine Publishing Co., 1965.

Tarn, John Nelson. *Five Per Cent Philanthropy: An Account of Housing in Urban Areas between 1840 and 1914*. London: Cambridge University Press, 1973.

Tarr, Joel. *Transportation Innovation and Changing Spatial Patterns in Pittsburgh*. Chicago: Public Works Historical Society, 1978.

Tarr, Joel and Gabriel Dupuy, eds. *Technology and the Rise of the Networked City in Europe and America*. Philadelphia: Temple University Press, 1988.

Taylor, Michael and Nigel Thrift, eds. *The Geography of Multinationals: Studies in the Spatial Development and Economic Consequences of Multinational Corporations*. London: Croom Helm, 1982.

Taylor, Ralph B. *Human Territorial Functioning: An Empirical Evolutionary Perspective on Individual and Small Group Territorial Cognitions, Behaviors, and Consequences*. Cambridge: Cambridge University Press, 1988.

Theodorson, George A., ed. *Urban Patterns: Studies in Human Ecology*. Rev. ed. University Park, PA: Pennsylvania State University Press, 1982.

Thomas, Jim, ed. "The Chicago School: The Tradition and the Legacy." Special issue of *Urban Life* 11 (January 1983).

Thomas, W. I. *W. I. Thomas on Social Organization and Social Personality*, ed. Morris Janowitz. Chicago: Phoenix Books, University of Chicago Press, 1966.

Thomas, W. I. and Florian Znaniecki. *The Polish Peasant in Europe and America*. 5 vols. Boston: Richard G. Badger, 1918–1920.

Thompson, Warren S. and David T. Lewis. *Population Problems*. New York: McGraw-Hill, 1965.

Timberlake, Michael, ed. *Urbanization in the World-Economy*. Orlando, FL: Academic Press, 1985.

Timms, Duncan. *The Urban Mosaic: Towards a Theory of Residential Differentiation*. Cambridge: Cambridge University Press, 1971.

Tobin, Gary, ed. *The Changing Structure of the City: What Happened to the Urban Crisis*. Vol. 16 of *Urban Affairs Annual Reviews*. Beverly Hills, CA: Sage Publications, 1979.

Tobin, Gary, ed. *Divided Neighborhoods: Changing Patterns of Racial Segregation*. Vol. 32 of *Urban Affairs Annual Reviews*. Newbury Park, CA: Sage Publications, 1987.

Toennies, Ferdinand. *Community and Society*. Trans. Charles Loomis. East Lansing, MI: Michigan State University Press, 1957. Originally pub. as *Gemeinschaft und Gesellschaft in 1887*.

Toffler, Alvin. *The Third Wave*. New York: Bantam Books, 1980.

Tolman, Edward C. "Cognitive Maps in Rats and Men." In Edward C. Tolman, *Collected Papers in Psychology*, pp. 241–264. Berkeley, CA: University of California Press, 1951. Originally in *Psychological Review* (July 1948).

Tringham, Ruth, ed. *Urban Settlements: The Process of Urbanization in Archaeological Settlements*. Andover, MA: Warner Modular Publications, 1973.

Tunnard, Christopher. *The Modern American City.* Princeton, NJ: D. Van Nostrand, Inc., 1968.

Ucko, Peter, Ruth Tringham, and G. W. Dimbleby, eds. *Man, Settlement and Urbanization.* London: Gerald Duckworth and Company, Ltd., 1972; Cambridge, MA: Schenkman Publishing Co., 1972.

U.S. Department of Commerce, Bureau of the Census. *The Black Population in the United States: March 1988.* Current Population Reports, PC Series P-20, No. 442. Washington, DC: Government Printing Office, 1989.

U.S. Department of Commerce, Bureau of the Census. *The Hispanic Population in the United States: March 1988.* Current Population Reports Series P-20, No. 431. Washington, DC: Government Printing Office, 1988.

U.S. Department of Commerce, Bureau of the Census. *Housing Opportunities for Black and White Households: Three Decades of Change in the Supply of Housing.* Special Demographic Analysis CDS-80–6. Washington, DC: Government Printing Office, 1982.

U.S. Department of Commerce, Bureau of the Census. *Patterns of Metropolitan Area and County Population Growth, 1980 to 1984.* Series P-25, No. 976. Washington, DC: Government Printing Office, 1985.

U.S. Department of Commerce, Bureau of the Census. *Population Profile of the United States, 1984/85.* Series P-23, No. 150. Washington, DC: Government Printing Office, 1987.

U.S. Department of Commerce, Bureau of the Census. *Projections of the Hispanic Population: 1983–2080.* Current Population Reports Series P-25, No. 995. Washington, DC: Government Printing Office, 1985.

U.S. Department of Commerce, Bureau of the Census. *The Social and Economic Status of the Black Population of the United States: An Historical Review, 1790–1978.* Current Population Reports. PC Series P-23, No. 80. Washington, DC: Government Printing Office, 1978.

U.S. Department of Commerce, Bureau of the Census. *Standard Metropolitan Statistical Areas and Standard Consolidated Statistical Areas: 1980.* PC80-S1–5. Washington, DC: Government Printing Office, 1981.

United Nations. *Demographic Yearbook.* Annual series.

United Nations. *Estimates and Projections of Urban and Rural Population 1950–2025: 1982 Assessment.* New York: United Nations, 1985.

United Nations. *Global Review of Human Settlements 1986.* Nairobi: United Nations Habitat, 1986.

United Nations. *Global Review of Human Settlements 1976.* New York: United Nations, 1976. Item 10 prepared by the United Nations Secretariat for United Nations Conference on Human Settlements.

United Nations. *The Growth of the World's Urban and Rural Population, 1920–2000.* New York: United Nations, 1969.

United Nations. *Patterns of Urban and Rural Population Growth.* New York: United Nations, 1981.

van Arsdol, Maurice, Jr., Santo Carmilleri, and Calvin Schmid. "The Generality of Urban Social Area Indexes." *American Sociological Review* 23 (June 1958), pp. 277–284.

van Til, Jon. *Living with Energy Shortfall: A Future for American Cities and Towns.* Boulder, CO: Westview Press, 1982.

Venkatarama Aiyar, C. P. *Town Planning in Ancient Dekkan.* Madras: Law Printing House, 1916.

Vesperi, Maria D. *City of Green Benches: Growing Old in a New Downtown.* Ithaca, NY: Cornell University Press, 1985.

Vidich, Arthur and Joseph Bensman. *Small Town in Mass Society: Class, Power, and Religion in a Rural Community.* Princeton, NJ: Princeton University Press, 1958; reissued Doubleday Anchor, 1960.

Vidich, Arthur, Joseph Bensman, and Maurice Stein, eds., *Reflections on Community Studies.* New York: John Wiley, 1964.

Vigil, James Diego. *Barrio Gangs: Street Life and Identity in Southern California.* Austin: University of Texas Press, 1988.

Wade, Richard C. *The Urban Frontier: The Rise of the Western Cities, 1790–1830.* Cambridge, MA: Harvard University Press, 1959.

Wakefield, D. *Island in the City: Puerto Ricans in New York.* New York: Citadel Press, 1960.

Walker, Richard A. "Two Sources of Uneven Development Under Advanced Capitalism—Spatial Differentiation and Capital Mobility." *Review of Radical Political Economics* 10 (1978), pp. 28–38.

Wallerstein, Immanuel. *The Modern-World System I: Capitalist Agriculture and the Origins of the European World-Economy in the Sixteenth Century.* New York: Academic Press, 1974.

Wallerstein, Immanuel. *The Modern-World System II: Mercantilism and the Consolidation of the European World-Economy 1600–1750.* New York: Academic Press, 1980.

Wallerstein, Immanuel. *The Modern World-System III: The Second Era of Great Expansion of the Capitalist World-Economy, 1730–1840s.* Orlando, FL: Academic Press, 1989.

Walton, John. "Community Power and the Retreat from Politics." In *New Perspectives on the American Community,* ed. Roland Warren and Larry Lyon. Homewood, IL: Dorsey Press, 1983.

Walton, John. "Discipline, Method, and Community Power: A Note on the Sociology of Knowledge." *American Sociological Review* 31 (October 1966), pp. 684–689.

Walton, John. "The New Urban Sociology." *International Social Science Journal* 33 (1981), pp. 374–390.

Ward, Barbara [Lady Jackson]. *The Home of Man.* Toronto: McClelland and Stewart, 1976.

Ward, David. *Cities and Immigrants: A Geography of Change in Nineteenth Century America.* New York: Oxford University Press, 1972.

Ward, David. *Poverty, Ethnicity and the American City, 1840–1925.* New York: Cambridge University Press, 1989.

Ware, Caroline. *Greenwich Village, 1920–1930.* Boston: Houghton Mifflin, 1935.

Warner, Sam Bass, Jr. *The Private City: Philadelphia in Three Periods of Growth.* Philadelphia: University of Pennsylvania Press, 1968.

Warner, Sam Bass, Jr.. *Streetcar Suburbs: The Process of Growth in Boston, 1870–1900.* Cambridge, MA: Harvard University Press and MIT Press, 1962.

Warner, Sam Bass, Jr.. *The Urban Wilderness.* New York: Harper & Row, 1972.

Warner, William Lloyd. *Yankee City.* New Haven, CT: Yale University Press, 1963.

Warner, William Lloyd and J. O. Low. *The Social System of a Modern Factory.* New Haven, CT: Yale University Press, 1947.

Warner, William Lloyd and Paul S. Lunt. *The Social Life of a Modern Community.* New Haven, CT: Yale University Press, 1941.

Warner, William Lloyd and Paul S. Lunt. *The Status System of a Modern Community.* New Haven, CT: Yale University Press, 1942.

Warner, William Lloyd and Leo Srole. *The Social Systems of American Ethnic Groups.* New Haven, CT: Yale University Press, 1945.

Waste, Robert J. *Community Power: Directions for Future Research.* Newbury Park, CA: Sage Publications, 1986.

Waste, Robert J. *The Ecology of City Policymaking.* New York: Oxford University Press, 1989.

Webber, Melvin. "Order in Diversity: Community Without Propinquity." As reprinted in R. Gutman and David Popenoe, eds. *Neighborhood, City, and Metropolis.* New York: Random House, 1970.

Webber, Melvin. "The Urban Place and the Nonplace Urban Realm." In M. Webber *et al., Explorations into Urban Social Structure.* Philadelphia: University of Pennsylvania Press, 1964.

Weber, Adna. *The Growth of Cities in the Nineteenth Century: A Study in Statistics.* Ithaca, NY: Cornell University Press, 1967.

Weber, Alfred. *Theory of the Location of Industries.* Trans. C. J. Friedrich. Chicago: University of Chicago Press, 1929.

Weber Max. *The City.* Ed. and trans. Don Martindale and Gertrud Neuwirth. New York: Colliers Books, 1962.

Weber, Max. *The Protestant Ethic and the Spirit of Capitalism.* New York: Charles Scribner's Sons, 1958.

Weiss, Marc. *The Rise of the Community Builders.* New York: Columbia University Press, 1987.

Weiss, Michael. *The Clustering of America.* New York: Tilden Press, 1988.

Wekerle, Gerda. *Vertical Village: The Social World of a Highrise Complex.* Ph.D. dissertation, Department of Sociology, Northwestern University, Evanston, IL: 1974.

Wekerle, Gerda. "Women in the Urban Environment." Special issue of *Signs.* Supplement 5 (1980), pp. S188–S214.

Wekerle, Gerda, David Morley, and Rebecca Peterson, eds. *New Space for Women.* Boulder, CO: Westview Press, 1980.

Wekerle, Gerda, and Brent Rutherford. "The Mobility of Capital and the Immobility of Female Labor: Responses to Economic Restructuring." In *The Power of Geography,* ed. Jennifer Wolch and Michael Dear, pp. 139–172. Boston: Unwin Hyman, 1989.

Welfeld, Irving. *Where We Live: The American Home and the Social, Political, and Economic Landscape, from Slums to Suburbs.* New York: Simon & Schuster, 1990.

Wellman, Barry. "East Yorkers and the Community Question." *American Journal of Sociology* 84 (1979), pp. 1201–1231.

Wellman, Barry and S. D. Berkowitz, eds. *Social Structures: A Network Approach.* Cambridge: Cambridge University Press, 1988.

Wellman, Barry and Scot Wortley. "Different Strokes from Different Folks: Which Types of Ties Provide What Kinds of Social Support?" Research Paper No. 174 (mimeo.). University of Toronto: Centre for Urban and Community Studies, July 1989.

Wendorf, Fred and Romuald Schild, "The Earliest Food Producers." *Archaeology* 34 (Sept.–Oct., 1981), pp. 30–36.

West, James (pseud. Carl Withers). *Plainville, U.S.A.* New York: Columbia University Press, 1945.

Wheatley, Paul. *The Pivot of the Four Quarters.* Chicago: Aldine, 1971.

White, Harrison *et al.* "Structural Equivalence of Individuals in Social Networks." *Journal of Mathematical Sociology* 1 (1971), pp. 49–80.

White, Michael J. *American Neighborhoods and Residential Differentiation.* New York: Russell Sage Foundation, 1987.

White, Morton and Lucia White. *The Intellectual versus the City.* New York: Mentor, 1962.

Whitt, J. Allen. *Urban Elites and Mass Transportation: The Dialectics of Power.* Princeton, NJ: Princeton University Press, 1982.

Whyte, William Foote. "The Slum: The Evolution of Street Corner Society." In *Reflections on Community Studies,* ed. Arthur Vidich, Joseph Bensman, and Maurice Stein. New York: John Wiley, 1964.

Whyte, William Foote. *Street Corner Society.* Chicago: University of Chicago Press, 1955.

Whyte, William Holly. *City: Rediscovering the Center,* New York: Doubleday, 1988.

Whyte, William Holly. *The Organization Man.* New York: Simon & Schuster, 1956.

Whyte, William Holly. *City: Rediscovering the Center.* New York: Doubleday, 1988.

Williams, Brett. *Upscaling Downtown: Stalled Gentrification in Washington, D.C.* Ithaca, NY: Cornell University Press, 1988.

Williams, Terry and William Kornblum. *Growing Up Poor.* Lexington, MA: D. C. Heath, 1985.

Wilson, William Julius. *The Declining Significance of Race.* Chicago: University of Chicago Press, 1978, 2nd ed. 1981.

Wilson, William Julius, ed. *The Ghetto Underclass: Social Science Perspectives.* Special issue of *Annals of the American Academy of Political and Social Science* 501 (January 1989).

Wilson, William Julius. *The Truly Disadvantaged.* Chicago: University of Chicago Press, 1987.

Winnick, Louis. "To House a Nation." *The Public Interest* (Winter 1989), pp. 137–141.

Wireman, Peggy. *Urban Neighborhoods, Networks, and Families: New Forms for Old Values.* Lexington, MA: D. C. Heath, 1984.

Wirth, Louis. "Urbanism as a Way of Life." *American Journal of Sociology* 44 (July 1938), pp. 1–24.

Wirth, Louis and Eleanor H. Bernert, eds., *Local Community Fact Book of Chicago.* Chicago: University of Chicago Press, 1949.

Wirth, Louis, with Margaret Furez and Edward Burchard. *The Local Community Fact Book.* Chicago, 1938.

Wittfogel, Karl. *Oriental Despotism: A Comparative Study of Total Power.* New Haven: Yale University Press, 1957.

Wolch, Jennifer and Michael Dear, eds. *The Power of Geography: How Territory Shapes Social Life.* Boston: Unwin Hyman, 1989.

Wong, Bernard. *Chinatown: Economic Adaptation and Ethnic Identity of the Chinese.* New York: Holt, Rinehart and Winston, 1982.

Wong, Bernard. *Patronage, Brokerage, Entrepreneurship and the Chinese Community of New York City.* New York: AMS Press, 1984.

Wood, Edith Elmer. *The Housing of the Unskilled Wage Earner: America's Next Problem.* New York: Macmillan Company, 1919.

Wood, Robert. *1400 Governments: The Political Economy of the New York Metropolitan Region.* Cambridge, MA: Harvard University Press, 1961.

World Bank, The. *World Development Report 1989.* New York: Oxford University Press, 1989.

Wright, Frank Lloyd. "Broadacre City: A New Community Plan." *Architectural Record* 74:4(April 1935), pp. 243–254.

Wright, Frank Lloyd. *The Disappearing City.* New York: W. F. Payson, 1932.

Wright, Frank Lloyd. *The Living City.* New York: Horizon Press, 1958.

Wright, Frank Lloyd. *When Democracy Builds.* Chicago: University of Chicago Press, 1945.

Wright, Gwendolyn Wright. *Building the Dream: A Social History of Housing in America.* Cambridge, MA: MIT Press, 1983.

Yago, Glenn. *The Decline of Transit: Urban Transportation in German and U.S. Cities, 1900–1970.* New York: Cambridge University Press, 1984.

Young, Michael and Peter Willmott. *Family and Kinship in East London.* London: Routledge & Kegan Paul, 1957.

Zald, Mayer and John D. McCarthy, eds. *The Dynamics of Social Movements: Resource Mobilization, Social Control and Tactics.* Cambridge, MA: Winthrop, 1979.

Zavella, Patricia. *Women's Work and Chicano Families: Cannery Workers of the Santa Clara Valley.* Ithaca, NY: Cornell University Press, 1987.

Zeitlin, Maurice. "Corporate Ownership and Control: The Large Corporation and the Capitalist Class." *American Journal of Sociology* 79 (1974), pp. 1073–1119.

Zerubavel, Eviatar. *Hidden Rhythms.* Chicago: University of Chicago Press, 1981.

Zinsser, Hans. *Rats, Lice and History.* Boston: Little, Brown, 1935.

Zoll, Seymour I. *Zoned America.* New York: Grossman Publishers, 1969.

Zorbaugh, Harvey. *The Gold Coast and the Slum.* Chicago: University of Chicago Press, 1929.

Zorbaugh, Harvey. "The Natural Areas of the City." *Publications of the American Sociological Society* 20 (1926), pp. 188–198. Reprinted in *Urban Patterns,* ed.

George A. Theodorson. Rev. ed. University Park, PA: Pennsylvania State University Press, 1982.

Zukin, Sharon. "A Decade of the New Urban Sociology." *Theory and Society* 9 (1980), pp. 575–602.

Zukin, Sharon. *Loft Living Culture & Capital in Urban Change*. Baltimore: Johns Hopkins University Press, 1982. Reissued New Brunswick: Rutgers University Press, 1989.

Index